ETERNAL LIFE AND HUMAN HAPPINESS IN HEAVEN

ETERNAL LIFE AND HUMAN HAPPINESS IN HEAVEN

PHILOSOPHICAL PROBLEMS, THOMISTIC SOLUTIONS

Christopher M. Brown

The Catholic University of America Press
Washington, D.C.

Copyright © 2021
The Catholic University of America Press
All rights reserved
The paper used in this publication meets the minimum requirements of
American National Standards for Information Science—Permanence
of Paper for Printed Library Materials, ANSI Z39.48-1984.
∞

Frontispiece: *Mary, Queen of Heaven*, c. 1485/1500. Master of the Saint Lucy Legend.
Courtesy of the Samuel H. Kress Collection, National Gallery of Art.

Cataloging-in-Publication Data available from the Library of Congress
ISBN 978-0-8132-3414-4

To my wife, Merry Elizabeth, and my sons,
Judah, Leo, and Thomas

I ... pray that You bring [us] ... sinner[s] to that ineffable banquet where You dwell with Your Son and Holy Spirit. You Who are for Your saints true light, complete fulfillment, eternal joy, consummate delight, and perfect happiness. Through the same Christ Our Lord. Amen.

THOMAS AQUINAS, "LONGER PRAYER AFTER COMMUNION"

CONTENTS

Acknowledgments	ix
List of Abbreviations	xi
Introduction	1

Part 1. Four Apparent Problems concerning Eternal Life

1. Contemporary Philosophy and Theology and Two Problems concerning the Nature of Heaven	7
2. Contemporary Philosophy and Theology and a Third Problem concerning the Nature of Heaven: Static or Dynamic Reality?	30
3. Contemporary Philosophy and Theology and the Problem of the Tedium of (Heavenly) Immortality	76

Part 2. St. Thomas on the Essential Reward in Heaven

4. Human *beatitudo* in Heaven: A Prolegomena	89
5. The Essential Reward I: The Essential Characteristics of the Beatific Vision	122
6. The Essential Reward II: The Primary and Secondary Objects of the Beatific Vision	141
7. The Essential Reward III: The Beatific Vision as Participation in God's Eternal Life	167
8. The Essential Reward IV: The Proper Accidents of the Beatific Vision	180

Part 3. St. Thomas on the Accidental Reward in Heaven

9. The Accidental Reward I: The Relative Importance of Embodiment for Human Happiness in Heaven ... 197
10. The Accidental Reward II: Resurrection Bodies ... 234
11. The Accidental Reward III: Glorified Bodies ... 282
12. The Accidental Reward IV: The Communion of the Saints, the Aureoles, and the Fruits ... 328
13. The Accidental Reward V: Nonhuman Material Beings in Heaven ... 339

Part 4. Thomistic Solutions to Four Apparent Problems concerning Eternal Life

14. A Thomistic Solution to PNH-I: The Goods of the Beatific Vision and the City of God, Rightly Ordered ... 391
15. A Thomistic Solution to PNH-II: Transfigured Human Embodiment ... 400
16. A Thomistic Solution to PNH-III: Heaven as Perfectly Dynamic ... 411
17. A Thomistic Solution to the Problem of the Tedium of Heavenly Immortality ... 420

Conclusion ... 445

Selected Bibliography ... 449
Scriptural Index ... 461
General Index ... 463

ACKNOWLEDGMENTS

There are many people to thank. The following people discussed with me topics central to the book, offered encouragement, or provided helpful comments on earlier drafts of the book or papers that are ancestors to the book: Leasha Allen, Spencer Atkins, Thomas Atkinson, Fiona Grooms Barker, Mark Barker, Gregory Beabout, Fr. Timothy Bellamah, OP, John F. Boyle, Matthew Braddock, Jeff Brower, Merry Brown, T. Ryan Byerly, Richard Cain, Calob Cohoe, Bryan Cross, Brandon Dahm, Jason Eberl, Lawrence Feingold, Jim Fieser, John Glass, Luke Henderson, Chris Hill, Nathan Howard, Art Hunt, Colin Johnson, Jahann Jones, Norman Lillegard, Mark Lister, Megan Long, Les Macdiarmid, Lydia Martin, Colleen McCluskey, Dan McDonough, Esaias McKinney, Laura Miller, Sarah Miller, Mixon Moore, Jack Mulder, Turner Nevitt, Emily Nuenke, Joe Ostenson, Tim Pawl, Garner Perkins, Sam Richardson, Callum Savage, Fr. Dennis Schenkel, Jeffrey Schlicter, John Schommer, Eric Silverman, Mark Spencer, Mallory Spisak, Eleonore Stump, Kevin Timpe, Patrick Toner, John G. Trapani Jr., Christina Van Dyke, Fr. Theodore Vitali, CP, Sam Webb, and Thomas Williams; participants in my upper-division classes on God and human happiness at the University of Tennessee at Martin in 2008, 2011, and 2017; members of the Martin Hobbit Club; participants at the 2008 American Maritain Conference; participants at St. Thomas paper sessions at the International Congress for Medieval Studies in Kalamazoo, Michigan, in 2014, 2015, and 2016; participants in the 2015 Interim State Writing Workshop in McCall, Idaho; and an anonymous reader for the Catholic University of America Press.

I also wish to thank the journal *Faith and Philosophy* for permission to use parts of my "Making the Best Even Better: Modifying Pawl and Timpe's Solution to the Problem of Heavenly Freedom."[1] Thanks to Routledge for permission to use parts of my "Friendship in Heaven:

1. *Faith and Philosophy* 32, no. 1 (2015): 63–80.

Aquinas on Supremely Perfect Happiness and the Communion of the Saints."[2]

Special thanks are due to my editor, John B. Martino, and all those at the Catholic University of America Press. In addition, thanks are owed to John's predecessor, James Kruggel, who first showed interest in the project. Thanks also to Paul Higgins, whose meticulous copy-editing greatly improved the book. Thanks to Mark Spencer, who gave me comments on two different drafts of the entire manuscript. The project was greatly improved in light of his detailed and philosophically astute commentaries. Work on this project greatly benefited from the Reagan Leave program at the University of Tennessee at Martin, as well as a Ray and Wilma Smith Award, neither of which would have been possible without the support of David Coffey and Lynn Alexander. I am grateful to John V. Glass for his friendship, prayers, and encouragement. For their love and support, I thank my father, Noel Brown (+), my mother, Patricia Brown, and my in-laws, Ed and Susan Hill. Finally, with great love, affection, and thanks, I dedicate this book to my wife, Merry, and my sons, Judah, Leo, and Thomas.

---

2. *Metaphysics and God: Essays in Honor of Eleonore Stump*, ed. Kevin Timpe (London: Routledge, 2009), 225–48.

ABBREVIATIONS

Works of St. Thomas Aquinas

CA	*Catena Aurea* (Matthew, 1262–64; Mark, Luke, and John, 1265–68)
CSA	*Collationes in Symbolum Apostolorum* (Lent 1273)
CT	*Compendium theologiae* (part I, 1265–67; part II, 1272–73)
DEE	*De ente et essentia* (1252–53)
DPN	*De principiis naturae, ad fratrem Sylvestrum* (1248–52 or 1252–56)
DR	*De regno* (1266–67)
In 1 Cor, etc.	*Expositio et lectura super Epistolas Pauli Apostoli* (1263–65)
In BDT	*Expositio super librum Boethii De trinitate* (1257–58 or 1259)
In DA	*Sententia libri De anima* (1267–68)
In DDN	*Expositio super librum Dionysii De divinis nominibus* (1265–68)
In Heb	*Super Epistolam ad Hebraeos* (1272–73)
In Is	*Expositio super Isaiam ad litteram* (1251–52)
In Jb	*Expositio super Iob ad litteram* (1263–65)
In Jn	*In Joannem* (1270–71 or 1272)
In LDC	*Expositio super librum De causis* (1272–73)
In Meta	*Sententia super Metaphysicam* (1270–73)
In Mt	*In Matthaeum* (1269–70)
In NE	*Sententia Libri Ethicorum* (1271–72)
In Phys	*Expositio Libri Physicorum* (1268–70)
In Pss	*Super Psalmos* (September–October 1273)
In Rom	*Super Romanos* (1271–72)
In SA	*In salutationem angelicam* (1268–72)

In Sent	*Scriptum super libros Sententiarum* (1252–56)
QDA	*Quaestio disputata de anima* (1266–67)
QDM	*Quaestiones disputatae de malo* (1269–71)
QDP	*Quaestiones disputatae de potentia* (1265–66)
QDSC	*Quaestio disputata de spiritualibus creaturis* (1267–68)
QDUVI	*Quaestio disputata De unione verbi incarnati* (1272)
QDV	*Quaestiones disputatae de veritate* (1256–59)
QQ	*Quaestiones de quodlibet* (VII–XI, 1256–59; I–VI and XII, 1268–72)
RJV	*Responsio ad magistrum Joannem de Vercellis* (Holy Thursday, April 2, 1271)
RLV	*Responsiones ad lectorem Venetum de 30 et 36 articulis* (1271)
SCG	*Summa contra Gentiles* (1259–65)
Sermo Beata gens	(Sermon, Happy the Nation): The Feast of All Saints, ca. 1256–59 or 1268–72?
Sermo Beati qui habitant	(Sermon, Happy are Those Who Live in Your House, O Lord): The Feast of All Saints, ca. 1256–59 or 1268–72?
Sermo Beatus vir	(Sermon, Happy the Man Whose Help Is from You): November 11, the feast of St. Martin, ca. 1256–59 or 1268–72?
Sermo Osanna filio David	(Sermon, Hosanna to the Son of David), December 1, 1269
ST	*Summa Theologiae* (Prima Pars [I], qq. 1–74, 1265–67; Prima Pars [I], qq. 79–119, 1267–68; Prima Secundae Partis [I-II], 1271; Secunda Secundae Partis [II-II], 1271–72; Tertia Pars [III], 1272–73; *Supplement* [*Suppl.*])

Works by Other Authors

DH	*Compendium of Creeds, Definitions, and Declarations on Matters of Faith and Morals*, 43rd edition (Denzinger)
NE	*Nicomachean Ethics* (Aristotle)

Arguments, Theses, and Logical Terms

Add.	Addition
AIHSS	The argument for the imperfect happiness of the separated soul

Abbreviations

AIPO	The argument from imperfect and perfect operation
APT	The animal and plant thesis
DREA	Development of REA (the removal of one of the ends of eating and sex argument)
DV	Dynamic view of the nature of heaven
EOC objection	The eternity of choices in heaven eclipses the choices of this life objection
G properties	Qualities characteristic of glorified human bodies
Givens thesis	The thesis that the Givens exist in heaven
HS	Hypothetical syllogism
MP	*Modus ponens*
MT	*Modus tollens*
PNH-I	The first problem concerning the nature of heaven
PNH-II	The second problem concerning the nature of heaven
PNH-III	The third problem concerning the nature of heaven
PTHI	The problem of the tedium of heavenly immortality
PTI	The problem of the tedium of immortality
R properties	Resurrection properties
REA	The removal of one of the ends of eating and sex argument
SV	Static view of the nature of heaven
TD	Totally dynamic view of the nature of heaven
Trans.	Transposition

ETERNAL LIFE AND HUMAN HAPPINESS
IN HEAVEN

Introduction

Thinking about problems concerning eternal life—and responding to them—has a long and celebrated history. Recall that near the end of Christ's public ministry, as Matthew, Mark, and Luke all report it, the Sadducees raise a problem concerning eternal life for Christ. How can human persons be resurrected from the dead if (a) the Mosaic law commands that a brother should marry his deceased brother's wife in a case where the dead man has no sons; (b) there is a family with seven brothers, and the oldest dies without having a son, and so the second brother marries the dead man's wife; (c) the second brother also dies without having a son, and so the third brother marries that same woman, etc., until the one woman is married to each of seven brothers at different times in this life? For, if all of those brothers rise from the dead, whose wife will she be at the resurrection? In effect, Christ responds to the problem raised by the Sadducees by questioning some of their assumptions about the nature of the afterlife.[1]

This book treats four apparent problems concerning eternal life in order to clarify our thinking about perfect human happiness in heaven. Just as Christ's response to the thought experiment of the Sadducees challenged some of the assumptions the Sadducees were making about the afterlife, so the teachings of St. Thomas Aquinas provide the basis for solutions to these four apparent problems about eternal life by calling into question common contemporary theological or philosophical presuppositions. Indeed, these Thomistic solutions often require us to think very differently from our contemporaries about God, human persons, and heaven. But thinking differently with St. Thomas is worth it: for these Thomistic solutions to problems are more satisfying, on both

---

[1]. See Mt 22:23–33, Mk 12:18–27, and Lk 20:27–40. Unless otherwise noted, I have used the New Revised Standard Version Catholic Edition of the Bible for scriptural references throughout this book.

theological and philosophical grounds, than a number of contemporary theological and philosophical approaches to solving such problems.[2]

The argument of the book is carried out in four parts. Part 1 lays out, in three chapters, four apparent problems concerning eternal life and explains how and why some important contemporary Christian theologians and philosophers resolve these problems, or, if those theologians or philosophers do not treat such problems directly, how such thinkers could resolve those problems.[3] Part 2 explains, in five chapters, St. Thomas's significant distinction between the essential reward of the saints in heaven and the accidental reward, and treats in detail his account of the *essential* reward, namely, the beatific vision and the proper accidents of the vision (delight, joy, and charity). Part 3 treats, in five chapters, St. Thomas's views on the multifaceted *accidental* reward in heaven, where the accidental reward includes, among other things, glorified human embodiment, participation in the communion of the saints, and the joy experienced by the saints in sensing God's "new heavens and new earth." Finally, part 4 argues, in four chapters, that St. Thomas's views allow for powerful solutions to four apparent problems about eternal life, solutions which possess virtues not possessed by the contemporary solutions canvassed in part 1.

St. Thomas's solutions to these four problems concerning eternal life are powerful for a number of reasons. First, unlike many contemporary solutions, St. Thomas's solutions are consistent with authoritative, Catholic Christian tradition. Second, St. Thomas's solutions make sense of a wide variety of different beliefs about heaven, namely: *heaven for hu-*

---

2. One cannot possibly in one book show that St. Thomas's views on eternal life in heaven—and solutions based on an interpretation of those views—are preferable to *all* conceivable approaches to solving apparent problems concerning heaven. Nonetheless, the book aims to show that Thomistic solutions to four apparent problems about heaven are preferable to a number of contemporary approaches insofar as St. Thomas's account of eternal life better takes into account all of the details of what scripture, Christian tradition, and human reason have to say about eternal life.

3. The book does not treat all of the apparent problems about heaven that theologians and philosophers have raised. For Thomistic solutions to two additional apparent problems concerning eternal life in heaven not treated in this book, see my "Some Advantages for a Thomistic Solution to the Problem of Personal Identity beyond Death," in *Paradise Understood: New Philosophical Essays about Heaven*, ed. T. Ryan Byerly and Eric J. Silverman (Oxford: Oxford University Press, 2017), 228–62, and "Making the Best Even Better: Modifying Pawl and Timpe's Solution to the Problem of Heavenly Freedom," *Faith and Philosophy* 32, no. 1 (2015): 63–80. Notably, my treatment in chapter 3 suggests ways of developing the argument in my 2015 article. In addition, for helpful responses to "four impediments" to receiving St. Thomas's teaching on heaven, see Reinhard Hütter, *Bound for Beatitude: A Thomistic Study in Eschatology and Ethics* (Washington, D.C.: The Catholic University of America Press, 2019), 49–71.

man persons is a perfect personal union with God and *heaven for human persons is a perfect society of creatures*; *heaven for human persons is a transcendent reality that sates the human desire for perfect goodness itself* and *heaven for human persons satisfies characteristically human desires*; and, finally, *heaven for human persons is an immutable participation in God's eternal life* and *heaven for human persons (eventually) includes perfect sensation and bodily movement in the new heavens and the new earth*. Third, St. Thomas's account of heaven knits together these different beliefs about heaven without raising any of the significant theological or philosophical problems that attend the contemporary theological and philosophical solutions examined in part 1. We do well, therefore, to take St. Thomas, the Common Doctor, as our guide in thinking about the nature of eternal life in heaven.

PART 1

FOUR APPARENT PROBLEMS CONCERNING ETERNAL LIFE

1

Contemporary Philosophy and Theology and Two Problems concerning the Nature of Heaven

What is heaven? As one becomes acquainted with the history of theological discussion of heaven, even just within the Christian tradition, one comes to realize that this is a very good question.[1] Indeed, where thinking about the *nature* of heaven is concerned, there are a number of questions we can reasonably ask. Is heaven a *place*? Is heaven at least *partly* a place? Or, is heaven merely a particularly intimate relation with God, an immaterial being, in the next life? In addition, is union with God in heaven merely a *private* union between a human soul and God? Or, does heaven rather consist in an intimate union between God and a perfect human community, that is, the church? Does heaven ever involve a bodiless existence? Is union with God in heaven qualitatively better with the body than without? And how should a *Christian* theologian or philosopher in particular respond to these sorts of questions?

This first chapter treats two apparent problems about the *nature* of eternal life in heaven. The first problem concerns the question: is heaven for human persons merely a private communion with God or, rather, is heaven a perfect community consisting not only of God and the soul, but also angels, other human persons, and (perhaps) other kinds of material creatures such as dogs, cats, rats, etc.? The second apparent

---

1. For some important treatments of (aspects of) the history of Christian theology on heaven, see, e.g., Colleen McDannell and Bernhard Lang, *Heaven: A History* (New Haven, Conn.: Yale University Press, 1988); Caroline Walker Bynum, *The Resurrection of the Body in Western Christianity, 200–1336* (New York: Columbia University Press, 1995); and Jeffrey Burton Russell, *A History of Heaven: The Singing Silence* (Princeton, N.J.: Princeton University Press, 1997).

problem focuses upon the related question regarding whether heaven is an entirely transcendent and spiritual reality or rather one that involves the resurrection of *human* bodies.

PNH-I: PRIVATE COMMUNION WITH GOD OR CITY OF GOD?

In reflecting on what the Christian scriptures, Christian tradition, and historically important Christian theologians have to say about the nature of heaven or eternal life, one notices certain apparent tensions in and between those sources. For example, one might think that in the sources of Christian teaching there is a tension between the importance of the individual human person's communion with God in heaven, on the one hand, and the importance of the human person's membership in a perfect community of embodied beings in heaven on the other. That is to say, when we examine the sources of Christian tradition, there seem to be two very different, competing accounts or *models* of what heaven will be like. As Christian philosopher Gilbert Meilaender remarks, "Christians have thought of ... eternal life in two somewhat different ways—as a 'beatific vision,' and as a 'new heaven and new earth.'"[2]

Meilaender's remark first suggests a potential "which one?" problem for the Christian theologian or philosopher where thinking about the nature of heaven is concerned. But, in light of Meilaender's remark, we can also formulate an apparent *dilemma* for the Christian theologian or philosopher. For we might think that perfect human happiness consists in the beatific vision alone; if heavenly joy consisted in a union with both God and creatures, that would problematically minimize the importance of the soul's union with God in heaven as the source of perfect human happiness. On the other hand, the scriptures and Christian tradition also speak about heaven as involving a union *between* creatures, for example, the communion of the saints, and such union between creatures in heaven is presumably a good thing for such creatures. Call this apparent dilemma *the first problem concerning the nature of heaven* (or PNH-I, for short). Here follows a formalization of the problem:

---

2. *Should We Live Forever? The Ethical Ambiguities of Aging* (Grand Rapids, Mich.: Eerdmans, 2013), 49.

(1) The notion that (a) heaven for an intellectual creature consists merely of the beatific vision is in conflict with the notion that (b) heaven includes the reality of "the new heavens and the new earth," which itself includes a perfect human community, and, at least eventually, perfected embodiment on the part of human persons in the next life [assumption].

(2) The notion that (c) heaven consists merely of a perfect cosmic community, that is, "the new heavens and the new earth," which includes a perfect human community, overseen by a good and gracious God, is in conflict with the notion that (d) God is absolutely perfect and infinitely good [assumption].

(3) (a) or (c) [assumption].

(4) (b) and (d) [assumption].

(5) Therefore, if (b), then ~ (a) and [from (1), Transposition (hereafter Trans.)].

(6) Therefore, ~ (a) [from (4) and (5), *modus ponens* (hereafter MP)].

(7) Therefore, if (d), then ~ (c) [from (2), Trans.].

(8) Therefore, ~ (c) [by MP from (4) and (7), MP].

(9) Therefore, ~ (a) and ~ (c) [from (6 and (8), by Addition (hereafter Add.)].

(10) Therefore, the traditional Christian account of heaven entails a contradiction [from (3) and (9)].

Motivating the Premises of PNH-I

PNH-I consists of four assumptions—premises (1), (2), (3), and (4)—and a series of logically valid inferences from those four assumptions. Why should one think that the assumptions in PNH-I are true? Because the four assumptions make mention of propositions (a), (b), (c), and (d), I will begin my investigation by examining the meaning of the crucial terms in these propositions. In order to understand proposition (a), it will help first to say a few things about proposition (d).

Proposition (d) simply affirms an important part of the classical understanding of God that we find in great philosophers and theologians such as Plotinus, St. Augustine, Dionysius, Boethius, St. Anselm, St. Bonaventure, St. Thomas Aquinas, and John Duns Scotus. If God is not absolutely perfect and infinitely good, then God can be better than he is. However, God cannot be better than he is. Therefore, anything that was less than absolutely perfect and infinitely good cannot rightly be considered to be God. Indeed, for Catholics, authoritative Christian tradition teaches that this is so.³

One can draw out another implication of God's absolute perfection and infinite goodness: a possible world that contains an absolutely perfect and infinitely good being and some being that is less than absolutely perfect and infinitely good is no better or more valuable than a possible world that contains only an absolutely perfect and infinitely good being. Because God is absolutely perfect and infinitely good, a possible world (such as the actual world) with God in it and some creature is no better or more valuable than a possible world that contains only the absolutely perfect and infinitely good God.⁴

Proposition (a) uses the expression, *the beatific vision*, which denotes a kind of unmediated union between a human soul (or human person, or angel) and God in heaven.⁵ Something like the idea is found in Plato's *Phaedrus*, where Plato describes the separated soul's vision of beauty itself in heaven.⁶ But the idea is contained in the New Testament too. In the Sermon on the Mount, Jesus teaches: "Blessed are the pure of heart, for they shall see God."⁷ In 1 Corinthians, St. Paul contrasts the partial knowledge of God Christians have in this life with the "face to face" knowledge of God the saints have in heaven.⁸ In addition, St. John teaches, "Beloved, we are God's children now; what we will be has not yet been revealed. What we do know is this: when he is revealed, we will be like him, for we will see him as he is."⁹

Note that all of these passages speak of "seeing" God: this is explicitly so in Matthew and 1 John, and implicitly so in the passage from 1 Corin-

---

3. See, e.g., Vatican Council I, *Dei Filius*, April 24, 1870, no. 3001: "The holy, catholic, apostolic and Roman church believes and acknowledges that there is one true and living God, creator and lord of heaven and earth, almighty, eternal, immeasurable, incomprehensible, infinite in will, understanding, and every perfection." In *Decrees of the Ecumenical Councils*, ed. Norman P. Tanner (London / Washington, D.C.: Sheed and Ward / Georgetown University Press, 1990), 2:805. See chapter 4 below for more about God's absolutely perfect and infinite goodness.

4. See, e.g., Robert Pasnau, *Thomas Aquinas on Human Nature: A Philosophical Study of Summa theologiae Ia. 75–89* (Cambridge: Cambridge University Press, 2002), 402–4.

5. For discussion of the nature of human persons and the human soul, see chapter 9 below and my "Some Advantages for a Thomistic Solution to the Problem of Personal Identity beyond Death."

6. *Phaedrus* 247c–e.

7. Mt 5:8.

8. 1 Cor 13:12.

9. 1 Jn 3:2.

thians. Insofar as seeing is a bodily activity that makes use of our eyes, we might think that this "seeing" is metaphorical, because "God is spirit,"[10] that is, God is an immaterial being, and so cannot be seen with the bodily eye.[11] Rather, seeing God in heaven—what the Christian tradition calls *the beatific vision*—is an intellectual, and not a bodily, apprehension of God. That is to say, God makes himself directly present to the intellect of the person in the beatific vision.[12] Thus Pope Benedict XII can speak of the union of the saints with God in heaven in the following terms:

> By this Constitution which is to remain in force forever, we, with apostolic authority, define the following: ... Since the passion and death of the Lord Jesus Christ, these souls [of the saints in heaven, already before they take up their bodies again and before the general judgment] have seen and see the divine essence with an intuitive vision and even face to face, without the mediation of any creature by way of object of vision; rather the divine essence immediately manifests itself to them, plainly, clearly, and openly, and in this vision they enjoy the divine essence.[13]

Suppose that heaven includes the beatific vision. But why must we also think that (a) is true, that is, that heaven consists *merely* in the beatific vision? One might think that heaven consists in whatever satisfies human desire altogether.[14] That is to say, a human person in heaven is a perfectly happy human person. But surely all by itself the greatest possible union with God—the beatific vision—satisfies human desire altogether. As St. Augustine famously says in the *Confessions*, "For Thou hast made us for Thyself, and our hearts are restless till they rest in Thee,"[15] and, as St. Augustine also affirms in that same work, the one who enjoys God

---

10. Jn 4:24.

11. For more discussion of the immateriality of God and the impossibility of seeing God directly with the bodily eye, see chapters 4 and 5 below.

12. For more discussion of the beatific vision, see below in this chapter. Chapters 5–8 below treat St. Thomas's account of the beatific vision in detail.

13. *Benedictus Deus*, no. 1000, January 29, 1336, in *The Christian Faith in the Doctrinal Documents of the Catholic Church*, ed. Jacques Dupuis, 6th ed. (New York: Alba House, 1996), 942–43. See chapters 4–7 below for more on the beatific vision, especially as St. Thomas understands it.

14. For now, let us not rule out the following: person S might be perfectly satisfied or happy in possessing some good G at a stage in S's life in heaven, while S is still able, in some sense, to grow in S's possession or appreciation of G in later stages of S's life in heaven. Thanks to Mark Spencer for pointing out the need to mention this possibility here. Chapters that follow argue that this proposition is false.

15. *Confessions* I.1, trans. Frank Sheed (Indianapolis, Ind.: Hackett, 2006), 3. For the thought that St. Augustine is here teaching us that perfect human happiness is found in God alone, see also Romanus Cessario, *Introduction to Moral Theology*, rev. ed. (Washington, D.C.: The Catholic University of America Press, 2013), 34.

alone has no less than he who enjoys some creature in addition to God.¹⁶

Let us call the position on perfect human happiness that union with God in the beatific vision is both necessary and sufficient for perfect human happiness, *the Augustinian Intuition*. The Augustinian Intuition is a corollary of a proposition such as (d). To see why, note that God is not just one good on a par with, or comparable to, other good things; God—the Father, the Son, and the Holy Spirit—is absolutely perfect and infinite goodness. Consider all of the ways in which the absolutely perfect and infinitely good God could have made a use of his free will. God could have chosen not to create. Although God chose to create, he could have created a different universe from the one he created. But no matter what God chooses to do, whether to create or not, whether to create this universe or another, God is not better or happier in one of these states of affairs than another, given his own absolutely perfect and infinite goodness.

It is plausible, then, to think that the Augustinian Intuition is true. For, just as God is no better (e.g., happier) in one possible state of affairs than another, the human person S who enjoys beatific union with God alone is perfectly happy and S is no less perfectly happy in that state of affairs than S in a state of affairs where S enjoys some creaturely good in addition to beatific union with God.

We can put this argument for the Augustinian Intuition in a different way. Heaven is that reality where the intellectual creature becomes perfectly *deiform*, like unto God.¹⁷ That is to say, intellectual creatures are made perfectly happy by coming to *participate* as perfectly as logically possible in God's own perfect happiness. Mark Spencer offers the following helpful account of what it is for one being to participate in another: "when one being 'participates' in another, the latter has certain characteristics essentially, and the former has these characteristics only through the latter's formal causality; the former receives a likeness to the [latter], but has this likeness only through a real relationship with the [latter]."¹⁸ That is to say, when x participates in y, for example, St. Paul

---

16. *Confessions* V.4.

17. For more on the deiformity or glorification of the Christian, and the degree of deiformity enjoyed by the saints in heaven in particular, see chapters 8 and 17 below.

18. "The Phenomenology and Metaphysics of Spiritual Perception: A Thomistic Framework," *New Blackfriars* 97 (2016): 683. Through personal correspondence with the author, Mark Spencer has noted that the passage cited here, with the words in the square brackets, is the correct reading of the passage. In thinking about participation in this manner, Spencer cites, for example, St. Thomas's

participates in God's perfect happiness such that St. Paul enjoys perfect human happiness in heaven, a feature F of x is *what* it is through F in y, for example, St. Paul's perfect human happiness in heaven is what it is through God's own perfect happiness, where F in x is a likeness of F in y, for example, St. Paul's perfect human happiness in heaven is a likeness of God's perfect happiness, and x has F as a likeness only through a real relationship with y, for example, St. Paul has perfect human happiness as a likeness of God's perfect happiness only through a real relationship with God in St. Paul's beatific vision. Let us adopt Spencer's account of participation. Now, consider that God's own perfect happiness is not increased by his creating, knowing, and loving creatures.[19] The beatific vision is a *participation* in God's perfect happiness that is as perfect as is logically possible, so that intellectual creatures are like unto God, which entails that their own happiness is not increased by knowing and loving creatures in addition to God. Therefore, a human person having the beatific vision is perfectly happy, and is not made more perfectly happy in knowing and loving creatures in addition to having the beatific vision.

But what about goods other than union with God, such as human friendships? Do these not also have a place in heaven? And if human friendships are genuine goods—as they surely are—would the lack of such things in heaven not make us less than perfectly happy there? The citations from St. Augustine mentioned above suggests he thinks the answer to this third question is "no." But in that case, we might think the answer to the second question is "no" as well. For there simply would be no need for goods other than God in heaven. The saints would be, at best, indifferent to such goods in heaven, and, at worst, such goods would distract the saints from focusing upon "the one thing needful" (Lk 10:42). Call proposition (a)—that heaven for an intellectual creature consists merely in the beatific vision—an *individualistic* model of the nature of heaven.

Proposition (c) captures a model of the nature of heaven alternative

---

Summa Theologiae [hereafter *ST*] I, q. 44, a. 1. He also cites Gregory Doolan's *Aquinas on the Divine Ideas as Exemplar Causes* (Washington, D.C.: The Catholic University of America Press, 2014), 195–212.

19. See, e.g., Vatican Council I, *Dei Filius* I, no. 3001, in *Decrees* (ed. Tanner), 2:805: "Since [God] is one, singular, completely simple and unchangeable spiritual substance, he must be declared to be in reality and in essence, distinct from the world, supremely happy in himself and from himself.... This one true God, by his goodness and almighty power, not with the intention of increasing his happiness, nor indeed of obtaining happiness, but in order to manifest his perfection by the good things which he bestows on what he creates, by an absolutely free plan, together from the beginning of time brought into being from nothing the twofold created order, that is the spiritual and the bodily."

to the individualistic account. In what we might call a *social* model of the nature of heaven, heaven consists of a number of nested relationships. According to the social model, perfect human happiness in heaven consists not only in a relationship with God, but also in relationships with other human persons and created beings, where these relationships are perfected versions of the relationships that human persons have with God and creatures in this life. The social model of heaven is thus less otherworldly than the individualistic model, emphasizing the notion that heaven consists of a "new heaven(s) and a new earth,"[20] where "the wolf shall live with the lamb."[21]

In their detailed account of the history of Christian talk about heaven, Colleen McDannell and Bernhard Lang note that Christian accounts of heaven have tended to one of two poles: a theocentric account of heaven and an anthropocentric account, what I have called the *individualistic* model—proposition (a)—and the *social* model—proposition (c)—respectively.[22] In addition, one detects in some scholars who write about heaven from a theological or historical perspective the tendency to think about early church or medieval or neo-Scholastic theories of heaven as embracing (a) whereas contemporary eschatological theories think about heaven in terms of (c).[23] That has strengthened the sense for some theologians and philosophers that a proposition such as premise (3) of PNH-I is correct, and furthermore, that contemporary theologizing about heaven has corrected early church or medieval or neo-Scholastic accounts of heaven.[24] It has corrected such accounts insofar as those older accounts owe more to Greek philosophical accounts of the soul than to scripture,[25] or focus overmuch on "the eternal fate of the individual,"[26] or are exces-

---

20. See, e.g., Is 65:17; 2 Pt 3:13; Rv 21:1.
21. Is 11:6.
22. See the entry under "heaven" in their index (*Heaven: A History*, 405). See also Jerry Walls, *Heaven: The Logic of Eternal Joy* (Oxford: Oxford University Press, 2008), 7.
23. See, e.g., Peter C. Phan, "Roman Catholic Theology," in *The Oxford Handbook of Eschatology*, ed. Jerry L. Walls (Oxford: Oxford University Press, 2008), 215–32, esp. 216–17.
24. See, e.g., J. Richard Middleton, *A New Heaven and a New Earth: Reclaiming Biblical Eschatology* (Grand Rapids, Mich.: Baker Academic, 2014).
25. See, e.g., Phan, "Roman Catholic Theology," 216. See also N.T. Wright, *Surprised by Hope* (New York: HarperOne, 2008), 173. For arguments from scripture in defense of the Christian tradition's talk of an (immortal) soul, see, e.g., John W. Cooper, *Body, Soul, and Life Everlasting: Biblical Anthropology and the Monism-Dualism Debate* (Grand Rapids, Mich.: Eerdmans, 1989), and Matthew Levering, *Jesus and the Demise of Death: Resurrection, Afterlife, and the Fate of the Christian* (Waco, Tex.: Baylor University Press, 2012).
26. Phan, "Roman Catholic Theology," 216 and 220.

sively otherworldly,[27] while contemporary theologians have retrieved the Hebraic, social, and this-worldly accounts of heaven offered in the Old and New Testaments. For those theologians and philosophers who think that early church or medieval or neo-Scholastic views of heaven are excessively philosophical, individualistic, or otherworldly, premise (3) is true because (c) is true.

Having said something about propositions (a), (c), and (d), and premise (3) of PNH-I, let us examine proposition (b), as premise (4) consists of a conjunction of propositions (b) and (d). Proposition (b) itself has two parts: the first part of proposition (b) states that heaven has a *communal* and *cosmic* dimension, whereas the second part of proposition (b) states that heaven, at least eventually, involves the resurrection of human bodies, where those bodies are perfected, that is, minimally, they cannot fall apart, they are not subject to disease, etc.

The scriptures and Catholic Christian tradition both undeniably teach the two component parts of (b). As for part one of proposition (b), the Hebrew scriptures—particularly, the Book of Psalms—often speak of the good life as *life in the city of David, the city of Zion, or the city of Jerusalem*[28] or *the people of God gathered in worship*.[29] The New Testament[30] and authoritative, Catholic Christian tradition[31] read those texts according to the spiritual sense as pointing to heavenly life as consisting of the New Jerusalem, which itself consists of the people of God gathered in worship.[32] In addition, the New Testament often uses the image of a wedding feast to describe the kingdom of heaven.[33] Even if some aspects of the wedding feast as an image of heaven should be taken metaphorically, we may think that heaven's consisting of a community of creatures is not one such aspect. More generally, both the Old Testament (Is 65:17) and the New Testament (2 Pt 3:13 and Rv 21:1) teach that heaven involves a perfect cosmic community. In addition, authoritative, Catholic Christian tradition teaches the first part of (b).[34]

---

27. Ibid., 218 and 220.
28. See, e.g., 2 Chr 5; Pss 48, 87, 137; Sir 51:12 (Hebrew text); Is 33:20, 60:14; Mi 4:10; Zec 8:3.
29. See, e.g., 2 Chr 30:1–26.
30. See, e.g., Heb 12:22 and Rv 3:12; 21.
31. See, e.g., *The Liturgy of the Hours according to the Roman Rite*, Week II, Tuesday Morning Prayer, Psalm 65 (New York: Catholic Publishing Group, 1975), 878.
32. See Rv 5. For a concise explanation of the literal and spiritual senses of scripture, see, e.g., St. Thomas, *ST* I, q. 1, a. 10.
33. See, e.g., Mt 9:5, 22:1–14, 25:1–12; Mk 2:19; Lk 5:34, 12:36; Rv 19.
34. See, e.g., Vatican Council II, *Lumen Gentium*, November 21, 1964, no. 48; *Gaudium et Spes*,

That the New Testament and authoritative, Catholic Christian tradition teach the resurrection of the human body is also clearly true. After all, orthodox Christianity teaches the resurrection of Jesus Christ from the dead and the notion that all human beings will one day be resurrected in virtue of Christ's resurrection, and thereby (literally) stand before the judgment seat of Christ.[35] In addition, because there will be no more death, disease, or suffering in heaven, the saints in heaven will not only eventually be embodied, but, like Christ after his resurrection, will also possess *perfected* bodies.[36] Christians therefore have good reasons to accept propositions (b) and (d), and so premise (4) of PNH-I.

Having said something about propositions (a), (b), (c), and (d), I am now in a position to assess reasons for accepting premises (1) and (2) of PNH-I. Let us begin with premise (1). As shown above, because the beatific vision is a "face to face" encounter with God, and God is an immaterial being, the beatific vision is not a bodily union with God, but an intellectual one. Indeed, as *Benedictus Deus* makes clear, separated souls before the general judgment or general resurrection[37] enjoy the beatific vision. We

---

December 7, 1965, no. 39 (both available at www.vatican.va); and the *Catechism of the Catholic Church*, 2nd ed. (Vatican City: Libreria Editrice Vaticana, 1994), nos. 1042–50. As we will see, this is the teaching of St. Thomas as well. See chapters 12 and 13 below.

35. See, e.g., 1 Cor 15; 2 Cor 5:10; Eleventh Council of Toledo, Symbol of Faith (675): "Thus, according to the example of our Head, we confess that there is a true resurrection of the body for all the dead. And we do not believe that we shall rise in an ethereal body or in any other body, as some foolishly imagine, but in this very body in which we live and are and move. After having given an example of this holy resurrection, our Lord and Savior by his ascension returned to the throne of his Father from which in his divine nature he had never departed. There, seated at the right hand of the Father, he is awaited till the end of time as judge of all the living and the dead. From there he shall come with all the holy [angels and human beings] to pass judgment and to render to each one the reward due to one, according to what each one has done while in the body, whether good or evil (*cf. 2 Cor 5:10*)." In *The Christian Faith* (ed. Dupuis), 940–41. See also the Fourth Lateran Council, Symbol of Lateran (1215): "He shall come at the end of time to judge the living and the dead and to render to each one according to his works, to the reprobate [*reprobis*] as well as the elect. All of them will rise again with their own bodies which they now bear," in *The Christian Faith* (ed. Dupuis), 16; and the Second Council of Lyons, "Profession of Faith of Michael Palaeologus" (1274): "we believe also in the true resurrection of this body which we now bear, and in the life eternal," in *The Christian Faith* (ed. Dupuis), 19.

36. See, e.g., Rv 21:4; *Lumen Gentium*, no. 49; *Gaudium et Spes*, no. 18; and Paul VI, *Solemni Hac Liturgia*, Apostolic Letter, June 30, 1968, par. 28 (available at www.vatican.va).

37. The *general judgment*, or *general resurrection*, is the time, at the end of time, when all souls (with the exceptions of Christ and the Virgin Mary, who already have their bodies in heaven) are resurrected from the dead and stand before the judgement seat of Christ. For texts from authoritative, Catholic Christian tradition on the general resurrection, see, e.g., 2 Cor 5:10; The Pseudo-Athanasian Symbol, *Quicumque* ("At his coming all human beings are to rise again with their bodies"), in *The Christian Faith* (ed. Dupuis), 13; Fourth Lateran Council, Symbol of Lateran (1215); Second Council of Lyons, "Profession of Faith of Michael Palaeologus" (1274); Benedict XII, *Benedictus Deus*; Pius XII, Apostolic Constitution *Munificentissimus Deus*, November 1, 1950, pars. 4–5; and the following judgment of the Sacred Congregation for the Doctrine of the Faith on Certain Questions

might therefore think that proposition (a) is logically inconsistent with the second part of proposition (b), that is, that heaven involves human embodiment at and after the general resurrection.

But there are reasons to think that proposition (a) is also inconsistent with the first part of proposition (b). For, whatever else we want to say about the beatific vision, it is a personal union between God and any created person in heaven, and so, if heaven consists merely in the beatific vision, then heaven does not consist of something such as a new heavens and a new earth or a perfect community of human persons. We might think that, if (a) were true, at best heaven would consist of a number of created persons, where each one of these persons would be having the beatific vision, and where such created persons would not have direct friendships with one another in heaven.

Why should one think that premise (2) is true? As I said above, heaven consists in that which satisfies human desire altogether. But if (c) is true, then heaven can be construed as a whole with integral parts, where union with God is only one, even if the most important, integral part of what makes for perfect human happiness in heaven. In that case, union with God (even in the beatific vision) alone would not satisfy human desire altogether. Union with God, in that case, would be on a par with any less-than-perfect, finite, or mundane good, at least insofar as union with God in heaven, like less-than-perfect, finite, or mundane goods, is not sufficient by itself to sate all human desire. To say such a thing seems to entail that God is less than absolutely perfect and infinitely good, that is, the denial of (d).

Recall also the defense of proposition (a) that I examined above. According to that defense of (a), the beatific vision is the greatest possible union between God and a human person, and such a union satisfies human desire altogether. We might ask, "why should one think that the beatific vision satisfies human desire altogether?" Perhaps the beatific vision satisfies human desire altogether because union with God in the beatific vision is union with a being that is absolutely perfect and

---

concerning Eschatology (Letter, *Recentiores episcoporum synodi*, no. 4656 [May 17, 1979]): "In teaching her doctrine about man's destiny after death, the Church excludes any explanation that would deprive the Assumption of the Virgin Mary of its unique meaning, namely, the fact that the bodily glorification of the Virgin is an anticipation of the glorification that is the destiny of all the other elect." In Heinrich Denzinger, *Compendium of Creeds, Definitions, and Declarations on Matters of Faith and Morals*, ed. Peter Hunermann, Robert Fastiggi, and Anne Englund Nash, 43rd ed. (San Francisco, Calif.: Ignatius Press, 2012) [hereafter DH], 1027.

infinitely good. But the person who knows the absolutely perfect and infinitely good God has her desires sated. Therefore, the defense of (a) given above also provides a reason for thinking that, if proposition (d) is true, then union with God in the beatific vision *does* satisfy human desire altogether. But, in that case, because proposition (c) entails that a human person's union with God is only a necessary, but not a sufficient, condition for that person's being perfectly happy, proposition (c) is inconsistent with proposition (d).

I have suggested reasons for thinking that premises (1)–(4) are true. But (10) follows logically from premises (1)–(4). It therefore appears as though the traditional Christian account of heaven entails a contradiction. As we have seen, some contemporary thinkers seem to resolve this apparent tension in the sources of the Christian tradition by rejecting (a) and (d). Alternatively, one might respond to PNH-I by rejecting premise (3), thereby proposing a third model of blessedness, one which combines the advantages of the previously mentioned models without entailing their weaknesses. I will now examine two very different contemporary approaches to PNH-I that advocate for a model of heaven alternative to the individualistic and social models.

Germain Grisez's Third Way: Beatitude in Heaven as Kingdom of God, Not God Alone

Germain Grisez argues that the individualistic model of heaven is deeply problematic from a Christian point of view—especially a Catholic Christian perspective—and that something such as a modified social model of heaven must replace it if we are to think correctly about eschatological matters. According to Grisez, the problematic character of the individualistic model of heaven is made particularly clear by the documents of the Second Vatican Council, which documents evince a recognition of doctrinal development with respect to the nature of human beings: human beings should be understood as *persons*. Rather than a human person's perfect happiness consisting in the beatific vision alone, perfect happiness in heaven for human persons consists in membership in the kingdom of God in heaven, which includes both the beatific vision and relations with other created things, especially other created persons.[38]

---

38. See especially his "The True Ultimate End of Human Beings: The Kingdom, Not God Alone," *Theological Studies* 69 (2008): 38–61, and "Natural Law, God, Religion, and Human Fulfillment," *American Journal of Jurisprudence* 46 (2001): 3–36.

Grisez on Why Perfect Human Happiness Does Not Consist in the Beatific Vision Alone

Grisez offers a number of arguments against the view that perfect human happiness in heaven consists in the beatific vision alone, a view Grisez attributes to St. Thomas Aquinas.[39] In one of these arguments, Grisez notes that, according to those who say perfect human happiness consists merely in the beatific vision, Mary and the other saints in heaven have all of their desires sated just in virtue of having the beatific vision. Therefore, if perfect human happiness consists in the beatific vision alone, then Mary and the other saints in heaven do not desire anything, as they already enjoy the beatific vision. But one cannot sincerely ask for something if one does not desire that thing. According to scripture and authoritative Catholic tradition, Mary and the other saints in heaven ask God for things on our behalf. Therefore, it is not the case that Mary and the other saints in heaven do not desire anything. Therefore, it is not the case that perfect human happiness consists in the beatific vision alone.[40]

In another argument, Grisez notes that authoritative Christian tradition teaches both that the saints in heaven who die before the general resurrection have the beatific vision and that Christians are to hope for the resurrection of the body. If perfect human happiness consists in the beatific vision alone, then disembodied human persons—or souls—having the beatific vision are perfectly happy and so have their desires sated. But to hope for something is to desire it. Therefore, disembodied saints having the beatific vision desire embodiment and so desire something they do not currently possess. Therefore, disembodied human persons—or souls—having the beatific vision cannot be perfectly happy in

---

39. "The True Ultimate End of Human Beings." Given the focus here on discussing how Grisez would respond to PNH-I, examining all of Grisez's arguments would take us too far afield. For additional responses to Grisez's arguments on the ultimate end of human persons, see, e.g., Brandon Dahm, "Distinguishing Desire and Parts of Happiness: A Response to Grisez," *American Catholic Philosophical Quarterly* 89 (2015): 97–114; Ezra Sullivan, "Seek First the Kingdom: A Reply to Germain Grisez's Account of Man's Ultimate End," *Nova et Vetera* (English edition) 8 (2010): 959–95; and Benedict Ashley, "Integral Human Fulfillment According to Germain Grisez," in his *The Ashley Reader: Redeeming Reason* (Naples, Fla.: Sapientia Press, 2006), 225–69. For a book-length argument that objections such as Grisez's are founded on an overly simplistic reading of St. Thomas's texts on the natural desire to see God, see Lawrence Feingold, *The Natural Desire to See God according to St. Thomas and His Interpreters*, 2nd ed. (Naples, Fla.: Sapientia Press, 2010). See also Denis Bradley's *Aquinas on the Two-Fold Human Good: Reason and Human Happiness in Aquinas's Moral Science* (Washington, D.C.: The Catholic University of America Press, 1997), 424–81.

40. "The True Ultimate End of Human Beings," 46–47.

the sense of not having desire. Therefore, it is not the case that perfect human happiness consists in the beatific vision alone.[41]

Grisez on Perfect Human Happiness in Heaven

Grisez describes his own account of perfect human happiness in terms of "integral communal fulfillment."[42] In order to understand what Grisez means, a few words about his philosophy of human action are in order. Grisez thinks that there are certain "fundamental goods" for human persons, knowledge of which are self-evident first principles of human action that "direct us indiscriminately toward the well-being and flourishing of ourselves and everyone else."[43] The fundamental goods include *life*, which itself includes health and bodily integrity, *skillful work*, *play*, *knowledge*, *aesthetic experience*, *harmony with God*, *harmony among human beings*, *harmony between one's own faculties* (e.g., harmony with one's own judgements, choices, feelings, and behavior), *marriage*, and *parenthood*.[44] Because grace perfects and does not set aside nature, the graced and perfect human life of heaven includes the perfection of all these fundamental goods for human persons.

In Grisez's view, Christian theologians have not always explicitly recognized the importance of all of these fundamental goods in offering their accounts of heavenly bliss. According to Grisez, "Vatican II takes into account elements of New Testament eschatology previously hardly considered in the church's teachings and explains how promoting and protecting any fundamental human good is relevant to the kingdom."[45] On Grisez's reading of the documents of Vatican II, the Council teaches that God alone is not the object of perfect human happiness, attained in the beatific vision. Rather, the object of perfect human happiness is "integral communal fulfillment in God's kingdom, which will be a marvelous communion of divine Persons, human persons, and other created persons."[46] In fact, perfect human happiness in heaven not only includes the fundamental good of relations to other persons, but also includes the perfection of the other fundamental goods, including knowledge, aesthetic experience, and play.[47]

41. Ibid., 49–51.
42. Ibid., 57.
43. Ibid., 54.
44. Ibid.
45. Ibid., 58.
46. Ibid., 58–59.
47. Ibid., 59.

What, then, is the logical relation between the beatific vision and perfect human happiness in heaven, according to Grisez? Because Grisez thinks there are component parts to perfect human happiness in heaven for human beings other than harmony with God in the beatific vision, union with God alone, in his view, is not that in which perfect human happiness consists. Nonetheless, Grisez can say, "the beatific vision will fulfill human persons. Integral communal fulfillment includes human persons' harmony with God, a fundamental good of human persons that can be realized less and more."[48] In addition, as blessed as Christians in this life are when they live in accord with the beatitudes, Grisez notes that "still more blessed are they, when purified, they see God: even before resurrection, they 'are truly blessed and have everlasting life and rest' (Benedict XII, *Benedictus Deus*, DS 1000)."[49] It is fair to say that Grisez takes the beatific vision and its effects on the soul to be a *central* component part of the perfect human good in heaven. In fact, Grisez is also at pains to note that his view does *not* entail that there are any aspects of human beatitude in heaven that human persons have apart from God. Even if perfect human happiness does not consist in the beatific vision alone, any fundamental goods distinct from God enjoyed by human persons in heaven are nonetheless possessed in heaven "in God" or "within ... their joyful intimacy with the divine Persons."[50]

48. Ibid., 59–60.
49. Ibid., 60.
50. Ibid., 61. For some development of Grisez's critique of the individualistic model of human happiness in heaven, see Christopher O. Tollefsen, "First- and Third-Person Standpoints in the New Natural Law Theory," in *Subjectivity: Ancient and Modern*, ed. R. J. Snell and Steven F. McGuire (Lanham, Md.: Lexington Books, 2016), 95–113. Tollefsen thinks that Grisez's rejection of the individualistic model of blessedness can be expressed as follows: the individualistic model of heaven (again, attributed to St. Thomas) is problematic insofar as it is a purely third-person account of desire and perfect human happiness, one that is blind to the first-person perspective, and acknowledgment of the first-person perspective of human persons, and their desires for *human* goods from such a perspective, is necessary in order to give a capacious account of perfect human happiness in heaven and reasons for desiring heaven in the first place. According to Tollefsen, Grisez's view that perfect human happiness consists in membership in the kingdom of God is a successful model of perfect human happiness insofar as it does take into account both first-personal and third-personal perspectives on human desire (thanks to Mark Spencer for pointing out Tollefsen's paper). For a critique of the idea that St. Thomas thinks about the satisfaction of desire only in terms of the third-person perspective, see Eleonore Stump, *Wandering in Darkness: Narrative and the Problem of Suffering* (Oxford: Clarendon Press, 2010), 85–128. For a critique of Tollefsen's emphasis on the importance of the first-person perspective in thinking about human desire and heaven, see Paul J. Griffiths, *Decreation: The Last Things of All Creatures* (Waco, Tex.: Baylor University Press, 2014), 222–40, and the discussion of Griffiths's arguments in chapter 2 below. Finally, see chapter 17 below for a Thomistic explanation of how perfect human happiness consisting essentially in the beatific vision can satisfy the desires of human persons, even given the kinds of desires human persons have in this life.

Grisez on PNH-I

How will someone with Grisez's views on beatitude in heaven respond to PNH-I? Recall the four assumptions at play in PNH-I:

(1) The notion that (a) heaven for an intellectual creature consists merely of the beatific vision is in conflict with the notion that (b) heaven includes the reality of "the new heavens and the new earth," which itself includes a perfect human community, and, at least eventually, perfected embodiment on the part of human person in the next life [assumption].

(2) The notion that (c) heaven consists merely of a perfect cosmic community, that is, "the new heavens and the new earth," which includes a perfect human community, overseen by a good and gracious God, is in conflict with the notion that (d) God is absolutely perfect and infinitely good [assumption].

(3) (a) or (c) [assumption].

(4) (b) and (d) [assumption].

Clearly, Grisez accepts (1) and (b) and so rejects (a). He also accepts (d) and thus accepts premise (4). In order to avoid contradiction, then, someone with Grisez's views needs to reject (c), and so premise (3), or needs to reject premise (2), that is, that (c) and (d) are inconsistent. Although Grisez's third way between the individualist and social models of heaven has him decidedly leaning in the direction of the social model—proposition (c)—Grisez accepts that human fulfillment in the kingdom of God in heaven requires union with the God who is absolutely perfect and infinitely good.

Problems for Grisez's Solution to PNH-I

There are at least two problems for Grisez's third way.[51] First, given his account of perfect human happiness as the perfect possession of the fundamental goods, Grisez will have to say something awkward about the nature of God. Whether someone with Grisez's views rejects proposition (c), and so premise (3), or rejects premise (2), we can revise premise (2) of PNH-I in a way that puts pressure on Grisez's third way. Consider the following revision of premise (2) of PNH-I:

---

51. Chapter 9 below contains defeaters for Grisez's criticisms of St. Thomas's views on perfect human happiness.

(2*) The notion that (c*) perfect happiness for human persons consists of the perfect possession of the set of fundamental goods for human persons, where the beatific vision is merely the central of these fundamental goods is in conflict with the notion that (d) God is absolutely perfect and infinitely good [assumption].

Grisez accepts (d). Although he would be at pains to reject (2*), it is not clear that he reasonably can. If God is absolutely perfect and infinitely good, then the Augustinian Intuition follows: the one who enjoys God alone is no less perfectly happy, all other things being equal, than one who enjoys some creature in addition to God. Therefore, it is not the case that perfect happiness for human persons consists of the perfect possession of the set of fundamental goods for human persons, where the beatific vision is merely the central of these fundamental goods. Therefore, (2*) is true. Because Grisez clearly accepts (c*), Grisez's third way entails the rejection of (d). However, not only does Grisez accept (d), and so his position is inconsistent with itself, but, as we have seen, (d) is proclaimed as true by authoritative, Catholic Christian tradition.

A second problem for Grisez's third way is that Grisez suggests that perfected versions of all the fundamental goods of human life exist in heaven.[52] But, according to authoritative Christian tradition, some of the fundamental human goods in this life do not exist in heaven. For example, Jesus says, "in the resurrection, they neither marry nor are given in marriage, but are like the angels in heaven."[53] Given the context, which is an answer to the thought experiment of the Sadducees—concerning a woman who has been lawfully married to seven brothers in this life, whose wife will she be in the resurrection?—Christ teaches here that there is no marriage in heaven. Grisez is thus wrong to think that heaven for human persons is the perfection of the members of that set of fundamental human goods that human persons enjoy in this life.[54]

---

52. See, e.g., "The True Ultimate End of Human Beings," 58.
53. Mt 22:30. See also Mk 12:25 and Lk 20:35–36.
54. Grisez is aware of the objection and responds to it in his *Way of the Lord Jesus*, vol. 2: *Living a Christian Life* (Quincy, Ill.: Franciscan, 1993): 607–9. But his response—that marriage endures in heaven insofar as all the saints in heaven enjoy a nonconjugal one-flesh communion with Christ and the other saints—appears to either change the subject or treat marriage as if it is not a fundamental good after all.

Katherin Rogers's Anselmian Third Way

In a recent article, Katherin Rogers has suggested an Anselmian way of responding to what I have defined as PNH-I.[55] Rogers begins by noting that although Christians can know some things about heaven by faith, given what is taught by scripture and authoritative, Christian tradition, the "traditional Christian doctrine regarding heaven is mysterious."[56] That being said, Rogers tentatively proposes an Anselmian response to a problem such as PNH-I. Rogers first makes clear that, in her view, St. Anselm clearly teaches that heaven consists in the beatific vision. So, insofar as we think that Christian tradition has proposed two different models of heavenly life, the beatific vision, on the one hand, and a perfected version of earthly life, on the other, she says, "it would be a mistake to place Anselm's heaven half way along the spectrum, since it very clearly consists in the beatific vision."[57]

But Rogers thinks that a problem such as PNH-I presents a false dichotomy insofar as the saints in heaven enjoy created goods such as the communion of the saints *through* enjoying the beatific vision. What does the saint in heaven see in the beatific vision? Not only God, but also what God creates. So, insofar as the saint sees God in the beatific vision, the saint in heaven also sees all creatures, including herself and the other saints, too.

It is not clear, however, that Rogers's middle way offers a complete solution to PNH-I. Let us grant the point that in having the beatific vision, one also knows the creatures that God has made. We might think it is one thing to know a creature in virtue of knowing God and another thing to experience that creature in and of itself. For all she has said, then, premise (1) may still be true. However, we might think that heaven also consists of a communion of the saints where human persons know and love one another *directly*, and not simply mediately by way of knowing the essence of God in the beatific vision. Or to put the point another way, heaven involves not just having objective knowledge of creatures in virtue of having a subjective experience of God, but subjective experiences of creatures themselves. Insofar as we believe that heaven consists of the

---

55. "Anselmian Meditations on Heaven," in *Paradise Understood* (ed. Byerly and Silverman), 30–47.
56. Ibid., 30.
57. Ibid., 33.

beatific vision and we also think that (b) is true, Rogers's middle way does not provide a perfect resolution to PNH-I.

PNH-II: OTHERWORLDLY HEAVEN OR THIS-WORLDLY PARADISE?

Consider another apparent tension in the Christian tradition. On the one hand, there is the Christian teaching that heaven is something transcendent or otherworldly insofar as heaven is an immaterial or incorruptible or impassible reality. On the other hand, there is the Christian teaching that human persons have *human*, that is, resurrected, bodies in heaven. This tension between the transcendent and the immanent will be particularly pronounced if we think with authoritative, Catholic Christian tradition that a human person in heaven not only has a human body in heaven, but also has numerically the same body that that human person possesses in this life.[58] We can thus formulate an apparent issue for the Christian tradition called *the second problem concerning the nature of heaven* (PNH-II):

(11) The notion that (e) heaven is otherworldly insofar as it involves *the beatific vision*, that is, an immaterial union between immaterial God and the immaterial soul, is in conflict with the notion that (f) human persons are essentially temporal beings or the notion that (g) the resurrected bodies of the saints in heaven are numerically and specifically the same as the bodies human persons have in this life, for example, bodies that are constantly changing, are corruptible, take up space, etc. [assumption].

(12) The notion that (h) heaven is otherworldly insofar as *the resurrected bodies of the saints in heaven are spiritual, incorruptible, and immortal in heaven* is in conflict with the notion that (g) the resurrected bodies of the saints in heaven are numerically and specifically the same as the bodies that human persons have in this life, for example, bodies that are constantly changing, are corruptible, take up space, etc. [assumption].

(13) Proposition (f) is true [assumption].

(14) Authoritative, Christian tradition affirms (e), (g), and (h) [assumption].

---

58. See, e.g., the texts cited in notes 35 and 37 above.

(15) Therefore, the Christian tradition's account of heaven entails a contradiction [from (11)–(14)].

Motivating the Premises of PNH-II

As with PNH-I, PNH-II has premises that contain propositions which require some explanation as to their meaning. The propositions that figure in the assumptions of PNH-II are (e), (f), (g), and (h). Let us begin with (e).

The nature of heaven in the Christian tradition has, at the very least, some otherworldly elements. I have already spoken of the beatific vision, which is the saint in heaven's direct and intuitive union with immaterial God. We might think that, because God is an immaterial being and seeing God involves a direct and intuitive union between the created person *qua* immaterial having the vision and immaterial God, even if an embodied person can enjoy the beatific vision, that person's body itself would play no role in the beatific vision. The beatific vision would then be a kind of out-of-body experience (even for those who are embodied).

In addition to the apparent otherworldly character of the beatific vision, Christian tradition teaches that the resurrected bodies of the saints are spiritual, immortal, and incorruptible.[59] But this-worldly human bodies are non-spiritual, mortal, and corruptible. Thus, as proposition (h) states, Christian tradition's account of the resurrection body is also otherworldly.

Whatever else we human persons are, we seem to be essentially temporal beings. That is, we are essentially beings that change and experience the passage of time. So says proposition (f). Proposition (f)—and so the truth of premise (13)—would thus seem to need no further explanation, or defense, than our everyday experience of ourselves. Of course, the experience of time is presumably decidedly different for those in "the new heavens and the new earth." (We might think that boredom is impossible there. Perhaps time is also measured differently.) But whatever the experience of human persons in heaven, presumably there is still something like the experience of before and after, and so time.

---

59. See, e.g., 1 Cor 15:42–53 and Rv 21:1–4. See also Christian creeds as early as ca. 348 A.D., which include a confession of belief in *the life everlasting*. Finally, the otherworldly quality of the resurrected bodies of the saints is even more pronounced for those theologians, such as St. Thomas Aquinas, who think the resurrected bodies of the saints are *glorified*, i.e., impassible, subtle, agile, and luminescent. See chapter 11 below for discussion of St. Thomas on glorified bodies.

The saints in heaven will eventually have *resurrected* bodies. Scripture[60] and Christian tradition[61] both clearly teach this doctrine. But Catholic Christian tradition also gives resurrection a more specific meaning, which is captured in proposition (g): a saint's resurrection body in heaven is specifically and numerically the same as that saint's body in this life.[62] To say that the saint's body in heaven is *specifically* the same body as the saint's body in this life is to say that the saint's body is a *human* body, and not a nonhuman body such as a body made of some otherworldly substance. To say that the saint's body in heaven is *numerically the same* body as the saint's body in this life is to say that the saint in heaven is not resurrected with a human body numerically distinct from the human body that saint possessed in this life. In other words, as Christian tradition has it, the resurrection of the saints conforms to the model of Christ's resurrection, and Christ's resurrected body is numerically the same body that suffered on the cross and was three days in the tomb.

I noted above some reasons for thinking that premise (13) of PNH-II is true. Should we accept premise (14)? We have seen that Christian tradition teaches the truth of propositions (g) and (h). But authoritative, Catholic Christian tradition has also not been silent on the beatific vision being a chief aspect of heavenly life for rational creatures such as ourselves.[63]

Consider two arguments in defense of premise (11) of PNH-II. First, we might wonder about the practical compatibility of a human person's enjoying the beatific vision and the possession of a this-worldly kind of bodily life in heaven. For as Plato, Jesus, and St. Paul all attest about human bodily life in this life, "the spirit is willing, but the flesh is weak." If heavenly life consists (essentially or chiefly) in a beatific vision, a perfect joining of the saint's mind to God in perpetual contemplation, from whence flows perfect joy, would a body like ours that hungers, thirsts,

---

60. See, e.g., 1 Cor 15:12–58.
61. See the texts cited in notes 35 and 37 above.
62. See the texts cited in notes 35 and 37 above.
63. See, e.g., Benedict XII, *Benedictus Deus*; General Council of Florence, Decree for the Greeks, no. 1305 (1439); Pope Leo XIII, *Divinum Illud*, Encyclical Letter, May 9, 1897, par. 3331; Pope Pius XII, *Mystici Corporis*, Encyclical Letter, June 29, 1943, par. 3815; Pope Paul VI, *Solemni Hac Liturgia*, par. 29; and the judgment of the Sacred Congregation for the Doctrine of the Faith, Letter (on Certain Questions concerning Eschatology), *Recentiores Episcoporum Synodi*, no. 4656 (May 17, 1979). See also the *Catechism of the Catholic Church*, nos. 1023–24, 1028, 1053, 1720–22, and 1726.

and desires not be, at best, superfluous, and at worst, a distraction? Proposition (e) appears to conflict with proposition (g).

Second, consider the possibility that the beatific vision is a kind of participation in God's eternal life. Such a view seems to conflict with the temporal mode of human existence—proposition (f). For human persons exist in time in this life. Being temporal is an essential feature of any substance that has that property, but the beatific vision as a kind of participation in God's eternal life is a nontemporal activity.[64] Therefore, there seems to be a conflict between the idea that human happiness in heaven consists in the beatific vision, at least insofar as it is construed as a participation in God's eternal life, and a basic truth about the nature of human persons. Because proposition (e) conflicts with (f) or (g), premise (11) is true.

Lynne Rudder Baker offers an argument in defense of premise (12). She begins her argument by noting that our bodies in this life are *human* bodies: they are mortal, corruptible, and cannot survive without food, drink, and oxygen. But our resurrection bodies are not human bodies, because, as St. Paul teaches (1 Cor 15:42–53), resurrection bodies will be *spiritual*, both immortal and incorruptible. Therefore, according to scripture, our bodies in this life and our bodies at and after the resurrection have different persistence conditions. But a thing's persistence conditions are among its essential properties. In addition, if x and y have different essential properties, then x and y are not numerically identical. Therefore, our bodies in this life are not numerically identical to resurrection bodies in the next life. Rudder Baker thus takes St. Paul quite literally when he contrasts this-worldly human bodies, which are biological, with the *spiritual* bodies of the next life.[65] There seems, therefore, to be a problem with thinking about *even our bodies* in heaven in this-worldly terms.

I have offered defenses of premises (11)–(14) of PNH-II, which premises, taken together, entail a contradiction. According to PNH-II, there appears to be a real tension between the otherworldly and this-worldly confessions of the Catholic Christian tradition concerning the nature of heaven.

---

64. As we will see, this is an aspect of St. Thomas's view of the beatific vision. See chapter 7 below.

65. See, e.g., "Persons and the Metaphysics of Resurrection," *Religious Studies* 43, no. 3 (2007): 333–48. For a similar view, see Uwe Meixner, "The Indispensability of the Soul," in *Die menschliche Seele: Brauchen wir den Dualismus?*, ed. Bruno Niederberger and Edmund Runggaldier (Heusenstamm: Ontos Verlag, 2006), 39.

Lynne Rudder Baker's Modified Traditionalism as a Partial Response to PNH-II

As we saw above, Lynne Rudder Baker accepts premise (12) and proposition (h) insofar as she thinks that the bodies of the saints in heaven will be spiritual, immortal, and incorruptible. In order to avoid contradiction, Baker rejects proposition (g). In what sense, then, is she a *traditionalist* Christian philosopher? In speaking about the resurrection of the body, Baker is careful to talk about time-honored Christian traditions with respect to the doctrine of the resurrection of the body. For example, she argues that a *Christian* way of speaking about the next life must include three elements. First, Christian belief about the next life requires belief that persons in this life are numerically identical to persons in the next; psychological *similarity* is not enough. Second, our life in the next life involves embodiment. Plato is wrong to think about heaven as a wholly immaterial reality. Third, the resurrection of the dead is not something natural, but miraculous.[66]

Is holding these three beliefs about the next life sufficient for a *traditional Christian* account of the next life? Possibly. Baker clearly defends traditional Christian beliefs about the next life. But her traditionalism is also clearly selective, because authoritative Catholic Christian tradition clearly also accepts the view that our *bodies* at and after the resurrection are specifically and numerically the same as our bodies in this life, which view Baker clearly rejects. Baker's selective appropriation of the Christian tradition on the nature of heaven is a significant limitation for her partial solution to PNH-II.[67]

---

66. "Persons and the Metaphysics of Resurrection," 339–40.
67. Assuming that Rudder Baker never commented upon a premise such as (11) in print, this chapter thus describes her solution to PNH-II as a *partial* solution.

2

Contemporary Philosophy and Theology and a Third Problem concerning the Nature of Heaven

STATIC OR DYNAMIC REALITY?

Some of our contemporaries worry that heaven would be boring, perhaps because heaven is often portrayed in the popular imagination as sitting on a cloud, playing a harp, and worshipping God.[1] David Byrne suggests he experiences such a worry in the late 1970s art-pop song "Heaven," when he sings, "heaven is a place where nothing, nothing ever happens."[2] However, perfect happiness for human persons requires that they are *doing* something *interesting*. To put the point in another way, heaven must, it seems, be a constantly changing, dynamic reality, rather than an immutable, static one. Because some Christian theologians have offered reasons for thinking that heaven is an immutable reality, at least in some sense, that suggests a third apparent problem concerning the nature of heaven, one which I will call *the third problem concerning the nature of heaven* (PNH-III):

(1) The notion that (i) heaven is static is in conflict with the notion that (b) heaven includes the reality of "the new heavens and the new

---

1. Of course, this popular picture is itself rooted in scriptural accounts of individual and corporate worship of God throughout the Old Testament (see, e.g., 2 Sm 6:5; 1 Kgs 10:12; 1 Chr 13:8; 1 Chr 15; 1 Chr 16:5; 1 Chr 25:1–7; 2 Chr 5:12; 2 Chr 9:11; 2 Chr 20:28; 2 Chr 29:25; Neh 12:27; 1 Mc 3:45; 1 Mc 4:54; 1 Mc 13:51; Ps 33:2; Ps 43:4; Ps 57:8; Ps 71:22; Ps 81:1–2; Ps 92:1–4; Ps 108:2; Ps 144:9; Ps 150:3; and Sir 39:12–15) and the Book of Revelation (see, e.g., 5:8, 14:2, 15:2). Perhaps we also have here a popular picture of the traditional Christian view that perfect human happiness in heaven consists essentially in the beatific vision.

2. Talking Heads, *Fear of Music*, Sire Records SRK-6076, 1979, compact disc. For an interesting discussion of the meaning of the song with David Byrne, one of the writers of the song, see Lisa Miller, *Heaven: Our Enduring Fascination with the After-Life* (New York: HarperCollins, 2010), 207.

earth," which itself includes a perfect human community, and, at least eventually, perfected embodiment on the part of human persons in the next life and the notion that (j) if there is a human person S in heaven, then S is flourishing [assumption].

(2) The notion that (k) heaven is dynamic, that is, not static, is in conflict with the notion that (a) heaven for intellectual creatures consists merely in the beatific vision and the notion that (l) human persons in heaven are perfectly happy [assumption].

(3) (i) is true or (k) is true [assumption].

(4) [(b) is true or (j) is true] and [(a) is true or (l) is true] [assumption].

(5) Therefore, [if (b), then ~ (i)] and [if (j), then ~ (i)] [from (1), by Trans.].

(6) Therefore, ~ (i) [from (4) and (5), by DE].

(7) Therefore, [if (a), then ~ (k)] and [if (l), then ~ (k)] [from (2), by Trans.].

(8) Therefore, ~ (k) [from (4) and (7), by DE].

(9) Therefore, ~ (i) and ~ (k) [from (6 and (8), by Add.].

(10) Therefore, the traditional Christian account of heaven entails a contradiction [from (3) and (9)].

Of course, PNH-III is only a potential problem for the Christian theologian or philosopher if she accepts premises (1)–(4). Should she?

MOTIVATING THE PREMISES OF PNH-III

In order to motivate premises (1)–(4) in PNH-III, we first need to understand the component propositions of those premises. Let us begin with propositions (i) and (k). In a very interesting recent article, philosopher Eric Silverman suggests we distinguish *static views* of heaven and *dynamic views* of heaven as follows:

Static views of heaven (SV): "conceptions of heaven that portray paradise as a place or state of existence where there is no further moral, aesthetic, epistemological, relational, and other change or progress for the inhabitants of heaven."[3]

Dynamic views of heaven (DV): "conceptions of heaven that depict

---

3. "Conceiving Heaven as a Dynamic Rather than Static Existence," in *Paradise Understood* (ed. Byerly and Silverman), 14. See also Tim Pawl and Kevin Timpe, "Paradise and Growing in Virtue," in ibid., 107.

paradise as a place or a state of existence where moral, aesthetic, epistemological, relational, and other changes or progress takes place."[4]

Silverman takes these accounts to be "mutually exclusive and jointly exhaustive."[5] But consider one natural way of reading SV and DV:

(SV*): *conceptions of heaven that portray paradise as a place or state of existence where* there is no further moral change or progress *and* there is no further aesthetic change or progress *and* there is no further epistemological change or progress *and* there is no further relational change or progress *and* there is no other change or progress *for the creaturely inhabitants of heaven.*

(DV*): *conceptions of heaven that depict paradise as a place or a state of existence where* there are moral changes or progress *and* there are aesthetic changes or progress *and* there are epistemological changes or progress *and* there are relational changes or progress *and* there are other changes or progress *for the creaturely inhabitants of heaven.*

However, SV* and DV* are *not* jointly exhaustive conceptions of heaven, as we may imagine possible conceptions of heaven where there are *only some* sorts of changes or progress in heaven, for example, consider a conception of heaven where there is *epistemological* change or progress there, but no *moral* change or progress. That conception would satisfy neither SV* nor DV*.

As both PNH-III and Silverman's discussion of the nature of heaven clearly trade on there being two mutually exclusive and jointly exhaustive accounts of heaven, let us interpret SV as SV* and modify DV as follows:[6]

(DV**): *conceptions of heaven that depict paradise as a place or a state of existence where* there are moral changes or progress *or* there are aesthetic changes or progress *or* there are epistemological changes or progress *or*

---

4. "Conceiving Heaven," 18.
5. Ibid., 18n2.
6. One may worry about using the word "static" to pick out the view described in SV and SV* insofar as "static," used as a word to describe reality, has a negative connotation, and, given the classical view of God, God's life is not characterized by change or progress of any kind, and God's life is a happy one if any being's is. Therefore, use of the word "static" to pick out a conception of heaven that does not involve change or progress is misleading at best and rhetorically pernicious at worst. For a contemporary philosopher who shares this concern, see Rogers, "Anselmian Meditations on Heaven," 38–39. For more discussion of this point, see this chapter, as well as chapters 4, 7, and 16 below.

there are relational changes or progress *or* there are other changes or progress *for the creaturely inhabitants of heaven.*[7]

I have offered some provisional definitions of "static views of heaven" and "dynamic views of heaven," and so have clarified the meanings of propositions (i) and (k). I have spoken about the meaning of propositions (a) and (b)—and reasons someone might think that those propositions are true—in chapter 1, above. I will now turn to examining propositions (j) and (l).

The meaning, and truthfulness, of proposition (j) is straightforward. However we conceive of the nature of heaven, if a human person exists in heaven, then that human person is happy, or is living a good human life, or is flourishing as a member of the human species. Proposition (j) states that *if there are human persons in heaven, then they are happy or flourishing*, while proposition (l) makes a stronger claim: human persons in heaven are not only happy or flourishing, they are *perfectly* happy. We might think that a human person is rightly described as *happy*, or *living a good life*, even though that person does not have everything she wants. For example, Sarah has a good and loving husband, her children are obedient, creative, and loving, she is healthy, and she helps to support her family financially by engaging in extremely fulfilling work. She prays deeply and habitually. She is living a good human life. Sarah is happy. Even so, she does not know everything she wants to know, she does not love as well as she wants to love, etc. She also realizes that her this-worldly happiness is fragile, as she might outlive her children, she might lose her own good health, or she might make some bad moral choices in the future. Although Sarah *is* happy, she is not *perfectly* happy. But whatever else is true about heaven, the following is true: human persons in heaven are perfectly happy, that is, they act, know, and love such that there is nothing else they would want to add to their acting, knowing, and loving, and they have no fear of losing the happiness they possess.

We are now in a position to examine some defenses of the assumptions of PNH-III. Let us begin with premise (1). If bodily existence is a feature of heavenly life, as proposition (b) of (1) states, then we may think that heavenly life involves movement and change, for human bodies necessarily move and change. That is *not* to say that human bodies in

---

7. Silverman seems to assume something such as DV** as the correct reading of his dynamic view of heaven. See "Conceiving Heaven," 18n2.

heaven would have to move and change in all the ways they do so in this life (e.g., perhaps resurrected bodies no longer need to breathe or circulate blood). But, if heavenly life involves the possession of *human bodies*, as Catholic Christian tradition suggests, then heaven involves some change or movement. Propositions (i) and (b) are *prima facie* logically inconsistent with one another.

Someone may suggest that it is false that human bodies necessarily move and change. Nonetheless, surely human bodies that did not move and change at all would be less than perfect *qua* human body. So if heavenly life involves the possession of *perfect* human bodies, then (i) is not true. The importance of *mutability* for a perfect human *bodily* life applies more generally to the notion that human *persons* are flourishing. We might think that not only does the possession of a perfect human body in heaven require a nonstatic heavenly existence, but also the psychological experience of a happy human person in heaven could not be static either. Whether because such a life would be boring or tedious, or for some other reason—for example, we may think human persons by nature always need new challenges in order to see their lives as worth living—a *flourishing* human life needs to be dynamic and not merely static. Thus, we have some reasons for thinking that propositions (i) and (j) are logically inconsistent. As (i) is apparently incompatible with both (b) and (j), premise (1) is apparently true.

Why should one think that premise (2) is true? Let us begin with the relevance of (a). A Christian philosopher may follow St. Augustine in thinking that the beatific vision is an immutable cognition of God.[8] For example, David Brown argues that in heaven, "man can ... partake in God's timelessness, and so it is meaningless to speak of any temporal measure of change."[9] But (we might think) an immutable cognition of S is a static experience.[10] Therefore, (k) and (a) are logically inconsistent.

As for the thought that (k) and (l) are logically inconsistent, consider the following argument: if a person named Susan is perfectly happy, then Susan's desires are entirely satisfied. If Susan's desires were entirely satisfied, then Susan would have no good reason to change. But if persons act such that they change in heaven, then they act with good reasons to change in heaven, if anywhere. Therefore, insofar as human persons are perfectly happy in heaven, they do not change.

---

8. See, e.g., *De trinitate* XV.
9. "No Heaven without Purgatory," *Religious Studies* 21 (1985): 447–56, esp. 448.
10. But see note 6 in this chapter above.

Alternatively, consider the following argument. We might think that if Theresa changes, then Theresa changes because she is aiming to acquire a good she does not currently possess. In that case, if Theresa's life in heaven is a dynamic and changing one, then Theresa not only aims at becoming happier in heaven through her actions, but she becomes happier the more time she spends in heaven. We might also think that if Theresa is happier at time t than she was at $t-1$, then she is not perfectly happy at $t-1$. Theresa, at $t-1$, either realizes that she will be happier at time t than she is at $t-1$ or she does not. If Theresa does not realize that at $t-1$ she will be happier at t than she is at $t-1$, then, at $t-1$, Theresa is ignorant of an important fact about herself. However, if Theresa is ignorant of an important fact about herself at $t-1$, then she is not *perfectly* happy at $t-1$. If Theresa does realize at $t-1$ that she will be happier at t, then, at $t-1$, Theresa desires something she does not yet possess at $t-1$, namely, the greater happiness she will possess at t. Therefore, if Theresa realizes that at $t-1$ she will be happier at t than she is at $t-1$, then Theresa is not perfectly happy at $t-1$. Therefore, if the life of a human person in heaven is a perpetually dynamic and changing one, then that person is never perfectly happy in heaven.[11] Therefore, (k) and (l) are logically inconsistent.

Premise (3) is necessarily true, at least on the assumption that heaven is real, because (i) and (k) are logical contraries. As far as premise (4) is concerned, I have already examined reasons for thinking propositions (a) and (b) are true in chapter 1. I take the truth of proposition (j) to be self-evident, in the sense that, as soon as one understands the meaning of the words in that proposition, one accepts the truth of that proposition.

What about proposition (l) in premise (4)? Even if one rejects the individualistic model of heaven—and so rejects (a)— one may very well think that a person in heaven enjoys whatever it is that will make that

---

11. Mark Spencer points out that some Eastern Church Fathers, e.g., St. Gregory of Nyssa, have an account of desire different from the account of desire assumed here. Whereas the argument above assumes that if John *desires x* at time t, then John is not perfectly happy at t—following the lead of Plato (see, e.g., *Symposium* 200b), St. Augustine, and St. Thomas (see, e.g., *ST* I, q. 19, a. 1, ad 2)—St. Gregory thinks that one could be perfectly happy in possessing God in heaven, while also desiring to grow ever closer to God. In this case, desire for greater union with God grows with one's growing satisfaction in possessing God. As God is the infinite good, the saint in heaven will never stop growing closer to, and so desiring greater union with, God. For some contemporary philosophers who draw on this Nyssian account of desire and apply it to talk about perfect human happiness in heaven, see, e.g., Pawl and Timpe, "Incompatibilism, Sin, and Free Will in Heaven," *Faith and Philosophy* 26 (2009): 398–419. See also their "Paradise and Growing in Virtue," 97–109. For a critique of this Nyssian view, see below in this chapter.

person perfectly happy, for example, the beatific vision plus another good G. Insofar as (b) and (j) are both true, and (a) or (l) is true, premise (4) is true.

A FIRST CONTEMPORARY SOLUTION TO PNH-III: ERIC SILVERMAN ON A DYNAMIC VIEW OF HEAVEN

In addition to distinguishing static and dynamic views of heaven, Eric Silverman also describes a particular understanding of dynamism in heaven such that the saints in heaven undergo perpetual moral *and* aesthetic *and* epistemological *and* relational progress in heaven, not only with respect to other creatures, but with respect to God as well.[12] I will call such an account of heaven a *totally dynamic* (TD) view of the nature of heaven. Silverman also offers interesting arguments for preferring a dynamic view of heaven, in general, to a static account, and he also appears to offer arguments for preferring a TD view of the nature of heaven to other dynamic accounts.[13]

Silverman on *Paradiso* XXXIII

Silverman begins his defense of a dynamic or TD view of heaven by noting that important theologians and philosophers have defended a dynamic view of heaven. For example, according to Silverman, Dante Alighieri offers a "Thomistic account of paradise [that] includes at least one very important dynamic element."[14] On the basis of *Paradiso* XXXIII.106–14, Silverman argues that Dante thinks that blessed souls in heaven are perpetually changed as they enjoy the beatific vision of the eternal and immutable one God in three Persons.[15]

---

12. "Conceiving Heaven."
13. Even if he does not intend to argue for the TD view, this chapter examines what I will call Silvermanian arguments for, and defenses of, a TD view of heaven, arguments that are developed in the spirit of Silverman's arguments in "Conceiving Heaven."
14. "Conceiving Heaven," 18.
15. One can argue that Silverman misreads Dante here. Dante's *Divine Comedy* is, among other things, a story about Dante the character being given the grace of taking a journey into the next world. Before being taken on the journey through heaven, Dante has already gone through hell (recorded in *Inferno*) and purgatory (in *Purgatorio*). Certainly, the journey has changed him for the better. But Dante the character remains through the course of his otherworldly journey a Christian who is *on the way*, i.e., someone who is not yet living *the next life*. In other words, Dante the character is not dead and does not experience hell, purgatory, or heaven in the same way the inhabitants of those abodes do. For Dante undergoes spiritual and moral transformation in hell and heaven, something that does not happen to any of the souls that inhabit those places (he also

Silverman's Philosophical Argument for a Dynamic (or TD) View of Heaven

In addition to citing great thinkers who articulate a dynamic view of heaven, Silverman also offers a philosophical argument in defense of a dynamic view. Silverman's argument can be summarized as follows. One cannot argue for the truth of a static or a dynamic view of heaven by way of empirical studies[16] or simply by way of an analysis of *a priori* concepts about heaven. Nonetheless, central features of paradise or heaven common to the conceptions of a number of important religious and philosophical traditions do not require a static existence in heaven. In addition, these central features of paradise provide four reasons for preferring a dynamic view of heaven to the static view.

What are these central features of paradise or heaven common to a number of different religious and philosophical traditions? Silverman notes that, when one examines a number of different religious and philosophical traditions, one finds four "features associated with paradise"[17] that are common to a diverse group of religious and philosophical traditions: (a) "paradise ... [is] an overwhelmingly good eternal existence ... [and one that is] unqualifiedly good";[18] (b) "the great goodness of heaven [is] rooted in the presence of the divine";[19] (c) there is no moral evil in heaven; and (d) the inhabitants of heaven do not suffer negative

---

arguably merits in purgatory, something the dead in purgatory can no longer do). As the passage from *Paradiso* that Silverman cites makes clear, Dante the character is changed when he is given a glimpse of God in heaven. But it does not follow that Dante the author thinks the *inhabitants* of heaven experience God in the way that Dante the character as traveler does. Although Silverman is correct to think that Dante, as a Thomist, has a dynamic view of heaven, i.e., that the saints undergo some changes in heaven, Silverman is wrong to conclude on the basis of XXXIII.106-14 that Dante conceives of the saints in heaven as undergoing perpetual spiritual transformation in their enjoying the beatific vision.

16. Mark Spencer makes the good point that some contemporary philosophers would disagree with Silverman that empirical studies have nothing of relevance to say about the lifeworld of heaven, if "empirical studies" is understood broadly enough to include studies based on our everyday experience of ourselves. For example, Spencer argues that we can say something about the nature of heaven based on what is essential to any kind of *human* experience. See his "What Is It Like to Be an Embodied Person? What Is It Like to Be a Separated Soul?," *Angelicum* 93 (2016): 219-46. See also the discussion of St. Thomas's views in chapter 17 below for an account of how God does not set aside what is essential to human experience in this life for the saints in heaven, despite heaven's otherworldly character.

17. "Conceiving Heaven," 19.
18. Ibid.
19. Ibid., 21.

psychological or physical states such as sadness and pain.[20] Call these four features common to a number of different religious and philosophical accounts of heaven or paradise, *heavenly goods*. Any concept of heaven that excluded any one of these heavenly goods would be a limited or problematic one.

Silverman on Heavenly Goods Not Requiring a Static Existence

Silverman attempts to show that a dynamic view of heaven can include the heavenly goods in two ways. First, he responds to the objection that a dynamic view of heaven is incompatible with the blessed in heaven having an absolutely perfect existence, where we might think that enjoying the heavenly good of an unqualifiedly and overwhelmingly good human existence entails enjoying an absolutely perfect existence. Second, he offers a description of a dynamic view of heaven, one that shows that such a view can include the four heavenly goods.

We might think that a dynamic view of heaven cannot include the heavenly good of an unqualifiedly and overwhelmingly good human existence for the following reasons:

(11) If human person S has an unqualifiedly and overwhelmingly good existence in heaven, then S's existence in heaven is absolutely perfect.

(12) If S's existence in heaven is absolutely perfect, then S does not change in heaven, as any change in an absolutely perfect being would be a change for the worse.

(13) Therefore, if human person S has an unqualifiedly and overwhelmingly good existence in heaven, then S does not change in heaven [from (11) and (12), hypothetical syllogism (hereafter HS)].

(14) According to a dynamic view of heaven, persons in heaven undergo changes [assumption].

(15) Therefore, according to a dynamic view of heaven, human persons in heaven do not enjoy an unqualifiedly and overwhelmingly good existence in heaven [from (13) and (14), by *modus tollens* (hereafter MT)].

Silverman offers challenges to both premises (11) and (12) in the argument above. In offering a challenge to premise (11), he notes that "many

---

20. Ibid., 21–22.

traditions are simply silent on the matter," and that "gives some reason to doubt ... heaven must be absolutely perfect."[21] But that human persons in heaven enjoy an unqualifiedly or overwhelmingly good existence is one of the heavenly goods. So that gives us some reason to doubt premise (11).

In addition, Silverman wonders whether the notion of an absolutely perfect human existence is even coherent. For consider the great goodness for a person named Susan of knowing a friend Sally in heaven. From the real goodness of friendship, it follows that heaven for Susan is better with Sally than without her. Therefore, a human life in heaven can always be improved, if only "by the addition of one more blessed friend."[22] That heavenly life is unqualifiedly or overwhelmingly good is beyond doubt. Insofar as the coherence of an absolutely perfect human existence is dubitable, that gives us an additional reason to doubt the truth of (11).

Even if we grant premise (11), Silverman argues that there is reason to reject premise (12). For let us say that perfect human existence in heaven is primarily constituted by one's relation to God in heaven, and such a lived relationship with God is itself constituted by a cluster of different activities, such as worship, prayer, and study. As it is not possible to engage in these activities simultaneously, *the saint's relation to God in heaven is a dynamic existence in the sense of an ever-changing one* insofar as it involves engaging in different activities at different times.

Silverman also argues that a dynamic view of heaven can include the heavenly goods by way of offering a description of a dynamic view of heaven that includes all of the heavenly goods. Silverman sees the challenge here as describing heaven in such a way that, at any given stage s of a human person's life in heaven, it is possible that the person enjoys an unqualifiedly or overwhelmingly good state of affairs, even though the person at s lacks certain goods, where lacking those goods is not an evil for the person. To see if this is possible, Silverman asks us to consider the following state of affairs: a human person's environment being beautiful such that it contains nothing ugly but nonetheless does not contain every possible beautiful thing (say, for example, that it does not yet contain a certain work of art by Leonardo da Vinci). Perhaps heaven is like that.

21. Ibid., 20.
22. Ibid., 21.

Although it is beautiful and contains nothing ugly, it becomes more and more beautiful as additional beauties continually are added to it, where when heaven at some stage of a created person's existence lacks such beauties, the overall beauty of heaven is not marred for that person.

Silverman on Four Advantages for a Dynamic View of Heaven

Silverman also argues that a dynamic view of heaven has four advantages over a static view of heaven. First, note that, intuitively, if there is a heaven, heavenly life is fulfilling and meaningful. However, life in heaven being fulfilling and meaningful is better *explained* on a dynamic view of heaven than on a static one. This is because, according to the former, "paradise can be eternally meaningful because there is always more that can be known and experienced of the infinitely rich being of God."[23]

It is worth noting that Silverman's argument here is also implicitly an argument that a TD view of heaven *better explains* the idea that heaven is fulfilling and meaningful than does a non-TD *dynamic* view of heaven (for example, a non-TD dynamic view that posits that a human person's relationship with God in heaven does not undergo development or progress). For it is clear to us that a relationship in this life that grows is more fulfilling than one than does not. Therefore, a TD view of heaven that involved human persons changing not only in their relations with creatures but also in relation to God better explains how heavenly life is fulfilling and meaningful than a dynamic view of heaven where one's relation with God does not change.

Second, Silverman argues that a dynamic view of heaven is better positioned to respond to Bernard Williams's famous complaint that immortality would necessarily be tedious for any human person.[24] A dynamic heavenly life characterized by perpetual spiritual, intellectual, and moral growth better explains how heaven can be fulfilling, meaningful, and non-tedious when compared to a static view that entails there is no such sort of growth.

This second reason seems also to show that a TD view is better positioned to respond to Williams's argument than a non-TD dynamic view. For, according to Silverman: "The quest for ever increasing enjoyment of

---

23. Ibid., 24.

24. For more discussion of Williams's argument and the problem of the tedium of (heavenly) immortality, see chapters 3 and 17 below.

Static or Dynamic Reality? 41

union with and knowledge of the infinite loving God is the best possible candidate for a continually meaningful eternity that would be completely immune to boredom."[25] Third, Silverman thinks that a dynamic view of heaven has the following advantage over a static view: "dynamic views of heaven ... cohere better with a wider range of beliefs about and metaphors for paradise across a wide range of traditions."[26] We might split Silverman's claim here into two parts:

(A) The dynamic view coheres better with a wider range of beliefs about and metaphors for paradise within the Jewish-Christian tradition or traditions.

(B) The dynamic view coheres better with a wider range of beliefs about and metaphors for paradise across a wide range of traditions, including not only Jewish-Christian tradition or traditions, but also Greek philosophical traditions and Islamic religious traditions.

Leaving a discussion of (B) to one side, let us see how Silverman defends (A). In defense of (A), Silverman mentions the Book of Revelation's portrayal of heaven as an eternal worship of God (Rv 4:8–11), its picturing heaven as an active city (Rv 22), the parable of the wedding banquet in the Gospel of Matthew (Mt 22:1–14), the parable of the talents in Matthew (Mt 25:14–30), all of which, according to Silverman, "portrays the afterlife as ... a place of blessed ongoing uncursed work and responsibilities"[27] in accordance with the Christian belief in the resurrection of the body (1 Cor 15). Although Silverman recognizes that the first example in the list above admittedly lends support to the static view of heavenly life, he thinks that the other examples in this list, even if they are to be read metaphorically, lend themselves more to supporting a dynamic view.

It is less clear whether this third way in which Silverman claims dynamic views are theoretically advantageous in relation to a static view of heaven lends any potential support to a TD view of heaven over against a non-TD dynamic view. For one way to put together all of the images and beliefs about heaven from scripture that Silverman lists is as a description of a non-TD *dynamic* view of heavenly life: whereas the saints in heaven enjoy a beatific vision that is eternal, timeless, and immutable (Rv 4), the saints (eventually) have bodies that move (1 Cor 15) and enjoy

25. "Conceiving Heaven," 25.
26. Ibid., 26.
27. Ibid.

a communion of the saints that involves dynamically changing relations between created persons (Mt 22 and 25; Rv 22).

Fourth, Silverman thinks that a dynamic view of heaven enjoys an advantage over the static view insofar as a dynamic view is *theoretically simpler* than a static view. According to Silverman, this is because, on a dynamic view, happiness in heaven is a perfected version of common conceptions of happiness in this life, which common conceptions of happiness in this life entail growing in knowledge, moral goodness, and depth of personal relationships, whereas according to the static view of heaven, happiness in heaven is quite dissimilar from common conceptions of happiness in this life.

Silverman's fourth listed advantage for a dynamic view over against a static view of heaven also suggests an additional theoretical advantage for a TD conception of the nature of heaven over against non-TD dynamic views of heaven. Even if we think about heaven as a dynamic reality, we might also think that the most important dimension of heavenly life is a timeless and immutable, and thus very otherworldly, cognition and love of God. Whatever else one may want to say in defense of such a view—and I will have much to say by way of defense of such a view in the chapters that follow—such a view of heaven is more difficult to motivate than a view of heaven that has it that heaven is essentially a perfected form of this-worldly human happiness.

Silverman on PNH-III

In speaking about Silverman's approach to PNH-III, let us first recall the four assumptions made in the argument:

(1) The notion that (i) heaven is static is in conflict with the notion that (b) heaven includes the reality of "the new heavens and the new earth," which itself includes a perfect human community, and, at least eventually, perfected embodiment on the part of human persons in the next life and the notion that (j) if there is a human person S in heaven, then S is flourishing [assumption].

(2) The notion that (k) heaven is dynamic, that is, not static, is in conflict with the notion that (a) heaven for intellectual creatures consists merely in the beatific vision and the notion that (l) human persons in heaven are perfectly happy [assumption].

(3) (i) is true or (k) is true [assumption].
(4) [(b) is true or (j) is true] and [(a) is true or (l) is true] [assumption].

Let us begin with what Silverman undoubtedly accepts and rejects. Silverman clearly accepts premises (1) and (3). He clearly accepts propositions (b), (j), and (k). Silverman also clearly rejects proposition (i), making his acceptance of premise (1) reasonable insofar as rejecting (i) is. Silverman also clearly rejects proposition (a).

Silverman can thus solve PNH-III in two ways, depending on his ultimate attitude toward proposition (l) in premise (2). First, if Silverman accepts proposition (l), he can reject premise (2) by making sense of it not being the case that (k) entails the falsity of proposition (l). As we have seen, Silverman thinks that even a perfect human existence in heaven is consistent with human persons engaging in different activities at different times.

Second, if Silverman rejects proposition (l), Silverman can reject premise (4), as he also rejects proposition (a). Why would he reject proposition (l)? As we have seen, Silverman sympathizes with the thought that an absolutely perfect human existence is a contradiction in terms insofar as *human* happiness in heaven could always be improved upon, for example, by adding another person to the communion of the saints, the presence of whom would increase every human participant's enjoyment of heaven.

Four Problems with a TD View of the Nature of Heaven

Silverman defends a dynamic view of the nature of heaven over against a static view. As we will see, St. Thomas, in particular, and authoritative Catholic Christian tradition more generally, also defend some kind of dynamic view of the nature of heaven. But given some things Silverman says, he also seems to favor a TD view of heaven over against non-TD dynamic views. Recall that the TD view of heaven entails, among other things, that human persons in heaven perpetually grow closer to God in heaven. But there are good reasons to think the blessed in heaven will not perpetually grow closer to God in heaven, and so good reasons for rejecting a TD view of heaven.

A first problem for thinking that human persons in heaven will perpetually grow closer to God in heaven is that this view is incompatible with one important traditional Catholic Christian account of the relation between one's moral character in heaven and beatitude in heaven. As theologian Ludwig Ott notes, it is a dogma of the Catholic church that "the degree of perfection of the beatific vision granted to the just is proportioned to each one's merits."[28] Therefore, we might think the orthodox Catholic should accept the following:

(16) If human persons in heaven have the ability to get ever closer to God in heaven, that is, to advance in the beatific vision or the essential reward,[29] then human persons in heaven have the ability to undergo moral improvement in heaven, that is, they can merit in heaven.

But eminent Catholic theologians reject the consequent of (16). Consider first a passage from scripture, John 9:4: "We must work the works of him that sent me while it is day; night is coming when no man can work."[30] In interpreting this passage, Ludwig Ott suggests, "the period of earthly life is the 'Day,' the time for work, the period after death is the 'Night,' when no man can work.'"[31] The person meriting therefore "must be ... here on earth."[32]

Other eminent twentieth-century Catholic theologians reject the consequent of (16). For example, theologian Karl Adam states: "death is the end of all creative moral initiative and meritorious activity."[33] And Dom Anscar Vonier rejects the view that human persons can undergo moral improvement in heaven: "Through death there comes a sudden and permanent standstill to that mighty forward movement of man's soul which has been produced by the grace of God. The period of spiritual change, of merit, of progress, is forever at an end."[34]

---

28. *Fundamentals of Catholic Dogma*, trans. Patrick Lynch (Rockford, Ill.: TAN Books, 1974), 479. In defense of this theological statement, Ott cites a decree from the Council of Florence, Session 6 (July 6, 1439): "Also, the souls of those who have incurred no stain of sin whatsoever after baptism, as well as those souls who after incurring the stain of sin have been cleansed whether in their bodies or outside their bodies, as was stated above, are straightaway [*mox*] received into heaven and clearly behold the triune God as he is, *yet one person more perfectly than another according to the difference of their merits*" (*Decrees*, ed. Tanner, 2:527–28; emphasis added). Ott also cites the Council of Trent, *Decree on Justification*, canon 32 (January 13, 1547).

29. According to St. Thomas, the essential reward in heaven is the beatific vision and those acts of will, such as delight, joy, and charity, that follow upon having the vision. The essential reward is contrasted with the accidental reward, e.g., being embodied, the communion of the saints, etc. See chapter 4 below.

30. See also 2 Cor 5:10 and Gal 6:10a.

31. *Fundamentals of Catholic Dogma*, 474.

32. Ibid., 266.

33. *The Spirit of Catholicism*, trans. Dom Justin McCann (Garden City, N.Y.: Image Books, 1954), 110.

34. "Death and Judgment," in *The Teaching of the Catholic Church*, ed. George D. Smith (New York: MacMillan, 1949), 2:1107.

Static or Dynamic Reality? 45

In addition, it is clear that St. Thomas Aquinas rejects the notion that a saint in heaven can make spiritual or moral progress in heaven. In one place, he states: "Merit and progress belong to this present condition of life.... Every rational creature is so led by God to the end of its beatitude, that from God's predestination it is brought even to a determinate degree of beatitude. Consequently, when that degree is once secured, it cannot pass to a higher degree."[35] As this passage shows, St. Thomas rejects the view that the saints in heaven can perpetually get closer to God in heaven. But the passage above also shows why he thinks so. For St. Thomas also accepts (16),[36] and so, given that "merit and progress belong to this present condition of life," it follows that the antecedent of (16) too is false. Therefore, insofar as we give weight to the judgments of St. Thomas, Ott, Adam, and Vonier, we should say that proposition (16) is true, its consequent is false, and so we should also reject its antecedent.[37]

Tim Pawl and Kevin Timpe have responded to this reason for thinking that human persons cannot get closer to God in heaven.[38] They note that at least one important theological authority, St. Gregory of Nyssa, teaches that the saints in heaven can get continuously and perpetually closer to God, and that St. Gregory's view has not been condemned by the church.[39] Assuming that St. Gregory of Nyssa's point of view—that is, that the antecedent of (16) is true—is a live theological option, then either proposition (16) is false or the consequent of (16) is true.

According to Pawl and Timpe, one way of making sense of St. Gregory of Nyssa's position is to agree that one's getting closer to God in heaven entails growing in merit in heaven, and so proposition (16) is correct, but to reject as false the view that the saints in heaven cannot grow in merit. Pawl and Timpe suggest the possibility that, by affirming that "saints merit only in this life," Catholic theologians such as Ludwig Ott and Karl

---

35. *ST* I, q. 62, a. 9, s.c. and resp.; trans. Fathers of the English Dominican Province (Allen, Tex.: Christian Classics, 1950), 311. See also *Scriptum super libros Sententiarum* [hereafter *In Sent*] IV, d. 45, q. 2, a. 2, q.c. 1, resp. (*ST Suppl.*, q. 71, a. 5, resp.); q.c. 4, ad 3 (*ST Suppl.*, q. 71, a. 8, ad 3); *Quaestiones disputatae de malo* [hereafter *QDM*], q. 5, a. 4, ad 5; *In Joannem* [hereafter *In Jn*] 9, lect. 1, n. 1307, and *Super Epistolam ad Hebraeos* [hereafter *In Heb*] 3, lect. 3, n. 187. See also the constant theme in St. Thomas's work that in this life human persons are *wayfarers*, whereas the saints in heaven have arrived at their proper place (see, e.g., *Compendium theologiae* [hereafter *CT*] I, chaps. 149–50).

36. See, e.g., *ST* I, q. 12, a. 6, and *ST* I-II, q. 5, a. 2. For more sources from the Catholic tradition on merit, see also the texts cited in note 53 below.

37. An earlier version of this objection can be found in my "Making the Best Even Better."

38. See their "Paradise and Growing in Virtue."

39. Ibid., 105–6.

Adam are simply trying to safeguard the church's view that the time for meriting *salvation* or *damnation* is in this life (i.e., they are affirming that one cannot be saved in hell and one cannot fall from heaven).

But as we have seen, theologian Karl Adam states: "death is the end of *all* creative moral initiative and meritorious activity."[40] Recall also Dom Anscar Vonier: "Through death there comes a sudden and permanent standstill to that mighty forward movement of man's soul which has been produced by the grace of God. The period of spiritual change, of merit, of progress, is forever at an end."[41] As the quotation above from *Prima Pars* shows, St. Thomas is clear that there is no meriting in heaven so as to change the degree of one's beatitude.

In an alternative attempt to defend St. Gregory of Nyssa's notion that human persons can grow closer to God in heaven, Pawl and Timpe also entertain the possibility that it is true that one cannot gain merit at all in the next life, but that proposition (16) is false. On this supposition, we can make sense of the rejection of (16), argue Pawl and Timpe, by noting that the initial placement of a saint S in heaven tracks S's merit at the end of this life, but that in heaven S gets closer to God independently of any growth or lack of growth in merit in heaven.[42] After all, argue Pawl and Timpe, authoritative, Catholic Christian tradition only affirms the connection between one's initial placement in heaven and merit in this life, but, assuming that getting closer to God in heaven is possible, authoritative, Catholic Christian tradition is silent about the connection between closeness to God and merit after a human person's initial placement in heaven.

That being said, a good argument can be made for (16) insofar as *one's degree of perfect happiness in heaven* is tied to *the degree of charity one has when one knows God in the beatific vision.*[43] In that case, St. Paul knows God better at one stage s of his life in heaven than he does at an earlier stage $s-1$ if, and only if, St. Paul has greater charity for God at s than $s-1$. But to increase in charity—and so to enjoy an increase in the reward of seeing God—is just to increase in merit. Putting such a defense of (16) together with the views of great theologians such as St. Thomas, Ott, Adam, and

---

40. *The Spirit of Catholicism*, 110; emphasis added.
41. "Death and Judgment," 1107.
42. Mark Spencer also suggested this possibility.
43. See, e.g., the discussion of St. Thomas's argument to this effect in chapter 8 below.

Vonier that the consequent of (16) is false, we have good reason to reject, by *modus tollens*, the antecedent of (16).[44]

A second reason for thinking that human persons cannot get ever closer to God in heaven deploys some assumptions about the relationship between the ability of human persons to get closer to God in heaven, the ability of human persons to undergo moral improvement in heaven, and the ability of human persons to make *morally weighty free choices* in heaven. Let us begin with some discussion of the possibility that the saints make morally weighty free choices in heaven.

In a very interesting recent paper, Tim Pawl and Kevin Timpe discuss the extent to which it makes sense to say that human persons in heaven act freely in a libertarian sense.[45] Pawl and Timpe argue, among other things, that human persons in heaven can make *morally weighty choices*, that is, they can exercise libertarian free will in heaven to make choices that are not simply like the following morally *trivial* choice: the choice to have one healthy cereal rather than a different, equally healthy, cereal for breakfast on a particular morning. Granted, Pawl and Timpe argue that, according to Christian tradition, human persons in heaven do not have the ability to make what Alvin Plantinga has famously labeled *morally significant choices*, that is, the ability to choose between good and evil,[46] whether because of their perfected moral characters, or for some other reason.[47] But nothing about having a perfected moral character, or a character such that it is impossible to will evil, necessarily rules out

---

44. Pawl and Timpe seem to be correct that one cannot make a *definitive* theological argument for (16) and the denial of (16)'s consequent from church documents. Furthermore, St. Gregory of Nyssa thinks that the saints in heaven get perpetually closer to God. Nonetheless, as we saw above, St. Thomas clearly accepts (16) and the denial of the consequent of (16). Now, St. Thomas is a Doctor of the church. Indeed, he is the Common Doctor: see, e.g., Pius XI, *Studiorum Ducem*, Encyclical Letter, June 29, 1923, par. 11, and Paul VI, *Lumen Ecclesiae*, Encyclical Letter, November 20, 1974, par. 2. So, if we are weighing authorities, St. Thomas trumps St. Gregory of Nyssa. Therefore, even if (16) and the denial of (16)'s consequent have not been dogmatically defined, and not all theological authorities accept (16), or deny the antecedent or consequent of (16), there are nonetheless strong arguments from authority as well as good theological arguments for both (16) and the falsity of the consequent of (16).

45. "Incompatibilism, Sin, and Free Will in Heaven." See also their "Paradise and Growing in Virtue" and my "Making the Best Even Better."

46. See, e.g., his *God, Freedom, and Evil* (Grand Rapids, Mich.: Eerdmans, 1977), 30. The expression *morally significant choice* is a term of philosophical art. The reader should therefore keep in mind the precise meaning of this expression in what follows. Similarly, with expressions such as *morally weighty choice, morally relevant choice*, etc.

47. "Incompatibilism, Sin, and Free Will in Heaven." For some sources in Christian tradition, see, e.g., St Augustine, *The City of God* X.30 and St. Thomas, *ST* I-II, q. 5, a. 4.

having the ability to choose between *this* good rather than *that* good in heaven, where one of these goods is objectively *better* than the other.

Pawl and Timpe go on to argue human persons in heaven can make morally *weighty* choices they call *morally relevant choices*. According to Pawl and Timpe, a free choice is morally relevant if and only if "the person is free to choose among at least two options, and at least two of the options, say, A and B, are related such that either A is better than B or B is better than A."[48] Because choosing good is better than choosing evil, all morally significant choices are morally relevant choices. But Pawl and Timpe note that not all morally relevant choices are morally significant choices. For the genus of morally relevant choices includes not only the species, *morally significant choices*, but the species of choices, *nonmorally significant, morally relevant choices*, for example, whether or not to perform supererogatory acts. If one chooses to perform a supererogatory act, then one chooses something better than choosing not to perform such an act, although choosing not to perform the supererogatory act would not count as an evil act. For example, say John sells everything he owns and gives the money to the poor. Had he not done this—let us assume for the sake of argument—John would not necessarily have done something morally wrong.[49] But John's deciding to follow one of the evangelical counsels is morally superior (given John's circumstances) to deciding not to do so. Hence, although John's choice whether or not to sell his possessions and give them to the poor is not *morally significant*, it certainly does have moral weight, and thus is a good example of *a nonmorally significant, morally relevant choice*.

One might wonder whether human persons *in heaven* have the ability to make any morally relevant choices. According to Pawl and Timpe:

It seems to us at least possible that a person can cling to the mean [of virtue] to such an extent that he can't fall from it, but he could nevertheless still cling tighter. If that is possible, then the redeemed in heaven are such that they are perfected in the first sense, being squarely on the mean, and perfected in the second sense insofar as they cling to the mean so tenaciously that they can't but remain there, but are nevertheless such that they could always cling tighter. Their morally relevant choices bring them to cling ever tighter to the mean, and

---

48. "Incompatibilism, Sin, and Free Will in Heaven," 416.
49. I assume (with Pawl and Timpe) that there are some actions that are morally better than others, but are not thereby morally obligatory actions.

we can judge them to be better for choosing supererogatory actions insofar as such choices bring them to cling more tenaciously to the mean.[50]

I am now in a position to lay out the assumptions in the background for some persons who maintain that human persons can get perpetually closer to God in heaven insofar as they can make morally weighty free choices. Consider the following propositions:

(16) If (i) human persons in heaven have *the ability to get ever closer to God in heaven*, that is, to advance in the beatific vision or the essential reward, then (ii) human persons in heaven have *the ability to undergo moral improvement in heaven*, that is, they can merit in heaven.

(17) If (iii) human persons in heaven have *the ability to make nonmorally significant, morally relevant choices*, then (ii) human persons in heaven have *the ability to undergo moral improvement in heaven*, that is, they can merit in heaven.

(18) If (ii) human persons in heaven have *the ability to undergo moral improvement in heaven*, that is, they can gain merit in heaven, then (i) human persons in heaven have *the ability to get ever closer to God in heaven*, that is, advance in the beatific vision or the essential reward.

(19) If (ii) human persons in heaven have *the ability to undergo moral improvement in heaven*, that is, they can merit in heaven, then (iii) human persons in heaven have *the ability to make nonmorally significant, morally relevant choices*.

I have already discussed reasons for accepting proposition (16) above. Some philosophers accept (17) and (18).[51] It seems someone who accepts (18) might accept (19). For the theologian or philosopher who accepts (16) and (19), as well as (17) and (18), it follows that:

(20) Human persons in heaven have *the ability to get ever closer to God in heaven*, that is, to advance in the beatific vision or the essential reward if, and only if, human persons in heaven have *the ability to make nonmorally significant, morally relevant choices*.

In addition, if we accept (20), then we might think:

---

50. "Incompatibilism, Sin, and Free Will in Heaven," 418.
51. See, e.g., ibid., 118.

(21) The way human persons get closer to God in heaven is by making, by grace, nonmorally significant, morally relevant choices to perform supererogatory acts.

I can therefore offer a second reason for thinking that human persons in heaven cannot get ever closer to God, assuming (20) and (21) are true, and that human persons in heaven have an infinite amount of time in which to make an infinite number of morally relevant choices. For, if a human person S in heaven can get closer to God in heaven, the way a human person gets closer to God in heaven is by making good morally relevant choices, and S has an infinite amount of time in which to make an infinite number of morally relevant choices, then the importance of the choices S makes during S's pre-heavenly existence, *at least where those choices have an effect on the degree to which S is happy in heaven*, would be problematically minimized. I will call this "the eternity of choices in heaven eclipses the choices of this life objection," abbreviated as the EOC objection.[52]

Say Samantha and Sarah die in a state of grace and so both go to heaven. Although Samantha dies possessing the habit of charity, Sarah's charity at the time of her death far outstrips that possessed by Samantha. Both Samantha and Sarah will be perfectly happy in heaven, as both get to eternally contemplate and delight in God. But according to Catholic Christian tradition, Sarah's happiness in heaven will be greater than Samantha's, as Sarah died with a greater love for God, and so God rewards Sarah with a greater degree of beatitude.[53] We might think that human persons in heaven exist for an infinite duration of time, where at any or all points on such a heavenly timeline Samantha or Sarah may or may not make a series of nonmorally significant, morally relevant choices.

---

52. An earlier version of this objection can be found in my "Making the Best Even Better."
53. For the doctrine that different human persons merit different degrees of beatitude in heaven in Catholic Christian tradition, see, e.g., Aphraates the Persian Sage, *Treatises* XXII.19; St. Jerome, *Against Jovian* II.32; St. Augustine of Hippo, *Sermons* LXXXVII.6; St. Augustine, *Homilies on John* LXVII.2; St. Augustine, *Enchiridion* XXIX.111; St. Gregory the Great, *Moralia* IV, 36, 70; and the Council of Florence, Session 6 (July 6, 1439): "Also, the souls of those who have incurred no stain of sin whatsoever after baptism, as well as those souls who after incurring the stain of sin have been cleansed whether in their bodies or outside their bodies, as was stated above, are straightaway [*mox*] received into heaven and clearly behold the triune God as he is, *yet one person more perfectly than another according to the difference of their merits*" (*Decrees*, ed. Tanner, 2:527–28; emphasis added). For discussion of the doctrine that different human persons merit different degrees of beatitude in heaven in St. Thomas, see chapter 8. For a compelling poetic expression of the doctrine, see Dante Alighieri's *Paradiso*.

Theoretically, then, Samantha might eventually outpace Sarah in choosing to perform more supererogatory acts in heaven. Therefore, given enough time, the choices Samantha and Sarah make in this life would eventually become irrelevant in heaven where the degree of their beatitude, that is, "their closeness to God" is concerned. But the choices human persons make in this life are vitally important, not only for whether such persons go to heaven, but also for determining how well placed such persons will be in eternity. Therefore, human persons cannot make morally relevant choices in heaven, and so cannot get ever closer to God in heaven.

Pawl and Timpe have responded to the EOC objection.[54] They propose that something such as the following principle is guiding the objection:

(P) "For any period of time t_1 such that it is before t_2, the opportunity to improve one's character in t_2 minimizes the importance of improving one's character in t_1."[55]

But there are clear counterexamples to P; Pawl and Timpe mention purgatory. The sanctification that a person S undergoes in purgatory does not render unimportant what S does in this life. But they also mention the this-worldly example of *a human person S's growing in virtue in May* not minimizing the importance of any moral growth S undergoes during the Lenten season of that same calendar year.

Indeed, P is false, and if the EOC objection depended upon P, then it would be unsound. But the objection does *not* depend upon principle P. The argument is not that just *any* moral growth in heaven would minimize what someone does in this life. Rather, the argument has it that any moral growth in this life becomes irrelevant for determining the relative degree of a saint's perfect happiness in heaven in light of an everlasting life that entails an *infinite* number of possible chances for moral growth in heaven.[56]

Pawl and Timpe also propose an additional response to the EOC objection. They say: "It is possible for two individuals to both increase infinitely along a trajectory without the one overtaking the other, just as two curves can infinitely approach a single asymptote without one line

---

54. "Paradise and Growing in Virtue," 103–5.
55. Ibid., 105.
56. Perhaps this point is not sufficiently emphasized in the version of the argument in my "Making the Best Even Better."

ever intersecting the other. So it is false that infinite growth in virtue entails that one saint would overtake another in heaven."[57]

In response, let us agree that if Samantha and Sarah are both infinitely growing closer to God in heaven, where Sarah was initially better placed in heaven than Samantha, *it does not logically follow* that Samantha will eventually overtake—or even match—Sarah in charity, merit, or closeness to God. However, given (21) and that Samantha and Sarah are continually making morally relevant choices to act, or not to act, in a supererogatory fashion in heaven, it is possible. And it is the mere possibility in an infinite stretch of time that Samantha catches or outpaces Sarah in charity that seems to dwarf, and eventually make irrelevant, what Samantha and Sarah freely choose to do in this life, at least where their degree of perfect happiness in heaven is concerned.

One might also suggest "an escalator analogy" as a possible response to the EOC objection.[58] In other words, begin again with our friends, Samantha and Sarah, where Sarah is initially better placed in heaven than is Samantha where such placement is based on the relative degree of charity in the souls of Samantha and Sarah when they die. We might imagine that Samantha and Sarah's growth in charity/getting closer to God is like Samantha and Sarah riding up an infinitely tall escalator, where Samantha and Sarah never go up on their own steam. Rather, they are both standing still on the escalator. Therefore, no matter where Samantha is on the escalator, Sarah is always higher up. So, if "going up the escalator" is a good analogy for how the saints in heaven get ever closer to God, then, though both Samantha and Sarah are perpetually getting ever closer to God in heaven, Sarah will always be closer to God than Samantha, thereby undermining the worry behind the EOC objection.

The escalator analogy may very well show how human persons in heaven can get perpetually closer to God without making irrelevant the choices of human persons in this life, all other things being equal. But insofar as one thinks that some person's making morally relevant choices in heaven draws that person closer to God in heaven and that the saints in heaven make such choices, the escalator model will not work as part of a response to the EOC objection. For if one thinks that some person's making morally relevant choices in heaven draws that person closer to

---

57. "Paradise and Growing in Virtue," 104.
58. Tim Pawl suggested this idea in conversation.

God in heaven and that the saints in heaven makes such choices, we can imagine that even though Sarah is better placed with respect to her essential reward than Samantha when they enter heaven, Samantha might very well choose to make more supererogatory acts than Sarah and so eventually get closer to God than Sarah in eternity.

To explain this, let us make additional use of the escalator analogy. If Sarah and Samantha can and do make morally relevant choices in heaven, where choosing to perform supererogatory acts in heaven is one way in which one gets closer to God in heaven, then Samantha might choose "to walk up the escalator," while Sarah chooses to "stand still on it," so that Samantha "passes Sarah on the escalator." In that case, Samantha "gets higher up the escalator" than Susan. Again, the worry arises that what human persons do in this life to affect their degree of happiness in heaven will in the course of an infinite amount of time simply become irrelevant if human persons in heaven can and do make morally relevant free choices in heaven that can change their degree of beatitude for the better. Thus, the escalator analogy fails to defuse the EOC objection.[59]

Consider a third reason for thinking that human persons in heaven cannot get ever closer to God. This third reason deploys from a certain understanding of *the nature of the beatific vision*. We might think with the Catholic Christian tradition that a human person's relation with God in heaven is essentially that person's beatific vision of the essence of God, and the love of God that results from that vision.[60] However, we might also think that the beatific vision is an eternal, timeless, and immutable

---

59. See my "Making the Best Even Better" for an argument that human persons in heaven do have the ability to make morally weighty libertarian free choices, even though human persons do not have the ability to make morally relevant choices in heaven and human persons cannot grow closer to God in heaven.

60. See, e.g., Benedict XII, *Benedictus Deus*, pars. 1000–1001: "By this Constitution which is to remain in force forever, we, with apostolic authority, define the following: ... Since the passion and death of the Lord Jesus Christ, these souls [of the saints in heaven, already before they take up their bodies again and before the general judgment] have seen and see the divine essence with an intuitive vision and even face to face, without the mediation of any creature by way of object of vision; rather the divine essence immediately manifests itself to them, plainly, clearly, and openly, and in this vision they enjoy the divine essence. Moreover, by this vision and enjoyment the souls of those who have already died are truly blessed and have eternal life and rest. Also the souls of those who will die in the future will see the same divine essence and will enjoy it before the general judgment.... Such a vision and enjoyment of the divine essence do away with the acts of faith and hope in these souls, inasmuch as faith and hope are properly theological virtues. And after such intuitive and face-to-face vision and enjoyment has or will have begun for these souls, the same vision and enjoyment has continued and will continue without any interruption and without end until the last Judgment and from then on forever" (*The Christian Faith*, ed. Dupuis, 942–43).

union with God. According to that traditional view, a human person does not grow closer to God in heaven insofar as the beatific vision is a participation in God's own eternal life, which participation is immutably as perfect for that person as is possible, given the extent to which that person cooperated with God's grace in this life.[61]

Here is a fourth reason to think that the saints in heaven cannot get perpetually closer to God. For if they can, heaven is in no sense a *novissimum* (a most new thing, and so, a *last* thing), a reality in which the human person is *quietus* (at rest). But heaven, among other things, is that reality where our hearts are at rest.[62] There is a good reason why we say *requiescat in pace* about those who die. One might think the notion, common enough among our contemporaries, that heavenly life must be ever progressing toward some goal is beholden to an overemphasis among our contemporaries to the domains of the psychological and the political.[63] Such a progressivist view of personal reality forgets that God himself is not on a journey. Heaven for human persons is not "more of this life, only better." Rather, it is the *culmination* of the project of *theosis* or becoming *deiform*, and God is absolutely immutable and perfect. I will have more to say about these matters in upcoming chapters.

I have suggested four reasons for thinking that the saints in heaven cannot get perpetually closer to God. However, the TD view of heaven entails that the saints in heaven can get perpetually closer to God. Therefore, if any of these four reasons are good ones, we have good reason to reject the TD view of heaven.

Some Problems for a Silvermanian Argument in Defense of the TD View of Heaven

Recall Silverman's philosophical argument in defense of a *dynamic* view of heaven. What of a *Silvermanian* philosophical argument in defense of a *TD view* of the nature of heavenly life? We can construct the following Silvermanian philosophical argument for the TD view of the nature of heaven based on Silverman's argument for a dynamic model of heaven:

---

61. For an articulation of, and arguments for, this view that the beatific vision is a timeless and immutable participation in God's own eternal life, see chapter 7 below.

62. See, e.g., St. Augustine's *Confessions* I.1: "our hearts are restless until they rest in thee" (*inquietum est cor nostrum donec requiescat in te*). See also Griffiths, *Decreation*, 216.

63. Of course, not *all* thinkers who believe that heaven involves perpetually growing closer to God do so because they have been overly influenced by the domains of psychology and politics. Thanks to Mark Spencer for pointing out the need to make this qualification.

(22) One cannot discover the nature of heaven on empirical grounds alone or simply by way of an analysis of *a priori* concepts [assumption].

(23) Therefore, if the static view of the nature of heaven is false and the common, central features of paradise or heaven, that is, the heavenly goods, do not entail a non-TD dynamic view, but instead provide four reasons for preferring the TD view to a non-TD dynamic view, then we should prefer a TD view to a non-TD dynamic view of the nature of heaven [from (22)].

(24) The static view is false and the common central features of paradise or heaven do not entail a non-TD dynamic view of heaven.

(25) There are four good reasons for preferring the TD view over non-TD dynamic views: (a) the TD view can more easily explain than a non-TD dynamic view how eternal life is desirable and meaningful; (b) the TD view is better positioned than a non-TD dynamic view to respond to Bernard Williams's dilemma concerning the tedium of immortality; (c) the TD view is consistent with a greater number of beliefs and images about heaven within the Christian tradition, broadly construed, than non-TD dynamic views; and (d) the TD view is theoretically simpler than a non-TD dynamic view [assumption].

(26) Therefore, we should prefer a TD view to a non-TD dynamic view of the nature of heaven [from (23)–(25), by MP].

There are a number of potential problems with the Silvermanian argument. First, there are good reasons for rejecting (Silvermanian defenses of) premises (24) and (25).

As we saw above, Silverman defends a dynamic view of heaven from the charge that it is inconsistent with commonly held notions about heaven, notions that treat what I have called *the heavenly goods*. For example, Silverman entertains an objection to a dynamic model of heaven that it cannot include the heavenly good of an unqualifiedly and overwhelmingly good human existence. The objection was formulated as follows:

(11) If human person S has an unqualifiedly and overwhelmingly good existence in heaven, then S's existence in heaven is absolutely perfect.

(12) If S's existence in heaven is absolutely perfect, then S does not change in heaven, as any change in an absolutely perfect being would be a change for the worse.

(13) Therefore, if human person S has an unqualifiedly and over-

whelmingly good existence in heaven, then S does not change in heaven [from (11) and (12), HS].

(14) According to a dynamic view of heaven, persons in heaven undergo changes [assumption].

(15) Therefore, according to a dynamic view of heaven, human persons in heaven do not enjoy an unqualifiedly and overwhelmingly good existence in heaven [from (13) and (14), by MT].

We can reframe the objection above specifically as a defeater for a TD view, that is, as an objection from someone who agrees that heaven is a nonstatic reality, but also thinks it is a non-TD dynamic reality, if only because heaven primarily consists in the beatific vision as an eternal and immutable union with God:

(11*) If human person S has an unqualifiedly and overwhelmingly good existence in heaven, then *there is an aspect A* of S's existence in heaven, for example, that saint's beatific vision, that is absolutely perfect—in other words, as perfect for that person as is logically possible, given facts about that person's this-worldly life, for example, the degree of the virtue of charity with which she dies.

(12*) If *there is an aspect A* of S's existence in heaven, for example, the saint's beatific vision, that is absolutely perfect (in the relevant sense), then, with respect to A, S does not change in heaven, as any change in A would be a change in S for the worse.

(13*) Therefore, if human person S has an unqualifiedly and overwhelmingly good existence in heaven, then, with respect to A, S does not change in heaven, as any change in A would be a change in S for the worse [from (11*) and (12*), HS].

(14*) According to a TD view of heaven, persons in heaven undergo changes in all aspects of their heavenly life [assumption].

(15*) Therefore, according to the TD view of heaven, persons in heaven do not enjoy an unqualifiedly and overwhelmingly good existence in heaven [from (13*) and (14*)].

How do Silverman's objections to (11) and (12) fare with respect to (11*) and (12*)? In offering a challenge to premise (11), recall that Silverman states: "many traditions are simply silent on the matter," and that "gives some reason to doubt ... heaven must be absolutely perfect."[64] However,

---

64. "Conceiving Heaven," 20.

this argument against (11) and (11*) suffers the following limitation: why should a Christian theologian or philosopher argue with ecumenical restrictions on a topic as important as the nature of heaven? Analogously, many non-Christian traditions are silent on the matter of the Trinity.[65] An orthodox Christian would not thereby conclude that this gives us a good reason to neglect or reject the doctrine of the Trinity. But, according to some theologians, the Christian notion of heaven is a revealed doctrine of the faith, just as is the doctrine of the Trinity.[66]

In addition, with respect to (11), Silverman wonders whether the notion of an absolutely perfect human existence is even coherent. For consider the great goodness for a person S of knowing a friend F in heaven. From the goodness of friendship, it follows that heaven for S is better with F than without F. Therefore, a human life in heaven can always be improved, if only "by the addition of one more blessed friend."[67]

But even granting that a creature's existence in heaven can always be better than it is (if only for the sake of argument), it does not follow that that creature's existence in heaven can, in all respects, be better than it is, let alone better in the most important respects. As I will argue in the coming chapters, one should distinguish, on the one hand, what is *essential* to heavenly life for a human person, for example, the human saint's beatific union with God and the love, joy, and delight that flows from such a union, and, on the other hand, what is *accidental* to heavenly life in the sense that it not necessary for perfect human happiness. Furthermore, what is essential to human happiness in heaven—the beatific vision and the delight that flows from it—is a good so great it is incommensurate with any goods that are accidental to human happiness in heaven.

It *may* be that what is accidental to heavenly life for the saints in heaven, including the communion of the saints, does change and grow, whereas what is essential to heavenly life for the saints does not.[68] But,

---

65. Indeed, many Christian traditions are silent concerning propositions that other Christian traditions take to be true and important, e.g., *that the existence of God can be proved by natural human reason apart from divine revelation*. Such silence does not provide good reason to doubt those propositions are true or important.

66. See, e.g., St. Thomas Aquinas's *ST* I, q. 1, a. 1, resp.

67. "Conceiving Heaven," 21.

68. Or perhaps the communion of the saints itself is an aspect of the happiness of the saints in heaven such that the relationship between the saints in heaven is immutably as *good* as it can be, even if the relationships between the saints undergo (non-value-enhancing) changes.

as I will argue, what is essential for the perfect happiness of a saint in heaven is as perfect as possible for that saint, given the manner in which that saint cooperated with God's grace in this life. Furthermore, the immutable aspect of a saint's happiness that is essential to it is a good of such value that it is incommensurate with any other goods the saint may or may not enjoy in heaven: therefore, it is what is essential to human happiness in heaven that chiefly explains why the saint in heaven's perfect happiness in heaven is unqualifiedly and overwhelmingly good. Silverman's argument against (11) does not defeat (11*).

Recall that Silverman also argues there is reason to reject premise (12), which states that an absolutely perfect human existence in heaven cannot change in any way. For Silverman thinks that it is possible that an absolutely perfect existence for human persons in heaven involves those human persons engaging in a variety of different activities in the presence of God, *all* of which involve perpetual growth and change. However, this argument against (12) does not address the possibility that, though there are many aspects of the saint's heavenly life that involve her undergoing change, there is at least one aspect—perhaps the most important aspect—of heavenly life that is immutable. As premise (12*) speaks merely of an *aspect* of the saint's life as absolutely perfect and immutable, we will need an argument against (12*) different from the ones Silverman offers.[69]

Indeed, there are reasons to think that (12*) is true. For we might think that:

(12**) If *there is an aspect A of* a human person S's existence in heaven, for example, the beatific vision, that is absolutely perfect (in the relevant sense), then S's desires are sated in heaven because of A.

(12***) If S's desires are stated in heaven because of A, then, with respect to A, S does not change in heaven, as any change in A would be a change in S for the worse.

(12*) Therefore, if *there is an aspect A of* S's existence in heaven, for example, the saint's beatific vision, that is absolutely perfect (in the relevant sense), then, with respect to A, S does not change in heaven, as any change in A would be a change in S for the worse [from (12**) and (12***), HS].

---

69. In "Conceiving Heaven."

As we will see in the chapters that follow, St. Thomas provides reasons for thinking that (12**) and (12***) are true, as well as responses to objections to (12**) and (12***). And by joining propositions (12*), (12**), and (12***) with propositions (11*) and (13*)–(15*), we get a defeater for premise (24) in the Silvermanian argument for the TD view of heaven.

However, given the possibility discussed above that human persons in heaven can grow in merit, a defender of the TD view of heaven might offer a defeater of my defeater of premise (24). A defender of the TD view of heaven could argue that (11*) can, and should, be disambiguated as follows.[70]

(11**) If human person S has an unqualifiedly and overwhelmingly good existence in heaven, then (a) *there is an aspect A of* S's existence in heaven, for example, that saint's beatific vision, that is absolutely perfect *simpliciter*, that is, as perfect for that person as is logically possible, given facts about that person's this-worldly life, for example, the degree of the virtue of charity with which she dies, or (b) (i) *there is an aspect A of* S's existence in heaven at a time t, for example, that saint's beatific vision, that is absolutely perfect at t, that is, as perfect for S as it is logically possible at t, (1) given facts about S's *this-worldly* life, for example, the degree of the virtue of charity with which S dies, or (2) given facts about S's *heavenly* life prior to t, for example, the degree to which S's merit has increased between death and time t or the morally relevant choices S makes in heaven before t, and (ii) *there is an aspect A1 of* S's existence in heaven at a time $t+1$, for example, S's degree of beatitude in the beatific vision, that is absolutely perfect at $t+1$, where S's perfect human happiness at $t+1$ is greater than S's perfect happiness at t, etc.

Now, if (11**) is true and if (b) is a possibility—which, as we have seen, is a position held by some Christian theologians and philosophers—then we will not be able to conclude to (13*), which would thereby defeat the proposed defeater of premise (24) in the Silvermanian argument for the TD view of heaven. Call this *the defeater of my defeater of premise* (24).

Of course, there are ways of responding to the defeater of my defeater of premise (24). For, if (b) is true, then human persons can get closer to God in heaven. But I have given four arguments above for why human

---

70. Mark Spencer suggested this objection.

persons do not have the ability to get closer to God in heaven. If any of those four arguments are sound, then (b) is false, and so the defeater of my defeater of premise (24) will itself be defeated.[71]

What about premise (25) in the Silvermanian argument for the TD view of the nature of heaven? Recall premise (25):

(25) There are four good reasons for preferring the TD view over non-TD dynamic views: (a) the TD view can more easily explain than a non-TD dynamic view how eternal life is desirable and meaningful; (b) the TD view is better positioned than a non-TD dynamic view to respond to Bernard Williams's dilemma concerning the tedium of immortality; (c) the TD view is consistent with a greater number of beliefs and images about heaven within the Christian tradition than non-TD dynamic views; and (d) the TD view is theoretically simpler than a non-TD dynamic view insofar as a defender of the TD view has to do less work than the defender of non-TD dynamic views to motivate its respective conception of heaven insofar as the TD view sees happiness in heaven as continuous with and analogous to happiness in this life whereas non-TD dynamic views of heaven involve otherworldly and strange ideas [assumption].

As I noted above when discussing Silverman's argument for a dynamic view of heaven over against a static view, (c) in (25) is false, as a non-TD dynamic view of heaven, just like the TD view, can make sense of the diverse group of images and metaphors in scripture that describe heavenly life.

As for (a), (b), and (d) in (25), they really reduce to one reason: it is easier for us to see how heaven is something desirable and perfectly fulfilling on the TD view than it is on non-TD dynamic views, because the TD view of heaven makes heaven more continuous with common notions of human happiness in this life than do non-TD dynamic views.[72] That

---

71. See also the discussion in chapter 1 of the beatific vision in heaven as sating all desire, coupled with the relevant Thomistic distinctions and defenses in chapters that follow, for another strategy for responding to the defeater of my defeater of premise (24).

72. Mark Spencer thinks that a stronger version of (a), (b), and (d) can, and ought to be, given as a reason for rejecting a non-TD dynamic view of heaven: not only is it *easier* to motivate the attractiveness of the TD view for beings such as ourselves, but given what is essential to human experience, e.g., temporality, it is metaphysically and logically *impossible* for a non-TD dynamic heaven to fulfill human persons. For a response to this sort of objection, see the Thomistic responses to apparent problems concerning eternal life in chapters 15–17 below.

certainly seems correct if a non-TD dynamic view includes something such as a timeless and immutable vision of God as its chief feature.[73]

The defender of a non-TD dynamic view of heaven thus bears a greater intellectual burden than the defender of the TD view. But insofar as there are good Catholic Christian theological and philosophical reasons for thinking that a non-TD dynamic view of heaven is true, this is a cross the Catholic Christian theologian or philosopher needs to bear. In addition, as we have seen, and will continue to see in what follows, there are good reasons to think that the TD view of heaven is false. Therefore, because (a), (b), and (d) in (25) merely suggest that the TD view of heaven has greater *persuasive* power than non-TD dynamic views of heaven, and only in the narrow sense that it has an immediate sort of sweetness for those hearing merely with contemporary ears, (a), (b), and (d) do not amount to strong reasons for preferring the TD view of heaven to non-TD dynamic views.

But we can say more. Heaven according to the TD view may appear more desirable to us than heaven on a non-TD dynamic view if one assumes that an immutable activity is something *static*. That is, (b) in (25) trades on maintaining the following:

(27) Dynamism or life entails change.

Silverman's philosophical argument for dynamic views of heaven and the Silvermanian argument for the TD view assumes (27).[74] Although I will have more to say about reasons to reject (27) in upcoming chapters, at this point we can recognize that any defender of classical theism has good reasons to reject (27), as the classical theist thinks that God is absolutely perfect and as happy as it is logically possible to be. Furthermore, God's life is eternal, timeless, and absolutely immutable. Assuming that a static life is not absolutely perfect, it follows that God's absolutely perfect, happy, eternal, timeless, and absolutely immutable life is rightly described as *dynamic*. The classical theist therefore has good reasons to reject (27). If we also think that the human person having the beatific vision timelessly and immutably participates in God's timeless and immutably perfect—and so meaningful—life, then we will have a reason not to accept (b) in (25).[75]

73. However, see the argument in chapter 17 below, which argument shows that there is continuity between a *graced* human person in this life and the numerically same human person in heaven enjoying the beatific vision.
74. Indeed, PNH-III itself seems to have (27) as a covert premise.
75. For an additional defense of these ideas from a Thomistic perspective, see chapters 4, 7, and 16 below. For an Anselmian defense, see Rogers, "Anselmian Mediations on Heaven."

That being said, there is perhaps no getting around (a) and (d) in (25). However, as I noted above, (a) and (d) do not confer a *significant* advantage for the TD view over non-TD dynamic views of the nature of heaven insofar as we have reasons for thinking the TD view is false or a non-TD dynamic view is true.

Before drawing this critique of a Silvermanian argument for the TD view of heaven to a close, I would like to also raise some potential problems for (the inference to) premise (23) in that argument. Recall propositions (22) and (23):

(22) One cannot discover the nature of heaven on empirical grounds alone or simply by way of an analysis of *a priori* concepts [assumption].

(23) Therefore, if the static view of the nature of heaven is false and the common, central features of paradise or heaven, that is, the heavenly goods, do not entail a non-TD dynamic view but instead provide four reasons for preferring the TD view, then we should prefer a TD view to a non-TD dynamic view of the nature of heaven [from (22)].

There are at least three possible reasons to reject (23) and the inference from (22) to (23). First, there may be teachings of an authoritative, Christian tradition, or, at the very least, eminent theologians from within such a Christian tradition, that tell against the TD view, but not against a non-TD dynamic view of the nature of heaven. I offered a number of such arguments above (and will have much more to say on this score in chapters that follow). In other words, say there are two views of heaven, A and B, where A is consistent with the heavenly goods (that Silverman identifies) and there are *noncompelling* reasons for thinking A is true, which reasons do not support the truth of B. Be that as it may, we may think there are other features of heaven identified by an authoritative, Christian tradition, or some eminent theologians from within that tradition, that support the truth of B over against A, where the tradition's authority supporting B trumps the noncompelling reasons given for A. That would give us a reason to reject the inference from (22) to (23).

Second, recall that Silverman argues for a dynamic view of heaven by privileging what a diverse number of religious and philosophical traditions, for example, Jewish, Christian, Islamic, and Greek, have to say about heaven over against views about heaven that are not shared by these various theological and philosophical traditions. But we may think that when it comes to a topic such as heaven—perhaps a topic that (a particular) divine revelation speaks to more clearly when compared to what human reason can say or what a number of religious traditions say in common—we should privilege what one religion R says over others. Similarly, our prayer and study may have brought us to the point where we think one theological or philosophical tradition T within R is wiser than the others are, and so think it quite reasonable to privilege what T has to say over against what the religious or philosophical traditions within R teach in common about the nature of heaven.

Third, even if it cannot be shown from the heavenly goods alone that we should prefer a non-TD dynamic view to the TD view, it may be that a tradition T has *other* arguments that entail the falsity of the TD view, which arguments do not entail the falsity of a non-TD dynamic view of the nature of heaven. Such arguments would give us reasons, if we accepted the authority of T, or the soundness of the arguments advanced by T, for preferring a non-TD dynamic view to the TD view. Again, the consequent of (23) does not follow from its antecedent.

In this part of the chapter, I have offered a number of defeaters for a Silvermanian philosophical argument for the TD view of heaven. In addition, I have advanced arguments that the TD view of heaven is false. I will have more to say about why a non-TD dynamic view of heaven is preferable to the TD view in chapters 4–8 and 16 below.

A SECOND CONTEMPORARY SOLUTION TO PNH-III: PAUL GRIFFITHS ON HEAVEN AS PARTICIPATION IN A PERFECT AND PERPETUAL LITURGY

A second account of the nature of heaven that will be useful to examine at this point is one put forward recently by the Catholic theologian Paul J. Griffiths, in his elegant and interesting book, *Decreation: The Last Things of All Creatures*.[76] According to Griffiths, heavenly life for angels and human persons is a minimally dynamic sort of existence insofar as the angels and human persons in heaven participate in an ever-repeating, perfect liturgy.

---

76. *Decreation: The Last Things of All Creatures* (Waco: Baylor University Press) 2014. This part of the chapter lays out in summary form the skeletal structure of Griffiths's account of heaven. The reader would do well to read, and reflect upon, Griffiths's beautiful book to garner the details.

In order to understand Griffiths's view of the nature of heaven, particularly for human persons, we need to examine four relevant positions that Griffiths takes up. First, Griffiths thinks that creatures are necessarily *temporal*. In thinking through the temporal nature of human persons, however, Griffiths distinguishes two different kinds of time (and duration): *metronomic* and *systolic*. Second, Griffiths thinks that all creatures have a last thing (*novissimum*) and, although there are three conceivable sorts of last things for human persons, in Griffiths's view, all created persons *in heaven* enjoy a last thing of a particular sort, namely, a minimally dynamic state of existence that he calls *repetitive stasis*. Third, Griffiths holds the view that heaven as a last thing consists centrally, if not exclusively, in the beatific vision, which itself has both intellectual and sensory dimensions. But heaven, according to Griffiths, is also a social reality for human persons insofar as they know and love other human persons, angels, nonhuman animals, and plants in heaven. Fourth, according to Griffiths, part of what it means to know and love in systolic rather than metronomic time is to know and love without reference to oneself.

Griffiths on the Nature of Time and the Temporal Nature of Human Persons

According to Griffiths, God is timeless, and only God is timeless.[77] Insofar as God creates x—and so x is not God—x is something that is by nature temporal.[78] Because anything that exists in time also exists in space, all creatures are also spatial or bodily beings (even if not all creatures, e.g., angels, or separated souls, have bodies of flesh and blood).[79]

Griffiths thinks that there are two kinds of *cosmic* time, that is, time as an ontological aspect of creatures.[80] There is cosmic time as it exists for fallen creatures in this life and, possibly, for fallen creatures in hell. He calls this sort of cosmic time, *metronomic* time. According to Griffiths, time is metronomic if and only if it is a *measurable* duration, and so a duration made up of discrete, regular periods.[81] In addition, metronomic time is *fallen* time. As Griffiths thinks that death is "an artifact of the

---

77. *Decreation*, 71–81.
78. Ibid., 69–70 and 81–87.
79. Ibid., 86–87.
80. Ibid., 89. As distinct from *psychic* time, i.e., time as creatures experience it.
81. Ibid., 91. Griffiths speaks of metronomic time as both a measure of duration that is measurable and temporal duration itself.

fall,"[82] he also has the view that time is metronomic if, and only if, it is a measureable duration of what tends toward annihilation or death.[83]

A second kind of cosmic time, according to Griffiths, is *systolic* time. This is time as it existed in Eden before the Fall, and as it exists in heaven.[84] Because systolic time is a form of time, it has duration. Nonetheless, systolic time is not a measurable duration. Whereas metronomic time measures being that tends toward annihilation or death, systolic time is a duration of what lives without dying or otherwise going out of existence. If we think of God's eternal duration as Boethius does, "the perfect possession of unlimited life all at once,"[85] systolic time is therefore a duration that more greatly participates in God's eternity than metronomic time.

According to Griffiths, systolic time breaks into this world of metronomic time paradigmatically in the passion, death, resurrection, and ascension of Christ. As the Mass is a representation of, and participation in, the passion, death, resurrection, and ascension of Christ, whenever and wherever the Mass takes place, that is a time and place in which systolic time is particularly transfiguring the metronomic.[86] Of course, until the general judgment, the systolic time of liturgical action exists in tension with metronomic time. Although we are sometimes fully engaged—and self-forgetful—in participating in the Mass in this life, we are often acutely aware of the passage of metronomic time and our own earthly concerns during the Mass.

In order further to understand the nature of systolic time according to Griffiths, we might think not only of particular this-worldly liturgies, but also of the liturgical *calendar*. Although the liturgical calendar occasionally makes reference to metronomic time—indeed, this is inevitable insofar as the kingdom of God is not yet fully consummated; in this life systolic time is always in tension with metronomic time—the liturgical calendar centers upon the times (systoles) of the most holy days of the Triduum, and "reaches back, temporally speaking, behind Easter to the time of Christmas and Advent, and reaches forward, in front of it,

82. Ibid., 92.
83. Ibid., 91–92.
84. Ibid., 95.
85. "Aeternitas igitur est interminabilis vitae tota simul et perfecta possessio." *The Consolation of Philosophy* V.6, in *Boethius: The Theological Tractates and the Consolation of Philosophy*, Loeb Classical Library 74 (Cambridge, Mass.: Harvard University Press, 1973).
86. *Decreation*, 96–99.

to Pentecost and the ascension."[87] And the church calendar continually repeats itself, no matter the metronomic time and place. Living one's life in accord with the church calendar can thus habituate one to living on systolic rather than metronomic time.

We can see a particularly powerful manifestation of what Griffiths is talking about in the manner in which the lives of the brothers or sisters of a monastic community are related to time (and insofar as the laity spend some time living and praying with that community, we experience it too, if only for a short span of metronomic time). For the brothers or sisters in a monastic community ideally live according to systolic time insofar as their daily activities are organized around the liturgy of the hours, itself a repetitive cycle of prayers. The operative question where time is concerned in a monastic community is not, "what time (in a metronomic sense) is it?" but rather, "what is it time for now?," for example, Lauds or Mass or work or study, etc.

Griffiths on the Last Things

Griffiths thinks of *the last thing* for a creature as referring to the *novissimum* (newest possible thing) for that creature. According to Griffiths, then, the *novissimum* for any creature is the state of that creature such that there is no longer any novelty possible for it; this is its "last thing."[88] Griffiths does think that it is *conceivable* that creatures do not have a last thing. Indeed, as we have seen, some Christian theologians and philosophers deny that there is a last thing for human persons insofar as they think that human life in heaven involves, among other things, a life of perpetual novelty. To think of human life in heaven in this way is to think of human persons in heaven existing in an *epektatic* state, one that is ever reaching forward to something.[89]

Griffiths himself rejects the view that human persons do not have a last thing.[90] For he thinks, with St. Augustine, that whatever else heaven is, it is a place of rest (*quies*).[91] But if heaven were not a *novissimum*, a last thing—if heaven involved perpetual intellectual, moral, and relational progress—it would not be a place of *quies*. As Griffiths notes, "under-

---

87. Ibid., 99.
88. Ibid., 7.
89. Ibid., 26.
90. Ibid., 27.
91. Ibid., 216.

standing ... heaven as *novissimum* is why we inscribe *requiescat in pace* on headstones and other memorials of death."[92]

According to Griffiths, there are three conceivable last things for human persons: annihilation, simple stasis, and repetitive stasis. A last thing may also be glorious (perfective) or inglorious. Griffiths takes absolute or permanent annihilation to be a last thing, as "it is an instance, perhaps the clearest possible instance, of a condition without future novelty."[93] As a Catholic theologian, however, Griffiths rejects the view that *human* persons can have annihilation as a *glorious* last thing.[94]

If human persons in heaven have a *simply static* last thing, then they enter a state such that they exist in systolic time, and do not change in any respect. Griffiths thinks many Christians have thought about heaven—particularly, after the general resurrection—on the model of simple stasis. Finally, there is the possibility that human persons in heaven have a *repetitively static* last thing. If that is the case, then human persons in heaven perpetually repeat the same kind of action or series of actions. In the case of this kind of last thing, there is change, but still no novelty. For example, it is possible that the saints in heaven endlessly repeat the Sanctus, and each time they do so, they do it just as (well as) they did the first time.

Griffiths on the Beatific Vision

As a Catholic theologian who wants to think with the church, Griffiths accepts that the saints in heaven have the beatific vision; indeed, the saints in heaven have the beatific vision before the general resurrection.[95] Nonetheless, for Griffiths, the beatific vision before the general resurrection is not a last thing, as "it is followed by something new (and longed for) that is the rejoining of the soul with its flesh, and that rejoining has effects upon the means by which the vision is had, and, thus, also upon the content of the vision."[96] When Griffiths offers his interpretation of what the beatific vision as last thing amounts to, he tends to

---

92. Ibid.
93. Ibid., 15.
94. Griffiths does think that annihilation is a coherent possibility for the damned, given Christian axioms (*Decreation*, 191–213 and 241–50). It is hard to see how this is true. However, adjudicating whether or not annihilation is a coherent possibility for the damned is beyond the scope of this book on heaven.
95. See, e.g., Benedict XII, *Benedictus Deus*.
96. *Decreation*, 218.

make one of a number of general points: (a) it is always experienced *sub species temporalis*;[97] (b) it involves both an intellectual dimension[98] and a sensory dimension, when (after the general resurrection) the saints see Christ the Lord in the flesh;[99] and, (c) unlike our intellectual and affective activity after the Fall, it does not involve a second-order experience of reality, that is, a person S's experience of reality such that S reflects on what it is like for S to experience reality.[100]

Griffiths also thinks that there is a social dimension to heaven for human persons insofar as the human saints in heaven know and love other human saints, angels, nonhuman animals, and plants in heaven's perpetually repeated and perfect liturgy. As we will see in chapter 13 below, where I treat this view of Griffiths's in more detail, Griffiths thinks that our healed relations with animals and plants are partly constitutive of the perfect life human persons enjoy in heaven. Therefore, heaven is more than the beatific vision; it also involves human knowledge and love of other persons, animals, and plants.

Griffiths on Experience in Heaven

Griffiths thinks that human experience in heaven is not self-referential. This claim is important for Griffiths's account of heaven as perfectly liturgical, as part of the function of liturgy in this life, Griffiths thinks, is to prepare us for the other-directedness of the perfect liturgy in heaven. In this life, when we engage in a token of some type of action we have performed many times, we often find ourselves distracted, thinking about our own experience of that action. Indeed, we sometimes focus our attention on our own experiences, rather than on some object outside ourselves. Griffiths thinks that such second-order experience is an artifact of the Fall and has no place in the life of the saints in heaven.[101]

More precisely, Griffiths thinks that all experience gives rise to qualia. When we look at something blue, we have the first-person experience or qualia of blue; certain circumstances or experiences give rise to experiences or qualia of emotions or feelings, for example, experiences of boredom or anger. But sometimes we experience *second*-order qualia,

---

97. Ibid., 144.
98. Ibid., 144, 218–19, and 308.
99. Ibid., 219–21 and 308.
100. Ibid., 222–38.
101. Ibid.

for example, we think about *what it is like to experience blue,* or John thinks about what it is like for *himself* to experience blue (Griffiths calls this sort of second-order experience *possessive* layering of experience), or we think about being appeared to bluely in order to categorize that experience as an experience of sensing color (Griffiths calls this sort of second-order experience *categorical* layering of experience). Griffiths notes that the recognition that human persons have second-order experiences has been an important part of the philosophy of mind since at least the seventeenth century. In addition, much of the "action" in modern novels takes places in the "theatres of the minds" of the central characters of those novels, as the authors of those novels inform readers about the second-order experiences had by those characters, with the characters of the novels themselves sometimes doing the narrating.

According to Griffiths, mental habit is the enemy of such second-order experience. So, the more we do some kind of thing A *habitually*, the more the doing of A does not give rise to second-order experiences, at least with respect to A. As Griffiths points out, some kinds of activity that many of us admire are done best when done habitually, such as writing, playing music, playing sports, speaking, acts of etiquette. But, according to Griffiths, the liturgy in particular is designed to eliminate second-order experience, habituating us to act such that we direct our attention to God and our neighbor, without reflecting upon what we are doing when we are, for example, worshiping God or doing something good for another human person. Because earthly liturgies habituate us to love of God and neighbor, gradually eliminating in us the tendency to self-absorption, and because earthly liturgies at their best participate in and prefigure the heavenly liturgy, Griffiths thinks that the heavenly liturgy in which the saints perpetually participate is devoid of second-order experiences such as thinking "what a joy it is to be here," or "this is sure a neat experience!"

Griffiths on Heaven as Perpetually Repeated and Perfect Liturgy

Griffiths claims that "liturgical action and liturgical agency provide, in the devastation, the fullest and best image of what heavenly action and heavenly agency will be like for human creatures."[102] As we have

102. Ibid., 104.

seen, this is because time in heaven is systolic and the Mass is a representation of, and participation in, the paradigmatic entrance of the systolic into the metronomic, namely, Christ's redemptive action. In addition, as Griffiths states elsewhere: "In its liturgical work the church provides the fullest foretaste of heaven to be had in the devastated world, and that is because the liturgy is where (and when) Christ the healer is most intensely present."[103] Of course, the liturgy itself is a cyclical action. As Griffiths writes: "An essential deep-structural feature of the liturgy here below is its cyclical repetitiveness. There is a cycle of the day, of the week, and of the year: the assembly, ideal-typically, does the same thing every sunrise and noon, every Friday and every Sunday, every Easter and every Christmas."[104] As heaven is liturgical, and an "essential deep-structural feature of the liturgy here below is its cyclical repetitiveness," this gives us reason to think that heaven, as a last end for human persons, is a repetitive stasis. Because time in heaven—and the ideal liturgy—is systolic, and heaven is perfectly fulfilling, this repetitive stasis cannot be boring, but rather involves perfect rest.

But why think that each reiteration of the liturgy in heaven is the same? That is certainly not true of earthly liturgies. Of course, as Griffiths points out, in this life there are differences between the tokens of any liturgical type. But Griffiths also notes that these differences are merely accidental and not essential to the liturgy being a liturgy, for "the goal toward which every liturgical celebration points and toward which it asymptomatically tends is indiscriminable identity of participation in what it is about, in the events that make it what it is."[105] Recall that Griffiths thinks that liturgical action—especially the Mass—is the best example of systolic, or heavenly, time breaking in to metronomic time. We can therefore conclude: "the end of human creatures in heaven is repetitively static."[106] Although there will be different tokens of the type(s) of liturgical action in heaven, these different tokens in heaven will be indiscriminable from one another, unlike in this life. Griffiths concludes:

Heaven's time . . . maintains and intensifies to the maximum the signs of temporal grace evident in the devastation [i.e., this life after the Fall], and removes all unendurability. This is to say that heaven's time is exclusively nonmetro-

103. Ibid., 251.
104. Ibid., 102.
105. Ibid., 103.
106. Ibid.

nomic.... What remains is the systole perfected, the tensive, gathered time of the liturgy now extended to infinity.... The [systolic] time of heaven is a constant, endless, back-and-forth of praise and love between the saints and the LORD, an inbreath and outbreath of gift-given and gift-received-by-being-returned. This endlessly repeated but temporally structured cycle is the temporal form of the beatific vision: it is how temporal creatures see the LORD, the maximal extent of creaturely participation in the LORD's eternity.[107]

Griffiths's View of Perfect Human Happiness in Heaven and PNH-III

How would someone with Griffiths's views respond to PNH-III? Recall the primary assumptions in PNH-III:

(1) The notion that (i) heaven is static is in conflict with the notion that (b) heaven includes the reality of "the new heavens and the new earth," which itself includes a perfect human community, and, at least eventually, perfected embodiment on the part of human persons in the next life and the notion that (j) if there is a human person S in heaven, then S is flourishing [assumption].

(2) The notion that (k) heaven is dynamic, that is, not static, is in conflict with the notion that (a) heaven for intellectual creatures consists merely in the beatific vision and the notion that (l) human persons in heaven are perfectly happy [assumption].

(3) (i) is true or (k) is true [assumption].

(4) [(b) is true or (j) is true] and [(a) is true or (l) is true] [assumption].

Someone with the views that Griffiths has with respect to heaven and time can respond to PNH-III in a couple ways, depending upon how we interpret certain of Griffiths's views. As we have seen, Griffiths portrays heaven as participation in heaven's perfect liturgy. Such activity counts as *a last thing*, and so does not involve any novelty. Rather, intellectual creatures such as human persons participate in a perpetually repeated perfect liturgy, which liturgy involves perpetual antiphonal responses between God and creatures, where each iteration of the liturgy is specifically the same. Because each cycle of the liturgy has different parts, creatures in heaven change insofar as they progress through the parts of a particular token of the heavenly liturgy. But each token of the liturgy is performed in precisely the same way. Therefore, Griffiths describes such

107. Ibid., 107–8.

a last thing for intellectual creatures in heaven as *repetitive stasis*. Given the way that I have defined *static* and *dynamic* views of heaven, Griffiths's view counts as a dynamic view. So an advocate of Griffiths's account of heaven accepts proposition (k) of PNH-III and so rejects proposition (i). We can also assume that an advocate of Griffiths's views would accept premise (1)—see my discussion of (1) above—and premise (3) of PNH-III. Because an advocate of Griffiths's views accepts propositions (b), (j), and (l) in that argument, she also accepts premise (4).

Given what I have said, if the advocate of Griffiths's view is to avoid a contradiction, she must reject premise (2). If she rejects premise (2), then she must think that heaven as perfect repetitive liturgy, and so, as dynamic reality—proposition (k)—is either *not* in conflict with the notion that heaven for intellectual creatures consists merely in the beatific vision—proposition (a)—*or* she must think that heaven as dynamic reality is *not* in conflict with the notion that human persons are perfectly happy in heaven—proposition (l). Griffiths clearly thinks the latter, that is, heaven as perfect repetitive liturgy is *not* in conflict with the notion that human persons are perfectly happy in heaven. Although the saint in heaven is undergoing changes within each cycle of the heavenly liturgy, she is not happier in one moment of the cycle than at another moment. It is participating in the ongoing liturgical cycle that makes the saint perfectly happy. Furthermore, each reiteration of the liturgy is specifically identical to the one that comes before. So she is not, for example, happier in the second reiteration of the liturgy than in her first participation in it. And the same goes for the third reiteration, etc. Because the changes that human persons in heaven undergo are not directed at obtaining further perfections on their part, the advocate of Griffiths's view can accept that heaven is a changing reality without rejecting the view that human persons in heaven are perfectly happy.

In addition, an advocate of Griffiths's views can also reject the idea that (k) entails the falsity of (a). For, according to Griffiths, perfect human happiness in heaven consists in a human person's participation in the perpetual and perfect liturgy of heaven. The beatific vision is clearly central to this liturgy and, according to Griffiths, the vision has two dimensions, an intellectual and (perhaps more important for Griffiths) a sensitive dimension (wherein the human person knows by acquaintance Christ the Lord by way of the senses). For Griffiths, unlike for St. Augustine, the beatific vision is a temporal activity. Therefore, proposition (k) does not conflict with (a). Nonetheless, although Griffiths thinks that the beatific vision is central to the heavenly liturgy, it is not identical to this liturgy. Therefore, an advocate of Griffiths's view of heaven rejects (a).

A Problem with Griffiths's Account

As helpful as Griffiths's account of human happiness in heaven is—indeed, I will seek to incorporate certain aspects of it into a Thomistic account of heaven in later chapters—there is a systematic flaw in it, namely, that it *underestimates* the extent to which intellectual creatures such an angels and human persons are *glorified* in heaven. There are two ways to see this limitation in Griffiths's account, given what I have said about it so far.

First, Griffiths thinks of heaven as, at least in part, recapitulating life in the Garden of Eden, that is, the state of innocence before the Fall. So, for example, heavenly time is Edenic time, namely, systolic time that cannot be measured and is not bounded by death or annihilation. According to Griffiths, therefore, we only have death in metronomic time, and metronomic time is time that can be measured, that is, has an end. However, clearly there was death *before* the Fall. For example, we might think, with St. Thomas, that animal predation is something natural for certain animals.[108] In addition, even in the state of innocence there was death insofar as Adam and Eve were eating plants and plant parts. At the very least, in consuming (parts of) plants, Adam and Eve would have killed living cells. Therefore, if time that involves death is metronomic, then time in the state of innocence was metronomic. However, in heaven, "there will be no more death" (Rv 21:4). Therefore, assuming Griffiths's account of cosmic time, there is a greater contrast between the glory of heavenly human life and the life human persons lived in the state of innocence than Griffiths recognizes. For heavenly life is a different kind of life than life in the state of innocence. Although human persons in the state of innocence enjoyed the preternatural gift of immor-

---

108. See, e.g., *Summa contra Gentiles* [hereafter *SCG*] II.41.12–13 and III.71; *CT* I, chap. 142; *ST* I, q. 22, a. 2, ad 2; q. 47, a. 2, resp.; q. 48, a. 2, resp. and ad 3; q. 49, a. 2, resp.; q. 96, a. 1, ad 2; *QDM*, q. 1, a. 3, ad 18, and q. 5, a. 5, ad 2. See also his commentary on Is 11:1–16 and 65:25, where St. Thomas reads passages such as "the wolf shall dwell with the lamb" (11:6) and "the lion shall eat straw like the ox" (11:7) figuratively as speaking of the spiritual and moral transformation of human persons in the advent of the kingdom of God. See *Commentary on Isaiah*, trans. Joshua Madden (Lander, Wyo.: The Aquinas Institute, 2017), available at aquinas.cc/la/en/~Isaiah.

tality,[109] life in general in the state of innocence, like life after the Fall, is a corruptible life, involving as it does the activities of eating, drinking, and generation. By contrast, the life of heaven is incorruptible: "For this perishable body must put on imperishability, and this mortal body must put on immortality" (1 Cor 15:53).

Even if we think that there is no death or corruption in the state of innocence, it seems as though time in the state of innocence still would have been metronomic. For, according to authoritative, Catholic Christian tradition, Adam and Eve, before the Fall, had the preternatural gift of immortality.[110] But that gift is understood such that God's design for human persons is that life in this world is temporary and finite, and so would eventually end, even if Adam, Eve, and their progeny never sinned. That is to say, even if human persons never sinned, they would eventually have been translated to a heavenly life so that they could enjoy the beatific vision. Notably, Adam and Eve clearly did not enjoy the beatific vision, because once one has this vision, one cannot sin.[111] So God's plan was that Edenic existence, in any case, would end. But a temporal duration that ends is metronomic. Therefore, time in the state of innocence was metronomic, where time in heaven is systolic, or at least, nonmetronomic. Because it is better to live according to systolic (or nonmetronomic) time than metronomic time, Griffiths underestimates the glory of heavenly life when compared to Edenic life.

The second way to see that Griffiths underestimates the glory of heaven is with his view that the beatific vision, whether for angels or human persons, is something temporal. God is eternal by nature. Although angels and human persons never become eternal *by nature*, they do (as

---

109. A *preternatural* gift G is something conferred by God on a being B such that B's possession and use of G is above and beyond B's nature, although it is not above and beyond all created natures. For example, the gift of immortality to Adam and Eve (as composite substances) is preternatural insofar as (1) it is not in the nature of spirit and matter to stay united forever, and so human persons as composites of spirit and matter are not naturally immortal; (2) Adam and Eve (and their progeny) would have remained immortal had they not sinned; and (3) angels are created substances that are immortal by nature. Preternatural gifts should not be confused with supernatural gifts, e.g., supernatural life or justifying grace. A *supernatural* gift G is something conferred by God on a being B such that B's possession and use of G is above and beyond all created natures. See, e.g., T. Scannell, "Supernatural Gift," in *The Catholic Encyclopedia* (New York: Robert Appleton, 1909), available at www.newadvent.org/cathen/06553a.htm.

110. See, e.g., Fifteenth (or Sixteenth) Council of Carthage (begun May 1, 418), canon 1; *Epistula tractoria* to the Eastern Churches, between June and August 418; Profession of Faith of Pope Vigilius (February 5, 552); and the Council of Trent, Session 5, Decree on Original Sin (June 17, 1546), no. 1.

111. For a discussion of the inability of the saints in heaven to choose evil, despite being able to make morally weighty free choices, see my "Making the Best Even Better."

I will articulate, and argue for, in later chapters), by the grace of God, come to participate in God's eternal life by engaging in a timeless and immutable *activity*, namely, the beatific vision. Because such an activity is greater than any temporal activity; because the saints in heaven *do* engage in such an activity; and because Griffiths denies that the saints engage in such an activity, it follows that Griffiths's account of heavenly life for angels and human saints in heaven underestimates the extent to which intellectual creatures are glorified in heaven.

3

Contemporary Philosophy and Theology and the Problem of the Tedium of (Heavenly) Immortality

> Our ancestors were afraid of Hell; we are afraid of Heaven. We think it will be boring.
> CAROL ZALESKI

In a famous paper, "The Makropulos Case," philosopher Bernard Williams argues that a meaningful *human* life must be a mortal life.[1] The title of Williams's paper is taken from a play by Karel Capek. The play tells the story of a woman named Elina Makropulos, who at the time of action is 342 years old (Makropulos, of course, has had many names, but all of them give her the initials "E.M."). What explains E.M.'s longevity? When E.M. was forty-two years old, her father, the court physician to a sixteenth-century emperor, gave her an elixir of life, which she drank. Drinking the elixir prolongs a person's life an additional three hundred years. In the story, if E.M. is to go on living, she must drink the elixir of life again. But her life has become joyless and full of boredom; she is indifferent and cold. In E.M.'s view, she has already lived life to its fullest. All of her present experiences are mere shadowy repetitions of past experiences. In E.M.'s view, her life no longer brings surprises or challenges. In the end E.M. refuses to take the elixir again; she dies and the formula is deliberately destroyed by another young woman, although

---

Epigraph is from Carol Zaleski, "In Defense of Immortality," *First Things* 105 (September 2000): 42.

1. Bernard Williams, "The Makropulos Case: Reflections on the Tedium of Immortality," in his *Problems of the Self* (Cambridge: Cambridge University Press, 1973), 82–100.

among the protests of some older men. According to Williams, E.M.'s story teaches a deep truth: given that human persons in this life necessarily desire finite goods, immortality would eventually become tedious for any human person. If there were persons for whom immortality was not something tedious, such persons could not be *human* persons.

I will offer a more formal presentation of Williams's argument for the conclusion that a meaningful human life is necessarily a mortal life. Williams argues that, if there can be persons that are immortal, then (a) there can be nonhuman immortal persons; or (b) there can be immortal human persons such that they have a *fixed* character, that is, Jane's character is fixed insofar as, for example, she immutably prefers the mountains to the beach, and the music of Duke Ellington to Count Basie; or (c) there can be immortal human persons who do not have a fixed character. Because a reflective person realizes that a human person cannot be numerically—or personally—identical to a nonhuman person, a reflective human person in this life cannot reasonably desire to be an immortal nonhuman person. But an immortal human person S who is numerically identical to a human person S_1 in this life whose character is fixed would eventually find an immortal life to be boring or tedious. Because for any human person S_1 in this life there are certain kinds of lives that S_1 would not want to live, S_1 cannot be certain that S_1 would want to live the life of an immortal human person whose character was not fixed. Therefore, at best, a reflective human person in this life cannot believe that an immortal human life *is* attractive or, at worst, she will find the prospect of an immortal human life positively unattractive. Call this problem for believing an immortal human life is meaningful *the problem of the tedium of immortality* (PTI).

Although in his paper Williams does not explicitly treat of traditional Christian notions of heaven, it is not difficult to turn PTI into a problem specifically aimed at traditional Christian understandings of eternal life in heaven. Indeed, contemporary philosopher Brian Ribeiro has done just that. In a recent development of Williams's paper, Ribeiro argues, among other things, that it does not make sense for human persons to desire to go to heaven because, given the radical differences between the psychological life of human persons in this life and that of supposed persons in heaven, no human person who desires heaven in this life could be personally—and so numerically—identical to a person in heaven. Perhaps some persons could be perfectly happy in heaven, but no person in heaven could be numerically identical to a *human* person in this life, given the kinds of things human persons in this life desire.[2] As we will see in later chapters, St. Thomas Aquinas holds the view that human beatitude in heaven consists essentially in a timeless act of contemplating the essence of God. Such a view of heaven is just the kind of view at which Ribeiro's development of Williams's PTI takes aim. Here follows a formulation of Ribeiro's argument:

(1) A human person S and a human person S1 are personally (and thus numerically) identical only if there is psychological continuity between the psychological stages of S and the psychological stages of S1 [assumption].

(2) There is psychological discontinuity between the psychological stages of any human person S in this life and the psychological stage or stages of any person in heaven enjoying the beatific vision, when the first stage of S's intellectual life is S's rationally desiring, that is, willing, things in this life [assumption].[3]

(3) Therefore, no human person in this life who rationally desires, that is, wills, things is personally—and so numerically—identical to a person having the beatific vision in heaven [from (1) and (2)].

(4) Therefore, no human person in this life who rationally desires things can go to heaven [from (3)].

(5) But it does not make sense for a human person to wish for something impossible, once that person is made aware of its impossibility [assumption].

(6) Therefore, no human person S in this life can sensibly desire to go to heaven, once S becomes aware of an argument consisting of propositions such as (1)–(6) [from (4) and (5)].

---

2. "The Problem of Heaven," *Ratio* 24 (2011): 46–64.

3. Regarding "when the first stage of S's intellectual life is S's rationally desiring things in this life": according to Catholic dogma, some human persons have their first rational desires, or acts of will, in heaven, e.g., a human person S1 who is baptized and dies before having her first rational desires or acts of will. In that case, S1's first rational desires occur in heaven when S1 begins having the beatific vision. See, e.g., Pope Benedict XII, *Benedictus Deus*. Let us assume that Ribeiro's argument is *not* designed to show that (a) it is impossible that a baptized human person, who dies before the age of reason, is personally and numerically identical to a human person in heaven whose first self-conscious psychological states are engaging in the beatific activity in heaven. If Ribeiro's argument *is* designed to show (a), it should be noted that he has not offered an argument for such a conclusion.

The Tedium of (Heavenly) Immortality

Call Ribeiro's argument above, the *problem of the tedium of heavenly immortality* (PTHI). PTHI is logically valid. Let us also grant premises (1) and (5) of PTHI to the objector, if only for the sake of argument.

But why would one think that a premise such as (2) is true? In order to defend a premise such as (2), and so the inference to a premise such as (3), Ribeiro distinguishes four different relevant kinds of psychological changes: *instantaneous* changes, *radical* changes, *unmixed* changes, and *changes in a person that are directed from without*. By an unmixed change, Ribeiro simply means a change only for the good, as opposed to a mixed change, one that involves changes for the good and the bad. By changes directed from without, Ribeiro means to draw attention to changes that are not—or are only to a minimal degree—under the self-direction and control of the person being changed.

Ribeiro seems willing to grant that the changes a human person would need to undergo in order to enjoy heaven need not be directed from without in his sense, that is, such changes could involve some sort of cooperation on the part of the human person undergoing those changes. Therefore, I will henceforward not mention this kind of change. Also, insofar as an unmixed change is one that is wholly for the best, the change a human person undergoes between death in this life and the beatific vision in heaven seems clearly unmixed. To round out a discussion of PTHI, then, we can note that Ribeiro thinks that the changes any human person would have to undergo in order to enjoy the beatific vision would have to be instantaneous and radical.

Although a person S can perhaps survive psychological changes that are unmixed and radical, but not instantaneous, or changes that are unmixed and instantaneous, but not radical, or changes that are radical and instantaneous, but mixed, Ribeiro thinks that a person S cannot survive a psychological change that is unmixed, instantaneous, *and* radical. Such a change would constitute such a large break in the psychology of a person that the person before such a change could not be numerically or personally identical to the person after the change. I can therefore complete my formal presentation of PTHI by including the following two propositions as premises in an argument for (2):

(7) The psychological change that a human person S who rationally desires things in this life would have to undergo in order to become a

person S1 who enjoys the beatific vision in heaven is unmixed, instantaneous, and radical [assumption].

(8) A psychological change that is unmixed, instantaneous, and radical is a discontinuous change [assumption].

CONTEMPORARY RESPONSES TO PTHI

There exists a voluminous literature responding to PTI.[4] But many of the responses in this literature, even if they count as good responses to PTI, nonetheless fail as satisfactory responses to PTHI.[5] For example, one argument John Martin Fischer brings against PTI is that it assumes that a meaningful, immortal life is one totally devoid of boredom. But Fischer notes that occasional experience of boredom is clearly compatible with a meaningful immortal life, just as it is compatible with a meaningful, mortal human life.[6] But, of course, a *heavenly* life is one that *is* totally devoid of boredom. For boredom is a negative psychological state, that is, a painful one. But the experience of negative psychological states is incompatible with a person being perfectly happy,[7] as scripture too seems to attest.[8] Therefore, a perfectly happy person is not—never is—bored. But a human person in heaven is perfectly happy. Therefore, a human person in heaven is not—never is—bored, even for a second. So Fischer's response to PTI fails as a satisfactory response to PTHI.

That being said, some work by contemporary theologians and philosophers offers some responses to PTI that also suggest ways of responding to PTHI. Let us turn to examining such responses, which, when combined with an account of St. Thomas's own detailed views of heavenly life in later chapters, will provide a satisfactory response to PTHI.[9]

---

4. See especially John Martin Fischer, "Why Immortality Is Not So Bad," *International Journal of Philosophical Studies* 2 (1994): 257–70; Timothy Chappell, "Infinity Goes Up on Trial: Must Immortality Be Meaningless?," *European Journal of Philosophy* 17 (2009): 30–44; and John Martin Fischer and Benjamin Mitchell-Yellin, "Immortality and Boredom," *The Journal of Ethics* 18 (2014): 353–72.

5. For this point, see also Gilbert Meilaender's *Should We Live Forever?*, 51.

6. "Why Immortality Is Not So Bad."

7. For a different view, see Adam C. Pelser, "Heavenly Sadness: On the Value of Negative Emotions in Paradise," in *Paradise Understood* (ed. Byerly and Silverman), 113–35.

8. See, e.g., Rv 21:1–5.

9. Because PTI and PTHI are versions of the same problem, and PTHI is a more difficult problem to solve than PTI, I assume that a satisfactory solution to PTHI is thereby also a satisfactory solution to PTI.

Chappell's "Infinity Goes Up on Trial"

In an article focused on responding to Bernard Williams's famous paper about the tedium of immortality, philosopher Timothy Chappell offers some interesting, although intentionally underdeveloped, responses to PTI, which responses may be used to respond to PTHI as well. Particularly interesting for my purposes, Chappell notes that Williams does not rule out the possibility that human immortality involves the enjoyment of timeless goods, or, more specifically, the timeless good which is union with the timelessly eternal God,[10] a taste for which some human persons develop in their activities even in this life, for example, in lovemaking, prayer, friendship, conversation, study, and contemplation. Chappell provocatively suggests that a logical requirement for boredom is timeboundedness.[11] Therefore, if human immortality for some involves the enjoyment of goods that are not bound by time, boredom would be impossible for such human persons. And if a human person S begins to develop a taste for timeless goods in this life, perhaps it is not too much of a stretch to think a person S1 enjoying a timeless good in heaven can be personally identical with S.

Gilbert Meilaender's *Should We Live Forever*?

In a recent book on the philosophy of aging, theological ethicist Gilbert Meilaender offers an insightful examination of PTI.[12] For example, taking a cue from Fischer's "Why Immortality Is Not So Bad," Meilaender wonders whether a number of inexhaustible finite goods, suitably arranged and spaced, would not make for a meaningful immortal human life. And if an omnipotent God were doing the arranging and spacing of these finite but inexhaustible goods, would human persons not find an

---

10. "Infinity Goes Up on Trial," 42. For this suggestion, see also Charles Taliaferro's "Why We Need Immortality," *Modern Theology* 6 (1994): 367–77, and Carol Zaleski, "In Defense of Immortality." For example, Zaleski remarks: "But adoration cannot be boring, for one is gazing at the face of the beloved, and the face of the beloved is inexhaustible. We find it hard to imagine the kind of happiness that might flow from a condition of perfection. The very idea of perfection has become alien to us. We prefer to speak of 'human flourishing,' an open-ended ideal that incorporates change and imposes no absolute standards. As an ideal, perfection produces anorexics and martinets, we think; only the 'spirituality of imperfection' can promote human flourishing. But this is to confuse perfection with perfectionism; *true* perfection is evergreen and alive, including within itself everything that we value about change" (42).

11. "Infinity Goes Up on Trial," 42.

12. *Should We Live Forever*? See esp. 42–56. Thanks to Matt Braddock for pointing me to Meilaender's work on PTI.

immortal life consisting of such goods quite satisfying? Of course, *some* human persons would find inexhaustible finite goods such as conjugal love and friendship tedious, but Meilaender thinks this would say more about those particular persons—that there exists in them some sort of moral deficiency—than for Williams's thesis that, necessarily, an immortal human life eventually becomes boring or tedious. As we will see in chapter 17, St. Thomas too thinks that not just anyone would enjoy eternal life with God, but only someone who is prepared by grace and charity.

One helpful aspect of Meilaender's treatment of PTI is that he mentions a couple of potential problems for human immortality that are different from, but closely related to, Williams's dilemma for a meaningful, immortal human life. For example, Meilaender discusses philosopher Christine Overall's claim that human immortality entails a "double axiological bind" insofar as human bodies and brains are finite. According to Overall, if a person S is a *human* person, an immortal life will eventually become, if not boring or tedious, *exhausting* for S, both physically and psychologically. For insofar as S has a finite human body and brain, S will eventually reach a point in S's immortal life where there is no more room for intellectual and moral growth, and this will be true whether S pursues ever-new self-exhausting pleasures, repeatable pleasures, or other-focused pleasures or desires. But if some person S1 lives a non-exhausting and non-exhausted immortal life, then S1 does not have a limited human body and so S1 is not a human person.[13]

Meilaender's helpful response to Overall's argument is that "we're not meant to live *this kind* of life forever." Indeed, "part of the point of this life is to draw us on to something still more fulfilling."[14] As St. Augustine says, "our hearts are restless till they rest in Thee."[15] And as we will see in future chapters, St. Thomas gives us a beautiful and profound description of human life in heaven, one that, although continuous with the psychological and bodily life of human persons in this life, is nonetheless a *new* human life. For such a heavenly human life is transformed and glorified, and is fully consistent with human lives being both immortal and fulfilling.

---

13. Christine Overall, *Aging, Death and Human Longevity: A Philosophical Inquiry* (Los Angeles: University of California Press, 2005), 124–82.
14. *Should We Live Forever?*, 47.
15. *Confessions* I.1 (trans. Sheed), 3.

In discussing PTI, Meilaender also mentions Martha Nussbaum's slightly different problem for the notion of a good, immortal human life. According to Nussbaum, immortality is incompatible with moral virtues the possession of which is necessary for *human* flourishing.[16] For, according to Nussbaum, a happy human life requires virtues such as courage whose possession only makes sense if we are fragile and mortal. Therefore, a happy immortal life cannot be a human life.

Sensitive to Nussbaum's point about the connection between human virtues and human mortality, Meilaender nonetheless helpfully points out that what is required for virtuous action in this life may be one thing, for example, courage in the face of the real possibility of death, whereas what is required for celebrating the virtuous actions of this life in heaven is something else altogether. As we will see in chapter 12 (almost as if St. Thomas foresaw an objection to an immortal life such as Nussbaum's), St. Thomas makes the fruit and aureoles of the virtues acted upon in this life an important aspect of the accidental reward of the saints in heaven insofar as the saints experience everlasting joy in heaven in their victories for the sake of the kingdom of God in this life.[17]

In responding to arguments against the idea that a human immortal life can be meaningful or good, Meilaender makes an additional argument. According to Meilaender, arguments against the idea that a human immortal life can be meaningful or good assume that there is some

---

16. Martha Nussbaum, *The Therapy of Desire: Theory and Practice in Hellenistic Ethics* (Princeton, N.J.: Princeton University Press, 1994). For additional discussion of Nussbaum's claim from a Thomistic perspective, see Thomas Hibbs, "Transcending Humanity in Aquinas," *Proceedings of the American Catholic Philosophical Association* 66 (1992): 191–202.

17. In addition, we might respond to Nussbaum by saying that, although the *material* aspects of the cardinal virtues (and the gifts of the Spirit) do not exist in an immortal being, e.g., the material aspect of the cardinal virtue of courage which is responding rationally to a fear of death and suffering is not found in an immortal being, the *formal* aspect of the cardinal virtues (and the gifts of the Spirit) can have a place in an immortal life, e.g., the formal aspect of the cardinal virtue of courage remains in the saint in heaven's irascible power being perfectly subject to reason (see, e.g., St. Thomas's *ST* I-II, q. 61, a. 5; q. 67, a. 1; q. 68, a. 6). In addition, it may be that some virtues, or *ways* of having virtues, do not have a place in an immortal life whereas they do play an important role as the means to the end of a happy immortal life. For example, St. Thomas argues that the theological virtues of faith and hope, as important as they are in this life for the sake of achieving the ultimate end in heaven, do not themselves exist in heaven (see, e.g., *ST* I-II, q. 67, aa. 4–6). Nonetheless, as the cardinal virtues in their material elements and the theological virtues of faith and hope are in some sense necessary for achieving the ultimate end for human persons, they still have a great significance. Finally, surely one reason that St. Paul says, "the greatest of these is love [i.e., charity]" (1 Cor 13:13) is that charity can exist as a virtue both in this life and the next. Therefore, from a Thomistic perspective, specifically, and a Christian perspective, more generally, we might think that Nussbaum does not sufficiently appreciate the importance of the virtue of charity for human flourishing, in this life and in the next.

sort of metaphysically neutral ground from which to discuss whether an immortal human life could be satisfying. But there is no such ground. For example, there is the contestable question, "what is a human person?" According to the Jewish and Christian traditions, we are created in the image and likeness of God, and so, given his neo-Platonic belief that all things desire to return to their source, St. Augustine thinks, "our hearts are restless till they rest in Thee." Someone who thinks from within such a metaphysical framework can agree with a philosopher such as Bernard Williams that an immortal human life that is aimed at securing finite goods will (even quickly) become tedious. For even a mortal human life aimed at finite goods is not satisfying for the Augustinian.

But where Williams and the Augustinian differ is on the nature of ultimate reality, for example, on whether there is a God who has created human persons to enjoy him forever. Like Chappell, Meilaender thinks that Williams does not rule out the possibility that what PTI really shows—worries about personal identity notwithstanding—is that human persons are not meant to be satisfied by an infinite parade of finite goods, but are rather meant to enjoy a transcendent and timeless good in heaven. As Meilaender notes, "any Augustinian would happily grant that finite beauties cannot bear the whole weight of the heart's longing, for they are shafts of the divine glory intended to direct our desire to ... God."[18] Or, as Meilaender artfully puts the point in another place,

Bernard Williams ... found ... no reason to suppose there could be anything or anyone "that could be guaranteed to be at every moment utterly absorbing." There is, I suppose, no indefeasible argument to persuade us that he is wrong and that, say, Dante's *Paradiso* is right. Nonetheless, if the search is on for an utterly absorbing object, some may find in Dante's classic depiction of the vision of God a deeper truth than Williams seems able to imagine (or, perhaps, hope for).[19]

Paul J. Griffiths and the Perfect Systolic Time of Heaven

In chapter 2, I discussed Paul Griffiths's view that heaven consists in a perpetual repetition of the perfect liturgy, with God himself presiding. One point Griffiths makes about the nature of heaven is relevant here for my discussion of PTHI. Recall that, according to Griffiths, all creatures exist in time. But there are two kinds of cosmic (that is, real rather

---

18. *Should We Live Forever?*, 44.
19. Ibid., 49–50.

than merely phenomenological) time: metronomic and systolic. Metronomic time is time that can be measured, whereas systolic time cannot be. Metronomic time is the temporal duration of hell and the temporal duration that characterizes this life after the Fall, except in those places (chiefly in the Mass) where the systolic is breaking in to the metronomic, transforming persons and places in this life and thereby making them fit for a heavenly, and so perfectly systolic, life. For, according to Griffiths, systolic time is the temporal duration of creatures in heaven.

On this analysis of the relation between human flourishing and immortality, Griffiths would agree with Williams that an eternity within the *metronome* would be tedious; in fact, it would be what Christians traditionally call hell. But the experience of boredom is not characteristic of a human person existing in systolic time. As the temporal duration of heaven is purely systolic—time cannot be measured in heaven—to be bored in heaven is a contradiction in terms.

But could a person for whom it is not possible to be bored be personally identical to a human person in this life, a person who routinely experiences the mental state of boredom? Yes. According to Griffiths, it is participation in the liturgy in this life—and, presumably other activities characterized by the systole such as prayer, study, and the doing of good works arising from charity—that prepare persons for the joy of measureless time in heaven. Therefore, to the extent that one's life is characterized by participating in Mass, prayer, study, and love in this life, one is prepared for an eternal systolic human life in heaven.

This brings the first part of the book to a close. I have noted what some contemporary theologians and philosophers have said regarding four problems concerning eternal life in heaven, or, if they have not addressed those problems directly, how those theologians and philosophers could respond to those four problems. Although I have certainly found some helpful suggestions in the literature surveyed, some of which I will draw upon later, I have also noted some problems or limitations with each of the positions under discussion. I now turn to the task of explaining, developing, and defending what St. Thomas Aquinas has to say about eternal life in the next two parts of this book, before showing, in the final part, how St. Thomas can respond to the four problems concerning eternal life in ways that are preferable to the contemporary solutions addressed hitherto.

PART 2

ST. THOMAS ON THE ESSENTIAL REWARD IN HEAVEN

4

Human *beatitudo* in Heaven

A PROLEGOMENA

Part 1 examined four apparent problems concerning the nature of eternal life as theologians and philosophers in the Christian tradition have talked about it. It also examined responses to these problems on the part of some contemporary theologians and philosophers. In order to offer Thomistic responses to these problems in part 4, the next two parts develop St. Thomas Aquinas's account of the logical parts of *beatitudo* for human persons in heaven. Part 2 treats in particular what St. Thomas in some places calls *the essential reward* of human persons in heaven. Part 3 treats the component parts of what St. Thomas sometimes calls *the accidental reward*. Parts 2 and 3 form the heart of the book. The details of St. Thomas's account of the nature of heaven and its various parts are interesting in themselves, but the Thomistic teaching on human happiness in heaven as consisting of an essential reward and an accidental reward in particular allows for sophisticated and convincing responses to the apparent problems about the nature of heaven that I have discussed. These Thomistic responses not only avoid the problems that plague the contemporary responses treated in part 1, but they allow for more detailed, and thus intellectually satisfactory, responses to such problems.

This chapter sets the stage for discussion of the details of the essential reward and the accidental reward in parts 2 and 3. Chapter 4 has three sections. The first section provides the context for St. Thomas's discussion of human *beatitudo* in heaven within the *Summa Theologiae*, his final and, in some ways, most detailed treatment of that subject, by offering a summary of the important logical moves that St. Thomas makes in *Prima Secundae*, qq. 1–2. The second section of the chapter explains some distinctions St. Thomas makes with respect to the various aspects of heavenly life for human persons, for example, his important distinction between *the essential reward* and *the accidental reward*. Because St. Thomas thinks about the essential reward as, among other things, a participation in God's eternal life, the third section offers a brief account of St. Thomas's views on the nature of God and God's eternal life.

THE IMMEDIATE CONTEXT OF ST. THOMAS'S DISCUSSION OF *BEATITUDO* IN *SUMMA THEOLOGIAE*

St. Thomas's last discussion of human happiness (*beatitudo*) in heaven comes at the beginning of *Summa Theologiae* I-II. Although St. Thomas discusses human *beatitudo* in some detail in earlier works,[1] his treatment here is his last detailed, even if incomplete, treatment. And as we will see, St. Thomas changes his mind about at least one important topic where human happiness is concerned by the time he writes this part of the *Summa*. For these reasons, it makes sense to write about St. Thomas's account of perfect human happiness in heaven from a *Summa*-centric point of view, even if we also consult other works. As the focus here is explaining and developing St. Thomas's views on human happiness in heaven, my account focuses on what St. Thomas says in I-II, qq. 3–5. Nonetheless, something needs to be said about the major logical moves that St. Thomas makes in qq. 1–2 in order to provide context for his treatment of perfect human happiness in heaven in qq. 3–5.

St. Thomas on Acts, Means, and Ends

The first question in the *Prima Secundae* consists of a discussion of what St. Thomas calls the "ultimate end" of human persons. This is an important expression for St. Thomas and it will pay some dividends to get clear on just what he means by it.

According to St. Thomas, every agent acts for an end. For, if an agent

---

1. Most notably, see *In Sent* IV, dd. 43–49 (*ST Suppl.*, qq. 73–96); *SCG* III.1–63 and IV.79–97; *CT* I, chaps. 149–74, and *CT* II, chaps. 8–10. When multiple passages from St. Thomas's oeuvre are cited in the footnotes, these are listed in chronological order, from earliest text to latest text. For the dating of St. Thomas's works, see Jean-Pierre Torrell, *The Person and His Work*, vol. 1 of *Saint Thomas Aquinas*, trans. Robert Royal, rev. ed. (Washington, D.C.: The Catholic University of America Press, 2005). For St. Thomas's Latin texts, see the online Latin collections at *Corpus Thomisticum*, ed. Enrique Alarcon, available at www.corpusthomisticum.org/iopera.html; and the Aquinas Institute, available at aquinas.cc/173/513/~182.

does not act for an end, then an agent acting in this or that way would be a matter of chance. In that case, there would be no reason why the agent acted as it did. In other words, the act would be unintelligible. But St. Thomas thinks that for any act A, A is intelligible. Therefore, every agent acts for an end.[2]

In St. Thomas's view, distinctively human actions stem from the workings of human intellect and will,[3] where the object of the power of the human intellect is the *intelligible* or *true* and the object of the power of the human will is the *human good (for the particular person whose will it is) insofar as the intellect apprehends it.*[4] For St. Thomas, the powers of intellect and will act in tandem so that willing always presupposes some sort of understanding, believing, knowing, or reasoning on the part of the intellectual agent, and intellectual activity often presupposes prior acts of will.[5] Therefore, the *end* of a characteristically human action is something (= *x*) such that a human person S believes or understands *x* to be a good or a goal for S. According to St. Thomas's action theory for rational beings, a *means to an end* refers to something (= *y*) such that one cognizes and wills *y* for the sake of something other than *y*. Notice, therefore, that some things, events, or activities can be both an end and a means to an end, albeit in different respects, for example, when a person S makes *mowing the lawn* an end or goal on a given day, for the accomplishing of which S engages in certain means, for example, *going to get some gas for the lawnmower* and *cleaning the mower*, but S also mows the lawn today because S wants to make S's property beautiful for a fitting celebration of Easter Sunday.

---

2. See, e.g., *SCG* III.2 and *ST* I-II, q. 1, a. 2. As with Aristotle, St. Thomas thinks that all actions are done for the sake of some end, even the actions of nonrational beings. Some philosophers charge Aristotle and St. Thomas with a kind of anthropomorphism here, namely, that they ascribe purposes or intentions to nonrational beings. The objector here is confused, thinking that Aristotle and St. Thomas identify final causes, ends, or goals, on the one hand, with purposes and functions on the other. Although all purposes and functions are ends, not all ends are functions or purposes for Aristotle and Thomas. For discussion, see Ed Feser, *Aquinas* (Oxford: Oneworld, 2009), 17.

3. See, e.g., *ST* I-II, q. 1, a. 1, resp.

4. The object of a power is that at which that power's characteristic activities aim. To take a few examples, the characteristic activities of the power of sight grasp color, and so the object of the power of sight is color. The characteristic activities of the power of hearing grasp sound, and so the object of the power of hearing is sound. To take an example of an appetitive power, the object of the concupiscible power is the simple good or bad (i.e., good or bad insofar as it is easy to obtain or avoid), insofar as it is presented to us by way of sense knowledge. For a helpful treatment of St. Thomas's philosophical psychology, see Steven Jensen, *The Human Person: A Beginner's Thomistic Psychology* (Washington, D.C.: The Catholic University of America Press, 2018).

5. See, e.g., *ST* I, q. 19, a. 1, and *ST* I-II, q. 9, a. 1.

But some ends are what St. Thomas calls "ultimate." An ultimate end is an end of action such that one desires it *merely* for its own sake, and not also as a means to some further end.[6] Now for St. Thomas, although wealth might be treated as an end relative to the means that a person employs to achieve it, it is obvious, upon reflection, that wealth is not *an* ultimate end, and even more clearly, wealth is not *the* ultimate end.[7] This distinction between *an* ultimate end and *the* ultimate end is important and does not go unnoticed by St. Thomas. He is willing to take seriously the question whether a human person can have several ultimate ends.[8] For example, we *might* think that knowledge, virtue, and pleasure are each ultimate ends of human life, that is, things we desire for their own sake and not also as a means to some further end. But St. Thomas thinks it is clear that a human person really has only one ultimate end. This is because the ultimate end—as St. Thomas understands the term—is more than something we seek for its own sake. We do not seek the ultimate end for the sake of something else; it is something that, all by itself, entirely satisfies one's desire.[9] One can make sense of the relation between the single ultimate end and those goods that are ends in themselves, but not the ultimate end, as follows. Say that both pleasure and virtuous activity are ends in themselves, pleasure and virtuous activity are not the same good, and there is a single ultimate end. In that case, pleasure and virtuous activity might be *component parts* of an ultimate end construed as a complex whole.

St. Thomas on Clarifying Ambiguities
Regarding the Meaning of *beatitudo*

So each and every human person has one ultimate end. But do all human persons have the *same* ultimate end? St. Thomas thinks so, and he believes that, in one sense, this is not at all controversial. For all human persons think of human *happiness* (*beatitudo*) as the ultimate end of human persons.[10] Of course, St. Thomas recognizes that to speak about

---

6. See, e.g., *SCG* III.2 and *ST* I-II, q. 1, aa. 4–8.
7. See, e.g., *SCG* III.30; *Sententia Libri Ethicorum* [hereafter *In NE*] I, lect. 5; *ST* I-II, q. 2, a. 1.
8. See, e.g., *ST* I-II, q. 1, a. 5.
9. See, e.g., *ST* I-II, q. 1, a. 5, and *In NE* I, lect. 9, n. 110.
10. *ST* I-II, q. 1, a. 7, s.c. St. Thomas sometimes uses *beatitudo* and sometimes uses *felicitas* to denote the ultimate end of human persons. In fact, *beatitudo* and *felicitas* are often used interchangeably by St. Thomas (see, e.g., *In Sent* II, d. 4, q. 1, a. 1, resp.; *SCG* III.25.14; *SCG* III.147; *ST* I, q. 26, a. 1, obj. 2; *CT* II, chap. 9; *ST* I-II, q. 2, a. 2, obj. 1). Although St. Thomas's translator tends to translate

the ultimate end as "happiness" is still to speak about the ultimate end in very abstract terms, or, as St. Thomas puts it, to speak merely of the "notion of the ultimate end" (*rationem ultimi finis*).[11] We can also think about the ultimate end as that in which human happiness is actually found.[12] Four people might agree that their goal in life is to be happy but disagree with one another greatly about what counts as a happy human life.

Although people certainly disagree about that in which happiness is found, St. Thomas maintains that there is only one object that can satisfy the desires and longings of human persons. If we take St. Thomas's method of treating human happiness in texts such as *Summa Contra Gentiles* and *Summa Theologiae* as demonstrative of his own position—what we have in those places, after all, are long chains of arguments—he thinks it is possible to offer a convincing argument for what fulfills a human person *qua* human person.[13] But St. Thomas also shows sensitivity to the role that our moral habits play in forming our beliefs—and so which arguments we will find convincing—regarding the nature of the good life for human persons.[14]

As we have seen, one ambiguity where the terms "ultimate end" or "happiness" are concerned is that between the *notion* of the last end—the last end in the abstract, that is, *human happiness*—and *that in which* the last

---

Aristotle's *eudaimonia* as *felicitas* in his rendering of *NE*, so that St. Thomas uses *felicitas* to denote the ultimate end in his commentary on Aristotle's *NE*, and St. Thomas usually uses *beatitudo* to denote perfect happiness in heaven, St. Thomas sometimes uses *beatitudo*, albeit imperfect beatitude (*beatitudo imperfecta*) to denote happiness in this life (see, e.g., *ST* I-II, q. 4, a. 5, resp.) and *felicitas* to speak of perfect happiness in heaven (see, e.g., *SCG* III.148). In fact, St. Thomas sometimes uses *felicitas* to denote God's happiness (see, e.g., *SCG* III.51.6). In his translation of and commentary on Aristotle's *Nicomachean Ethics* [hereafter *NE*] (Indianapolis, Ind.: Hackett, 1999), contemporary classicist and philosopher Terence Irwin argues that Aristotle uses *makarios* and *eudaimonia* as interchangeable expressions in that work (318). If Irwin is correct, then St. Thomas's use of *beatitudo* and *felicitas* as roughly equivalent expressions parallels Aristotle's use of *makarios* and *eudaimonia* in *NE* as roughly equivalent. Finally, note that it is customary to translate both *beatitudo* and *felicitas* as "happiness" despite the fact that "happiness" in English connotes merely a positive mood or feeling, where such a feeling or mood is, for St. Thomas, at best merely a proper accident of *beatitudo* or *felicitas*. One should therefore also think of *beatitudo* or *felicitas* as *well-being* (see, e.g., *CT* II, chap. 9), or *flourishing*.

11. See, e.g., *ST* I-II, q. 1, a. 7, resp.

12. Ibid.

13. See, e.g., *SCG* III.25–37; *ST* I-II, q. 2; *In NE* I, lect. 10. It is important to emphasize here that, if one thinks that there are ways in which all of us must live if we are to be counted as genuinely happy, e.g., by displaying and acting in accord with the virtues, then one can also think that there are a number of different ways of life in which we can manifest those virtues, e.g., as mothers, fathers, farmers, doctors, lawyers, teachers, artists, mechanics, engineers, priests, religious, lay persons, etc.

14. See, e.g., *ST* I-II, q. 1, a. 7.

end or happiness *is actually realized*. St. Thomas thinks that the expression *beatitudo* is ambiguous in other ways. For example, he thinks it is one thing to speak about the happiness that human persons can possess in this life, what St. Thomas sometimes calls *imperfect* human happiness, and another thing to speak about the happiness possessed by God, the blessed angels, and human persons in heaven, which happiness St. Thomas considers to be *perfect*.[15] Although St. Thomas is primarily interested in perfect human happiness, it is worth noting that he also says quite a bit about imperfect happiness in this life throughout his corpus.

One reason that St. Thomas speaks about imperfect happiness in this life is that he wants to show that what Aristotle says about happiness, for example, in *Nicomachean Ethics*, is compatible with the Catholic Christian notion that perfect happiness consists in a next-worldly vision of God. St. Thomas notes that, after identifying the general characteristics of happiness in I.7—that happiness is perfect and self-sufficient in the sense that the happy person has all her desires sated—Aristotle goes on to note in I.10 that human persons cannot be happy, absolutely speaking, or perfectly, in this life. This is because, in this life, human persons can lose their happiness, and human persons naturally desire happiness that cannot be lost. Thus St. Thomas notes that Aristotle himself thinks of human happiness in this life as imperfect in light of the conditions laid out in I.7.[16]

A second reason that St. Thomas speaks quite a bit about this-worldly, imperfect happiness in his works is that a certain kind of this-worldly, imperfect happiness is the typical means to achieving the end of perfect happiness in the next life.[17] To see this, note that St. Thomas distin-

---

15. See, e.g., the sermon *Beati qui habitant* 1.1; *Expositio super librum Boethii De trinitate* [hereafter *In BDT*], q. 6, a. 4, ad 3; *ST* I, q. 62, a. 1; *ST* I-II, q. 3, a. 5, resp.; q. 4, a. 5, resp.; q. 4, a. 7, resp.; q. 5, a. 4, resp.; *In NE* I, lect. 10, n. 129; *Super Psalmos* [hereafter *In Ps/Pss*] 32. Of course, St. Thomas thinks that God's perfect happiness is uncreated and unparticipated whereas the perfect happiness of the blessed angels and saints is a created participation in God's uncreated perfect happiness (see, e.g., *SCG* III.51.6, 53.2, 58.1; *ST* I, q. 26, a. 2, resp.; *In Matthaeum* [hereafter *In Mt*] 25, lect. 2, n. 2054). It should also be noted that St. Thomas sometimes speaks of the imperfect happiness of the wayfarer as a participation in, or share of, the perfect happiness of the saints (see, e.g., *In Sent* IV, d. 49, q. 1, a. 1, q.c. 4; a. 2, q.c. 2, ad 5; *SCG* III.48.9; *ST* I-II, q. 2, aa. 2 and 6). For a detailed discussion of St. Thomas's notion of imperfect happiness and its relation to St. Thomas's reading of Aristotle, see Bradley, *Aquinas on the Two-Fold Human Good*, 395–423.

16. See, e.g., *In Sent* IV, d. 49, q. 1, a. 1, q.c. 4; *SCG* III.48.9; *ST* I-II, q. 3, a. 2, ad 4; q. 5, a. 4, resp.; *In NE* I, lects. 9 and 16; X, lect. 13, n. 2136.

17. It is the *typical means* because St. Thomas thinks that baptized infants who die before the age of reason go to heaven; he thinks that baptized infants before the age of reason are virtuous in the sense that they possess the habits of the infused virtues. But insofar as they cannot act on

guishes two different kinds of imperfect human happiness in this life. First, there is this-worldly, imperfect happiness *apart from grace*. This is what we might call *merely natural* imperfect happiness, that is, happiness in this life devoid of grace, but involving the activation of the human virtues of justice, courage, moderation, and wisdom.[18] Second, there is *graced* imperfect happiness in this life. This is *supernatural* imperfect happiness, that is, happiness in this life, at the center of which is the activation of the theological virtues of faith, hope, and charity, the infused versions of the cardinal virtues, and the gifts of the Holy Spirit.[19]

St. Thomas agrees with Aristotle that this-worldly happiness consists in the soul's activity expressing virtue, in a complete life,[20] that is, a life of continuous and prolonged virtuous activity, where the virtuous life involves contemplative activity, primarily, and, secondarily, practical activity.[21] But St. Thomas also thinks that "happiness is the reward of virtue,"[22] or, as he puts it in other places, virtue is the means to,[23] or is ordered to[24] beatitude, that is, perfect human happiness in heaven. Elsewhere, St. Thomas notes that rectitude of the will, or virtuous dispositions or actions on the part of the will, are necessary for happiness.[25] But the perfect beatitude of heaven is a grace.[26] Therefore, it is by the grace

---

those virtues, and happiness in this life is the soul's activity expressing virtue, such infants, though virtuous and heaven-bound, are not actually happy in this life. See, e.g., *ST* III, q. 68, a. 9, ad 3.

18. According to St. Thomas, human persons can acquire virtues that perfect human beings *according to their natural end* by repeatedly performing the kinds of acts a virtuous person performs, that is, by habituation. St. Thomas calls such virtues *human* (see, e.g., *ST* I-II, q. 54, a. 3; q. 55, aa. 1–3; q. 61, a. 1, ad 2) in order to distinguish them from *infused* (or, to use concepts Thomas finds in Aristotle, *godlike*, *heroic*, or *superhuman*) virtues, which are virtues we have only by way of a gift from God, not by habituation. For example, we can imagine that, apart from grace, Socrates is humanly courageous in the sense that Socrates acquires the ability to habitually say "yes" to pains that are in accord with right reason in much the same way that athletes or musicians voluntarily become more skilled or proficient in what they do through practice, i.e., by doing (or at least approximating) what good athletes and virtuosi do. By contrast, *infused* virtues are gifts from God that enable the saints to do more than lead a naturally perfect human life; they are graced dispositions that enable human persons to perform acts that merit the reward of perfect human happiness in heaven.

19. See, e.g., *ST* I-II, q. 54, a. 3, resp.; q. 55, aa. 1–4; q. 58, a. 3, ad 3; q. 61, a. 5; q. 62, aa. 1–3; q. 63, aa. 2–4; q. 68. See also the entirety of *ST* II-II.

20. See, e.g., *In NE* I, lect. 10, nn. 129–30; lect. 19, n. 224; X, lect. 9.

21. See, e.g., *ST* I-II, q. 3, a. 5, resp.; *In NE* X, lect. 11, n. 2104; lect. 12, n. 2111. For more discussion of contemplative and practical activity, see chapter 5 below.

22. See, e.g., *SCG* IV.54.7; 91.2; *ST* I, q. 62, a. 4, resp.; q. 4, a. 6, s.c.; *In NE* I, lect. 14, n. 169; *Collationes in Symbolum Apostolorum* [hereafter *CSA*], a. 12.

23. See, e.g., *In Sent* IV, d. 49, q. 1, a. 2, q.c. 5; *SCG* III.58.4; *CT* I, chap. 172; *ST* I-II, q. 1, prol.; q. 6, prol.; q. 4, a. 6, s.c.; *In NE* X, lect. 1, n. 1953.

24. See, e.g., *SCG* III.27; *CT* I, chap. 172; *In Jn* 13:17.

25. See, e.g., *CT* I, chap. 172; *ST* I, 62, a. 4; *ST* I-II, q. 4, a. 4; q. 5, a. 7.

26. See, e.g., *In Sent* I, prol., a. 1; *Quaestiones disputatae de veritate* [hereafter *QDV*], q. 14, a. 10; *ST* I, q. 1, a. 1, resp.; q. 12, aa. 4–6; *ST* I-II, q. 5, a. 5; *ST* II-II, q. 2, a. 3.

of infused virtue that one is rewarded with perfect beatitude. Given St. Thomas's interest as a Dominican priest and theologian in preaching and teaching the Word of God so as to facilitate the salvation of his hearers and readers, one reason that he spends time speaking about this-worldly happiness—again, the soul's activity expressing virtue, in a complete life—is because he thinks it is the means to achieving, by the grace of God, perfect happiness in heaven.[27]

There is another ambiguity where *beatitudo* is concerned to which St. Thomas often draws our attention. He recognizes two different kinds of questions we might wish to raise when we think about the nature of perfect human happiness. When asking about the nature of perfect human happiness, we might be asking about what is true *of the person* who is happy. As St. Thomas puts it, this is to focus our attention on the *use*, *possession*, or *attainment* of perfect happiness. But in asking about the perfect happiness of human persons, we might rather be asking about the *cause* or *object* of happiness, or as St. Thomas puts it, "the thing itself in which is found the aspect of good."[28] To speak about perfect human happiness in the sense of *attainment* is to make claims about the soul of the person who is happy, for example, that it is an *activity* of the soul and not merely a state of the soul or an emotion,[29] that it is a *speculative* rather than a practical activity,[30] etc. On the other hand, to speak about the *cause* or *object* of perfect human happiness is to make claims about that good, the attainment of which makes a human person perfectly happy. Following the lead of St. Thomas, Josef Pieper illustrates the difference between happiness as object and happiness as attainment as follows: the end of a thirsty man in the sense of the *object* of his desire is *drink*; the end of the thirsty man in the sense of *attainment* is *drinking*.[31]

For St. Thomas, then, a person's possession of happiness is not necessarily the same as the object of that person's happiness. In fact, this is strikingly the case for St. Thomas when it comes to perfect human hap-

---

27. See, e.g., *ST* I-II, q. 69, a. 2, resp. and ad 3.
28. *ST* I-II, q. 1, a. 8, resp. (trans. English Dominicans, 588). For the distinction between the *object* of perfect happiness and the *attainment* of perfect happiness, see also *In Sent* II, d. 38, q. 1, a. 2; *In Sent* IV, d. 49, q. 1, a. 1, q.c. 2, resp.; a. 2, q.c. 1, resp.; *QDV*, q. 5, a. 6, ad 4; *SCG* III.25.1-2; *ST* I, q. 26, a. 3, resp. and ad 2; *In Mt* 6, lect. 3, n. 585; *ST* I-II, q. 2, a. 7, resp.; q. 3, a. 1, resp.; a. 8, ad 2; q. 5, a. 2, resp.
29. See, e.g., *ST* I-II, q. 3, a. 2.
30. See, e.g., *ST* I-II, q. 3, a. 5.
31. *Happiness and Contemplation*, trans. Richard Winston and Clara Winston (South Bend, Ind.: St. Augustine's Press, 1998), 32–33.

piness, as the attainment of perfect happiness exists as an accident *in* the soul of the human person whereas the object of perfect human happiness is God.[32] In this sense (as well as others), St. Thomas rejects the Stoic idea that *perfect human* happiness is a matter of becoming self-sufficient.

St. Thomas on the Object of Perfect Human Happiness in Heaven

Whereas *ST* I-II, q. 1, provides a conceptual framework for talking sensibly about the ultimate end of rational beings such as ourselves, q. 2 goes on to discuss with precision the nature of the *object* of perfect human happiness—that thing, the acquisition of which causes beings such as ourselves to be perfectly happy. St. Thomas's account here takes a cursory look at some of the candidates for human happiness discussed by historically important sources such as Aristotle, Cicero, St. Augustine, and Boethius. The candidates for object of human happiness include wealth (*divitiae*),[33] honor (*honor*),[34] fame or glory (*fama sive gloria*),[35] power (*potestas*),[36] some good of the body,[37] pleasure (*voluptas*) or delight (*delectatio*),[38] some good of the soul,[39] or some created good.[40] St. Thomas offers various reasons for rejecting each of these as plausible candidates for the object of human happiness in the places cited. He argues instead from authority and from reason that

(1) God alone makes human persons perfectly happy.

He asserts, or defends his acceptance of, (1) in many places.[41] As for his arguments from authority in support of (1), St. Thomas cites many pas-

---

32. See, e.g., *ST* I-II, q. 2, a. 7, resp.; q. 3, a. 1, resp.
33. See a. 1 and *SCG* III.30; *In NE* I, lect. 5.
34. See a. 2 and *SCG* III.28; *De regno* [hereafter *DR*] I, chap. 8 (chap. 7 in some editions), and *In NE* I, lect. 5.
35. See a. 3 and *SCG* III.29; *DR* I, chap. 8 (chap. 7 in some editions).
36. See a. 4 and *SCG* III.31; *DR* I, chap. 8 (chap. 7 in some editions); *In Mt* 5, lect. 2, n. 404; *CT* II, chap. 9.
37. See a. 5 and *In Sent* IV, d. 49, q. 1, a. 1, q.c. 1; *SCG* III.32; *In NE* I, lect. 10; *CT* II, chap. 9.
38. See a. 6 and *In Sent* IV, d. 44, q. 1, a. 3, q.c. 4, ad 3 and ad 4 (*ST Suppl.*, q. 81, a. 4, ad 3 and ad 4); *SCG* III.27 and III.33; *In NE* I, lect. 5.
39. See a. 7.
40. See a. 8 and *In Sent* IV, d. 49, q. 1, a. 2, q.c. 1; *SCG* III.17 and IV.54; *CT* I, chap. 108; *ST* I, q. 12, a. 1, resp.; *DR* I, chap. 9 (chap. 8 in some editions); *ST* I-II, q. 3, a. 1; *CT* II, chap. 9; *In Ps* 32.
41. See, e.g., *SCG* IV.54; *Expositio et lectura super Epistolas Pauli Apostoli* [hereafter *1 Cor*, etc.], *In 1 Cor* 15, n. 950; *In Eph* 1, lect. 1, n. 8; *CT* I, chap. 108; *DR* I, chap. 9 (chap. 8 in some editions); *ST* I, q. 26, a. 3, resp.; *In Mt* 5, lect. 2, n. 412; 24, lect. 4, n. 2003; *ST* I-II, q. 2, a. 8; q. 3, a. 1; q. 4, a. 8; *CSA*, a. 12; *CT* II, chap. 9; *In Ps* 32. As Michael Pakaluk rightly points out, we can also see St. Thomas's

sages of scripture through his corpus.⁴² In one place St. Thomas cites St. Augustine's *The City of God* XIX.26, which itself cites a passage of scripture: "As the soul is the life of the body, so God is man's life of happiness: of Whom it is written: 'Happy is that people whose God is the Lord' (Ps 143:15)."⁴³

St. Thomas also offers philosophical arguments for his acceptance of (1). *ST* I-II, q. 2, a. 8, contains an argument defending the thesis that *no created thing* can be the object of perfect human happiness, and so by implication that God alone is the object of human happiness. The argument runs as follows: perfect happiness is the perfect good for a rational being, that is, it is one that satisfies the appetites of a rational being altogether. But just as the object of an intellect is *the universal true*, the object of the will is *the universal good*. In contrast to those creatures that merely enjoy goods that are sensed or imaginable—and so have no desires for what lies beyond these particular objects of sense or imagination—intellectual creatures can conceive, at least abstractly, the notion of *knowing everything that can be known*, and in turn, *having every conceivable and realistic good*. So the human good cannot consist in *this* particular good—*unless* this particular good can provide every conceivable and realistic good. The acquisition of any good short of the universal good will leave us in the state of still desiring something more. Any creature or set of creatures is simply a certain finite participation of the universal good. Therefore, no created good can be that in which perfect human happiness consists.⁴⁴ For St. Thomas (as for St. Augustine), God is the perfect good,⁴⁵ the universal good,⁴⁶

---

agreement with (1) in his prayers, e.g., *Adoro te devote*. See Pakaluk's lecture, "Grisez's Critique of Aquinas on the Ultimate End of Human Life," The Thomistic Institute, Duke University (April 11, 2019), available at www.academia.edu/38785923/Grisez_Critique_of_Aquinas_on_the_Ultimate_End_of_Human_Life?auto=download.

42. St. Thomas cites the following passages of scripture in defense of (1): Gn 15:1 in *CSA*, a. 12; Ps 15:5 in *In Ps* 15; Ps 15:16 in *CSA*, a. 12; Ps 16:15 in *In Ps* 32:12; Ps 33:12 in the sermon *Beate gens*; Ps 72:25–28 in *ST* I-II, q. 4, a. 7, s.c. and *CT* II, chap. 9; Ps 84:5 in the sermon *Beati qui habitant*; Ps 94:12 in the sermon *Beatus vir* 1.3; Ps 102:5 in *ST* I-II, q. 2, a. 8, resp. and *CSA*, a. 12; Ps 143:15 in *ST* I-II, q. 2, a. 8; Ps 147:14 in *CT* II, chap. 9; Prv 16:4 in *SCG* III.17.10; Wis 7:11 in *ST* I-II, q. 4, a. 8, s.c.; Mt 13:44–45 in *In Mt* 13, lect. 4, n. 1194; Mt 25:21 in *In Mt* 25, lect. 2, n. 2054 and *CSA*, a. 12; Jn 14:8 in *In Sent* IV, d. 49, q. 1, a. 1, q.c. 2, s.c. and *In Jn* 14, lect. 3, n. 1883; Jn 17:3 in *In Sent* IV, d. 49, q. 1, a. 1, q.c. 2, s.c.; Rv 14:13 in *ST* I-II, q. 4, a. 5, s.c.; Rv 22:13 in *SCG* III.17.10.

43. *ST* I-II, q. 2, a. 8, s.c. (trans. English Dominicans, 595).

44. *ST* I-II, q. 2, a. 8, resp. See also the sermon *Beatus vir*; *SCG* III.25 and IV.54; *CT* I, chap. 108; *ST* I, q. 12, a. 1; *DR* I, chap. 9; *CT* II, chap. 9; *CSA*, a. 12; *In Ps* 32.

45. *ST* I-II, q. 2, a. 8.

46. Ibid.

goodness itself,[47] and infinite goodness.[48] Therefore, God is the object of perfect human happiness.

But presumably there are genuine goods that one does not get simply by knowing and loving God, such as the good of taking pleasure in hitting a home run. Insofar as finite goods such as taking pleasure in hitting a home run are real goods, how can even the good of knowing and loving God in heaven really be the universal, perfect, or infinite good that sates all human desire? St. Thomas entertains an objection of this sort.[49] In *ST* I, St. Thomas asks whether beatitude in God includes all beatitudes.[50] For example, there are desirable things that are corporeal, such as wealth and riches.[51] Therefore, it seems that God's beatitude or the beatitude of a human person having the beatific vision does not embrace all beatitudes.

St. Thomas's response to such an objection has two parts. First, whatever creaturely good is desired—riches, sexual congress, etc.—preexists (*praeexistit*) in God.[52] Second, whatever finite good a creature desires, exists in God in a more eminent degree (*eminentius*).[53] Therefore, a human person enjoying God in the beatific vision is not only a necessary but a sufficient condition for that human person's desires being sated.

Let us begin with the first claim in St. Thomas's response to the objection: whatever creaturely good we desire in this life *preexists* in God. St. Thomas defends this notion by way of the principle of causality. There cannot be more in an effect than in its cause or causes. But God alone is the primary efficient and exemplar formal cause of all created effects. Therefore, whatever perfection or good exists in a creature preexists in God.[54]

As far as God being the primary *efficient* cause of creaturely goods is concerned, the perfection of a creaturely good preexists in God insofar

---

47. See, e.g., *ST* I, q. 6, aa. 2–4; q. 13, a. 1, ad 2.
48. See, e.g., *ST* I, qq. 5 and 7.
49. See, e.g., *ST* I, q. 26, a. 4, obj. 2. See also *SCG* I.102 and *CSA*, a. 12.
50. *ST* I, q. 26, a. 4.
51. *ST* I, q. 26, a. 4, obj. 2.
52. See, e.g., *ST* I, q. 26, a. 4, resp.; q. 4, a. 2.
53. *ST* I, q. 26, a. 4, resp. and ad 2. See also *ST* I, q. 13, a. 2, resp.
54. See, e.g., *In Sent* I, d. 2, a. 2; *QDV*, q. 2, a. 1; *SCG* I.28 and 31; *CT* I, chaps. 21–22; *ST* I, q. 4, a. 2; *Expositio super librum Dionysii De divinis nominibus* [hereafter *In DDN*], chap. 5, lects. 1–2. Of course, St. Thomas thinks that creatures are secondary causes of some created effects, e.g., two rabbits are genuine secondary efficient causes of another rabbit coming into existence. But God is also the primary efficient cause of the being and activity of the secondary causes.

as God has the perfect power to bring that good into existence as well as conserve it in existence. So the perfection of a creaturely good preexists in God insofar as God has the perfect power to bring and conserve any creaturely good in existence we might desire.[55]

In addition, God is the exemplar formal cause of any creature.[56] Because God knows and wills the existence of all created things, and God knows things other than himself in virtue of knowing himself, God has ideas of the creatures he knows and wills to exist. Therefore, a creaturely perfection exists in God insofar as God has the idea of such a creature. Therefore, the perfection or goodness of a created thing desired preexists in God as a divine idea of such a creature.

Someone might object at this point: "what I want is friendship with a particular person, or sexual congress (with a particular person) in heaven. I do not see how having God alone in heaven can sate my desires for those things." St. Thomas anticipates this objection by arguing that, not only do all creaturely perfections preexist in God, they preexist in God in a more eminent way. St. Thomas notes that things preexist more eminently in God insofar as God is the absolutely perfect creator and sustainer of all finite goods.[57] However, we might speak about two different ways that goods preexist more eminently in God, as there are *unmixed* goods and *mixed* goods. If G is an *unmixed* good, then a being B's possessing G does not imply metaphysical imperfection on the part of B. For example, knowing and loving are unmixed goods. For a being to love or know does not necessarily imply a metaphysical limitation on the part of the being that knows or loves. Unmixed finite goods preexist in God such that the words we use to signify them also substantially and literally can be said of an absolutely and infinitely perfect being, that is, God, albeit in a manner analogous to the way we apply such words to imperfect and finite goods.[58]

---

55. See, e.g., *In Sent* I, d. 2, a. 2; *QDV*, q. 2, a. 1; *SCG* I.28 and 31; *CT* I, chaps. 21–22; *ST* I, q. 4, a. 2; *In DDN*, chap. 5, lects. 1–2.

56. See, e.g., *In Sent* I, d. 36, q. 2, aa. 2 and 3; *QDV*, q. 3, aa. 2–8; *Quaestiones disputatae de potentia* [hereafter *QDP*], q. 1, a. 5, ad 11; *ST* I, q. 15, a. 3; *In DDN*, chap. 5, lect. 3.

57. See, e.g., *ST* I, q. 4, a. 2.

58. See, e.g., *ST* I, q. 13, a. 2, resp. For St. Thomas, words we use to refer to *unmixed* goods "signify the divine substance, but in an imperfect manner, even as creatures represent it imperfectly. So when we say, *God is good*, the meaning is not, *God is the cause of goodness*, or *God is not evil*; but the meaning is, *Whatever good we attribute to creatures, preexists in God*, and in a more excellent and higher way. Hence it does not follow that God is good, because He causes goodness; but rather, on the contrary, He causes goodness in things because He is good; according to what Augustine says (*De Doctr. Christ.* i, 32), *Because He is good, we are.*" *ST* I, q. 13, a. 2, resp. (trans. English Dominicans, 61). See also *In Sent* I, d. 2, a. 2; *SCG* I.31; *QDP*, q. 7, a. 5; *ST* I, q. 13, a. 5, resp.

On the other hand, if some good G is a *mixed* good, then a being B's possessing G implies an imperfection on the part of B, whether that imperfection is merely a metaphysical imperfection or limitation in B, or also a moral imperfection in B. For example, the possession of the good, *hitting a home run*, implies a metaphysical (although not necessarily a moral) imperfection on the part of the being that possesses that good. This is because a being that hits a home run is a bodily being that changes, and a being that changes has a cause of its existence. But a being that has a cause of its existence cannot be the absolutely and infinitely perfect being. Therefore, the perfection *hitting a home run* cannot be said literally of an absolutely and infinitely perfect being. Such a created perfection preexists in God insofar as God is the primary efficient and exemplar formal cause of that created perfection.

So how do unmixed and mixed goods preexist in God in a more eminent manner? Consider first unmixed goods. As the possession of such goods does not imply imperfection on the part of the being that possesses that good, words used to denote unmixed goods can be predicated substantially and literally, albeit analogously, of God and creatures. But because God is the absolutely perfect creator, an unmixed good must preexist in a higher and more excellent way in God than in creatures. For example, take the creaturely good of loving. Because loving is an unmixed good, "loving" can be applied substantially and literally, but analogously, to God. Now God is the absolutely perfect creator, and so God loves in a manner that is more perfect than creatures. Therefore, our desire to love and to be loved by any creature is more than sated in loving and being loved by God in the beatific vision.

What of mixed goods such as sexual congress or hitting a home run? How do such goods preexist in God in a more eminent manner such that enjoying God in the beatific vision is sufficient for perfect human happiness? Let us suggest the following:

(2) A mixed good G, for example, *materiality*, preexists more eminently in God than creatures insofar as: (a) G is a species or mode of an unmixed good G_1, for example, *being*, (b) there is some *unmixed* good G_2, for example, *immateriality*, that is a species of G_1 or a mode of G_1 or identical to G_1, (c) and G_2 is more desirable or more perfect than G such that, if one possesses G_2, one's desire for G is sated in having G_2.

For example, consider the creaturely perfection *feeling pleasure in the conjugal act*. First, feeling pleasure in the conjugal act is a *mixed* good as feeling such a pleasure requires being embodied, and an embodied being is a created being.

Second, assuming the truth of (2), feeling pleasure in the conjugal act preexists in God in a more eminent way because, first, feeling pleasure in the conjugal act is a species or mode of the unmixed good, *delight*. In addition, *taking delight in union with God in the beatific vision* is another species or mode of delight to which we can reasonably compare *taking pleasure in the conjugal act*. Third, *union with God in the beatific vision* is perfective of the person S who enjoys it such that S's desire for feeling pleasure in the conjugal act in this life is more than sated if S enjoys union with God in the beatific vision instead.

So, for example, St. Thomas says in one place:

Everlasting life is the full and perfect satisfying of every desire; for there every blessed soul will have to overflowing what he hoped for and desired. The reason is that in this life no one can fulfill all his desires, nor can any created thing fully satisfy the craving of man. God only satisfies and infinitely exceeds man's desires; and, therefore, perfect satiety is found in God alone.... Whatever is delightful will be there in abundant fullness. Thus, if pleasures are desired, there will be the highest and most perfect pleasure, for it derives from the highest good, namely, God: "Then shalt thou abound in delights in the Almighty" [Jb 22:26]. "At the right hand are delights even to the end" [Ps 15:10]. Likewise, if honors are desired, there too will be all honor. Men wish particularly to be kings, if they be laymen; and to be bishops, if they be clerics. Both these honors will be there: "And hath made us a kingdom and priests" [Rv 5:10]. "Behold how they are numbered among the children of God" [Wis 5:5]. If knowledge is desired, it will be there most perfectly, because we shall possess in the life everlasting knowledge of all the natures of things and all truth, and whatever we desire we shall know. And whatever we desire to possess, that we shall have, even life eternal: "Now, all good things come to me together with her" [Wis 7:11]. "To the just their desire shall be given" [Prv 10:24].[59]

Insofar as beatific union with God by itself sates our desires—as he says in the above passage, "God infinitely exceeds man's desires"—St. Thomas can say with St. Augustine, "the one who enjoys God has no less than he

---

59. *CSA*, a. 12, in *Catechetical Instructions of St. Thomas Aquinas*, trans. Joseph Collins (Fort Collins, Colo.: Roman Catholic Books, 1939), 63–64. See also *ST* I, q. 26, a. 4, resp.

who enjoys some creature in addition to God."[60] Notice that it does not follow from this thesis that finite goods are not genuine goods, or that finite goods have no role to play in the heavenly life of human persons. What St. Thomas maintains is that creatures are not the object of perfect human happiness. As we will see in later chapters, St. Thomas does think that creatures or finite goods themselves nonetheless have a proper place in the heavenly life of human persons.

St. Thomas on the Attainment of Perfect Human Happiness

As we have seen, St. Thomas argues that God alone is the *object* of perfect human happiness. Let us now begin a treatment of St. Thomas's views on the *attainment* of perfect human happiness in heaven, which St. Thomas treats, for example, in *ST* I-II, qq. 3–5. In many places, St. Thomas states:

(3) The attainment of perfect human happiness in heaven consists in the beatific vision, that is, a saint's immediate intellectual union with the essence of God, and the love, joy, or delight that necessarily accompanies such a vision.[61]

But, as we will see, St. Thomas also accepts the following:

(4) The beatific vision and the delighting in it is a *nonbodily, individual* union with the essence of God.

St. Thomas also holds that:

(5) (a) Some souls in heaven are already embodied, e.g., the souls of Christ and the Virgin Mary,[62] and (b) all souls in heaven eventually will be embodied, and (c) after the general judgment, heaven will consist of a communion between God, the blessed angels, and blessed human persons.

---

60. See, e.g., *Confessions* V.4. St. Thomas cites this very passage in *ST* I, q. 26, a. 3, resp., when he argues that only God is the object of human beatitude. He also cites the passage approvingly in *Beata gens* 2.3.1; *QDM*, q. 5, a. 1, obj. 4 and ad 4; *ST* I-II, q. 5, a. 2, ad 3; *In Heb* 1, lect. 6, n. 86.

61. See, e.g., *ST Suppl.*, q. 13, a. 2, ad 1; *In Sent* IV, d. 45, q. 2, a. 2, q.c. 4, ad 3 (*ST Suppl.*, q. 71, a. 8, ad 3); *In Sent* IV, d. 49, q. 2, a. 1 (*ST Suppl.*, q. 92, a. 1); *ST Suppl.*, q. 96, a. 1; *Quaestiones de quodlibet* [hereafter *QQ*] X, q. 8; *QDV*, q. 8, a. 1; *SCG* III.51, 54, 57; *ST* I, q. 12, a. 1; q. 95, a. 4, resp.; *CT* I, chaps. 104 and 106; *In Mt* 5, lect. 2, n. 408; *In Mt* 25, lect. 2, n. 2053; *ST* I-II, q. 1, a. 8, resp.; q. 3, a. 8; q. 4, a. 1; a. 5, resp.; a. 8, resp. and ad 1; q. 5, a. 1, resp.; a. 3, resp.; a. 4, resp.; a. 5, resp.; q. 69, a. 3, resp.; *In Jn* 1, lect. 11, n. 212; *CT* II, chap. 9; *In Ps* 32.

62. See, e.g., *In Sent* IV, d. 43, q. 1, a. 3, q.c. 1, obj. 2 and ad 2 (*ST Suppl.*, q. 77, a. 1, obj. 2 and ad 2) and *In salutationem angelicam* [hereafter *In SA*].

Statements (3), (4), and (5) seem to be incompatible with one another. For if the heavenly reward sates all human desire, and all human desire is sated in union with God in heaven, there would seem to be no reason for embodiment or the communion of saints in heaven. We might think, then, that the conjunction of (3), (4), and (5) is another way of formulating PNH-I.[63]

Although St. Thomas's views about the attainment of beatitude undergo some development through the course of his life, he accepts (3), (4), and (5) throughout his teaching career. In addition, St. Thomas consistently makes sense of the conjunction of (3), (4), and (5), at least in part, by making a distinction between, on the one hand, *the essential reward* or *the essence of perfect happiness in heaven*—what Catholic theologians have sometimes referred to as *essential beatitude*[64]—and on the other hand, *the accidental reward* or what is *accidental* to perfect happiness in heaven—sometimes called in the Catholic tradition *accidental beatitude*.[65] Before offering the details of St. Thomas's account of the attainment of perfect human happiness, we need to make more precise St. Thomas's distinction between the essential reward and the accidental reward.

ST. THOMAS ON THE LOGICAL STRUCTURE OF PERFECT *BEATITUDO QUA* ATTAINMENT

Just as Aristotle distinguishes what is *essential* to human happiness in this life, that is, the soul's activity expressing virtue, from those human goods that merely add decoration to human happiness (e.g., the goods of fortune),[66] so St. Thomas sometimes speaks of the *essential* heavenly reward in contrast to the *accidental* reward.[67] He uses this way of speaking

---

63. See chapter 1 above.
64. See, e.g., Arthur Devine, *A Manual of Ascetical Theology; Or, the Supernatural Life of the Soul on Earth and in Heaven* (New York: Benzinger, 1902), 522; J. Hontheim, "Heaven," in *The Catholic Encyclopedia*, available at http://www.newadvent.org/cathen/07170a.htm; Reginald Garrigou-Lagrange, *Life Everlasting*, trans. Patrick Cummins (St. Louis, Mo.: Herder, 1952), 247, and Ott, *Fundamentals of Catholic Dogma*, 476–78.
65. Ibid.
66. See, e.g., *NE* I.10.1100b25–27 and X.7.1177b25–26. For St. Thomas on the distinction in Aristotle, see, e.g., *In NE* I, lect. 13, n. 163; lect. 14, n. 173; lect. 16, n. 194; *In NE* X, lect. 11, n. 2104.
67. See, e.g., *In Sent* II, d. 5, q. 2, a. 2, resp.; d. 11, q. 2; d. 29, q. 1, a. 3, ad 5; d. 40, q. 1, a. 3, resp. and ad 2; III, d. 29, q. 1, a. 8, q.c. 2, resp.; d. 31, q. 2, a. 4, ad 3; IV, d. 8, q. 1, a. 2, q.c. 1, ad 2; d. 12, q. 2, a. 1, q.c. 2, resp.; d. 15, q. 4, a. 6, q.c. 2, ad 3; d. 17, q. 3, a. 5, q.c. 2, ad 2; d. 20, q. 1, a. 2, q.c. 3, ad 1; a. 5, q.c. 3, ad 1; d. 33, q. 3, a. 3, ad 3; d. 44, q. 3, a. 3, q.c. 3, ad 8; d. 45, q. 1, a. 3, ad 10; q. 2, a. 2, q.c. 1, resp.; d. 47, q. 1, a. 2, q.c. 3, ad 3; d. 49, q. 5, a. 1, arg. 1, ad 2, and resp.; a. 1, q.c. 1, arg. 3; a. 2,

throughout his career; especially early in the *Sentences* commentary,⁶⁸ but also at least two times in *ST* I,⁶⁹ at least two times in *ST* II,⁷⁰ and three times as late as the composition of *ST* III.⁷¹

According to St. Thomas, the *essential reward* consists in the beatific vision and anything related to that vision as a concomitant or proper accident, for example, the delight that the saint experiences in the beatific vision. Notice, then, that St. Thomas also thinks that the essential reward itself is logically complex: on the one hand there is the beatific vision, which is the *essence* of the essential reward, and there are those features of the essential reward which are logically related to the essence as its concomitant or proper accidents, such as delight, joy, and love in the vision.

St. Thomas distinguishes the essence of the essential reward from what is nonessential but nonetheless an aspect of the essential reward in many places.⁷² For example, in answering the question regarding whether the beatitude of human persons consists in pleasure or delight (in *ST* I-II), St. Thomas responds that, for a thing x such that we can distinguish in it an essence and its proper accidents, we distinguish its essence from its proper accidents such that the essence of x is the formal cause of x's proper accidents.⁷³

St. Thomas gives as an example the relationship between the essence

---

q.c. 2, arg. 2 (*ST Suppl.*, q. 96. a. 3, obj. 2); a. 2, q.c. 3, ad 2; a. 3, q.c. 2, ad 3; a. 4, q.c. 3, arg. 1; a. 4, q.c. 2, ad 2; a. 5, q.c. 3, resp.; *ST Suppl.*, q. 10, a. 2, ad 2; q. 13, a. 2, ad 1; q. 25, a. 2, ad 2; q. 27, a. 3, ad 1; q. 41, a. 4, ad 1; q. 71, a. 1, resp.; *In Sent* IV, d. 45, q. 2, a. 2, q.c. 1, resp. (*ST Suppl.*, q. 71, a. 5, resp.); a. 2, q.c. 4, ad 3 (*ST Suppl.*, q. 71, a. 8, ad 3); *ST Suppl.*, q. 89, a. 2, ad 5; a. 3, ad 3; *In Sent* IV, d. 49, q. 2, a. 5, resp. (*ST Suppl.*, q. 92, a. 3, resp.); *ST Suppl.*, q. 93, a. 3, ad 3; *ST Suppl.*, q. 96, a. 1; a. 2, ad 3; a. 4, ad 2; a. 9; a. 10; a. 13, resp.; *In Sent* IV, d. 50, q. 2, a. 1, q.c. 6, resp. (*ST Suppl.*, q. 98, a. 6, resp.); *ST Suppl.*, Appendix I, q. 2, a. 4, ad 4; *QDV*, q. 12, a. 13, resp.; q. 26, a. 6, ad 8; q. 29, a. 7, ad 5; *ST* I, q. 62, a. 9, ad 3; q. 95, a. 4, resp.; II-II, q. 152, a. 4, ad 1; q. 182, a. 2, ad 1; *QDM*, q. 2, a. 2, ad 8; q. 5, a. 1, obj. 5 and ad 5; q. 7, a. 11, obj. 6; *Super Romanos* [hereafter *In Rom*] 8, lect. 5, n. 677; *ST* III, q. 59, a. 6, resp. and ad 1; q. 89, a. 5, ad 3.

68. See, e.g., *ST Suppl.*, q. 10, a. 2, ad 2; q. 13, a. 2, ad 1; q. 25, a. 2, ad 2; q. 27, a. 3, ad 1; q. 41, a. 4, ad 1; q. 71, a. 1, resp.; *In Sent* IV, d. 45, q. 2, a. 2, q.c. 1, resp. (*ST Suppl.*, q. 71, a. 5, resp.); a. 2, q.c. 4, ad 3 (*ST Suppl.*, q. 71, a. 8, ad 3); *ST Suppl.*, q. 89, a. 2, ad 5; a. 3, ad 3; q. 93, a. 3, ad 3; q. 96, a. 1; a. 2, ad 3; a. 8, ad 1; *In Sent* IV, d. 50, q. 2, a. 1, q.c. 6, resp. (*ST Suppl.*, q. 98, a. 6, resp.); *ST Suppl.*, Appendix I, q. 2, a. 4, ad 5.

69. See, e.g., *ST* I, q. 62, a. 9, ad 3; q. 95, a. 4, resp.

70. See, e.g., *ST* II-II, q. 152, a. 4, ad 1; q. 182, a. 2, ad 1.

71. See, e.g., *In Rom* 8, lect. 5, n. 677; *ST* III, q. 59, a. 6, resp. and ad 1; q. 89, a. 5, ad 3.

72. See, e.g., *In Sent* IV, d. 44, q. 1, a. 3, q.c. 4, ad 3 and ad 4; d. 49, q. 1, a. 1, q.c. 2, resp.; a. 3, q.c. 4, ad 1; q. 4, a. 5, q.c. 1; *QQ* VIII, q. 9, a. 1; *SCG* III.26.15; *CT* I, chap. 107; *In 1 Cor* 15, lect. 3, n. 937; *ST* I, q. 26, ad 2; *In Mt* 5, lect. 2, n. 408; 25, lect. 2, n. 2053; *In NE* X, lect. 6, nn. 2030–31; *ST* I-II, q. 2, a. 6; q. 3, a. 3; a. 4, resp. and ad 2; q. 3, a. 8; q. 4, a. 1, resp.; aa. 2–4; q. 11, a. 3, ad 3; *In Jn* 14, n. 1854.

73. From q. 2, a. 6, resp. and ad 1.

of a human person, that is, *being a mortal, rational animal*, and a proper accident of a human person, such as *being risible*. The latter is not the formal cause of the former but rather the reverse. In other words, the reason that a human person is risible is because she is a mortal, rational animal; she is not a mortal, rational animal because she is risible. St. Thomas goes on to apply the distinction between the essence of a thing and the proper accidents of a thing to human beatitude. At best, pleasure (*voluptate*)[74] or delight (*delectatio*)[75] is a proper accident of beatitude, as the reason a human person is delighted is that she has a fitting good; she does not have the fitting good that delights her because she is delighted. But a fitting good, if it is the perfect good, is the beatitude of a human person. Pleasure or delight is therefore not the essence of perfect happiness, but at best a proper accident of it.

Whereas St. Thomas thinks that delight in the beatific vision is a *proper* accident of the essence of the essential reward, the *accidental reward* consists of any good in heaven added to the essential reward as a *nonproper* accident. To make sense of those claims, it will be helpful to say something at this point about the different kinds of accident. For example, in one place, St. Thomas posits there are three different kinds of accidents. First, there are *proper* accidents, such as risibility, which are accidents caused by the principles of the species of a thing. That is, John's having the proper accident of (having the root cause of) risibility is caused by John's being a rational animal. Second, there are nonproper accidents that are *inseparable* accidents. These are accidents that are caused by the principles of the individual substance. These accidents are not effects of the principles of the species of a thing, but rather flow from the individual form and matter of an individual substance such that they have a permanent cause in the individual substance that is the subject of such accidents. St. Thomas's examples of inseparable accidents are *the masculine and the feminine*. Third, there are those nonproper accidents that are *separable* accidents, that is, those nonproper accidents that are not permanently caused by the form and matter of the individual substance, such as sitting or walking.[76]

So how do these distinctions apply in the case of the proper accidents

---

74. Ibid.
75. Ibid.
76. *Quaestio disputata de anima* [hereafter *QDA*], a. 12, ad 7; see also *De ente et essentia* [hereafter *DEE*], chap. 5, n. 105.

of the beatific vision and those nonproper accidents that are component parts of the accidental reward? First of all, in an *analogous* way, because we are comparing the component parts of human happiness in heaven, on the one hand, and the accidents of a material substance, on the other. The proper accidents of the beatific vision, for example, delight in the vision, are analogous to the proper accidents of a material substance. Whereas the proper accidents of a material substance are caused by the principles of the species of a thing, for example, Socrates's risibility is caused by his rational animality, the proper accidents that are component parts of the essential reward are caused by the essence of the essential reward of the saint in heaven, that is, the saint's being united to God as the object of perfect human happiness in the beatific vision.

The component parts of the accidental reward of the saints in heaven are analogous to the inseparable and separable accidents of a material substance. As we shall see, some of the component parts of the accidental reward are analogous to the *inseparable* accidents of a material substance. Just as the inseparable accidents of a material substance, for example, Socrates's masculinity, are not caused by the essence of Socrates, that is, his rational animality, although Socrates is always found with them, so there are component parts of the accidental reward that a saint always has, for example, communion with other creatures, but such parts of the heavenly reward are not a part of the essential reward insofar as those goods do not have God as their object and so they are not required for human persons to be perfectly happy. Other component parts of the accidental reward, for example, embodiment, are analogous to the separable accidents of a material substance, for example, Socrates's being tan. Not only do such component parts of the accidental reward not count as parts of the essential reward because they do not have God as their object, but the saints in heaven do not always possess these goods.

As far as goods enjoyed by saints other than the essential reward—and so forming part of the accidental reward—St. Thomas mentions, for example: (a) seeing God indirectly in bodies, not only the heavenly and earthly bodies of the new heavens and the new earth, but chiefly in the glorified bodies of the saints, and most especially in the body of Christ;[77]

---

77. See, e.g., *In Sent* IV, d. 48, q. 2, a. 1, resp. (*ST Suppl.*, q. 91, a. 1, resp.); *In Sent* IV, d. 49, q. 2, a. 2, resp. (*ST Suppl.*, q. 92, a. 2, resp.) and ad 6 (*ST Suppl.*, q. 92, a. 2, ad 6); *Expositio super Iob ad litteram* [hereafter *In Jb*] 19, lect. 2; *In Mt* 5, lect. 2, n. 434.

(b) joy in heaven in any created good;[78] (c) the removal of temporal punishment in purgatory;[79] (d) the remission of venial sin in purgatory;[80] (e) rejoicing in the good of others in the communion of the saints;[81] (f) teaching and being taught by other creatures in heaven;[82] (g) the voluntary poor judging with Christ the rich at the general judgment;[83] (h) the aureoles (crowns or halos), in the specific sense of the joy taken by the martyrs, virgins, and doctors of the church in their victories in this life (characteristic of martyrdom, virginity, and teaching, respectively) which especially conform to Christ's perfect victory;[84] (i) the glory of one's own resurrected body, that is, its impassibility, subtlety, agility, and clarity;[85] (j) spiritual fruit in the sense of a reward given to those saints who, in a particular way, withdraw from carnality in this life;[86] (k) the joy taken in works of charity done in this life;[87] and, (l) in seeing the damned, the delight the saints have in the justice of God.[88]

What generalizations can we draw from St. Thomas's texts about the accidental reward in comparison to the essential reward? For one thing, St. Thomas clearly states that the essential reward is invariable,[89] whereas, at least until the general judgment, the accidental reward (and its attendant joy) can increase,[90] for example, as more human persons join the church triumphant.[91] As the essential reward is immutable, the increase of the accidental reward does not change the extent to which one enjoys the essential reward.[92] Second, the essential reward picks out

78. See, e.g., *ST Suppl.*, q. 93, a. 3, ad 3; *ST* I, q. 95, a. 4, resp.; *In Rom* 8, lect. 5, n. 677.
79. See, e.g., *ST Suppl.*, q. 10, a. 2, ad 2; q. 25, a. 2, ad 2; q. 71, a. 1, resp.
80. See, e.g., *ST Suppl.*, Appendix I, q. 2, a. 4, ad 4.
81. See, e.g., *ST Suppl.*, q. 71, a. 1, resp.; *In Sent* IV, d. 45, q. 2, a. 2, q.c. 4, ad 3 (*ST Suppl.*, q. 71, a. 8, ad 3); *ST* I, q. 62, a. 9, ad 3.
82. See, e.g., *In Sent* IV, d. 49, q. 2, a. 5, resp. (*ST Suppl.*, q. 92, a. 3, resp.).
83. See, e.g., *ST Suppl.*, q. 89, a. 2, ad 5.
84. See, e.g., *ST Suppl.*, q. 89, a. 3, ad 3; q. 96, a. 1, resp.; a. 2, ad 3.
85. See, e.g., *ST Suppl.*, q. 96, a. 1, resp.
86. See, e.g., *ST Suppl.*, q. 96, a. 2, ad 3; aa. 3-4.
87. See, e.g., *ST* III, q. 89, a. 5, ad 3.
88. See, e.g., *In Sent* IV, d. 50, q. 2, a. 4, q.c. 3 (*ST Suppl.*, q. 94, a. 3); *QQ* VIII, q. 7, a. 1, ad 1; *In Ps* 36.
89. See, e.g., *In Sent* IV, d. 45, q. 2, a. 2, q.c. 1 (*ST Suppl.*, q. 71, a. 5); a. 2, q.c. 4, ad 3 (*ST Suppl.*, q. 71, a. 8, ad 3); d. 50, q. 2, a. 1, q.c. 6, resp. (*ST Suppl.*, q. 98, a. 6, resp.); *QDM*, q. 5, a. 1, obj. 5 and ad 5.
90. See, e.g., *In Sent* IV, d. 49, q. 2, a. 5, resp. (*ST Suppl.*, q. 92, a. 3, resp.); d. 50, q. 2, a. 1, q.c. 6, resp. (*ST Suppl.*, q. 98, a. 6, resp.); *ST* I, q. 62, a. 9, ad 3; *ST* II-II, q. 182, a. 2; *QDM*, q. 5, a. 1, obj. 5 and ad 5.
91. See, e.g., *In Sent* IV, d. 45, q. 2, a. 2, q.c. 4, ad 3 (*ST Suppl.*, q. 71, a. 8, ad 3).
92. Ibid. and *QDM*, q. 5, a. 1, ad 4 and ad 5.

what is necessary for man's perfect happiness, which consists in a perfect operation, whereas the accidental reward, at best, adds to the glory of perfect happiness.[93] Third, the accidental reward pales by comparison to the essential reward.[94] In one place, St. Thomas calls the essential reward "true beatitude" (*vera beatitudo*),[95] while the accidental reward is a certain likeness of beatitude (*quaedam similitudinaria beatitudo*).[96] This is because the essential reward is fixed upon the uncreated good alone whereas the accidental reward consists of goods enjoyed by the saints in addition to the essential reward, that is, that reward that "is fixed upon some created good."[97]

In concluding these introductory remarks on the logical structure of *beatitudo*, it is important to emphasize that St. Thomas sometimes uses a different terminology in speaking about the essential reward and the accidental reward, distinguishing rather between perfect happiness in heaven (= the essential reward) and the well-being (*bene esse*) of perfect happiness (= the essential reward *plus* the accidental reward). Although St. Thomas uses the distinction between perfect happiness and the well-being of perfect happiness throughout his scholarly life, he uses it more in the later part of his career, particularly when composing *ST* I-II and his *Commentary on Aristotle's* Nicomachean Ethics.[98] As we have seen, St. Thomas uses the distinction between the essential reward and the accidental reward throughout his scholarly career, including up until the very end of his life.[99]

ST. THOMAS ON GOD'S ETERNAL LIFE

As we will see in chapter 7, St. Thomas takes the essential reward of the saints in heaven to be a certain kind of participation in God's eternal life: a *participated eternity*. Therefore, we need to know something about St. Thomas's views on *God's eternal life* in order to make sense of the es-

---

93. *ST Suppl.*, q. 96, a. 1.
94. Ibid. See also *QDV*, q. 12, a. 13, resp.; q. 26, a. 6, ad 8.
95. *QDM*, q. 5, a. 1, ad 5.
96. Ibid.
97. *QDM*, q. 5, a. 1, obj. 5 and ad 5; see *QDM*, q. 2, a. 2, ad 8.
98. See, e.g., *In Sent* IV, d. 49, q. 4, a. 2, ad 1 (*ST Suppl.*, q. 96, a. 1, ad 1); *ST* I-II, q. 4, a. 5; a. 6, resp.; a. 6, ad 1; a. 7, ad 3; a. 8, resp.; q. 5, a. 2, ad 3; *In NE* I, lect. 13, n. 163; lect. 14, n. 173; lect. 16, n. 194; X, lect. 11, n. 2104.
99. See the texts cited in notes 67–71 above.

sential reward, as St. Thomas understands it. Much ink has been spilled in presenting the details of St. Thomas's philosophical theology.[100] As the focus here is presenting and defending St. Thomas's views on human happiness in heaven, this part of the chapter treats only enough of St. Thomas's views on the nature of God to explain and motivate his account of the essential reward. Such an account of God includes St. Thomas's philosophical analysis of the immutability and eternity of God, as well as his account of the reasonableness of predicating "life" and "love" of God the creator.[101]

On God's Absolute Immutability

St. Thomas thinks that God is absolutely immutable. One reason that St. Thomas gives for speaking this way about God begins from the distinction between act and potency in things that change.[102] Thus, in order to understand St. Thomas's argument here, we need to understand St. Thomas's view that substances that change are composed of *act* and *potency*. Here follows a short primer on composition of act (or actuality) and potency (or potentiality).

First, in speaking about composition of act and potency, St. Thomas is thinking that act and potency are *parts* of a certain kind.[103] That is to say, there is a part of a substance S that explains why it is actually F, and there is a different part of S that explains why it is potentially not-F. Of course, the most obvious sense of "part" is a *quantitative* part, that is, a part of a whole that has dimensions and is smaller than the whole of which it is a part. Act and potency are not parts in that sense. Nonetheless, act and

---

100. For helpful recent studies of St. Thomas's philosophical theology, see, for example, Norman Kretzmann, *The Metaphysics of Theism* (Oxford: Clarendon Press, 1997); Eleonore Stump, *Aquinas* (London: Routledge, 2003) and *The God of the Bible and the God of the Philosophers* (Marquette, Wis.: Marquette University Press, 2016); and Rudi te Velde, *Aquinas on God: The "Divine Science" of the Summa Theologiae* (London: Routledge, 2006). On explaining and motivating St. Thomas's Boethian view of the eternity of God, see especially Stump, *Aquinas*, chap. 4.

101. Interestingly, when St. Thomas treats of the beatific vision, he typically confines himself to speaking of what the saints in heaven will know of God *qua* God in the vision (for an exception, however, see *SCG* IV.1.5). But we certainly could also speak of St. Thomas's view of the beatific vision as involving a knowing and delighting in the one God in three Persons, the second Person having assumed a human nature, as, for example, the Thomist Dante Alighieri does in *Paradiso* (see, e.g., XXXIII.115–32).

102. See, e.g., *ST* I, q. 9, a. 1, resp.; see also *In Sent* I, d. 8, q. 3, a. 1; *In BDT*, q. 5, a. 4, ad 2; *SCG* I.13–14 and II.25; *QDP*, q. 8, a. 1, ad 9; *CT* I, chap. 4.

103. See, e.g., *De principiis naturae, ad fratrem Sylvestrum* [hereafter *DPN*], chaps. 3–4; *SCG* II.54; *QDA*, a. 1, ad 13; *In Met* VII, lect. 21, n. 1095.

potency are rightly called *parts* of a mutable substance insofar as they are intrinsic to that substance and are not identical to one another.[104]

Second, if *x* is *actually* F (or in act with respect to F), then *x* is F right now. If *x* is *potentially* F, then x is not F right now, but can become F. For example, let us say Socrates is tan right now. We could put the same point in the language of act and potency: *Socrates is actually tan* (or *tan in act*). Now, although Socrates is actually tan at time *t*, it is also true at *t* that he can become non-tan (say, in winter). To put that claim in the language of act and potency: *Socrates is potentially non-tan* (or *tan in potency*). We can also contrast Socrates with an oak tree. An oak tree is neither actually nor potentially tan; an oak tree is not the sort of thing that can be, or become, tan.

According to St. Thomas, we can also use the language of act and potency to explain the nature of material substances as beings capable of *substantial* change, that is, the coming into existence or going out of existence of a substance.[105] We can make sense of the nature of material substances as composites of act and potency insofar as they are capable of undergoing substantial change by way of an analogy to substances undergoing *accidental* change, as accidental change is easier to imagine than substantial change. Consider, then, what is required for a substance to undergo accidental change. An accidental change is a change where numerically the same substance gains or loses a property, for example, Socrates changes such that he is tan at time *t* and not tan at *t*+1. Any change involves a *subject* or *matter* of the change. This is what is changed in a change. Any change also requires features or forms that are gained/lost in the change.[106] For an accidental change such as Socrates becoming tan, Socrates (a substance) is the subject or matter of the change, and *being tan/being non-tan* are the accidental forms gained/lost in that change. To put this in the language of potency and act, anything that undergoes accidental changes is composed of a principle of potentiality, such as a substance that is not actually, but potentially, configured by an acciden-

---

104. For more detailed discussion of composition of act and potency in mutable substances in St. Thomas's thought, see, e.g., Ed Feser, *Aristotle's Revenge: the Metaphysical Foundations of Physical and Biological Science* (Neunkirchen-Seelscheid: Editiones Scholasticae, 2019).

105. See, e.g., *DPN*, chaps. 1–2. The complication is ignored here that, for Aristotle and St. Thomas, there are material substances, i.e., the heavenly bodies, that cannot undergo substantial change.

106. See, e.g., *DPN*, chap. 1.

tal form not-F, and a principle of actuality, for example, an accidental form F.

Now, consider substantial change. As anything that can change is composed of act and potency, a thing that can undergo substantial change is composed of act and potency. A substance is the principle of potentiality in an accidental change. Therefore, the principle of potency in a being that can undergo substantial change is a nonsubstance. St. Thomas calls this principle, a portion of *prime matter*.[107] The prime matter of a substance that can undergo substantial change explains that that substance is corruptible. A substance is actually a substance of substantial kind F; its prime matter explains why that substance is corruptible such that that prime matter is potentially part of a substance of substantial kind not-F. As the forms gained or lost in a substantial change are forms intrinsic to a substance that cause a substance to be one substance of a certain kind rather than some numerically different (kind of) substance, St. Thomas calls the principle of actuality in a substantial change (or, in a substance that can undergo substantial change) *a substantial form*. The substantial form of a corruptible substance is the principle intrinsic to that substance that explains that a substance is actually a substance of a certain kind, rather than some numerically different (kind of) substance.

Finally, St. Thomas extends Aristotle's doctrine of the composition of act and potency in material substances to all creatures, even those that are substantially incorruptible, such as the angels. According to St. Thomas, all creatures are composed of act and potency insofar as they are composed of *actus essendi* (an act of being) and a *form* or *essence*.[108] To say that a being is composed of act and potency in the sense of being composed of *actus essendi* and form or essence is just to say that such a being actually exists, but does not have to exist. Even as actually existing, any being composed of act and potency does not have existential inertia. Such a being is a *contingent* being, both in the sense that it might not have existed at all, and in the sense that it depends for its existence, at every moment it exists, on some cause conserving it in existence.

With this primer on composition of act and potency in creatures in the background, we are now in a position to see why St. Thomas thinks

---

107. See, e.g., *DPN*, chaps. 1–2.
108. See, e.g., *SCG* II.54.

that God is absolutely immutable. What follows from the doctrine of act and potency is that a being composed of act and potency is a being capable of change or is a being that need not exist or is a being that depends for its existence on some extrinsic cause. But a being that is capable of change or need not exist or depends for its existence on some extrinsic cause cannot be the *first* being, that is, a being whose existence is uncaused and is the primary cause of the existence of all things that have a cause of their existence. For a being that can change, or need not exist, or depends for its existence on some extrinsic cause, has a cause of its existence. Therefore, if there is actually a first being whose existence is uncaused and is the cause of the existence of things whose existence is caused, then that being is not composed of act and potency.

Let us suppose that God, who is the first being, actually exists.[109] Given what I have said above, God is not composed of act and potency. As potency without act does not actually exist, it follows that God is pure actuality. But if something x can change, then x is composed of act and potency. As God is in no way in potency, God cannot change in any way; he is absolutely immutable.

Notice the reason that God is absolutely immutable: he is pure act. We could think about it this way: *God is pure activity*. God's inability to change exemplifies a *perfection* in God and *not* a limitation. Theologian Thomas Weinandy puts the point helpfully: "God is unchangeable not because he is inert and static ... but for the opposite reason. He is so dynamic, so active that no change can make him more active. He is act pure and simple."[110]

According to Weinandy, God's immutable being is *dynamic*. In fact, God is "so dynamic, so active that no change can make him more active." As we saw in chapter 2, some theologians and philosophers think that a dynamic reality is, by definition, a reality that changes. But Weinandy, who is influenced on this score by St. Thomas, has a different way of thinking about the relationship between mutability, activity, and the dynamic. This Thomistic way of thinking about such things is worth exploring here, however briefly.

Some dynamic realities are clearly mutable, for example, organisms

---

109. For exposition, defense, and development of St. Thomas's arguments for the existence of God, see Kretzmann, *The Metaphysics of Theism*; Feser, *Aquinas*; Edward Feser, *Five Proofs of the Existence of God* (San Francisco, Calif.: Ignatius Press, 2017).

110. *Does God Suffer?* (Notre Dame, Ind.: University of Notre Dame Press, 2000), 124.

and their vegetative actions. But St. Thomas thinks there are examples of even mundane dynamic realties that are, in and of themselves, immutable. For, according to St. Thomas, acts of delight, understanding, and willing are not in and of themselves successive, and so such activities are not in and of themselves in time. Although Socrates's acts of delight, understanding, and willing—for example, his act of understanding the nature of triangularity—can be spoken about as being in time and successive in an extended sense, this is only because those activities are the end (perfection) of a process (which is successive and in time) that a material substance goes through leading up to that activity.[111] Nonetheless, activities of delight, understanding, and willing, in and of themselves, are not successive or in time. But if x is mutable, then x exists in time. Therefore, in and of themselves, acts of delight, understanding, and willing are immutable. Now activities such as understanding, willing, and delighting are dynamic realities insofar as they are activities. Therefore, even some mundane activities of human persons in this life, those of understanding, willing, and delighting, are dynamic immutable realities, at least in and of themselves.

Granted, these dynamic immutable realities are not substances. In St. Thomas's view, however, the most perfect and dynamic realities are substances that engage in acts of understanding and willing, where those substances, insofar as they are substances, are immutable. As we will see below, this is how St. Thomas thinks about the angels. But more to the present point, insofar as God is an absolutely immutable being that understands, delights, and wills, God, in Weinandy's words, "is so dynamic, so active that no change can make him more active."

God's Eternality

St. Thomas follows Boethius in defining *eternity* as it is rightly said of God as "the unlimited and perfect possession of life, all at once" (*aeternitas est interminabilis vitae tota simul et perfecta possessio*).[112] Note first that God's eternal life is *interminabilis*, that is, it has no beginning or end. However, although God's eternal life is interminable, there is more to God's eternity than that. That is because there are conceivable realities

---

111. *ST* I-II, q. 31, a. 2. Thanks to Mark Spencer for pointing me to this text. See also *In Sent* IV, d. 49, q. 1, a. 2, q.c. 3, resp.; q. 3, a. 1, q.c. 3; *Sententia libri De anima* [hereafter *In DA*] I, lect. 10, nn. 157–60; *In DA* III, lect. 12, nn. 765–67.

112. See, e.g., *In Sent* I, d. 8, q. 2, a. 1; *ST* I, q. 10, a. 1; *Expositio super librum De causis*, lect. 2.

that are interminable, but not eternal in Boethius's sense. For example, St. Thomas notes that Aristotle conceives of the physical universe as a whole as interminable. But even if Aristotle were correct about the nature of the physical universe, there would still be a significant ontological difference between the physical universe and God.[113] For God's eternity is not only interminable but also *total simul* (often translated, *all at once*). What could this mean? A first approximation is that, unlike the physical universe—whether or not the physical universe had a beginning in time—God's being cannot be measured by time; God's being is timeless.

To see why St. Thomas thinks that God's being cannot be measured by time, note that St. Thomas follows Aristotle in defining time as "the measure of movement with respect to before and after."[114] Therefore, to deny that a being is mutable is to deny such a being can be measured by time. But God is absolutely immutable. Therefore, God's being is absolutely timeless.[115]

But to say that God's being is *eternal*—or perhaps to say God's being is *total simul*—is also to say more than *God's being cannot be measured by time*. For St. Thomas also thinks that the substantial being of the angels cannot be measured by time and that angelic being is not eternal in the Boethian sense. Rather, the substantial being of the angels is measured by what St. Thomas calls *aeveternity* (*aeviternitas*). As aeveternity is a measure of creaturely being, God being eternal is also a denial that God's being is measured by aeveternity.

In order to understand the meaning of this denial, we need to understand *aeveternity*. According to St. Thomas, aeveternity is a mean between eternity and time.[116] Furthermore, because eternity is the measure of an absolutely permanent or immutable being,[117] insofar as x is not absolutely permanent or immutable, x differs in its mode of being from a being that is eternal.[118] Now time is the measure of the duration of beings that *are in no sense* immutable. Therefore, aeveternity is the measure of

---

113. See, e.g., *ST* I, q. 10, a. 4.
114. *ST* I, q. 10, a. 1, resp.
115. See, e.g., *In Sent* I, d. 19, q. 2, a. 1; *SCG* I.15; *QDP*, q. 3, a. 17, ad 23; *CT* I, chaps. 5 and 8; *ST* I, q. 10, a. 2, resp.
116. See, e.g., *ST* I, q. 10, a. 5, resp. See also *In Sent* I, d. 8, a. 2; d. 19, q. 2, a. 1; II, d. 2, q. 1, a. 1; *QQ* X, q. 2; *QDP*, q. 3, a. 14, ad 18.
117. See, e.g., *ST* I, q. 10, a. 5.
118. *ST* I, q. 10, a. 5, resp.: "cum aeternitas sit mensura esse permanentis, secundum quod aliquid recedit a permanentia essendi, secundum hoc recedit ab aeternitate."

the duration of beings that are immutable in some ways but mutable in others. As eternity, aeveternity, and time are measures of beings that are absolutely immutable, partly immutable, or entirely mutable, respectively, we can get a clearer understanding of aeveternity—and so eternity in the Boethian sense—by examining with St. Thomas the different ways in which things can be mutable, and so immutable.

St. Thomas notes that a thing can be mutable in two ways.[119] First, a thing x can be mutable because of a power y possesses, where y is not identical to x.[120] According to St. Thomas, all creatures depend for their existence, from moment to moment, on God's conserving them in existence. If God withheld his power to keep a creature in existence at some time, then that creature would be reduced to nothing at that time. Therefore, *all* creatures are mutable in the sense that the possibility of their going from existing to nonexisting is in the power of another, namely, God. But God exists by nature and nothing causes God to exist or can cause God not to exist. So, whereas all creatures are mutable insofar as they can be changed such that they can cease to exist because of the power of God, God himself is not mutable in that sense.[121]

Second, x can be mutable because of powers or properties intrinsic to x. According to St. Thomas, all creatures are mutable in this way too (whereas God is not mutable in this sense either). Now there are two ways that a thing can be mutable because of its intrinsic powers or properties. First, some things are mutable insofar as they are *substances*. For example, substances such as plants and animals are mutable insofar as they can die. Call such substances *corruptible* substances.[122] More precisely, a corruptible substance S is a substance such that S can undergo a *substantial* change, that is, S's prime matter can be configured by a substantial form F at one time, but configured by a substantial form F1 at another time, where F is not numerically identical to F1. For example, Fido the dog is a substance configured by a doggie substantial form F and prime matter M at time t, Fido gets hit by a car and killed at $t+1$ so that M is no longer configured by F at $t+1$. As Fido's substantial form goes out of existence when M is no longer configured by it at $t+1$, and Fido depends

---

119. See, e.g., *ST* I, q. 9, a. 2, resp.
120. See ibid.
121. See ibid.
122. Although St. Thomas thinks that human persons are animals and so are corruptible substances, there is a sense in which human persons are incorruptible substances. See chapter 9 below for my treatment of that complication.

for Fido's existence on his substantial form configuring matter, Fido goes out of existence at $t+1$. Fido is mutable because of his own intrinsic powers or properties in the sense that, as a substance, he is corruptible.

A second way that a thing can be mutable because of its own intrinsic powers or properties is with respect to its *accidental* features. For example, corruptible substances are not only mutable in their substance, but also undergo accidental changes, for example, Rex the dog is barking at one time and is not barking at another time, where Rex survives such a change. Compare with the Fido case above, where Fido does not survive the change. The case involving Rex is an accidental change; the case involving Fido is a substantial change. So we can say corruptible substances are mutable insofar as they are subject to both substantial and accidental changes.

By contrast to corruptible substances, some created substances, St. Thomas thinks, are mutable because of their intrinsic features only accidentally, and not substantially. St. Thomas calls these substances *incorruptible*. We should note that *corruptible* and *incorruptible* are technical terms for St. Thomas; as we have seen, all existing created substances are potentially nonexistent insofar as their continued existence from moment to moment depends upon God, as their creating and sustaining cause, causing them to exist from moment to moment. Of course, some created substances are potentially nonexistent because of the actions of other creatures, that is, corruptible substances. However, the only way that an *incorruptible* substance is mutable with respect to its substance is in relation to God; no creature could move an *incorruptible* substance from existence to nonexistence.

According to St. Thomas, angels are incorruptible substances, and angels are incorruptible because they are wholly immaterial substances (St. Thomas thinks the heavenly bodies are incorruptible substances too; but they are incorruptible not because they are immaterial, but because they are composed of a special kind of matter that is not in potency to a substantial form other than the substantial form God has given them). Because angels are incorruptible substances, they enjoy a relative kind of immutability insofar as they are substances.[123] Nonetheless, whereas the angels in their substance are not subject to time and change, time and change are added (*adiunctam*) to angelic being insofar as angels engage

---

123. See ibid.

in different activities at different times, for example, Gabriel applies his intellect to one thing T he already knows at time *t* and Gabriel applies his intellect to a numerically different thing T1 he already knows at time $t + 1$.[124] In addition, angels are not created in heaven or hell. Therefore, angels are mutable insofar as each is, in its first moment of existence, confronted with a choice: either to will (by the grace of God) in accord with God's will, or to will to reject God's will. Those angels that choose to will in union with God go from not having the beatific vision in the first moment of their existence, but potentially having it or potentially being damned, to actually having the beatific vision in the next moment of their existence, whereas those angels that choose to will in discord with God's will go from not having the beatific vision in the first moment of their existence, but potentially having it or potentially being damned, to being damned in the next moment.[125]

We are now in a position to understand what St. Thomas means by saying that God's eternal mode of being transcends not only time but also aeveternity. Recall that, for St. Thomas, aeveternity is a measure between time and eternity. In addition, St. Thomas thinks that we can understand

---

124. See, e.g., *QDP*, q. 3, a. 14, ad 18. As St. Thomas puts it in *ST* I, q. 10, a. 5, resp.: "Now some things recede from permanence of being ... forasmuch as ... they have change annexed to them either actually, or potentially. This appears in the heavenly bodies, the substantial being of which is unchangeable; and yet with unchangeable being they have changeableness of place. The same applies to the angels, who have an unchangeable being as regards their nature with changeableness as regards choice; *moreover they have changeableness of intelligence, of affections, and of places, in their own degree*" (trans. English Dominicans, 43-44; emphasis added). *ST* I, q. 10, a. 5, ad 1: "spiritual creatures [such as angels] as regards successive affections and intelligences, are measured by time. Hence also Augustine says (*Gen. ad lit.* viii, 20, 22, 23) that to be moved through time is to be moved by affections. But as regards their nature they are measured by aeveternity; whereas as regards the vision of glory, they have a share of eternity" (trans. English Dominicans, 44). See also *ST* I, q. 58, a. 1, resp.; q. 65, a. 1, ad 1; q. 66, a. 4, ad 3. It should be noted that angelic affections (*affectiones*) are not bodily states for St. Thomas, but rather acts of will (see, e.g., *ST* I, q. 57, a. 4, resp.; q. 59, a. 3, ad 2; q. 63, a. 2, resp.; a. 6, ad 4; q. 65, a. 1, ad 1; q. 82, a. 5, ad 1). Although, as we will see below, immaterial beings, such as God and the angels, do not have emotions, passions, or feelings, as having emotions, passions, or feelings entails possessing a body, such beings can have appetites or affections understood as *acts of will*. Here is St. Thomas at *ST* I, q. 82, a. 5, ad 1: "Love, concupiscence, and the like can be understood in two ways. Sometimes they are taken as passions—arising, that is, with a certain commotion of the soul. And thus they are commonly understood, and in this sense they are only in the sensitive appetite. They may, however, be taken in another way, as far as they are simple affections without passion or commotion of the soul, and thus they are acts of the will. And in this sense, too, they are attributed to the angels and to God" (trans. English Dominicans, 417). Thanks to Mark Spencer for showing me the need to make explicit this point that affections (*affectiones*) in God and the angels are acts of will for St. Thomas.

125. See, e.g., *QDP*, q. 3, a. 14, ad 18; *ST* I, q. 10, a. 5, resp. and ad 1; q. 58, a. 1, resp.; q. 62, aa. 1-5. As we will see in the chapters that follow, once a person S has the beatific vision, S cannot lose that vision.

why any of these measures apply to a substance insofar, and to the extent that, a substance is immutable. Corruptible substances such as plants and nonhuman animals are measured by time, as such substances are in no sense immutable; they not only undergo *accidental* changes but their substantial being too is mutable. Angelic being is measured by aeveternity because, though angels are immutable and permanent with respect to their substantial being, they nonetheless undergo accidental changes and so "before" and "after" are said truly of them, for example, Gabriel delivers a message to Zechariah *before* he delivers a message to the Virgin Mary. Whereas before and after are said of substances measured by time and aeveternity, albeit in different ways, God's being is absolutely permanent and immutable and so "before" and "after" cannot be said of God in any sense. Again, this is no imperfection in God, but a mark of his absolute perfection, and an implication of his pure actuality. Consider again Weinandy's wise words: "God is so dynamic ... so active, that no change could make Him more active." We could put this point differently: "God's eternity is so perfect, that no change, whether in time, or in some other manner, could make Him more perfect than He is by nature."

God's Life

Recall that for St. Thomas, following Boethius, eternal being is not only *interminable* and *total simul*, but involves the "perfect possession of life." We might wonder, however, insofar as God is immaterial, and not an organism, how "life" can rightly be said of God. St. Thomas argues that life exists in God in the highest possible way.[126] This is because a thing is said to live insofar as it acts *from itself* (*ex seipso*), and not by way of being changed by another.[127] Therefore, the more something acts from itself, or in virtue of itself, rather than being changed by another, the more perfectly life is found in that thing. For example, although both plants and animals are living things, life is found more perfectly in animals than in plants because, as beings that cognize the world, animals can be said to move themselves to act more so than plants. But because God is pure act, and not in any way in potency, he cannot be changed by another, and so acts only of himself.[128] Therefore, life belongs to God

---

126. See, e.g., *SCG* I.97–98 and IV.11; *ST* I, q. 18, a. 3, resp.; *In Jn* 14, lect. 2, n. 1869.
127. See the texts cited in the note immediately above.
128. 1 Jn 4:8 and 4:16. Someone might think that God acting from or of himself (*ex seipso*) means that God's act is *self-caused*. But St. Thomas, as an advocate of divine simplicity, thinks that

most perfectly. Indeed, as we have seen, God's life is eternal, absolutely immutable, and perfect.[129]

God Is Love

So says the Apostle John.[130] St. Thomas therefore thinks it right to predicate "love" of God.[131] Indeed, as St. Thomas argues, God loves all created things. For what is it to love x, but to will good to x? But existence is a good, and all created things have their existence from God's willing that they exist. Therefore, God loves all created things.[132] However, as St. Thomas is quick to note, God does not love in the way we love.[133] For our love arises—is called forth—from things outside of us that appear to us to be good. In seeing or hearing or knowing something we perceive to be good, we *desire* that perceived good, if we do not already have it, and if we already enjoy some union with that good, we *desire* to preserve that union. As St. Thomas notes, God does not love in those ways. God does not love in the sense of desiring or wanting. As Plato has Socrates put the point in *Symposium*, love in the sense of *eros* or desire is the *philosopher's* way of loving—the way someone who lacks wisdom loves. But the gods are not philosophers, for they already possess the true object of desire, namely, wisdom.[134] As St. Thomas puts it, God's love is pure delight in himself as perfect goodness possessed,[135] such that creatures exist and enjoy other goods as a freely chosen effect of his perfect love for himself.[136] We can also put St. Thomas's point in Christian Trinitarian terms: God's love *ad intra* is a perfect, immutable, and eternal exchange of love between the three divine Persons. God's love *ad extra* is a function of God's free choice in willing that creatures exist and enjoy other goods

---

there is no distinction between substance and accident in God. Therefore, God is identical to his activity (see, e.g., *ST* I, q. 3, aa. 3, 6, 7). Because God's existence is uncaused, God's acting only of or from himself, i.e., God's acting without in any way being changed by another, does not imply that God's activity is self-caused for St. Thomas. Thanks to Mark Spencer for pointing out the need to address this complication. For clarification and defense of St. Thomas's doctrine of divine simplicity, see the authors and texts cited in note 100 above.

129. For a detailed discussion of "life" as predicated of God, see Carlo Leget, *Living with God: Thomas Aquinas on the Relation between Life on Earth and 'Life' After Death* (Leuven: Peeters, 1997), 20–47.

130. 1 Jn 4:8 and 1 Jn 4:16.

131. See, e.g., *SCG* I.91 and IV.19; *ST* I, q. 20, a. 1, s.c.; *In DDN*, chap. 4, lect. 9.

132. *ST* I, q. 20, a. 2, resp.

133. Ibid.

134. *Symposium* 203e–204a.

135. See, e.g., *ST* I, q. 19, a. 1, ad 2. See also *In Sent* I, d. 45, a. 1, ad 1, and *QDV*, q. 23, a. 1, ad 8.

136. See, e.g., *ST* I, q. 19, a. 2.

as effects of God's love *ad intra*, including, in some cases, coming to participate in God's eternal life in the beatific vision in heaven.

Finally, human love is often accompanied, or colored, by a *feeling*, or *emotion*, or *passion*[137] that we denote by the word "love." This sense of "love" is so important for us that we sometimes forget—perhaps some human persons have *never* known—that there are any other senses of love. But God is not, and does not love, in the sense of a passion, feeling, or emotion. For passions, feelings, and emotions are always connected with bodily states.[138] But God is not a bodily being. Therefore, God does not love in the sense of a passion, emotion, or feeling.[139] His love is entirely a matter of his *willing* what he knows to be perfectly good, namely, himself. As I have said, God's willing is never a *desire*, but rather a *delighting in* the perfect good as possessed, which willing has the good of creatures as freely willed effects of his delight in his own perfect goodness.[140] God does not therefore love human persons by compassion (*compassio*); rather, God loves us by bringing about goods for us, beginning with our very existence, but including, by grace, that we participate in his own perfection insofar as that is logically possible, given our own free choices. God *is* a perfect act of love that has every creature and every creaturely good as its freely willed effect.

Having said something about St. Thomas's views on God as the object of perfect human happiness, the distinction between the essential reward in heaven and the accidental reward, and God's eternal life, we are now in a position to examine in detail St. Thomas's views on the essential reward in heaven, particularly the beatific vision. It is to that subject that I now turn.

---

137. The words "passion," "feeling," and "emotion" are used interchangeably here.

138. See, e.g., *ST* I, q. 20, a. 1, ad 1.

139. See, e.g., *In Sent* III, d. 32, a. 1, ad 1; *SCG* I.91; *ST* I, q. 20, a. 1, ad 1 and ad 2; q. 82, a. 5, ad 1. For St. Thomas on scripture attributing passions, emotions, or feelings to God *metaphorically*, see, e.g., *SCG* I.91; *In Eph* 4, lect. 10, n. 263; *ST* I, q. 3, a. 2, ad 2; q. 20, a. 1, ad 2; q. 59, a. 4, ad 1; I-II, q. 47, a. 1, ad 1. Of course, it is important to keep the relevant orthodox Christological doctrines in mind here: the second Person of the Trinity, Jesus Christ, does love in the sense of a passion, feeling, or emotion, but he does so *qua* his human nature (perhaps more so than any human person ever has). It also is important to keep in mind that, as I go on to say below, love exists in God as an act of will.

140. See, e.g., *In Sent* III, d. 32, a. 1, ad 1; *SCG* I.91; *ST* I, q. 20, a. 1, ad 2 and ad 3; q. 82, a. 5, ad 1.

5

The Essential Reward I

THE ESSENTIAL CHARACTERISTICS
OF THE BEATIFIC VISION

In chapter 4, I offered a preliminary explanation of the distinction between the essential reward and the accidental reward in heaven. In addition, I said something about God's eternal life according to St. Thomas. This chapter begins a detailed examination of St. Thomas's views on *the essential reward* by focusing on the *essence* of the essential reward, what St. Thomas sometimes calls *the beatific vision*.[1] St. Thomas thinks that the beatific vision is that which constitutes the essence of the essential reward in heaven.[2] But what exactly does St. Thomas mean by the beatific vision, or as he usually refers to it, the vision of the essence of God?

First, St. Thomas thinks that the beatific vision is something *created*. As we saw in the previous chapter, it is true that the *object* of perfect human happiness—what, the possession of which, causes humans to be perfectly happy—cannot be a creature. But the beatific vision is not itself the object of human happiness; rather the beatific vision is the intellectual creature's *attainment* of the essence of perfect human happiness.[3] The attainment of the essence of perfect human happiness or the es-

---

1. See, e.g., *In Sent* IV, d. 49, q. 2, a. 1, resp. (*ST Suppl.*, q. 92, a. 1, resp.), where St. Thomas uses the expression *visio beatificans*. At *ST* II-II, q. 175, a. 3, obj. 2, St. Thomas uses the expression *"visio... beatum"* and at *ST* III, q. 9, a. 2, ad 3, the expression, *"visio... beata."* At *ST* III, prol., q. 10, he uses the expression *de scientia beata, quae in Dei visione consistit*.

2. See, e.g., *In Sent* IV, d. 44, q. 1, a. 3, q.c. 4, ad 3 and ad 4; d. 49, q. 1, a. 1, q.c. 2, resp.; a. 3, q.c. 4, ad 1; q. 4, a. 5, q.c. 1; *QQ* VIII, q. 9, a. 1; *SCG* III.26.15; *CT* I, chap. 107; *In 1 Cor* 15, lect. 3, n. 937; *ST* I, q. 26, a. 2; *In NE* X, lect. 6, nn. 2030–31; *In Mt* 5, lect. 2, n. 408; *ST* I-II, q. 2, a. 6; q. 3, a. 3; a. 4, resp. and ad 2; a. 8; q. 4, a. 1, resp.; aa. 2–4; q. 11, a. 3, ad 3; *In Jn* 14, lect. 1, n. 1854.

3. See, e.g., *ST* I-II, q. 3, a. 8. See also *QDV*, q. 8, a. 1; *QQ* X, q. 8; *ST* I, q. 12, a. 1; *CT* I, chap. 104; *In Mt* 5, lect. 2; *In Jn* 1, lect. 11; *CT* II, chap. 9.

sence of the essential reward in heaven is an accident of a human person, and human persons are creatures. Because an accident of a creature must itself be a creature, the beatific vision itself is something created.[4]

A second feature of the beatific vision, according to St. Thomas, is that it is an *operation* or *activity* of the soul.[5] In *ST*, St. Thomas argues for this thesis as follows: a thing is perfect to the extent that it is in act, that is, x is actually F rather than potentially F, where F is a feature perfective of members of the *infima* species to which x belongs.[6] But the attainment of the essence of perfect human happiness is a human person's supreme perfection. Therefore, the attainment of the essence of perfect human happiness consists in a human person's most perfect act.

Now, there are (at least) three ways for something x to be in act, where the second is more perfect than the first, and the third more perfect than the second. In a first way that something is actual, x actually is a *substance* that belongs to some species S, but x only potentially has an *ability* to Q, where to Q is an ability perfective of members of S, for example, baby Socrates of Athens *actually* is a *substance* belonging to the species *human person*, but baby Socrates of Athens only *potentially* has the ability to *philosophize*.

In a second way that something is actual, a way of being actual more perfect than the first way, x actually is a substance that belongs to some species S, x actually has an ability to Q, but x at time t is only potentially and not actually Q-ing, for example, the adult Socrates at time t is actually a substance belonging to the species *human person* and actually has the ability to philosophize. But Socrates is not philosophizing at t.

Finally, we can mention a third way that something is in act, a way of being actual that is more perfect than the second way: x actually is a substance that belongs to some species S, x actually has the ability to Q, and x is actually engaged in the activity of Q-ing as we speak, for example, the adult Socrates is an actual human person engaged in the activity of philosophy as we speak (he is actually refuting Polus). Therefore, because it is evident that *operation* or *activity* is the most perfect act—for it

---

4. See, e.g., *In Sent* IV, d. 49, q. 1, a. 2, q.c. 1; *ST* I, q. 26, a. 3; I-II, q. 2, a. 7, resp.; q. 3, a. 1, resp.
5. See, e.g., *In Sent* IV, d. 49, q. 1, a. 2, q.c. 2; *SCG* I.100 and III.25; *ST* I-II, q. 3, a. 2; *In NE* I, lect. 10; *Sententia super Metaphysicam* [hereafter *In Meta*] IX, lect. 8.
6. The *infima* species of a substance x, e.g., Socrates of Athens, is the most particular species of x, e.g., *human person* or *rational animal*; any other true descriptions of Socrates of Athens pick out some genus of Socrates, e.g., *animal* or *substance*, or a component part of the *infima* species of Socrates, e.g., *rational*, or some kind of accidental feature of Socrates, e.g., *being risible*, *male*, or *tan*.

implies that something actually is a substance, which actually possesses an ability, which is actually being used—the essence of perfect happiness or the essential reward is an activity or operation (and not simply a state, power, or habit, let alone a feeling).

Because the essence of the essential reward consists in the beatific vision, St. Thomas therefore thinks that the beatific vision is an activity. This is particularly instructive for us. It is easy for us to hold fast to the idea that the beatific vision is something that merely *happens* to the saints in heaven. But, in saying that the beatific vision is an *activity*, St. Thomas helps to ward off such a misimpression. The attainment of perfect happiness is something intellectual creatures are *doing*; it is not simply something done to them.

According to St. Thomas, the beatific vision is an *intellectual* and not in any way a bodily activity.[7] Of course, the locutions *vision of the divine essence* or *beatific vision* obviously trade on a comparison with the activity of the sense of sight, and intentionally so, given that the sense of sight is naturally, of all the senses, the most productive of knowledge.[8] Nonetheless, St. Thomas thinks that the beatific vision is not an activity of the senses.[9] As we will see, even after the general resurrection, the beatific vision itself remains a purely nonbodily activity for human persons, according to St. Thomas. As the beatific vision is a nonsensory activity, *a fortiori*, it cannot be a bodily activity such as eating, drinking, or copulating. It must therefore be an activity of the intellectual part of us.

If the object of human happiness in heaven were a good of the body, then it would make perfect sense to think that the essence of the essential reward in heaven would involve some activity of the senses, or of the body more generally. But the object of human happiness is God. Now, God is not a composite of matter and form. But if something is not composed of matter and form, then it cannot be cognized *directly* by way of a sense faculty. But, as we will see below, the beatific vision is the most direct and unmediated union with immaterial God logically possible for a creature. Therefore, the attainment of God in the beatific vision itself is not an activity of the bodily senses.[10]

---

7. See, e.g., *SCG* III.33; *In 1 Cor* 13, lect. 4, n. 802; *In NE* I, lect. 10; *ST* I-II, q. 3, a. 3; *In Jn* 1, lect. 11, n. 213; *CT* II, chap. 9.
   8. See, e.g., *In Meta* I, lect. 1, nn. 5–8.
   9. See, e.g., *ST* I-II, q. 4, a. 5.
   10. See *ST* I-II, q. 3, a. 3, resp. See also *SCG* III.33; *In NE* I, lect. 10; *CT* II, chap. 9.

Someone may object: but *we* know that human intellectual activity depends upon brain activity. Because brain activity is bodily activity and the beatific vision is a human intellectual activity, St. Thomas is wrong to think that the beatific vision is not in any way a bodily activity. It is true for St. Thomas that *this-worldly* or *natural* human intellectual activity depends upon the activity of the senses, and this is true in a number of different ways. For example, St. Thomas thinks in order for a human person in this life to cognize *what* something is, the person must receive from a sensible object the form of the object sensed as a spiritual immutation by way of an external sense organ.[11] St. Thomas calls this form "the sensible species." The sensible species is then cognized by way of what St. Thomas calls the interior senses,[12] and becomes what St. Thomas calls a *phantasm* so that the agent is conscious of the object sensed. Only then can the intellect of the agent abstract the quiddity of the object sensed so that intellectual activity culminates in what St. Thomas calls *simple apprehension*. The form or quiddity of the object sensed—what the object is—as it exists in the intellect St. Thomas calls "the intelligible species."[13] Even if the intellect and the intelligible species do not exist in matter, there is no principled reason why a Thomist cannot agree that external sense activity and interior sense activity naturally involve, or even require, brain activity. Therefore, because this-worldly intellectual activity depends upon external and interior sense activity, this-worldly human intellectual activity does depend upon brain activity.

However, there are two reasons that the objection above nonetheless fails. First, even this-worldly intellectual activity, in and of itself, does not make use of a bodily organ (as the external and interior senses clearly do). Take the act of simple apprehension, that is, cognizing what something is. Although, as we have seen, the act of simple apprehension naturally depends upon the external and interior senses to provide it with that from which it abstracts the quiddity or whatness of a thing, the act of simple apprehension itself is a wholly immaterial act. This is because the act of simple apprehension cognizes universals, such as

---

11. See, e.g., *ST* I, q. 78, a. 3.
12. See, e.g., *ST* I, q. 78, a. 4.
13. See, e.g., *ST* I, q. 84, a. 7. In order for a human person S to be conscious that the quiddity or intelligible species by which S understands is not simply a separately existing form, S's intellect returns to the phantasm from whence the intelligible species was abstracted so that S recognizes that the quiddity is the quiddity of an individual material thing (see, e.g., *ST* I, q. 84, a. 7).

triangularity. If the act of simple apprehension were not a wholly immaterial activity, for example, if it made use of a bodily organ such as a brain, then it would only ever cognize particulars, for example, *this* acute triangle, and not universals. But we do know universals (such as triangularity), which universals cannot be reduced to some imagined object.[14] Therefore, an intellectual act such as simple apprehension is a wholly immaterial activity.[15]

Second, the beatific vision is not a this-worldly or natural human intellectual activity. As we will see in what follows, St. Thomas thinks that the human person having the beatific vision cognizes, by way of a special grace, the essence of God in a particularly unmediated manner. Because God is an immaterial being, if the beatific vision were an intellectual activity that involved the body, the beatific vision would not be a cognition of the very essence of God. Therefore, St. Thomas thinks that the beatific vision is an intellectual activity that does not make use of the body.

All that being said, St. Thomas thinks there is a sense in which the activity of the bodily senses *pertains* (*pertinere*) to human happiness in heaven.[16] In explaining how that is so, St. Thomas distinguishes three different ways that something x might *pertain* to y: essentially (*essentialiter*), antecedently (*antecedenter*), and consequently (*consequenter*).[17] St. Thomas has the following meanings in mind by these technical terms:

(3)(a) x pertains to y *essentially* if and only if x picks out (part of) *what y is*. For example, *being rational* pertains essentially to Socrates of Athens, where *being risible* or *being an Athenian* does not.

(3)(b) x pertains to y *antecedently* (*antecedenter*) if and only if (a) x is not (part of) the essence of y and either (b) x is a temporal prerequisite for something z's possessing y, that is, for any z, in order for z to possess y at time t, z possesses x at some time before t, for example, Glenn Gould's having piano teachers pertains *antecedently* to his being a virtuoso pianist or (c) x is a logical prerequisite for y, for example, Aristotle's having

---

14. Consider that any sensed or imagined triangle is necessarily an acute, or an obtuse, or a right triangle (but not all three). But triangularity is neither acute, nor obtuse, nor right. For if triangularity were any of these, it could not be applied to all of these. What is true of triangularity is true of other universals such as acute triangularity or animality. Therefore, universals cannot be reduced to objects that can be sensed or imagined. I owe this method of argumentation to Feser, *Aquinas*, 144.
15. See, e.g., *ST* I, q. 75, a. 5, resp.
16. See, e.g., *ST* I-II, q. 3, a. 3, resp.
17. See ibid.

friends pertains antecedently to Aristotle being a successful politician.[18]

(3)(c) *x* pertains to *y* consequently (*consequenter*) if and only if (a) *x* is not (part of) the essence of *y* and either (b) *y* does not always possess *x*, but *y* will possess *x* eventually, for example, assuming that Socrates's soul is not now embodied, Socrates's soul will be embodied at the general resurrection or (c) *x* is a concomitant or proper accident of *y*, for example, *risibility* pertains consequently to a rational animal such as Socrates of Athens.[19]

Not only does St. Thomas make it clear that the activity of the senses is not the *essence* of the essential reward, he also posits that such activity is not any part of the essential reward. As he says, "two things are needed for happiness: one, which is the essence of happiness: the other, that is, as it were, its proper accident, i.e., the delight connected with it."[20] But such delight is an act of the will and not an act of the body.

Nonetheless, St. Thomas thinks that the activity of the senses pertains to human persons in heaven *consequently* in the sense of (3)(a)–(b).[21] Not all the saints in heaven are embodied now (although the Virgin Mary is), but all the saints in heaven will *eventually* be embodied at the general resurrection, and at that point they will make a perfect use of their sense faculties.[22] Therefore, St. Thomas says that the activity of the senses pertains to perfect happiness, or the essential reward, *consequently*.[23]

As an intellectual activity, the essential reward involves the operation of the two intellectual powers for St. Thomas: the intellect and the will. The idea that the essential reward involves both acts of intellect and will for St. Thomas is supported by texts across the span of his body of work.[24] That being said, the *essence* of the essential reward consists in

---

18. See also *ST* I-II, q. 3, a. 4, ad 1; q. 4, aa. 4 and 6. At *ST* I-II, q. 4, a. 1, resp., St. Thomas speaks of *x*'s being required for *y* as a "preamble" (*praeambulum*) or "preparation" (*praeparatorium*) for *y*, e.g., as teaching is required for science. It seems that *x*'s being required for *y* as a preamble or preparation is logically equivalent to (2)(a)–(b).

19. For an example of St. Thomas's use of *consequenter* in sense (3)(a)–(c), see *ST* I-II, q. 3, a. 4, ad 1.

20. *ST* I-II, q. 3, a. 4, resp. (trans. English Dominicans, 598). See also *ST* I-II, q. 2, a. 6; q. 4, a. 5.

21. *ST* I-II, q. 3, a. 4.

22. See chapters 11 and 13 below for a development of this point.

23. See, e.g., *ST* I-II, q. 3, a. 3, resp.

24. See, e.g., *ST Suppl.*, q. 13, a. 2, ad 1; *In Sent* IV, d. 45, q. 2, a. 2, q.c. 4, ad 3 (*ST Suppl.*, q. 71, a. 8, ad 3); d. 49, q. 2, a. 1 (*ST Suppl.*, q. 92, a. 1); *ST Suppl.*, q. 96, a. 1; *QQ* X, q. 8; *QDV*, q. 8, a. 1; *SCG* III.51, 54, 57; *ST* I, q. 12, a. 1; q. 95, a. 4, resp.; *CT* I, chaps. 104 and 106; *In Mt* 5, lect. 2, n. 408; *ST* I-II, q. 1, a. 8, resp.; q. 3, a. 8; q. 4, a. 1; a. 3, resp.; a. 5, resp.; a. 8, resp. and ad 1; q. 5, a. 1, resp.; a. 3, resp.; a. 4, resp.; a. 5, resp.; *ST* I-II, q. 69, a. 3, resp.; *In Jn* 1, lect. 11, n. 212; *CT* II, chap. 9; *In Ps* 32.

the beatific vision, according to St. Thomas, whereas the love, joy, and delight that follow upon the beatific vision are proper accidents of that vision.[25] As we saw above, St. Thomas thinks that "two things are needed for happiness: one, which is the essence of happiness: the other, that is, as it were, its proper accident, i.e., the delight connected with it."[26]

As the text from *ST* cited above makes clear, according to St. Thomas, the essence of the essential reward is not an act of will but rather an act of intellect. How does St. Thomas argue for this view? The argument that St. Thomas employs in *ST*[27]—as well as many other places[28]—runs as follows:

(4) Where the attainment of the end is concerned,[29] there are two species of willing: (a) willing x in the sense of *desiring x*, that is, willing such that one wants to achieve a good one does not already possess and (b) willing x in the sense of *delighting in x*, that is, willing such that one rests in and enjoys a good already possessed [assumption].

(5) Therefore, if the attainment of the ultimate end is an act of will, then either (i) the attainment of the ultimate end consists in *desiring* the ultimate end (which is absent in the one so desiring), or (ii) the attainment of the ultimate end consists in *taking delight in* the ultimate end insofar as the ultimate end is already possessed [from (4)].

(6) But not (i), because a desire for the ultimate end is not the attainment of the ultimate end but is rather a movement *toward* attaining the ultimate end [assumption].

(7) But not (ii), because one delights in the ultimate end insofar as it is attained; one does not delight in the ultimate end and thereby attain it. That is, delight pertains to attaining the ultimate end *consequently* insofar as delight in attaining the ultimate end is a concomitant or proper accident of that act whereby the ultimate end is attained, just as *risibility* pertains consequently to a rational animal such as Socrates of Athens

---

25. See, e.g., *In Sent* IV, d. 49, q. 1, a. 1, q.c. 2, resp.; a. 2, q.c. 2, ad 3; a. 3, q.c. 4, ad 1; *QQ* VIII, q. 9, a. 1; *SCG* III.26; *In 1 Cor* 15, lect. 3, n. 937; *ST* I, q. 26, a. 2, ad 2; *CT* I, chap. 107; *In Mt* 5, lect. 2, n. 408; *ST* I-II, q. 2, a. 6; q. 3, a. 4, resp. and ad 2; q. 4, a. 1; a. 2, resp.; a. 3; a. 4; q. 11, a. 3, ad 3; *In NE* X, lect. 6, nn. 2030–31; *In Jn* 14, lect. 1, n. 1854.

26. *ST* I-II, q. 3, a. 4, resp.

27. Ibid.

28. See, e.g., *In Sent* IV, d. 49, q. 1, a. 1, q.c. 2, resp.; *QQ* VIII, q. 9, a. 1; *SCG* III.26; *CT* I, chap. 107; *ST* I, q. 26, a. 2, ad 2; *ST* I-II, q. 4, aa. 1–4.

29. St. Thomas identifies other species of willing that do not have to do with attaining the end, e.g., *consent, choice,* and *use* (see, e.g., *ST* I-II, qq. 14–16). Thanks to Mark Spencer for pointing out the need to make this point explicit.

as a concomitant or proper accident of Socrates's rational animality [assumption].

(8) Defense of (6) and (7): the covetous person is delighted because he has money in his hand, he does not have money in his hand because he is delighted that he has money in his hand. We first *desire* to attain an intelligible good, and we then attain that good and delight in its attainment as a logical consequence of attaining the good; we do not delight in an intelligible good attained and consequently attain the good delighted in [assumption].

(9) Therefore, it is *not* the case that the attainment of the ultimate end comes by way of an act of will [from (5), (6), and (7) by MT].

(10) A human person S attains the ultimate end if and only if S attains the essence of the essential reward [assumption].

(11) Therefore, it is not the case that the attainment of the essence of the essential reward comes by way of an act of will [from (9) and (10)].

(12) Because the attainment of the essence of the essential reward is an intellectual activity, it is either an act of *intellect* or an act of *will* [assumption].

(13) Therefore, the attainment of the essence of the essential reward is an act of the intellect [from (11) and (12), disjunctive syllogism].

Although according to St. Thomas the essence of the essential reward is an act of intellect and not an act of will, he argues that the act of will which is love, delight, or joy in attaining the ultimate end is a concomitant or proper accident of the essence of the essential reward.[30] Therefore, it is a component part of the essential reward.[31] Here we can con-

---

30. For a slightly different way of speaking about St. Thomas on the relationship between the beatific vision and the delight that logically follows upon the vision, see Joseph Stenberg, "Aquinas on the Relationship between the Vision and Delight in Perfect Happiness," *American Catholic Philosophical Quarterly* 90, no. 4 (2016): 665–80. Stenberg makes an interesting case for the view that St. Thomas thinks that both the beatific vision and delight are component parts of the essence of perfect happiness, the vision nonetheless being more important than delight. Stenberg's article cannot be treated with the detail it deserves here. However, it seems the thesis that *the beatific vision is the essence of the essential reward* and *delight is that part of the essential reward that is a proper accident of the beatific vision* does greater justice to texts across St. Thomas's corpus than Stenberg's interpretation (see the texts cited in note 25 above and in note 72 in chapter 4). Nonetheless, Stenberg is correct that St. Thomas thinks that the essential reward or perfect happiness involves both acts of intellect and will.

31. *ST* I-II, q. 3, a. 4, resp. Indeed, sometimes St. Thomas speaks of delight in the beatific vision as a quasi-formal completion of the essence of beatitude, something that supervenes on the essence of beatitude (see, e.g., *In Sent* IV, d. 49, q. 1, a. 1, q.c. 2, ad 2, and *In NE* X, lect. 6, n. 2031), a completion or decoration of beatitude (see, e.g., *In Jn* 17, lect. 1, n. 2186), even a perfection of the essence of beatitude (see, e.g., *In Sent* IV, d. 49, q. 1, a. 2, q.c. 2, ad 3; a. 3, q.c. 4, ad 1; *ST Suppl.*, q. 95,

trast the act of will that is delight in the attainment of the essence of the essential reward in heaven with goods in heaven such as embodiment and the communion of the saints. For delight is a part of the *essential* reward as a proper accident of the beatific vision whereas embodiment and the communion of the saints are component parts of the *accidental* reward in heaven.

Given that the essence of the essential reward is the beatific vision and the beatific vision is an act of intellect, an additional feature of the beatific vision worth emphasizing in St. Thomas's view is that the beatific vision is an act of *speculative* or *theoretical* intellect and not an act of *practical* intellect.[32] As St. Thomas points out, Jesus says to contemplative Mary rather than practical Martha: she "has chosen the better part, which will not be taken away from her" (Lk 10:32).[33]

The distinction between speculative and practical intellect is, of course, Aristotle's. St. Thomas understands the distinction in Aristotelian terms: "the speculative intellect ... directs what it apprehends, not to operation, but to the consideration of truth; while the practical intellect is that which directs what it apprehends to operation."[34] And elsewhere, St. Thomas states: "the object of [the practical intellect] ... is some true, contingent thing, that can be made or done."[35]

St. Thomas offers three arguments in *ST* for the view that perfect happiness is essentially an act of speculative rather than practical intellect.[36] St. Thomas's first argument begins with the supposition that, if perfect happiness is an operation or activity, then *perfect* happiness must consist in the most noble of human activities. But a human person's most noble activity is an activity of a human person's highest power, that is, the intellect, thinking about the noblest being, that is, God. Therefore,

---

a. 5, resp.; *CT* I, chap. 107; *In NE* X, lect. 6, n. 2031). In other places, St. Thomas speaks of beatitude as consisting in two things, vision and delight (see, e.g., *In 1 Cor* 15, lect. 3, n. 937, and *In Jn* 14, lect. 1, n. 1854).

32. See, e.g., *In Sent* IV, d. 49, q. 1, a. 1, q.c. 3; *SCG* IV.83.24; *Catena Aurea* [hereafter *CA*], Lk 10, lect. 10; *ST* I-II, q. 3, a. 5; *In NE* X, lect. 10, nn. 2087–97.

33. See, e.g., *SCG* IV.83.24, trans. Charles J. O'Neil (Notre Dame, Ind.: University of Notre Dame Press, 1975), and *CA*, Lk 10, lect. 10. In these texts St. Thomas reads Lk 10:32 with Pope St. Gregory the Great as teaching that, according to a spiritual sense of the passage, Mary represents the contemplative life while Martha represents the active life, and while the contemplative life goes on in heaven (it "shall not be taken away from her"), the active life comes to a halt at the end of this life.

34. *ST* I, q. 79, a. 11, resp. (trans. English Dominicans, 406).

35. *ST* II-II, q. 4, a. 2, obj. 3 (trans. English Dominicans, 1185).

36. *ST* I-II, q. 3, a. 5, resp.

the attainment of perfect happiness for a human person consists of that human person thinking about God.³⁷ But the object of a practical use of intellect is a particular human action or product. Of course, God himself is neither a human action nor a human product. Therefore, God himself cannot be the object of a practical use of the intellect. It therefore follows that the attainment of perfect happiness does not consist in a practical use of intellect.³⁸ But an act of intellect is either speculative or practical. Therefore, the act of intellect in which the attainment of the essence of perfect happiness consists is an act of speculative intellect.

St. Thomas's second argument takes its start from the supposition that the intellectual activity which constitutes the essence of perfect happiness is not itself a means to an end. But contemplation, that is, the speculative act of thinking about a truth already known, *is* an activity that can be an end in itself and not a means to some further end. In contrast, a practical use of intellect, even if we treat it as an end in itself, is always a means to an additional end, namely, the bringing about of some action or product. Therefore, the activity that is the essence of perfect happiness is an act of speculative and not practical intellect.³⁹

Finally, St. Thomas argues that the attainment of perfect human happiness in heaven is a function of making human persons like unto God and the angels insofar as they themselves are happy.⁴⁰ But God and the angels are happy insofar as they contemplate God. Therefore, human happiness in heaven consists essentially in the contemplation of God. But an act of contemplation is a speculative and not a practical use of intellect. Therefore, the essence of the attainment of perfect human happiness in heaven consists in a speculative and not a practical use of intellect.⁴¹

Why should one think that divine and angelic beatitude is contemplative? First, consider God's perfect happiness. God is the object of his own happiness; otherwise, he would be perfected by something other than himself, which is impossible. In addition, for the same reason that

---

37. Ibid. See also *In NE* X, lect. 10, n. 2087.
38. *ST* I-II, q. 3, a. 5, resp. See also *In Sent* IV, d. 49, q. 1, a. 1, q.c. 3, s.c.; *In NE* X, lect. 10, n. 2087.
39. *ST* I-II, q. 3, a. 5, resp. See also *In Sent* IV, d. 49, q. 1, a. 1, q.c. 3, s.c. and resp.; *In NE* X, lect. 10, n. 2097.
40. See also *ST* I, q. 26, a. 2, resp. Chapters 8 and 17 below develop the notion in St. Thomas's thought that perfect human happiness is a function of making human persons *deiform*, i.e., like unto God.
41. *ST* I-II, q. 3, a. 5, resp.

the essence of perfect human happiness consists in an intellectual activity and not in an act of the will, it is fitting that God is called *perfectly happy* in virtue of his intellectual activity (x is delighted in virtue of attaining the perfect good; it is not the case that x's taking delight in attaining the perfect good causes x to attain the perfect good).[42] Now, practical intellectual activity aims at realizing a good outside the agent. Therefore, God's intellectual activity is speculative (again, if God's perfect happiness consisted in practical intellectual activity, then God would be perfected by something other than himself). Speculative intellectual activity consists either in an act of scientific inquiry or in an act of contemplation. But if a being B engages in scientific inquiry, then B does not know everything. God knows everything. Therefore, God's intellectual activity is rightly spoken of as contemplative activity. However, angels are made perfectly happy by participating in God's beatitude. Therefore, angelic beatitude is essentially contemplative too.

The last argument offers us a chance to emphasize a further detail regarding St. Thomas's account of the beatific vision as the essence of the attainment of perfect human happiness in heaven. St. Thomas thinks that the attainment of perfect happiness in thinking about God does not consist in just any kind of speculative activity, but specifically consists in an act of *contemplation*.

For, as we have seen, we can distinguish two different kinds of *speculative* intellectual activity, that is, intellectual activity whose proximate end is thinking about truth: first, there is *contemplation* of truth, which is thinking about truth already known; second, there is *inquiry*, which is searching for truth not yet known. But the attainment of perfect happiness in heaven is an activity that is merely an end in itself and not also a means to an end. Scientific inquiry is speculative activity not done simply for its own sake; it is also a means to the end of the activity of contemplation of the truth. Therefore, scientific inquiry is not the sort of activity that is done *merely* for its own sake. Therefore, the attainment of the essence of perfect human happiness consists not only in a speculative use of intellect, but more specifically in a contemplative use of speculative intellect rather than an act of scientific inquiry.[43]

---

42. See, e.g., *ST* I, q. 26, a. 2. Of course, given the divine simplicity, God's being, intellect, and will are distinct only in our way of understanding them, and not in God. Nonetheless, God's intellectual activity is *logically* prior to his willing.

43. See, e.g., *In NE* X, lect. 10, n. 2092. For other places where St. Thomas argues that perfect

The essence of the essential reward in heaven is a speculative activity, and more precisely, a *contemplative* one. As we have seen, God is the object of perfect human happiness. Therefore, the essence of the essential reward consists in some sort of contemplative union with God.[44] But what is the nature of such a contemplative union?

In *ST*, St. Thomas argues that the attainment of the essence of perfect human happiness consists in the beatific vision, that is, an act of contemplating the *essence* of God.[45] St. Thomas's argument for this view in *ST* trades on the notion that (as Aristotle points out in the *Metaphysics*) human persons are creatures that wonder. When we encounter a phenomenon that puzzles us, or causes us to wonder, we want to know what causes it. Although we may know *that* the phenomenon in question has a cause, we want to know more than that. We naturally desire to know the *nature* of the cause, that is, its essence, or the answer to the question *quid est*? This is because the perfection of a power is determined by its characteristic object. Just as the characteristic object of sight is color, so that the perfection of the power of sight is seeing and distinguishing colors well, the characteristic object of understanding is the essences of things and so the perfection of the power of understanding is knowing well the essences of things. When a person S knows the essence of an effect, thereby knowing the effect has a cause, S still does not necessarily know the essence of the cause of that effect. In addition, the person who has an unfulfilled desire is not perfectly happy. Therefore, if a person S knows the essence of an effect, knowing it has a cause, she naturally

---

happiness consists of contemplative activity, see, e.g., *In Sent* IV, d. 49, q. 1, a. 1, q.c. 3; *SCG* III.37; *ST* I-II, q. 3, a. 5; *In NE* X, lect. 10, nn. 2088, 2090–91, 2093–96.

44. See, e.g., *SCG* III.37. St. Thomas also argues that the activity in which the essence of the essential reward consists is not (a) the contemplation of truths *gained through speculative science* (see, e.g., *In BDT*, q. 6, a. 4, resp.; *SCG* III.48.2; *CT* I, chap. 104; *ST* I-II, q. 3, a. 6) or (b) *primarily* the contemplation of truths about *angels*—although, as we will see, contemplation of truths about angels belongs to the secondary object of the essential reward and is an aspect of the accidental reward; see, e.g., *In BDT*, q. 6, a. 4, ad 3; *SCG* III.59; *ST* I, q. 64, a. 1, ad 1; *ST* I-II, q. 3, a. 7.

45. *ST* I-II, q. 3, a. 8. See also *In Sent* II, d. 4, q. 1, a. 1; d. 23, q. 2, a. 1; d. 49, q. 2, a. 1 (*ST Suppl.*, q. 92, a. 1); the sermon *Beata gens* 2.3.1; *QDV*, q. 8, a. 1; *QQ* X, q. 8, a. 1; *SCG* III.51, 54, 57; *CT* I, chap. 104; *ST* I, q. 12, a. 1; a. 4, ad 3; *In Mt* 5, lect. 2, nn. 408, 412, 428, 433–34; *ST* I-II, q. 5, a. 1; *In 1 Tm* 6, lect. 3; *In Jn* 1, lect. 11; 6, lect. 4, n. 927; 17, lect. 1, n. 2186; *CT* II, chaps. 8 and 9. See also *SCG* III.38–48, where St. Thomas argues in stages that the essence of perfect human happiness cannot consist in (a) the general knowledge human persons have of God in this life (chap. 38), (b) knowledge of God by way of a scientific demonstration (chap. 39), (c) knowledge of God by way of faith (chap. 40), (d) knowledge of God by way of knowing the separate substances (chaps. 41–46), (e) knowledge of the essence of God in this life—as we cannot know God's essence in this life (chap. 47), or (f) anything in this life (chap. 48). Therefore, St. Thomas concludes that the only possible alternative is that the essence of the essential reward consists in knowing the essence of God in the next life, i.e., the beatific vision (*SCG* III.51).

desires to know the essence of the cause of the said effect. Therefore, if she does not know the essence of the cause of the said effect, she is not perfectly happy. Because what human persons know in this life are the created effects of God, knowing that God is their first cause, human persons therefore naturally want to know the essence of God. Therefore, human persons will not be *perfectly* happy unless they know the essence of God (although they may be *imperfectly* happy, i.e., happy insofar as one can be happy apart from grace, knowing less than the essence of God). As we have already seen, the attainment of the essence of perfect human happiness consists in an act of contemplation. Therefore, attainment of the essence of perfect human happiness requires contemplating the essence of God, that is, the beatific vision.[46]

But why is having the beatific vision a *sufficient* condition for perfect human happiness so that we can say that the essence of the essential reward in heaven precisely consists in contemplating the essence of God in heaven? Recall that St. Thomas argues that God alone is the object of human happiness. Human persons, because they are rational beings, desire the perfect good, which will completely satisfy the appetite. The object of the human will is the perfect good, just as the object of the intellect is the perfectly true. But God alone is the uncreated good, and so the unparticipated good and true, by which all other things are good and true by participation. At most, then, any created good approximates, but is not identical to, the perfect good that God is. Therefore, God alone can satisfy the human desire for the perfect good.[47] But human persons are most perfectly united to the object of their desire, God, by way of the vision of the divine essence. Therefore, having that vision is not only a necessary, but a sufficient condition, for attaining the essence of perfect human happiness.

In addition, as we will see below, in contemplating the essence of God in heaven intellectual creatures also know the essences of all creatures. Therefore, insofar as human persons want to know the essences of creatures, that is, they desire some creaturely good, human persons have that desire satisfied in virtue of having the beatific vision.

---

46. *ST* I, q. 3, a. 8, resp. See also *ST* I, q. 12, a. 1, resp.; *CT* I, chap. 104; *In Mt* 5, lect. 2, n. 434; *In Jn* 1, lect. 11, n. 212; *In Heb*, chap. 11, lect. 1, n. 553.

47. *ST* I-II, q. 3, a. 8, resp.: "And thus it will have its perfection through union with God as with that object, in which alone man's happiness consists, as stated above [see, e.g., *ST* I-II, q. 1, a. 7; q. 2, a. 8]" (trans. English Dominicans, 602).

St. Thomas also thinks that scripture clearly teaches that the essence of the essential reward in heaven consists in contemplating the essence of God. For example, there are passages such as "Blessed are the pure of heart, for they will see God" (Mt 5:8),[48] "Take care that you do not despise one of these little ones; for, I tell you, in heaven their angels continually see the face of my Father in heaven" (Mt 18:10),[49] "And this is eternal life, that they may know you, the only true God, and Jesus Christ whom you have sent" (Jn 17:3),[50] "For now we see in a mirror dimly, but then we will see face to face" (1 Cor 13:12),[51] and "When He is revealed, we will be like Him; for we will see Him as He is" (1 Jn 3:2).[52] But "to see God as He is" or "to see God face to face" or "to know [God]" all mean "to contemplate the essence of God." Assuming that these passages show us that in which the essence of the essential reward consists, it follows that the essence of the essential reward consists in contemplating the essence of God.[53]

But St. Thomas notes that there are passages in scripture that suggest that human persons cannot see the essence of God. For example, "No one has ever seen God" (Jn 1:18), "No one has ever seen God" (1 Jn 4:12), "he ... dwells in unapproachable light, whom no one has ever seen, or can see" (1 Tm 6:16), and "For no one shall see me and live" (Ex 33:20). I will close this chapter by showing how St. Thomas resolves this apparent contradiction in scripture.

St. Thomas points out that the locution *seeing God* has a number of different possible meanings (in scripture), and it is only according to some, and not all, of these meanings that human persons cannot see the essence of God. First, by *a human person S sees God*, someone might mean, "S *comprehends* God in the sense of knowing everything that God knows."

---

48. See, e.g., *SCG* III.25; *CA*, Mk 13, lect. 5; *In Mt* 5, lect. 2, n. 434; *In Mt* 18, lect. 1, nn. 1505–6; *In Mt* 24, lect. 1, n. 1965; *In Mt* 28, lect. 1, n. 2452; *ST* I-II, q. 4, a. 4, s.c.; *In Jn* 1, lect. 11, n. 212; 5, lect. 5, n. 789; 14, lect. 1, n. 1854.

49. See, e.g., *In Sent* IV, d. 45, q. 3, a. 1, obj. 4 and ad 4; *SCG* III.48; *In Mt* 11, lect. 1, n. 914; 18, lect. 1, nn. 1505–6; *In Jn* 1, lect. 11, n. 210; 7, lect. 3, n. 1062; *In Heb* 1, lect. 6, n. 86.

50. See, e.g., *In Jn* 1, lect. 11, n. 212.

51. See, e.g., *ST Suppl.*, q. 92, a. 1, s.c.; *SCG* III.51.5; *In Mt* 5, lect. 2, n. 434; 18, lect. 1, n. 1505; *In Jn* 7, lect. 3, n. 1062.

52. See, e.g., *ST Suppl.*, q. 92, a. 1, s.c.; *QDV*, q. 8, a. 1, s.c.; *SCG* III.51.6; *ST* I, q. 12, a. 1, s.c.; *In Mt* 5, lect. 2, n. 434; *ST* I-II, q. 3, a. 8, s.c.; *In Jn* 1, lect. 11, n. 212; 7, lect. 3, n. 1062; 17, lect. 1, n. 2186.

53. For additional authorities cited by St. Thomas and additional arguments from authority that the essence of the essential reward consists in the beatific vision, see, e.g., *ST Suppl.*, q. 89, a. 3, obj. 3 and ad 3; q. 91, a. 4, resp.; q. 92, a. 1, s.c.; *QQ* X, q. 8, a. 1; *QDV*, q. 8, a. 1, s.c and resp.; *SCG* III.51.6 and 57.5; *ST* I, q. 12, a. 1, resp.; q. 98, a. 2, ad 1; q. 108, a. 8, resp.; *CA*, Lk 20, lect. 4; *In Mt* 5, lect. 2, n. 412; *ST* I-II, q. 3, a. 5, resp.; II-II, q. 24, a. 3, obj. 3; *In Jn* 1, lect. 11, nn. 210–13; *ST* III, q. 76, a. 7, obj. 3.

St. Thomas argues God cannot be understood *comprehensively*, that is, human persons—no creatures—can know God the way God knows himself, even in heaven.[54] Therefore, a human person cannot see God in the sense of *comprehending* God, that is, knowing everything about God. *That no creature can comprehend God* is one possible interpretation of passages such as John 1:18 and 1 Timothy 6:16.[55] But, as we will see, St. Thomas does not take a human person's having the beatific vision to entail that one comes to know everything that God knows. Therefore, the scriptural teaching that the saint's attainment of beatitude consists in seeing the essence of God (in passages such as Mt 5:8, Mt 18:10, Jn 17:3, 1 Cor 13:12, and 1 Jn 3:2) does not contradict the scriptural teaching that human persons cannot see God in the sense of comprehending God.

Second, by *a human person S sees God* one might mean, "S sees God *qua* God[56] directly *by way of the corporeal eye*."[57] But God *qua* God cannot be seen directly with the corporal eye, as God *qua* God is an immaterial being (see Jn 4:24, "God is spirit"), and an immaterial being cannot be seen directly by way of a corporeal eye.[58] That God *qua* God cannot be seen directly with the corporeal eye is another interpretation that can be given to John 1:18 and 1 Timothy 6:16.[59] Now, according to St. Thomas, a saint S having the beatific vision in heaven does not entail that S sees God *qua* God directly with the corporal eye. The apparent contradiction in scripture is therefore resolved.

---

54. See, e.g., *In Sent* IV, d. 49, q. 2, a. 1, ad 1 (*ST Suppl.*, q. 92, a. 1, ad 1); *In 1 Cor* 13, lect. 4, n. 802; *In 1 Tm* 6, lect. 3, n. 270; *In Mt* 5, lect. 2, n. 434; 11, lect. 3, nn. 965–66; 18, lect. 1, n. 1505; *In Jn* 1, lect. 11, nn. 213–14. See chapter 6 below for more discussion of this point.

55. See, e.g., *In 1 Tm* 6, lect. 3, n. 270; *In Mt* 5, lect. 2, n. 434; *In Jn* 1, lect. 11, n. 214.

56. The use of the expression "God *qua* God" is necessary because of the Catholic Christian understanding of Christ. According to that teaching, Christ is one divine person with two natures, which natures, although unmixed, are nonetheless hypostatically united in the one divine person, Jesus Christ. In order to guard the dogma of the hypostatic union, the church has taught that it is appropriate to say things such as "God died on the cross." But that statement can be given both orthodox and unorthodox readings. For example, "Jesus, who is God, suffered death in his human nature" would be an orthodox reading of the statement "God died on the cross." But "God *qua* God died on the cross" would be an unorthodox way to read the statement "God died on the cross." Similarly, "God does not have a body" should be understood as "God *qua* God does not have a body." But God does have a body in the sense that Jesus Christ, who is God, has a body *qua* his human nature. For detailed discussion and defense of Catholic Christology, see Timothy Pawl's *In Defense of Conciliar Christology: A Philosophical Essay* (Oxford: Oxford University Press, 2016) and *In Defense of Extended Conciliar Christology: A Philosophical Essay* (Oxford: Oxford University Press, 2019).

57. See, e.g., *In Sent* IV, d. 49, q. 2, a. 1, ad 1 (*ST Suppl.*, q. 92, a. 1, ad 1); *SCG* III.51.5; *In 1 Tm* 6, lect. 3, n. 270; *In Mt* 5, lect. 2, n. 434; *In Jn* 1, lect. 11, nn. 213–14.

58. See, e.g., *In Sent* IV, d. 49, q. 2, a. 2 (*ST Suppl.*, q. 92, a. 2), and *In Jn* 1, lect. 11, nn. 213–14.

59. See, e.g., *In 1 Tm* 6, lect. 3, n. 270; *In Mt* 5, lect. 2, n. 434; *In Jn* 1, lect. 11, n. 214.

Third, by *a human person S sees God* one might mean, "S sees the essence of God by one's natural intellectual powers, without the aid of grace." But no human person can cognize the essence of God apart from grace.[60] St. Thomas thinks that this is clear from scripture: "No one knows the Father except the Son and anyone to whom the Son chooses to reveal Him" (Mt 11:27) and "Flesh and blood has not revealed this to you" (Mt 16:17).[61] Here we have, according to St. Thomas, another possible interpretation of the passages that say we cannot see God.[62] But, as we shall see, the beatific vision of the saints in heaven is a *supremely graced* intellectual union with God. Therefore, scripture does not entail a contradiction regarding the human ability to see God.

Fourth, by *a human person S sees God* one might mean, "S sees the essence of God in this life such that (a) S is embodied with what St. Thomas calls a human *animal* body, rather than a human *spiritual* or *glorified* body, and (b) S knows the essences of things by the intellect abstracting the essences of things from phantasms produced by the senses."[63] Although *Christ* saw the essence of God in this life, while embodied with a human animal body, knowing the essences of things by the intellect abstracting the essences of things from phantasms produced by the senses,[64] no *human person* S can see the essence of God in that way.[65]

Why can no *human person* S see the essence of God in this life while S is embodied with a human animal body, knowing the essences of things by S's intellect abstracting the essences of things from phantasms produced by the senses? Consider that if a human person S knows the essence of

---

60. See, e.g., *In Sent* II, d. 4, a. 1; d. 23, q. 2, a. 1; IV, d. 49, q. 2, a. 6; *QDV*, q. 8, a. 3; *SCG* I.3.3; III.49 and 52; *In 1 Tm*, chap. 6, lect. 3, n. 270; *ST* I, q. 12, a. 4; q. 64, a. 4, ad 2; *QDA*, a. 17, ad 10; *ST* I-II, q. 5, a. 5.
61. See, e.g., *In 1 Tm* 6, lect. 3, n. 270.
62. Ibid.
63. "Animal body" here refers to a nonglorified *human* body, i.e., a *human* body that is mortal, corruptible, and apt to require nourishment, grow, and aid in reproductive activity. According to St. Thomas, the glorified body is still an animal body metaphysically, i.e., it is a human body that moves and senses. See chapter 11 below for details.
64. See, e.g., *QDV*, q. 10, a. 11, ad 3, and *In 1 Tm* 6, lect. 3, n. 270. St. Thomas thinks Christ, a *divine* person, has knowledge of the essence of God, i.e., the beatific vision, *qua* his human nature, in this life, from the moment of conception (see, e.g., *In Sent* III, d. 14, a. 3, q.c. 6, resp.; *QDV*, q. 20, a. 2, resp.; *CT* I, chap. 216; *ST* III, q. 34, a. 4).
65. See, e.g., *In Sent* III, d. 27, q. 3, a. 1; d. 35, q. 2, a. 2, q.c. 2; IV, d. 49, q. 2, a. 7; *QDV*, q. 13, aa. 2–4; *In 2 Cor* 12, lect. 1; *In 1 Tm* 6, lect. 3, n. 270; *SCG* III.47; *ST* I, q. 12, a. 11; *In Mt* 5, lect. 2, n. 434; *ST* II-II, q. 175, aa. 3–6; *In Jn* 1, lect. 11, nn. 213–14. It is worth noting that, because, according to St. Thomas, Christ had the beatific vision from the moment of conception, he would have had a glorified body in this life if he did not will to possess a passible body for the sake of suffering for our redemption (see, e.g., *ST* III, q. 14, a. 1, ad 2).

God in this life, then S knows the essence of God naturally or supernaturally. But, as we saw earlier in this chapter, for human persons, all *natural* cognition begins in sensation so that knowledge of immaterial things comes *indirectly* through inference from some knowledge of material things. But to know the essence of God is to know God in a particularly *direct* and *unmediated* way, and so one cannot know the essence of God by way of making inferences from some knowledge possessed of material things.[66] Therefore, one cannot have natural knowledge of the essence of God in this life. In addition, awareness of material things in this life through the senses hinders contemplation, and so human persons cannot reach the summit of contemplation in this embodied life.[67] But seeing the essence of God constitutes the summit of contemplative activity.[68] Furthermore, St. Thomas argues that a person S being *miraculously* elevated to seeing the essence of God in the wayfaring state would require that S be withdrawn from the senses.[69] Therefore, it is not possible to see the essence of God in this life *supernaturally* while also knowing material things through the senses with a human animal body.[70] It follows, then, that no *human person* S can see the essence of God in this life with a human animal body while S is embodied and knowing the essences of things by S's intellect abstracting the essences of things from phantasms produced by the senses. According to St. Thomas, this fourth way of understanding the meaning of "one cannot see God" is another

---

66. See, e.g., *SCG* III.47.9; *ST* I, q. 12, a. 11, resp.; *In Jn* 1, lect. 11, n. 211.

67. See, e.g., *ST* I-II, q. 4, a. 6, resp.: "we must say that perfect disposition of the body is necessary ... antecedently ... for that Happiness which is in all ways perfect.... As Augustine says (*Gen. ad lit. xii*, 35), *if the body be such, that the governance thereof is difficult and burdensome, like unto flesh which is corruptible and weighs upon the soul, the mind is turned away from that vision of the highest heaven*. Whence he concludes that, *when this body will no longer be 'natural,' but 'spiritual,' then will it be equaled to the angels, and that will be its glory, which erstwhile was its burden*" (trans. English Dominicans, 607).

68. See, e.g., *SCG* III.47.2 and *In Jn* 1, lect. 11, n. 213.

69. See, e.g., *In Sent* IV, d. 49, q. 2, a. 7, ad 4. St. Thomas argues: when S is *miraculously* elevated such that one engages in an act A, one cannot simultaneously be engaged in a natural action contrary to A. For example, when St. Peter was miraculously walking on water, thereby participating in the agility of the spiritual body of the saints, his body was not at that time naturally subject to gravity. Therefore, when Moses or St. Paul were miraculously having a temporary share in the beatific vision of the saints, they were not also engaged in natural cognitive acts such as sensing.

70. But, in that case, how do the saints in heaven enjoy the beatific vision after the general resurrection? The short answer: the bodies of the saints in heaven are glorified and spiritual, i.e., they are (a) perfected by the soul having the beatific vision, (b) which soul has a different mode of being, (c) so that those bodies do not distract the saints from the beatific vision but rather support the saints in having the beatific vision. Chapter 11 below says more about glorified bodies and the beatific vision. It is also worth noting here St. Thomas's judgment that Adam and Eve did not have the beatific vision in the state of innocence (see, e.g., *In Sent* II, d. 23, q. 2, a. 1; *QDV*, q. 18, a. 1; *ST* I, q. 94, a. 1).

possible interpretation of passages such as "For no one shall see me and live" (Ex 33:20) and John 1:18.[71] But, as we will see, the beatific vision in heaven is an *otherworldly* union with God (and not a this-worldly union as in the fourth interpretation) *enjoyed by the separated soul alone*, or by a human person whose soul beatifies the body so that the human body *is no longer animal but spiritual* (again, in contrast to the fourth interpretation of "one cannot see God"). Hence, scripture does not contradict itself on the subject of the human ability to see God.

Fifth, by *a human person S sees God* one might mean, "S is *caught up in rapture in this life*, thereby knowing the essence of God, not habitually, but only temporarily insofar as S is separated for a time from the influence of the senses."[72] This is the way St. Thomas understands the experience that St. Paul relates in 2 Corinthians 12:3.[73]

As we will see in more detail in what follows, St. Thomas thinks that in order to see the essence of God we need a special grace from God called the *lumen gloriae* (light of glory), which grace disposes and raises up the created intellect so that God can join the created intellect to himself in the beatific vision.[74] Now, there are two ways that one can receive the grace of the light of glory. First, one can receive the *lumen gloriae* as an immanent form (*modum formae immanentis*) such that the glorified soul permanently cognizes the essence of God and the glorified soul beatifies the body. Such a beatified human body is *spiritual* rather than *animal* so that the human person can simultaneously enjoy the vision of the essence of God and know things by way of the bodily senses. Second, one can receive the *lumen gloriae* as a certain transient passion (*modum cuiusdam passionis transeuntis*) such that one *temporally* cognizes the essence of God in such a way that, while having the vision, one is separated from this life insofar as one loses the ability to know things by way of the senses.[75] It is in this second sense that St. Thomas thinks that Moses and St. Paul saw the essence of God, and he does not think that the scriptural passages that speak of human persons not being able to see God have in

---

71. See, e.g., *In 1 Tm* 6, lect. 3, n. 270; *In Mt* 5, lect. 2, n. 434; *In Jn* 1, lect. 11, n. 214.
72. See, e.g., *In 2 Cor* 12, lect. 1, nn. 448–54; *ST* I, q. 12, a. 11, ad 2; II-II, q. 180, a. 5; *QQ* I, q. 1.
73. See, e.g., *In Sent* IV, d. 49, q. 2, a. 7, ad 5; *In 2 Cor* 12, lect. 1; *ST* II-II, q. 175, aa. 3–6 (see esp. a. 4); *In Jn* 1, lect. 11, n. 213.
74. Chapter 8 below has more to say about the *lumen gloriae*.
75. See, e.g., *ST* II-II, q. 175, a. 3, ad 2. Earlier in his career, St. Thomas apparently thinks the miracle of temporarily seeing the essence of God in this life does not involve the *lumen gloriae* (see, e.g., *QDV*, q. 10, a. 11, resp.), a view he rejects by the time he writes *ST* II-II.

mind these rare cases where, by a miracle, a human person is given a temporary glimpse of the essence of God, causing them to take leave of their senses.[76]

Sixth, by *a human person S sees God* one might mean "S has a permanent, direct, and unmediated intellectual union with God in heaven." According to St. Thomas, various scriptural passages (such as Mt 5:8, Mt 18:10, Jn 17:3, 1 Cor 13:12, and 1 Jn 3:2) speak of seeing God in this sense.[77] On the other hand, passages such as John 1:18[78] and 1 Timothy 6:16[79] do not speak of seeing God in the sense of the beatific vision in heaven. Again, we can see that there is no contradiction in scripture regarding the human ability to see (or not see) God, as long as the different meanings of "seeing God" are distinguished.[80]

In this chapter, we have examined some of the essential features of the beatific vision according to St. Thomas. In his view, the beatific vision is the essence of the essential reward of intellectual creatures in heaven. More specifically, the beatific vision is a created, nonbodily, graced, otherworldly, permanent, intellectual act of contemplating the essence of God in heaven. The next chapter explores St. Thomas's views on just what and how intellectual creatures know (about) God in the beatific vision.

---

76. See, e.g., *In Sent* IV, d. 49, q. 2, a. 7, ad 4 and ad 5; *QDV*, q. 10, a. 11, resp.; *ST* I, q. 12, a. 11, ad 2; II-II, q. 180, a. 5; *QQ* I, q. 1.

77. See, e.g., notes 48–52 above.

78. See, e.g., *In Jn* 1, lect. 11, nn. 210–12.

79. See, e.g., *In 1 Tm* 6, lect. 3, nn. 260–70.

80. For discussion of St. Thomas, the beatific vision, and scripture on seeing God, with special attention to St. Thomas's treatment of the Greek Fathers, see Hutter, *Bound for Beatitude*, 392–97.

6

The Essential Reward II

THE PRIMARY AND SECONDARY OBJECTS
OF THE BEATIFIC VISION

According to St. Thomas, the essence of the essential reward for human persons in heaven consists in the beatific vision. However, St. Thomas thinks that the saints who see God's essence do not only see God himself as he is, they also see creatures in God insofar as God is their primary cause. Therefore, we can distinguish, where the beatific vision is concerned, what theologians have referred to as the *primary object* of the beatific vision, namely, God himself as he is, and the *secondary object* of the beatific vision, creatures insofar as they are cognized in virtue of seeing the essence of God.[1] This chapter explores both the primary and secondary objects of the beatific vision in order to explain in greater detail how the beatific vision is perfective of human persons.

THE PRIMARY OBJECT OF THE BEATIFIC VISION:
GOD HIMSELF AS HE IS

We can begin with a question: What precisely does it mean to know the essence of God as the primary object of the beatific vision? At least three things. Knowing the essence of God as the primary object of the beatific vision means *knowing God by simple apprehension, knowing God in a way that surpasses in its perfection all the ways in which human persons can know God in this life,* and *knowing God such that God makes it be the case that God himself is that by which the one who is blessed sees the essence of God.*

---

1. See, e.g., Devine, *A Manual of Ascetical Theology*, 506; Garrigou-Lagrange, *Life Everlasting*, 125–27; and Hontheim, "Heaven," in *The Catholic Encyclopedia*.

The Beatific Vision as Knowing God by Simple Apprehension

To know the essence of God as primary object of the beatific vision is *to know God by simple apprehension*. To know the essence of a thing is to know *what* that thing is. So, to know the essence of God is to know *what* God is. Now, in speaking about the cognition of a thing's essence—what it is—we could be speaking of one of two things. For we sometimes cognize a thing's essence by way of what we might call *a simple act of understanding* or *an act of simple apprehension*, for example, John sees something approaching and, by way of John's intellect and its power to abstract the essence of things from their material conditions, John knows that what is approaching is *a human person*. But in some cases our understanding of a thing's essence in this life is more precise: in such a case we can cognize a thing *x*'s essence *by way of offering a definition of that x's essence by composing and dividing terms*, that is, by placing *x* in a genus and distinguishing the species to which *x* belongs from other species by finding the relevant difference, for example, John comes to know about the something that is approaching, not only that it is a human person, but that what is approaching is, say, *a rational animal*. How does this distinction apply to knowing God's essence?

God cannot be defined by composing and dividing terms. God cannot be defined in this way because God is an absolutely simple being.[2] Rather, as St. Thomas notes, the beatific vision involves God's gracing us with the ability to see God's essence by an act of simple apprehension.[3]

The Beatific Vision as Knowing God in a Way That Surpasses Earthly Knowledge of God

To know the essence of God as the primary object of the beatific vision is also *to know God in a way that surpasses in its perfection all the ways in which human persons can know God in this life*. To see this point, let us examine a representative sample of different ways human persons can know God in this life. These include: (a) knowledge by way of *philosophical argument*; (b) knowledge by *faith*; (c) knowledge by *a gift of the Holy Spirit* such as *un-*

---

2. See, e.g., *DEE*, chap. 6; *In Sent* I, d. 8, q. 4, a. 2; d. 19, q. 4, a. 2; *SCG* I.25; *CT* I, chap. 12; *ST* I, q. 3, a. 5; II-II, q. 1, a. 2, ad 3.

3. See, e.g., *ST* II-II, q. 1, a. 2, ad 3.

derstanding; (d) knowledge by *preternatural gift prior to the Fall*;[4] (e) knowledge by the gratuitous grace of *prophetic inspiration*; and (f) knowledge by the gratuitous grace of temporally being given a glimpse of the essence of God in this life, that is, by *rapture*. According to St. Thomas, the beatific vision of the saints in heaven differs from all of these this-worldly forms of knowledge of God insofar as it is permanent and is the most direct and unmediated cognition of God that it is possible for a creature to have.

Consider the ways in which *philosophical* knowledge of God by way of a demonstrative argument is limited in comparison to knowledge of God by way of the beatific vision. First, although St. Thomas thinks that human persons can know significant truths about God by way of philosophical argument,[5] philosophical knowledge of God is nonetheless limited in what it can show to be true about God. This is because such knowledge takes its start from what we know by way of the bodily senses. For example, the great truths of the Catholic faith, such as the Trinity and the incarnation, cannot be demonstrated by philosophical argumentation.[6] By contrast, the beatific vision affords the person who possesses it the greatest possible knowledge of God that a creature can have, a knowledge which includes the truths of the faith.

Second, consider those truths that it is possible for human persons to know about God by philosophical argument. Very few human persons actually know God in this way—only a few theologians and some philosophers—and those who do, do so only late in life. In addition, even those theologians and philosophers who come to know truths about God by way of philosophy late in life, do so only in a fallible way, that is, with the real possibility of an admixture of error.[7] But the beatific vision is an infallible form of knowledge of God, available to all who die in a state of grace, even to the baptized who die before they reach the age of reason.[8]

Third, knowledge of God by way of philosophical argument is *indirect* and *mediated* knowledge of God in ways that the beatific vision is not. To see how, note that in one place St. Thomas distinguishes three ways in which knowledge of things can be mediated.[9] First, there is a medium

---

4. See chapter 2, note 109 above for a definition of *preternatural gift*.
5. See, e.g., *In BDT*, q. 1. a. 2; *SCG* I.3 and IV.1; *ST* I, q. 12, a. 12, resp.; q. 32, a. 1; *In Rom* 1, lect. 6, nn. 114–22.
6. See, e.g., *SCG* I.3; *ST* I, q. 1, a. 8; q. 32, a. 1.
7. See, e.g., *SCG* I.4 and *ST* I, q. 1, a. 1, resp.
8. See, e.g., *ST* III, q. 69, a. 6, resp.
9. *QDV*, q. 18, a. 1, ad 1. For a similar set of distinctions, spoken about somewhat differently,

under which (*sub quo*) something is cognized. For example, in seeing with the corporeal eye, the medium *under which* is light; in natural intellectual knowledge St. Thomas sometimes speaks of the medium *under which* as the natural light of human reason.[10] Second, there is a medium *by which* (*quo*) something is cognized. For example, St. Thomas thinks that we see a material object *by which* what he calls "the sensible species" of the object seen. In intellectual knowledge, the medium *by which* something is cognized is the intelligible species of the object cognized. Third, there is the medium *from which* (*a quo*) one obtains knowledge. For example, if John sees Jane in a mirror, then the mirror is a medium *from which* John cognizes Jane.

According to St. Thomas, when human persons know God by way of philosophical argument, they know God by way of a medium *from which*.[11] Why? All natural human knowledge begins in sensation of material creatures.[12] Because God is immaterial, insofar as we come to know about God philosophically, we do so by inference from our direct knowledge of material creatures. In other words, we know God in this life by way of "the intellectual mirror" of creatures.[13]

It may be helpful to note that there are three different ways that we know God through creatures as a medium *from which*, according to St. Thomas.[14] One way is insofar as we know God to be the uncaused cause of the existence and perfection of creatures. Arguments for the existence of God are an example of this sort of knowledge. A second way is insofar as we deny of God any imperfections that attach to creatures insofar as he is the uncaused cause. For example, we can know that God is not a

---

see, e.g., *In 1 Cor* 13, lect. 4, n. 800. By such talk of mediation, the reader should not draw the conclusion that St. Thomas thinks that what we primarily know are our ideas. Rather, St. Thomas thinks we primarily know external reality through the intentional forms of things (see, e.g., *ST* I, q. 85, a. 2).

10. See, e.g., *SCG* I.3.

11. See, e.g., *QDV*, q. 18, a. 1, ad 1, and *In 1 Cor* 13, lect. 4, nn. 800–801. See also *In Sent* III, d. 27, q. 3, a. 1, resp.; *In BDT*, q. 1. a. 2; *SCG* I.3; *ST* I, q. 12, a. 12; q. 86, a. 2, ad 1. Eleonore Stump thinks that second-person experiences—experiences where persons encounter persons *qua* persons—have as a necessary condition that such experiences be *direct* and *unmediated*. However, as she explains, this does not rule out second-person experiences being mediated by pieces of technology, e.g., computers, eyeglasses, etc. (*Wandering in Darkness*, 75–76). Given that second-person experiences can be mediated by pieces of technology, our knowing God by way of a medium *from which* is *a fortiori* compatible with such knowledge counting as second-personal in Stump's sense (see also *Wandering in Darkness*, 538n39).

12. See, e.g., *SCG* I.3.3 and IV.1.1; *ST* I, q. 12, a. 12, resp.

13. See, e.g., *SCG* III.47 and *In 1 Cor* 13, lect. 4, nn. 800–801.

14. See, e.g., *In BDT*, q. 1, a. 2; *SCG* IV.1; *ST* I, q. 12, a. 12, resp.; *In Rom* 1, lect. 6, nn. 114–22.

bodily thing, a temporal being, etc. A third way we know God by way of creatures as a medium *from which* is insofar as we predicate words analogously of God and creatures. In doing so, although we reasonably attribute to God perfections enjoyed by creatures, such perfections exist in God in a manner that is more excellent than the manner in which they exist in creatures. Furthermore, we must admit that such perfections exist in God in a way that we cannot understand in this life.[15]

By contrast with philosophical knowledge of God, the blessed in heaven know God in the beatific vision without a medium *from which* (*a quo*). This is part of what it means to say that the beatific vision is a knowledge of the *essence* of God.[16] St. Thomas thinks that, in contrast to philosophical knowledge of God, the beatific vision also does not involve knowing God by way of a medium *by which* (*quo*). Rather, God causes it to be the case that the blessed are united to himself such that God functions, as it were, as the intelligible species of the beatific vision. Because all philosophical knowledge requires a medium *by which*, both by way of some sensible species and an intelligible species of the sensible objects cognized, the beatific vision is a less mediated, and so a more perfect, form of knowledge of God than any philosophical knowledge of God.

According to St. Thomas, the knowledge human persons have of God in this life *by divine faith* is more perfect than knowledge by way of philosophical argument in some ways,[17] but less perfect in others.[18] Knowledge by faith too is an imperfect form of knowledge of God when com-

---

15. See, e.g., *ST* I, q. 13, a. 2, resp. and ad 3; a. 3, resp.
16. See, e.g., *In Sent* II, d. 23, q. 2, a. 1; *In BDT*, q. 1, a. 2; *SCG* IV.1.8; *QDV*, q. 18, a. 1, ad 1; *ST* I, q. 86, a. 2, ad 1; q. 94, a. 1.
17. It is more perfect in at least three ways: first, faith requires a graced illumination of the intellect that is more powerful than the natural light of reason (see, e.g., *QDV*, q. 14, a. 9, ad 2, and *ST* I, q. 12, a. 3, resp.). The light of faith and the natural light of reason are examples of what St. Thomas calls a medium *under which* (*sub quo*) (*QDV*, q. 18, a. 1, ad 1). Second, human persons can know more true propositions about God by divine faith than by way of philosophical demonstration (see, e.g., *SCG* I.3; *ST* I, q. 1, a. 8; q. 32, a. 1), and, third, that which is known by faith is more certain *qua* cause than what we know about God by the natural light in a philosophical demonstration insofar as the cause of what we believe by faith is the infallible testimony of God and the cause of what we believe by philosophical argument is fallible human reason (see, e.g., *ST* II-II, q. 4, a. 8, resp.).
18. Believing by faith is less perfect than what we believe on the basis of the natural light of reason by demonstrative philosophical argument insofar as what we believe by faith is less certain *qua* our *understanding* of what we believe than what we know on the basis of the natural light of reason by demonstrative philosophical argument. For the more that S's intellect grasps or understands a thing it cognizes the more certain it is. But what we believe by faith we believe on the basis of what God understands and what we believe on the basis of the natural light of reason by demonstrative philosophical argument we believe because of what we understand (see, e.g., *ST* II-II, q. 4, a. 8, resp.).

pared to knowledge of God in the beatific vision. In speaking of the ways in which knowledge by faith is imperfect in comparison to the perfect knowledge of God in the beatific vision, we can note three ways in which knowledge by faith is indirect or mediated in ways that the beatific vision is not.

First, as with knowledge by way of philosophical demonstration, knowledge by faith involves creatures as a medium *from which* (*a quo*), as the propositions that human persons believe by faith are inevitably interpreted in light of what they know by way of their natural knowledge of material creatures.[19] But, as we saw above, the beatific vision does not involve this sort of mediation.

Second, there is the sort of mediation St. Thomas calls mediation *by which* (*quo*). Just as we know a material thing by the natural light of reason by way of a form in the intellect (recall St. Thomas calls the form of a material object *qua* intentional object, "the intelligible species"), so we know God by way of faith through *propositions* presented to us for belief.[20] But in the beatific vision, the blessed do not see God by way of a created species or by way of a proposition.[21] As I will speak about in greater detail below, St. Thomas thinks that God brings it about that God himself takes the place of a medium *by which* in the beatific vision of the blessed.

Third, St. Thomas thinks that knowledge of God by divine faith is indirect or mediated in another sense. When it comes to knowing that *p* scientifically by the natural light of reason, we are compelled to believe that *p*, given the strength of evidence available to our intellect that *p*.[22] It is otherwise with what we believe by faith. Certainly, the intellect of a human person S who makes an act of faith is illumined by the grace of the light of faith so that S knows which propositions S should believe.[23] In addition, what a Catholic believes by faith may have great evidential support.[24] Nonetheless, if S believes that *p* by divine faith, then S does not assent to *p* because S fully understands *p* or because S knows why *p* is true or because S is compelled by the evidence available to S to believe

---

19. See, e.g., *QDV*, q. 10, a. 11, ad 9, and *SCG* IV.1.4.
20. See, e.g., *ST* II-II, q. 1, a. 2.
21. See, e.g., *QDV*, q. 10, a. 11, resp., and *ST* II-II, q. 1, a. 2, ad 3. For additional texts, see below in this chapter.
22. See, e.g., *QDV*, q. 14, a. 2; a. 9; *ST* II-II, q. 1, a. 4, resp.; q. 4, a. 1.
23. See, e.g., *QDV*, q. 14, a. 9, ad 1; *ST* II-II, q. 1, a. 4, ad 3; q. 2, a. 3, ad 2.
24. See, e.g., *SCG* I.6; *ST* II-II, q. 1, a. 5, ad 2; q. 2, a. 10; *CSA*, prol.

that *p*. Rather, if S believes the propositions presented to S for belief by divine faith, S does so on the basis of trusting in the testimony of God,[25] whether immediately in the case of Adam (before the Fall), the prophets, and the apostles, or mediately, in the case of the rest of us, insofar as we believe what the church teaches.[26] As the term "beatific vision" suggests, whereas those who believe by faith know what they know on the basis of believing what someone else knows, the blessed enjoying the beatific vision see with their own intellects that what they believe is true.[27] Therefore, in contrast to the number of ways that those who believe things about God by divine faith have a knowledge of God that is mediated, the blessed knowing God by the beatific vision possess as direct a knowledge of God as is possible for creatures.[28]

In addition to knowledge of God by way of the grace of the infused virtue of faith, there is also another kind of knowledge by habitual grace in this life, St. Thomas thinks—namely, knowledge by way of *the gifts of the Holy Spirit such as understanding*.[29] One way St. Thomas thinks that the gifts of the Holy Spirit are distinguished from infused virtues such as faith is that the latter perfect *human reason* with respect to its inclinations to perfect happiness in heaven whereas the former specifically make human persons *responsive to the continual inspirations of the Holy Spirit in concrete situations* in order better to facilitate achieving our supernatural end.[30] The gift of understanding in particular conduces to a kind of intimate knowledge of things, penetrating below the surface level of reality, whether that reality be a natural substance or a text, such as a text of scripture.[31] For example, we can come to know many things by way of historical biblical scholarship about a text in Matthew's Gospel. But what we can know in this way has its definite limits. One reason that God gives the baptized the gift of understanding is so they can know things about scripture that human persons could not know simply by the natural light of reason,

---

25. See, e.g., *In Sent* III, d. 24, a. 2, q.c. 1; *QDV*, q. 14, a. 9; *ST* I, q. 1, a. 2; q. 12, a. 13, ad 3; *ST* I-II, q. 1, a. 4, ad 3; q. 67, a. 3; *In Heb* 11, lect. 1, n. 558.
26. See, e.g., *QDV*, q. 17, a. 3, resp., and *ST* II-II, q. 6, a. 1.
27. See, e.g., *ST* II-II, q. 1, a. 5, resp.
28. See, e.g., *QDV*, q. 18, a. 1, ad 1; *In BDT*, q. 1, a. 2; *SCG* IV.1.8; *ST* I, q. 86, a. 2, ad 1.
29. See, e.g., *In BDT*, q. 1, a. 2, resp.; *ST* I-II, q. 68; II-II, q. 8. This chapter cannot give an exhaustive treatment of St. Thomas's views on the gifts of the Holy Spirit. It offers enough of St. Thomas's account of the gift of understanding to shed some light on the gifts of the Holy Spirit as an additional kind of graced knowledge of God human persons possess in this life.
30. See, e.g., *ST* I-II, q. 68, a. 2, resp. and ad 2.
31. See, e.g., *ST* II-II, q. 8, a. 1.

particularly insofar as such understanding is conducive to salvation.[32] Furthermore, the gift of understanding is distinguished from other gifts having to do with the perfection of intellect insofar as understanding gives us a deep penetration and grasping of what is proposed to human persons to believe by faith.[33]

In a question where St. Thomas speaks of the relationship between faith and understanding, he makes a few distinctions which are particularly important for my discussion of the relative degree of perfection of human knowledge of God in this life.[34] St. Thomas first distinguishes two parts of faith: what *directly* comes under faith, for example, articles of faith such as the doctrine of the Trinity and the incarnation, and what *indirectly* comes under faith, for example, what Matthew says that Jesus did in Galilee in a certain period of his public ministry. St. Thomas next makes a distinction between two ways of understanding: *perfectly*, for example, when we know the essence of a thing or when we understand why a proposition we believe is true, and *imperfectly*, for example, even though we do not know the essence of a thing T or the reason why a proposition p is true, we nonetheless understand that nothing else we know contradicts what we do know about T or p, for example, Jane does not understand why the doctrine of the Trinity is true, but she does understand that there are good reasons to trust the church that proposes we believe the doctrine and that there are no good reasons to reject the doctrine.

With these two distinctions in mind, St. Thomas explains how understanding as a gift of the Holy Spirit adds, and does not add, to human knowledge of God by faith in this life.[35] First, although we cannot understand perfectly what directly comes under faith in this life, we can imperfectly understand what directly comes under faith in this life insofar as we can understand how to refute arguments against what directly comes under faith. Second, we can perfectly understand what comes under faith indirectly. For example, the Holy Spirit might move us to believe by the gift of understanding that St. Augustine rather than St. Jerome has the more plausible understanding of a particular passage in

---

32. See, e.g., *ST* II-II, q. 8, a. 4, resp.
33. See, e.g., *ST* II-II, q. 8, a. 6, resp.
34. *ST* II-II, q. 8, a. 2, resp.
35. It is worth noting that, like some of the virtues, e.g., charity and the moral virtues, the gifts of the Holy Spirit remain in heaven, although their acts manifest differently in this life and in heaven (see, e.g., *ST* I-II, q. 68, a. 6).

scripture, or, alternatively, that both interpretations are equally plausible, and that those interpretations do not contradict each other so that we can believe that scripture means both of those things, etc. Indeed, we might think that St. Thomas's own commentaries on scripture are fruits of his being moved by the Holy Spirit to understand the scriptures aright in this sense.

As should be clear, human knowledge of God by way of a gift of the Holy Spirit such as understanding is limited in ways analogous to the ways divine faith is limited as a form of knowledge of God. First, whatever understanding of God we gain by way of the gift of the Holy Spirit in this life will fall short of knowledge of the essence of God, as such knowledge by way of understanding will be mediated *from which* (*a quo*) insofar as such knowledge will necessarily make reference to creatures and sense images. The knowledge of the blessed having the beatific vision is not limited in this way. In addition, the blessed see the essence of God, by God himself joining them to his essence, whereas knowledge by understanding in this life comes through a created medium *by which* (*quo*). Finally, the blessed having the beatific vision enjoy a perfect understanding of the articles of faith such as the Trinity of Persons and the incarnation whereas the person of faith in this life enjoying the gifts of the Holy Spirit does not have such a perfect understanding of the articles of faith.

St. Thomas thinks that in the state of innocence, Adam and Eve have a preternatural knowledge of God not possessed by human persons after the Fall, and this preternatural knowledge of God is superior to a knowledge of God that begins with a sense knowledge of creatures.[36] Such prelapsarian knowledge is akin to the natural knowledge the angels possess by nature of the existence and nature of God insofar as it is a kind of intuitive rather than inferential knowledge of the existence and nature of God.[37] However, this prelapsarian knowledge of God is imperfect in comparison to the beatific vision in the following way. Whereas the prelapsarian knowledge of God is a kind of mediated knowledge *by which* (*quo*) insofar as Adam knows God through a kind of intelligible effect of God, the knowledge of the blessed in the beatific vision is not mediated in that manner.[38]

36. See, e.g., *In Sent* II, d. 23, q. 2, a. 1; *QDV*, q. 18, aa. 1–2; *ST* I, q. 94, a. 1, resp.
37. See, e.g., *QDV*, q. 18, a. 1, ad 1, and *ST* I, q. 94, a. 1.
38. See ibid.

There are two additional forms of knowledge of God in this life that I can mention and contrast with the beatific vision: *prophecy* and *rapture*. Knowledge of God by prophecy is a gratuitous grace wherein God reveals to certain human persons things that are far removed from natural human knowledge.[39] Knowledge of God by rapture is a gratuitous grace wherein the soul of a human person is carried away to God in order to know divine things.[40] These two forms of knowledge have a number of things in common. First, unlike the infused virtue of faith and the gift of understanding, not all persons of faith enjoy the gifts of prophecy and rapture.[41] Second, and more importantly for my purposes, both of these kinds of knowledge are not habitual but transitory.

The transitory nature of prophecy and rapture is a significant way in which these forms of knowledge are imperfect in relation to knowledge of God by the beatific vision.[42] St. Thomas admits the possibility that Moses and St. Paul in this life saw the essence of God in rapture. However, this vision of God by rapture did not beatify their souls, insofar as it was transitory, and the beatific vision is a permanent grace in the souls of the blessed.[43] As we saw in chapter 5, another way in which the vision of God by rapture is imperfect in comparison to the beatific vision is that the vision of God by rapture disenables sense activity so that while Moses and St. Paul had their visions, they could not also engage in sense activity. By contrast, as we will see in coming chapters, the blessed in heaven who are embodied simultaneously enjoy the beatific vision and that part of the accidental reward that is sensing "the new heavens and the new earth."

The Beatific Vision as Involving No Medium *by Which* (*quo*)

So far, I have mentioned two things that St. Thomas thinks are entailed by the beatific vision understood as knowing God himself as the primary object of vision: it is a graced *simple apprehension of the essence of God* and it is *a way of knowing God that far surpasses the ways that we can know God in this life*. Here, I focus on a detail that sheds additional light on what it means to say that *God is the primary object of the beatific vision*, namely, that

---

39. See, e.g., *ST* II-II, q. 171, a. 1.
40. See, e.g., *ST* II-II, q. 175, a. 1, ad 1 and ad 2.
41. See, e.g., *ST* II-II, proem. to qq. 171–89.
42. See, e.g., *ST* II-II, q. 171, a. 2; q. 175, a. 3, ad 2.
43. See, e.g., *ST* II-II, q. 175, a. 3, ad 2.

God makes it be the case that God himself is that by which (*quo*) the one who is blessed sees the essence of God.

St. Thomas argues that if the essence of God were mediated by the medium of a created likeness, by which (*quo*) God were seen, for example, an idea of God generated in light of the experience of some creature, then it would not be the essence of God that would be seen in the beatific vision, but some created likeness of God.[44] But the primary object of the essence of the essential reward is God alone apprehended by way of the beatific vision. Therefore, the essential reward for human persons in heaven requires that God make it be the case that God himself functions, as it were, as the intelligible species by which created persons see the essence of God in the beatific vision.

Why should one think that the beatific vision—that in which the essence of the essential reward consists—requires that God unite created persons to himself so that the essence of God functions as the intelligible species of such an act of intellect? As we have seen,[45] when a human person S comes to know *what* a *material* object is that S is perceiving, for example, a donkey, S does so by way of an intelligible species of the donkey, which intelligible species is abstracted by S's agent intellect from a phantasm, where the phantasm itself is produced from a sensible species that S receives by way of S's sense faculties from the extrasensory object. S knows *what* it is that S perceives because the substantial form of the donkey (the form of a donkey as it exists in matter) and S's intelligible species of a donkey (the form of a donkey abstracted from matter) are identical in species.[46]

But any created likeness of God, whether it be some material object such as a donkey, an immaterial substance such as an angel, or an idea of God in a human intellectual soul, is not identical in species to God's form or essence, because God's form or essence is uncreated and things such as donkeys, angels, and an intelligible species in a creature's mind are created things. As St. Thomas puts it in a passage from *QDV*, if S knows the absolutely simple creator by way of a created similitude, S would know God, at best, by analogy.[47] But if a created person S knows *x* by

---

44. See, e.g., *In Sent* III, d. 14, a. 1, q.c. 3; *In Sent* IV, d. 49, q. 2, a. 1; *QQ* VII, q. 1, a. 1; *QDV*, q. 8, a. 1; q. 10, a. 11; *In BDT*, q. 1, a. 2; *SCG* III.49 and 51; *In 1 Cor* 13, lect. 4, n. 803; *CT* I, chap. 105; *ST* I, q. 12, a. 2, resp.; *In DNN*, chap. 1, lect. 1; *In Jn* 1, lect. 11, n. 211; *CT* II, chap. 9.
45. In chapter 5 above.
46. See, e.g., *SCG* III.49.5.
47. *QDV*, q. 8, a. 1, resp. For a different argument for why creatures cannot give us knowledge

analogy, then S does not know the essence of *x*; at best, S knows some truth about S that falls short of knowing *x*'s essence. As we have seen, the essence of the essential reward consists in nothing less than a vision of the essence of God. Therefore, if something nonidentical in species with God's essence functions as the intelligible species in a saint S's act of knowing God in heaven, it then follows that S does not enjoy the essential reward of perfect happiness in heaven. But the saints in heaven do enjoy the essential reward of perfect happiness in heaven. Therefore, God himself makes it be the case that his own essence functions, as it were, as the intelligible species in a saint's contemplative act of knowing God's essence in heaven.[48] Considering that God makes it be the case that God himself functions as the intelligible species of knowing the essence of God in the beatific vision, we might say that there is no logically possible union between God and a creaturely person that is as intimate as that of the beatific vision.

St. Thomas on Making Sense of the Beatific Vision as Involving No Medium *by Which* (*quo*)

In *SCG* III, St. Thomas offers a way of making sense of God's causing it to be the case that created intellects in heaven are united to God so as to enjoy a union with God that does not involve a medium *by which* (*quo*).[49] St. Thomas lays out his explanation as to how a created person can know the essence of God in three stages.

First, in order for a created person S to understand the essence of a thing *y*, S needs to receive the form of a material object *y* *intentionally* (rather than *materially*).[50] As we have seen, St. Thomas calls the intentional form of *y*, whereby S understands the essence of *y*, the *intelligible species*. Typically, what serves as the intelligible species of *y* in S is something other than *y*, that is, it is some likeness of *y*. But for reasons that I have outlined above, St. Thomas thinks that perfect human happiness

---

of God's essence, based on the divine simplicity and the identity of God's attributes, see *CT* II, chap. 9.

48. See, e.g., *In Sent* III, d. 14, a, 1, q.c. 3; IV, d. 49, q. 2, a. 1 (*ST Suppl.*, q. 92, a. 1); a. 2, a. 6; *QDV*, q. 8, a. 1, resp.; q. 10, a. 11, resp.; *QQ* VII, q. 1, a. 1; *In BDT*, q. 1, a. 2; *SCG* III.51 and IV.7.15; *In 1 Cor* 13, lect. 4, nn. 800–804; *CT* I, chap. 105; *In DDN*, chap. 1, lect. 1; *ST* I, q. 12, a. 2; *In Jn* 1, lect. 11, n. 211; 14, lect. 2, n. 1880; *CT* II, chap. 9.

49. In chap. 51. See also *In Sent* IV, d. 49, q. 2, a. 1, resp. (*ST Suppl.*, q. 92, a. 1, resp.).

50. If *x*, e.g., a human person, *materially* receives the form F of *y*, e.g., the form of a house, then *x* would, *per impossible*, become a house.

requires that we possess a more intimate union with God than can be afforded by knowledge of God by way of some likeness of God. What St. Thomas therefore contends is that God can unite the intellect of a creaturely person to himself such that the essence of God functions as (or like) an intelligible species of the essence of God in the blessed enjoying the beatific vision.

Second, St. Thomas makes a case for God being able to function as (or like) an intelligible species for the blessed. Now, if God were a composite of matter and form, then God could not be the form of something other than God. For the form of a matter/form composite is limited to being the form of the matter which it configures. But God is a pure form and a pure form x can be the form of another thing y, at least insofar as y can participate in x. But if a being z cannot be participated in by another—as is, for example, the case with purely material beings or the substantial forms of nonintellectual beings—then z cannot be the form of something other than z.

Third, St. Thomas has an example of a form that can be participated in by another ready to hand, namely, the human soul. According to St. Thomas, the human soul is unlike other substantial forms of material beings in that the human soul is a substantial form that has its own act of being, which it can share with matter so that the result is a human person existing in her natural conditions, that is, as a form/matter composite.[51] Therefore, according to St. Thomas, one can draw an analogy between the manner in which the substantial being of the human soul can be participated in by prime matter such that what is produced is the composite human person and God's joining to himself the created intellect such that what is produced is the intellectual creature knowing the essence of God.

There is an important difference, however, between the soul sharing its being with matter to bring about the composite human person and God uniting intellectual creatures to his essence to bring about the beatific vision in the blessed. In the former case matter participates in the soul *substantially* so that what comes to exist is a composite *substance*. In the latter case, the created intellect participates in the essence of God *intentionally* so that what exists is a created act of *knowing* God, that is, the

---

51. See, e.g., *SCG* II.68. For more on St. Thomas on substantial form and prime matter, see chapter 9 below, my *Aquinas and the Ship of Theseus: Solving Puzzles about Material Objects* and my "Some Advantages for a Thomistic Solution to the Problem of Personal Identity beyond Death."

beatific vision in the soul of the saint. Because God's form is possessed by a creature's intellect *intentionally* and not *substantially* in the beatific vision, God can thus make it so an intellectual creature knows God directly in the beatific vision while still maintaining the substantial, that is, existential, distinction between God and those creatures enjoying the beatific vision.

This may all sound quite abstract, but one must remember St. Thomas is here using the tools of philosophy (which are, of course, being pushed to the limit) in order to help elucidate a traditional interpretation of scripture. As St. Thomas points out in *SCG*, St. Paul says in 1 Corinthians 13:12: "For now we see in a mirror, dimly, but then we will see face to face."[52] As God is incorporeal, "face to face" is clearly a metaphorical way of speaking.[53] By seeing "face to face," St. Thomas reads St. Paul as teaching that the blessed in heaven will know the essence of God without a medium *by which* (*quo*). If we are inclined to say that St. Paul is describing in 1 Corinthians 13 the intimacy with which the blessed know God, St. Thomas supplies us with a way of thinking about this intimacy that also takes seriously the radical metaphysical difference between the nature of God and human persons.

Indeed, St. Thomas finishes *SCG* III.51 with another argument from scripture.[54] In the beatific vision, intellectual creatures become maximally assimilated to God, thereby participating in God's own perfect happiness. For God himself understands his own substance through his own substance, and this is his felicity. But it is said in 1 John 3:2: "When He is revealed, we will be like Him, because we will see Him as He is." Therefore, in heaven created persons are perfectly happy because, like God, they know absolutely happy God without a medium by which (*quo*).

St. Thomas on God's Self-Knowledge and the Creature's Knowledge of God's Essence

The beatific vision is thus a remarkably intimate cognition of God. St. Thomas nonetheless clearly distinguishes God himself from those intellectual creatures that have a direct cognition of God's essence in the beatific vision by noting that creatures possess God's form intentionally and not substantially. In addition, although the perfect happiness

---

52. *SCG* III.51.5. See also *In 1 Cor* 13, lect. 4, nn. 800–804, and *In Mt* 18, lect. 1, n. 1505.
53. *SCG* III.51.5.
54. *SCG* III.51.6.

of created persons is a function of knowing God in the way God knows himself—through his essence—St. Thomas has a number of ways of distinguishing a creature's knowledge of the essence of God in the beatific vision from God's knowledge of himself. Let us examine three.

First, creatures cannot *naturally* know the *essence* of God. For example, even Adam and Eve before the Fall did not naturally know the essence of God.[55] In addition, the angels in their first moment of existence did not *naturally* know the essence of God.[56] What goes for Adam in the prelapsarian state and angels according to their natural mode of cognition goes for any creature. For, as we have seen, if we know God through a medium by which (*quo*), then we do not know the essence of God. But the only way for a creature to know the essence of God without a medium *by which* is if God, by his grace, joins that creature to himself such that God functions as the intelligible species in the beatific vision of that creature. This is because God is infinite, absolutely perfect, and simple.[57] Therefore, if a created person S comes to know God's essence, this is by way of a supernatural gift of grace whereby God joins S's intellect to himself so that S sees God's essence by way of God's essence, rather than through some created medium *by which*.[58] Of course, God knows his essence by nature.[59] Therefore, the knowledge of a creature having the beatific vision is therefore distinct from, because less perfect than, God's own knowledge of his essence.

That brings us to a second way in which God's knowledge of himself differs from the vision of the essence of God on the part of the blessed. Recall that we can speak of different kinds of media necessary for some kinds of cognition. For example, there is the medium by which (*quo*) something is cognized, for example, the sensitive species in the eye as the form received in the eye is a medium by which the agent sees a visible object. There is also the medium under which (*sub quo*) something is cognized, for example, light from the sun is the medium under which an agent sees a visible object. Now, as we have seen, the blessed do not

---

55. See, e.g., *QDV*, q. 18, a. 1, and *ST* I, q. 94, a. 1.
56. See, e.g., *In Sent* II, d. 4, a. 1; IV, d. 49, q. 2, a. 6, ad 1; *QDV*, q. 8, a. 3; *ST* I, q. 56, a. 3, ad 2; q. 62, a. 1.
57. See, e.g., *ST* I, q. 12, a. 4.
58. See, e.g., *In Sent* II, d. 4, a. 1; d. 23, q. 2, a. 1; IV, d. 49, q. 2, a. 6; *QDV*, q. 8, a. 3; q. 18, a. 1; *SCG* I.3; III.49 and 52; *In 1 Tm* 6, lect. 3; *ST* I, q. 12, a. 4; q. 64, a. 1, ad 2; *QDA*, a. 17, ad 10; *ST* I-II, q. 5, a. 5. Chapters 8 and 17 below have more to say about the graciousness of the beatific vision.
59. See, e.g., *QDV*, q. 18, a. 1, ad 1.

require a created medium by which in order to see the essence of God insofar as God joins the intellect of the blessed to himself immediately. But, according to St. Thomas, in order for the intellect of the blessed to be joined to God in this manner, the intellect of the blessed itself must be properly disposed, that is, there must be in the intellect of the blessed a medium *under which* the essence of God is cognized.[60] This medium *sub quo* is what Catholic tradition calls the *lumen gloriae* (light of glory).[61] The *lumen gloriae* is the grace that God creates in the intellect of the blessed, which disposes and raises up the created intellect so that God can join the created intellect to himself in the beatific vision.[62] But God knows his own essence without a medium under which.[63] Because creatures require the *lumen gloriae* as a medium under which to see the essence of God, God's knowledge of his own essence is distinct, and more perfect than, any creature's knowledge of the essence of God.

A third way that St. Thomas distinguishes the blessed creature's cognition of the essence of God from God's cognition of his own essence is that the blessed creature cannot, but God can, *comprehend* God.[64] Consider that Jane can know *what* Susan is—Susan is a human person, and human persons are distinguished from other beings insofar as they are mortal, rational, dependent animals—without knowing everything there is to know about her, such as knowing that she is temperamentally shy. Similarly, St. Paul's cognizing the essence of God—knowing what God is—does not entail that St. Paul knows everything there is to know about the infinite God.

But perhaps it seems as if, given other things that St. Thomas believes, the saints in heaven do comprehend God. Consider the following argument to that effect:

---

60. See, e.g., *In Sent* IV, d. 49, q. 2, a. 6, ad 4. See also *In Sent* III, d. 14, a. 1, q.c. 3; *QDV*, q. 8, a. 3; q. 18, a. 1, ad 1; q. 20, a. 2; *QQ* VII, q. 1, a. 1; *SCG* III.53–8; *CT* I, chap. 105; *ST* I, q. 12, a. 5, resp. and ad 2.

61. That the blessed need the *lumen gloriae* to see the essence of God in heaven was declared dogmatically at the Council of Vienne (1311–12); in *Decrees*, ed. Tanner, 2:28.

62. See, e.g., *In Sent* III, d. 14, a. 1, q.c. 3; IV, d. 49, q. 2, a. 6; *QQ* VII, q. 1, a. 1; *QDV*, q. 8, a. 3; q. 18, a. 1, ad 1; q. 20, a. 2; *SCG* III.53 and 54; *CT* I, chap. 105; *ST* I, q. 12, a. 5. Chapter 8 below treats the *lumen gloriae* in greater detail.

63. See, e.g., *QDV*, q. 18, a. 1, ad 1.

64. See, e.g., *In Sent* III, d. 14, a. 2, q.c. 1; d. 27, q. 3, a. 2; IV, d. 49, q. 2, a. 3; *QDV*, q. 2, a. 1, ad 3; q. 8, a. 2; q. 20, a. 5; *SCG* III.55; *In Eph* 5, lect. 3, n. 280; *In 1 Tm* 6, lect. 3; *CT* I, chap. 106; *ST* I, q. 12, aa. 7–8; *In DDN*, chap. 1, lect. 1–2; *ST* I-II, q. 4, a. 3, ad 1; *In Jn* 1, lect. 11, nn. 213–14; *ST* III, q. 10, a. 1. It is worth noting that *comprehendere* can mean at least two things in the sources that St. Thomas is reading: (a) to comprehend *x* is to know *x* as perfectly as *x* can be known; (b) to comprehend *x* is to attain *x* (see, e.g., *ST* I, q. 12, a. 7, ad 1, and *ST* I-II, q. 4, a. 3, ad 1). The saints in heaven do comprehend God in sense (b). But it is sense (a) of *comprehendere* that is at issue here.

(1) If God is absolutely simple, then God is identical to God's essence [assumption].

(2) If S knows God's essence, then S knows everything God knows [from (1)].

(3) If S knows everything God knows, then S comprehends God [assumption].

(4) Therefore, if S knows God's essence, then S comprehends God [from (2) and (3), HS].

(5) The saints know God's essence [assumption].

(6) Therefore, the saints comprehend God [from (4) and (5), MP].

As we have seen, St. Thomas rejects the conclusion of this argument. He also accepts premises (1)[65] and (5). Because (4) follows logically from (2) and (3), that leaves premises (2) and (3) and the inference to (2) from (1) as possibly problematic. Indeed, St. Thomas rejects both (2) and the inference from (1) to (2). He also rejects premise (3). Hence, he can, and does, reject (4).

First, St. Thomas thinks that (3) is false. Even if S knows everything there is to know about x, it does not thereby follow that S *comprehends x*. For St. Thomas thinks that to comprehend x (in the relevant sense) is to know x *in the most perfect way possible*. But S might know everything there is to know about x, but not know x in the best way possible. For example, God knows everything that there is to know about triangularity simply by timelessly knowing himself. Socrates, in this life, might know everything there is to know about triangularity, but come to know this only later in his life. But knowing x timelessly is a better way of knowing x than coming to know x. Furthermore, Socrates never knows all that there is to know about triangularity, all at once. But because God knows what God knows timelessly, God does know everything there is to know about triangles, all at once. Therefore, God's *way* of knowing triangularity is perfect in comparison to the less than perfect manner in which Socrates knows triangularity.[66] So, even *if* the saints were to know everything God knows in seeing the essence of God, they would not thereby comprehend God in seeing the essence of God. This is because, as we have seen, the

---

65. See, e.g., *ST* I, q. 3, a. 3.
66. See, e.g., *In Sent* III, d. 14, a. 2, q.c. 1; d. 27, q. 3, a. 2; IV, d. 49, q. 2, a. 3; *QDV*, q. 2, a. 1, ad 3; q. 8, a. 2; q. 20, a. 5; *SCG* III.55; *In Eph* 5, lect. 3, n. 280; *In 1 Tm* 6, lect. 3; *CT* I, chap. 106; *ST* I, q. 12, a. 7; *In DDN*, chap. 1, lect. 1–2; *ST* I-II, q. 4, a. 3, ad 1; *In Jn* 1, lect. 11, nn. 213–14; *ST* III, q. 10, a. 1.

saints do not know the essence of God in the perfect way that God knows himself. For creatures know the essence of God by way of a created medium *under which*, the *lumen gloriae*, but God does not. Furthermore, the saints come to know the essence of God by grace instead of knowing it naturally and immutably. In addition, the saints know the essence of God by way of a finite intellect instead of as an infinite one,[67] and as a creature and not as the creator.[68]

Second, St. Thomas both rejects (2) and that (2) follows logically from (1). The saints do not know everything there is to know about God in virtue of knowing the essence of God.[69] Nor does it follow from God's simplicity that if S knows the essence of God, then S knows everything there is to know about God. One way St. Thomas can show that a proposition such as (2) is false and that (2) does not follow from a proposition such as (1) is as follows. God's essence is infinite and a thing is knowable to the extent that it is. Therefore, God's essence is infinitely knowable. Now, the beatified person S knows the essence of God in virtue of God uniting S's intellect to God so that God takes the place of the medium *by which* in S's cognition of God. But this is possible only insofar as God creates in S's intellect a medium *under which*, namely, the *lumen gloriae*, under which S's intellect can see the essence of God. Because the *lumen gloriae* is a created disposition to know the essence of God, it is finite. Of course, no finite intellect—even with the aid of the created *lumen gloriae* by which a creature knows the essence of God in the beatific vision—can know the infinite God *qua* infinite, as the finite cannot know the infinite *qua* infinite. Therefore, no creature can know the essence of God perfectly.[70] Therefore, it is not the case that, if S knows the essence of God, then S knows everything there is to know about God. Premise (2) is false.

Furthermore, because a created intellect knows the essence of God in proportion to the amount of the *lumen gloriae* God creates in that created intellect, and some of the blessed know the essence of God better

---

67. See, e.g., *QDV*, q. 2, a. 2, ad 5; *SCG* III.55.3; *In 1 Tm* 6, lect. 3, n. 269; *ST* I, q. 12, a. 7, resp.
68. See, e.g., *SCG* III.55.5 and *ST* I, q. 12, a. 7, resp.
69. See, e.g., *In Sent* II, d. 11, q. 2, a. 2; III, d. 14, a. 2, q.c. 2; IV, d. 45, q. 3, a. 1; d. 49, q. 2, a. 5 (*ST Suppl.*, q. 92, a. 3); *SCG* III.56; *ST* I, q. 12, aa. 7–8; q. 57, a. 5; q. 106, a. 1, ad 1.
70. See, e.g., *In Sent* III, d. 27, q. 3, a. 2; IV, d. 49, a. 2, a. 3; *QDV*, q. 2, a. 2, ad 5–7; q. 8, a. 2; q. 20, a. 5; *SCG* III.55.3; *CT* I, chap. 106; *ST* I, q. 12, a. 7, resp.; q. 62, a. 9, resp.; *In Jn* 1, lect. 11, nn. 211 and 213.

than others, it does not follow from the divine simplicity that, if S knows the essence of God, then S knows everything there is to know about God.[71] The inference from (1) to (2) incorrectly conflates God's mode of knowing the essence of God, which is simple, infinite, and absolutely perfect, and the intellectual creature's mode of knowing the essence of God, which is something created, finite, and less than absolutely perfect.

St. Thomas has a number of ways of making sense of the difference between God's comprehension of his own essence and the intellectual creature's noncomprehensive knowledge of the essence of God. First, as we shall see below, intellectual creatures know things other than God in virtue of knowing the essence of God. However, these things other than God are known as effects are known through their cause, as the essence of God is the cause of creatures. Now the more perfectly a cause is seen, the more that cause's effects are seen, whether possible or actual. Applying that axiom to knowledge of the essence of God, it is possible to know the essence of God more or less perfectly insofar as one knows more or less of the actual or possible effects of the essence of God. But we might think that creatures cannot know everything that an absolutely perfect God can do, or could have done. Because God does know everything he can do, or could have done, creatures do not know everything there is to know about God just in virtue of seeing the essence of God.[72]

Indeed, because the divine power is infinite and the created intellect is finite, the created intellect cannot know all the things that are possible for God's divine power. But God knows whatever God knows in virtue of knowing God's essence and God knows what is possible for his power. Therefore, not knowing the extent of God's power as perfectly as God does in knowing the essence of God, creatures do not know all that God knows in virtue of knowing the essence of God.[73]

There is also a second way that St. Thomas distinguishes God's comprehension of his own essence and the creature's less than comprehensive mode of knowing the essence of God. S does not know what a voluntary agent S1 (where S and S1 are not numerically identical) wills simply

---

71. See, e.g., *In Sent* IV, d. 49, q. 2, a. 4; *SCG* III.58; *ST* I, q. 12, a. 6; a. 7, resp.; q. 62, a. 9; I-II, q. 5, a. 2, resp. and ad 3.

72. See, e.g., *In Sent* IV, d. 49, q. 2, a. 5, resp.; *ST* I, q. 12, a. 8, resp.; q. 106, a. 1, ad 1; III, q. 10, a. 2.

73. See, e.g., *SCG* III.56.4. See also *ST* I, q. 12, a. 8, resp., and III, q. 10, a. 2, resp.

from S knowing the essence of S1, as the will is free and not necessitated. However, God wills things and knows everything he wills. Therefore, not knowing the essence of God as perfectly as God does, the creature does not know everything that God knows in virtue of the creature knowing the essence of God in the beatific vision.[74]

Finally, St. Thomas sometimes argues as follows that God knows more about God's essence than do creatures, and so a creature does not know everything there is to know about God just in virtue of seeing the essence of God. The beatified angels know the essence of God, but they do not know future contingent things or the secret thoughts of intellectual creatures. But God does know these things. Again, God knows his essence more perfectly than creatures. Therefore, creatures do not know everything that God knows in virtue of knowing the essence of God.[75]

THE SECONDARY OBJECT OF THE BEATIFIC VISION:
A PERFECT COGNITION OF CREATURES

St. Thomas thinks that a saint S in heaven's having the beatific vision entails that S has the most intimate union with God himself that it is logically possible for S to enjoy, given the degree to which S receives the *lumen gloriae*.[76] But in seeing the essence of God, St. Thomas thinks that created intellects also know *creatures* indirectly insofar as God is their cause.[77] Perhaps I can put the point in less technical terms: not only are the saints united to God in the most intimate way in heaven, but, just in virtue of this union with God, they know the answers to all those questions that perplexed them in this life about the world God has made. We can collectively call the things other than God himself the saints know in virtue of having the beatific vision *the secondary object* of the beatific vision.

What kinds of things other than God do the saints in heaven know

---

74. *SCG* III.56.5.
75. *ST* I, q. 12, a. 8, s.c. See also *ST* I, q. 57, aa. 4–5.
76. Chapter 8 below explains the importance of the parenthetical remark, where both the *lumen gloriae* and the thesis that some intellectual creatures are happier than others is discussed in detail.
77. See, e.g., *In Sent* II, d. 11, q. 2, aa. 1–2; III, d. 14, q. 1, a. 2; IV, d. 45, q. 3, a. 1; d. 49, q. 2, a. 5 (*ST Suppl.*, q. 92, a. 3); *QDV*, q. 8, a. 4; q. 20, aa. 4–6; *SCG* III.56 and 59; *ST* I, q. 12, aa. 8–10; q. 57, a. 5; q. 106, a. 1, ad 1; III, q. 10, a. 2.

in virtue of having the beatific vision? St. Thomas often answers that question in the context of responding to another question: "whether those who see the essence of God see all things?"[78] St. Thomas's answer to that question requires that we disambiguate "all things."[79] Given what St. Thomas says throughout his body of work, there are at least three possible ways to interpret "all things" in the question, "whether created intellects know *all things* in virtue of seeing the essence of God?":

(a) *All things* = the genera,[80] species,[81] proper accidents,[82] and powers[83] of all *substances* in the created universe, including the individual things falling under those species,[84] as well as the order of the universe as a whole.[85]

(b) *All things* = the genera, species, proper accidents, and powers of all *created beings*, past, present, and future, including the individual things falling under those species, for example, *all the secret thoughts of human persons*,[86] as well as the order of the universe as a whole. In other words, "all things" includes all that God knows by his "knowledge of vision."[87]

(c) *All things* = the genera, species, proper accidents, and powers of all created beings, past, present, and future, including the individual things falling under those species, for example, all the secret thoughts of human persons, as well as the order of the universe as a whole. In other words, "all things" includes all that God knows by his "knowledge of vision." *However, it also includes (i) all possible creatures*,[88] (*ii*) *all the rea-*

---

78. See, e.g., *In Sent* III, d. 14, q. 1, a. 2, q.c. 2; IV, d. 49, q. 2, a. 5 (*ST Suppl.*, q. 92, a. 3); *QDV*, q. 8, a. 4; q. 20, aa. 4–5; *SCG* III.56 and 59; *ST* I, q. 12, a. 8; III, q. 10, a. 2.
79. See especially *QDV*, q. 8, a. 4; *SCG* III.59.6; *ST* III, q. 10, a. 2, resp.
80. See, e.g., *SCG* III.56.1 and *ST* I, q. 12, a. 8, ad 4.
81. See, e.g., *QDV*, q. 8, a. 4, ad 1; *SCG* III.56.1; *ST* I, q. 12, a. 8, ad 4.
82. See, e.g., *SCG* III.56.6.
83. See, e.g., *SCG* III.56.1.
84. See, e.g., *SCG* III.56.6.
85. See, e.g., *SCG* III.56.1.
86. See, e.g., *QDV*, q. 20, a. 4, resp., and *ST* III, q. 10, a. 2, resp.
87. St. Thomas distinguishes God's "knowledge of vision" (*cognoscere notitia visionis*), i.e., God's knowledge of what he actually creates, in our past, in our present, and in our future, from God's knowledge of necessary truths and what God could do, i.e., God's "knowledge of simple intelligence" (*cognoscere notitia simplicis intelligentiae*). See, e.g., *In Sent* IV, d. 49, q. 2, a. 5, resp. (*ST Suppl.*, q. 92, a. 3, resp.), and *QDV*, q. 20, a. 4, ad 1. Later, the great Jesuit scholastic Luis de Molina (1535–1600) will defend the thesis that God has a kind of knowledge in between these two kinds of knowledge, God's so-called middle knowledge, i.e., knowledge of what free creatures would do in all circumstances within every possible world (where "free" is meant in a libertarian sense of "free").
88. See, e.g., *In Sent* IV, d. 49, q. 2, a. 5, resp. (*ST Suppl.*, q. 92, a. 3, resp.), and *SCG* III.56.8.

sons why God makes actual creatures,[89] *and (iii) all the things that depend upon the will of God alone, for example, why God creates this universe rather than another.*[90]

St. Thomas thinks that if (a) is what we have in mind by "all things," then all created intellects in heaven do in fact know all things in virtue of seeing the essence of God in the beatific vision. One reason St. Thomas offers for thinking that all created intellects in heaven know all things in God in sense (a) is that a being that possesses the power of intellect has a natural desire to know all things in sense (a). As God alone is the ultimate end of human persons, which end is attained in the beatific vision, it follows that in having the beatific vision, the saint knows all things in sense (a).[91]

According to St. Thomas, the soul of Christ knows *all things* in the beatific vision in sense (b).[92] St. Thomas employs various arguments in defense of this thesis. For example, he offers the following argument based on the view that Christ's soul is the most perfect of created intellects: all creatures proceed from God insofar as God creates them, and, in virtue of having a nature from God, they are naturally inclined "to return to God," that is, to act in such a way that approximates, or participates in, the perfection of their cause, to the extent that they are able. For example, nonintellectual creatures are inclined to approximate or participate in God's activity insofar as they are inclined to act perfectly in accord with their kind, for example, plants and nonhuman animals are inclined to perform the perfect act of contributing to the reproduction of their species. By contrast, intellectual creatures are inclined naturally and characteristically to approximate or participate in God's activity by acts of perfect knowing and loving. In order for an intellectual creature to be perfect, that creature must know all the things a creature

---

89. See, e.g., *SCG* III.56.9.

90. See, e.g., *SCG* III.56.10.

91. See, e.g., *SCG* III.59.1 and *ST* I, q. 12, a. 8, ad 4. In *QDV*, q. 8, a. 4, resp., St. Thomas argues that, even if all saints know all things in sense (a), it is also the case that some creatures know more about God's creation than others. For example, "the soul of Christ, which sees God more perfectly than all other creatures do, is said to know all things, present, past, and future. Other creatures however, do not have this knowledge. Each one of them sees more or fewer effects of God [above and beyond what is contained in (a)] in proportion to the knowledge he has of Him." *Truth*, trans. Robert W. Mulligan (Indianapolis, Ind.: Hackett, 1994), 1:334.

92. See, e.g., *In Sent* IV, d. 49, q. 2, a. 5, resp. and ad 12 (*ST Suppl.*, q. 92, a. 3, resp. and ad 12); *QDV*, q. 8, a. 4, resp.; q. 20, a. 4, resp.; *CT* I, chap. 216; *ST* III, q. 10, a. 2, resp. and ad 2.

can know. Now, there are two kinds of things a creature can know: those things that are a part of the natural order, and those things that are part of the order of grace. As Christ's soul is the perfection of created intellects, Christ knows all things in the order of nature *and* all things in the order of grace. That is, Christ's soul knows in virtue of the beatific vision all things in sense (b).[93]

In *ST*, St. Thomas offers a theological argument that Christ's soul knows all things in sense (b).[94] A created intellect sees more things in the essence of God, or the Word, the more perfectly it sees the essence of God. But every beatified intellect knows all things that pertain to itself. But all things in sense (b) pertain to Christ because all things in sense (b) are subject to him. In addition, he is the judge of all men, and so he must know all of their secret thoughts. Hence, Christ, in his soul, knows all things in sense (b) in virtue of his seeing the essence of God.

Although not all created intellects know all things in sense (b) in knowing the essence of God,[95] some intellectual creatures know more things in virtue of having the beatific vision than what is contained in (a). This is because some angels and human souls know more things in knowing the essence of God than others insofar as they have a clearer beatific vision, where an intellectual creature's clarity of beatific vision is proportional to the amount of *lumen gloriae* God creates in their intellect.[96] Nonetheless, save in the case of the soul of Christ, no created intellect knows all things in sense (b) in virtue of the beatific vision,[97] because an intellectual creature *qua* intellectual creature's knowing such things is not a function of a natural desire to know on the part of that intellectual creature; nor does it pertain to them.[98]

But if "all things" is taken in sense (c), then no created thing, not even the soul of Christ, can know all things in virtue of having the beatific vision. This is because in order to know, for example, (i) all possible created things, the angel or saint or soul would have to comprehend

---

93. See, e.g., *QDV*, q. 20, a. 4, resp.
94. *ST* III, q. 10, a. 2, resp. See also *CT* I, chap. 216.
95. Or "in the Word" (*in verbo*), as St. Thomas sometimes puts it in this context (see, e.g., *ST* III, q. 10, a. 2).
96. See, e.g., *QDV*, q. 8, a. 4, resp. and ad 3, ad 4; *CT* I, chap. 216; *ST* I, q. 12, a. 8, resp.; q. 54, a. 5, resp.; q. 106, a. 1, ad 1. Chapter 8 below explains what St. Thomas means by saying different created intellects have more or less clear knowledge of God in the beatific vision.
97. See, e.g., *QDV*, q. 8, a. 4, resp.
98. *ST* I, q. 12, a. 8, resp.

(the power of) God. But, as we saw above, comprehending God (and God's power) is only possible for God.[99] In addition, in order to know (ii), one would have to comprehend the divine goodness and wisdom. But creatures cannot do that.[100] Neither can creatures know (iii), for, as St. Thomas notes, St. Paul teaches the following at 1 Corinthians 2:11: "For what human being knows what is truly human except the human spirit that is within? So also no one comprehends what is truly God's except the Spirit of God."[101]

But we might wonder *how* any created intellect knows things other than the essence of God in virtue of having the beatific vision. As St. Thomas notes, some have compared *seeing created things in virtue of seeing the essence of God* to *seeing things in a mirror*.[102] St. Thomas himself seems to have had mixed reactions to that comparison. In *QDV*, St. Thomas mentions the mirror as a metaphor for the manner in which things other than God are seen in virtue of seeing the essence of God. However, he states a preference for thinking about knowing created things in God as effects are known in virtue of knowing their cause, that is, two persons S and S1 might both know that x is a cause of things other than x in virtue of knowing the essence of x, but not know the same number of effects of that cause.[103] For example, John and Jane both know what a triangle is, but John does not know that a triangle inscribed in a circle has a smaller area than does the circle, whereas Jane does know this.

Why does St. Thomas prefer the model of knowing effects virtually within their cause to the model of seeing things reflected in a mirror? According to St. Thomas, the mirror model, and not the cause and effect model, implies that the saints actually see two distinct objects in seeing the essence of God, namely, God and created things (the mirror, and those things reflected in the mirror), which St. Thomas thinks is not the case. For although created things are substantially distinct from God, and the saint seeing God and knowing things in virtue of seeing God knows that God and creatures are distinct (just as God does), things other than

---

99. See, e.g., *In Sent* IV, d. 49, q. 2, a. 5, resp. (*ST Suppl.*, q. 92, a. 3, resp.); *QDV*, q. 20, a. 4, resp.; a. 5, resp.; *SCG* III.59.8; *CT* I, chap. 216; *ST* III, q. 10, a. 2, resp.
100. See, e.g., *SCG* III.59.9.
101. *SCG* III.59.10.
102. See, e.g., *QDV*, q. 8, a. 4, resp.
103. See ibid. and also *QDV*, q. 20, a. 4, resp.; *SCG* III.56.2; *ST* I, q. 12, a. 8, resp.

God do not exist *in the essence of God* as actually distinct from God, given divine simplicity.[104]

However, in the fourth book of his *Sentences* commentary (composed just prior to *QDV*), St. Thomas employs the mirror metaphor in talking about the saints knowing things other than God in virtue of seeing the essence of God, while emphasizing ways in which God's essence is not like a *material* mirror. In fact, in this text he combines the mirror model and the knowing effects through their mutual cause model:

> We may also reply that in a material mirror both object and mirror are seen under their proper image; although the mirror be seen through an image received from the thing itself, whereas the stone is seen through its proper image reflected in some other thing, where the reason for seeing the one is the reason for seeing the other. But in the uncreated mirror a thing is seen through the form of the mirror, just as an effect is seen through the image of its cause and conversely.[105]

Finally, we might wonder how *important* it is for human persons in heaven to know things other than God in virtue of having the beatific vision. As we have seen, St. Thomas thinks that possessing such knowledge in heaven answers to a natural desire insofar as a being has an intellect. But in a passage from *ST*, St. Thomas argues that, although the saints in heaven *do* know all things in virtue of having the beatific vision, insofar as human persons have a natural desire for such knowledge, even if a person S knew the essence of God without also knowing all things, S's natural desire would be satisfied. Here is the text of St. Thomas:

> Yet if God alone were seen, Who is the fount and principle of all being and of all truth[,] He would so fill the natural desire of knowledge that nothing else would be desired, and the seer would be completely beatified. Hence Augustine says (*Confess.* v): *Unhappy the man who knoweth all these* (that is, all creatures) *and knoweth not Thee! But happy whoso knoweth Thee although he know not these. And whoso knoweth both Thee and them is not the happier for them, but for Thee alone.*[106]

---

104. See, e.g., *QDV*, q. 8, a. 4, resp.; q. 20, a. 4, resp.
105. *ST Suppl.*, q. 92, a. 3, ad 6 (trans. English Dominicans, 2956). See also *In Sent* IV, d. 49, q. 2, a. 5, ad 6.
106. *ST* I, q. 12, a. 8, ad 4 (trans. English Dominicans, 56). See also the sermon *Beata gens* 2.3.1; *ST* I, q. 26, a. 3, resp.; *QDM*, q. 5, a. 1, obj. 4 and ad 4; *ST* I-II, q. 5, a. 2, ad 3; *In Heb* 1, lect. 6, n. 86.

As he does in other places, we can see St. Thomas here emphasizing the view that knowing God himself in the beatific vision is not just a necessary, but also a sufficient, condition for a human person attaining perfect happiness.[107]

[107]. One can usefully compare what St. Thomas says here about the relevance of *a created person S knowing the secondary object of the beatific vision* for attaining perfect human happiness with what St. Thomas says about the relevance of human friendship for attaining perfect happiness in *ST* I-II, q. 4, a. 8, ad 3: "Perfection of charity is essential to Happiness, as to the love of God, but not as to the love of our neighbor. Wherefore if there were but one soul enjoying God, it would be happy, though having no neighbor to love. But supposing one neighbor to be there, love of him results from perfect love of God. Consequently, friendship is, as it were, concomitant with perfect Happiness" (trans. English Dominicans, 608).

7

The Essential Reward III

THE BEATIFIC VISION AS PARTICIPATION
IN GOD'S ETERNAL LIFE

In continuing my discussion of St. Thomas's views on the essential reward in general, and the beatific vision in particular, this chapter explores St. Thomas's understanding of the meaning of "eternal" (*aeternam*) in the Vulgate translation of a scriptural passage such as John 17:3: "and this is eternal life, that they may know you, the only true God, and Jesus Christ whom you have sent." As we will see, St. Thomas thinks that the intellectual creature's beatific vision is an immutable participation in God's own eternal life, one that transcends both time and aeveternity.[1]

ST. THOMAS'S EARLY WORK ON THE BEATIFIC VISION AS PARTICIPATED ETERNITY

In examining St. Thomas's views on the meaning of *eternal life*, I begin with texts from his earliest systematic treatment of the beatific vision. In his *Sentences* commentary, St. Thomas asks whether human beatitude is the same as eternal life.[2] In responding to that question, he distinguishes between eternal life as *perpetual*, that is, unending but temporal life, and

---

1. For another examination of St. Thomas's views on eternal life as it applies to human persons in heaven—one which includes an examination of the commentary tradition on St. Thomas's views—see C. J. Peter, *Participated Eternity in the Vision of God. A Study of the Opinion of St. Thomas Aquinas and His Commentators on the Duration of the Acts of Glory* (Rome: Gregorian University Press, 1964). For the views of St. Thomas's teacher, St. Albert the Great, on eternity and time, see Henryk Anzulewicz, "Aeternitas – Aevum – Tempus. The Concept of Time in the System of St. Albert the Great," in *The Medieval Concept of Time: Studies on the Scholastic Debate and its Reception in Early Modern Philosophy*, ed. Pasquale Porro (Leiden: Brill, 2001), 83–130.

2. *In Sent* IV, d. 49, q. 1, a. 2, q.c. 3.

eternal life as transcending time and the *aevum*, and he favors the latter way of understanding the true meaning of *eternal life*. To see this, consider the following objection that St. Thomas entertains: "further, whatsoever endures perpetually participates, in a way, in eternal life, if 'eternal' be taken to mean 'perpetual.' But the damned endure perpetually, sent into eternal fire, as is evident from Matthew 25:41. However, they have not beatitude."[3] St. Thomas responds:

> To the fourth, it should be said that the eternal life the saints will have is spoken of according to a participation of eternity, not merely with regard to lacking an end (in which manner even the punishment of the damned is called "eternal"). But further with regard to the removal of all change, not only in act, which an "age" [*aevum*] too excludes, but even in potency. For the saints, through clinging to God, will obtain such stability from the divine gift that they cannot be changed—a stability God has by his nature, by reason of which he is eternal.[4]

As St. Thomas claims here, the punishment of the damned is eternal only in the sense that it lacks an end. By contrast, the eternal life of the saints is not simply without end, it is "a participation of eternity" (*participationem aeternitatis*). What does that mean? As St. Thomas notes in his answer to the objection, the eternal life of the saints involves the removal of all change, not just in act, but also in potency. It also transcends the *aevum*. So, as St. Thomas states in the body of the article:

> The vision of God ... cannot be an action measured by time in and of itself, since it is not successive; nor can it be measured by time on the part of the seer or on the part of the seen, since both are outside motion; hence it can be measured neither by time nor by the instant, which is the terminus of time. It cannot even be measured by an age [*aevo*], for an age [*aevum*], insofar as it is distinguished from eternity, pertains to immutable creatures, whereas the vision exceeds the natural power of the creature, since no creature by its natural endowments is capable of arriving at it; hence its proper measure is eternity itself [*ipsa aeternitas*].[5]

But at this point, one might object (with an objection from the *Sentences* commentary) as follows: an eternal being, by definition, cannot be measured by time. Because the being of every human person was at some

---

3. Ibid., obj. 4; trans. Peter A. Kwasniewski, Thomas Bolin, and Joseph Bolin, *On Love and Charity: Readings from the Commentary on the Sentences of Peter Lombard* (Washington, D.C.: The Catholic University of America Press, 2008), 359.

4. *In Sent* IV, d. 49, q. 1, a. 2, q.c. 3, ad 4 (361).

5. *In Sent* IV, d. 49, q. 1, a. 2, q.c. 3, resp. (360). See also *QQ* X, q. 2, a. 1, resp. Note that St. Thomas composed *Quodlibet* X just a little later than the *Sentences* commentary.

point measured by time, if a human person comes to enjoy the vision of God's essence in heaven, then there was a time in which that human person began enjoying that vision. Therefore, the beatific vision cannot participate in eternity in the sense of being an act that transcends time and the *aevum*.[6]

St. Thomas responds to this objection by granting that a human person cannot become eternal. That would be tantamount to becoming God, which is a contradiction in terms. The conclusion that a human person cannot become an eternal being follows from the premises of the objection, St. Thomas thinks. But it does not follow from those premises that a non-eternal being cannot, by a gift of grace, come to engage in an activity that is a *participation* in the activity of an eternal being in the sense that that participating activity transcends both time and aeveternity. God is eternal by nature, and because he is identical with his activity, only God is measured by eternity *simpliciter*. But human persons nonetheless *participate* in God's eternal activity insofar as they are gifted the beatific vision, an activity that transcends all change, both actual and potential. The beatific vision is thus an activity that transcends both time and aeveternity.[7]

What could it mean for a creature such as a human person to *participate* in the eternal activity of God the creator? Recall that the beatific vision is a created activity for St. Thomas, and so is an accident of a substance, namely, an intellectual creature. Furthermore, whereas there is no real difference between God's nature and God's act of intellect and will, there *is* a difference between the nature or substance of any human person and the actions of that human person. So St. Paul enjoying the beatific vision does not become eternal *qua* his nature or substance, for the nature or substance of St. Paul is such that he has a past. Furthermore, there is a time in which St. Paul begins to enjoy the beatific vision. But St. Paul's act which is the beatific vision itself cannot be measured *as a whole* by time or aeveternity. This is because the act (or operation) which is the beatific vision, once it begins in the soul of a saint, does not involve succession (time and change), but rather occurs all at once. Nor can it change. St. Thomas thus conceives of a human person's beatific vision as that creature's sharing *qua* activity in God's own perfect eternal

---

6. *In Sent IV*, d. 49, q. 1, a. 2, q.c. 3, obj. 3.
7. *In Sent IV*, d. 49, q. 1, a. 2, q.c. 3, ad 3.

activity. The beatific vision is measured by neither time nor aeveternity. It is rather a participated eternity.

ST. THOMAS'S MIDDLE-PERIOD WORK ON THE BEATIFIC VISION AS PARTICIPATED ETERNITY

I will consider now some texts from the middle period of St. Thomas's oeuvre. He treats the nature of the beatific vision where its relationship to time is concerned in *SCG* III.60–62. In III.60, St. Thomas offers arguments for his view that what is seen in the divine vision is seen all at once (*simul*), and not successively. His first argument defending that view can be read as follows:

(1) The created intellect, enjoying the vision of the divine substance, not only sees God as primary object of the vision, but all the species of things too as its secondary object.

(2) But the created intellect, having the beatific vision, understands all the species of things, not under an idea or similitude distinct from the essence of God, but in virtue of seeing the divine essence itself in the one beatific vision (proved in III.59).

(3) A vision corresponds to the principle of vision [self-evident].

(4) Therefore, if x and y are understood by numerically the same idea, then x and y are understood simultaneously through one act of knowing [from (3)].

(5) Therefore, if God as primary object and the species of all things as secondary object are understood by seeing the essence of God in the one beatific vision, then God as primary object and the species of all things as secondary object are understood simultaneously (*simul*) and not successively [from (4)].

(6) Therefore, God as primary object and the species of all things as secondary object are understood simultaneously and not successively [from (1), (2), and (5), MP].[8]

What does this argument have to do with the thesis that the beatific vision itself is not a successive experience of God? We might think that, for all this argument shows, St. John knows God and the species of all things

---

8. *SCG* III.60.1. See also *In Sent* II, d. 3, q. 3, a. 4; III, d. 14, a. 2, q.c. 4; *QDV*, q. 8, a. 4, ad 14 and ad 15; a. 14, resp.; *QQ* VII, q. 1, a. 2; *ST* I, q. 12, a. 10, resp.; q. 54, a. 2, resp.

simultaneously at time *t*, and St. John knows God and the species of all things simultaneously at *t*+1, and also at *t*+2, *ad infinitum*.

One way of showing that reading of the text is problematic is by drawing out a different implication from premise (3). Consider the following proposition, which follows from (3):

(4*) If an act A of knowing in person S is such that its object O and that by which O is understood are numerically identical, where O is eternal (in the Boethian sense), then S in A does not understand O successively [from (3)].

(5*) If the beatific vision in a created intellect is such that its object, that is, the essence of God, is numerically identical to that by which it understands the essence of God, where the essence of God is eternal (in the Boethian sense), then the created intellect in the beatific vision does not understand the essence of God successively [from (4*)].

Because, as we have seen in chapter 6, St. Thomas has reasons to think the antecedent of (5*) is true, he can conclude to the consequent of (5*).

Indeed, St. Thomas argues in just this sort of way in *SCG* III.61, which discusses the notion "that through the vision of God one becomes a partaker of eternal life."[9] St. Thomas notes that if an action exists in time, then this is either because the principle (i.e., starting point) of the action is something that exists in time or the terminus of the action exists in time. So, if the beatific vision in any sense exists in time, then the principles of the beatific vision in some sense exist in time, or that in which the beatific vision terminates (i.e., the object of the beatific vision) exists in time.

Now, the terminus of the beatific vision is the essence of God, which is eternal in the sense that it totally transcends time and aeveternity. But there are two principles of the creature's beatific vision: *God*, insofar as God raises the intellect up by grace so that it can see God himself by way of God (rather than by way of some mere created likeness of God)—as we saw in chapter 6, the beatific vision does not involve a medium *by which*—and the created intellect that experiences the vision. Of course, God's being transcends time and aeveternity. According to St. Thomas, the created intellect also is not in time. This is because the human intel-

---

9. "Quod per visionem Dei aliquis fit particeps vitae aeternae," trans. Vernon J. Bourke (Notre Dame, Ind.: University of Notre Dame Press, 1975) 3.1:200.

lect or soul has, like an angel, an incorruptible mode of being, and so the being of the intellect or soul, like the being of an angel, is aevaternal and so timeless. But we can also add, as St. Thomas does not here, that the human intellect or soul seeing God is given the grace of the *lumen gloriae* so that it has a disposition such that it can see the eternal God. In that case, it would seem to follow that the created intellect as principle of the beatific vision is raised even above aeveternity. That view corresponds with St. Thomas's conclusion of the argument here: "Therefore, this vision consists in a participation in eternity, as completely transcending time."[10] Recall that aeveternity does not completely transcend time, as time is compatible with it. Therefore, the beatific vision transcends both time and aeveternity.

In another argument in *SCG* III.61, St. Thomas begins by distinguishing temporal being from eternity: where temporal being necessarily involves succession, eternity is simultaneously whole. But the beatific vision does not involve temporal succession but rather occurs all at once. So St. Thomas concludes that the beatific vision is "a participation [*participatione*] in eternity." Now, the manner in which a creature can participate in eternity is intellectual (and so volitional). But intellectual activity is the activity of something that lives. Thus, the beatific vision consists in a participation in eternity that we can speak of as *eternal life*.

By speaking of a saint's participation in eternity as a kind of *life*, St. Thomas forestalls a possible objection to the idea that the beatific vision is an activity that transcends time, change, and aeveternity. For someone might aver that a timeless and immutable experience of God would necessarily be static and inert. But a static and inert experience of God would not be pleasant for a human person and so could not be essential to the attainment of perfect human happiness.

There are at least two ways that St. Thomas can respond to this sort of objection, given other things I have argued so far. Here is a first way of responding. Let us grant for the sake of argument that a static and inert existence would be less than satisfying for an intellectual creature. It does not follow from the fact that the beatific vision transcends time, change, and aeveternity, that it is static and inert. For the beatific vision is essentially an intellectual *activity*. But an activity is not inert or static

---

10. "Est igitur visio illa secundum aeternitatis participationem, utpote omnino transcendens tempus" (trans. Bourke, 201).

but dynamic. Furthermore, an *intellectual* act is the act of a *living* being. But the act of a living thing is not inert and static but *dynamic*. Finally, the beatific vision is an intellectual activity whereby the human person knows *God in the most intimate way possible*. However, an intellectual activity whereby the human person knows God in the most intimate way possible is not inert and static but dynamic. So the objection fails.

St. Thomas has a second way of responding to the objection above. For St. Thomas specifically, and the Catholic Christian tradition more generally,[11] God is timelessly eternal and absolutely immutable. But God is perfectly happy. Let us, for the sake of argument, take those views as givens. It follows that either a static and inert existence is compatible with the perfect happiness of an intellectual being, or, if a static and inert existence is incompatible with the perfect happiness of an intellectual being, then a timelessly eternal and absolutely immutable existence is not a static and inert existence, but rather a dynamic one. Now, the beatific vision of a human person is a participation in God's eternal activity. Furthermore, the beatific vision is the essence of the attainment of perfect human happiness. Therefore, either the beatific vision as static and inert is compatible with its being the essence of the attainment of perfect human happiness or, if what constitutes the essence of the attainment of perfect human happiness cannot be static and inert, then the beatific vision is not a static and inert reality, but rather a dynamic one. Therefore, because Catholics already believe that God's perfectly happy life is timelessly eternal and absolutely immutable, we can reasonably believe that the beatific vision, as a participation in God's eternal life and activity, is one that conduces to perfect human happiness.[12]

Consider next an argument that St. Thomas offers in *SCG* III.62. In this chapter, he offers arguments that those who come to participate in God's eternal life in heaven will never depart from it. His first argument for this thesis is relevant for our purposes. His argument begins from the assumption that, if one can lose the beatific vision once one comes to en-

---

11. See notes 3 and 19 in chapter 1, above.
12. Given that the human person's experience of God in heaven, *qua* the essential reward, is timeless and immutable, one might wonder whether human persons in heaven can be numerically identical with human persons in this life insofar as we take continuity of psychological experience to be a necessary condition for preserving personal identity through time and change, and insofar as our experience in this life is bounded by time. In addition, one might wonder whether any of our this-worldly experiences can help us to make sense of the beatific vision as an immutable, yet perfectly dynamic, reality. Chapter 17 below addresses these sorts of concerns.

gage in it, then the beatific vision is measured by time. But, St. Thomas continues, the beatific vision is in eternity (*in aeternitate*) and not in time. Therefore, it is impossible (*impossible*) for the blessed to lose the beatific vision once they begin to engage in it.

Again, we find St. Thomas affirming the view that the beatific vision of a creature is outside of time. But a variation on the argument above also shows that the beatific vision transcends aeveternity. Consider that aeveternity is the measure of what is immutable in some senses but mutable in others. For example, St. Thomas thinks that the angels are aeveternal beings, for they are substantially immutable (as immaterial beings they cannot undergo substantial change) but change and time can be added to them in the sense that they are capable of undergoing certain kinds of accidental changes.

What sort of accidental changes? For one, St. Thomas thinks that God created all of the angels in a state of grace, without the beatific vision. Some angels chose to remain in grace in that first moment of their existence and were immediately granted the beatific vision; those who chose not to remain in grace in that first moment were damned in the next.[13] St. Thomas has another example of an aeveternal being that is useful for my purpose of clarifying what an aeveternal being is. St. Thomas thinks that the heavenly bodies are aeveternal because they cannot undergo substantial change even though they do undergo accidental changes of place. So an aeveternal being is a being B that is immutable in some ways but capable of change in others. Now consider the beatific vision itself. It is in no sense capable of change; therefore, it is not aeveternal. Of course, because it begins at a certain point in the intellect of the intellectual creature, the beatific vision is not eternal *simpliciter*. Rather, as St. Thomas says in *SCG*, the beatific vision is "a participation in eternity" (*in aeternitate ... particeps*).

Another important source for St. Thomas's views on the nature of eternal life and the beatific vision where time is concerned is his *Compendium Theologiae*, a text that is roughly contemporaneous with *SCG*. In *CT* I, no. 149, St. Thomas argues that a person S having the beatific vision entails immutability in both S's intellect and will. Engaging in the beatific vision entails immutability in the intellect, as the intellect's questing comes to an end in knowing the essence of God. It entails immutability

---

13. See, e.g., *ST* I, q. 62, aa. 1–5; q. 63, a. 6.

in the will because, in seeing the essence of God, there is nothing left to be desired. But the will is subject to change because it desires what it does not yet possess.

As St. Thomas goes on to show in *CT* I, no. 150, the immutability of intellect and will in the beatific vision means that that vision is a participation in God's eternal life, understood as the perfect possession of unlimited life all at once. For without change, there is no time. But if there is no time, then there is no before and after. Therefore, if there is no change in the intellect and will of the saints where the beatific vision and its proper accidents are concerned, then there is no before and after in the beatific vision and its proper accidents.[14]

Now, as we saw in chapter 3, even the mode of being between eternity and time, aeveternity, depends upon the existence of time, as aeveternity is the mode of being of something x, where x is incorruptible and such that the gaining and losing of accidental features can be attributed to it. The beatific vision, though not a substance, is a perpetual—and so we might say *incorruptible*—activity to which accidental features cannot be predicated. Thus, as St. Thomas goes on to say in *CT* I, no. 150, in the intellect and will of the saint in heaven, "nothing remains but eternity, which is simultaneously whole [*tota simul*]. Therefore in his final consummation man attains eternal life, not only in the sense that he lives an immortal life in his soul—for this is a property of the rational soul by its very nature, as was shown above—but also in the sense that he is brought to the perfection of immobility."[15]

ST. THOMAS'S LATER WORK ON THE BEATIFIC VISION AS PARTICIPATED ETERNITY

Finally, let us look at what St. Thomas's later writings have to say about the nature of eternal life where its relation to time and aeveternity are concerned. Two sets of texts from *ST* will serve to represent St. Thomas's final views on the subject of time, aeveternity, eternity, and

---

14. St. Thomas is narrowly focused in this text on eternal life *qua* the essential reward. As chapters 9–13 below make clear, from the fact that the essential reward of the saints in heaven is immutable and timeless, it does not follow that all aspects of the heavenly reward of the saints are immutable and timeless. As we will see in those chapters, some aspects of the accidental reward involve the passage of time (albeit not as we experience it now).

15. Trans. Cyril Vollert, in *Light of Faith: The Compendium of Theology* (Manchester, N.H.: Sophia Institute Press), 168.

the beatific vision. The first set of texts comes from *ST* I, q. 10, which treats the divine eternity. In the third article of that question, St. Thomas asks whether to be eternal belongs to God alone. St. Thomas answers the question by noting that a thing is eternal to the extent that it is immutable. Now, God alone is altogether immutable and so, if one means by *eternal*, "eternal in the truest and most proper sense," then God alone is eternal.

But things other than God share in the eternity of God insofar as they are immutable. St. Thomas distinguishes four different ways in which something might participate in God's immutability and eternity. First, there are those things that are immutable and eternal in the sense that they do not—or will not—cease to exist. St. Thomas's example here is the earth, and he cites Ecclesiastes 1:4 to this effect. In other places, St. Thomas maintains that the angels,[16] human souls,[17] and the heavenly bodies,[18] respectively, are also immutable—and so eternal—in the sense that, once created, they will never cease to exist. Second, things can be said to share in God's eternity insofar as they last a long time, for example, mountains, rivers, hills. The third way something x can share in God's eternity is insofar as x is immutable in being, for example, as are the angels, human souls, composite human persons after the general resurrection, and the heavenly bodies. But the fourth way something can share in God's eternity and immutability is the greatest: insofar as something engages in the eternal and immutable operation of the beatific vision, enjoyed by the angels and the blessed in heaven. St. Thomas makes this clear by citing a favorite passage from St. Augustine's *De trinitate* XV, "As regards that vision of the Word, no changing thoughts exist in the Saints," and a passage from the Gospel of John, "This is eternal life, that they may know Thee the only true God" (17:3).[19] St. Thomas's con-

16. See, e.g., *ST* I, q. 50, a. 5.
17. See, e.g., *ST* I, q. 75, a. 6.
18. See, e.g., *CT* I, chaps. 170–71.
19. As cited in *ST* I, q. 10, a. 3, resp. (trans. English Dominicans, 42). See also *QDV*, q. 8, a. 4, obj. 15 and ad 15: "The beatific vision is measured by eternity, and for this reason is called eternal life. Now, since there is no 'before' or 'after' in eternity, these sequences are not in the beatific vision either. Hence, [in the vision] something cannot be known which was not known previously.... The beatific vision is that by which God is seen through His essence and things are seen in God. There is no succession in this vision, nor do angels make any progress in it or in beatitude. But they can progress in their vision of things through innate species or through the illumination of superior angels; and this vision is measured, not by eternity, but by time—not by that time which is the measure of the first mobile thing's motion, about which the Philosopher speaks—but by non-continuous time, such as that by which creation is measured. This is nothing other than

trast here between the substantial being of the angels and saints, on the one hand, and the beatific vision of the angels and saints, on the other hand, counts as another text where St. Thomas shows that he thinks the beatific vision is not only timeless, but also is a reality that transcends aeveternity.[20]

Now, let us say, for the sake of argument, that the substance of human persons in heaven is measured by aeveternity. But our question is not so much about the measurement of human persons *qua* substance in heaven as it is with the measurement of that *activity* in which the attainment of the essence of perfect human happiness consists, namely, the beatific vision. In one place, St. Thomas explicitly makes this sort of contrast between an intellectual creature's substantial nature and activity in heaven. In the context, St. Thomas is responding to the following objection: "It seems that aeveternity is the same as time. For Augustine says (*Gen. ad lit.* viii, 20, 22, 23), that *God moves the spiritual through time.* But aeveternity is said to be the measure of spiritual substances. Therefore time is the same as aeveternity."[21] Here is St. Thomas's answer: "Spiritual creatures as regards successive affections and intelligences are measured by time. Hence also Augustine says (*Gen. ad lit.* viii, 20, 22, 23) that to be moved through time, is to be moved by affections. But as regards their nature they are measured by aeveternity; whereas as regards the vision of glory, they have a share of eternity [*participant aeternitatem*]."[22] St. Thomas thus makes it clear that, in his view, the measurement of the beatific vision itself is not aeveternity, but something greater than it: insofar as angels and human persons have the vision of glory, they participate in God's eternal and immutable activity, and in a way that transcends both time and aeveternity.

The second set of texts representative of St. Thomas's last known views on time, eternity, and the beatific vision come from *ST* I-II. In q. 5,

---

the difference between 'before' and 'after' in the creation of things or in the succession of acts of understanding had by angels" (trans. Mulligan, 331 and 338). As we have seen, something such as "the succession of acts of understanding had by the angels" are those times "annexed" to angels such that angels exist in aeveternity. Thus, the beatific vision, which is "measured by eternity," transcends aeveternity.

20. *ST* I, q. 10, a. 3, resp.: "Quaedam autem amplius participant de ratione aeternitatis, inquantum habent intransmutabilitatem vel secundum esse, vel ulterius secundum operationem, sicut Angeli et beati, qui verbo fruuntur."

21. *ST* I, q. 10, a. 5, obj. 1 (trans. English Dominicans, 43).

22. *ST* I, q. 10, a. 5, ad 1 (trans. English Dominicans, 44). For St. Thomas on the affections (*affectiones*) of the angels, see note 124 in chapter 4, above.

a. 4, St. Thomas asks a now-familiar question, "can happiness, once possessed, be lost?" When it comes to perfect happiness, St. Thomas answers "no." He gives two reasons for this view. First, it follows from the general notion of happiness. For, if perfect happiness could be lost, then the saints would necessarily fear losing such happiness. But fear is an evil that is incompatible with perfect happiness. Second, it follows from that in which the attainment of the essence of perfect happiness specifically consists, namely, the beatific vision. For, if St. John, who is perfectly happy, were to lose such happiness, this would be on account of something St. John does, something God does, or because of what something x does, where x is neither St. John nor God.

But it is psychologically impossible for St. John to no longer will to know God—and so to sin—after he comes to have the vision of God's essence, for this vision satisfies St. John's every desire. Furthermore, God's taking the beatific vision from St. John could only be by way of a just punishment. But St. John having the beatific vision necessarily wills in accord with God's will. Finally, and importantly for our purposes, something other than God or St. John could not take the beatific vision away from St. John. This is because "the mind that is united to God is raised above all other things: and consequently no other agent can sever the mind from that union. Therefore it seems unreasonable that as time goes on, man should pass from happiness to misery, and vice versa; because such like vicissitudes of time can only be for such things as are subject to time and movement" (*subiacent tempori et motui*).[23] The last line in the text implies what we have seen in earlier texts. The beatific vision cannot be lost because it is not subject to change. The beatific vision is clearly, then, not in time. But the aeveternal too is subject to change insofar as accidental features can be annexed to it. Therefore, the beatific vision is also not measured by aeveternity. In the beatific vision, the intellectual creature participates in God's own eternal and immutable activity.

St. Thomas's answer to the first objection (in q. 5, a. 4) represents a nice summary of his teaching on the nature of the beatific vision where time and change are concerned. The objector argues that human persons can lose perfect happiness because happiness is a perfection, perfections

---

23. *ST* I-II, q. 5, a. 4, resp. (trans. English Dominicans, 612). Compare with the parallel argument from *SCG* III.62.1–2.

exist in a thing perfected according to the mode of the thing perfected, and human persons are by nature mutable. St. Thomas answers the objector, first, by noting that perfect happiness differs from other sorts of perfection insofar as it excludes any possible defect, for example, being able to lose said perfection. Furthermore, St. Thomas does not deny the premise in the objection that human persons, by nature, are mutable. But human persons are made perfectly (and so unchangeably) happy in the beatific vision by divine power, "which raises man to the participation of eternity which transcends all change."[24]

As we have seen, St. Thomas teaches consistently throughout his career that the beatific vision is a participation in God's own eternal life. As we have seen, this means that, although human persons in heaven are not eternal according to their substantial being, they do engage in an activity, the beatific vision, which cannot be measured by either time or aeveternity. Rather, the beatific vision, like God's perfect being, is a reality that is simultaneously whole. Just as, in Boethius's definition, eternity is the unlimited and perfect possession of life, all at once, the beatific vision is *participated* eternal life: a participated, unlimited, and perfect possession of life, all at once. Thus, as St. John says: "Beloved, we are God's children now; what we will be has not yet been revealed. What we do know is this: when he is revealed, we will be like him, for we will see him as he is" (1 Jn 3:2).

---

24. "Faciente hoc virtute divina, quae hominem sublevat in participationem aeternitatis transcendentis omnem mutationem." *ST* I-II, q. 5, a. 4, ad 1 (trans. English Dominicans, 612).

8

The Essential Reward IV

THE PROPER ACCIDENTS OF THE
BEATIFIC VISION

I have explored St. Thomas's views concerning the essence of the essential reward—the beatific vision—in some detail. Before we leave the topic of St. Thomas on the essential reward, there are three additional aspects of the essential reward that require some explicit treatment: the proper accidents of the beatific vision; the *lumen gloriae* as medium *under which* (*sub quo*) the saints in heaven see the essence of God; and the view that some intellectual creatures have a greater beatific vision than others, and so are more perfectly happy in heaven than others.

THE PROPER ACCIDENTS OF THE BEATIFIC VISION: DELIGHT, JOY, LOVE, AND RIGHT WILLING

Although the beatific vision is the *essence* of the essential reward, the essential reward *also consists* of those acts of will that follow as a consequence of enjoying the beatific vision.[1] St. Thomas thinks that the saints necessarily engage in such acts of will, as they result from being united in the beatific vision to the perfect good.[2] Those acts of will, or perhaps, in some cases, effects of acts of will,[3] that are component parts of the essential reward include the following: delight (*delectatio*),[4] en-

---

1. See the texts cited in note 72 in chapter 4, above.
2. See, e.g., *In Sent* IV, d. 49, q. 3, a. 1, q.c. 4, resp.
3. See ibid.
4. *In Sent* IV, d. 49, q. 1, a. 1, q.c. 2; a. 2, q.c. 4, resp.; a. 3, q.c. 4, ad 1; q. 3; *ST Suppl.*, q. 95, a. 5; the sermon *Beata gens* 2.3.3; *SCG* III.26.12; *In 1 Cor* 15, lect. 3, n. 937; *CT* I, chaps. 107 and 165; *ST* I,

joyment (*frutio*),⁵ love (*amare* or *dilectio*),⁶ charity (*caritas*),⁷ joy (*gaudium*),⁸ peace (*pax*),⁹ benevolence (*benevolentia*),¹⁰ rightness of will (*rectitudo voluntatis*, i.e., willing in accordance with God's will and the eternal law),¹¹ and praise (*laus*).¹² Although many of the names of these intellectual appetites correspond with the names of sensitive appetites, that is, passions, emotions, or feelings, those appetites that are aspects of the essential reward are intellectual appetites, that is, acts of will, and not passions, emotions, or feelings, in the strict sense of those terms.¹³ This is because, for St. Thomas, passions, emotions, or feelings, in the strict sense, are linked with bodily activities¹⁴ and the essential reward, as we have seen, does not involve bodily activity (although glorified bodily activities are compatible with the essential reward, and will accompany it at, and after, the general resurrection).

That act of will that is a component part of the essential reward St. Thomas most often speaks about is *delight* (*delectatio*). For St. Thomas, the *delectatio* of the saints is a resting (*quietatio*) of the will in the ultimate end as a reality attained.¹⁵ St. Thomas often contrasts *delectatio* as an act of will with intellectual *desire*. If Sam *desires* (*desiderat*) a thing, he wants that thing but does not possess it. But if Sam *delights* in a thing, he possesses the object of his love and wills to rest in the possessing of it.¹⁶

St. Thomas has three different, but logically compatible, ways of speaking about the logical relation between the beatific vision and the delight that results from it. First, the beatific vision and the delight that

---

q. 20, a. 1, resp.; the sermon *Osanna filio David* 3.3; *ST* I-II, q. 2, a. 6, resp. and ad 1; q. 3, a. 4, resp.; q. 4, aa. 1 and 2; *In NE* X, lect. 6, n. 2031; *In Jn* 14, lect. 1, n. 1854.

5. See, e.g., *CT* I, chap. 165; *ST* I-II, q. 3, a. 1, resp.; II-II, q. 27, a. 8, resp.

6. For *amare*, see, e.g., *SCG* III.26.12; *ST* I, q. 20, a. 1, resp.; I-II, q. 4, a. 4, resp.; II-II, q. 27, a. 2, resp. For *dilectio* see, e.g., *CT* I, chap. 165; *In Mt* 5, lect. 2, nn. 433 and 436; *ST* I-II, q. 3, a. 4, ad 4.

7. See, e.g., *In Sent* IV, d. 49, q. 1, a. 1, q.c. 2, ad 3; *ST* I-II, q. 4, a. 2, ad 3; q. 67, a. 6, ad 3; II-II, q. 24, a. 7, ad 3.

8. See, e.g., *In Sent* IV, d. 49, q. 1, a. 1, q.c. 2, s.c.; *ST* I, q. 20, a. 1, resp.; I-II, q. 3, a. 4, resp.; II-II, q. 28, a. 1.

9. See, e.g., *ST* I, q. 29, a. 3; I-II, q. 3, a. 4, ad 1.

10. *ST* II-II, q. 27, a. 2, resp.

11. See, e.g., *ST* I-II, q. 3, a. 4, ad 5; q. 4, a. 4, resp.; q. 67, a. 1.

12. See, e.g., *In Sent* IV, d. 49, q. 4, a. 5, q.c. 1, ad 6 (*ST Suppl.*, q. 95, a. 5, ad 6).

13. See, e.g., *In Sent* IV, d. 49, q. 3, a. 1, q.c. 1.

14. See, e.g., ibid. and *ST* I, q. 20, a. 1, ad 1 and ad 2.

15. See, e.g., *In Sent* IV, d. 49, q. 3, a. 1, q.c. 4, resp.; *SCG* III.26.15; *CT* I, chap. 107; *ST* I-II, q. 2, a. 6, ad 1; q. 4, a. 2, resp.

16. See, e.g., *In Sent* IV, d. 49, q. 1, a. 1, q.c. 2, resp.; *SCG* III.26.12; *ST* I, q. 19, a. 1, ad 2; I-II, q. 3, a. 4, resp.

results from it are related, he thinks, as a formal cause to its effect.[17] Because a cause ranks higher than its effect, this is one reason St. Thomas offers for why the beatific vision, and not delight, is the essence of the essential reward.[18]

Second, St. Thomas sometimes describes *delectatio* as a quasi-formal completion (*quasi formaliter complens*) of the *ratio* of beatitude,[19] where the substance (*substantia*) of beatitude is the beatific vision[20] and delight supervenes (*supervenit*) on the beatific vision, perfecting and decorating it (*perficiens et decorans eam*).[21] In saying this—note his use of *quasi*—St. Thomas makes it very clear that the addition of *delectatio* to the beatific vision does not change, or cause, the species of the beatific vision.[22] To explain what he has in mind, St. Thomas is fond of citing Aristotle's example of the logical relation between youth and beauty (or vigor). As beauty (or vigor) is a fitting decoration of a young person, but it is not the essence of what it means to be young, so delight is a fitting decoration of the beatific vision, but it is not the essence of perfect beatitude.[23]

Third, in later texts, St. Thomas often refers to delight as a concomitant accident of,[24] or as a proper (*per se*) accident of,[25] or as following as a logical consequence of[26] the attainment of the essence of perfect happiness, that is, the beatific vision. Just as risibility is a proper accident of, although not itself the essence of, a human person, so the essence of perfect human happiness is the beatific vision, whereas delight in the vision is like a proper accident of the beatific vision (and so not itself the essence of perfect human happiness or the essential reward).

---

17. See, e.g., *SCG* III.26.12; *CT* I, chap. 165; *ST* I-II, q. 4, a. 2, s.c. and resp.
18. See, e.g., *ST* I-II, q. 4, a. 2, s.c. and resp.
19. See, e.g., *In Sent* IV, d. 49, q. 1, a. 1, q.c. 2, resp. and ad 2.
20. See ibid. See also *In Sent* IV, d. 49, q. 1, a. 3, q.c. 4, ad 1; *ST Suppl.*, q. 95, a. 5, resp.; *CT* I, chap. 107; *ST* I-II, q. 4, a. 1, ad 3; a. 2, ad 1; *In NE* X, lect. 6, n. 2031.
21. See, e.g., *In Sent* IV, d. 49, q. 1, a. 1, q.c. 2, ad 5; *CT* I, chap. 107; *ST* I-II, q. 4, a. 1, ad 3; *In NE* X, lect. 6, n. 2031.
22. See, e.g., *ST* I-II, q. 4, a. 2, ad 1.
23. See, e.g., *In Sent* IV, d. 49, q. 1, a. 1, q.c. 2, ad 2; *SCG* III.26.3; *ST* I-II, q. 4, a. 2, ad 1; *In NE* X, lect. 6, n. 2031.
24. See, e.g., *SCG* III.26.19; *CT* I, chap. 107; *ST* I-II, q. 4, a. 1 and ad 3; a. 2, ad 1. See also *CT* I, chap. 165; *ST* II-II, q. 175, a. 3, ad 4.
25. See, e.g., *ST* I-II, q. 2, a. 6, resp.; q. 3, a. 4, resp. In the passage in *ST* I-II, q. 3, a. 4, resp., St. Thomas calls delight "the quasi-proper accident" (*quasi per se accidens*) of the beatific vision, thereby emphasizing the close connection between the beatific vision as essence of the essential reward and delight and other acts of will as nonessential component parts of the essential reward.
26. See, e.g., *ST* I-II, q. 2, a. 6, resp.; q. 3, a. 4, ad 1 and ad 3; q. 4, a. 1, ad 2; a. 2, s.c. and ad 1, ad 3.

A couple of final points about willing in heaven.[27] First, it is worth noting that, for St. Thomas, (acts of) the powers of intellect and will always come and go together.[28] Therefore, insofar as an act of will such as love, joy, or delight is a concomitant or proper accident of the beatific vision, and the beatific vision is an activity of a created intellect that transcends both time and aeveternity, those acts of will in heaven that are component parts of the essential reward also transcend both time and aeveternity.[29]

Second, that certain acts of will are concomitant accidents of the vision of the essence of God has interesting implications. Because the primary object of the beatific vision is the essence of God, which is perfect goodness, the saint that sees the essence of God cannot but will rightly as a consequence of seeing the essence of God. In other words, the saint enjoying the beatific vision cannot sin.[30] Here follows a formalization of a first argument for that thesis:

(1) If a person S's perfect happiness can come to an end, then S can be perfectly happy and S is ignorant of the fact that S's perfect happiness can come to an end, or S can be perfectly happy and S is not ignorant of the fact that S's perfect happiness can come to an end [self-evident].

(2) If S is not ignorant of the fact that S's perfect happiness can come to an end, then S would be anxious about losing perfect happiness, and such anxiety is itself incompatible with S's perfect happiness [assumption].

(3) Therefore, it is not the case that S can be perfectly happy and S is not ignorant of the fact that S's perfect happiness can come to an end [from (2)].

(4) Therefore, if a person S's perfect happiness can come to an end, then S can be perfectly happy and S is ignorant of the fact that S's perfect happiness can come to an end [from (1) and (3)].

(5) But, if S is ignorant about the fact that S's perfect happiness can come to an end, then S is ignorant about an important fact about S's existence and such ignorance is inconsistent with S being perfectly happy [assumption].

---

27. For more on willing in heaven, see, e.g., my "Making the Best Even Better" and Pawl and Timpe, "Incompatibilism, Sin, and Free Will in Heaven."
28. See, e.g., *ST* I, q. 19, a. 1, resp.
29. See, e.g., *CT* I, chaps. 149–50.
30. See, e.g., *SCG* IV.92; *CT* I, chap. 166; *ST* I-II, q. 4, a. 4, resp.

(6) Therefore, it is not the case that S can be perfectly happy and that S is ignorant of the fact that S's perfect happiness can come to an end [from (5)].

(7) Therefore, a person S's perfect happiness cannot come to an end [from (4) and (6), MT].[31]

(8) Perfect happiness is intellectual and volitional union with God, who is perfect goodness, which, minimally, means that the person S who is perfectly happy does not sin, as sinning entails not willing in union with God [assumption].

(9) Therefore, if S sins, then S is not perfectly happy [from (8)].

(10) Therefore, if a perfectly happy person S can sin, then S's perfect happiness can come to an end [from (9)].

(11) Therefore, the person who is perfectly happy cannot sin [from (7) and (10)].

(12) Therefore, it follows that, if S has the beatific vision, then S cannot sin [from (8) and (11)].[32]

There is a second argument to support the position that those who have the beatific vision cannot sin. We necessarily will our happiness; we cannot will not to be happy. But the person S who has the beatific vision knows that God is the object of perfect human happiness insofar as S knows that God is perfect goodness. Seeing and willing perfect goodness as the saint does, no apparent good that entailed sinning could hold the remotest psychological interest for the saint. Therefore, the person having the beatific vision cannot sin.[33]

ST. THOMAS ON THE *LUMEN GLORIAE*

According to St. Thomas, the essential reward, or the attainment of perfect human happiness, in heaven consists of the beatific vision and the delight that flows from it. Although St. Thomas thinks that God prepares the saints for the beatific vision by imparting graces to them *in*

---

31. For the argument in premises (1)–(7), see, e.g., *SCG* III.62; *CT* I, ch. 166; *ST* I-II, q. 5, a. 4, resp.

32. For arguments like the one consisting of premises (8)–(12), see, e.g., *SCG* IV.92 and *CT* I, chap. 166.

33. See, e.g., *SCG* IV.92; *CT* I, chap. 166; *ST* I-II, q. 4, a. 4, resp. For a defense of this thesis against objections, see my "Making the Best Even Better" and Pawl and Timpe, "Incompatibilism, Sin, and Free Will in Heaven."

this life—indeed, as one of the beatitudes puts it, "blessed are the pure in heart, for they will see God" (Mt 5:8)[34]—the saints' having the beatific vision also requires that God give the saints an additional special grace *in heaven*, one that perfects their intellects so as to make it possible for them to engage in the beatific vision. This special grace is called the light of glory (*lumen gloriae*).

To begin my discussion of the *lumen gloriae*, recall that St. Thomas thinks that many forms of cognition are mediated in various ways. Some forms of cognition involve a medium *under which* (*sub quo*). For example, in seeing with the corporeal eye, the medium *under which* is light. Other forms of cognition also involve a medium *by which* (*quo*), that is, some sort of intentional likeness of the object cognized. For example, St. Thomas thinks that, when it comes to intellectual knowledge in this life, the medium *by which* human persons cognize something is an intelligible species of the object cognized. Finally, there is sometimes a medium *from which* (*a quo*) one obtains knowledge. For example, if John sees Jane in a mirror, then the mirror is a medium *from which* for John's cognition of Jane.[35] According to St. Thomas, the *lumen gloriae* is the medium *under which* the essence of God is seen. It is a created supernatural disposition in an intellectual creature requisite for joining that creature to God so that no medium *by which*—no created concept—is required for the beatific vision.[36]

Note the connection between the *lumen gloriae* and the beatific vision being a cognition of the essence of God without a medium *by which*. As we have seen, St. Thomas thinks that nothing short of an intellectual apprehension of the essence of God such that God unites the soul of the human person to God without a medium *by which* will make human persons perfectly happy. But being united to God in this radical way is beyond the natural powers of intellectual creatures and requires that God prepare the intellect of such intellectual creatures in heaven by grace such that God can play the role in the cognition of the essence of God that concepts—creatures of some sort—play in natural ways of creaturely knowing. The *lumen gloriae* is the grace that God gives to a saint in heaven

---

34. See, e.g., *In Mt* 5, lect. 2, nn. 407–8, 412, 433–35. Chapter 17 below says more about how St. Thomas thinks that God prepares human persons for the beatific vision by imparting graces to human persons in this life.

35. See, e.g., *QDV*, q. 18, a. 1, ad 1.

36. See, e.g., *In Sent* IV, d. 49, q. 2, a. 6, resp. and ad 4; *ST* I, q. 12, a. 2, resp.; a. 5, resp.

that disposes the intellect of the saint such that God can play the role in the beatific vision that concepts play for human persons in this life.[37]

Is the *lumen gloriae* something created? Yes, because in order for something x to perform an act that exceeds x's natural powers, x needs added to it a disposition that enables x to act in this manner. Recall that the beatific vision is an act of the saint in heaven. In addition, the beatific vision is an act that is not natural for *any* intellectual creature. It is therefore, a supernatural act. Therefore, if the saint in heaven is to engage in the beatific vision, that saint needs a supernatural disposition added to her intellect "in order that it may be raised up to such a great and sublime height."[38] Because the *lumen gloriae* is a disposition of the created intellect of the saint who sees God, the *lumen gloriae* is itself a creature.

In talking about the *lumen gloriae*, St. Thomas sometimes employs another way of speaking: the *lumen gloriae* is that created grace which makes the saints in heaven disposed to becoming perfectly *deiform*, that is, perfectly like unto God in seeing the essence of God.[39] As St. Thomas points out, this is what the Apostle John teaches: "when he is revealed, we will be like him, for we will see him as he is" (1 Jn 3:2).[40]

---

37. See ibid.

38. *ST* I, q. 12, a. 5, resp. (trans. English Dominicans, 53). See also *SCG* III.53.

39. See, e.g., *ST* I, q. 12, a. 5, resp. and ad 3. See also *Beata gens* 2.31. Chapter 17 below says more about St. Thomas on the deiform nature of Christians and growth in deiformity as culminating in the beatific vision in heaven. For a detailed treatment of St. Thomas's doctrine of deiformity, see, e.g., A.N. Williams, *The Ground of Union: Deification in Aquinas and Palamas* (New York: Oxford University Press, 1999), and Daria Spezzano, *The Glory of God's Grace: Deification According to St. Thomas Aquinas* (Ave Maria, Fla.: Sapientia Press, 2015). See also Andrew Hofer, "Deification in the Dominican Tradition: Albert, Thomas, and Catherine," in *Called to be Children of God: The Catholic Theology of Human Deification*, ed. David Meconi and Carl E. Olson (San Francisco, Calif.: Ignatius Press, 2006), 101–17.

40. See, e.g., *ST* I, q. 12, a. 5, resp. St. Thomas also sometimes speaks of the referent of the *lumen gloriae*, following a long tradition, as one of three dowries (*dotes*) of the soul (see, e.g., *In Sent* IV, d. 49, q. 4, a. 5, q.c. 1, resp., found in *ST Suppl.*, q. 95, a. 5, resp.) conferred on the saints in heaven insofar as the church—and each individual saint—is the bride of Christ the bridegroom. See, e.g., *In Sent* I, d. 1, a. 1, resp.; *In Sent* IV, d. 49, q. 4, a. 4 (*ST Suppl.*, q. 95, a. 4); *ST* I, q. 12, a. 7, ad 1; I-II, q. 4, a. 3; *In Heb* 1, lect. 6, n. 88. As the dowries of carnal marriage are meant to ease the burden of such marriage, according to St. Thomas's reception of Christian tradition, the *heavenly* dowries of the soul refer to graced dispositions in the souls of human persons in heaven given by God to facilitate the saints in heaven taking delight in God in the beatific vision; see, e.g., *In Sent* IV, d. 49, q. 4, a. 1, resp. (*ST Suppl.*, q. 95, a. 1, resp.) and a. 5, q.c. 1, resp. (*ST Suppl.*, q. 95, a. 5, resp.). The *lumen gloriae* corresponds with the dowry of the soul known as *visio*, the dowry of *visio* being the disposition in the human soul that enables the saint to delight in the beatific vision itself; see, e.g., *In Sent* IV, d. 49, q. 4, a. 2, resp. and ad 3 (*ST Suppl.*, q. 95, a. 2, resp. and ad 3); a. 5 (*ST Suppl.*, q. 95, a. 5, resp.). The other two dowries of the soul are *delectio* (or *fruitio* in other authors), which dowry of the soul is a disposition in the beatified soul facilitating affection for God as fitting object of perfect human

Why do intellectual creatures need the disposition of the *lumen gloriae* in order to be united to God without a medium *by which*? One argument that St. Thomas offers goes as follows. Just as a being that does not have intellect cannot cognize universals, or a soul joined to matter cannot naturally know intellectual substances directly, so no intellectual creature can naturally know the essence of God. This is because intellectual creatures are composite beings (composites of essence and *esse*) and so naturally know composite beings, that is, things that need not exist. But God is absolutely simple, or "subsisting Being itself" (*ipsum esse subsistens*). Therefore, intellectual creatures cannot naturally know the essence of God. It therefore follows that if intellectual creatures are to see the essence of God they must be given a special grace in order to do so, which tradition calls the *lumen gloriae*, whereby the created intellect is made deiform so as to be able to see the essence of God.[41]

Although intellectual creatures such as human persons cannot naturally see the essence of God, St. Thomas nonetheless thinks that intellectual creatures *qua* intellectual creatures can know the essence of God, if God gives them the supernatural power to do so. St. Thomas argues for that view in *SCG* as follows:

> The divine substance is not beyond the capacity of the created intellect in such a way that it is altogether foreign to it, as sound is from the object of vision, or as immaterial substance is from sense power; in fact, the divine substance is the first intelligible object and the principle of all intellectual cognition. But it is beyond the capacity of the created intellect, in the sense that it exceeds its power, just as sensible objects of extreme character are beyond the capacity of sense power. Hence, the Philosopher says that "our intellect is to the most evident things, as the eye of the owl is to the light of the sun." So, a created intellect needs to be strengthened by a divine light in order that it may be able to see the divine essence.[42]

---

happiness, and *comprehensio* (or *fruitio* in some other authors), which dowry is a disposition in the beatified soul facilitating delight in the union between God and the soul in the beatific vision; see, e.g., *In Sent* IV, d. 49, q. 4, a. 5, q.c. 1, resp. (*ST Suppl.*, q. 95, a. 5, resp.). Finally, St. Thomas recognizes that the Christian tradition sometimes also speaks of dowries of the body (see, e.g., *In Sent* IV, d. 49, q. 4, a. 5, q.c. 2, resp.) and sometimes speaks of the four characteristic properties of glorified bodies, namely, impassibility, subtlety, agility, and clarity, as the dowries of the body (see, e.g., *In Sent* IV, d. 49, q. 4, a. 5, q.c. 3, resp.). See chapter 11 below for a detailed treatment of the four characteristic properties of the glorified body.

41. See, e.g., *In Sent* III, d. 14, q. 1, a. 1, q.c. 3; IV, d. 49, q. 2, a. 6; *QDV*, q. 8, a. 3; q. 18, a. 1, ad 1; q. 20, a. 2; *SCG* III.52–53; *CT* I, chap. 105; *ST* I, q. 12, a. 4, resp.; a. 5, resp.; II-II, q. 175, a. 3, ad 2.

42. *SCG* III.54.8, trans. Bourke, 3.1:184. See also *ST* I, q. 12, a. 4, ad 3.

Because intellectual creatures have intellect, they are capable, if given the requisite graced disposition by God, of seeing the essence of God in the beatific vision without a medium *by which*, God himself functioning, as it were, as the intelligible species of the beatific vision. According to St. Thomas, this requisite grace in the created intellect is the *lumen gloriae*.[43]

But if God himself functions, as it were, as the concept by which the saints apprehend the essence of God in the beatific vision, why cannot God simply function, as it were, as the disposition perfecting the intellect in the beatific vision? One way of showing the need for the *lumen gloriae* is as follows: without positing the *lumen gloriae* as a disposition in the created intellect having the beatific vision, there is no principled way of distinguishing God and the intellectual creature having the beatific vision.

To see this, first consider God's cognition of his essence. Because God's intellectual activity is identical to himself,[44] God's cognition of himself is wholly direct and unmediated. Therefore, God requires no medium *from which* to know himself (unlike human persons in this life after the Fall, who invariably know God in creatures functioning as a kind of mirror of the creator). Given the divine simplicity, God also does not require a medium *by which* to know his essence (as we have seen, God makes it possible for intellectual creatures to see the essence of God by way of the essence of God too).[45] Finally, given the divine simplicity, God also knows his essence without a medium *under which*. According to St. Thomas, God is the light under which he sees himself.[46] God's knowledge of himself is therefore distinguished from that of all creatures, including those intellectual creatures having the beatific vision, insofar as God's knowledge of himself does not, whereas any creature's knowledge of God does, require a medium *under which* the essence of God is seen. But in speaking of a medium *from which*, a medium *by which*, and

---

43. St. Thomas thinks that the idea is scriptural. He cites, for example, Ps 35:10 [36:9], "In your light we see light" (trans. English Dominicans, 52) in *In Sent* IV, d. 49, q. 2, a. 4, s.c.; a. 6, resp.; *QDV*, q. 8, a. 3, resp.; q. 18, a. 1, ad 1; *SCG* III.53.7; *In 2 Cor* 12, lect. 1, n. 455; *CT* I, chap. 105; *ST* I, q. 12, a. 2; a. 5, s.c.; *QQ* I, q. 1, resp.; *ST* II-II, q. 175, a. 3, ad 2. He also cites Rv 21:23, "The glory of God hath enlightened it [i.e., the society of the blessed who see God]" (trans. English Dominicans, 53), in *ST* I, q. 12, a. 5, resp.; and finally makes reference to Rv 22:5, "The city [i.e., of the blessed] hath no need of the sun, nor of the moon ... for the glory of God hath enlightened it" (trans. Bourke, 3.1:182), in *SCG* III.53.7.
44. See, e.g., *SCG* I.45; *CT* I, chap. 31; *ST* I, q. 14, a. 4; *In Meta* XII, lect. 11.
45. See, e.g., *QDV*, q. 18, a. 1, ad 1; *SCG* I.45; *CT* I, chap. 31; *ST* I, q. 14, a. 4; *In Meta* XII, lect. 11.
46. See, e.g., *QDV*, q. 18, a. 1, ad 1.

a medium *under which*, we have exhausted the ways in which knowledge involves a medium.[47] Therefore, God's knowledge of himself is distinguished from that of the intellectual creature having the beatific vision as follows: God's knowledge of himself is *completely* direct and unmediated, whereas the knowledge of the intellectual creature having the beatific vision, although less indirect or mediated than any other possible sort of creaturely knowledge of God, does require a medium *under which*, namely, the *lumen gloriae*, in order to see the essence of God.

Now we are in a position to see the importance of the *lumen gloriae* as a created disposition in the intellectual creature, enabling the beatific vision. For consider the following proposition:

(13) In the beatific vision of an intellectual creature C, (a) C sees the essence of God without a medium *from which* and (b) God joins C to the essence of God such that God functions, as it were, as the medium *by which* C knows the essence of God (so that, given the divine simplicity, C knows God without a medium *by which*), and (c) God joins C to the essence of God such that God functions, as it were, as the medium *under which* C knows the essence of God (so that, given the divine simplicity, C knows God without a medium *under which*).

Given what I have said about God's cognition of God's essence and the various media whereby some forms of cognition take place, if (13) is true, then the creature is, or becomes, God. But no creature is God, nor can a creature become God. Therefore, (13) is false. Because, as we have seen, St. Thomas offers good reasons for thinking that both (a) and (b) in (13) are true, it makes sense to say with St. Thomas that (c) in (13) is false. Positing the *lumen gloriae* as a created disposition in the intellectual creature whereby the creature sees the essence of God by way of a medium *under which* is crucial to preserving the distinction between God and the intellectual creature having the beatific vision.

But someone might object: why do we need to posit the *lumen gloriae* as a created disposition in the intellectual creature having the beatific vision? Why not distinguish God and the intellectual creature having the beatific vision as follows: God by nature knows his essence by way of himself whereas creatures are gifted with God functioning as the me-

---

47. Alternatively, we can reasonably assume the following: if there is any kind of a medium M for knowledge other than a medium *from which*, *by which*, or *under which*, neither God's knowledge of himself nor the intellectual creature's knowledge of God in the beatific vision involves M.

dium *by which* the essence of God is known in the beatific vision? With this distinction between God by nature knowing his essence by his essence and creatures knowing God's essence not by nature, but by gift, we can distinguish God and intellectual creatures having the beatific vision without positing the *lumen gloriae*.

St. Thomas has a number of ways of responding to an objection such as this. For example, St. Thomas argues that in order for an *x* and a *y* to be united in a certain way W, where *x* and *y* were not originally united in way W, *x* or *y* must change. But God does not (typically) create intellectual creatures having the beatific vision. Because God is absolutely immutable, in order for the saints in heaven to have the beatific vision, the intellects of those creatures coming to have the beatific vision must be changed. That change in the created intellect is the introduction of the *lumen gloriae*.[48]

In another place,[49] St. Thomas argues that, where an activity takes place in a potency, for example, a subject, it only takes place in a potency that is suited for that act. For example, not just any matter can be the matter for the intellectual soul of a human person: for example, according to the order of nature, such matter is the fusion of a human sperm cell and a human ovum.[50] But the beatific vision is an act of seeing the essence of God such that God functions, as it were, as the intelligible species by which the creature sees the essence of God. Such an act requires a subject suitable for that act. But God is not in potency. Therefore, in order for a created intellect to engage in the beatific vision, that intellect must take on a created disposition that makes the intellect suited for the vision. But this cannot be a natural (or preternatural) disposition in the

---

48. *SCG* III.53.4. St. Thomas goes on to argue that even if a creature were created having the beatific vision, it would still require a created disposition enabling the possibility of the vision. For that intellect would still be in potency to the vision in the sense that it is not necessary that it have such a vision. Therefore, in order to explain why a creature actually has the beatific vision, its intellect needs a created disposition such that it is a suitable subject for the vision. This is not an idle question for St. Thomas, for as we have seen, he thinks the soul of Christ has the beatific vision from its very beginning (see, e.g., the texts cited in chapter 5, note 64, above).

49. *QDV*, q. 8, a. 3, resp.

50. For arguments in defense of such a Thomistic embryology, see Samuel B. Condic and Maureen L. Condic, *Human Embryos, Human Beings: A Scientific and Philosophical Approach* (Washington, D.C.: The Catholic University of America Press, 2018). Of course, God, as the author of nature, can bring about human bodies fit for the infusion of human souls miraculously (see, e.g., *ST* I, q. 92, a. 4, resp.). Nonetheless, as grace does not destroy or set aside nature, a miraculous infusion of the human soul into matter requires matter that is fit for such infusion, e.g., a human soul cannot configure an automobile.

soul. Thus, it is a supernatural disposition in the soul. The supernatural disposition in the created intellect that perfects the intellect so that it can see the essence of God is the *lumen gloriae*.

St. Thomas can also respond as follows. In the beatific vision, God makes intellectual creatures *deiform*, that is, like unto God. But in doing that, he must bring about some change in the intellectual creature, rather than doing all the work himself extrinsic to the creature. Therefore, St. Thomas gives to human persons the *lumen gloriae*, a disposition that is the medium *under which* they engage in the *act* of the beatific vision, thereby becoming perfectly deiform.[51]

ST. THOMAS ON THE DEGREES OF PERFECT HUMAN HAPPINESS IN HEAVEN

According to St. Thomas, the essential reward in heaven is, in one sense, the same for all. The essential reward is the same for all created persons in heaven insofar as it consists in the beatific vision and the proper accidents such as delight and love that follow upon that vision. But, in another sense, the essential reward is not the same for all insofar as some of the saints in heaven enjoy a more perfect beatific vision—and thereby greater happiness—than others.[52] Why does St. Thomas hold this position?

First, he finds the doctrine in scripture and other *auctoritates*. St. Thomas follows Pope St. Gregory the Great in thinking that Matthew 20:10 teaches that all the saints in heaven enjoy the same essential reward in the sense that *they all enjoy the beatific vision* and St. Augustine of Hippo in thinking that John 14:2 teaches that some saints enjoy a greater essential reward or perfect happiness than others insofar as *some have a more perfect vision of God than others*.[53]

In addition, there is 1 Corinthians 15:41: "Star differs from star in glory." St. Thomas thinks that St. Paul speaks here of the clarity of the

---

51. Compare with St. Thomas's argument that God gives to human persons in this life dispositions, i.e., the gifts of the Holy Spirit, to facilitate the Holy Spirit moving us to act because we are agents and not simply instruments (see, e.g., *ST* I-II, q. 68, a. 3, ad 2).

52. See, e.g., *In Sent* IV, d. 49, q. 2, a. 4; *SCG* III.58; *ST* I, q. 12, a. 6; q. 62, a. 9; I-II, q. 5, a. 2, resp.; *In Jn* 1, lect. 1, nn. 1853–55. See also the discussion in chapter 6 above of St. Thomas's account of the secondary object of the beatific vision, which has it that not all intellectual creatures see the same things other than God in the beatific vision, but some see more or less.

53. See, e.g., *In Mt 20*, lect. 1, n. 1640; *ST* I-II, q. 5, a. 2; *In Jn* 1, n. 1855.

glorified bodies of the saints. Because star differs from star in glory, the clarity of some glorified bodies is greater than others. But, as we will see below in chapter 11, St. Thomas thinks that the degree of clarity in a saint S's glorified body is a reflection of the degree of glory in the soul of S in heaven, which itself is a function of the degree of charity in S's soul in heaven. In addition, the more a soul is glorified—the more *lumen gloriae* there is in the soul—the greater the beatific vision of the saint. Of course, the more clearly a saint sees the essence of God, the greater is that saint's perfect happiness. Therefore, some saints are more perfectly happy than others in heaven.[54]

Finally, there is the teaching of Dionysius the Areopagite. St. Thomas notes that Dionysius teaches in the *Celestial Hierarchy* that different angels see God more or less clearly, and so are more or less perfectly happy in heaven.[55] But Matthew (22:30b) and Luke (20:35b) teach that human persons will be as the angels in heaven. Therefore, human persons will be more or less perfectly happy in heaven according to the degree of clarity with which they apprehend the essence of God in heaven.

St. Thomas also offers a theological argument for the view that some saints enjoy a greater perfect happiness than others.[56] He first notes that one saint S does not see the essence of God more clearly than another saint S1 because S has a better similitude by which S sees God more clearly than S1.[57] As we have seen, St. Thomas thinks that the beatific vision does not involve mediation *by which*, for in the beatific vision God unites the creature to himself so that the saints in heaven see the essence of God by the essence of God. We have also seen that the saints cannot enjoy the beatific vision without receiving a special supernatural grace from God that St. Thomas calls the *lumen gloriae*. Because the *lumen gloriae* is a created disposition or habit in the intellect of the saint, it can admit of degrees more or less. But the amount of the *lumen gloriae* that a saint receives is relative to that saint's desire to see God in heaven. This is because the more a saint longs to see God, the more that saint is apt

---

54. See, e.g., *In Sent* IV, d. 49, q. 2, a. 4, s.c.; *In 1 Cor* 15, lect. 6, n. 978; *In Mt* 18, lect. 1, n. 1487; *ST* I, q. 12, a. 6, s.c.

55. See, e.g., *In Sent* IV, d. 49, q. 2, a. 4, s.c.

56. See esp. *ST* I, q. 12, a. 6, resp. See also *In Sent* IV, d. 49, q. 2, a. 4, resp.; *In Mt* 18, lect. 1, n. 1491; *In Jn* 1, lect. 1854. For a helpful personalist way of thinking about the different degrees of perfect human happiness among the saints in heaven, one that is consistent with St. Thomas's expression of the doctrine, see Stump, *Wandering in Darkness*, 390–92.

57. See, e.g., *ST* I, q. 12, a. 6, resp.

to receive the object desired. Therefore, the more a saint desires God in heaven, the greater the degree of *lumen gloriae* God gives to that saint's soul. Because the more a saint has the *lumen gloriae* the more perfect that saint's vision of God, the more a saint desires God the greater that saint's beatific vision of the essence of God in heaven.

But the degree to which a saint longs to see God in heaven is relative to the amount of charity for God the saint has when the saint dies. For St. Thomas thinks the charity of the saints does not vary in heaven; change with respect to degree of charity in heaven would mean meriting in the next life, and there is no meriting in the next life.[58] Therefore, the relative degree of perfection of a saint's vision of the essence of God in heaven is relative to the amount of charity the saint has at the end of her earthly life. Because the essential reward in heaven or the attainment of perfect happiness consists in the beatific vision and the delight that flows from having the vision, the greater the vision of the essence of God and its concomitant delight, the more perfectly happy the saint is in heaven. Therefore, the greater the charity in the soul of the saint at the time of her death, the greater will be that saint's perfect happiness in heaven. Given that some saints die with greater charity for God than others,[59] some saints enjoy a greater essential reward or perfect happiness than others in heaven.[60]

---

58. See, e.g., *ST* I, q. 62, a. 9; *QDM*, q. 5, a. 4, ad 5; *ST* II-II, q. 24, a. 7, obj. 1 and ad 1. See also *CT* I, chaps. 149–50, where St. Thomas argues that there is immobility in the intellect and will with respect to the essential reward.

59. For St. Thomas's arguments that charity admits of degrees so that a person S can have more charity at one time than another and that S can have more or less charity than another person, see, e.g., *ST* II-II, q. 24, aa. 4–12.

60. The Catholic church at the Council of Florence (1439) dogmatically teaches the doctrine that different saints enjoy different degrees of happiness in heaven. For the text from the Council of Florence and the textual tradition of this teaching in the Church Fathers, see chapter 2, note 53 above.

PART 3

ST. THOMAS ON THE ACCIDENTAL REWARD IN HEAVEN

9

The Accidental Reward I

THE RELATIVE IMPORTANCE OF EMBODIMENT
FOR HUMAN HAPPINESS IN HEAVEN

Having treated in detail St. Thomas's account of the essential reward in part 2, part 3 explains and defends St. Thomas's intricate account of what he sometimes calls "the accidental reward" for human persons in heaven. This chapter treats the question of the relative importance of embodiment for human happiness in heaven in four sections. The first section offers a brief sketch of St. Thomas's philosophical anthropology,[1] which is necessary for appreciating St. Thomas's approach to understanding perfect human happiness in heaven (St. Thomas's philosophical anthropology also happens to offer us a helpful middle position between materialism and substance dualism). The second section examines a number of texts from St. Thomas's earlier works, in which he argues that perfect human happiness requires embodiment. The third section shows that St. Thomas's treatment of the relative importance of embodiment for perfect human happiness undergoes a significant development by the time he writes *ST* I-II, his final, detailed treatment of the subject. For in that place St. Thomas defends the view that embodiment is not required for perfect human happiness, but rather is required for the well-being (*bene esse*) of perfect human happiness. The fourth part defends St. Thomas's later position against an objection, namely, if the separated soul in heaven *desires* reunion with the body, as St. Thomas admits, then he inconsistently says that the separated soul is *perfectly happy*.

---

1. For a more detailed account of St. Thomas's philosophical anthropology, including all of the relevant texts in St. Thomas, and discussion of his views in light of some contemporary work in philosophical anthropology, see my *Aquinas and the Ship of Theseus*. See also my "Some Advantages for a Thomistic Solution."

ST. THOMAS'S PHILOSOPHICAL ANTHROPOLOGY

St. Thomas rejects both a Democritean *materialism* that fails to recognize that compound material objects can count as substances too[2] and at least two varieties of *substance dualism*, where substance dualism, as St. Thomas understands the position, treats the intellect or human soul as an immaterial substance and the human body as a separate material substance.[3] He offers his own philosophical anthropology within an Aristotelian hylomorphic conceptual framework. According to such a philosophy of material substance, the human person is ever and always one substance naturally composed of parts, which parts are not themselves substances.[4] Furthermore, substances such as human persons are normally, if not necessarily, composed of two different kinds of parts. First, there are the ordinary kinds of parts we attribute to human persons, such as atoms, molecules, hands, feet, etc. Call these *quantitative* parts.[5] Second, a substance such as a human person S is also normally, if not necessarily, composed of two *metaphysical* parts, S's substantial form, that is, the human soul, and S's prime matter (matter which, in and of itself, has no substantial form).[6]

A few words about substantial form and prime matter are in order. The substantial form of a material substance is the *intrinsic formal* cause of that substance's (a) existence, both at a time and through time and

---

2. See, e.g., *DPN*, chap. 1 (2–3), chap. 2 (14); *QDA*, a. 18, ad 5; *ST* I, q. 50, a. 5, resp.; *Quaestio disputata de spiritualibus creaturis* [hereafter *QDSC*], a. 1, resp.; *In Meta* VII, lect. 2, n. 1292; IX, lect. 9, n. 2289.

3. See, e.g., *ST I*, q. 76, a. 1. In this text, St. Thomas recognizes two varieties of substance dualism: the *simple* substance dualism of Plato (i.e., the person is identical to the immaterial soul) and what we might call *compound* substance dualism: the human person is naturally and necessarily composed of an immaterial substance (i.e., the mind or soul), and also naturally, but not necessarily, composed of a material substance (i.e., the human organism). See my "Some Advantages for a Thomistic Solution" for the details.

4. Although some of the actual parts of the human person are potential substances, i.e., they become actual substances when they are no longer parts of the human person. For the details and texts, see my *Aquinas and the Ship of Theseus*.

5. St. Thomas distinguishes between (a) those quantitative parts of substances whose properties we can observe when they compose a substance, e.g., arms, legs, organs, etc., and (b) those parts of substances whose properties we do not observe, but still exist by power (*virtute*) in the properties of the wholes which they compose, i.e., the way in which the elements—the most fundamental kind of material substance for St. Thomas—exist in mixed bodies. For more on this distinction, see my *Aquinas and the Ship of Theseus*, 87–98. For the sake of simplicity, henceforward, the expression "quantitative parts" refers to both kinds of parts of substances.

6. See, e.g., *DPN*, chap. 3 (17); chap. 4 (22); *SCG* II.54; *QDA*, a. 1, ad 13; *In Meta* VII, lect. 21, n. 1095. For the adjective "metaphysical" in *metaphysical parts*, see Eleonore Stump, *Aquinas*, 35.

change, and (b) its belonging to an *infimae* species (which includes being the intrinsic formal cause of that substance's characteristic features, powers, and quantitative parts). The prime matter of a material substance explains that that substance belongs to a kind of substance whose members are generated and corrupted, that is, such substances come into existence from other material substances and such substances can suffer the natural change of going out of existence, or, in the case of living substances, death.[7]

According to St. Thomas, a human person S is a material substance whose substantial form is called *the intellectual soul*, which soul enables S, if S is mature and healthy, to engage in characteristically human acts, namely, intellectual acts of *simple apprehension*, that is, grasping the natures of things; *judgment*, that is, possessing propositional attitudes, such as believing or knowing certain propositions are true; and *reasoning*, that is, drawing conclusions from other things that S believes or knows. As we have seen, intellectual and volitional acts come and go together for St. Thomas, and so, if S is mature and healthy, S also engages in acts of will, such as delighting in, loving, and choosing, all done in light of S's intellectual activity. According to St. Thomas, human persons naturally and normally engage in intellectual and volitional acts as embodied beings. Furthermore, as we have seen, human knowledge in this life begins with, and naturally makes constant reference to, sense knowledge. Nonetheless, human intellectual and volitional acts, in and of themselves, do not make use of bodily organs and so are purely immaterial activities.[8] But purely immaterial activities require a subject that is purely immaterial. Therefore, the immaterial human soul is the subject of these purely immaterial activities.

Because it engages in acts that do not make use of bodily organs, there are two ways in which the human soul is not like other substantial forms. First, where other substantial forms do not in any sense themselves engage in actions, the human soul does engage in actions, at least derivatively. That is to say, although St. Thomas thinks it is the human person, properly speaking, who understands and wills,[9] it is nonethe-

---

7. As we shall see below in this chapter and in chapter 10, there is an added complication where the corruption of human persons is concerned, as human persons do not go out of existence when they die.

8. See, e.g., *ST* I, q. 75, a. 5, resp.

9. See, e.g., *ST* I, q. 75, a. 2, ad 2.

less the case that the human person understands and wills by way of the human soul engaging in certain activities. Because the human soul engages in activities, it is a *hoc aliquid*, a *this something*.[10] Just as an eye is a *this something* by which the human person sees, but it is not really the eye that sees but the human person who sees by way of her eye, so the human soul is an (immaterial) *this something* by which the human person understands and wills, and yet it is not really the human soul that understands and wills, but the human person who understands and wills by way of the human soul. So although the human soul is a substantial form for St. Thomas, as it performs the functions of a substantial form, it is also like a quantitative part of a substance in that it is a *this something*.

Second, as a thing's operation flows from its way of being, and the human soul does things without the body (i.e., understand and will), the human soul does not depend for its existence upon the body. Therefore, unlike other kinds of substantial forms, the human soul can survive the death of the body.[11]

But just as the human soul is unlike other substantial forms, the human soul is also unlike the quantitative parts of the human person (in more than just the obvious way in which the human soul is something *immaterial* and quantitative parts are not). For the quantitative parts of a human person have their existence and identity from the whole to which they belong. For example, when a molecule M of some sort is a part of a human person, M is not a substance. Therefore, when that human person dies, and M is released from the causal influence of the human soul, M becomes a substance in its own right. Because an actual substance is not numerically identical to what is not an actual substance, M as a quantitative part of the human person is not numerically identical to M after it becomes an actual substance. The human soul is not like quantitative parts in this regard. The human soul is always and ever a metaphysical part of a substance; it is not potentially a substance, even though it can survive apart from the composite human person.

There is another way in which the human soul is *sui generis* as a kind of part, thinks St. Thomas. He distinguishes the act of being (*esse*) of a substance and the essence or form of a substance. Whereas the essence or form of a substance is the principle of a substance that explains *what* it

10. See, e.g., *ST* I, q. 75, a. 2.
11. See, e.g., *ST* I, q. 75, a. 6.

is, the act of being of a substance explains *that* the substance exists. Now, whereas the act of being of a whole is *not* numerically identical to the act of being of any of its *quantitative* parts, the act of being of the human soul *is* numerically identical to the act of being of the whole to which the human soul belongs, namely, the human person.[12] That is to say, the human soul is a metaphysical part of the human substance that is capable of preserving the existence and identity of the human substance of which it is a part, even beyond death.

St. Thomas explains his view in the following way. The human soul has its own act of being, which, from the very beginning of the soul's existence, it naturally shares with prime matter so that what results is the composite human person.[13] The *composite* human person is composed of the human soul and prime matter, and as a result of such composition, the human person is also composed of various quantitative parts at different times (e.g., fewer parts when she is a zygote, more kinds of parts around ten days later, etc.). Because the human soul can survive death, and the human soul's act of being is numerically identical to the act of being of the composite, the human person survives her death as a disembodied soul, albeit in a metaphysically truncated form, as it is normal and natural for a human person to exist as embodied. Although St. Thomas makes it clear throughout his career that the human person is not—never is—identical to the human soul, he thinks that a human person S can be—and is during the interim state—composed of S's soul alone.[14] As we will see, the fact that the human person can survive as a disembodied soul is one reason that St. Thomas distinguishes the essential reward and the accidental reward. For, whereas the human person without the body can already enjoy the essential reward, there are aspects of the accidental reward that the human person cannot enjoy when the human person is not embodied. As we will also see in what follows, St. Thomas believes, as a Catholic Christian, that all human persons will be restored to metaphysical, if not moral, perfection at the general resurrection by the power of Christ's resurrection. But in rising from the dead, the saints in heaven get to enjoy those aspects of the accidental re-

---

12. See, e.g., *In Sent* IV, d. 44, q. 1, a. 1, ad 1 (*ST Suppl.*, q. 79, a. 2, ad 1); *SCG* II.68.3–5 and IV.81.11; *ST* I, q. 76, a. 1, ad 5; I-II, q. 4, a. 5, ad 2.

13. See, e.g., *SCG* II.68.3.

14. See, e.g., *SCG* IV.81.11; *ST* I, q. 76, a. 1, ad 5; I-II, q. 4, a. 5, ad 2. For a defense of St. Thomas's view that composition is not identity, see my *Aquinas and the Ship of Theseus* and "Some Advantages for a Thomistic Solution."

ward that require embodiment, for example, sensing the "new heavens and the new earth."

Now, the interpretation or development of St. Thomas's views I have presented here is controversial. There is currently some very active and philosophically interesting debate about just how to interpret St. Thomas on the ontological status of human persons in the interim state, and so on his views about personal identity beyond death. In addition, there is also the theological or philosophical question: "what position should a contemporary Thomist adopt, given St. Thomas's principles and the teaching of the church?" Those who read St. Thomas as a *human survivalist* take him to think—or, those, like me, who adopt a human survivalist *development* of St. Thomas's thought think—that, strictly speaking, the human person, although never identical to the human soul, nevertheless exists in the interim state such that she is composed of her soul alone.[15] Human survivalists take the ability of the human person to be composed of her soul alone while not being identical to her soul when she is composed of her soul alone to be one example of a general metaphysical truth to which St. Thomas is committed, namely, that composition (or constitution) is not identity. On the other hand, those who read St. Thomas as a *corruptionist* hold that St. Thomas thinks that, for any human person S, S does not exist without S's body. As most human persons do not have bodies in the interim state, most human persons do not exist in the interim state (although the *souls* of such human persons do exist in the interim state).[16] Some of the texts cited in this third part of the

---

15. For arguments that St. Thomas holds the human survivalist view, see, e.g., my *Aquinas and the Ship of Theseus*, 68–79; Eleonore Stump, "Resurrection, Reassembly, and Reconstitution: St. Thomas on the Soul," in *Die menschliche Seele* (ed. Niederberger and Runggaldier), 151–71; Jason T. Eberl, "Do Human Persons Persist between Death and Resurrection?," in *Metaphysics and God* (ed. Timpe), 188–205. For a defense of human survivalism as a fruitful *development* of St. Thomas's views insofar as Thomistic human survivalism provides a helpful solution to the problem of personal identity beyond death, see my "Some Advantages for a Thomistic Solution." See also David S. Oderberg, *Real Essentialism* (New York: Routledge, 2007), 255–60; David S. Oderberg, "Survivalism, Corruptionism, and Mereology," *European Journal for Philosophy of Religion* 4 (2012): 1–26.

16. For arguments that St. Thomas holds the corruptionist view, see, e.g., Brian Davies, *The Thought of Thomas Aquinas* (Oxford: Clarendon Press, 1992), 212–20; Pasnau, *Thomas Aquinas on Human Nature*, 380–93; Christina van Dyke, "Human Identity, Immanent Causal Relations, and the Principle of Non-repeatability: Thomas Aquinas on the Bodily Resurrection," *Religious Studies* 43 (2007): 373–94; Patrick Toner, "Personhood and Death in St. Thomas," *History of Philosophy Quarterly* 26 (2009): 121–38, and "St. Thomas Aquinas on Death and the Separated Soul," *Pacific Philosophical Quarterly* 91 (2010): 587–99; Turner Nevitt, "Survivalism, Corruptionism, and Intermittent Existence in St. Thomas," *History of Philosophy Quarterly* 31 (2014): 1–19; Patrick Toner, "St. Thomas Aquinas on Gappy Existence," *Analytic Philosophy* 56 (2015): 94–110; and Turner Nevitt, "Aquinas on the Death of Christ: A New Argument for Corruptionism," *American Catholic Philosophical Quarterly* 90 (2016):

book clearly lend support to interpreting St. Thomas as a human survivalist, but (it must be admitted) there certainly are recalcitrant texts that lend some support to the corruptionist interpretation. That being said, this book assumes that a human survivalist development of St. Thomas's views is the correct philosophical and theological approach to thinking about human existence and identity beyond death. Such a human survivalist development of St. Thomas's thought is consistent with all of St. Thomas's theological and philosophical principles,[17] particularly his rejection of Platonic substance dualism.[18]

As we have seen, according to St. Thomas's account of human persons (or my development of St. Thomas's philosophical anthropology), the soul of a human person S is by itself sufficient to preserve the existence and identity of S. Why is St. Thomas's philosophical anthropology not then an instance of substance dualism? All substance dualists believe that the immaterial soul and the human body are two distinct substances. St. Thomas rejects that view for at least two reasons. First, the human soul is not a substance, even in the interim state. A substance is a *hoc aliquid* that is complete in species whereas the human soul is not—never is—complete in species.[19] Second, the prime matter of a human person is not a substance. The human person is ever and always one

---

77–99. For an interesting argument that St. Thomas is neither a human survivalist nor a corruptionist, but rather a nonhuman survivalist, see Jeffrey E. Brower, *Aquinas's Ontology of the Material World: Change, Hylomorphism, and Material Objects* (Oxford: Oxford University Press, 2014), 279–310. For attempts at carving out a middle position between corruptionism and human survivalism as an interpretation of St. Thomas's views different from Brower's, see Melissa Eitenmiller, "On the Separated Soul according to St. Thomas Aquinas," *Nova at Vetera* (English edition) 17 (2019): 57–91, and Daniel D. De Haan and Brandom Dahm, "Thomas Aquinas on Separated Souls as Incomplete Human Persons," *The Thomist* 83 (2019): 589–637.

17. For an argument that human survivalism is consistent with St. Thomas's theological and philosophical principles—even if it is not consistent with everything St. Thomas says—see Mark Spencer, "The Personhood of the Separated Soul," *Nova et Vetera* 12, no. 3 (2014): 863–912.

18. For good arguments that the texts that are sometimes used to defend a corruptionist interpretation of St. Thomas do not have anything like the survivalist/corruptionist debate in view but merely show St. Thomas is arguing against a Platonist philosophical anthropology and that the contemporary Thomist should adopt the human survivalist view, see Stump, "Resurrection, Reassembly, and Reconstitution"; Oderberg, "Survivalism, Corruptionism, and Mereology," 12–13n34; and Ed Feser, "Aquinas on the Human Soul," in *The Blackwell Companion to Substance Dualism*, ed. Jonathan J. Loose, Angus J. L. Menuge, and J. P. Moreland (Oxford: Wiley-Blackwell, 2018), 88–101.

19. A *hoc aliquid* H is complete in species just in case one can define H without making reference to some *hoc aliquid* H1, where H and H1 are not numerically identical. For example, one can define a human person as a member of the species *rational animal*. This definition makes no reference to a concrete individual distinct from the human person being defined. But the human soul is that part of a human person—here I make reference to a *hoc aliquid* that is not identical to the soul—which is that intrinsic formal cause of the numerical and specific identity of a human person.

substance composed of a part or parts that are not themselves substances. St. Thomas's philosophical anthropology is therefore a perspicuous account of human persons that, unlike crude materialism or some sort of substance dualism, explains the substantial unity of human persons through time and change, even beyond the radical change that is biological death.

ST. THOMAS ON THE SIGNIFICANCE OF EMBODIMENT FOR HUMAN HAPPINESS IN HEAVEN: AN EARLY VIEW

In the fourth book of his *Sentences* commentary, St. Thomas asks whether the happiness of the saints will be greater after the general judgment than before.[20] Given that embodiment at, and after, the general judgment is a good not enjoyed by the saints in the interim state, that is, the state between death and the general judgment,[21] St. Thomas's simple answer to this question is "yes." But St. Thomas goes on to explain the *significance* of such an increase in beatitude. At this point in his theological career, he argues that there are at least two ways in which the happiness of the saints increases after the general resurrection.

First, the happiness of the saints will increase *in extent* after the general resurrection, because "their happiness will then be not only in the soul but also in the body."[22] One way of thinking about what St. Thomas says here is that there will be *more* of a human person to enjoy God after the general resurrection—when all the saints are again embodied—than before the general resurrection. This is because before the general resurrection the saints' enjoyment of God does not include the good of embodiment (excepting the Virgin Mary), whereas after the general resurrection it does. The idea that the happiness of the saints increases *in extent* after the general resurrection is one that St. Thomas consistently teaches throughout his corpus.[23]

Second, St. Thomas goes on to say that the soul's happiness after the general resurrection increases *in intensity* (*intensive*). By the soul's happiness increasing in intensity after the general resurrection, St. Thomas

---

20. Stated in d. 49, q. 1, a. 4, q.c. 1 (*ST Suppl.*, q. 93, a. 1).
21. The interim state is sometimes called *the intermediate state*.
22. *ST Suppl.*, q. 93, a. 1, resp. (trans. English Dominicans, 2957). See also *In Sent* IV, d. 49, q. 1, a. 4, q.c. 1, resp.
23. For a late text that includes this teaching, see, e.g., *ST* I-II, q. 4, a, 5, ad 5.

seems to mean that the soul's essential reward is greater in degree after the general resurrection than before.[24] That is to say, just as we have seen that St. Thomas thinks that some persons in heaven have a greater degree of happiness than others, so he seems to say here that St. Paul enjoys a greater degree of perfect happiness after the resurrection than before. To see this, note St. Thomas's extended argument for this thesis:

(1) The human soul is merely a component part of the human person, that is, the soul is not identical to a human person [assumption].

(2) A part p is less perfect in its natural being when separated from the whole of which p is naturally a part when compared to p when p is joined to the other parts that are naturally a part of the whole of which p is a natural part [assumption].

(3) Therefore, the soul is more perfect in its natural being when it exists in the whole which includes soul and body, that is, when the soul configures matter, than when it exists just by itself [from (1) and (2)].

(4) The more perfect that a thing is in its natural being, the more perfect is its operation [assumption].

(5) If all in a human body that hampers the activity of the human soul is removed after the general resurrection, then the soul configuring matter after the general resurrection has a more perfect operation than the separated soul [from (3) and (4)].

(6) After the general resurrection, all that hampers the activity of the human soul is removed insofar as the saints will have glorified bodies [assumption].

(7) Therefore, all of the operations of the soul configuring matter after the general resurrection are more perfect operations than those of the separated soul [from (5) and (6)].

(8) Beatitude consists in an operation, that is, the beatific vision [assumption].

(9) Therefore, the soul's beatitude after the general resurrection will be more perfect than before [from (7) and (8)].

(10) Every imperfect thing naturally desires its perfection [assumption].

---

24. *In Sent* IV, d. 49, q. 1, a. 4, q.c. 1, resp. (*ST Suppl.*, q. 93, a. 1, resp.). In *ST* III, q. 1, a. 4, St. Thomas says that *greater* is said in two ways: x can be greater than y *intensively*, as one instance of whiteness might be said to be more intense than another, or x can be greater than y *extensively*, as *this* surface might be greater in whiteness than *that* surface because *this* surface is larger than *that* surface.

(11) Therefore, the separated soul naturally desires to be embodied at and after the general resurrection so as to enjoy a more perfect beatitude [from (9) and (10)].

(12) If the separated soul naturally desires to be embodied at and after the general resurrection so as to enjoy a more perfect beatitude, then the embodied soul's beatitude at and after the general resurrection is more intense than the separated soul's beatitude [assumption].

(13) Therefore, the embodied soul's beatitude at and after the general resurrection is more intense than the separated soul's beatitude [from (11) and (12)].[25]

Call this argument *the argument from imperfect and perfect operation* (AIPO) that the separated soul of a saint is less intensely happy than the embodied saint at and after the general resurrection.

Given that St. Thomas argues in the *Sentences* commentary that happiness is greater in extent *and* intensity after the general resurrection than before, what implications does this have for the question whether embodiment belongs to the essential reward or the accidental reward? It appears that embodiment at and after the general resurrection forms a part of both the essential and the accidental reward in the *Sentences* commentary. Embodiment is a part of the accidental reward insofar as embodiment at and after the general resurrection constitutes an acquisition of that good that is a human person's beatitude increasing *in extent* insofar as both the soul and the body are glorified. This amounts to an increase in the accidental reward of the saint in heaven because the acquisition of the good in question is a good other than and in addition to the beatific vision and its proper accidents, that is, the good that is the glory of the soul flowing into the body to make the body glorified.

On the other hand, St. Thomas also argues in the *Sentences* commentary that beatitude is greater *intensively* after the general resurrection than before. The human person is a composite—and so an embodied—being by nature. But an operation is perfect to the extent that the being that operates is perfect. So, as St. Thomas notes, "the body's glory will conduce to the intensity of the joy that refers to God, in so far as it will conduce to the more perfect operation whereby the soul tends to God: since the more perfect is a becoming operation, the greater the delight

---

25. *In Sent* IV, d. 49, q. 1, a. 4, q.c. 1, resp. (*ST Suppl.*, q. 93, a. 1, resp.).

[see *ST* I-II, q. 32, a. 1], as stated in Ethic. x, 8."²⁶ Insofar as embodiment conduces to a more intense operation on the part of the soul seeing God when compared to the separated soul's seeing God in the interim state, embodiment plays a role in the *essential* reward of the saints. This is because *embodiment is an instrumental cause* for a beatific vision that is more intense than that experienced by the separated soul.²⁷

But it also seems reasonable to argue as follows:

(14) If an embodied soul's beatitude at and after the general resurrection is more intense than the separated soul's beatitude, then embodiment is required for perfect happiness [assumption].

(15) Therefore, embodiment is required for perfect human happiness [from (13) and (14)].

So we can also say that, at the time St. Thomas composes the fourth book of his *Sentences* commentary, he maintains that embodiment is necessary as an instrumental cause of the soul being perfectly happy in God. Of course, this suggests that embodiment plays a very significant role for St. Thomas where perfect human happiness is concerned at this early point in his teaching career.

A few years later, St. Thomas offers an argument in *SCG* similar to AIPO. In the context of arguing that there will be a general resurrection, St. Thomas offers the following argument for a proposition similar to (15):

(16) The ultimate happiness (*felicitas ultima*) or perfect happiness (*felicitas perfectio*) of x is the perfection of x [assumption].

(17) A being that desires something it does not have is not perfect [assumption].

(18) A being existing in an imperfect condition desires something it does not have, namely, its own perfection [assumption].²⁸

(19) A being existing in an imperfect condition is not perfect [from (17) and (18)].

(20) Therefore, a being existing in an imperfect condition does not enjoy ultimate or perfect happiness [from (16) and (19)].

(21) But a part p existing apart from the whole of which p is naturally

---

26. *ST Suppl.*, q. 93, a. 1, ad 4 (trans. English Dominicans, 2958). See also *In Sent* IV, d. 49, q. 1, a. 4, q.c. 1, ad 4.

27. *In Sent* IV, d. 49, q. 1, a. 4, q.c. 1, ad 3 (*ST Suppl.*, q. 93, a. 1, ad 3).

28. Compare with premise (10) above.

a part exists imperfectly in comparison to *p* when it is not separate from the whole of which *p* is naturally a part [assumption].

(22) But the human soul is naturally a part of complete human nature [assumption].

(23) Therefore, the separated human soul exists imperfectly when compared to the embodied human soul, that is, the human soul, as it exists at and after the general resurrection [from (21) and (22)].[29]

(24) Therefore, ultimate (*ultima*) or perfect (*perfectum*) happiness cannot be possessed by the separated soul, but rather only by the embodied soul at and after the general resurrection [from (20) and (23)].[30]

We can call the argument above *the argument for the imperfect happiness of the separated soul* (AIHSS). Although there are some similarities between AIHSS and AIPO, we can also note a key difference. Whereas AIPO has as its conclusion that the happiness of the soul *is more intense* after the general resurrection than before, AIHSS has as its conclusion that the separated soul cannot be ultimately or perfectly happy. Nonetheless, as we have seen, it seems a simple logical step to move from a proposition such as (13) to a proposition such as (24).[31]

Let us examine a couple of additional arguments that are roughly contemporaneous with AIHSS in *SCG* IV. For example, in *QDP*, St. Thomas offers the following argument that the separated soul is not perfectly happy (call this argument *the argument from the natural union of the soul and body*):

(25) There can be no perfection of happiness (*perfectio beatitudinis*) where [the] nature [of the soul] is not perfect [assumption].

(26) The union of the human soul and the body is natural [assumption].

(27) Therefore, the nature of the human soul is not perfect when it is separated from the body [from (26)].

(28) Therefore, the separated human soul cannot be perfectly happy [from (25) and (27)].[32]

St. Thomas makes it clear here that the happiness he is speaking about is the perfect happiness or essential reward of the separated soul and

---

29. Note that the argument composed of propositions (21)–(23) resembles the argument composed of propositions (1)–(3).
30. *SCG* IV.79.11. See also *ST Suppl.*, q. 75, a. 1, resp.; a. 2, *resp*.
31. See the argument above consisting of propositions (13)–(15).
32. *QDP*, q. 5, a. 10, resp.

not simply the accidental reward, for he continues by saying, "For this reason Augustine (*De Gen. ad lit.* xii, 35) says that the souls of the blessed do not as perfectly enjoy the sight of God before the resurrection as after: wherefore the human body will need to be united to the soul in the final state of beatitude."[33]

Although the language of St. Thomas is a bit different here, he seems to be defending the same position in this passage from *QDP* that he defends in *Sentences* IV: the happiness of the separated soul is less intense than that of the embodied soul, that is, the essential reward of the embodied soul is greater than the essential reward of the separated soul. In addition, because the separated soul's beatific vision is not as perfect as it could be, the separated soul cannot be perfectly happy.

Consider also two arguments found in *CT* I, nos. 150–51. Here again St. Thomas argues that the separated soul requires the body in order to enjoy perfect happiness (*perfectam beatitudinem*). In the first of these, St. Thomas argues as follows:

(29) Perfect human happiness is eternal life [assumption].

(30) Eternal life is a participation in God's eternal life [assumption].

(31) Therefore, perfect human happiness is a participation in God's eternal life [from (29) and (30)].

(32) A participation in God's eternal life is immutable [assumption].

(33) Therefore, perfect human happiness is immutable [from (31) and (32)].[34]

(34) Perfect happiness consists in acts of intellect and will [assumption].

(35) Therefore, if the separated soul in heaven can be perfectly happy, then the acts of the will of the separated soul that are aspects of perfect happiness in heaven are all immutable [from (33) and (34)].

(36) If the acts of the will of the separated soul that are aspects of perfect happiness in heaven are all immutable, then the will of the separated soul in heaven is perfectly at rest (*perfecta quietatio voluntatis*), that is, the separated soul in heaven has no desire to change [assumption].

(37) If the will of the separated soul in heaven is perfectly at rest, that is, the separated soul in heaven has no desire to change, then every natural desire of the separated soul in heaven is satisfied [assumption].

---

33. Trans. English Dominicans (Eugene, Ore.: Wipf and Stock, 2004), 2:148.
34. *CT* I, chap. 150.

(38) If x is naturally united with y, then x and y are naturally inclined to be united one with the other [assumption].

(39) But the human soul is, by nature, the substantial form of a human body [assumption].

(40) Therefore, the human soul has a natural inclination to be united to a human body [from (38) and (39)].

(41) If something rational w has a natural inclination for z, then w has a natural desire for z [assumption].

(42) Therefore, the separated soul in heaven has a natural desire for embodiment that is not satisfied [from (40) and (41)].[35]

(43) Therefore, it is not the case that the will of the separated soul in heaven is perfectly at rest, that is, the separated soul in heaven has a desire to change [from (37) and (42), MT].

(44) Therefore, it is not the case that the acts of the will of the separated soul that are aspects of perfect happiness are all immutable [from (36) and (43), MT].

(45) Therefore, the separated human soul in heaven cannot be perfectly happy [from (35) and (44), MT].[36]

Let us call the argument above "the argument from disquiet in the will." St. Thomas has a second argument in *CT* I in defense of the thesis that ultimate or perfect human happiness requires embodiment. Let us call this argument *the argument from first perfection*.

The argument begins from the premise:

(46) The final perfection (*finalis perfectio*) of a being x requires that x enjoy its first perfection (*primam perfectionem*) [assumption].[37]

It continues as follows:

(47) The first perfection of x requires that x is perfect in its nature [assumption].

(48) No part of a whole is perfect in its nature unless it exists in the whole of which it is naturally a part [assumption].

(49) The separated human soul does not exist in the whole of which it is naturally a part [assumption].

---

35. See also *In 1 Cor* 15, lect. 2, n. 924.
36. *CT* I, chap. 151.
37. As St. Thomas makes clear in *SCG* II.46.3, x's *first* perfection includes its being and nature whereas x's *second* perfection include x's actions or operations.

(50) Therefore, the separated human soul is not perfect in its nature [from (48) and (49)].

(51) Therefore, the separated human soul cannot enjoy its first perfection [from (47) and (50)].

(52) Therefore, the separated human soul cannot enjoy its final perfection [from (46) and (51)].

(53) The final perfection of x is x's attaining its ultimate end [assumption].

(54) Therefore, the separated human soul cannot attain its ultimate end [from (52) and (53)].

(55) The ultimate end for a rational thing such as the separated human soul is ultimate *happiness* [assumption].

(56) Therefore, the separated human soul cannot enjoy ultimate happiness (*ultimam beatitudinem*) [from (54) and (55)].

Notice that the heart of the argument from first perfection—propositions (48)–(50)—is similar to (1)–(3) in AIPO and (21)–(23) in AIHSS. In addition, like many of the arguments that we have been examining, the conclusion of the argument from first perfection is that the separated human soul cannot enjoy final, ultimate, or perfect happiness.

As we have seen, St. Thomas also explicitly defends the view early in his career (in the *Sentences* commentary and *QDP*) that the embodied human soul at, and after, the general resurrection is more *intensely* happy than the separated soul in heaven insofar as the embodied human soul's joy in the beatific vision will be greater than the joy of that numerically same separated soul. That view has the following implications:

(57) The *essential* reward of an embodied soul S is greater than that of S when S is separated from the body.

(58) Embodiment at and after the general resurrection is an aspect of the essential reward insofar as it is an instrumental cause of the perfect happiness of the embodied saint.

Insofar as the glorified body—that is, the resurrected body of a saint—is an instrumental cause of a beatific vision that is more perfect than the beatific vision on the part of the numerically same soul when separated from the body, and the essence of the essential reward consists in the beatific vision, it follows that embodiment at and after the general resurrection is an aspect of the essential reward.

There is, however, a serious objection to attributing (57) and (58) to St. Thomas in the earlier part of his career: it is inconsistent with other things that he says about the essential reward at this time. For if the essential reward is more intense in the embodied human soul at and after the general resurrection than it is in the separated human soul, then the essential reward is variable, mutable, and in time. But St. Thomas teaches throughout his career—including in his early works—that the essential reward is invariable, immutable, and timeless.[38] At the very least, there seems to be an ambiguity or a tension in St. Thomas's early treatment of the beatitude of the separated human soul.[39]

ST. THOMAS ON THE SIGNIFICANCE OF EMBODIMENT FOR HUMAN HAPPINESS IN HEAVEN: A LATER VIEW

St. Thomas's last systematic discussion of the significance of embodiment for perfect human happiness comes in *ST* I-II. St. Thomas argues that perfect happiness (*beatitudinem perfectam*) does *not* require embodiment. Indeed, he notes that "some have maintained that [perfect happiness] is not possible to the soul separated from the body; and have said that the souls of saints, when separated from their bodies, do not attain to that Happiness until the Day of Judgment, when they will receive their bodies back again. And this is shown to be false, both by authority and by reason."[40] St. Thomas's argument from authority is taken from statements St. Paul makes in 2 Corinthians 5. The argument from authority is itself composed of two arguments. In the first argument St. Thomas aims to show from St. Paul's text:

(59) If a saint S is at home in the body, then S is absent from the Lord [2 Cor 5:6].

St. Thomas thinks that St. Paul believes a proposition such as (59) for the following reasons:

(60) If a saint S is at home in the body, then S walks by faith and not by sight [2 Cor 5:7].

---

38. See chapter 4, note 89, and chapter 7, above.
39. Indeed, St. Thomas seems to teach his "later view" on the relative importance of embodiment for perfect happiness in *In Sent* IV, d. 44, q. 1, a. 3, q.c. 4, obj. 3 and ad 3 (*ST Suppl.*, q. 81, a. 4, obj. 3 and ad 3).
40. See q. 4, a. 5, resp. (trans. English Dominicans, 605).

(61) If S walks by faith and not by sight, then S is not having the beatific vision [assumption].

(62) If S is not having the beatific vision, then S is absent from, that is, not present to, the Lord [assumption].

(63) Therefore, if S walks by faith and not by sight, then S is absent from, that is, not present to, the Lord [from (61) and (62), HS].

And from proposition (60)—2 Corinthians 5:7—and proposition (63) we get proposition (59), or 2 Corinthians 5:6 (by HS). That is, in the first argument St. Thomas shows, from the authority of the Apostle Paul, that saints in this life are absent from the Lord, that is, they do not have the beatific vision, and so are not perfectly happy.

In the second argument in 2 Corinthians 5, St. Thomas notes that St. Paul's text continues as follows:

(64) If a saint in heaven S is separated from the body, then S is present to the Lord [2 Cor 5:8].

We can assume—as St. Paul's text suggests we do—as follows:

(65) If S is present to the Lord, then S walks by sight, that is, S enjoys the beatific vision.

In that case it follows that:

(66) If a saint in heaven S is separated from the body, then S enjoys the beatific vision [from (64) and (65), by HS].

Finally, as St. Thomas notes:

(67) If a saint in heaven S enjoys the beatific vision, then S is perfectly happy [proved at ST I-II, q. 2, a. 8, and q. 3, a. 8].

It therefore follows:

(68) If a saint in heaven S is separated from the body, then S is perfectly happy [from (66) and (67), HS].[41]

Note that, in the argument presented above, St. Thomas maintains a thesis that he denies early in his career, namely, that the separated human soul enjoys perfect (*perfectam*) or true (*vera*) happiness (*beatitudo*).

---

41. See also *In 2 Cor* 5, lect. 2, n. 167; *In Phil* 1, lect. 3, nn. 32–35; *ST* I-II, q. 4, a. 5, s.c.: "It is written (Apoc. 14:13): 'Happy are the dead who die in the Lord'" (trans. English Dominicans, 605).

In arguing that embodiment is not a requirement for perfect happiness (*ST* I-II, q. 4, a. 5, resp.), St. Thomas also offers an argument *per rationem*. The argument can be formulated as follows:

(69) The human intellect does not require the body for its operation, save on account of the phantasms, from whence it abstracts the intelligible species of material objects; but the act of simple apprehension itself is a wholly immaterial activity [proved at *ST* I, q. 75, a. 5, resp., and q. 84, a. 7].

(70) Now it is evident that the divine essence cannot be seen by means of phantasms, as God is immaterial [proved at *ST* I, q. 12, a. 3].

(71) Therefore, if human persons can see the divine essence, then they do not need the body to do so [from (69) and (70)].

(72) Human persons can see the divine essence [proved at *ST* I, q. 12, a. 1].

(73) Therefore, human persons do not need the body to see the divine essence [from (71) and (72), MP].

(74) The attainment of perfect human happiness consists in the vision of the divine essence [proved at *ST* I-II, q. 2, a. 8, and q. 3, a. 8].

(75) Therefore, the attainment of perfect human happiness does not require embodiment [from (73) and (74)].

Someone may object here that, above, I argued that St. Thomas thinks that the attainment of perfect human happiness or the essential reward consists in both the beatific vision and the proper accidents of the will that flow from the vision, for example, delight, charity, joy, etc., whereas *ST* I-II, q. 4, a. 5, resp., has it that the attainment of perfect human happiness or the essential reward consists merely in the vision of the divine essence. However, St. Thomas sometimes uses "consists" (*consistat*) in a narrow sense to pick out what counts as the essence of a thing.[42] In that narrow sense of "consists," the attainment of perfect human happiness or the essential reward consists in the beatific vision.[43] For, as we have seen, St. Thomas argues that the *essence* of perfect human happiness *qua* attainment or the *essence* of the essential reward is the beatific vision. That being said, St. Thomas thinks the acts of will concomitant with the vision are nonetheless aspects of the essential reward and so the attain-

---

42. See, e.g., *ST* I-II, q. 3, a. 4, resp.
43. Ibid.

ment of perfect happiness or the essential reward *consists* of them in a broader sense.[44]

All that being said, because the acts of will that flow from the beatific vision do not themselves require the body, the argument consisting of propositions (69)–(75) can be reformulated in order to show that the attainment of perfect happiness or the essential reward as a whole does not require embodiment by simply adding the following premises to the argument above:

(74a) Human acts of will are coordinated with characteristic intellectual acts [assumption; see, e.g., *ST I*, q. 80, a. 2].

(74b) Therefore, human acts of will do not require embodiment [from (69) and (74a)].

(74c) Those human acts of will that are concomitant with the beatific vision especially do not require embodiment because the act of the intellect that is the beatific vision is immaterial [from (73)].

(74d) The attainment of perfect human happiness or the essential reward includes only (a) the essence of perfect human happiness *qua* attainment or the concomitant accidents that flow from having the vision, that is, acts of will such as delight, love, and joy [proved at *ST* I-II, q. 2, a. 8; q. 3, aa. 4 and 8].

(75) Therefore, the attainment of perfect human happiness does not require embodiment [from (73), (74b), (74c), and (74d)].

Given St. Thomas's early view, what St. Thomas says here in *ST* I-II, represents, at the very least, a change in the way he expresses his views on the happiness of the separated soul. According to his early view, he thinks that *perfect human happiness requires embodiment*. Here, he denies such a claim.

If it is clear from scripture and theological argument that perfect human happiness in heaven does not require embodiment, how does St. Thomas make sense of the fact that some theologians—apparently even St. Thomas himself earlier in his career—teach that perfect human happiness requires the body? He does so by going on to make a distinction between the *essence* of perfect happiness and *the well-being* (*bene esse*) of perfect happiness (in *ST* I-II, q. 4, a. 5). Whereas the former does not

---

44. See, e.g., *ST* I-II, q. 3, a, 4; q. 4, a. 1 (esp. ad 1); q. 4, a. 2, and my discussion of those texts (and others) in chapters 4–5, above.

require embodiment, the latter does. This Aristotelian way of speaking of the essence of happiness versus its well-being is one that St. Thomas uses throughout his teaching career, but he applies it to a discussion of the relative importance of embodiment for perfect happiness only in this later stage of his life.[45]

To help us understand the significance of the difference between *perfect* human happiness in heaven and the *bene esse* of perfect human happiness, we might consider a this-worldly use of the distinction. Consider the relationship between the beauty (or health) of the human body and the kind of imperfect human happiness possible in this life. We might think with St. Thomas that the essence of this-worldly imperfect happiness consists in graced virtuous activity, that is, acts of faith, hope, charity, wisdom, justice, courage, and temperance, as acting in concert with the Holy Spirit's inspirations (enabled by the gifts of the Holy Spirit). Someone who lived a life characterized by such actions, even if they did not enjoy beauty (or health) of body would be happy. But we might also admit that beauty (or health) of the body is a real good. We might say that such goods are part of the well-being of the imperfect kind of happiness human persons can possess in this life.

In order to understand the significance of St. Thomas's relegation of embodiment to the well-being of perfect human happiness in heaven, let us begin with how St. Thomas understands the distinction between the *essence* of happiness and *the well-being* of happiness in Aristotle. For St. Thomas's increased use of such a distinction in *ST* I-II probably owes to his concurrently authoring the commentary on the *Nicomachean Ethics*.[46] For example, in one place in that commentary St. Thomas argues that Aristotle distinguishes the *essence* of happiness, which consists in the soul's activity expressing virtue, from secondary goods. Some of these secondary goods are necessary for a certain *decoration* (*decorum*) of happiness, whereas others are necessary *instrumentally* (*instrumentaliter*) for attaining the essence of happiness.[47]

---

45. St. Thomas uses the distinction between perfect happiness and the well-being of perfect happiness at least one time in the *Sentences* commentary when speaking of the distinction in Aristotle. See, e.g., *In Sent* IV, d. 49, q. 5, a. 1, ad 1 (*ST Suppl.*, q. 96, a. 1, ad 1) and several times in *ST* I-II (see, e.g., q. 4, a. 5, resp.; a. 6, resp. and ad 1; a. 7, ad 3; a. 8, resp.; q. 5, a. 2, ad 3). See also his commentary on Aristotle's *NE* (I, lect. 13, n. 163; lect. 14, n. 173; lect. 16, n. 194; X, lect. 11, n. 2104) for places where he distinguishes happiness, on the one hand, and an enrichment or adornment (*decorum*) or the well-being (*bene esse*) of happiness, on the other hand.

46. See Torrell, *Saint Thomas Aquinas*, 328.

47. *In NE* I, lect. 14, n. 173; lect. 16, n. 194.

If St. Thomas has this distinction in mind (in *ST* II, q. 4, a. 5), then by speaking of embodiment as part of the *well-being* of perfect happiness, St. Thomas certainly means that embodiment is a kind of decoration (*decorem*) of perfect happiness, as he denies that embodiment is necessary as an instrument for attaining the essence of perfect happiness. Indeed, St. Thomas makes clear—even as early as the *Sentences* commentary—that by the expression, *well-being of perfect happiness* (*bene esse beatitudinis*), he means perfect happiness to which "a non-instrumental decoration of perfect happiness" is added.[48] Therefore, embodiment as a component part of the well-being of perfect happiness is not an instrumental good but rather a good of decoration. As a decoration of perfect happiness is clearly a nonproper accident of perfect happiness, St. Thomas thinks (at the time he authors *ST* I-II) that embodiment is part of the *accidental* reward and not the *essential* reward.[49]

Returning to *ST* II, q. 4, a. 5, resp., St. Thomas concludes by invoking an argument that we have seen him use earlier in his career. He argues that embodiment is not a part of the essence of perfect happiness but a part of the well-being of perfect happiness. Because the perfection of a thing's operation depends upon a thing's nature and the human soul's nature is more perfect insofar as it configures matter (as it is part of the nature of the human soul to do that), so the human soul's operation is more perfect insofar as the soul is embodied.

Does this mean that embodiment is an aspect of the essential reward? St. Thomas's use of a citation from St. Augustine suggests not: "the souls of the dead separated from their bodies ... cannot see the Unchangeable Substance, as the blessed angels see It; either for some other more hidden reason, or because they have a natural desire to rule the body."[50] The context of this citation from St. Augustine suggests that St. Thomas thinks St. Augustine *has* indeed hit upon the reason that there is a difference between the blessed angels and separated human souls: the accidental reward of the latter is incomplete in a sense in which the accidental reward of the former is not, for separated souls wish to rule their bodies in heaven whereas angels (not naturally having bodies) do not have such a desire.[51]

---

48. *In Sent* IV, d. 49, q. 5, a. 1, ad 1 (*ST Suppl.*, q. 96, a. 1, ad 1).
49. See also *ST* I-II, q. 4, a. 6, ad 1 and ad 2. For discussion, see Leget, *Living with God*, 225.
50. Trans. English Dominicans, 606.
51. See also *ST* I-II, q. 4, a. 5, ad 6.

Why the *accidental* reward? The human soul's desire to rule the body—or to see the body participate in the beatific vision—is a desire for a *created* good, and such desires form a part of the accidental reward for St. Thomas.[52] In addition, recall that the essential reward consists in the beatific vision and whatever is related to the beatific vision as a proper accident of the vision. But any goods enjoyed by the saints that are related to the beatific vision as nonproper accidents, for example, features not always possessed by the saints such as the good which is the human soul's glory flowing into the resurrected body, are constitutive parts of the accidental reward.

There is additional evidence that St. Thomas thinks, in the later part of his teaching career, that embodiment is an aspect of the accidental reward of the saints and not the essential reward. For St. Thomas treats the society of created friends in heaven as a part of the well-being of perfect happiness rather than as an aspect of the essence of perfect happiness.[53] But the society of *created* friends is clearly part of the accidental reward.[54] But the following principle seems plausible:

(76) For any parts x and y of the well-being of perfect happiness that are not required for perfect happiness, if x is a part of the accidental reward, then y is a part of the accidental reward.

Given that embodiment in heaven is an aspect of the well-being of perfect happiness not required for perfect happiness, the truth of (76), and the fact that for St. Thomas the communion of the saints is both an aspect of the well-being of human happiness and part of the accidental reward, it follows that St. Thomas thinks that embodiment in heaven is an aspect of the accidental and not the essential reward.

As we have seen, St. Thomas arguably treats embodiment as an aspect of the essential reward in some of his earlier works insofar as, at that time, he thinks that the body is an instrumental cause of the operation of the beatific vision being perfect. Because what St. Thomas says in *ST* implies that embodiment is part of the accidental reward, St. Thomas

---

52. Also, as we will see below in chapters 11 and 13, one way that the glorified body participates in the beatific vision, according to St. Thomas, is that it senses "the new heavens and the new earth" in such a way that it is obvious to the saint that such things are effects of God. Although such cognition is God-directed, it still forms part of the accidental reward because it is a good distinct from the beatific vision and the proper accidents of the vision.

53. *ST* I-II, q. 4, a. 8, resp. and ad 3.

54. Ibid.

changes his mind about the relative importance of embodiment for human happiness by the time he authors *ST*.

For further evidence that St. Thomas changes his mind about the relative importance of embodiment for perfect human happiness by the time he authors *ST* I-II, consider some of the objections and replies contained in q. 4, a. 5. The first objection begins by noting that the perfection of virtue and grace, in which beatitude consists, presupposes the perfection of nature. The first objection continues as follows: a part is imperfect when separated from the whole. Because the human soul is a part of human nature, the separated human soul does not possess the perfection of nature. Therefore, the human soul without the body is not able to be perfectly happy (*beata*).

The first thing to notice about this objection is that it is nearly identical to St. Thomas's argument from first perfection in *CT*, which argument resembles the argument from imperfect happiness and the argument from the natural union of the soul and body. It appears as though this text (*ST* I-II, q. 4, a. 5, obj. 1) is an argument that St. Thomas himself thought sound earlier in his teaching career.

How does St. Thomas respond to the first objection—and so an argument such as the argument from first perfection in *CT*? St. Thomas's central point in his response is that the perfection of the human soul is twofold, as the human soul is both something that naturally has powers that transcend the body and something that naturally (if not necessarily) is the substantial form of a living body. As long as the human soul is perfected with respect to its intellectual activities, which transcend the body, that human soul is perfectly happy. Therefore, even though the separate human soul does not possess the perfection of the nature *qua* substantial form, it does possess the perfection of nature *qua* possessor of intellect, the possession of which is sufficient for perfect happiness.

St. Thomas, by the time he writes *ST* I-II, therefore finds a need to disambiguate premises in arguments that he previously thought to be sound. For example, premises (2)[55] and (4)[56] in AIPO are ambiguous because the separated human soul retains the perfection of its natural being insofar as it is intellectual, even if it does not retain it insofar as it is

---

55. A part *p* is less perfect in its natural being when separated from the whole of which *p* is naturally a part when compared to *p* when *p* is joined to the other parts that are naturally a part of the whole of which *p* is a natural part.

56. The more perfect a thing is in its natural being, the more perfect is its operation.

substantial form of the body. In addition, premise (21)[57] in AIHSS is ambiguous because, although the separated human soul exists imperfectly as a part *qua* substantial form of a body, it does not exist imperfectly *qua* possessor of intellect. Premises (25)[58] and (27)[59] in the argument from the natural union of the soul and body are also ambiguous. This is because the separated human soul can be perfect in nature *qua* possessor of intellect if not *qua* substantial form of the body. Finally, premises (47)[60] and (48)[61] in the argument from first perfection are ambiguous because, although the separated human soul is not perfect in nature *qua* part of the form/matter composite, it is perfect in nature *qua* possessor of intellect.

How can disambiguating such premises help St. Thomas to avoid the conclusions of arguments he rejects by the time he authors *ST* I-II? To see how, let us take a look at the argument from first perfection. First, where premise (48) is concerned, St. Thomas would want to distinguish the following:

(48*) For any part p of a whole that is a substantial form, p is not perfect in its nature *qua* part of the composite unless p exists in the whole of which p is naturally a part.

(48**) For any part p of a whole that possesses an intellect, p is not perfect in its nature *qua* possessor of an intellect unless p exists in the whole of which p is naturally a part.

Note that St. Thomas, given what he argues in *ST* I-II, would think that (48**) is false. That introduces just enough of an ambiguity in the argument composed of (47)–(51) that the argument from first perfection would have to be entirely reconstructed, perhaps as an argument that simply shows that the separated human soul does not enjoy the *well-being* of perfect happiness. St. Thomas, at the time he composes *ST* I-II, can say something similar with respect to AIPO, AIHSS, and the argument from the natural union of the soul and body.

Having said something about *ST* I-II, q. 4, a. 5, obj. 1, let us turn to the

---

57. But a part p existing apart from the whole of which p is naturally a part exists imperfectly in comparison to p when it is not separate from the whole of which p is naturally a part.

58. There can be no perfection of happiness (*perfectio beatitudinis*) where [the] nature [of the soul] is not perfect.

59. The nature of the human soul is not perfect when it is separated from the body.

60. The first perfection of x requires that x is perfect in its nature.

61. No part of a whole is perfect in its nature unless it exists in the whole of which it is naturally a part.

second objection. The second objection goes as follows: for any part *p*, *p* is imperfect in being (*esse*) when separated from the whole of which *p* is naturally a part; therefore, the human soul separated from the body is not perfect in being. Because the degree to which an operation is perfect is relative to the perfection of the being of that which operates, it follows that the separated human soul cannot have a perfect operation. But perfect happiness is a perfect operation. Therefore, the separated human soul cannot be perfectly happy.

Of course, we have seen an argument like this already, namely, AIPO in the *Sentences* commentary. How does St. Thomas respond to the second objection? By pointing out that the objector does not fully appreciate the manner in which the human soul is *sui generis* as a kind of part. As St. Thomas notes, generally speaking, when it comes to the part/whole relation, for any given part P, one of two things will happen when P is separated from the whole to which P belongs, or the whole to which P belongs is corrupted. One possibility is that P will cease to exist when P is separated from the whole to which P once belonged, for example, as the eyes of an animal cease to exist when that animal dies (as they are no longer apt to function as eyes).

Another possibility is that, if P does survive the corruption of the whole to which P belonged, then the being of P will not be identical to the being of the whole to which P once belonged. For example, consider a case where a log that is not currently a part of a log cabin and a log that once was a part of a log cabin are numerically identical. In such a case, the log's being is obviously not numerically identical to the being of the log cabin of which that log was once a part. Now, for St. Thomas, the human soul *is* a part of a human person that can survive the death of the composite human person, while at the same time preserving the being, identity, and individuality of that *composite* human person. Because the human soul's activity of knowing and loving God in heaven does not require use of the body—as we have seen, the vision of God's essence in heaven is entirely an intellectual and not a bodily sort of seeing—the separated human soul's act of seeing God's essence is no less perfect than that of the embodied soul.

Nonetheless, the separated human soul does not possess the perfect nature of the human species, as human persons are naturally (if not necessarily) embodied beings. As in his answer to the first objection,

St. Thomas therefore answers the second objection by making a distinction: the separated human soul is perfect *qua* being and operation but it is not perfect *qua* possessing the complete nature of the species. As perfect happiness is an operation, operation follows being, and the separated human soul has perfect being, the separated human soul can be perfectly happy even if it does not enjoy the perfection of possessing the complete nature of the species (which perfection is part of the accidental reward).

St. Thomas's response to the second objection suggests how he would respond to some of his earlier arguments. For example, he would *reject* premise (4)[62] of AIPO because the human soul is not less perfect in its being and operation when separated from matter than when the human soul is configuring matter. In reconstructing those arguments in light of such ambiguities, the most one could argue is that the separated human soul cannot enjoy the *well-being* of perfect happiness, which is consistent with what St. Thomas argues in *ST* I-II.

Consider now the fourth objection to q. 4, a. 5. The objection begins with an Aristotelian premise: the operation of bliss is not hindered. It continues with a citation from St. Augustine's *Literal Commentary on Genesis*: "[the soul] has a natural desire to rule the body, the result of which is that it is held back, so to speak, from tending with all its might to the heavenward journey [i.e., to the vision of the divine essence]."[63] Therefore, the separated soul is held back or hindered with respect to the operation of bliss. Therefore, the separated soul cannot be perfectly happy.

St. Thomas responds to this fourth objection by noting that there are at least two ways that something can be hindered. A thing can be hindered by *opposition* or *defect*. The former prevents someone from being perfectly happy but the latter does not. For example, the soul that still has evil inclinations, and so is hindered by *opposition*, is such that it cannot be perfectly happy. On the other hand, the separated human soul of a saint has the *defect* of lacking matter to configure. Although this hinders such a separated human soul from being perfect in every way—and so enjoying what St. Thomas in the body of this article calls *the well-being of perfect happiness*—it does not prevent such a separated human soul from enjoying perfect happiness, which it possesses just in virtue of enjoying the beatific vision. In interpreting the text from St. Augustine, St. Thom-

---

62. The more perfect a thing is in its natural being, the more perfect is its operation.
63. Trans. English Dominicans, 605.

as says that the appetite (*appetitus*) of the separated human soul is sated in the beatific vision. Nonetheless, the soul is hindered from tending with all its might to the beatific vision because it would still wish (*vellet*) that the body participate in the beatific vision insofar as it can, namely, by receiving an overflow of beatitude from the soul, that is, that the body be glorified, and so, be impassible, subtle, agile, and luminescent.

ST I-II, q. 67, helps to clarify what St. Thomas has in mind here by saying that a defect in the separated human soul of the saint is consistent with that saint being perfectly happy. The text is St. Thomas's answer to an objection, which objection has someone defending the thesis that the virtue of hope can exist in the souls of the blessed. The objector defends the thesis as follows:

(77) If there can be *desire* for a future good in the soul of the blessed, then there can be *hope* for some future good in the soul of the blessed.

(78) But there can be desire for a future good in the soul of the blessed, because (a) St. Augustine thinks that there can be a desire in the souls of the blessed for the glory of the body, and (b) scripture (Sir 24:29) teaches that there can be desire in the souls of the blessed for the glory of the soul.[64]

In St. Thomas's view, the theological virtue of hope cannot exist in the souls of the blessed because hope is a virtue that facilitates our tending toward God as not possessed (*non habetur*) and human persons in heaven, even before the general resurrection, possess God insofar as they have the beatific vision.[65]

He responds, then, to the objection above by first denying that the souls of the blessed have a desire for the glory of the soul (78b). This is because desire looks to some good to be possessed in the future not yet possessed; because the souls of the blessed enjoy the glory of the soul just in virtue of having the beatific vision;[66] and because there is no succession—and so no future—in the beatific vision.[67] The scriptures that speak of desire (for glory) in the soul do so, thinks St. Thomas, as a way of communicating that the soul will never tire of heavenly glory.[68]

---

64. *ST* I-II, q. 67, a. 4, obj. 3.
65. See, e.g., *ST* I-II, q. 67, a. 3, resp.
66. *ST* I-II, q. 67, a. 4, ad 3.
67. *ST* I-II, q. 67, a. 4, ad 2.
68. *ST* I, q. 67, a. 4, ad 3.

Second, St. Thomas notes that there is indeed a desire for *the glory of the body* in the separated soul, but that such a desire is unlike hope, no matter how we understand the word *hope*. If we understand *hope* as the theological virtue, the desire of the separated human soul for the glorified body is unlike hope because hope has *God for its object* and the separated human soul's desire for embodiment has a *created good* for its object. If we understand hope in a looser sense such that its object is *something difficult to obtain*, a saint's desire for embodiment before the general resurrection is also unlike hope, as the saint knows she will, one day, be embodied.[69] Because the desire of the separated human soul for the glory of the body is radically unlike hope, premise (77) is false.

The takeaway from this text for my purposes is that St. Thomas clearly teaches here that the separated human soul's desire for the glory of the body *is not a part of the essential reward*, but rather a part of the accidental reward. This is because such a desire is a rational desire for a *created* good in addition to the beatific vision and its proper accidents.

Coming back, then, to St. Thomas's response (to *ST* I-II, q. 5, a. 4, obj. 4), the separated soul is perfectly happy having the beatific vision, even though it suffers the defect of not having a glorified body. But the separated soul's having such a defect is consistent with its being perfectly happy because the attainment of perfect happiness (or the essential reward) consists in the beatific vision, the object of which is God, whereas the object of the desire for the glorified body is a created good, and therefore the saint's having a glorified body is an aspect of the accidental reward.

St. Thomas's response to the fourth objection shows how he would respond to the argument from disquiet in the will: when premise (36)[70] is disambiguated, either the argument from disquiet in the will is invalid or else premise (36) is false. First, note that perfect happiness in that argument is equivalent to the essential reward, otherwise, proposition (33), and at least one of the premises in the argument consisting of propositions (29)–(33), will be false, because St. Thomas, throughout his corpus, thinks that, at the very least, the general resurrection occasions a change in the happiness of the saint or separated soul in heaven. In

---

69. Ibid.
70. If the acts of the will of the separated soul that are aspects of perfect happiness are all immutable, then the will of the separated soul in heaven is perfectly at rest (*perfecta quietatio voluntatis*), i.e., the separated soul in heaven has no desire to change.

light of the distinction between the desire for perfect happiness as sated by the beatific vision and the desire for the well-being of perfect happiness, which is satisfied by the addition of certainly creaturely goods to the good of the beatific vision and the acts of will that follow upon the vision, we can disambiguate premise (36) as follows:

(36*) If the acts of the will of the separated soul that are aspects of perfect happiness, that is, the essential reward, are all immutable, then the will of the separated soul in heaven is perfectly at rest (*perfecta quietatio voluntatis*) with respect to the essential reward, that is, the separated soul in heaven has no desire to change *with respect to the essential reward*.

(36**) If the acts of the will of the separated soul that are aspects of perfect happiness, that is, the essential reward, are all immutable, then the will of the separated soul in heaven is perfectly at rest (*perfecta quietatio voluntatis*) with respect to the well-being of perfect happiness or the accidental reward, that is, the separated soul in heaven has no desire to change *with respect to the well-being of perfect happiness or the accidental reward*.

Consider the version of the argument from disquiet in the will that includes (36*). Premise (36*) is true, but the argument that consists of (36*), (43),[71] and (44)[72] is logically invalid. It does *not* follow that *it is not the case that the separated soul's acts of will that are aspects of perfect happiness, that is, the essential reward, are all immutable* simply because the separated soul has unsated desires for creatures, for example, the resurrection of the separated soul's body. This is because St. Thomas thinks that perfect happiness, or the essential reward, has God alone as its object.[73] For the same sort of reason, (36**) is false because it does not follow that, if S's acts of will are immutable with respect to perfect happiness or the essential re-

---

71. Therefore, it is not the case that the will of the separated soul in heaven is perfectly at rest, i.e., the separated soul in heaven has a desire to change; from (37) and (42), MT.

72. Therefore, it is not the case that the acts of the will of the separated soul that are aspects of perfect happiness are all immutable; from (36) and (43), MT.

73. In addition, there is good evidence for thinking that St. Thomas believes that created persons in heaven enjoy multiple modes of cognition. Those acts that constitute aspects of the attainment of perfect human happiness or the essential reward, i.e., the beatific vision and the acts of will that are proper accidents of the vision, are timeless and immutable. But those cognitive acts that are part of the accidental reward—and so part of the well-being of perfect happiness—take place in time, e.g., willing to move the glorified body from one place to another, or willing to look at *this* celestial body right now (rather than another), thereby delighting in God's wisdom in fashioning the new creation. See, e.g., *In Sent* IV, d. 49, q. 2, a. 2, resp. and ad 6 (*ST Suppl.*, q. 92, a. 2, resp. and ad 6) and *SCG* IV.86. See also the discussion of St. Thomas on human cognition in heaven other than the beatific vision in chapters 11 and 13 below.

ward, that S's desire for the well-being of perfect happiness is satisfied.

Returning to *ST* I-II, q. 4, a. 5, the fifth objection is similar to the fourth objection insofar as it also has to do with desire. The objection goes as follows: perfect happiness sates all desire. But, as St. Augustine notes, the separated human soul desires to be united to the body. Therefore, the separated human soul is not perfectly happy.

St. Thomas responds to this objection by making a distinction between two ways that a soul's desire might be at rest. First, a soul S's desire might be at rest insofar as S possesses the object O that lulls S's desire. Second, a soul S's desire might be at rest insofar as S possesses O in every manner in which S might wish to possess O. The soul that has its desires lulled in the first sense is perfectly happy. According to St. Thomas, the separated human soul does not have its desires lulled in the second way—as it desires that the body would share in the soul's beatitude. But recall that the essential reward is a wholly immaterial union between the human soul and God. Therefore, the desire that the body might share in beatitude—that the human person can enjoy God indirectly through the body—is a desire to obtain an aspect of the accidental reward or the well-being of perfect happiness, namely, the glorification of the body. Therefore, the separated human soul is perfectly happy, or enjoys the essential reward, even if it does not enjoy the well-being of perfect happiness, or all aspects of its accidental reward. And so St. Thomas goes on to note that the embodied soul of a saint is *not* more intensely happy than is the separated soul of a saint—note here an explicit departure from his early view in the *Sentences* commentary.

Rather, perfect happiness only increases in extent at the general resurrection insofar as the body too participates in the perfect happiness of the soul's beatific vision. All of this makes sense in light of what we have seen St. Thomas say: the desire for embodiment is a desire for a good that is a part of the accidental reward, and not a desire for (an aspect of) the essential reward. The human person who possesses the essential reward—as does the separated human soul of the saint—is perfectly happy *in possessing God* in the greatest logically possible way in the beatific vision, even if that saint's accidental reward is not all that it can be, for example, insofar as it lacks *the created good* of having a glorified body in heaven.[74]

---

74. See also *QDM*, q. 5, a. 1, ad 4: "A created good added to an uncreated good does not make it a good greater nor cause greater happiness. The reason for this is that if two participants are conjoined, that of which they are participants can be augmented in them; but if a participant

Given St. Thomas's way of responding to the fifth objection, he would obviously reject some of the premises in arguments he gave earlier in his career for the thesis that the separated human soul is not perfectly happy. By the time he authors *ST* I-II, St. Thomas rejects the position that the saint in heaven is more intensely happy at and after the resurrection of the body than before the resurrection. Due to this rejection, St. Thomas has to reject one of the premises of AIPO. We have already seen that St. Thomas has reasons to reject premise (2) of that argument by the time he authors *ST* I-II. But his answer to the fifth objection shows that he would also reject premise (12)[75] of AIPO because he now thinks that the human soul's beatific vision without the body is just as perfect as it is with the body.

PERFECT HUMAN HAPPINESS AND ITS WELL-BEING

St. Thomas thinks that, in order to make sense of scripture and authoritative, Catholic Christian tradition on human happiness in heaven, we need to distinguish the essential reward (= the attainment of perfect human happiness) and the accidental reward (= the attainment of the composite of goods that is added to perfect human happiness to make for the attainment of the well-being of perfect human happiness). One might wonder, however, whether it makes any sense to say that a separated human soul is perfectly happy if that human soul lacks goods that make for the well-being of perfect human happiness. Should we not simply say that the separated human soul is not perfectly happy after all? As we saw in chapter 1, this is an objection that Catholic theologian Germain Grisez raises for St. Thomas's account of perfect human happiness in heaven.[76]

---

is added to that which is such essentially, it does not cause it to be greater, for example, two hot things joined to one another can result in greater heat, but if there were such a thing as essentially subsistent heat, it would not become hotter by the addition of any hot object. Since then God is the very essence of goodness, as Dionysius says, and all other things are good by participation, God does not become a greater good by the addition of any good because the goodness of every other thing is contained in Him. Hence since happiness is nothing other than the attainment of the perfect good, any other good whatsoever added to the divine vision or enjoyment will not cause greater happiness; otherwise God would have become happier by making creatures," trans. Jean Oesterle (Notre Dame, Ind.: University of Notre Dame Press, 1995), 212–13.

75. If the separated soul naturally desires to be embodied at and after the general resurrection so as to enjoy a more perfect beatitude, then the embodied soul's beatitude at and after the general resurrection is more intense than the separated soul's beatitude.

76. Recall that Grisez also raises an objection to a view such as St. Thomas's from the theological

There are a number of ways to show the coherence of St. Thomas's views that *the essential reward is a good that wholly satisfies human desire* and *the accidental reward consists of genuine human goods*. The beatific vision, along with its concomitant accidents of delight, love, and joy, are sufficient to sate the desire of an intellectual creature, as the beatific vision and its proper accidents consist of God's gracing the intellectual creature such that that creature becomes perfectly *deiform*, like unto God, in the greatest logically possible way. For that creature is taken up into God's own perfect eternal life and happiness so that the creature engages in the perfect and simultaneously whole act of seeing the essence of God in the most direct and unmediated way for a creature. In virtue of knowing the essence of God in the beatific vision in this intimate way, the intellectual creature is also granted the greatest logically possible creaturely knowledge of creatures. Therefore, the goodness of the beatific vision is simply incommensurate with any other creaturely good.

Consider also that an absolutely and infinitely perfect God is no happier in a state of affairs where there are creatures than in a state of affairs where creatures do not exist. It follows that, if a human person S, with a degree of charity C, enjoys the good of beatific union with God, and a human person S1, with a degree of charity C, has a creaturely good G1 in addition to the good of beatific union with God, S1 is no more *intensely* happy than S. Or, we might also say, to employ another way that St. Thomas speaks, S1 is no more *perfectly* happy than S, keeping in mind the real difference between perfect happiness, on the one hand, and the well-being of perfect happiness, on the other. St. Thomas thus preserves what I have called the Augustinian Intuition about God and human happiness.[77]

That being said, Christian tradition teaches that the saints in heaven (eventually) enjoy goods other than God in heaven, including human embodiment and the communion of the saints. If the aspects of the accidental reward are not necessary for perfect happiness, how should we speak about the goods that make up the accidental reward? Ezra Sullivan offers one way. He speaks of the parts of the accidental reward, and the resurrection of the body in particular, as *gratuitous* goods.[78] Let us say that

---

fact that the saints intercede for us: for, if a person S asks for something for person S1, then S has an unmet desire. What this chapter says about the separated human soul's desire for embodiment, despite that soul being perfectly sated in the beatific vision, also provides an answer to this objection of Grisez's.

77. See chapter 1 above.
78. "Seek First the Kingdom," esp. 979.

a gratuitous good G is a good that a person S would not miss if S did not possess G, but S is nonetheless thankful for G if or when S does possess G.[79] For example, Jane offers to pay for her friend Sally's lunch. Sally did not need this good, nor did Sally expect it. But given Jane's insistence, Sally gratefully accepts Jane's offer to pay for her lunch. Jane's friend buying her lunch is a gratuitous good for Sally.

Similarly, the aspects of the accidental reward are gratuitous goods. As the saints in heaven are perfectly happy having the beatific vision, they would not miss the loss of any of those aspects of the accidental reward they already enjoy, such as a certain kind of direct fellowship with the angels and other saints. Nor is their perfect happiness affected by not having those parts of the accidental reward they know they will one day possess, for example, glorified bodies and the more human communion of the saints that comes with possessing that good. Although these goods are not aspects of their perfect happiness or essential reward, they are (or will be) thankful for them nonetheless. Hence, the component parts of the accidental reward, such as the communion of the saints, human embodiment, and sensing the beauty of the new heavens and the new earth, make for, as St. Thomas sometimes puts it, the attainment of the *bene esse* of perfect human happiness.

Consider a second way of talking about (some of) those goods that are aspects of the accidental reward in heaven. As we are animals of a certain sort, some of the goods that are aspects of the accidental reward are *fitting* or *appropriate* goods for creatures such as ourselves to enjoy in heaven, even if they are not necessary for perfect happiness. To understand that claim, let us say that a good G is *fitting* or *appropriate* for a creature C if and only if the perfection of C does not require G, but, given C's nature, the possession of G would be a real good for C.[80] For example, Sam could live a good human life, even if he never hears (with some understanding) Chick Corea or Herbie Hancock play the piano with a jazz trio (say he lives before either Corea or Hancock were born). But Sam's hearing Corea (or Hancock) play the piano with a jazz trio (with some understanding), if it were possible, would count as real goods for Sam (assume

---

79. Fr. Sullivan does not define *gratuitous good*; he supplies the lovely English word, and this chapter supplies the definition in light of Michael Pakaluk's lecture, "Grisez's Critique of Aquinas on the Ultimate End of Human Life."

80. This chapter uses "fitting" in a slighter weaker sense than St. Thomas's *conveniens*, which is often translated as "fitting" (see, e.g., *ST* III, q. 1, a. 2).

with us that, given human nature, beautiful music is a good for human persons, and that the music of both Corea and Hancock is important and quite distinctively beautiful).

Now, consider that each one of the component parts of the accidental reward is a *fitting* or *appropriate* addition to the essential reward in heaven in the sense specified. The saints in heaven therefore can be perfectly happy without any of the component parts of the accidental reward. Nonetheless, each component part of the accidental reward, such as embodiment, would be, if it were possessed by the saints in heaven, a genuine good for human persons. Therefore, human persons are perfectly happy, or enjoy the essential reward, in the beatific vision and its concomitant accidents alone. One way to think about what St. Thomas means by *the well-being of perfect happiness* is as follows: that happiness of the saints that includes not just the essential reward, but also the accidental reward, namely, that set of goods each one of which, although not necessary for the attaining of perfect human happiness, is nonetheless a fitting or appropriate good for human persons to enjoy.

We can make sense of the distinction between the good of the essential reward in heaven and the good that is the accidental reward for human persons in still another way, drawing upon the work of philosopher Brandon Dahm. Dahm distinguishes between *desires-from-fulfillment* and *desires-from-lack*.[81] *Desires-from-lack* are the more ordinary sort of desires. A person S's possession of such desires entails that S is not perfectly happy. Although all human persons in this life suffer desires-from-lack, no human person in heaven suffers such desires, even the human person who is disembodied. This is because human persons in heaven are having the beatific vision, and to see God in that way is to see the essence of goodness itself. But there can be no more desires-from-lack on the part of such a seer.

On the other hand, *desires-from-fulfillment* are desires that arise not from a lack in the desirer, but rather from a perfection in the agent such that she wills to share the perfection she has with another. Dahm's this-worldly example of a desire-from-fulfillment is the father who rushes to tell his family and friends—even any strangers he happens to meet along the way—about the birth of his child. He does so not so much

---

81. See his "Distinguishing Desire and Parts of Happiness: A Response to Grisez." For a similar distinction, see Michael Pakaluk's lecture, "Grisez's Critique of Aquinas on the Ultimate End of Human Life," 11–12.

out of an unsatisfied need, but rather because he desires to share a great good with others.[82]

Dahm goes on to apply the distinction between desires-from-lack and desires-from-fulfillment to the case of the separated human soul in heaven.[83] A separated soul S in heaven no longer has, and never will have, any desires-from-lack. This is because S is as perfectly united to the essence of God in intellect and will as S can be, given the amount of charity S has when S dies, and God is perfect and infinite goodness. Nonetheless, S can still desire to share its beatitude with its body and with friends. Such desires are not desires-from-lack, but rather desires-from-fulfilment. Here is St. Thomas speaking similarly: "For the [separated] soul desires to enjoy God in such a way that the enjoyment also may overflow into the body, as far as possible. And therefore, as long as it enjoys God, without the fellowship of the body, its appetite is at rest in that which it has, in such a way, that it would still wish the body to attain to its share."[84] In addition, St. Thomas notes, "after the body has been resumed [at the general resurrection], happiness [in the human person in heaven] increases not in intensity [*instensive*], but in extent [*extensive*]."[85]

The essential reward of the saint therefore satisfies all of the saint's desires-from-lack, but that is consistent with that saint's having desires-from-fulfillment. The accidental reward, which when added to the essential reward is the attainment of the well-being of perfect happiness, consists in the expression of certain desires-from-fulfillment, for example, for embodiment and the communion of the saints.[86]

---

82. As Dahm points out ("Distinguishing Desire and Parts of Happiness," 108), one can always interpret such a desire as a lack in the one who desires, just as one can always interpret an altruistic act as motivated by some selfish desire on the part of one who does a good turn for another. In addition, in this life, we might think that charitable acts arise from both a concern for oneself and a concern for another. Likewise, any candidate for desire-from-fulfillment in this life is likely to be both a desire-from-lack *and* a desire-from-fulfillment. Nonetheless, this is to say enough to motivate the idea that there is such a thing as pure desire-from-fulfillment for human persons in heaven.
83. "Distinguishing Desire and Parts of Happiness."
84. *ST* I-II, q. 4, a. 5, ad 4 (trans. English Dominicans, 606).
85. Ibid., ad 5.
86. Mark Spencer suggests a possible parallel between Dahm's distinction between *desires-from-lack* and *desires-from-fulfillment*, as a way of making sense of St. Thomas's views, and St. Gregory of Nyssa's view that, at any moment in heaven, the human person in heaven is perfectly happy in having the beatific vision, but nonetheless grows in her enjoyment of God from moment to moment as she grows ever closer to God throughout eternity. But there is an important difference between Dahm's distinction, used as a way of interpreting St. Thomas's views, and the views of St. Gregory of Nyssa. For using Dahm's terminology to interpret St. Thomas, the separated soul does

Consider also that God is absolutely perfect and yet has willed to create. God does not will to create out of some lack in himself, as perhaps some neo-Platonists and Hegelians have believed. Rather, God freely wills to create so as to share his goodness with creatures. We might then say that, although God cannot have desires-from-lack, God has desires-from-fulfillment insofar as God freely chooses to will his own goodness such that the existence and flourishing of creatures is the result. Recall that St. Thomas argues that the saint having the beatific vision is made perfectly deiform. That makes an apt analogy between, on the one hand, a perfect God having no desires-from-lack but willing creatures to exist and, on the other hand, the separated soul having its desires-from-lack sated in the beatific vision while also wishing to share its perfection with the body and friends.

CONCLUSION

How significant is embodiment for human beatitude according to St. Thomas? As we have seen, St. Thomas changes his mind on how to answer this question over the course of his career. First of all, by the time he composes *ST* I-II, St. Thomas no longer thinks, as he did at the time of composing the *Sentences* commentary, that the essential reward or perfect happiness of the saints in heaven—the beatific vision and its proper accidents—is more intense at and after the resurrection of the dead than before. That, by itself, significantly reduces the importance of embodiment for human beatitude.

Second, St. Thomas changes the manner in which he speaks about the happiness of the separated human soul. Where according to his early view he claims that *the separated human soul cannot be perfectly happy*, by the time he composes *ST* I-II he denies this claim. In this later text, St. Thomas prefers to speak of the separated human soul's defect in human happiness as a lack in the attainment of the well-being of perfect happiness rather than as a lack of perfect happiness. As we have seen, however,

---

not have desires-from-lack because the separated soul already enjoys *the essential reward*, where the essential reward of the saint in heaven is immutable, but the separated soul does have desires-from-fulfillment, as the soul wishes that the body too could participate in the beatific vision. But the body's participation in the beatific vision is an aspect of *the accidental reward* for St. Thomas. Assuming that St. Gregory of Nyssa's views entail that *the essential reward* gets better for the saints in heaven from moment to moment, there is an important sense in which St. Gregory's views do not parallel the views of Dahm and St. Thomas.

the lack of embodiment—or any aspect of the accidental reward—in the separated human soul is consistent with the soul's being perfectly happy because embodiment is a genuine human good that is not necessary, but rather gratuitous, fitting, or appropriate, where perfect happiness is concerned. To put the point another way, embodiment is a genuine human good that satisfies a desire-from-fulfillment rather than a desire-from-lack.

Finally, whereas according to St. Thomas's early view embodiment is clearly an aspect of both the essential and accidental rewards, St. Thomas's later view implies that embodiment at and after the general resurrection is a part of the accidental reward only. Why does St. Thomas change his mind? A speculation: given that (a) St. Thomas thinks throughout his career that the essential reward is invariable, timeless, and unchanging, and (b) if embodiment increases the essential reward (as St. Thomas's early view implies), then the essential reward is variable, timebound, and changing, it seems that St. Thomas's later view more greatly coheres with other things he says about the next life than does his early view.

10

The Accidental Reward II

RESURRECTION BODIES

According to St. Thomas, all human persons will be resurrected at the end of time[1] when Christ comes again,[2] with the exception of the Virgin Mary, whose body has already been assumed into heaven.[3] In addition, all resurrected bodies—whether those in heaven or those in hell—will have certain properties *qua* resurrected bodies.[4] Call these properties *resurrection properties*, or "R properties." St. Thomas thinks that the following properties are among the R properties: (a) being a body of a human person that is immortal;[5] (b) incorruptibility;[6] (c) being specifically identical to a human body that existed in this life;[7] (d) being numerically identical to a particular human body that existed in this life;[8] (e) enjoying specific integrity of parts,[9] that is, being such that

---

1. See, e.g., *In Sent* IV, d. 43, q. 1, a. 1, q.c. 2 (*ST Suppl.*, q. 75, a. 2); *SCG* IV.79 and 81.15. It is worth noting that, by the time St. Thomas is teaching, the view that all human persons will rise from the dead—with bodies numerically identical to the ones that they possessed in this life—was already dogmatically defined at Lateran Council IV, Dogmatic Constitution *De Fide Catholica* (1215).

2. See, e.g., *In Sent* IV, d. 43, q. 1, a. 3, q.c. 1, resp. (*ST Suppl.*, q. 77, a. 1, resp.) and *SCG* IV.79.

3. See, e.g., *In Sent* IV, d. 43, q. 1, a. 3, q.c. 1, obj. 2 and ad 2 (*ST Suppl.*, q. 77, a. 1, obj. 2 and ad 2) and *In SA*. Christ already has his resurrected human body in heaven, but Jesus Christ is a *divine* person who rises from the dead *qua* his human nature. See chapter 5, note 56, above. Of course, we must also keep in mind the communication of the idioms and the hypostatic union when speaking about Christ (see, e.g., *ST* III, q. 16).

4. See, e.g., *In Sent* IV, d. 44, q. 1 (*ST Suppl.*, qq. 79–81); *SCG* IV.82–85 and 86.1; *CSA*, chap. 11.

5. See, e.g., *SCG* IV.82 and *In 1 Cor* 15, lect. 3, n. 944.

6. See, e.g., *In Sent* IV, d. 44, q. 3, a. 2, q.c. 2 (*ST Suppl.*, q. 86, a. 2); *QQ* VII, q. 5, a. 1; *SCG* IV.85 and 89; *ST* I, q. 97, a. 1; *CT* I, chap. 177; *In 1 Cor* 15, lect. 3, nn. 931 and 934; lect. 8, n. 1003; lect. 9, n. 1012; *QDM*, q. 5, a. 5; *Responsiones ad lectorem Venetum de 30 et 36 articulis*, a. 20; *Responsio ad magistrum Joannem de Vercellis*, aa. 24 and 25; *In Rom* 5, lect. 3; 8, lect. 2, n. 633; *CSA*, a. 11.

7. See, e.g., *In Sent* IV, d. 44, q. 1, a. 1, q.c. 1 (*ST Suppl.*, q. 79, a. 1); *QQ* XI, q. 6; *SCG* IV.80–81; *CT* I, chap. 153; *In 1 Cor* 15, lect. 5, nn. 970–71; lect. 9, nn. 1012–15; *QDA*, a. 19, ad 13; *In Jb* 19, lect. 2.

8. See all texts mentioned in the note immediately above.

9. See, e.g., *In Sent* IV, d. 44, q. 1, a. 2 (*ST Suppl.*, q. 80, aa. 1–5); q. 3, a. 2, q.c. 1 (*ST Suppl.*, q. 86,

the body has the same kinds of quantitative parts as a mature, healthy human body in this life; (f) being numerically identical in stature;[10] (g) being identical in biological sex;[11] (h) being a body of a perfect age;[12] and (i) being such that it does not give rise to animal actions such as eating, sleeping, drinking, and sexual union.[13] Let us consider each of these R properties in detail.

ON NUMERICAL, SPECIFIC, AND PERSONAL IDENTITY BEYOND DEATH

The Christian tradition teaches that, with the exception of the Virgin Mary, all human persons are resurrected at the last day.[14] According to St. Thomas, if Socrates is *resurrected* from the dead, then Socrates at and after the general resurrection is specifically and numerically identical to Socrates in this life. In addition, if Socrates at and after the general resurrection is numerically identical to Socrates in this life, then Socrates's human body and human soul at and after the general resurrection are specifically and numerically identical to Socrates's body and soul, respectively, in this life. Finally, if Socrates at and after the general resurrection is numerically identical to Socrates in this life, then Socrates's human body at and after the general resurrection is *specifically* identical to Socrates's body in this life.[15] In defense of this account of the general resurrection, St. Thomas cites Job 19:25-27 ("For I know that my Redeemer lives, and that at the last he will stand upon the earth; and after my

---

a. 1); *QQ* VII, q. 5, a. 2; VIII, q. 3; *SCG* IV.84, 88.2, 89.2; *QDP*, q. 5, a. 10; *ST* I, q. 119, a. 1; *CT* I, chaps. 157, 176, 238; *In Mt* 10, lect. 2, nn. 877-78; *In Jn* 20, lect. 4-6; *QQ* V, q. 3, a. 1; *ST* III, q. 54.

10. See, e.g., *In Sent* IV, d. 44, q. 1, a. 3, q.c. 2 (*ST Suppl.*, q. 81, a. 2).

11. See, e.g., *In Sent* IV, d. 44, q. 1, a. 3, q.c. 3 (*ST Suppl.*, q. 81, a. 3); *SCG* IV.88; *In Eph* 4, lect. 4, n. 216; *CA*, Mt 22, lect. 3; *In Mt* 22, lect. 3, n. 1801.

12. See, e.g., *In Sent* IV, d. 44, q. 1, a. 3, q.c. 1 (*ST Suppl.*, q. 81, a. 1); *SCG* IV.88.5; *In Eph* 4, lect. 4, n. 216; *ST* III, q. 46, a. 9, ad 4; *CSA*, a. 1.

13. See, e.g., *In Sent* IV, d. 44, q. 1, a. 3, q.c. 4 (*ST Suppl.*, q. 81, a. 4); *In Jb* 19, lect. 2; *SCG* IV.83; *ST* I, q. 97, a. 3; *CT* I, chap. 156; *In 1 Cor* 15, lect. 5, n. 965; *In Mt* 22, lect. 3, n. 1800. Although one might think that eating, drinking, and venery are *vegetative* actions, St. Thomas, as we shall see, consistently calls them *animal* actions. He does this because the vegetative actions he is speaking about are vegetative actions as performed by human *animals*, e.g., not *simply taking in nourishment* and *reproducing*, but *eating*, *drinking*, and *procreating*. Thanks to Mark Spencer for showing the need to make this point explicit.

14. For texts from the tradition, see chapter 1, note 37 above.

15. See, e.g., *In Sent* IV, d. 44, q. 1, a. 1, q.c. 1 (*ST Suppl.*, q. 79, a. 1); *QQ* XI, q. 6; *SCG* IV.80-81; *CT* I, chap. 153; *In 1 Cor* 15, lect. 6, n. 976; lect. 9, nn. 1012-15; *In Jb* 19, lect. 2; *QDA*, a. 19, ad 13; *ST* III, q. 54, a. 1, resp.

skin has been thus destroyed, then in my flesh I shall see God, whom I shall see on my side, and my eyes shall behold, and not another. My heart faints within me!"),[16] 1 Corinthians 15:53 ("For this perishable body must put on imperishability, and this mortal body must put on immortality"),[17] as well as the positions of various Church Fathers, including St. John Damascene,[18] Pope St. Gregory the Great,[19] and St. Augustine of Hippo.[20]

St. Thomas is well aware of alternative ways of thinking about life after death for human persons. In his *Sentences* commentary, for example, he notes that some ancient philosophers teach that human souls are *naturally* reunited to bodies in another life. For St. Thomas, this view differs from resurrection in the Christian sense, because, according to Christian tradition, the resurrection is something miraculous, an event that occurs by way of power that goes beyond the powers of nature.[21]

St. Thomas knows of other views of bodily life in the next life that are problematic insofar as they entail that resurrected bodies are *nonhuman* bodies or human bodies that are *not numerically the same* as the human bodies that resurrected persons possessed in this life. Before discussing these views, it will be helpful to say something about St. Thomas's notion of what a human body is and what explains why human body B is numerically the same as human body B2. Let us begin with a discussion of the meaning of *human body*.

Some philosophers and theologians think that a human body is a

---

16. See, e.g., *In Sent* IV, d. 44, q. 1, a. 1, q.c. 1, s.c. and resp. (*ST Suppl.*, q. 79, aa. 1–2, s.c. and resp.); *SCG* IV.84.8; *In Jb* 19, lect. 2; *CSA*, a. 11.

17. See, e.g., *SCG* IV.85.7; *In 1 Cor* 15, lect. 9, n. 1014; *CSA*, a. 11.

18. See, e.g., *In Sent* IV, d. 44, q. 1, a. 1, q.c. 1, s.c. (*ST Suppl.*, q. 79, a. 1, s.c.).

19. See, e.g., *In Sent* IV, d. 44, q. 1, a. 1, q.c. 1, resp. (*ST Suppl.*, q. 79, a. 1, resp.).

20. See, e.g., *In Sent* IV, d. 44, q. 1, a. 1, q.c. 2, s.c. (*ST Suppl.*, q. 79, a. 2, s.c.).

21. See, e.g., *In Sent* IV, d. 44, q. 1, a. 1, q.c. 1 (*ST Suppl.*, q. 79, a. 1). See also *CT* I, chap. 154; *In 1 Cor* 15, lect. 2, n. 914; lect. 5, n. 969; *CSA*, a. 11. St. Thomas thinks that there are four *infimae* species of the genus *miracle* (see, e.g., *QDP*, q. 6, a. 2, ad 3): (a) miracles that nature in no way can produce that have things acting in a way A, where nature inclines them to actions non-A, e.g., Shadrach, Meshach, and Abednego not being burned in the fiery furnace; (b) miracles that nature in no way can produce that do not belong to species (a), e.g., God bringing about the incarnation of the Word; (c) miracles nature can bring about, absolutely speaking, but not in *this* or *that* particular matter, e.g., a person regaining his sight after going blind; and (d) miracles (call them the *m*s) belonging to a kind K of event such that nature can bring about members of K, but God brings about the *m*s apart from causes in nature, e.g., Christ healing St. Peter's mother-in-law. According to St. Thomas, resurrection is an example of miracle species (c) (see, e.g., *SCG* III.101.3; *QDP*, q. 6, a. 1, resp.; *ST* I, q. 105, a. 8, resp.). For discussion of a Thomistic definition of a miracle and these different *infimae* species of miracle, see my unpublished manuscript, "St. Thomas Aquinas on the Nature of Miracles."

physical substance distinct from the immaterial substance that is the human soul, as perhaps Plato teaches. St. Thomas does not think that there are human bodies in that sense. As we have seen, St. Thomas thinks that the human person is always and ever one substance, normally and naturally, if not necessarily, composed of two metaphysical parts—the human soul as substantial form and some prime matter—as well as the quantitative parts that result from the union of the human soul and prime matter. None of these parts of human persons is itself a substance.

There are a number of ways that an Aristotelian such as St. Thomas might use the word "body" in the expression *human body*. But there seems to be one meaning of *human body* that is particularly prominent in those places where St. Thomas discusses the resurrected body. In this sense of *human body*, the human body of a human person S is contrasted with S's soul in the sense that S's human body is everything about S that is physical, much of which can (in principle) be observed by way of the five senses, whereas S's soul, as a substantial form, is the immaterial part of S and so is among those features of a human person that cannot directly be observed by way of the five senses. Use of the expression *human body* in that sense has St. Thomas thinking about the collection of the natural, quantitative parts of the human person, such as heads, hearts, blood, flesh, etc. The human body in this sense is not a substance. Rather, it is merely a convenient way of speaking about the physical aspects of human persons that result from some prime matter being configured by a human substantial form.[22]

Recall that a substantial form is the intrinsic formal cause of a substance's species-specific properties, powers, and parts.[23] In the case of living substances such as human persons, this means that the substantial form of such a substance causes it to have certain bodily parts, organs, and systems, arranged in various shapes, at certain times, all other things being equal, for example, as long as some other substance does not prevent that substance from possessing those parts, organs, etc., at those times.[24] As we will see, the resurrected human body is a biologi-

---

22. See, e.g., *SCG* IV.81–96 and *ST* I, qq. 75–76.
23. See, e.g., *ST* I, q. 76, a. 8, resp.; q. 77, a. 6, resp.
24. The human person is a type of animal organism that develops through a number of different stages, e.g., zygote, embryo, fetus, newborn, infant, etc. Of course, at each of these stages it is normal and natural for an embodied human person to have certain sorts of quantitative parts, organs, and systems (and not others), where, among other things, those parts, organs, and systems are arranged in certain shapes. Assuming what we now know about human embryology, we can

cally mature, healthy, adult human body. Therefore, St. Thomas thinks that a *human body* in the next life is a body of flesh, blood, and bones, with various sorts of quantitative parts (e.g., arms, legs, torso, and head) with various sorts of organs (e.g., sexual organs, lungs, stomach, a brain), where those parts, organs, etc., exist in specifically the same spatial relations with one another as they do in biologically mature and healthy human bodies in this life. Any body in heaven that failed to conform to the above pattern would not be a *human* body in heaven and therefore would not have a human substantial form as its formal cause.[25]

Before moving on to speak about additional problematic views of the resurrection in St. Thomas's view, it will be helpful to say something about what makes a human body B and a human body B1 numerically identical. Recall that St. Thomas thinks that the intrinsic formal cause of the existence of human person S's body is S's human soul as substantial form configuring some prime matter. Therefore, the identity of S's human body will be tied to the identity of S's human soul and prime matter. In that case, a human person S's body B is numerically identical to a human person S1's body B1 if and only if S's soul is numerically identical to S1's soul, (b) S's prime matter is numerically identical to S1's prime matter, and (c) S's soul configures S's prime matter.

But what explains the numerical identity of a human person's soul and prime matter? Although St. Thomas thinks that a human soul, which is a substantial form, is individuated when it configures prime matter at the beginning of that soul's existence, a human soul nonetheless remains numerically the same as long as it exists.[26] As we have seen, the human soul is naturally immortal. Therefore, Socrates's soul after death is naturally numerically the same as Socrates's soul in this life.

I stated above that a human soul is individuated when it configures prime matter at the beginning of its existence. I can now be more precise: a material substance S's substantial form (e.g., a human soul), is individuated by the designated matter that S's substantial form configures when S's substantial form comes into existence.[27] Hence, designated

---

reasonably assert that the human soul as substantial form is the intrinsic formal cause of all of these features, starting at the very beginning of a human person's existence at the stage of the zygote. For arguments to this effect, see, e.g., Condic and Condic, *Human Embryos*.

25. See below for possible minor exceptions in the case of martyrs.
26. See, e.g., *QDA*, aa. 1–2, and *ST* I, q. 76, a. 2, ad 2.
27. See, e.g., *In BDT*, q. 4, a. 2, and *SCG* II.83.34.

matter, that is, matter that can be pointed at with a finger, is the principle (ultimate explanation) of individuation for material substances such as human persons.[28]

A few words of explanation regarding St. Thomas's views on designated matter are in order. First, designated matter is a *portion* of prime matter, that is, prime matter with the addition of the accidental form of *unterminated* quantity under three dimensions.[29] Second, the dimensions of some matter or material substance can be considered as either *terminated* or *unterminated*.[30] If the dimensions of some matter or material substance x are considered as terminated, then those dimensions are being considered according to the precise figure that x has at some time t. However, a material substance x is by its very nature something spread out in space—having quantity in three dimensions—and therefore x excludes any substance not-x from being where x is at any given time. To observe that two things x and y cannot exist in the same place at the same time (where x is not a proper part of y, or vice versa), without concern for the precise (terminated) dimensions of those two things, is to acknowledge that matter can be considered simply insofar as it is spread out in different places, that is, that different portions of prime matter or different material substances have different matter under unterminated dimensions.

Third, St. Thomas thinks that most accidents are individuated by the substances they characterize, for example, Socrates's tan is distinct from Plato's tan because Socrates's tan is a feature of Socrates, Plato's tan is a feature of Plato, and Socrates is numerically distinct from Plato.[31] In his commentary on Boethius's *De trinitate*, St. Thomas notes there is

---

28. *In BDT*, q. 4, a. 2, and *SCG* II.83.34. Understanding St. Thomas's account of the individuation of human persons involves a number of difficult interpretative matters that cannot be treated here. Suffice it to say the interpretation of St. Thomas's views offered here is controversial. For some detailed discussion of the interpretative issues, see, e.g., Jeffrey Brower, "Matter, Form, and Individuation," in *The Oxford Handbook of Aquinas*, ed. Brian Davies and Eleonore Stump (Oxford: Oxford University Press, 2012), 85–103; John F. Wippel, *The Metaphysical Thought of Thomas Aquinas: From Finite Being to Uncreated Being* (Washington, D.C.: The Catholic University of America Press, 2000), 362–75; and Lawrence Dewan, "The Individual as a Mode of Being according to Thomas Aquinas," *The Thomist* 63 (1999): 403–24. For additional sources, and additional defense of the position expressed here, see my *Aquinas and the Ship of Theseus*, 124–30, and my "Aquinas on the Individuation of Non-Living Substances," *Proceedings of the American Catholic Philosophical Association* 75 (2001): 237–54.

29. *In BDT*, q. 4, a. 2, and *SCG* II.83.34.

30. See, e.g., *In BDT*, q. 4, a. 2, resp.

31. See, e.g., *In Sent* I, d. 9, q. 1, a. 1, resp.; *QDP*, q. 9, a. 1, ad 8; *QDSC*, a. 3, ad 19; *In Meta* X, lect. 4, n. 2007; *ST* I, q. 29, a. 1, resp.; q. 39, a. 3, resp.; II-II, q. 24, a. 5, ad 1; III, q. 77, aa. 1–2.

an interesting difference between unterminated dimensions and other kinds of accidents.[32] Whereas unterminated dimensions—when found in matter—are principles of individuation, all other kinds of accidents are not.[33] There is therefore a difference between the accidents of unterminated dimensions and all other sorts of accidents, as accidents other than unterminated dimensions are individuated by the substances in which they inhere—which is the general rule where accidents are concerned—whereas unterminated dimensions are not so individuated. Rather, designated matter, or this portion of prime matter, is individuated in and of itself, and so designated matter is the *principle* of individuation for material substances. Even though Socrates's substantial form (his intellectual soul) is an individual thing distinct from other things once it configures designated matter, and so retains its numerical identity even when it does not configure its designated matter (e.g., in the interim state), the ultimate reason that it is distinct from other human souls is because Socrates's soul is individuated to begin with on account of its configuring some designated matter. Hence, designated matter is the *principle* of individuation insofar as it is the ultimate explanation as to why anything counts as an individual within a species.[34]

Fourth, St. Thomas thinks that in order for Socrates to rise as numerically the same human person at the general resurrection, Socrates's soul, which survives his death and is naturally immortal, must be joined miraculously to numerically the same designated matter that Socrates's soul configured in this life, where Socrates's designated matter has been configured by other substantial forms during the interim state.[35]

To conclude, we can say that, for St. Thomas, a human body B is numerically identical to human body B1 if and only if (a) human body B is the human body of human person S, (b) B1 is the human body of human person S1, (c) S and S1 are composed of numerically the same human soul as substantial form, and (d) S and S1 are composed of numerically the same designated matter, where, if (e) S and S1 are composed of numerically the same human soul as substantial form and numerically

---

32. *In BDT*, q. 4, a. 2.
33. *In BDT*, q. 4, a. 2, resp. and ad 3.
34. St. Thomas thinks that angels are not individuals within a species, but that story cannot be told here.
35. See, e.g., *In Sent* IV, d. 44, q. 1, a. 1, q.c. 1, ad 3 (*ST Suppl.*, q. 79, a. 1, ad 3); *SCG* IV.81.6; *In 1 Cor* 15, lect. 9, n. 1015.

the same designated matter, then (f) S and S1 are numerically the same human person.[36]

With St. Thomas's views on what makes a body *human* and the identity conditions for human bodies in the background, I can continue my treatment of those views of bodily life in the next life that St. Thomas finds to be problematic. St. Thomas notes that some ancient philosophers held the view that human souls can be united to bodies numerically, and in some cases specifically, different from the bodies to which they are united in this life.[37] According to St. Thomas, this mistaken view is rooted both in a problematic account of the nature of human persons and a problematic view of the nature of intellect. For some ancient philosophers wrongly thought that the soul could be united to a numerically or specifically different body because they thought that the soul is only *accidentally* united to the body in the sense that the body is never an essential part of us. In that case, the soul could preexist the human body, be joined to a numerically different human body, or even be joined to a nonhuman body. But, as we have seen, St. Thomas thinks that the soul stands to the body not simply as mover to thing moved but as substantial form to matter. Soul and matter form a substantial unity and not an accidental union of two different substances.

In addition, some ancient philosophers failed to see that intellect is different in kind from the senses. These philosophers therefore thought that there was no problem in principle with a human person who misused her cognitive powers in this life being born again as a kind of being that lacked an intellectual power in any sense, such as a wolf or a bee. But, as St. Thomas notes, intellect and the senses differ in kind, because the intellect is a wholly immaterial power whereas the senses are powers that require bodily organs functioning as the matter of such powers in

---

36. Insofar as the correct way to develop St. Thomas's views with respect to personal identity beyond death is to say that *a human person* can survive the death of the body, i.e., the loss of her designated matter, (e) is not also a necessary condition for (f). Rather, the existence of a human person S's soul is a necessary and sufficient condition for the existence of S. Nonetheless, if S is embodied in the next life, S must be composed of the designated matter that composed S in this life. Notice also that nothing I have said suggests that St. Thomas thinks that Socrates's resurrected body has to be composed of numerically the same atoms or quanta as Socrates's body in this life. For one reason that St. Thomas is an Aristotelian hylomorphist is that he realizes that it is possible that numerically the same organism is composed of numerically different quantitative parts at different times; it is identity of *metaphysical* parts that grounds numerical identity through time for St. Thomas, not numerical identity of *quantitative* parts (as it is for the atomist).

37. See, e.g., *In Sent* IV, d. 44, q. 1, a. 1, q.c. 1 (*ST Suppl.*, q. 79, a. 1).

order to act.³⁸ Anything without (the root capacity for) an intellect, for example, a wolf or a bee, could not be numerically identical to an intellectual substance such as a human person.

St. Thomas also mentions the views of some heretics, some of whom repeat the mistakes of the ancient philosophers, while others posit that resurrection bodies are made up of heavenly bodies, or are bodies like the wind. St. Thomas refutes these views by noting that scripture speaks the language of resurrection when treating of the afterlife, and not merely the assumption of a body, let alone a numerically different body.³⁹ Indeed, the assumption of a numerically different body in the afterlife would not, properly speaking, be a resurrection from the dead but rather an instance merely of reincarnation.

In *SCG*, St. Thomas offers a number of possible reasons that heretics have come to take the position that the human soul is joined to a specifically different—and thus numerically different—body at the resurrection.⁴⁰ One reason that heretics have adopted this view, thinks St. Thomas, is because human bodies are composed of contraries, and bodies composed of contraries are liable to corrupt. But resurrection bodies are incorruptible.⁴¹ A second reason that heretics adopted the view is because they misread 1 Corinthians 15:44: "It is sown a natural body; it shall rise a spiritual body."⁴² Finally, St. Thomas notes two other passages from 1 Corinthians that heretics have cited in defense of their view that we rise with specifically different kinds of bodies, namely, 15:40—"There are bodies celestial and bodies terrestrial"—and 15:50—"Flesh and blood cannot possess the kingdom of God."⁴³

St. Thomas has a number of arguments that show that these heretical interpretations cannot be correct. The first argument is a scriptural one. St. Paul teaches that our resurrection conforms to the resurrection of Christ. For, as it says in Philippians: "He will reform the body of our lowness, made like to the body of His glory" (3:21).⁴⁴ But after his resur-

---

38. Ibid.
39. Ibid.
40. I assume with St. Thomas that, for any x and any y, if x is *specifically* different from y, then x is *numerically* distinct from y.
41. *SCG* IV.84.1.
42. *SCG* IV.84.2 (trans. O'Neil, 320).
43. Ibid.
44. *SCG* IV.84.3 (trans. O'Neil, 321). See also *In Eph* 1, lect. 7, n. 57 (where St. Thomas cites Rom 8:17, Phil 3:20–21, and Rv 3:21); *In Phil* 3, lect. 3, n. 145; *In Rom* 8, lect. 3, nn. 649–51.

rection, Christ had a body that one could touch and a body composed of flesh and bones, for as St. Luke records: "Handle and see; for a spirit hath not flesh and bones as you see me to have" (24:39).[45] Therefore, when human persons rise at the last day, they too will have tangible human bodies composed of flesh and bone.

One might object that Christ rose from the dead with a human body but ascends into heaven (or exists in heaven) with a nonhuman body. But as St. Thomas points out, Christ must have ascended into heaven with the same (kind of) body, forever keeping it, as Romans 6:9 says that "Christ having risen again from the dead dieth no more." But death is the separation of the soul from the body. If Christ puts on another body after the resurrection, then he is separated from his resurrected body. If he is separated from his resurrection body, then he dies again after the resurrection.[46]

Another of St. Thomas's arguments relies on an Aristotelian philosophy of nature.[47] The human soul is united to a body as substantial form to prime matter. Furthermore, the prime matter to which the human soul is united is the prime matter of a certain kind of substance at the time the human person comes to be.[48] For example, a human soul cannot be united to an acorn so as to make a human person. Likewise, a human soul cannot be united to a heavenly body at the resurrection. In addition, prime matter is such that a certain kind of body results from its union with a *human* substantial form, that is, one with blood, bones, and flesh.[49] But even the heretic admits that the human soul is the same in species at the resurrection. Therefore, the matter that the rational soul configures is the same in species at the resurrection. It thus follows that the human body at the resurrection consists of flesh, blood, bone, etc., just as it did in this life.

Another argument begins with the premise that there is a greater difference between two specifically different bodies than two numerically distinct human bodies.[50] Therefore, if the human soul at the resurrection cannot be joined to a body numerically different from the one it

---

45. *SCG* IV.84.3 (trans. O'Neil, 321).
46. *QDP*, q. 5, a. 10, s.c.
47. *SCG* IV.84.4.
48. Prime matter in this sense is sometimes called matter *ex qua* (See, e.g., *DPN* I, 3).
49. See also *CT* I, chap. 153.
50. *SCG* IV.84.6.

configured in this life and retain its numerical identity, then the human soul at the resurrection cannot be joined to a body specifically different from a body in this life. But the human soul at the resurrection cannot be joined to a body numerically different from the one it configured in this life. This is because, as we saw above, *designated matter* is the principle of individuation such that one human soul is distinct from another insofar as a soul configures *this* rather than *that* matter at the beginning of its existence.[51] Now, the individual human soul can exist apart from the matter that individuates it, because once the soul is individuated, it is individuated in and of itself. However, it is not possible for the individual human soul to configure designated matter that is numerically distinct from the designated matter that it configures at the beginning of its existence.[52] Given that the body to which the soul is "joined" is caused by the human soul configuring designated matter, if it is possible for the human soul to be joined to a numerically different body, then it is possible for the human soul to configure designated matter that is numerically distinct from the designated matter that it configures at the beginning of its existence. Therefore, the human soul cannot be joined to a body *numerically* different from the one it configured in this life.[53] It thus follows that a human soul at the resurrection cannot be joined to a body *specifically* different from the body it possessed in this life.[54]

But how does St. Thomas understand St. Paul's text that says "flesh and blood cannot inherit the kingdom of God" (1 Cor 15:50)? St. Thomas's most detailed exegesis of this text comes in his own commentary on that text. He argues that St. Paul cannot mean in this passage that "the *substance* of flesh and blood cannot inherit the kingdom of God," as that interpretation flatly contradicts what scripture plainly says in other places, for example, in the conjunction of Philippians 3:21 ("He will transform the body of our humiliation so that it may be conformed to the body of his glory") and Luke 24:39 ("Touch me and see; for a ghost does not have flesh and bones as you see that I have").[55] St. Thomas thinks

---

51. See, e.g., *SCG* II.83.34.
52. See, e.g., *SCG* II.74.4; IV.80.2 and 81.6; *QDSC*, a. 9, ad 4. If, *per impossibile*, a human soul configured designated matter at the resurrection numerically distinct from the designated matter it configured in this life, it would become a numerically different soul.
53. See also *CT* I, chap. 153.
54. *SCG* IV.84.6. See also the rest of *SCG* IV.84, where St. Thomas offers additional *reductio* arguments for the heretical positions he mentions at the beginning of this chapter.
55. *In 1 Cor* 15, lect. 7, nn. 999–1000.

rather that St. Paul's "flesh and blood cannot inherit the kingdom of God" in 1 Corinthians 15:50 should be read metaphorically. He suggests three possible interpretations along these lines.[56] First, St. Paul may mean "*those devoting themselves to flesh and blood,* namely, men given to vices and lusts, cannot inherit the kingdom of God."[57] As St. Thomas points out, St. Paul uses "flesh" in this sense in other places in his letters, such as Romans 8:9 ("But you are not in the flesh, you are in the Spirit, if in fact the Spirit of God dwells in you").[58] A second possible interpretation: St. Paul means that "*the works of flesh and blood* cannot inherit the kingdom of God," that is, eating, drinking, and sexual congress.[59] As we will see, this interpretation is natural for St. Thomas given other things he sees in scripture, for example, that bodily life in the next life will be a very different kind of life, a bodily life in a "new heavens and a new earth" (Is 65:17–18 and Rv 21:1).[60] St. Thomas offers a third possible interpretation of the passage. St. Paul means: "*the corruption* of flesh and blood cannot possess the kingdom of God, that is, after the resurrection."[61] St. Thomas defends such a reading by noting that St. Paul goes on to say in the same verse that "neither shall corruption possess incorruption" (1 Cor 15:50b), while going on to interpret this passage as follows: "nor can the corruption of mortality, which is expressed here by the term *flesh,* inherit incorruption, that is, the incorruptible kingdom of God, because we will rise in glory: *because the creation itself will be set free from its bondage to decay and obtain the glorious liberty of the children of God* (Rom 8:21)."[62]

ON RESURRECTED BODIES AS POSSESSING SPECIFIC INTEGRITY OF BODILY PARTS

According to St. Thomas, all human bodies will enjoy *specific integrity* of bodily parts at the resurrection. That is, human bodies at the resur-

---

56. *In 1 Cor* 15, lect. 7, n. 1000. See also *In Sent* IV, d. 44, q. 1, a. 2, q.c. 3, ad 1 (*ST Suppl.*, q. 80, a. 3, ad 1), and *ST* III, q. 54, a. 3, ad 1.
57. *In 1 Cor* 15, lect. 7, n. 1000, trans. F. R. Larcher, B. Mortensen, and D. Keating, ed. J. Mortensen and E. Alarcón (Lander, Wyo.: Aquinas Institute for the Study of Sacred Doctrine, 2012), 376; emphasis added.
58. Ibid.
59. Ibid.; emphasis added.
60. See, e.g., *SCG* IV.97.8.
61. *In 1 Cor* 15, n. 1000 (emphasis added).
62. Ibid.; emphasis added. Chapter 11 below explains how St. Thomas understands 1 Cor 15:40 and 44.

rection have all of the same *kinds* of bodily parts at the resurrection they possessed in this life. More precisely:

> A human person S at and after the general resurrection is composed of (a) all of the non-sex-specific kinds of quantitative parts that naturally compose a mature and healthy human body, for example, arms, legs, head, torso, a heart, a brain, etc., (b) all of the sex-specific kinds of quantitative parts that compose a mature and healthy human body of the sex S possessed in this life, and (c) every stuff-kind that naturally makes up a mature and healthy human body, such as, blood, bone, flesh, hair, etc.

So, not only will a human person's body at and after the general resurrection be the same *kind* of body she possessed in this life, that is, a human one, it will also be a *complete* human body.[63]

Before examining St. Thomas's reasons for accepting (a), (b), and (c) above, there are three preliminary points worth mentioning here. First, the theses under consideration here should not be confused with the very different thesis that *all the matter that ever composed a human person will come to compose that human person at the resurrection*.[64] St. Thomas denies this latter thesis, as he sees no reason to believe it[65] and, as we shall see below, it conflicts with a doctrine that St. Thomas does have reason to believe, namely, that the human body at and after the general resurrection, insofar as it is a perfect *human* body, has a certain range of possible *statures*.

Second, as is the case with a number of the bodily perfections that I will discuss in this chapter, specific integrity of bodily parts is a perfection enjoyed, St. Thomas thinks, by both the blessed and the damned. We might think that the damned will not, in any sense, have perfect bodies. Indeed, St. Thomas entertains objections of just this sort.[66] But, as St. Thomas reminds us, there must be some perfection—at least the perfection of existence—in the damned, otherwise the damned would not exist at all. In addition, certain absurdities regarding the punishments of the damned would result if the damned did not enjoy specific integrity

---

63. See, e.g., *In Sent* IV, d. 44, q. 1, a. 2 (*ST Suppl.*, q. 80, aa. 1–5); q. 3, a. 1, q.c. 1 (*ST Suppl.*, q. 86, a. 1); *QQ* VII, q. 5, a. 2; VIII, q. 3; *SCG* IV.84, 88.2, 89.2; *QDP*, q. 5, a. 10; *ST* I, q. 119, a. 1; *CT* I, chaps. 157, 176, 238; *In Mt* 10, lect. 2, n. 877; *In Jn* 20, lect. 4–6; *QQ* V, q. 3, a. 1; *ST* III, q. 54.
64. See, e.g., *In Sent* IV, d. 44, q. 1, a. 2, q.c. 5 (*ST Suppl.*, q. 80, a. 5), and *In Mt* 10, lect. 2, n. 877.
65. Ibid.
66. See, e.g., the objections that St. Thomas fields in *In Sent* IV, d. 44, q. 3, a. 1, q.c. 1 (*ST Suppl.*, q. 86, a. 1).

of bodily parts at the resurrection.⁶⁷ Therefore, St. Thomas thinks that the damned too enjoy the perfection of human nature in the sense that human nature in the damned is restored, all other things being equal, to its original natural integrity, which includes specific integrity of bodily parts.⁶⁸ The key difference between the bodies of the damned and bodies of the blessed lies in the fact that the former are resurrected with certain *natural* qualities of the human body, such as the qualities of passibility, carnality, heaviness, and being darksome, whereas the blessed are resurrected with the *glorified* qualities of impassibility, subtlety, agility, and clarity.⁶⁹

Third, we should distinguish two different kinds of parts at issue in these three different theses. Theses (a) and (b) treat parts that we might call the *quantitative* parts of a material substance, such as atoms, molecules, cells, arms, legs, and brains.⁷⁰ Quantitative parts are not substances as long as they belong to the substances of which they are parts, according to St. Thomas.⁷¹ Nonetheless, each quantitative physical part is a *hoc aliquid*, a *this* something.⁷² The important thing to note here, for our purposes, is that the quantitative parts of a substance are individual things.

By contrast with (a) and (b), thesis (c) treats those parts of a substance that are less clearly individual things. For example, whereas arms, legs, and heads are all clearly individual things, the referents of the *flesh* and *blood* of a human person appear not to be individual things, but rather *masses* or *stuffs*. Call such part-kinds of human persons *stuff-parts*.⁷³

Turning to St. Thomas's own discussion of the specific integrity of

---

67. See, e.g., *In Sent* IV, d. 44, q. 3, a. 1, q.c. 1 (*ST Suppl.*, q. 86, a. 1).

68. See ibid. (*ST Suppl.*, q. 86, a. 1, resp.); *QQ* VII, q. 5, a. 2; *SCG* IV.89.2; *CT* I, chap. 176. I say "all other things being equal" because there are some aspects of original human nature that are incompatible with the incorruptible nature of the next life. For example, resurrected human persons do not engage in the natural *actions* of eating, drinking, and sex. Also, resurrected human persons in heaven do not even have natural *desires* for such things. For detailed discussion of these topics, see below in this chapter and in chapter 11.

69. Chapter 11 below treats in detail the properties characteristic of glorified human bodies in heaven.

70. St. Thomas sometimes refers to such quantitative parts of a substance such as hands and hearts as "parts of a substance" (see, e.g., *QQ* IX, q. 2, a. 1, resp., and *ST* I, q. 75, a. 2, ad 1).

71. See, e.g., *SCG* IV.49; *CT* I, chap. 211; *Quaestio disputata De unione verbi incarnati*, a. 2, resp.; *QDA*, q. 1, a. 1, resp.; *ST* I, q. 75, a. 2, ad 1; a. 4, ad 2; III, q. 2, a. 2, ad 3.

72. See, e.g., *ST* I, q. 75, a. 2, ad 1. For more discussion of St. Thomas on quantitative (sometimes called *integral*) parts, see my *Aquinas and the Ship of Theseus*, 87–94.

73. For more discussion of masses or stuffs and stuff-parts from contemporary and Thomistic philosophical perspectives, see my *Aquinas and the Ship*, 32–44 and 176–81.

bodily parts at and after the general resurrection, St. Thomas's scriptural touchstone is Deuteronomy 32:4 ("The works of God are perfect"). St. Thomas argues that, because the resurrection is a work of God—and, we might add, a work of God possessing a kind of finality at that—resurrected bodies will be made perfect in all their members.[74]

One philosophical argument that St. Thomas offers for (a), (b), and (c) begins from the assumption that human persons rise with perfect human bodies. For insofar as the body at and after the general resurrection reflects the degree of perfection in the soul, the body will be restored to *natural* (if not graced) perfection insofar as the soul at the time of the resurrection is so perfected, both in the blessed and the damned.

This requires some explanation. In St. Thomas's Aristotelian philosophy of nature, there is a sense in which the substantial form of a living organism is not only the formal and final cause of that organism, but also its efficient cause. That is, one reason that we give the substantial form of a living organism a special name—*soul*—is because the substantial form of a living organism is an efficient cause of the growth and maturity of that substance. Therefore, just as the parts of a work of art are, in a sense, in the artisan even before she makes that work of art, so the parts of an organism are found implicitly in the soul of the organism. Therefore, just as a work of art would be imperfect if it lacked anything that was contained in the idea of the work of art in the artisan, so the human body would be lacking if it lacked anything that exists implicitly in the soul *qua* soul. But, at the resurrection, the soul is *naturally* perfect *qua* soul, that is, as the substantial form of a living thing, and the body corresponds to the condition of the soul at the resurrection.[75] Therefore, resurrected bodies are composed of every kind of bodily member that naturally composes a mature and healthy human body in this life, such as hands, feet, hairs, etc.[76]

St. Thomas entertains a number of objections to the truth of views such as (a) and (b). Let us consider one of these in particular. There seem

---

74. *ST Suppl.*, q. 80, a. 1, s.c. (trans. English Dominicans, 2882). See also *In Sent* IV, d. 44, q. 1, a. 2, q.c. 1, s.c.

75. St. Thomas does not mean here that souls are perfect *qua* acquired or infused virtue, as he says that the souls of both the blessed and the damned are perfect in the relevant sense, and the damned lack the virtues. Hence, every soul at the resurrection is, at the very least, *naturally* perfect *qua* soul as substantial form.

76. See, e.g., *In Sent* IV, d. 44, q. 1, a. 2, q.c. 1, resp. (*ST Suppl.*, q. 80, a. 1, resp.). See also *In Sent* IV, d. 44, q. 1, a. 2, q.c. 2, resp. (*ST Suppl.*, q. 80, a. 2, resp.), and *CT* I, chap. 157.

to be reasons for thinking that human bodies will not have certain quantitative parts at the resurrection. For example, as we will discuss in detail below, St. Thomas does not think that human persons at the resurrection will make use of the generative organs for generative purposes or the organs that eliminate waste for the purposes of eliminating waste, as there is no eating, drinking, or sexual union in the next life. But the organs of our body are related to the act or use of those organs as means to end. Furthermore, if one takes away the end for which something is a means, it does not make sense to restore the means. Therefore, it does not make sense that human persons will rise with the generative organs of the human body or the organs that eliminate waste.[77]

In answering this kind of objection, St. Thomas notes that the quantitative parts of an organism are related to the soul of that organism in two ways: either as matter to form or as instruments to an agent cause. But if we think about the organs of a body as the matter of their formal cause, that is, the soul, then the end of those organs is not operation, as is assumed in the objection, but rather the greater perfection of the species, that is, the perfection of the human person as a kind of bodily being.[78] Therefore, insofar as the organs of the human body are related to the human soul as matter to form, the human body will be perfected at the resurrection as a result of the human soul being perfected *qua* substantial form, and insofar as a perfect human body has all its members, it follows that resurrected human bodies are composed of all the organs that naturally compose a human body in this life, including those that do not have an operation in the next life, such as the generative and waste-disposing organs.[79]

On the other hand, if we consider the quantitative parts of a human body as related to the human soul as instruments to an agent cause, then the end of its quantitative parts, such as the generative and waste-disposing organs, is their operation. That being said, insofar as we think about the organs of the human body as related to the human soul as instruments to an agent cause, we still have reason to think that the human body at the resurrection will possess those quantitative parts of the

---

77. See, e.g., *In Sent* IV, d. 44, q. 1, a. 2, q.c. 1, obj. 1 (*ST Suppl.*, q. 80, a. 1, obj. 1) and q.c. 3, obj. 2 (*ST Suppl.*, q. 80, a. 3, obj. 2).

78. *In Sent* IV, d. 44, q. 1, a. 2, q.c. 1, ad 1 (*ST Suppl.*, q. 80, a. 1, ad 1).

79. Ibid. See also *In Sent* IV, d. 44, q. 1, a. 2, q.c. 3, ad 2 (*ST Suppl.*, q. 80, a. 3, ad 2); *SCG* IV.88.2; *QDP*, q. 5, a. 10, ad 9; *CT* I, chap. 157.

human body that will not operate in the next life (as least in accord with their this-worldly purposes). This is because such organs will not be useless at the resurrection, for instruments are useful not only as an aid in operation, but also as that which helps demonstrate the virtue of the agent cause. Hence, although the generative and waste-producing organs do not operate in the next life, it is proper that they form part of the resurrected body insofar as they show forth the virtue of the soul's powers in this life in the bodily instruments of the soul, thereby illuminating the wisdom of God in creating such bodies.[80] Although some bodily parts no longer function in the next life in accord with their natural this-worldly purposes, those parts nonetheless continue to show forth the wisdom of God's this-worldly plan, for example, in God's wise and beautiful way of bringing about human persons through procreation in this life through the complementarity of man and woman. Although human persons cannot sense those reproductive actions in the next life, they can nonetheless know of the activity of such parts by remembering such actions, or by being told by others, or, in the case of the saints in heaven, by seeing such actions in the beatific vision as effects of God as their cause.

St. Thomas's philosophical arguments for (a) and (b) suffice as sample Thomistic arguments for (c). But St. Thomas offers a number of arguments from authority throughout his corpus specifically designed to show the truth of (c). A couple of these are worth mentioning. For example, if Christ's body at the resurrection does not have a stuff-kind such as blood, then wine is not changed into the blood of Christ in the sacrament of the altar.[81]

In *SCG*, St. Thomas offers the conjunction of two passages from St. Paul as evidence from authority that resurrected bodies will have the same kind of bodily parts as human persons in this life, some of which part kinds are stuff-kinds.[82] For, in Philippians 3:21, St. Paul says: "He will reform the body of our lowness, made like to the body of His glory."[83] But, as St. Thomas also notes, the Gospel of Luke has Jesus say to the apostles, after his resurrection, "Handle and see; for a spirit hath not

---

80. *In Sent* IV, d. 44, q. 1, a. 2, q.c. 1, ad 1 (*ST Suppl.*, q. 80, a. 1, ad 1). See also *In Sent* IV, d. 44, q. 1, a. 2, q.c. 3, ad 2 (*ST Suppl.*, q. 80, a. 3, ad 2).
81. *In Sent* IV, d. 44, q. 1, a. 2, q.c. 1, ad 1 (*ST Suppl.*, q. 80, a. 1, ad 1).
82. *SCG* IV.84.3.
83. Ibid. (trans. O'Neil, 321).

flesh and bones as you see me to have" (24:39).[84] In addition, St. Thomas cites Job 19:26–27: "Once again I shall be clothed with my skin, and in my flesh I shall see my God. Whom I myself shall see and not another."[85] But flesh and skin are stuff-kinds. Therefore, human persons at and after the resurrection will be composed of specifically the same sorts of stuff-kinds as in this life.[86]

One objection to a thesis such as (c) that St. Thomas entertains in a number of places begins with St. Paul's teaching in 1 Corinthians 15:50 that "flesh and blood will not inherit the kingdom of God."[87] But, as we have seen above, St. Thomas can respond to an objection of this sort by denying that St. Paul means to say that the *substances* of flesh and blood inherit the kingdom of God; rather, St. Paul means "the works of flesh and blood, that is, evil deeds," or "the works of flesh and blood that are animal rather than spiritual," that is, acts of eating, drinking, and sexual union, or "the works of flesh and blood as works of a corruptible rather than an incorruptible body."[88] Indeed, this is how St. Thomas tends to respond to the objection, namely, that the objector misinterprets St. Paul.[89]

There is a detail of St. Thomas's doctrine with respect to specific integrity of bodily parts that I have yet to mention. Human bodies at and after the general resurrection not only have all of the same kinds of parts as human bodies in this life, they also have them in the right quantities and shapes, and in the right *order* and *positions* (we can presume that no resurrected human bodies will have arms on top of heads or bones outside the flesh!).[90] In that case, we can append to theses (a), (b), and (c) above another thesis with respect to specific integrity of bodily parts at and after the general resurrection, namely, (d) the parts that compose human bodies at the resurrection have specifically the same quantities, shapes, order, and positions as the parts that compose healthy and mature human bodies in this life.

As it turns out, however, we need to make a slight modification to (d) in light of the theological fact that the resurrected body of Christ and

---

84. Ibid. See also *QDP*, q. 5, a. 10, s.c., and *CT* I, chap. 238.
85. *SCG* IV.84.8 (trans. O'Neil, 322).
86. Ibid.
87. See, e.g., *In Sent* IV, d. 44, q. 1, a. 2, q.c. 3, obj. 1 (*ST Suppl.*, q. 80, a. 3, obj. 1); *SCG* IV.84.2 and *QDP*, q. 5, a. 10, obj. 1.
88. See the discussion of numerical and specific identity above.
89. See, e.g., *In Sent* IV, d. 44, q. 1, a. 2, q.c. 3, ad 3 (*ST Suppl.*, q. 80, a. 3, ad 1), and *QDP*, q. 5, a. 10, ad 1.
90. See, e.g., *In Sent* IV, d. 44, q. 1, a. 2, q.c. 4, resp. (*ST Suppl.*, q. 80, a. 4, resp.).

the resurrected bodies of some of the martyrs possess the scars of their martyrdom in heaven.[91] In support of this view that Christ rose with the scars of his crucifixion, St. Thomas cites scripture—Lk 24:39: "Look at my hands and my feet; see that it is I myself"[92] and Jn 20:27: "Put your finger here and see my hands. Reach out your hand and put it in my side. Do not doubt but believe"[93]—and the fact that both St. Augustine and Pope St. Gregory the Great teach that Christ ascends into heaven with his scarred body, keeping such scars on his body forever in heaven.[94]

As one might imagine, St. Thomas entertains objections to the view that some human bodies in heaven have scars.[95] For, if the bodies of Christ and the martyrs have scars in heaven, then it is not the case that human bodies are perfect in heaven, as, for example, there will be a lack of continuity in the flesh of some human bodies in the next life, for example, there will be holes in Christ's wrists, where the standard for the proper position of flesh is a healthy, mature human body.[96] St. Thomas responds to objections of this sort by noting that the greater beauty of glory (*maiorem decorum gloriae*) communicated by these wounds more than makes up for the little lack of bodily integrity in the bodies of Christ and the martyrs at the resurrection.[97]

As St. Thomas notes, Church Fathers such as Augustine, Bede, and Pope Gregory the Great also mention a number of reasons it was fitting for Christ's body to rise and ascend to heaven bearing the scars of his crucifixion: as a sign of Christ's own glory; to confirm for the disciples that he had indeed risen from the dead; that Christ would perpetually

---

91. See, e.g., *ST* III, q. 54, a. 4.
92. See, e.g., *In Jn* 20, lect. 4, n. 2533.
93. See, e.g., *ST* III, q. 54, a. 4, s.c.
94. See, e.g., *ST* III, q. 54, a. 4, ad 3. See also *CT* I, chap. 238, and *In Jn* 20, lect. 4, n. 2533. In this latter passage, St. Thomas argues that Christ's body keeps his scars in heaven so that those in glory can see them, citing two passages from the Gospel of John: "Those who love me will keep my word, and my Father will love them" (14:23); "and I will manifest myself to him and I will ... reveal myself to them" (14:21). In *In Jn* 20, lect. 6, n. 2558, St. Thomas notes, citing St. Augustine's *The City of God* XXII, that the martyrs too will rise with their scars, the spiritual beauty of which making up for any physical imperfection in those resurrected bodies. Those who were decapitated or suffered amputation will rise with their limbs restored, although there will be scars on those limbs signifying the manner and glory of their martyrdom.
95. See, e.g., *CT* I, chap. 238; *In Jn* 20, lect. 6; *ST* III, q. 54, a. 4, objections.
96. See, e.g., *ST* III, q. 54, a. 4, obj. 2.
97. *ST* III, q. 54, a. 4, ad 2. See also *CT* I, chap. 238, where St. Thomas also notes that, although bodily integrity is the proper condition of the incorruptible body, God provides a dispensation for Christ's body, as his scars provide a proof for the disciples that Christ has indeed risen from the dead.

show the Father the manner of death he endured for us; that the blessed would have a perpetual sign of Christ's great mercy toward them, and that the condemned, in seeing Christ's scarred body, would be suitably upbraided for their lack of faith.[98] And as St. Thomas also states, rather than suggesting corruption or defect in Christ's body, the scars in his glorified body belong "to the greater increase of glory, inasmuch as they are the trophies of his power" (*pertinent . . . sed ad maiorem cumulum gloriae, inquantum sunt quaedam virtutis insignia*).[99]

Where does that put St. Thomas's views on the specific integrity of bodily parts at the resurrection? Perhaps with something such as the following:

A human person S at and after the general resurrection is composed of (a) all of the non-sex-specific kinds of quantitative parts that naturally compose a mature and healthy human body, such as arms, legs, head, torso, a heart, a brain, etc., (b) all of the sex-specific kinds of quantitative parts that compose a mature and healthy human body of the sex S possessed in this life, (c) every stuff-kind that naturally makes up a mature and healthy human body, such as blood, bone, flesh, etc., and (d) all other things being equal, the parts that compose human bodies at the resurrection have specifically the same order, quantities, shapes, and positions as the parts that compose healthy and mature human bodies in this life.

Nonetheless, there are exceptions to (d), namely, where the presence of scars in the resurrected bodies of Christ and the martyrs function as a fitting way in which to signify the perfection, glory, and beauty of their martyrdom.[100]

---

98. See, e.g., *In Jn* 20, lect. 6, n. 2557, and *ST* III, q. 54, a. 4, resp.

99. *ST* III, q. 54, a. 4, ad 1 (trans. English Dominicans, 2311).

100. There is a large and growing literature on the question regarding whether certain so-called disabilities are compatible with—and for any human person S who has certain so-called disabilities in this life, where those disabilities are understood as constitutive of S's personal identity, perhaps even required for—the resurrection of the body or heavenly life. There is not sufficient space here to treat these questions with the detail they deserve. For a Thomistic argument that all disabilities will be healed in heaven, as disabilities are privations of powers, properties, or parts in a normally-functioning human person and loss of a disability in heaven does not prevent numerically the same person from rising again, see, e.g., Terrence Ehrman, "Disability and Resurrection Identity," *New Blackfriars* 96 (2015): 723–38. For a critique of Ehrman's paper, see Kevin Timpe, "Defiant Afterlife: Disability and Uniting Ourselves to God," in *Voices from the Edge: Centering Marginalized Perspectives in Analytic Theology*, ed. Michelle Panchuk and Michael Rea, Oxford Studies in Analytic Theology (Oxford: Oxford University Press, 2020), 206–31. See also the relevant papers by Timpe and others in *The Lost Sheep in Philosophy of Religion: New Perspectives on Disability, Gender, Race, and Animals*, ed. Blake Hereth and Kevin Timpe (New York: Routledge, 2020). For a recent articulation and defense of the view that disabilities will be healed in heaven, one which engages the work of

ON THE AGE OF THE RISEN

In discussing the age (*aetas*) of the risen, St. Thomas means to talk of the age of the body with which the dead are resurrected.[101] St. Thomas thinks that all human persons will rise with the *body* of someone who is approximately thirty years old, that is, one that is youthful and biologically mature, rather than the body of a child or an old person.[102] Nonetheless, St. Thomas notes that such bodily equality in the next life does not set aside every kind of psychological difference between persons in the next life. Indeed, some will be owed reverence for the divine wisdom of the experience of old age, thinks St. Thomas.[103]

Why a youthful body, as opposed to the body of a child or the body of an old person? The youthful body is a body that is physically perfected.[104] Although there is a sense in which the body of a child is more powerful than the body of a youth, as the body of a child grows more than the youthful body, the body of a child is not yet mature, while the body of a youth has reached maturity without yet passing it by.[105]

But why think that all will be resurrected with a physically mature body? St. Thomas has two arguments, one from scripture and tradition, as well as a philosophical argument. The argument from scripture and tradition takes its start from a passage from St. Paul read according to the eschatological sense: "Until we all meet ... unto a perfect man, unto the measure of the age of the fullness of Christ" (Eph 4:13). Now Christ rose from the dead in a youthful age, at about thirty years, as St. Augustine says in *The City of God* XXII.15. Therefore, all human persons will rise with youthful bodies.[106]

Timpe and other contemporary philosophers of disability, see Bryan R. Cross, "A Thomistic, Non-Ableist Conception of Impairment and Disability," *The National Catholic Bioethics Quarterly* 20, no. 2 (2020): 233–42. Finally, interested readers should also examine recent work on disability and the next life by philosophers (and scholars of medieval philosophy) Richard Cross, Christina van Dyke, Michael Waddell, and Scott Williams.

101. See, e.g., *In Sent* IV, d. 44, q. 1, a. 3, q.c. 1, ad 2 (*ST Suppl.*, q. 81, a. 1, ad 2).

102. See, e.g., *In Sent* IV, d. 44, q. 1, a. 3, q.c. 1, s.c (*ST Suppl.*, q. 81, a. 1, s.c.). See *In Eph* 4, lect. 4, n. 216, where St. Thomas says more specifically that Christ—and so every human person at the resurrection—has the bodily stature of a thirty-year-old. In *CSA*, a. 11, St. Thomas says that the perfect age is thirty-two or thirty-three years old.

103. See, e.g., *In Sent* IV, d. 44, q. 1, a. 3, q.c. 1, ad 1 (*ST Suppl.*, q. 81, a. 1, ad 1).

104. *In Sent* IV, d. 44, q. 1, a. 3, q.c. 1, ad 3 (*ST Suppl.*, q. 81, a. 1, ad 3).

105. Ibid.

106. *ST Suppl.*, q. 81, a. 1, s.c. (trans. English Dominicans, 2889). See also *In Sent* IV, d. 44, q. 1, a. 3, q.c. 1, s.c.; *In Eph* 4, lect. 4, n. 216; *ST* III, q. 46, a. 9, ad 4; *CSA*, a. 11.

The philosophical argument that each of the resurrected will rise with a youthful body begins from the premise that human persons were originally created in a state of perfection, that is, without defect. Therefore, the restoration of human nature in the next life also requires a lack of defect in human nature. But defect in body is of two kinds: the defect of not yet having arrived at bodily perfection and the defect of receding from bodily perfection. Therefore, in the resurrection, human persons will rise with a youthful body, that age of the body in which the growth of the body of a child terminates and from which the body has yet to recede, as in old age.[107]

ON RESURRECTION BODIES AS BEING IDENTICAL IN STATURE TO THIS-WORLDLY BODIES

Despite the fact that all human persons will rise in the bloom of youth, St. Thomas thinks that not all human persons will be equal *in stature* at the resurrection. By the *stature* of human bodies St. Thomas is thinking about the shape, size, and proportions of particular human bodies, which, although he does not mention it, would also include the particularities of human faces.

One might think that human bodies in the next life would be equal in stature, as each human body is perfect.[108] Just as there is a perfect age for the human body, there is a perfect stature for the human body, which all human bodies will then possess.[109] Rather, St. Thomas thinks there are a range of sizes (and shapes) of the human body, and all bodies falling within that range are consistent with the physical perfection of the human body.[110] That being said, there are, St. Thomas thinks, some sizes and shapes of the human body that fall outside of the range of bodily perfection. As we have already seen, the bodies of children and old persons fall outside this range. So if a person dies in childhood, God presumably resurrects that person with the youthful bodily stature that that person would have had, had that person reached the age of youth. In addition, we might think that a person who is overweight in this life is

---

107. *In Sent* IV, d. 44, q. 1, a. 3, q.c. 1, s.c. and resp. (*ST Suppl.*, q. 81, a. 1, s.c. and resp.). See also *SCG* IV.88.5; *In Eph* 4, lect. 4, n. 216; *CSA*, a. 11.
108. See, e.g., *In Sent* IV, d. 44, q. 1, a. 3, q.c. 2, obj. 2 (*ST Suppl.*, q. 81, a. 2, obj. 1).
109. See, e.g., *In Sent* IV, d. 44, q. 1, a. 3, q.c. 2, obj. 1 (*ST Suppl.*, q. 81, a. 2, obj. 2).
110. See, e.g., *In Sent* IV, d. 44, q. 1, a. 3, q.c. 2, resp. (*ST Suppl.*, q. 81, a. 2, resp.).

resurrected with the numerically same body, albeit with a bodily weight that he would have had in this life, if he had had a healthy weight.[111] St. Thomas also thinks that some physical maladies are not essential to the bodily life of an individual person. He mentions dwarfism and those who are immoderately large.[112]

One argument that St. Thomas offers for these theses regarding the stature of human bodies at the resurrection begins with the premise that, as we have seen, our bodies have an individual and not simply a specific nature in this life, that is, each of us has not only a *human* body, but a *particular* human body, one that differs numerically from all other human bodies. As we have seen, human person S's soul at the resurrection can only configure the particular human body S possessed in this life. But individual human bodies in this life have particular statures, which statures differ one from another (indeed, every human face is distinctive). Therefore, the stature of a human person S's body in this life will be the stature of S's resurrection body. As the statures of bodies differ from one another in this life, the statures of the resurrection bodies of the saints will differ from one another.

Of course, St. Thomas is aware of the fact that the shape, size, or stature of a particular human body undergoes changes through time. In addition, some human persons die prior to reaching biological maturity, whereas others die in old age, when their bodies are not what they used to be. So, for any human person S, what will be the precise stature of S's resurrected body? St. Thomas thinks that, for any human person S, there is a definite body size or stature D to which S's individual body is inclined by nature to grow, which S's body will reach at the time of biological maturity, unless some other cause or causes get in the way. The resurrected human body will rise with stature D. Of course, the dimensions of D will not be the same for all human bodies. Therefore, the stature of the human body will not be the same for all resurrected bodies.[113]

Consider an important epistemological implication of the identity of body shape and stature between this life and the next. A human person's body, particularly that person's face, has a distinctive shape, one that

---

111. See ibid.
112. See, e.g., *In Sent* IV, d. 44, q. 1, a. 3, q.c. 2, ad 3 (*ST Suppl.*, q. 81, a. 2, ad 3). Here too development of St. Thomas's thought in light of deeper reflection on the relationship between disability and the next life may be in order. See note 100 above.
113. See, e.g., *In Sent* IV, d. 44, q. 1, a. 3, q.c. 2, s.c. and resp. (*ST Suppl.*, q. 81, a. 2, s.c. and resp.).

distinguishes that body or face from every other human body or face. Such distinctive sizes, statures, or shapes of bodies and faces play a very important role in how human persons recognize and interact with one another in this life. As we will see, friendship and other forms of human community are important features of next-worldly life, at least as aspects of the accidental reward of the saints. Because the recognition of the identity of, and differences between, human bodies and faces are necessary conditions for the existence of certain kinds of human community in the next life, for example, rejoicing in seeing and so recognizing the body or face of an old friend, St. Thomas is right to insist on identity of bodily stature between this world and the next.

ON HUMAN PERSONS RISING WITH BIOLOGICAL SEX

Although it seems obviously mistaken to us, there is a strong current in classical thought that regards the members of the female sex as fundamentally flawed.[114] Consider, for example, the Gnostic Gospel of Thomas: "Simon Peter said to him, 'Let Mary leave us, for women are not worthy of life.' Jesus said, 'I myself shall lead her in order to make her male, so that she too may become a living spirit resembling you males. For every woman who will make herself male will enter the kingdom of heaven.'"[115] To pick another example, St. Thomas, in an objection to his own view that biological sex is indeed preserved at the resurrection, cites a passage from Aristotle's *On the Generation of Animals* II.3: "the female is a misbegotten male."[116]

Given such a view of women and St. Thomas's view that resurrected bodies are perfected bodies, it is natural to draw the conclusion that all human persons rise as male. Such a view should not be confused with the belief that only human persons who are males rise from the dead.

---

114. Of course, not all classical sources have this view of women. Famously, Plato has Socrates defend a more egalitarian view in *Republic* V.451c–457b. In addition, as one interpreter of Aristotle has put it, despite some of his remarks about women, Aristotle's account of the best sort of life "is neither inherently masculine nor inherently exploitative. Instead, ... his ideal is worthy of emulation by both women and men." Marcia L. Homiak, "Feminism and Aristotle's Rational Ideal," in *A Mind of One's Own: Feminist Essays on Reason and Objectivity*, ed. Louis M. Antony and Charlotte Witt, 2nd ed. (New York: Routledge, 2018), 4.

115. Logion 114, trans. Thomas O. Lambdin, in *The Nag Hammadi Library*, ed. James M. Robinson, rev. ed. (San Francisco, Calif.: HarperCollins, 1990), available at www.earlychristianwritings.com/text/thomas-lambdin.html.

116. See, e.g., *In Sent* IV, d. 44, q. 1, a. 3, q.c. 3, obj. 3 (*ST Suppl.*, q. 81, a. 3, obj. 3).

Rather, as suggested by the passage from the Gnostic Gospel of Thomas, the idea is rather that all human persons, some of whom were biologically female in this life, are resurrected as males.

St. Thomas himself knows of the position that all human persons will rise with male bodies and unequivocally rejects it.[117] He offers a number of arguments throughout his corpus that there are indeed female bodies in the next life. One of his arguments from authority begins from the premise that God restores at the resurrection what he makes at creation. But St. Thomas notes that the Book of Genesis teaches that, in the beginning, God creates both man and woman.[118]

One of the philosophical arguments that St. Thomas offers for his view that human persons rise with the sex they possessed in this life trades on the account of bodily life we have seen him develop in other places. For it is not just the *species* of a person S's body in this life that S must possess at and after the general resurrection if S is to be resurrected as numerically the same person, but the *individual* human body that S possessed in this life. Of course, some human persons are biologically female in this life. If such human persons were not raised with a female body, it would follow that those human persons would not rise as numerically the same human persons. But all human persons rise numerically the same at the general resurrection. Therefore, some human persons will rise with bodies that are biologically female.[119]

But one might wonder: why not think that *being a female* or *being a male* are accidental forms analogous to *being overweight*? Just as *being overweight* is an accidental form such that, if S is overweight in this life, S is nonetheless resurrected with a numerically identical body that has a healthy weight, so accidents of gender such as *being male* or *being female* are such that, if S is female in this life, S need not be female at the resurrection in order to rise as numerically the same person.

St. Thomas can respond to such an objection by noting there are different kinds of accidents. Recall that St. Thomas posits there are three different kinds of accidents. First, there are *proper* accidents, such as risibility, which are accidents caused by the principles of the species of a thing. That is, John's having the proper accident of (having the root

---

117. See, e.g., *In Sent* IV, d. 44, q. 1, a. 3, q.c. 3 (*ST Suppl.*, q. 81, a. 3); *CA*, Mt 22, lect. 3; *SCG* IV.88; *In Eph* 4, lect. 4, n. 216; *In Mt* 22, lect. 3, n. 1801.
118. See, e.g., *In Sent* IV, d. 44, q. 1, a. 3, q.c. 3, s.c. (*ST Suppl.*, q. 81, a. 3, s.c.).
119. See, e.g., *In Sent* IV, d. 44, q. 1, a. 3, q.c. 3, resp. (*ST Suppl.*, q. 81, a. 3, resp.).

cause of) risibility is caused by John's being a human person. Second, there are *inseparable* accidents. These are accidents that are caused by the principles of the individual substance. These accidents are not effects of the principles of the species of a thing, but rather flow from the individual substantial form and designated matter of the individual substance such that they have a permanent cause in the individual substance that is the subject of such accidents. St. Thomas's examples of inseparable accidents are *the masculine and the feminine*. Third, there are *separable* accidents, that is, those accidents that are not permanently caused by the form and matter of the individual substance, such as sitting or walking.[120] *Being overweight* is a separable accident, so that, if S is overweight in this life, S can be resurrected with a healthy weight. But by hypothesis *being female* is an inseparable accident of a human person S who is a female in this life. Therefore, St. Thomas can consistently teach that, if S at the resurrection is numerically the same as S in this life, then S is resurrected as a female.

Of course, someone might wonder why we should treat accidents of gender as inseparable accidents. For present purposes, I can simply record my conviction that St. Thomas is correct to treat accidents of gender in this manner. Although accidents of gender are certainly not proper accidents, the relation between a human person S and S's gender seems to be stronger than that between a substance and a separable accident. What is important to see here is that St. Thomas has a principled way of distinguishing between an accident such as *being female* and a separable accident such as *being overweight* so that he can say that the former characterizes a person both in this life and at and after the general resurrection, whereas the latter does not. *Being female* is so rooted in the substantial form and designated matter of the individual substance S that possesses it in this life that, whenever S exists, S possesses the accident *being female*. That means that if S is (really) female in this life, S is female at and after the resurrection. But *being overweight* is not like *being female*. It is not the sort of accident that always characterizes a human person. Therefore, if someone is overweight in this life, numerically the same person can have a healthy weight at the resurrection.[121]

St. Thomas has a second philosophical argument that human per-

---

120. *QDA*, a. 12, ad 7; see also *DEE*, chap. 5, n. 105.
121. For a defense and development of St. Thomas's metaphysics of gender, see, e.g., John Finley, "The Metaphysics of Gender: A Thomistic Approach," *The Thomist* 79 (2015): 585–614.

sons rise with the biological sex they possessed in this life. The argument has as a key premise a view we have seen him defend in another context: human bodies rise from the dead with *specific integrity of bodily parts* in the sense that they rise with human bodies containing the same kinds of quantitative parts and stuff-parts their bodies (should have) possessed in this life. But human bodies in this life (should) possess the generative organs.

As we have seen, and as I will discuss in greater detail below, St. Thomas does not think that the generative organs will be used for the purposes of sexual union in the next life. But this is no reason to think that such organs are not found in resurrected bodies. For, if there were no generative organs in the next life for the reason that such quantitative parts do not function as they do in this life, then, for the same reason, none of the quantitative parts of human persons that serve the purpose in this life of taking in nutrients would exist in resurrected bodies. But if any of these quantitative parts were lacking in the resurrected body, that body would seriously lack bodily integrity (think, for example, how misshapen resurrected bodies would be if they lacked all of the organs that serve reproductive and nutritive purposes in this life). Therefore, even though the generative parts do not serve the function at and after the general resurrection they do in this life, their presence is not in vain, as this presence serves the purpose of completing the integrity of the human body and showing forth the wisdom of God the creator.[122]

ON THE IMMORTALITY AND INCORRUPTIBILITY OF RESURRECTION BODIES

Throughout his corpus, St. Thomas offers a number of arguments, both theological and philosophical, for the following related views: first, human persons in the next life cannot die again and are therefore immortal;[123] second, all human persons will, in fact, be raised from the

---

122. *SCG* IV.88.2. According to St. Thomas, at the general resurrection God restores to perfection any deficiencies in nature (see, e.g., *SCG* IV.88.1). Assuming that any human person S is either male or female (and not both), in those cases where a human person S is born without some sexual organs corresponding to S's sex or with some sexual organs that do not correspond to S's sex, S will rise only with the perfected set of sexual organs that correspond with S's sex. For some discussion of St. Thomas's views on gender and the intersex condition, see Finley's "The Metaphysics of Gender."

123. See, e.g., *SCG* IV.82 and *CT* I, chap. 155.

dead;[124] and, third, all human persons and their bodies will be incorruptible at and after the general resurrection.[125] We might wonder why St. Thomas sometimes speaks about *the inability of humans to die* (i.e., immortality) in the next life, and sometimes speaks about *incorruptibility* in the next life. For are they not logically equivalent?

Presumably one reason St. Thomas treats both the immortality and incorruptibility of human persons at and after the general resurrection is because St. Paul does. For example, see 1 Corinthians 15:53: "This corruptible must put on incorruption, and this mortal must put on immortality."[126] Perhaps a second reason has to do with St. Thomas's attention to the details of history and scripture. When St. Thomas speaks about human persons as *immortal*, he is either addressing texts from scripture that speak of the end of death, that is, the immortality of human persons,[127] or a position defended by some pagans, as related by St. Augustine or Aristotle, for example, that human persons will live the same lives over and over again, *ad infinitum* (which position, because it implies human persons die an infinite number of times, contradicts the Christian notion of immortality that after the resurrection human persons will no longer die).[128]

But when St. Thomas speaks of the *incorruptibility* of the human body after the resurrection, he is often commenting upon, or thinking about, 1 Corinthians 15:53a: "This corruptible must put on incorruption."[129] Of course, Aristotle also speaks about incorruptible and corruptible substances, and so it would be natural for St. Thomas to think about the contrast between this-worldly human bodies and next-worldly human bodies by using the language of *corruptibility* and *incorruptibility*, respectively.

---

124. See, e.g., *SCG* IV.79 and *CTI*, chap. 151.

125. See, e.g., *SCG* IV.85 and *In 1 Cor* 15, lect. 6, n. 980; lect. 9, n. 1013. Recall that "human body" for St. Thomas is typically a convenient way of speaking about the physical dimensions of human existence and not some material substance in addition to the human soul. See discussion of the meaning of "human body" for St. Thomas in the section on numerical, specific, and personal identity above.

126. *SCG* IV.85.7 (trans. O'Neil, 324).

127. See *SCG* IV.82, where St. Thomas cites Rom 5:15 ("Not as the offence, so also the gift. For if by the offence many died, much more the grace of God, and the gift, by the grace of one man, Jesus Christ, has abounded unto many"), Hos 13:14 ("O death, I will be thy death"), 1 Cor 15:26 ("The enemy death shall be destroyed last"), Rom 6:9 ("Christ rising again from the dead dieth now no more"), Is 25:8 ("The Lord shall cast death down headlong forever"), and Rv 21:4 ("Death shall be no more") (trans. O'Neil, 308–11).

128. *SCG* IV.82.

129. *SCG* IV.85.7 (trans. O'Neil, 324).

As St. Thomas usually speaks about the *incorruptibilitas* of next-worldly bodies rather than human persons as *immortales*,[130] henceforward I will focus on the sense, or senses, in which human souls, human persons, and human bodies are *incorruptible* according to St. Thomas, especially at and after the general resurrection.

According to St. Thomas, *all* human bodies will be *incorruptible* at and after the general resurrection. St. Thomas is fond of citing St. Paul on this score: "This corruptible must put on incorruption, and this mortal must put on immortality" (1 Cor 15:53).[131] St. Thomas interprets St. Paul as teaching not only the universality of the general resurrection, but that all resurrected bodies will be incorruptible; see 1 Corinthians 15:21–22: "For since death came through a human being, the resurrection of the dead has also come through a human being; for as all die in Adam, so all will be made alive in Christ."[132]

But what does St. Thomas mean by "incorruptible" here? St. Thomas distinguishes a number of senses of "incorruptibility" throughout his corpus. It will be helpful to examine these in order to understand the precise sense, or senses, in which human persons and their bodies are incorruptible at and after the general resurrection. According to a first sense of "incorruptibility" that St. Thomas recognizes, something can be incorruptible *due to its matter or lack thereof*.[133] Angels and human souls are good examples of things that are incorruptible due to their lack of matter. According to their God-given nature, angels and human souls are such that, once created, the only way they could cease to exist is if God ceased to sustain them in existence, that is, if God annihilated them.[134]

In fact, given that St. Thomas thinks that human persons survive their death insofar as their souls do, *there is a sense* in which all *human persons* are *naturally incorruptible* due to their souls not having matter, as human souls are themselves things (if not substances) that are naturally incorruptible due to their not having matter.[135] Most material substances go out of existence when their substantial forms are separated from their matter. Indeed, most living things go out of existence when they die, that

---

130. See, e.g., the texts cited in notes 5 and 6 above.
131. *SCG* IV.85.7 (trans. O'Neil, 324). See also *CSA*, a. 11.
132. See, e.g., *In 1 Cor* 15, lect. 3, nn. 931 and 934; lect. 8, n. 1003; lect. 9, n. 1012.
133. See, e.g., ST I, q. 97, a. 1, resp.
134. See, e.g., ST I, q. 75, a. 6.
135. See the section on St. Thomas's philosophical anthropology in chapter 9 above.

is, when their souls as substantial forms are separated from matter. But recall that human persons, as they are intellectual creatures, have a special sort of substantial form that preserves the existence, identity, and individuality of the composite human person during the interim state.[136] Although a human person S is not—and never is—identical to S's soul, S nonetheless continues to exist when S is composed of S's soul alone between S's death and the general resurrection. But when S is composed of S's soul alone, S exists in a metaphysically truncated and unnatural state. For S does not exist in this state as a composite of soul and matter, which is the natural state for human persons.

Note, then, that this means there are two senses in which we might speak of a human person *being corrupted*. First, we might speak of a human person being corrupted at death in the sense that her soul is separated from matter. Here, "the corruption of the human person" simply means: the human soul is separated at death from matter, to which the soul is naturally (if not necessarily) united. Call this sort of corruption of the human person, *composite of soul and matter corruption*. In this sense, human persons are naturally corruptible. This is because, although human souls are naturally incorruptible, it is natural for composites of soul and matter to corrupt.[137] But, importantly, a human person S survives composite of soul and matter corruption insofar as S's soul survives such corruption and the human soul is by itself sufficient to preserve the existence, identity, and individuality of S.

Second, we might speak of a human person S being corrupted at death in the sense that S's soul is separated from matter such that S goes out of existence. Here, "corruption" means: the human soul is separated from matter, to which the soul is naturally united, and the whole to which the soul naturally, if not necessarily, belongs goes out of existence. Call this sort of corruption of the human person, *existence corruption*. It is in the sense of existence corruption that human persons are naturally incorruptible due to their souls being naturally incorruptible, where the souls of human persons are sufficient to preserve the existence of

---

136. Again, see the section on St. Thomas's philosophical anthropology in chapter 9 above for the details.

137. See the discussion, and texts from St. Thomas cited, below regarding the preternatural gift of immortality where those in the state of innocence are concerned, which implies that material substances such as human persons are not *naturally* incorruptible *qua* composites of substantial form and matter.

human persons even after those human persons do suffer composite of soul and matter corruption at death.[138]

Some things are therefore naturally incorruptible because of their lack of matter: for example, angels, human souls, and even human persons in the sense that their souls naturally preserve their existence after human persons suffer composite of soul and matter corruption at death. According to St. Thomas's Aristotelian cosmology, the heavenly bodies are a good example of things that are incorruptible *due to their matter*. Though composed of matter, the heavenly bodies have matter that is not in potency to a substantial form other than the substantial form that currently configures that matter.[139] According to certain popular presentations of contemporary particle physics, physical simples have the kind of matter St. Thomas ascribes to the heavenly bodies: Carl Sagan was fond of speaking of human persons as being composed of "star stuff."

So far, I have spoken about kinds of incorruptibility where things are incorruptible due to their matter or lack thereof, and such things are naturally incorruptible in the sense that they have a God-given nature such that they are incorruptible.[140] However, material things also can be incorruptible due to their form but not due to their matter.[141] In order to understand what St. Thomas has in mind here by a material thing's being incorruptible due to its form rather than its matter, it will help first to say something more about the notion that some material things are naturally corruptible due to their matter. For St. Thomas, a material substance such as an insect is naturally corruptible due to its matter insofar as it is composed of matter that is in potency to being configured by a different substantial form from the one that currently configures it. For example, at some point after an insect is eaten by a bear, that insect's

---

138. A hypothesis: corruptionists, i.e., those who think, or read St. Thomas as thinking, *if a human person S does not have matter as a part, then S does not exist*, fail to distinguish, but rather conflate, these two ways of speaking about the corruption of human persons.

139. See, e.g., *CT* I, chap. 95. In addition, there is also talk in the Christian tradition about the empyrean heaven—the most perfect of all corporeal *places*—as naturally incorruptible. According to tradition, the empyrean heaven is the proper place to which the beatified angels are present, and as that incorruptible place present from the beginning of creation also prefigures the incorruptibility of "the new heavens and the new earth" (see, e.g., *ST* I, q. 61, a. 4; q. 66, a. 3; q. 68, a. 4, resp.; q. 102, a. 2, ad 1). I discuss St. Thomas on the empyrean heaven in greater detail in chapter 13 below.

140. Of course, a being B's being naturally incorruptible is compatible with God being the primary creating and conserving cause of B's existence at every moment in which B exists; only God is incorruptible, absolutely speaking (see, e.g., *ST* I, q. 3, a. 4, and *In 1 Tm* 6, lect. 3, n. 268).

141. See, e.g., *ST* I, q. 97, a. 1.

matter in the stomach of the bear comes to have substantial forms other than that of an insect. For example, the insect's matter might take on the substantial forms of various nonliving compounds that are themselves soon corrupted insofar as the matter of such compounds becomes part of the bear that originally ate the insect. For St. Thomas, for a material substance or body to be naturally incorruptible *qua* matter is for that material substance or body to be such that its matter cannot naturally come to have another substantial form.

St. Thomas thinks that the human body is naturally corruptible. What is the significance of the adverb "naturally" here? According to St. Thomas, the elements (i.e., earth, air, fire, and water) which compose all mixed bodies, including human bodies, are, according to their God-given nature, corruptible, which makes those mixed bodies naturally corruptible too. As human bodies are composed of quantitative parts that are corruptible, human bodies are naturally corruptible as far as their matter is concerned.[142] But God might make it be the case that, at some point in time, what is corruptible according to its God-given nature becomes incorruptible insofar as God gives its form *a non-natural power*, where that power is either preternatural or supernatural.[143]

We are now in a position to make sense of St. Thomas's view that embodied human persons at and after the resurrection are incorruptible due to their form and not due to their matter.[144] According to St. Thomas, resurrected human bodies are incorruptible (and resurrected human persons are incorruptible *qua* composites of soul and matter) on account of their forms insofar as the substantial forms of human persons in the next life, by a non-natural gift from God, have such a hold over the matter they configure that it is no longer possible for the matter they configure to come to be configured by different substantial forms. But the kind of power given by God to the souls of human persons in the next life differs for the blessed and the damned. That gives us our next two senses of "incorruptibility."

---

142. See also *CT* I, chap. 152.
143. See chapter 2, note 109 above for definitions of *preternatural* and *supernatural*.
144. Given what I have said above, one might argue that human persons are naturally incorruptible *qua existence corruption* due to their forms and not due to their matter. But notice that here I am speaking about the incorruptibility of human persons *qua* composites of form and matter, and not *qua* existence. That is, I am speaking here of *composite of soul and matter corruption* and not *existence corruption*. And St. Thomas does not think that human persons are *naturally* incorruptible in the sense of composite of soul and matter corruption.

According to the sense of "incorruptibility" that applies to the bodies of the blessed, a human body is incorruptible due to its human soul as substantial form and not due to its matter, where the cause of the human soul's power to confer incorruptibility is a graced (i.e., supernatural) disposition in the soul, which disposition is caused by the soul having the beatific vision.[145] Only embodied human persons in heaven have incorruptible human bodies in this sense. This sense of incorruptibility seems to be a synonym for the glorified body's gift of *impassibility* (discussed below in chapter 11).[146]

St. Thomas is clear that even the damned have incorruptible bodies at and after the general resurrection because of the perfection of their souls *qua* substantial form.[147] This brings us to the sense in which all human bodies at and after the resurrection are incorruptible, where a body is incorruptible *qua* resurrected body due to its human soul as substantial form and not due to its matter, and where the cause of the human soul's power to confer incorruptibility is a preternatural disposition in the soul, which disposition is caused by the resurrection of Christ.[148] All human bodies are incorruptible in this sense at and after the resurrection, both those of the blessed and those of the damned.

According to an additional sense of incorruptibility, a thing is incorruptible due merely to an efficient cause acting upon that thing. According to St. Thomas, this is the sense in which human persons were immortal or incorruptible in the state of innocence.[149] Compare and contrast the incorruptibility enjoyed by human persons in the next life with the incorruptibility of those in the state of innocence. To take one point of comparison, in both cases human persons have a substantial form, the human soul, that itself is incorruptible according to its God-given nature. In addition, embodied human persons in the next life and those in the state of innocence both have bodies that are composed of quantitative parts that are naturally corruptible.

A key difference between embodied human persons in the next life

---

145. See, e.g., *ST* I, q. 97, a. 1, resp.
146. St. Thomas calls the impassibility of the glorified body *a mode of incorruptibility* in *In Sent* IV, d. 44, q. 3, a. 1, q.c. 2, resp. (*ST Suppl.*, q. 86, a. 2, resp.).
147. See, e.g., *SCG* IV.89.7.
148. See, e.g., *In Sent* IV, d. 44, q. 2, a. 1, q.c. 1, resp. (*ST Suppl.*, q. 82, a. 1, resp.); *SCG* IV.79, 82.2, 82.4, 86.1; *In Jb* 19, lect. 2; *ST* III, q. 14, a. 4, ad 1.
149. See, e.g., *ST* I, q. 97, a. 1.

and human persons in the state of innocence is that the incorruptibility of human bodies in the next life is due to a preternatural or supernatural disposition in the soul, given by God, whereas human persons in the state of innocence have preternaturally incorruptible bodies simply because of the extrinsic miraculous action of God. In other words, the incorruptibility of bodies in the next life has an intrinsic cause, that is, the soul's having such power that the matter configured by the soul cannot come to be configured by another substantial form *and* an extrinsic efficient cause (God's giving such power to the soul in virtue of the beatific vision or in virtue of the resurrection of Christ) whereas the incorruptibility of bodies in the state of innocence has merely a sustaining, extrinsic, efficient cause, that is, God's giving the preternatural gift of immortality to those in the state of innocence, as long as they freely will to remain in the state of innocence.

Where the soul of the resurrected person has been given a power such that *it* causes the body to be incorruptible, the soul of the person in the state of innocence does not have such a power. Rather, as long as those in the state of innocence did not sin in this life, *God alone* would miraculously keep those human persons from dying. Compare the preternatural gift of immortality with the miracle of Shadrach, Meshach, and Abednego not being burned in the fiery furnace. Nothing about their souls *qua* substantial form explains why the bodies of Shadrach, Meshach, and Abednego are not burned; rather, God simply miraculously prevents their bodies from being burned. It is in an analogous way that human bodies in the state of innocence were incorruptible. By contrast, in the case of resurrected bodies, there is a metaphysical disposition given to the souls of the resurrected that partly explains the incorruptibility of those bodies.

Interestingly, St. Thomas does note that even in the state of innocence there is a sense in which human persons *qua* composites of soul and matter are *naturally* incorruptible, namely, insofar as God created those in the state of innocence to remain in such a state until the time they would be transferred to heaven and begin enjoying the beatific vision. Insofar as they freely willed to remain in the state of innocence, God would preserve their bodies from corruption by way of continuing to give those in the state of innocence the gift of incorruptibility. That being said, St. Thomas thinks that human *bodies* in the state of innocence were not naturally incorruptible insofar as human bodies have a natural tendency to corrupt.[150]

So human bodies are incorruptible at and after the general resurrection insofar as God gifts human souls with a disposition that keeps human bodies, which bodies are naturally corruptible, from corrupting. What reasons does St. Thomas have for thinking that all human bodies are incorruptible in the next life? St. Thomas has arguments both from authority and from reason for this thesis.

For example, in his commentary on 1 Corinthians, St. Thomas offers three reasons why St. Paul teaches that "this corruptible must put on incorruption" (1 Cor 15:54).[151] First, for the sake of the completion of human nature. Citing St. Augustine, St. Thomas notes that the soul apart from the body exists in an imperfect state.[152] Second, all human bodies need to rise as incorruptible for the sake of divine justice. Because human persons do good works or evil deeds in the body, human persons should not only be perpetually rewarded or punished in their souls, but in their bodies too.[153] A third reason that St. Paul teaches that "the corruptible must put on incorruption" is so all the members of the body of Christ will be conformed to Christ.[154]

One compelling theological argument that St. Thomas offers for the immortality of human persons and the incorruptibility of human bodies after the resurrection in *SCG* is the following:

---

150. See, e.g., *QDM*, q. 5, a. 5, and *CT* I, chap. 152. It is worth noting at this point that St. Thomas does *not* defend the view that *there was no corruption in the state of innocence*. Indeed, there presumably would have been killing in the state of innocence, for example, human persons eating plants or plant parts and some animals killing other animals (although there would have been no corruption in human persons). See, e.g., *In Sent* IV, d. 48, q. 2, a. 5 (*ST Suppl.*, q. 91, a. 5); *SCG* IV.97.5; *CT* I, chap. 170; *ST* I, q. 48, a. 2, ad 3; q. 49, a. 2, resp.; q. 102, a. 2, ad 2; *QDM*, q. 5, a. 4, ad 2 and ad 8. Given what we know about early life on this planet by way of the biological sciences, this makes St. Thomas's views on the state of innocence more defensible than the views of those theologians who link *all* death with Adam's original sin.

151. *In 1 Cor* 15, lect. 9, n. 1013 (trans. Larcher et al., 382).

152. Ibid. St. Thomas goes on to note here that the separated soul therefore does not enjoy perfect beatitude (*beatitudine perfecta*) in heaven. As we have seen, we find St. Thomas speaking about the beatitude of the separated soul in this way in early texts such as the *Sentences* commentary, *SCG*, *QDP* (q. 5, a. 10), and *CT*, but not in the later *ST* I-II. Of course, the commentaries on St. Paul's first and second Letters to the Corinthians belong to the earlier stage of St. Thomas's career (see Torrell, *Saint Thomas Aquinas*, 340 and 431). Nonetheless, St. Thomas maintains the notion, even in the later part of his career, that the separated soul, even if it does not lack perfect happiness, nonetheless exists in an unnatural state and experiences a "desire-from-fulfillment" that the soul's human happiness would extend to that of the composite, both soul and body.

153. *In 1 Cor* 15, lect. 9, n. 1013.

154. Ibid.

(1) If a human person can die after the general resurrection, experiencing a second death, then (a) a human person can die after the general resurrection, experiencing a second death, and will rise again after this second death or (b) a human person can die after the general resurrection, experiencing a second death, and will not rise after this second death [law of the excluded middle].

(2) If (b) a human person can die after the general resurrection, experiencing a second death, and will not rise again after the second death, then (c) a human person can die after the general resurrection, experiencing a second death, and a human soul will, after the second death, be perpetually without the body [self-evident].

(3) A human soul, although naturally immortal, is also by nature the substantial form of a human body [assumption].

(4) Therefore, it is contrary to the nature of the human soul to be without the body [from (3)].

(5) Nothing that is contrary to nature can be perpetual (or, given the goodness of God, God would not allow the soul to exist perpetually in a state contrary to nature) [assumption].[155]

(6) Therefore, it is not the case that (c) a human person can die after the general resurrection, experiencing a second death, and a human soul will, after a second death, be perpetually without the body [from (4) and (5)].

(7) Therefore, it is not the case that (b) a human person can die after the general resurrection, experiencing a second death, and will not rise again after the second death [from (2) and (6), MT].

(8) If (a) a human person can die after the general resurrection, experiencing a second death, and will rise again after the second death, then (d) a human person can die after the general resurrection, experiencing a second death, and rise after dying this second death, never to die again, or (e) a human person can die after the general resurrection, experiencing a second death, and die and rise again an infinite number of times [assumption].

(9) The same reason a human person must rise after dying the second death, never to die again, explains why a human person cannot undergo a second death in the first place in the next life [assumption].

(10) If (d), then not (d) [from (9)].

---

155. For premises (3)–(5), see *SCG* IV.79.10.

(11) Therefore, it is not the case that (d) [from (10), negation introduction].

(12) If (e), then (f) there is a motion that is an end in itself [assumption].

(13) All motion is for an end that is not in motion [assumption].

(14) Therefore, not (f) [from (13)].

(15) Therefore, not (e) [from (12) and (14), MT].

(16) Therefore, not (a) [from (8), (11), and (15), MT].

(17) Therefore, it is not the case that a human person can die after the general resurrection, experiencing a second death; that is, human persons are immortal and have incorruptible bodies after the general resurrection [from (1), (7), and (16), MT].[156]

St. Thomas thinks, reasonably enough given the premises above, that all human bodies in the next life will be incorruptible. Note, as well, St. Thomas's reason for thinking we will be embodied in the next life: the soul, by nature, is inclined to configure matter.

In discussing the meanings of incorruptibility above, I noted that St. Thomas speaks about God's giving supernatural or preternatural dispositions to the human soul as the cause of the incorruptibility of resurrected bodies. Earlier in his career, however, he offers an additional explanation for how human bodies are made incorruptible in the next life: the absence of the motion of the heavenly bodies in the next life. According to St. Thomas's interpretation of Aristotelian cosmology, the motion of the heavens is an efficient cause of the corruption of the quantitative parts of human bodies. But at the end of the world, at which occurs the resurrection of the dead, the motion of the heavenly bodies will cease.[157] Therefore, the quantitative parts that compose the human body are rendered incorruptible, leaving the resurrection body composed of those parts incorruptible too.[158]

---

156. *SCG* IV.82.5. Mark Spencer raises the worry that an argument of this sort makes the resurrection necessary and naturally knowable, rather than a graced and miraculous act. For a Thomistic strategy for responding to this sort of worry, namely, that we cannot know premise (5) by natural reason with certainty, see Feingold, *The Natural Desire to See God*, 362–64. In addition, St. Thomas thinks that, apart from faith, it is difficult to maintain confidence in the immortality of the soul—and so premise (3)—given that the soul is naturally the substantial form of the body (see *In Cor 15*, lect. 2, n. 924).

157. See, e.g., *In Sent* IV, d. 44, q. 3, a. 2, q.c. 2 (*ST Suppl.*, q. 86, a. 2); *QDP*, q. 5, a. 5; *CT* I, chap. 171.

158. See esp. *In Sent* IV, d. 44, q. 3, a. 2, q.c. 2 (*ST Suppl.*, q. 86, a. 2). There is no explicit mention of this cause of incorruptibility in the later *SCG*, at least in those places one would expect to find it

Resurrection Bodies

Of course, we do not share the details of St. Thomas's cosmology here. Nonetheless, an argumentative strategy for defending the incorruptibility of human bodies at and after the resurrection can be drawn from what St. Thomas says here:

(18) Human bodies are corruptible only because the quantitative parts of which they are composed (call them "the xs") are corruptible, where the xs are not necessarily corruptible [assumption].

(19) If the xs that compose human bodies are rendered incorruptible, then human bodies are incorruptible [assumption].

(20) The xs that compose human bodies in this life are corruptible only because of the actions of things (call them "the ys") other than the xs [assumption].

(21) Therefore, if the action of the ys is suppressed, then the xs that compose human bodies are incorruptible [from (20)].

(22) Therefore, if the action of the ys is suppressed, then human bodies are incorruptible [from (18), (19), and (21)].

(23) God suppresses the action of the ys at and after the general resurrection [assumption].

(24) Therefore, human bodies are incorruptible at and after the general resurrection [from (22) and (23), MP].

Now, St. Thomas identifies candidates for the ys in the argument above, namely, the motion of the heavenly bodies. Though St. Thomas's Aristotelian empirical physics is outmoded on this score, St. Thomas's interest in using his understanding of physics to make sense of the faith is noteworthy. Presumably, *we* cannot (currently) identify candidates for the ys from contemporary physics. But that does not mean that the argument above is not useful at all.

Let us assume, for all we know (e.g., by contemporary physics), that premises (18), (19), (20), and (23) are true. We could posit there are some ys, which substances are currently directly unobserved, the actions of which explain the corruptibility of human bodies. If the action of these ys were suppressed, as by hypothesis it would be at and after the gener-

---

(see, e.g., *SCG* IV.85 and 86.7), despite the fact that St. Thomas continues to believe that the motion of the heavens will cease after the general resurrection (see *SCG* IV.97). However, St. Thomas does mention the cessation of motion in the heavens as a cause of the incorruptibility of the damned in *CT* I, chap. 177, which is typically dated as slightly later than *SCG* IV (see, e.g., Torrell, *Saint Thomas Aquinas*, 332 and 349).

al resurrection, then human bodies would be rendered incorruptible. Of course, such an argument would be significantly different from St. Thomas's argument insofar as his argument has an actual candidate for the ys whereas the reconstructed argument posits the ys as an occult cause.

That being said, nothing that we know about physics suggests that the laws of nature (or, if there are no laws of nature, their nonlaw-like equivalents) are necessarily true,[159] and so nothing we know about physics rules out thinking that (these laws of) nature could be altered by divine omnipotence in "the new heavens and the new earth." In that case, although human bodies are corruptible in this life, they will not be so in the next. We could thus offer the following modification of St. Thomas's argument above:

(18) Human bodies are corruptible only because the xs are corruptible, where the xs are not necessarily corruptible [assumption].

(19) If the xs that compose human bodies are rendered incorruptible, then human bodies are incorruptible [assumption].

(20*) If God can and does render the xs incorruptible at and after the general resurrection, for example, by changing certain nonessential features of the xs, then human bodies at and after the general resurrection are incorruptible [from (18) and (19)].

(21*) God can and does render the xs incorruptible at and after the general resurrection, for example, by changing certain nonessential features of the xs [assumption].

(22*) Therefore, human bodies at and after the general resurrection are incorruptible [from (20*) and (21*), MP].

Now, nothing we know by faith or physics shows that (18), (19), or (21*) are false. Therefore, if we grant (18), (19), and (21*), human bodies are incorruptible at and after the general resurrection.

In contrast to arguing that God removes a primary principle of corruption as a cause of incorruptibility in the afterlife, St. Thomas also argues, as we saw above, for the incorruptibility of resurrected bodies by positing that God *hinders* the principle of corruption in things (without needing to *remove* the principle of corruption altogether) by giving to the

---

159. See, e.g., Stephen M. Barr, *Modern Physics and Ancient Faith* (Notre Dame, Ind.: University of Notre Dame Press, 2003), 77.

souls of human persons a preternatural or supernatural disposition that keeps the matter that those souls configure from being corrupted. More specifically, in the next life all human bodies will be hindered from corruption by divine power through the merit of Christ's resurrection from the dead.[160] In addition, all glorified bodies in heaven will be hindered from corruption insofar as matter informed by a beatified soul renders the human body impassible. Therefore, the soul of any human person at and after the general resurrection has a preternatural or supernatural disposition from God such that the matter that the soul configures cannot come to be configured by some other substantial form.[161] Therefore, there is an efficient cause of the incorruptibility of the resurrected body (i.e., God) and a formal cause, that is, the perfected human soul of the resurrected human person where that soul is perfected by possessing a preternatural or supernatural disposition by a gift from God. If we assume that nothing St. Thomas says in this second argument (that human bodies will be incorruptible at and after the general resurrection) contradicts what we know by contemporary physics, then in that case, his second argument offers a possible way that God brings about the incorruptibility of human bodies at and after the general resurrection.

ON FOOD, DRINK, AND SEX IN THE AFTERLIFE

As we have seen, St. Thomas thinks that all human persons will rise numerically (and thus specifically) the same in the next life, with integrity and perfection of bodily parts. Despite such real similarities between this-worldly and next-worldly bodies, we have also seen that St. Thomas thinks that bodily life in the next life is very different for human persons too, as human persons and their bodies in the next life are incorruptible. This part of the chapter underscores some other ways that this-worldly bodily life differs from next-worldly bodily life according to the doctrine of St. Thomas. For in his view, there will be no eating, drinking, and sexual union in the next life.

St. Thomas often speaks in general terms of the bodily life of human

---

160. See the texts cited in note 148 above.
161. See, e.g., *QDP*, q. 5, a. 10, ad 3. In *SCG* IV.85.6–7 and 86.1 and *CT* I, chaps. 155 and 177. St. Thomas makes explicit that divine power is the efficient cause of the incorruptibility of the body for all human persons in the next life, whereas the human soul is the formal cause at *SCG* IV.85.7 and 86.1 and *CT* I, chap. 155.

persons in this life as an *animal* life. By implication, next-worldly-bodily life for human persons is a nonanimal life. So, for example, in his commentary on the *Sentences*, St. Thomas can ask about next-worldly bodily life: "will all rise to an animal life so as to exercise the generative and nutritive functions?"[162] The reader should note that the use of "animal" and "nonanimal" in this context do not amount to *metaphysical* descriptions, as St. Thomas thinks that human persons are essentially animals. Rather, the terms are used, as we will see, to describe *the kind of life* that human persons live in this life and the next.[163]

St. Thomas offers quite a few arguments throughout his corpus for the view that human persons no longer live an animal life at and after the general resurrection.[164] Let us focus on expressing and defending just one of these arguments. Call this argument, *the removal of one of the ends of eating and sex argument* (REA).

REA goes as follows. When an end is removed, the means ordered to that end will also be removed. But eating, drinking, and sexual activity are means that serve the ends of mortal life, such as preserving individuals insofar as they lose nutrients and the preservation of the human species in generation, respectively. But in the next life, human persons will no longer be mortal. In that case the ends of the mortal life are removed. Therefore, there are no longer the sorts of acts that are means to (or serve as their primary purpose the aiming to realize) these ends of a mortal life in the next life. Therefore, there is no eating, drinking, or sexual activity in the next life.[165]

We might object to REA on *personalist* grounds. First, eating and sexual union are not simply nutritive or generative acts, respectively. Both have a secondary, or perhaps even another primary, purpose: being the efficient and formal causes of (the perfection of) friendship. Second, the primary purpose of sex as preserving the species should not be thought of simply in terms of the generation of new human persons, but also in terms of educating them into the good life. For sexual union can especially serve, albeit indirectly, the end of educating children in the good life insofar as sexual union can facilitate friendship of the couple, which

---

162. See, e.g., *In Sent* IV, d. 44, q. 1, a. 3, q.c. 4 (*ST Suppl.*, q. 81, a. 4): "Videtur quod resurgent in vita animali, ut scilicet utantur actu nutritivae et generativae."

163. See also note 13 above.

164. See, e.g., *In Sent* IV, d. 44, q. 1, a. 3, q.c. 4 (*ST Suppl.*, q. 81, a. 4); *SCG* IV.83; *CT* I, chap. 156; *CA*, Mk 12:25, lect. 3; *In Mt* 22, lect. 3, n. 1800.

165. *CT* I, chap. 156. See also *CA*, Mk 12:25, lect. 3.

friendship of the couple in turn aids the couple in giving their offspring an education in virtue. But we can reformulate—and thereby strengthen—REA by taking these personalist concerns into account.

Consider the following development of REA (call this argument DREA):

(25) If, in performing an act A, one does not respect every one of the natural ends or purposes of A, given the kind of action to which A belongs, then one does what is morally wrong in performing A [assumption].

(26) Although there are secondary, or perhaps additional primary, ends or purposes for eating and sexual union other than nutritive and generative ones (such as perfecting friendship and growing in charity), maintenance of the human body and preservation of the species—and in the case of sexual union that means not only the generating of offspring but also the working to help those offspring flourish, where sexual union particularly facilitates a friendship that is conducive to helping the couple better educate their offspring in virtue—are primary purposes of eating and sexual union [assumption].

(27) Therefore, if (a) the next life is a context where maintenance of the body and preservation of the species are no longer rational ends or purposes of any human life, or there is no need—or it is no longer possible—to engage in sexual union in order to facilitate a friendship that itself facilitates growing in charity so as to help one's offspring develop the virtues, that is, as St. Thomas puts it, "the ends of mortal life are removed," then it is morally wrong to engage in acts of eating or sexual union in the next life [from (25) and (26)].

(28) If human bodies in the next life are immortal and incorruptible, then the next life is a context where maintenance of the human body and preservation of the species are no longer rational ends or purposes for any human life [self-evident].

(29) Human bodies in the next life are immortal and incorruptible [proved above].

(30) Therefore, the next life is a context where maintenance of the human body and preservation of the species are no longer rational ends or purposes for any human life [from (28) and (29), MP].

(31) The next life is a context where there is no need—or it is no longer possible—to engage in sexual union in order to facilitate a friendship

that itself facilitates growing in charity so as to help one's offspring develop the virtues [assumption].

(32) Therefore, it is morally wrong to engage in acts of eating or sexual union in the next life [from (27), (30), and (31), MP].

(33) Human persons in the next life will not engage in acts that are morally wrong [assumption].

(34) Therefore, human persons in the next life will not engage in acts of eating or sexual union [from (32) and (33)].

I cannot defend all of the assumptions in DREA here.[166] However, I will address premises (31) and (33). With respect to premise (31) there are two things to say. First, there is no need for the saints in heaven to engage in sexual union to facilitate friendship, for human persons will know each other in much deeper ways in heaven. For they will know each other (i) indirectly as a part of the secondary object of the beatific vision and (ii) directly within the communion of the saints that is an aspect of the accidental reward, which may include activities such as communal worship, stargazing, music-making, and conversation.[167] And although human persons married in this life do not engage in the conjugal act in heaven, there is every reason to believe that the uniqueness of the friendships they cultivated within marriage in this life are preserved forever in heaven.[168] Second, it is not possible for human persons in the next life to grow, or diminish, in virtue. Therefore, sexual union cannot serve the purpose of helping parents grow in charity so as to facilitate helping their children grow in virtue, and thus premise (31) is true.

As we have seen, St. Thomas argues that it is not possible for human persons in heaven to do what is morally wrong.[169] We might think that

---

166. In particular, there is not sufficient space here to defend premises (25) and (26) above. For good discussion and defenses of premises such as (25), see, e.g., J. Budziszewski, *On the Meaning of Sex* (Wilmington, Del.: ISI Books, 2012), and Ed Feser, "In Defense of the Perverted Faculty Argument," in his *Neo-Scholastic Essays* (South Bend, Ind.: St. Augustine's Press, 2015), 378–415. For discussion and defense of a premise such as (26), see Budziszewski, *The Meaning of Sex*, and Karol Wojtyla (Pope St. John Paul II), *Love and Responsibility*, trans. H.T. Willetts (San Francisco, Calif.: Ignatius Press, 1993); see esp. 45–69.

167. See chapters 12 and 13 below for more on the development of a Thomistic account of the communion of the saints as an aspect of the accidental reward.

168. That St. Thomas thinks that the circumstances, relationships, and friendships of this life are partly constitutive of the accidental reward in heaven, see my discussion of the aureoles and fruits in chapter 12. For a poetic expression of the idea that the circumstances, relationships, and friendships of this life are partly constitutive of the accidental reward in heaven, see Dante's *Paradiso*.

169. See chapter 8 above.

part of God's mercy toward those in hell is that God puts them in circumstances where they cannot do evil so as to become more miserable than they already are.[170] In addition, we might think that, just as there is no meriting in heaven, there is no demeriting in hell, and thus premise (33) is true.

Someone might object to the inference to (27) from premises (25) and (26) as follows. If that inference were correct, then would the following proposition not also follow from (25) and (26)?

(27*) Therefore, if (a*) post-menopausal sexual union, or sex during that part of a woman's cycle where she is infertile, or sex between partners at least one of whom is sterile, do not have the preservation of the species as a rational end or purpose of those sexual unions, then (b*) post-menopausal sex is necessarily morally wrong or sex during that part of a woman's cycle where she is infertile is necessarily morally wrong or sex between partners at least one of whom is sterile is necessarily morally wrong [from (25) and (26)].

The objection continues with the following premises:

(28*) Post-menopausal sex, or sex during that part of woman's cycle where she is infertile, or sex between partners at least one of whom is sterile, do not have the preservation of the species as a rational end or purpose of those sexual unions.

(29*) Therefore, post-menopausal sex is necessarily morally wrong or sex during that part of a woman's cycle where she is infertile is necessarily morally wrong or sex between partners at least one of whom is sterile is necessarily morally wrong [from (27*) and (28*)].

But Catholic moral teaching rejects (29*).[171] Assuming that the argument consisting of (25), (26), (27*), (28*), and (29*) is analogous to the argument consisting of (25)–(32), then DREA proves too much.

But (27*) is false, (27*) is not logically analogous to (27), and (27*) does not follow from (25) and (26). First, (27*) is false. Catholic moral teaching has it that an act of sexual union is morally wrong if it does not respect

---

170. For helpful discussion of God's care for the damned, see, e.g., Stump's *Wandering in Darkness*, 196–226.
171. See, e.g., Pope St. Paul VI, *Humanae Vitae*, Encyclical Letter, July 25, 1968, par. 11; *Code of Canon Law* (Washington, D.C.: Canon Law Society of America, 1999), c. 1084, § 3. For some discussion of this point, see Feser, "In Defense of the Perverted Faculty Argument."

the generative purpose of the sexual act.[172] But it does not require that each and every sexual act intend the good of procreation.[173]

In addition, (27*) is not logically analogous to (27), and (27*) does not follow from (25) and (26). One important way in which (27*) is not logically analogous to (27) so that it makes sense to accept (27) but reject (27*) is that (a) and (a*) are importantly different; (a) in (27) states that "the next life is a context where maintenance of the body and preservation of the species are no longer rational ends or purposes of *any* human life." But, importantly, (a*) treats only of the rational intentions of some human persons regarding sexual union. Whereas (a) describes the next life as a new life that does not include preservation of the species as a rational end of any human activity, (a*) simply describes what some adult human persons reasonably intend, in some select circumstances, with respect to sexual union in this life, without denying that preservation of the species is a rational end of sexual activity in general in this life.

There are additional important ways in which (27) and (27*) are not logically analogous so that (27*) does not follow from (25) and (26). For example, sexual unions in cases where couples are (temporarily) infertile or sterile can respect the generative purpose of sexual union insofar as sexual union facilitates a friendship between the spouses that helps them educate their children (whether biological or adopted offspring) in virtue, thereby fulfilling the primary purpose of sex to preserve the species (as preservation of the species involves not only generating offspring, but helping such offspring flourish long enough to contribute to the preservation of the species themselves). But as human persons in the next life are immortal and do not grow or diminish morally, sex cannot serve such a purpose in the next life. Premise (27*) is false and does not follow from (25) and (26); premise (27) is true and does follow from (25) and (26).

In addition, sexual union between (temporarily) infertile or sterile couples can serve in this life the secondary or additional primary purpose of drawing that couple into deeper friendship. But, as we have seen, the

---

172. For example, homosexual sex or contracepted sex or any kind of sex where the male (intentionally) ejaculates outside of his partner's vagina are examples of sexual acts that, by their very nature, do not respect the generative purpose of the sexual act and so are necessarily morally wrong. For a good defense of these views, see Feser, "In Defense of the Perverted Faculty Argument."

173. See, e.g., Pope St. Paul VI, *Humanae Vitae*, par. 11.

blessed in heaven no longer need sex to draw closer to one another, for they now enjoy much greater gifts, such as the beatific vision and the communion of the saints in heaven. Also, it may be that the (self-inflicted) absence of any sort of friendship is part of the punishment of those in hell.

Although sex between infertile or sterile couples in this life can be morally praiseworthy, sexual union in the next life would be immoral and in heaven nonsensical. As premise (27*) is not, therefore, analogous to premise (27), and (27*) does not follow from (25) and (26)—or any of the other premises in DREA—the objection from (27*), (28*), and (29*) to DREA fails.

REA and DREA both emphasize the lack of continuity between this life and the next life as a reason for thinking that eating, drinking, and sexual union have no place in—or do not make any sense as aspects of—the next life. Consider also an argument that is similar to REA and DREA that there will be no eating, drinking, and sexual union in the next life. St. Thomas believes, with the Christian tradition meditating upon Matthew 22:30, Mark 12:25, and Luke 20:35, that no human persons are married in the next life in the sense that *there are no persons married to each other in the carnal sense*[174] *in the next life.*[175] As the traditional wedding vow goes: "til death do us part." Let us assume that is true. But sex outside of marriage is morally wrong. Persons in the next life do not engage in morally wrong actions. Therefore, there is no sexual union in the next life.

Why is there no sexual union and marriage in the next life? The next life is a radically different sort of life, where sexual union and marriage no longer serve their very good, but this-worldly, purposes. For similar reasons, eating and drinking do not exist in the next life. Therefore, there is no eating, drinking, or sexual union in the next life.

St. Thomas fields a number of objections to the view that acts of eating, drinking, and sexual union cease in the next life. I will mention two here. A first objection: the primary purpose—or *a* primary purpose—of the generative and nutritive organs is begetting and eating, respectively. But we will rise with the generative and nutritive organs. Therefore, lest

---

174. Of course, St. Thomas thinks that there is marriage according to a spiritual sense in the next life, i.e., the church's marriage—and each individual soul's marriage—to Christ is consummated in heaven. See discussion of the communion of the saints in chapter 12 below.

175. For additional discussion of these passages and additional reasons for thinking that the saints in heaven, in particular, will not eat, drink, or engage in acts of sexual union at and after the general resurrection, see chapter 11 below.

those organs have no purpose at the resurrection, we will engage in acts of generation and eating after the resurrection.[176]

As we have seen, St. Thomas answers this objection by arguing that the nutritive and generative organs are restored at the general resurrection for the sake of bodily integrity, both specifically, for example, all human beings will have stomachs for the sake of *human* bodily integrity, and individually, for example, males will be resurrected with male generative organs and females with female generative organs for the sake of *individual* bodily integrity. Therefore, although such organs are not used for their natural this-worldly purposes at and after the resurrection, it does not thereby follow they do not serve a purpose in the next life. For the existence of such organs in the next life lends itself to the perfection and beauty of next-worldly bodies.[177]

A second objection begins with the premise that our resurrection will conform to that of Christ's resurrection. But as scripture teaches (see, e.g., Lk 24:43, Jn 21, and Acts 10:40–41), Christ ate after the resurrection. Therefore, we too will eat after the general resurrection. But, if we eat, then we will also beget. Therefore, we will eat and beget after the general resurrection.[178]

In responding to this objection, St. Thomas notes the reason why Christ eats after the resurrection: not because he needed to, say for the sake of maintaining his resurrection body, but rather in order to demonstrate to the apostles that he did indeed have a true human nature, that is, that he was not a ghost or simply a spirit. But such proof will not be necessary for human persons at and after the general resurrection. In other words, Christ's eating after his resurrection is a dispensation from or exception to the general rule that no one eats after the resurrection, which exception is necessary to teach the apostles that he has a true human nature, given their this-worldly state of mind. Therefore, Christ's eating does not indicate the kind of life Christ lives after the resurrection and so it does not follow that human beings after the resurrection live an animal life.[179]

---

176. See, e.g., *In Sent* IV, d. 44, q. 1, a. 3, q.c. 4, obj. 2 (*ST Suppl.*, q. 81, a. 4, obj. 2).

177. See, e.g., *In Sent* IV, d. 44, q. 1, a. 3, q.c. 4, ad 2 (*ST Suppl.*, q. 81, a. 4, ad 2).

178. See, e.g., *In Sent* IV, d. 44, q. 1, a. 3, q.c. 4, obj. 1 (*ST Suppl.*, q. 81, a. 4, obj. 1), and *SCG* IV.83.16.

179. See, e.g., *In Sent* IV, d. 44, q. 1, a. 3, q.c. 4, ad 1 (*ST Suppl.*, q. 81, a. 4, ad 1); *SCG* IV.83.19; *CT* I, chap. 238; *QQ* III, q. 2, a. 3 (thanks to Turner Nevitt for pointing out this passage); *ST* III, q. 54, a. 2, ad 3.

St. Thomas thinks that all resurrected bodies will have certain features. For example, they are numerically and specifically identical to the bodies that human persons possessed in this life. Resurrected bodies also enjoy a kind of natural perfection, and so they possess all of the kinds of parts that human bodies in this life possess. Despite the continuity of resurrected human bodies and human bodies in this life, resurrected human bodies are in many ways very different from human bodies in this life. For example, they are incorruptible. Because they are incorruptible, no human persons in the next life will eat, drink, or engage in acts of sexual union. Having said something about St. Thomas's views on resurrected bodies *qua* resurrected bodies, the next chapter turns to detailing the characteristic features of human bodies in heaven.

11

The Accidental Reward III

GLORIFIED BODIES

In the previous chapter, we saw that, according to St. Thomas, all resurrected bodies—whether those in heaven or those in hell—have certain properties *qua* resurrected bodies. I called these properties *resurrection properties*, or R properties. Following a long tradition,[1] St. Thomas thinks that, in addition to R properties, the bodies of the human blessed in heaven, because they are *glorified*, have the following four characteristic properties: impassibility (*impassibilitas*), agility (*agilitas*), clarity (*claritas*), and subtlety (*subtilitas*).[2] Call these qualities characteristic of glorified human bodies, G properties. This chapter explores what St. Thomas has to say about the G properties.[3]

THE IMPASSIBILITY OF THE GLORIFIED BODY

There are at least four meanings of impassibility that St. Thomas discusses in the context of talking about the characteristic properties of the glorified body. In the strongest sense of impassibility, an impassible

---

1. For some historical discussion of the characteristic properties of glorified bodies in the Christian tradition, see, e.g., Bynum, *The Resurrection of the Body in Western Christianity, 200–1336*.

2. See, e.g., *In Sent* IV, d. 44, q. 2, aa. 1–4 (*ST Suppl.*, qq. 82–85); *In Sent* IV, d. 49, q. 4, a. 5, q.c. 3, resp.; *SCG* IV.86; *CT* I, chap. 168; *In 1 Cor* 15, lects. 6–9; *ST* III, q. 45, a. 1, obj. 3 and ad 3; *CSA*, a. 11. Like the bodies of the blessed in heaven, the bodies of the damned have all of the R properties. In contrast to the bodies of the blessed in heaven, the bodies of the damned are passible, darksome, weighed down, and carnal. See, e.g., *In Sent* IV, d. 44, q. 3, a. 1 (*ST Suppl.*, q. 86); *SCG* IV.89; *CT* I, chaps. 176–77; *CSA*, a. 11.

3. In presenting the G properties, this chapter follows the order in which St. Thomas treats them in the *Sentences* commentary, which is the text where he offers the most detailed account of the G properties in his oeuvre. It is interesting to note that, although St. Thomas treats the G properties in a number of different works, he rarely treats them in the same order twice.

body is not in any way passive with respect to the physical world external to the body.[4] If the glorified body were impassible in that strong sense, then it could not receive data from the external world for the sake of sensing the world.[5] According to a slightly weaker sense of impassibility, the glorified body is impassible in the sense that, although it can be receptive in relation to the external world of bodies (e.g., in sensing the world), its receptivity with respect to the external world of bodies cannot alter the natural perfection of the human body such that the body can suffer pain or suffer damage or be corrupted.[6] In a third sense of impassibility, though an impassible body can sense the external world and suffer pain, it cannot suffer physical damage or be corrupted.[7]

Of the three senses of impassibility discussed so far, we might think St. Thomas's view is that the bodies of the blessed are impassible in the second sense. Such bodies can and will undergo changes that perfect the blessed with respect to their accidental reward, such as receiving by way of the senses what is requisite for forming sense images of God's "new heavens and new earth," or coming to experience pleasure at seeing or touching things not seen or touched previously, etc. But glorified bodies sense the world without the body suffering any pain as a result, without any threat to the integrity of their bodies,[8] and without altering the natural qualities of the human body, for example, such sensations will not make the human body colder or warmer than it ideally is.

That being said, in his commentary on Matthew 22:30b, St. Thomas states that glorified bodies will be impassible in a fourth sense—a sense stronger than the second sense but weaker than the first. According to St. Thomas's interpretation of this passage from the Gospel, glorified bodies will be raised above the passions, as are the angels.[9] However, such a passage can be given both a strong and a weak reading. On the strong reading, St. Thomas means that the glorified human body is the

---

4. See, e.g., *In Sent* IV, d. 44, q. 2, a. 1, q.c. 1 (*ST Suppl.*, q. 82, a. 1).

5. See, e.g., *In Sent* IV, d. 44, q. 2, a. 1, q.c. 3–4 (*ST Suppl.*, q. 82, aa. 3–4).

6. See, e.g., *In Sent* IV, d. 44, q. 2, a. 1, q.c. 1 (*ST Suppl.*, q. 82, a. 1); *In Sent* IV, d. 44, q. 2, a. 1, q.c. 2, obj. 2 (*ST Suppl.*, q. 82, a. 2, obj. 1); *In Sent* IV, d. 49, q. 4, a. 5, q.c. 3, resp.; *SCG* IV.86.4.

7. See, e.g., *In Sent* IV, d. 44, q. 3, a. 2, q.c. 3 (*ST Suppl.*, q. 86, a. 3).

8. See, e.g., *In Sent* IV, d. 44, q. 3, a. 2, q.c. 1, 3, 4 (*ST Suppl.*, q. 86, aa. 1, 3, 4); *SCG* IV.86; *CT* I, chap. 168; *In 1 Cor* 15, lect. 6, n. 980. Incidentally, the bodies of the damned are impassible in the third sense spoken about above. Although the bodies of the damned cannot be damaged or corrupted, they can suffer pain and receive sense data from the external world of bodies. See, e.g., *In Sent* IV, d. 44, q. 3, a. 2, q.c. 3 (*ST Suppl.*, q. 86, a. 3).

9. *In Mt* 22, lect. 3, n. 1800. See also *ST* I, q. 98, a. 2, ad 1, and *ST* I-II, q. 61, a. 5, resp.

body of a person who does not experience passions, emotions, or feelings at all. In that case, St. Thomas thinks:

(a) The glorified body is impassible in the sense that, although the glorified body can be receptive of sense data from the external world, the glorified body can neither suffer passions in the sense of feelings, suffer changes in its natural bodily dispositions, suffer pain, suffer damage, nor undergo corruption.

St. Thomas could also mean, as the context might suggest, that the embodied saints will not experience passions for the sorts of things humans share with other animals, such as eating, drinking, and sexual union. That would be the weaker reading of that passage. In that case, St. Thomas would think about the impassibility of the glorified bodies as follows:

(b) The glorified body is impassible in the sense that, although the body can be receptive of sense data from the external world and undergo passions, feelings, or emotions for spiritual goods, the glorified body can neither suffer passions for food, drink, or sex, suffer changes in its natural bodily dispositions, suffer pain, suffer damage, nor undergo corruption.

Arguments That Glorified Bodies Will Be Impassible

Why should one think that glorified bodies will be impassible in the sense of either (a) or (b) above? In various places, St. Thomas cites passages from scripture, including, as we saw above, Matthew 22:30b. He also cites 1 Corinthians 15:42 ("It is sown in corruption; it shall rise in incorruption"),[10] 1 Corinthians 15:43 ("It is sown in dishonor; it is raised in glory"),[11] Revelation 7:16 ("Never again will they hunger; never again will they thirst")[12] and Revelation 21:4 ("He will wipe every tear from their eyes. There will be no more death or mourning or crying or pain, for the old order of things has passed away").[13]

Of course, St. Thomas also offers theological arguments for the impassibility of glorified bodies. In a first argument, St. Thomas begins with the premise that bodies are passible only insofar as something can

---

10. See, e.g., *ST Suppl.*, q. 82, a. 1, s.c. (trans. English Dominicans, 2893; *In Sent* IV, d. 44, q. 2, a. 1, q.c. 1, s.c.). See also *SCG* IV.86.4; *In 1 Cor* 15, lect. 6, n. 980; *CT* I, chap. 168.
11. *CSA*, a. 11.
12. *In 1 Cor* 15, lect. 6, n. 980.
13. *CSA*, a. 11.

overcome them, for example, break them, corrupt them, or cause their possessors to experience pain or suffering. Although human bodies can be harmed in this life, this is not the case in the next life, according to 1 Corinthians 15:43 ("It is sown in weakness, it is raised in power"). Because there is nothing in heaven that is both stronger than the bodies of the saints and such that it would will to harm such human bodies—the great strength of the glorified body being a result of the soul's hold on the body in virtue of the soul's having the beatific vision—the bodies of the saints will be impassible.[14]

In *SCG*, St. Thomas offers a different argument. He argues from the premise of the perfect relationship between the human soul and human body in heaven, which itself is caused by the perfect relationship between the human soul and God in heaven. In virtue of having the beatific vision, the human soul has its every desire fulfilled in seeing the essence of God. But one thing a human person desires is the removal of every evil, including evils that can be suffered in the body. Although St. Thomas does not say so here, we might specify such evils that can be suffered in the body as the kinds identified in propositions (a) or (b) above, namely: suffering a passion that would interfere—or be inconsistent—with the soul's having the beatific vision; suffering a passion for food, drink, or sex in a context where acting on such a passion was morally wrong or insensible; suffering the loss of the human body's natural dispositions; suffering pain; suffering some damage to the body; and suffering death. Therefore, the body of the saint is impassible in the sense of proposition (a) or proposition (b) above.[15]

The Cause(s) of the Impassibility of Glorified Bodies in Heaven

What explains why the bodies of the blessed will be impassible? Before examining St. Thomas's own preferred explanation of what causes glorified bodies to be impassible, it will be helpful to examine some alternative explanations that he rejects.[16] St. Thomas notes that some theo-

---

14. Ibid. See also *In Sent* IV, d. 44, q. 2, a. 1, q.c. 1, resp. (*ST Suppl.*, q. 82, a. 1, resp.).
15. *SCG* IV.86.4. See also *CT* I, chap. 168.
16. Examining the details of all of the positions on the cause of the glorified body's impassibility St. Thomas considers and rejects would take us too far afield. This chapter examines only those aspects of explanations alternative to St. Thomas's that help shed some light on St. Thomas's own views. In some cases, the arguments presented rely upon Aristotle's theory of elements and mixed bodies. However, discussing that theory would also take us too far afield (for some expla-

logians suggest that the elements that compose human bodies remain in the resurrected body with respect to their substance but lack their proper accidents, such as their active and passive qualities. St. Thomas rejects that explanation because, if the elements existed without their active and passive qualities, then they would exist in a state less perfect than in this life. But the parts of the glorified human body do not exist in a state less perfect than in this life.[17]

Other theologians propose that the elements remain as substances with their proper accidents, but lack their proper activities.[18] This way of making sense of the impassibility of glorified bodies is problematic, St. Thomas thinks, for two reasons. First, the actions and passions that follow upon the active and passive qualities of the elements are a necessary condition for the existence of mixed bodies such as blood, bone, flesh, hair, etc. Therefore, if glorified bodies are impassible due to the suppression of these actions and passions, then glorified bodies are not composed of such mixed bodies. Of course, such bodies would not be *human* bodies, for human bodies are composed of mixed bodies such as flesh, blood, and bone. Second, if the glorified body were impassible due to the suppression of the actions and passions proper to the elements, then this would be due to the power of God. But in that case, St. Thomas argues, the glorified body would not be impassible itself, but rather would be impassible simply because God prevents it from suffering passion, for example, by a miracle. According to tradition, impassibility is a *gift* (*dos*) of the glorified body, and so it is a quality that the glorified body itself possesses.[19]

St. Thomas notes that some other theologians argue that glorified bodies are impassible on account of being composed of a fifth element—or some otherworldly matter—which element (matter) causes the body itself to be impassible.[20] St. Thomas thinks that this position is unten-

---

nation, discussion, and citations from the literature on St. Thomas on elements and compounds, see my *Aquinas and the Ship of Theseus*, 94–98). Therefore, in some places St. Thomas's arguments are stated not to illuminate the Aristotelian theory of elements and compounds, but rather to magnify aspects of St. Thomas's views on the impassibility of the glorified body.

17. *In Sent* IV, d. 44, q. 2, a. 1, q.c. 1, resp. (*ST Suppl.*, q. 82, a. 1, resp.). See also *QDP*, q. 5, a. 7, ob. 2 and ad 2.

18. *In Sent* IV, d. 44, q. 2, a. 1, q.c. 1, resp. (*ST Suppl.*, q. 82, a. 1, resp.).

19. Ibid.

20. Ibid. See also *In 1 Cor* 15, lect. 6, n. 988. Of course, we no longer believe in the so-called fifth element. However, there are contemporary theologians and philosophers who do think resurrected bodies will be composed of a kind of matter entirely different from the matter that

able for both scriptural and, as we have already seen, philosophical reasons. As for scriptural reasons, St. Thomas notes the Pauline teaching that resurrection bodies are glorified by the power of Christ and not because of some natural power,[21] citing 1 Corinthians 15:48[22] and Philippians 3:21[23] to this effect. As for his philosophical reasons, St. Thomas argues that a body that was composed of heavenly bodies would not be human—and the glorified bodies of human persons are human bodies.[24] In addition, St. Thomas thinks that heavenly bodies do not have the power to eliminate the tendencies in the elements to separate themselves from one another.[25]

St. Thomas thinks that there are two causes of the impassibility of a glorified body, namely, God and the human soul having the vision of the essence of God. The beatified soul is the *formal* cause of the impassibility of the glorified body as follows. The passibility of the body B of a human person S is due to the possibility that some agent A so weakens the hold that S's soul as substantial form has over S's matter that B is subject to corruption or harm. But the matter of a human person in heaven will be so subject to the human soul that it will not be possible for an agent to weaken the soul's relation with respect to the matter that composes a human person in heaven.[26] Why will the embodied human soul in heaven be such that it has such a hold over its matter? The human soul is so perfected in virtue of having the beatific vision, that when the soul configures its designated matter again at the resurrection, the union of the human soul and matter is also perfected such that the resurrected body of the saint is impassible.[27] Of course, the beatific vision itself is caused by God. Therefore, whereas the beatified human soul is the intrinsic formal cause of impassibility in glorified bodies, God is the *extrinsic efficient*

---

composes human bodies in this life, i.e., an otherworldly matter (see chapter 1, note 65 above). Henceforward, when St. Thomas speaks of *the fifth element*, that expression is rendered as "otherworldly matter."

21. *In Sent* IV, d. 44, q. 2, a. 1, q.c. 1, resp. (*ST Suppl.*, q. 82, a. 1, resp.).
22. Ibid. See also *In 1 Cor* 15, lect. 7, n. 997.
23. *In Sent* IV, d. 44, q. 2, a. 1, q.c. 1, resp. (*ST Suppl.*, q. 82, a. 1, resp.). See also *In Phil* 3, lect. 3, n. 145.
24. *In Sent* IV, d. 44, q. 2, a. 1, q.c. 1, resp. (*ST Suppl.*, q. 82, a. 1, resp.).
25. Ibid.
26. See ibid.; *In Sent* IV, d. 49, q. 4, a. 5, q.c. 3, resp.; *SCG* IV.86; *CT* I, chap. 168; *In 1 Cor* 15, lect. 6, n. 988.
27. Dom Anscar Vonier suggests the detail that the human soul has this power with respect to the body not *qua* substantial form of the body but *qua* spiritual being having the beatific vision (see *The Human Soul and Its Relations with Other Spirits*, 168–70).

cause of impassibility insofar as it is God that perfects the soul in the beatific vision such that the soul can be the intrinsic formal cause of the glorified body's impassibility.[28]

What Kind of Sensitive Life Do Human Persons in Heaven Enjoy?

As we have seen, St. Thomas thinks that the manner in which glorified bodies are impassible is consistent with the saints having sense experiences in heaven. Indeed, St. Thomas argues that, if the embodied saints in heaven did not have sense experiences, then their bodily life would be more like those who are asleep. But to be awake and active is a more perfect state than being asleep. Therefore, a bodily life that does not involve actual sensation would not be consistent with the perfect life of the blessed.[29]

Although "everyone holds" (*omnes ponunt*)[30] that glorified bodies sense, St. Thomas notes some of his near-contemporaries offer accounts of the impassibility of glorified bodies that have it that those bodies are not changed by way of external objects in sensing. As St. Thomas points out, some try to explain the impassibility of glorified bodies such that the sense organs of the glorified bodies do not receive sense impressions from without, but rather produce them from within. St. Thomas rejects this approach, as it entails that the sense powers in glorified bodies are active powers rather than passive ones. But human bodies in this life have sense powers that are passive powers and, just as matter cannot become form and remain the same kind of thing, neither can a passive power become an active power and remain specifically the same. Therefore, if the sense powers of the glorified bodies are active powers instead of passive ones, then glorified bodies are not specifically the same kind of body as bodies in this life. But, as we have seen, glorified bodies are specifically the same kind of body as bodies in this life.[31]

St. Thomas mentions, only to reject, another theory of how glorified bodies sense things. Like the theory mentioned above, this theory has

---

28. St. Thomas puts the point here in a complementary and Christocentric way in his commentary on Philippians: the glorification of the bodies of the saints, who share in Christ's passion, participate in Christ's glorified body, which itself is glorified because of his divinity (*In Phil* 3, lect. 3, n. 145).
29. *In Sent* IV, d. 44, q. 2, a. 1, q.c. 3, resp. (*ST Suppl.*, q. 82, a. 3, resp.). See also *SCG* IV.86.4.
30. *In Sent* IV, d. 44, q. 2, a. 1, q.c. 3, resp. (*ST Suppl.*, q. 82, a. 3, resp.).
31. Ibid.

the agent alone activating the sense powers, but, according to the present theory, this is not done by the sense powers themselves, but rather by a higher cognitive power (e.g., the imagination). The problem with this theory, according to St. Thomas, is that true sensation is caused by objects external to the agent that senses. Indeed, the difference between a madman (or, for example, someone who is hallucinating) and one who is sane (and does not have her sense organs impeded by a drug or physical problem) lies in the fact that the latter senses external objects whereas the former only *seems* to sense external objects.[32] In St. Thomas's own view, as glorified bodies are perfect human bodies, perfect human bodies are such that they enable human persons to sense things, and true sensation entails receiving sense impressions from objects external to the agent who senses, it follows that glorified bodies are human bodies that enable the saints in heaven to receive sense impressions from objects external to them.

But there are two ways in which the senses can be in act by way of being changed by things external to the agent, only one of which is consistent with other things St. Thomas believes he can prove by way of theological argument about glorified bodies. Sometimes the sense organs themselves take on a quality of the object sensed, for example, when the hand touches a hot object and itself becomes hot as a result. St. Thomas calls this *natural transmutation*. As we have seen, St. Thomas thinks that the glorified body cannot be changed in this way, as glorified human bodies constantly enjoy the natural qualities of the human body (e.g., the ideal heat).

At other times—in fact, in most instances of sensation—the sense organs receive the sensible quality of an object as a sensible species and not as it exists in the external object sensed. For example, when we see an object as white, our pupil does not itself get white, but rather we receive whiteness in a spiritual sense. St. Thomas calls this way of receiving the quality of an external object *spiritual* transmutation.[33] The glorified body can be changed in this manner, thinks St. Thomas. In addition, St. Thomas argues that only spiritual transmutation of the sense organ resulting in the organ receiving a sensible species counts as genuine

---

32. Ibid.
33. By *spiritual* transmutation, Eleonore Stump thinks that St. Thomas is speaking of what could be understood as receiving the quality of the object sensed as encoded information. See her *Aquinas*, 253.

sensation.³⁴ So the glorified body's inability to undergo natural transmutation is no strike against its perfection.

St. Thomas fields two objections to his view that the saints in heaven receive sensible species from external objects based on his belief that the essence of perfect happiness consists in the beatific vision. In responding to them, St. Thomas offers us interesting details about how he thinks the various aspects of human life are integrated in heaven.

In the first of the two objections, the objector argues that if x has actual sensations in heaven, then x comes to have new judgments. But in heaven there will be no new judgments, because, as St. Augustine says, "our thoughts will not then be changeable."³⁵ St. Thomas responds to the objection by denying its validity, for although he accepts the premises of the argument, he says that human persons will form new judgments, not intellectually, but in the common sense.³⁶ As he notes, even in this life we sometimes see something that we already know intellectually. For example, Susan might know what a bird is, though she has never seen an individual example of one. In addition, St. Augustine is speaking of coming to know things intellectually in the passage cited.³⁷ So, although St. Paul's seeing the new heavens and the new earth does not give him a new understanding of the new heavens and the new earth, as he already understands the new heavens and the new earth in virtue of having the beatific vision,³⁸ St. Paul does have a novel experience of the new creation in *sensing* God's new creation, and a new, or different way of cognizing the glory of God.³⁹

---

34. *In Sent* IV, d. 44, q. 2, a. 1, q.c. 3, resp. (*ST Suppl.*, q. 82, a. 3, resp.).

35. *De Trinitate* XV.16. See *ST Suppl.*, q. 82, a. 3, obj. 3 and ad 3 (trans. English Dominicans, 2895; *In Sent* IV, d. 44, q. 2, a. 1, q.c. 3, obj. 3 and ad 3). See also *In Sent* IV, d. 44, q. 2, a. 1, q.c. 4, ad 4 (*ST Suppl.*, q. 82, a. 4, ad 4).

36. *The common sense* is one of four interior senses; it coordinates the input from the exterior senses (see, e.g., *ST* I, q. 78, a. 4).

37. *In Sent* IV, d. 44, q. 2, a. 1, q.c. 3, ad 3 (*ST Suppl.*, q. 82, a. 3, ad 3).

38. See chapter 6 above for discussion of created things as the secondary object of the beatific vision.

39. See, e.g., *ST Suppl.*, q. 92, a. 2, resp. (*In Sent* IV, d. 49, q. 2, a. 2, resp.): "[by the power of sensation the embodied saint] will see [God] as an object of indirect vision, because on the one hand the bodily sight will see so great a glory of God in bodies, especially in the glorified bodies and most of all in the body of Christ, and, on the other hand, the intellect will see God so clearly, that God will be perceived in things seen with the eye of the body, even as life is perceived in speech. For although our intellect will not then see God from seeing His creatures, yet it will see God in His creatures seen corporeally. This manner of seeing God corporeally is indicated by Augustine (*De Civ. Dei* xxii), as is clear if we take note of his words, for he says: *It is very credible that we shall so see the mundane bodies of the new heaven and the new earth, as to see most clearly God everywhere present, governing all corporeal things, not as we now see the invisible things of God as understood by those that are made, but as when we see men ... we do not believe but see that they live*" (trans. English Dominicans, 2953).

Although St. Thomas does not argue in this way, it seems possible also to say that glorified human persons will know things in heaven in all the ways they know things in this life, and in a manner that does not draw the saints away from the beatific vision, but in a way that is supportive of it. For St. Thomas thinks that the following proposition is true:

(1) In his human nature, Christ possesses multiple forms of cognition, for example, he has acquired, infused, and beatific knowledge;[40] the blessed angels too possess a natural mode of cognition in addition to the beatific vision.[41]

By analogy with Christ and the blessed angels, we can think that:

(2) The saints in heaven enjoy multiple modes of cognition and willing, for example, there is the timeless and immutable act which is the beatific vision, and the acts of will that flow from it, that is, the essential reward, but, as a part of the accidental reward of the saints, there are also all those acts of cognition and willing analogous to acts of cognition and willing in which many of the redeemed were engaged in this life, for example, a saint's seeing with her glorified body the body of Christ and a saint's willing her body to travel to Mars.[42]

Again, St. Thomas does not explicitly endorse a proposition such as (2). However, there does not seem to be anything in his account of heaven inconsistent with it. In addition, St. Thomas does sometimes speak of acts of will in the separated soul (in heaven) distinct from those acts of will that are proper accidents of the beatific vision. For example, in *SCG*, St. Thomas states:

The soul's will, therefore, will be immovable regarding a desire for the ultimate end.... Now, on the ultimate end the entire goodness or wickedness of the will depends, for whatever goods one wills in an order toward a good end he wills well; whatever evil he wills in an order toward an evil end he wills badly. Therefore, there is not in the separated soul a will changeable from good to evil, although it is changeable from this object of will to that so long as the order to the same ultimate end is preserved.[43]

---

40. See, e.g., *ST* III, q. 9.
41. See, e.g., *ST* I, q. 58, aa. 1–2; q. 62, a. 7; *In Mt* 18, lect. 1, n. 1505.
42. Indeed, in enjoying multiple modes of cognition in heaven, the saints "are like the angels in heaven" (Mt 22:30b).
43. *SCG* IV.95.5–6 (trans. O'Neil, 344). See also *ST* III, q. 18, a. 4, ad 3: "The will of Christ, though determined to good, is not determined to this or that good. Hence it pertains to Christ,

In the passage above St. Thomas notes that the separated soul, including the separated soul in heaven, is immutable with respect to the ultimate end, so that it "cannot change from good to evil." In the case of the separated soul in heaven, this is the soul's acts of will that are proper accidents of the beatific vision. But St. Thomas goes on to note that the will "is changeable from this object of will to that so long as the order of the same ultimate end is preserved." As Melissa Eitenmiller argues, St. Thomas is here speaking about "changeability in the soul with regard to the desire of lesser things that are ordered to whichever ultimate end the soul had previously chosen."[44] Such acts of will are acts of will other than those that are a part of the essential reward. It stands to reason that if St. Thomas thinks there are acts of will other than those that are aspects of the essential reward, he also thinks that there are acts of intellect in the separated soul other than the beatific vision, insofar as acts of will follow upon acts of intellect for St. Thomas. In addition, there is no reason to think there will be no acts of intellect and will that are aspects of the accidental reward at and after the general resurrection. Indeed, there is every reason to think such acts do exist insofar as embodied saints can, for example, will their bodies to move from here to there.

The second of the two objections having to do with the compatibility of the saints experiencing the beatific vision, and the saints having bodies in heaven such that their senses are in act, begins with the premise that when one of the soul's powers is intensely in act, the other powers cannot be actively employed. But the souls of the saints will be supremely intent on contemplatively knowing the essence of God in the beatific vision. Therefore, the senses cannot be actively employed by the saints in heaven.[45]

St. Thomas offers two responses to this objection. In his first response, St. Thomas begins from a general psychological principle: when x is the type of y, consideration of y does not hinder consideration of x, and vice versa. To illustrate the principle, he offers the example of a physician considering a urine sample. Thinking about the sample does not hinder, but actually helps, his simultaneous consideration of the physi-

---

even as to the blessed, to choose with a free-will confirmed in good" (trans. English Dominicans, 2122).
44. "On the Separated Soul," 78.
45. *In Sent* IV, d. 44, q. 2, a. 1, q.c. 3, obj. 4 (*ST Suppl.*, q. 82, a. 3, obj. 4).

cian's rules concerning what the various colors of urine signify about the health of the patient. In other words, the physician is simultaneously looking at the urine sample and thinking about what the color of the urine sample means for the health of the patient. But, in the beatific vision, God is known as the type of all things known or done by the saints in heaven.[46] Therefore, the saints sensing external objects, or thinking about things other than God, or moving their bodies from here to there, in no way hinders the saints in their experience of God in the beatific vision, or vice versa.[47]

St. Thomas has a second way of responding to the objection. The reason why one power is often hindered by the intensity of another power's act is that these powers are not perfect. But in heaven, the powers of the saints will be most perfect,[48] just as Christ in this life had perfect powers operating simultaneously.[49]

So far, we have seen that St. Thomas thinks that the impassibility of glorious bodies does not rule out those bodies having organs that receive sense impressions from objects external to them. But are all of the senses in act in heaven? Some of St. Thomas's contemporaries think not. St. Thomas notes that some think that only sight and touch will be in act, as the other senses will not have a suitable medium in heaven in order to be active. Nonetheless, the glorious body will still contain the sense organs of hearing, smelling, and touch in order that the human body should be complete in its integrity and show forth the wisdom of the creator.[50]

St. Thomas maintains that there are no good reasons to think the senses of hearing and smelling will not be in act in heaven, as hearing and smelling, like sight, have air as their proper medium. Although there will be no tasting things in heaven caused by eating or drinking (as there is no eating or drinking in heaven), St. Thomas does not rule out the possibility that we taste things in some other way.[51] Furthermore, scripture and tradition indicate that the embodied saints will hear and smell things.[52] Finally, St. Thomas mentions some positive philosophical

---

46. For more discussion of this point, see chapter 6 above.
47. *In Sent* IV, d. 44, q. 2, a. 1, q.c. 3, ad 4 (*ST Suppl.*, q. 82, a. 3, ad 4).
48. Ibid.
49. See, e.g., *ST* III, q. 9.
50. *In Sent* IV, d. 44, a. 1, q.c. 4, resp. (*ST Suppl.*, q. 82, a. 4, resp.).
51. Ibid.
52. Ibid.

reasons that all the senses will be in act in heaven.[53] The sense powers are more like the human soul than is the body. But the blessed and the wicked will be rewarded or punished in their bodies in accordance with the merits or demerits of the soul. Therefore, how much more will the blessed and the wicked be rewarded or punished by way of their sensing, which sensing requires that the sense powers be in act.[54]

ST. THOMAS ON THE SUBTLETY, SPIRITUALITY, AND SEXUALITY OF THE GLORIFIED BODY

I will now explain St. Thomas's views concerning the traditional attribute of the glorified body known as subtlety (*subtilitas*). I begin with his most detailed treatment, which can be found in his *Sentences* commentary.

In discussing what tradition means in ascribing subtlety to glorified

---

53. St. Thomas sometimes speaks of knowing God by way of five *spiritual* senses. For example, in commenting on Phil 2:5 ("Let the same mind be in you that was in Christ Jesus") St. Thomas notes we should have this mind in five ways, which five ways correspond to the five senses. We should *see* his glory in order to be enlightened and so conformed to him, *hear* his wisdom in order to be made happy, *smell* the grace of his meekness in order to run to him, *taste* the sweetness of his mercy that we may always be in God, and *touch* his power in order to be saved (see *In Phil* 2, lect. 2, n. 52; *In Sent* III, d. 13, *expositio textus*; *In Ps* 33 [34]—thanks to Mark Spencer for pointing out these texts). The saints in heaven could also have perfected forms of these spiritual senses. For a Thomistic development of the notion of human persons having spiritual senses, see Spencer, "The Phenomenology and Metaphysics of Spiritual Perception."

54. *In Sent* IV, d. 44, a. 1, q.c. 4, s.c. (*ST Suppl.*, q. 82, a. 4, s.c.). Christina van Dyke wonders whether St. Thomas still thinks that active sensation is a part of heavenly life by the time he composes *ST*: see her "Aquinas's Shiny Happy People: Perfect Happiness and the Limits of Human Nature," *Oxford Studies in the Philosophy of Religion* 6 (2014): 269–91. It is true that St. Thomas does not later investigate the question in the detail he does in the *Sentences* commentary (presumably, he would have treated the topic in detail again, had he finished *ST* III). But nothing that St. Thomas says in his later discussions of perfect human happiness in heaven rules out that he continues to think human persons actually sense the new heavens and the new earth at and after the general resurrection. Perhaps one reason van Dyke has this worry, as well as others about St. Thomas's account of human happiness in heaven, is because she fails sufficiently to emphasize the importance of the distinction between the *essential* reward (perfect happiness, i.e., the beatific vision and its proper accidents) and the *accidental* reward (that which is added to perfect happiness to make the well-being of perfect happiness). As we have seen, actually sensing the new heavens and the new earth is not part of the essential reward for St. Thomas, but rather is an aspect of the accidental reward. In addition, as suggested above, it seems consistent with St. Thomas's conception of the essential reward and the accidental reward to say that human persons in heaven not only enjoy the supernatural activities that constitute the essential reward in heaven, but also perfected forms of the natural acts of intellect and will as aspects of the accidental reward, e.g., directly knowing and loving creatures in heaven through natural ways of knowing. That thesis makes sense particularly insofar as both Christ in his human nature and the angels enjoy multiple modes of cognition, both supernatural and natural. Finally, it is worth remembering that St. Thomas continues to think about human happiness in heaven in terms of the essential reward and the accidental reward at the time he composes *ST* (see chapter 4, notes 67–71, above).

bodies,[55] St. Thomas notes that the word subtlety comes from the notion of the power to penetrate.[56] But there are two causes of something having the power to penetrate: a body's being small in depth and breadth, though not in length, or a body's paucity of matter. As St. Thomas remarks, a needle has the power to penetrate for the first reason whereas we say that rare (*rara*) things, such as fires, have the power to penetrate for the second reason.[57] Now, rare bodies have the power to penetrate— and so are called subtle—insofar as the form rather than matter predominates (*forma praedominatur materiae magis*) in that rare thing. Therefore, the word "subtlety" is used metaphorically of a body such that its matter is perfectly subject to its form so as to be perfected by it. According to the Aristotelian cosmology that St. Thomas accepts, heavenly bodies are such that their matter is always perfectly subject to their form and so count as good examples of subtle bodies.

St. Thomas speaks of some additional extended senses of subtlety.[58] For example, insofar as we think of subtlety as a paucity of matter and quantity, immaterial substances, which have no matter or quantity at all, have been spoken of as subtle, and this is so, St. Thomas notes, not only with respect to their substance, but also in the manner in which they employ their powers. Thus insofar as a body is subtle because it can penetrate things, an intellect is spoken of, by extension, as subtle because it can understand the hidden (intrinsic) principles or causes of a thing. Similarly, St. Thomas notes that we speak of persons having subtle sight if they can see very small things that others cannot see.[59]

According to St. Thomas, it is the extended sense of *subtlety* as *form predominating the matter it configures* that is crucial for understanding what it means to say that glorified bodies are *subtle*. For heretical and otherwise problematic ways of thinking about the subtlety of the glorified body have it that, for example, the glorified body is *wholly immaterial* or *composed wholly of subtle bodies such as wind and air* or *composed partly of some otherworldly matter*.[60] St. Thomas says that we should rather think about

---

55. *In Sent IV*, d. 44, q. 2, a. 2 (*ST Suppl.*, q. 83).
56. *In Sent IV*, d. 44, q. 2, a. 2, q.c. 1, resp. (*ST Suppl.*, q. 83, a. 1, resp.).
57. In St. Thomas's Aristotelian account of the elements, fire is the *rarest* of the elements whereas earth is the *densest*.
58. *In Sent IV*, d. 44, q. 2, a. 2, q.c. 1, resp. (*ST Suppl.*, q. 83, a. 1, resp.).
59. Ibid.
60. Ibid. See also *SCG* IV.86.5 and 96.5; *In 1 Cor* 15, lect. 6, n. 984; lect. 7, nn. 999–1000; *In Jn* 20, lect. 6, n. 2559; *ST* III, q. 54, a. 3 (a. 2 in some editions), resp.; *CSA*, a. 11. See also note 20 above.

the glorified body's subtlety as the quality of that body being perfectly subject to the *beatified* human soul, the formal cause of which is the beatified soul being a benevolent lord over the body. In fact, he notes that this is why the glorified body is said to be *spiritual*—because the spirit or soul predominates in the embodied human person in heaven.

But St. Thomas thinks that there are two ways in which the glorified body can be perfectly *subject to the beatified soul*. The *primary* sense in which the glorified body is perfectly subject to the beatified soul is with respect to *the body's participating in the specific being of the substance*, as matter (the body) is subject to its substantial form (the soul). It is according to this primary way in which the glorified body is perfectly subject to the beatified soul that it is said to be *subtle*.

There is a secondary sense in which the body is said to be subject to the soul. This is with respect to *the powers of a substance*, as the soul is also the principle of movement in a substance.[61] The properties of impassibility, agility, and clarity are particular instances of the second way in which the glorified body is subject to the beatified soul, that is, as that which is moved. For example, it is in the glorified body's being perfectly subject to the soul as a principle of movement with respect to the body *sensing* that the glorified body is *impassible*. It is in the glorified body's being perfectly subject to the soul as a principle of movement with respect to *changing its place* that the glorified body is *agile*. Finally, it is in the glorified body's being perfectly subject to the soul as principle of movement with respect to *changing its degree of brightness* that the glorified body is *luminescent*.

But what does it mean to say that the subtlety of the glorified body is a function of its being perfectly subject to the soul as substantial form of the body? Begin with the causes of the subtlety of the glorified body. As with the impassibility of the glorified body, the causes of the subtlety of the glorified body are twofold. Because the subtlety of the glorified body is partly a function of its participation in the glory of the beatified soul as substantial form, the *beatified* soul is the formal cause of the glorified body's subtlety. But the human soul's being beatified has as an efficient cause God's giving to the human soul the *lumen gloriae*, thereby enabling the soul to see the essence of God. Therefore, the efficient cause of the

---

61. *In Sent* IV, d. 44, q. 2, a. 2, q.c. 1, resp. (*ST Suppl.*, q. 83, a. 1, resp.). See also *In Sent* IV, d. 49, q. 4, a. 5, q.c. 3, resp.

subtlety of the glorified body is God insofar as God beatifies the souls of the blessed.[62]

Recall Mark Spencer's Thomistic account of participation: "when one being 'participates' in another, the latter has certain characteristics essentially, and the former has these characteristics only through the latter's formal causality; the former receives a likeness to the [latter], but has this likeness only through a real relationship with the [latter]."[63] But, according to St. Thomas, the subtlety of the glorified body is the human body's participating in the glory of the beatified soul as substantial form. As we have seen, the beatified soul is perfectly in union with God's goodness. Therefore, St. Thomas thinks that the beatified soul *qua* substantial form existing in the predominating relation with matter means that the human body in heaven participates in the goodness of the beatified soul. For example, just as the beatified soul is perfectly in union with God's will, so, in participating in the beatified soul, the inclinations of the glorified body are perfectly in union with the inclinations of the beatified soul. Where our souls in this life and the souls of the damned are subject to inclinations that contradict the inclinations of God or reason, the beatified soul, in configuring matter, predominates in the human person so that the glorified body does not give rise to inclinations that are inconsistent with those of the human person having the beatific vision.

I can put this last point another way. The glorified body is a part of a human person where the beatified soul predominates in the person so that the body is spiritual, that is, a body that does not war with the soul or spirit. But, as we have seen, the primary sense of the soul's existing in the predominating relation with matter in the human person is known as its subtlety. Therefore, the glorified body's being subtle is the primary reason for thinking the glorified body is spiritual, as St. Paul says. In contrast, the glorified body's being agile, being impassible, and being such that it enjoys clarity, associated as each of these properties of the glorified body are with the secondary sense in which the glorified body is subject to the soul, constitute only secondary reasons for thinking of the glorified body as spiritual.[64]

62. See, e.g., *SCG* IV.86.5.
63. "The Phenomenology and Metaphysics of Spiritual Perception," 683.
64. *In Sent* IV, d. 44, q. 2, a. 2, q.c. 1, resp. (*ST Suppl.*, q. 83, a. 1, resp.). See also *In Sent* IV, d. 44, q. 2, a. 3, q.c. 1, resp. (*ST Suppl.*, q. 84, a. 1, resp.), and *ST* III, q. 54, a. 1, ad 2.

St. Thomas on 1 Corinthians 15:44

One of St. Thomas's favorite passages of scripture regarding the subtlety of the glorified body is 1 Corinthians 15:44: "it is sown an animal [*animale*] body, it is raised a spiritual body."[65] In explaining the meaning of this Pauline text, St. Thomas consistently argues that for the glorified body to be subtle or spiritual as opposed to animal means at least this much:

(3) The glorified body is perfectly subject to the soul in heaven such that it does not hinder the soul in its characteristic and essential activity of contemplating the essence of God.[66]

Sometimes, St. Thomas suggests that the glorified body being subtle or spiritual *also* entails:

(4) The glorified body is perfected in its union with the beatified soul such that it "will share in what is the soul's very own characteristics so far as possible, in the perspicuity of sense knowledge, in the ordering of bodily appetite, and in the all-around perfection of nature; for a thing is the more perfect in nature, the more its matter is dominated by its form. And for this reason the Apostle says: 'It is sown a natural [*animale*] body, it shall rise a spiritual body' (1 Cor 15:44)."[67]

We can add a third dimension to the glorified body's being subtle or spiritual at which St. Thomas sometimes hints, namely:

(5) The glorified body engages only in acts that support the soul's directly knowing and loving God, and not in acts that are directed at supporting the animal body and the generation of human persons.

As St. Thomas states in his commentary on 1 Corinthians:

It must be said that what the Apostle touches on here pertains to the mark of subtlety, when he says, *It is sown a natural [animale] body, it is raised a spiritual body* (1 Cor. 15:44).... In the resurrected state the animal activities by the body will

---

65. St. Thomas cites this passage when discussing the subtlety of the glorified body in the following places: *In Sent* IV, d. 44, q. 2, a. 2, q.c. 1, s.c. (*ST Suppl.*, q. 83, a. 1, s.c.); *SCG* IV.86.5; *CT* I, chap. 168; *In 1 Cor* 15, lect. 6, nn. 983–88; *ST* III, q. 54, a. 1, ad 2; *CSA*, a. 11.

66. See, e.g., *In Sent* IV, d. 44, q. 2, a. 2, q.c. 1, resp. (*ST Suppl.*, q. 83, a. 1, resp.); *SCG* IV.86.5; *CT* I, chap. 168; *ST* I-II, q. 4, a. 6, resp.; ad 2 and ad 3; *ST* III, q. 54, a. 1, ad 2; *CSA*, a. 11.

67. *SCG* IV.86.5 (trans. O'Neil, 326). See also *In Sent* IV, d. 49, q. 2, a. 2, resp. (*ST Suppl.*, q. 92, a. 2, resp.); *ST* I, q. 12, a. 3, ad 2; III, q. 54, a. 1, ad 2.

cease, because there will be no generation, or growth or nourishment, but the body without any impediment and weariness will unceasingly serve the soul in its spiritual activities: *blessed are those who dwell in your house, Lord* (Ps 84:4). Therefore, just as our body is now animal, then it will be truly spiritual.[68]

We can therefore say with precision that, in St. Thomas's view, the subtlety of the glorified body is the human body in heaven (a) being perfected by the soul having the beatific vision insofar as the glorified body is (b) subject to the soul as substantial form of the glorified body. In addition, for St. Thomas, the subtle body is (c) a spiritual body in St. Paul's sense. St. Thomas understands that to mean that (d) not only does the body not hinder the contemplation of God in heaven, but (e) the body actually participates in the beatified soul's contemplation of the essence of God in what it does, insofar as that is possible, rather than being engaged in characteristically animal activities such as eating, drinking, and sexual union. In addition, the glorified body (f) does not hinder the beatific vision by giving rise to inclinations that contradict the will of God or reason. The glorified body participates in the beatified soul so as (g) to enjoy a graced and perfected kind of sense knowledge of "the new heavens and the new earth." Finally, the glorified body (h) does not give rise to inclinations for eating, drinking, and sexual union. Rather, (i) just as the beatified soul is focused on contemplating God, the glorified body gives rise to inclinations to engage in bodily activities that are contemplative, such as sensing the beauty of the "new heavens and the new earth," and perhaps engaging in good conversation with fellow saints and playing music.

---

68. *In 1 Cor* 15, lect. 6, nn. 984–87 (trans. Larcher et al., 371–72). See also *ST* I, q. 98, a. 2, ad 1; *ST* I-II, q. 4, a. 7, resp. and ad 1–3. See also the discussion of St. Thomas on the lack of eating, drinking, and sexual union in heaven later in this chapter. That St. Thomas thinks subtle bodies are spiritual in the senses he gives to St. Paul's text in 1 Cor 15:44 can also be seen by examining what St. Thomas says about the resurrected bodies of the damned. In contrast to the glorified bodies of the saints in heaven, the bodies of the damned are not subtle, but *carnal*. As St. Thomas argues in *SCG* IV.89.3, because the wills of the damned are "turned away from God, and deprived of [their] own end, their bodies will not be spiritual, that is to say, entirely subject to the spirit; rather, by [their] affection[s] their soul[s] will be carnal" (trans. O'Neil, 330). Although St. Thomas does not use *subtilitas* here, the context demands that this is the glorified quality to which *carnalis* is opposed, as he goes on to talk about the bodies of the damned as passible, lacking in agility, and darksome. On carnality in the bodies of the damned as opposed to subtlety in the bodies of the blessed, see also *In Sent* IV, d. 44, q. 3, a. 2, q.c. 1, resp. (*ST Suppl.*, q. 86, a. 1, resp.); *CT* I, chap. 176; *CSA*, a. 11.

St. Thomas on Some Problematic Ways of Thinking about the Subtlety of the Glorified Body

St. Thomas recognizes that not everyone has understood the subtlety and spirituality of the glorified body in the way that he does. Furthermore, St. Thomas notes that some thinkers have attributed to the subtle or spiritual body in and of itself the ability to pass through other bodies, as Christ did when the disciples were locked away in the Upper Room. St. Thomas thinks that these various heretical or otherwise problematic ways of thinking about the glorified body can be traced to some of the extended senses of subtlety that I have mentioned above.

St. Thomas points out that some theologians have erred—indeed, taught heresy[69]—in taking the *subtlety* of the glorified body to mean that the blessed in heaven are transformed into pure spirits.[70] Recall that some have taken immaterial substances to be *subtle* in an extended sense of that term insofar as something is subtle because it has a paucity of matter. Defenders of this interpretation cite 1 Corinthians 15:44, St. Thomas notes. But this position is untenable, St. Thomas thinks, and is also a poor interpretation of St. Paul.

According to St. Thomas, the position itself is problematic for a number of reasons. First, if a body could be changed into a spirit, then there would have to be some matter common to both to function as the subject for such a change. But pure spirits do not have matter.[71] Second, even if it were possible for the body to be changed into a spirit, what would result would not be a human person, as human persons are naturally composed of soul and body.[72]

But St. Thomas thinks that the view that human bodies are turned into spirits in heaven is also a problematic interpretation of St. Paul. As St. Thomas notes, if we read St. Paul's expression "spiritual body" simply as *spirit*, then we should likewise read St. Paul's expression "animal [*animale*] body" simply as *soul* (*anima*).[73] Of course, St. Paul does not think that the animal body—that is, the human body in this life—is reducible to a soul. Likewise, we should not think that St. Paul means to reduce

---

69. See, e.g., *In Sent* IV, d. 44, q. 2, a. 2, q.c. 1, resp. (*ST Suppl.*, q. 83, a. 1, resp.).
70. See ibid. See also *SCG* IV.96.5; *In 1 Cor* 15, lect. 6, n. 984; *CSA*, a. 11.
71. *In Sent* IV, d. 44, q. 2, a. 2, q.c. 1, resp. (*ST Suppl.*, q. 83, a. 1, resp.).
72. Ibid.
73. Ibid. See also *SCG* IV.86.5 and *In 1 Cor* 15, lect. 6, n. 984.

human existence in the next life to that of a spirit. Rather, we should think that saints in the next life are embodied, at least eventually, albeit with bodies that have a different set of qualities than do human bodies in this life. Thus, St. Thomas does not take the Latin word *spirituale* that translates St. Paul's adjective to offer a *substantial* description of the glorified human body in the next life. Rather, *spirituale* is either a *practical* or a *qualitative* description of the body, that is, it says something about the *uses to which the saint in heaven puts the body in the next life* (and, as is very relevant here, the uses to which a saint in heaven does not put the body),[74] or it says something of the *qualities* of glorified bodies, which bodies are nonetheless numerically and specifically the same kinds of bodies that human persons possess in this life.[75]

According to St. Thomas, there is a second heretical understanding of the subtlety and spirituality of the glorified body. According to this heretical viewpoint, although the blessed do have bodies in heaven, these bodies will be made subtle by undergoing a process of rarefaction, so that glorified bodies will be subtle like the air or wind.[76] St. Thomas offers two arguments against this position. First, if the glorified body were subtle as are the wind or the air, then the glorified body would be impalpable. But Christ's glorified body, presented to the apostles after the resurrection, was both supremely subtle and palpable.[77] Second, the glorified body is a body of flesh and bones. In defense of this premise St. Thomas cites some of his favorite passages, such as Luke 24:39 ("Touch me and see; for a ghost does not have flesh and bones as you see that I have") and Job 19:26 ("in my flesh I shall see God"). But such a body is not subtle like the wind or the air.[78]

Other theologians, St. Thomas notes, grant that the bodies of the glorified saints are composed of flesh, blood, and bone, but go on to explain the subtlety of the glorified body by arguing that the human body in heaven exists in some new relation with some otherworldly matter.

---

74. So, for example, in the *Sentences* commentary, St. Thomas can ask about next-worldly bodily life: "will all rise to an animal life so as to exercise the generative and nutritive functions?" (*Videtur quod resurgent in vita animali, ut scilicet utantur actu nutritivae et generativae*). See, e.g., *In Sent* IV, d. 44, q. 1, a. 3, q.c. 4 (*ST Suppl.*, q. 81, a. 4).

75. Compare with St. Thomas's interpretation of St. Paul's claim, "flesh and blood will not inherit the kingdom" (1 Cor 15:50), discussed in chapter 10 above.

76. See e.g., *In Sent* IV, d. 44, q. 2, a. 2, q.c. 1 (*ST Suppl.*, q. 83, a. 1); *SCG* IV.86.5; *In 1 Cor* 15, lect. 6, n. 984; *In Jn* 20, lect. 6, n. 2559; *ST* III, q. 54, a. 3 (a. 2 in some editions), resp.

77. *In Sent* IV, d. 44, q. 2, a. 2, q.c. 1, resp. (*ST Suppl.*, q. 83, a. 1, resp.).

78. Ibid. See also *In Jn* 20, lect. 6, n. 2559.

St. Thomas rejects this view for the following reasons. For, if the glorified body is subtle due to a relation to some otherworldly matter, then (a) glorified bodies in heaven are composed of this otherworldly matter such that glorified bodies are larger in heaven than in this life due to the presence of the otherworldly matter in the glorified body or (b) glorified bodies are composed of some otherworldly matter and some of the quantitative parts that compose human bodies in this life are missing in glorified bodies in order to make room for the addition of this otherworldly matter, or (c) glorified bodies are subtle insofar as some otherworldly matter—external to the glorified body—predominates over glorified bodies in heaven in a manner it does not in this life. But (a) is false because, as we saw in chapter 10, glorified bodies *qua* resurrected bodies have the same stature as they do in this life. Option (b) too is false, as glorified bodies *qua* resurrected bodies have all of the same kinds of parts that this-worldly human bodies possess.[79] In addition, if the human body were subtle on account of the dominion of some otherworldly matter over the human body, then a quality of glory would have a natural cause, which is absurd, as a quality of glory is something supernatural, and thus not natural. Therefore, (c) too is false.[80] Therefore, it is not the case that the glorified body is subtle due to a relation to some otherworldly matter.

St. Thomas also notes that some theologians have thought that the subtlety of the glorified body entails that such a body is *impalpable*, that is, such a body does not resist other bodies, for example, as air does not resist other bodies. After all, there is the passage in the Gospel of John where Christ presents himself to the apostles, although the door is shut and locked (Jn 20:19–26). Although St. Thomas believes that this passage teaches that Christ did literally pass through a shut and locked door, he does not think that glorified bodies *qua* subtle bodies are able to pass through doors, that is, are impalpable.[81] In fact, citing Pope St. Gregory the Great, St. Thomas regards as heretical the position that it is in the nature of the glorified body to be impalpable.[82] In St. Thomas's view, it is in the nature of a glorified body, because it is a human *body*, that is, one

---

79. *In Sent* IV, d. 44, q. 2, a. 2, q.c. 1, resp. (*ST Suppl.*, q. 83, a. 1, resp.).
80. Ibid.
81. See, e.g., *In Sent* IV, d. 44, q. 2, a. 2, q.c. 2, ad 1 (*ST Suppl.*, q. 83, a. 2, ad 1), and *In 1 Cor* 15, lect. 6, n. 983.
82. *In Sent* IV, d. 44, q. 2, a. 2, q.c. 6, s.c. (*ST Suppl.*, q. 83, a. 6, s.c.).

having quantified dimensions,⁸³ to be palpable. Nonetheless, the glorified body is *subtle*, which entails that it is perfectly subject to the power of the beatified soul. Therefore, God has ordained that insofar as the saint wills, God by a *miracle* will render the saint's glorified body impalpable for a time, just as Christ miraculously rendered his body impalpable so that he could pass through the closed door leading to the Upper Room.⁸⁴

Spirituality, Subtlety, and Sex: St. Thomas on Sexual Union in Heaven

As we have seen, according to St. Thomas all human persons will rise with numerically (and so specifically) the same body they possessed in this life, along with perfection and specific integrity of the quantitative parts of the human body. Against Gnostic tendencies to the contrary, St. Thomas also defends the Christian tradition's view that sexual identity is retained in heaven, which means, among other things, that for any human person S, S's resurrection body has the sexual organs that correspond with S's sex in this life. Despite such similarities between this-worldly human bodies and glorified human bodies, St. Thomas thinks that bodily *life* in heaven will be quite different from this-worldly bodily life. For example, St. Thomas argues that human persons in the next life do not use the stomach, the intestines, and the sexual organs for the purposes for which they are designed to function in this life. This is because such animal functions belong to *the corruptible order* of growing and begetting rather than *the incorruptible order* of the next life. In chapter 10, I examined St. Thomas's arguments defending the conclusion that no human persons, neither the blessed nor the damned, will eat, drink, and engage in acts of sexual union in the next life. But St. Thomas also has arguments for why the blessed in particular do not eat, drink, and engage in the conjugal act in the next life. In examining some of St. Thomas's reasons for thinking that glorified bodies in particular do not live an animal life, his views on the nature of the subtlety and spirituality of the glorified body come into sharper focus.⁸⁵

---

83. See, e.g., *In Jn* 20, lect. 4, n. 2527.
84. See, e.g., *In Sent* IV, d. 44, q. 2, a. 2, q.c. 6 (*ST Suppl.*, q. 83, a. 6); *In 1 Cor* 15, lect. 6, n. 983; *QQ* I, q. 10, aa. 1–2; *In Jn* 20, lect. 4, n. 2527; *ST* III, q. 54, a. 1, ad 1 and ad 2.
85. There is not sufficient space to present, let alone defend, all of the arguments St. Thomas offers for the thesis that there is no eating, drinking, or sexual union in heaven. Nonetheless, this chapter explains and defends most of the different *kinds* of approaches St. Thomas takes up in arguing for that thesis.

A first kind of argument that St. Thomas sometimes employs in demonstrating that glorified bodies will not engage in acts of sexual union begins from the premise that the activities of animal life are by nature directed to, cause, or preserve the *first* perfection of human persons, that is, the *imperfect* happiness human persons can have in this life. The body and its activities are found in the saints in heaven only insofar as they are necessary for the acquisition of the ultimate end of human persons, that is, God. Although the *resurrection* of human persons is necessary for perfect human happiness, those natural activities that are directed to, or cause, or preserve the first perfection of human persons are not necessary for perfect human happiness. Therefore, there are no characteristic animal acts in heaven.[86]

Notice that St. Thomas's first kind of argument that embodied saints in heaven do not live an animal life assumes St. Thomas's early view on the relative importance of embodiment for perfect human happiness (the text comes from the early *Sentences* commentary). But we can recast the first kind of argument in terms that conform to St. Thomas's more mature understanding of the relative importance of embodiment in heaven for perfect happiness as follows (the changes are in brackets):

(6) The activities of animal life are by nature directed to, cause, or preserve the *first* perfection of human persons, that is, the *imperfect* happiness that human persons can have in this life.

(7) The body and its activities are found in the saints in heaven only insofar as they are necessary for [the well-being of] *perfect* human happiness [or the accidental reward], which glorified body and its activities subserve the human acquisition of the ultimate end of human persons, that is, God.

(8) Although the *resurrection* of human persons is necessary for [the well-being of] perfect human happiness [or the accidental reward], those natural activities which are directed to, cause, or preserve the first perfection of human persons are not necessary for [the well-being of] perfect human happiness [or the accidental reward in heaven].

(9) The natural activities that are directed to, cause, or preserve the first perfection of human persons include the animal activities of eating, drinking, and sexual union.

---

86. *In Sent* IV, d. 44, q. 1, a. 3, q.c. 4, resp. (*ST Suppl.*, q. 81, a. 4, resp.).

(10) Therefore, there will be no eating, drinking, and sexual union in heaven.

Someone might think that insofar as Christ elevates some kinds of eating, drinking, and sexual union to the status of sacraments, that is, the Eucharist and marriage, which sacraments have an eternal and supernatural significance, those kinds of activities do not simply serve the first perfection of human persons as premises (6) and (9) suppose. Rather, they serve, among other things, to prefigure the beatific vision.[87]

In response, I grant the point. But we can modify (6), (8), and (9) to take the point into account such that (10) still follows from the modified premises:

(6*) The activities of animal life are by nature directed to, cause, or preserve the *first* perfection of human persons, that is, the *imperfect* happiness that human persons can have in this life or, when functioning as the matter of sacraments such as the Eucharist and marriage, they serve as the matter for sacraments that confer grace upon us for the sake of getting us to heaven and serve as signs pointing us to the great goodness and beauty of (the well-being of) perfect human happiness in heaven.

(8*) Although the *resurrection* of human persons is necessary for the well-being of perfect human happiness or the accidental reward, those natural activities which are directed to, cause, or preserve the first perfection of human persons, or serve as the matter for sacraments that confer grace on us for the sake of getting us to heaven and serve as signs pointing us to the great goodness and beauty of (the well-being of) perfect human happiness in heaven, are not necessary for the well-being of perfect human happiness or the accidental reward in heaven.

(9*) The natural activities which are directed to, cause, or preserve the first perfection of human persons, or serve as the matter for sacraments that confer grace on us for the sake of getting us to heaven and serve as signs pointing us to the great goodness and beauty of (the well-being of) perfect human happiness in heaven, include the animal activities of eating, drinking, and sexual union.

This revised version of the first kind of argument above suggests an additional reason that a Thomist can take up for there being no sexual union in heaven. The argument begins with the following assumption: if some

---

87. Mark Spencer made this point.

kind of act A signifies some greater reality so that, once the greater reality signified by an A kind of act is achieved or realized in heaven, it would no longer be fitting or sensible or enjoyable to perform an A kind of act in heaven. Now, consider the nature of a sacrament, which according to St. Thomas simultaneously points us to a *past* event, that is, the passion, death, and resurrection of Christ, which event is the source of saving grace, a *future* event, that is, the glory of heaven, so that the reception of the sacraments is a foretaste of heavenly joy, and a *present* reality, that is, the graces conferred on the one who worthily receives the sacrament.[88] As wonderful as receiving a sacrament is, especially the Eucharist, it would not be fitting to have the Eucharist in heaven, as the future reality signified by receiving the Eucharist—direct union with the Trinity, as opposed to the union we have with God in the Eucharist by faith—is actually experienced by the saints in heaven in the beatific vision.[89]

Now consider the sacrament of marriage and the conjugal act, which, like the Eucharist, are signs of the consummation of the kingdom of God in heaven (and, even if some people, even some Christians, who go to heaven do not know this about the sexual act in this life, they certainly do know this in heaven). That is to say, the sacrament of marriage and the conjugal act are, among other things, signs that point human persons to the beatific vision, the resurrection of the body in heaven, and the communion of the saints. Even if the conjugal act is not *only* a figure for the consummation of the kingdom of God, such a spiritual meaning of the conjugal act, we might think, is at least one of its primary meanings. Therefore, when the greater goodness of intimate union with God in the beatific vision, the resurrection of the body of the saints in heaven, and the communion of the saints is realized, which realities sexual union signifies, it will not be fitting or sensible to engage in that act anymore. Therefore, as the saints will not want to do what is unfitting or insensible, there will be no desire to engage in the conjugal act in heaven. As no one in heaven wants to engage in sexual union, there is no sexual union in heaven.[90]

---

88. See, e.g., *ST* III, q. 60, a. 3.

89. Hence, St. Thomas writes in *Adoro te devote* (in the wonderful English translation of Gerard Manley Hopkins): "Jesu, whom I look at shrouded here below / I beseech thee send me what I thirst for so / Some day to gaze on thee face to face in light / And be blest for ever with thy glory's sight." *The Major Works* (Oxford: Oxford University Press, 2002), 105.

90. For detailed development of the notion that marriage and the conjugal act are signs of the beatific vision, the resurrection of the body in heaven, and the communion of the saints, and

Speaking of marriage and sexual union as a sign of the consummation of the kingdom of God in heaven suggests another possible argument that there is no sexual union in heaven. According to Jesus and St. Paul, some Christians give up the great good of marriage—and so sexual union—for the sake of the greater good of the kingdom of God.[91] Although there may be many reasons why the celibate life is conducive to advancing the kingdom of God, consider that one important reason is that the celibacy of priests and religious is a sign for all of us in this life that heaven is real. How does it do that? By testifying to the character of heavenly life, that is, one that does not involve the commonly sought after this-worldly goods of marriage and sexual union. With respect to his or her commitment not to engage in sexual union, the celibate priest or religious is living in this life like the angels and the saints in heaven, and is therefore a sign in this world of the reality, and nature, of heaven.[92] Therefore, to admit sexual union in heaven would be to make nonsense of one important and traditional way in which clerical and religious celibacy is a sign in this life of the reality of heaven.

St. Thomas deploys a second kind of argument that the saints in heaven do not engage in animal acts such as eating, drinking, and sexual union. That argument has as its primary premise that the character of embodied life in heaven is an overflowing of the human soul's beatific vision into the body. That is to say, embodied life in heaven is a reflection of the essential reward, and the essential reward is an act of contemplation and the delight that follows from it. Therefore, embodied life in heaven is not characteristically *animal*, but *contemplative*.

For example, in one place St. Thomas argues that the animal activities of eating, drinking, and sexual union do not belong to human persons *qua* human persons and, therefore, that the perfection of the human body in heaven does not consist of such animal activities. Rather, the happiness of the human body occurs by way of an overflow (*redundatia*) from the graced perfection of that by which a human person is a human person—reason.[93] As we saw above, the beatified soul configuring mat-

---

so marriage and the conjugal act are not parts of the heavenly life, see Pope St. John Paul II, General Audiences from December 2, 1981, through July 14, 1982, in *Man and Woman He Created Them: A Theology of the Body*, trans. Michael Waldstein (Boston: Pauline Books and Media, 2006), 387–457.

91. Mt 19:12 and 1 Cor 7:38.

92. For development of the idea that celibacy is a sign of the character of heavenly life, see Pope St. John Paul II, General Audience of March 24, 1982 (*Man and Woman He Created Them*, 419–22).

93. *In Sent* IV, d. 44, q. 1, a. 3, q.c. 4, ad 3 (*ST Suppl.*, q. 81, a. 4, ad 3). For the idea that the

ter causes the glorified body and its actions to participate in the soul's beatific vision. As the soul's beatific action is a contemplative act, so the actions of the body in heaven are contemplative, for example, sensing the goodness and beauty of the "new heavens and the new earth." As the (very good) human animal actions of this life are not contemplative actions, there is no eating, drinking, and sexual union in heaven.

St. Thomas has a third kind of argument that there is no eating, drinking, or sexual union in heaven, similar to the second kind.[94] The argument begins with the assumption that acts of eating, drinking, and sexual union belong to the *active* rather than the *contemplative* life. So, if the heavenly life is purely contemplative, then it does not include acts of eating, drinking, and sexual union, which kinds of acts are at least partially active or practical[95] by their very nature. Consider that, as we have seen, the glorified body and its actions are a participation in the activity of the beatified soul. But the activity of the beatified soul is purely contemplative.[96] Therefore, the activity of the glorified body is purely contemplative. Therefore, there is no eating, drinking, or sexual union in heaven.

In *SCG* IV, St. Thomas is content to cite texts from scripture to defend the purely contemplative nature of the heavenly life. Let us focus on St. Thomas's interpretation of Luke 10:42. St. Thomas thinks that it is to Mary's contemplation that Christ is referring when Christ says that she "hath chosen the best part which shall not be taken away from her" (Lk 10:42),[97] implying that Mary's contemplative life continues to exist in heaven, whereas the active life, symbolized by Martha's practical activity,

---

beatification of the body is a kind of overflowing (*per quamdam redundantiam*) from the beatification of the soul (when the beatified soul configures matter), see also *In Sent* IV, d. 44, q. 2, a. 3, q.c. 1, resp. and ad 2; a. 4, q.c. 1, resp. and ad 4; d. 45, q. 1, a. 3, ad 10; d. 49, q. 2, a. 2, ad 6; q. 4, a. 5, q.c. 2, resp.; q.c. 3, ad 3; q. 5, a. 4, q.c. 3, resp.; *SCG* IV.86; *In 1 Cor* 15, lect. 6, n. 988; *CT* I, chaps. 231 and 237; *In Mt* 6, lect. 5, n. 616; *ST* I-II, q. 3, a. 3, resp. and ad 3; q. 4, a. 5, ad 4; a. 6, resp.; II-II, q. 25, a. 5, ad 2; a. 12, resp. and ad 2; q. 26, a. 5, resp.; q. 175, a. 4, ad 1; III, q. 28, a. 2, ad 3; q. 45, a. 2, resp. and ad 1; q. 46, a. 8, resp.; q. 54, a. 2, ad 2; q. 57, a. 3, resp. In *ST* I-II, q. 4, a. 6, resp., St. Thomas shows that, in using the metaphor of *overflowing*, he is taking a cue from St. Augustine. Also, we might note that the overflow of the happiness of the soul into the body is an application of the general theological principle for St. Thomas that, according to the divine order, "lower beings receive an overflow of the excellence of the higher" (*ST* II-II, q. 83, a. 11, resp. [trans. English Dominicans, 1540]).

94. *SCG* IV.83.24. See also *ST* I-II, q. 3, a. 2, ad 4.

95. That is, *practical* in the Aristotelian sense, i.e., an action that (is supposed to) aim(s) not directly at happiness but directly at the production of an object or a further action.

96. *ST* I-II, q. 3, a. 5. See chapter 5 above for discussion of St. Thomas's three arguments for this view.

97. *SCG* IV.83.24 (trans. O'Neil, 319–20).

will be taken away at death. The heavenly life is a purely contemplative one. St. Augustine and Pope St. Gregory the Great's interpretations of Luke 10:42 appear to be in the background for St. Thomas's own interpretation of the passage. For example, in the *Catena Aurea* St. Thomas cites the following text of St. Augustine's on Luke 10:42:

> Now mystically, by Martha's receiving our Lord into her house is represented the Church which now receives the Lord into her heart. Mary her sister, who sat at Jesus' feet and heard His word, signifies the same Church, but in a future life, where ceasing from labor, and the ministering to her wants, she shall delight in Wisdom alone. But by her complaining that her sister did not help her, occasion is given for that sentence of our Lord, in which he shows that Church to be anxious and troubled about much service, when there is but one thing needful, which is yet attained through the merits of her service; but He says that Mary hath chosen the good part, for through the one the other is reached, which shall not be taken away.[98]

Perhaps even more telling is a passage St. Thomas cites from Pope St. Gregory's *Moralium*, where Gregory comments on Luke 10:42 as follows:

> Or by Mary who sat and heard our Lord's words, is signified the contemplative life; by Martha engaged in more outward services, the active life. Now Martha's care is not blamed, but Mary is praised, for great are the rewards of an active life, but those of a contemplative are far better. Hence Mary's part it is said will never be taken away from her, for the works of an active life pass away with the body, but the joys of the contemplative life the rather begin to increase from the end.[99]

So the active concerns of this world will have no place in the life of the saints in heaven; bodily life in heaven reflects and supports the purely contemplative life of the essential reward. As acts of eating, drinking, and sexual union belong by definition, at least partially, to the active life, the saints in heaven do not engage in such acts.

In a fourth kind of argument, one that focuses on the lack of sexual union in heaven, St. Thomas assumes—having proved it elsewhere[100]— that sexual union does not exist in heaven for the sake of generation. In this fourth kind of argument, he aims to demonstrate that the experience of pleasure in the conjugal act cannot be the reason that acts of

---

98. *CA*, Lk 10, lect. 10, trans. St. John Henry Newman (Boonville, N.Y.: Preserving Christian Publications, 2009), 381.

99. *CA*, Lk 10, lect. 10 (trans. Newman, 381–82).

100. See, e.g., *In Sent* IV, d. 44, q. 1, a. 3, q.c. 4, s.c. (*ST Suppl.*, q. 81, a. 4, s.c.); *SCG* IV.83.2, 5–8; *CT* I, chap. 156; *CA*, Mk 12:25, lect. 3; *In Mt* 22, lect. 3, n. 1799; *CSA*, a. 11.

sexual union constitute a component part of human happiness in heaven. Lacking reasons and desire to engage in the conjugal act, the saints in heaven will not engage in acts of sexual union in heaven. St. Thomas develops a number of different arguments across his corpus that can be usefully classified as a species of this fourth kind of argument, some of which arguments can be modified also to show that there is no eating in heaven either.

In a first argument, St. Thomas notes that Aristotle teaches that only spiritual pleasures are pleasures simply speaking, or pleasures to be sought for their own sake. Therefore, bodily pleasures either are to be enjoyed for medicinal purposes, that is, as a remedy for weariness in the soul, or bodily pleasures are enjoyed inordinately. But there is no inordinate desire in heaven; neither is there any weariness of soul there. Therefore, the saints in heaven do not engage in animal acts such as eating, drinking, and sexual union for the sake of pleasure.[101]

In a second argument of the fourth kind, St. Thomas begins with the assumption that the life of the saints in heaven is more harmonious and orderly than are the lives of human persons in this life. But bodily pleasure is not a proper end in itself, but rather pleasure is necessarily connected with acts of eating and drinking in animals so that animals will not desist from such activities insofar as such acts are necessary for the preservation of nature and animal species. Therefore, those who eat and engage in sexual activity for the sake of pleasure in this life act viciously. *A fortiori*, human persons in heaven will not eat and engage in sexual acts for the sake of pleasure.[102]

As we saw in chapter 10, such an argument can be modified in order to take into account a view that both eating and sexual union have as a secondary, or even another primary, purpose the facilitating, or the being constitutive of, friendship between human persons. That being said, St. Thomas's point in the second argument of the fourth kind still stands: as it is morally vicious to make bodily pleasure an end in itself, the saints' taking pleasure in eating or sexual union cannot be the reason that those activities exist in heaven, if they do.

A different and third argument of the fourth kind derives from St. Thomas's exegesis of Matthew 22:30 ("For in the resurrection they shall

---

101. *In Sent* IV, d. 44, q. 1, a. 3, q.c. 4, ad 4 (*ST Suppl.*, q. 81, a. 4, ad 4).
102. *SCG* IV.83.10. See also *CT* I, chap. 156.

neither marry nor be married, but shall be as the angels of God in heaven").[103] St. Thomas takes the phrase "[they] shall be as the angels of God in heaven" to mean that human persons in heaven will, like the angels, have no passions, or more specifically, no desires for engaging in the conjugal act.[104]

Of course, this makes sense. If the sensible and morally permissible context for sexual union is marriage and marriage is no more in heaven, which is a traditional interpretation of Matthew 22:30, then it is not sensible or morally permissible to engage in sexual union in heaven. But there are no (desires for) insensible or morally impermissible acts in heaven. Therefore, there is no (desire for) sexual union in heaven.

No Eating, Drinking, or Sexual Union in Heaven: Some Objections

I have treated in chapter 10 above (replies to) some objections to St. Thomas's view that, after the resurrection, no human persons use their resurrected body *qua* resurrected body to eat, drink, and engage in sexual union. Here I treat objections that St. Thomas fields that purport to show that the blessed in heaven in particular engage in characteristically animal acts, along with St. Thomas's replies to such objections.

In a first objection, St. Thomas notes that the whole human person is beatified in heaven, and the whole human person includes both the soul and the body. But beatitude is a kind of happiness and happiness requires perfect operation. Therefore, all bodily powers are in act in heaven. As the generative and nutritive organs are part of the body in heaven, human happiness in heaven involves generative and nutritive activity.[105]

In response to this first objection, St. Thomas notes with Aristotle that perfect human happiness consists only in those bodily activities that

---

103. *In Mt* 22, lect. 3, n. 1800, trans. Paul M. Kimball (Camillus, N.Y.: Dolorosa Press, 2012), 720.
104. Ibid. See also *In Sent* IV, d. 44, q. 1, a. 2, q.c. 1, obj. 1 and ad 1 (*ST Suppl.*, q. 80, a. 1, obj. 1 and ad 1); d. 48, q. 2, a. 4, resp. (*ST Suppl.*, q. 91, a. 4, resp.); *SCG* IV.83.13; *In Eph* 4, lect. 4, n. 216; *QDP*, q. 6, a. 7, resp.; *CA*, Mt 22, lect. 3 (see esp. St. Thomas's first citation of St. Hilary, continuing with the citations from St. John Chrysostom, Pseudo-Chrysostom, St. Jerome, Dionysius, and St. Augustine's *The City of God* XX.17); *ST* I, q. 98, a. 2, obj. 1 and ad 1; q. 108, a. 8, resp.; *CA*, Lk 20, lect. 4; *ST* I-II, q. 3, a. 2, ad 4; II-II, q. 24, a. 3, obj. 3; III, q. 76, a. 7, obj. 3; *CSA*, a. 11. It is also interesting to note in this context that the lack of desire for engaging in the conjugal act in the saints in heaven directly contrasts with the embodied life of the damned according to St. Thomas. Whereas the resurrected life of the blessed is characterized by the gift of subtlety, the resurrected life of the damned is carnal, i.e., the life of the damned is still subject to animal desire, such as the desire to engage in the conjugal act, although the damned are not able to engage in such acts.
105. See, e.g., *In Sent* IV, d. 44, q. 1, a. 3, q.c. 4, obj. 3 (*ST Suppl.*, q. 81, a. 4, obj. 3).

belong to human persons insofar as they are embodied *rational* beings (St. Thomas argues here that Aristotle was of the view that not even human happiness in this life consists in characteristically animal actions). But the animal acts of eating, drinking, and sexual union are not characteristically rational activities, as brute animals engage in them too. Combining Aristotle's insight with an Augustinian way of speaking, St. Thomas puts the point as follows: "the human body will be glorified by an overflow from the reason whereby man is man, inasmuch as the body will be subject to reason."[106] To speak in accord with St. Thomas's later views, although some bodily actions constitute a part of the accidental reward—to make for the *bene esse* of perfect human happiness—the bodily actions that constitute part of the accidental reward must be consistent with the kind of purely contemplative existence the blessed in heaven enjoy. But acts of eating, drinking, and sexual union are not consistent with the kind of purely contemplative existence that human persons enjoy in heaven. Therefore, not even the accidental reward consists of acts of eating, drinking, and sexual union.

Consider a second objection that St. Thomas fields. There is perfect happiness in the blessed after the resurrection (or, as St. Thomas says in his most mature treatment in *ST*, after the resurrection the blessed enjoy the well-being of perfect happiness).[107] Boethius says that happiness is "a state rendered perfect by the accumulation of all goods,"[108] and to be perfect is to lack nothing that is due. One kind of good is pleasure and there is great pleasure in the generative and nutritive acts. Therefore (the well-being of) perfect happiness includes the pleasures of animal life, and perhaps even more so in those who will have bodies that are less spiritual.[109]

In responding to this second objection St. Thomas notes what Aristotle points out in *NE* VII and X: not all pleasures are pleasures, absolutely speaking. In fact, bodily pleasures are not pleasures, absolutely speaking, but rather pleasant to virtuous people in order to help remove the weariness of work, and pleasant to vicious people as the best of all goods. So it does not follow that bodily pleasures exist in heaven, for example,

---

106. *ST Suppl.*, q. 81, a. 4, ad 3 (trans. English Dominicans, 2892; *In Sent* IV, d. 44, q. 1, a. 3, q.c. 4, ad 3).
107. See, e.g., *ST* I-II, q. 4, a. 5, resp.
108. *De Consol.* III.
109. See, e.g., *In Sent* IV, d. 44, q. 1, a. 3, q.c. 4, obj. 4 (*ST Suppl.*, q. 81, a. 4, obj. 4).

pleasures in eating, drinking, sleeping, and sex, as there will be no weariness or evil in heaven. Rather, the pleasures that Aristotle speaks about as absolute pleasures, for example, pleasure in virtuous activities such as contemplation, are the kind of pleasures that attend beatitude.[110]

We should note that St. Thomas is not saying here that *bodily* pleasure is inconsistent with human beatitude. As we have seen him say, human persons in heaven engage in certain bodily actions, for example, sensing the "new heavens and the new earth," and presumably experience great pleasure in thereby sensing the beauty, glory, and wisdom of God in creation. But if we have reason to think that a certain kind K of bodily action has no place in the purely contemplative life of heaven, the beatitude of human persons is not lacking if they lack the pleasures of engaging in actions that belong to K. But we have good reasons to think that there is no eating, drinking, or sexual union in heaven. Therefore, the beatitude of human persons is in no way lacking for not enjoying the pleasures of such activities.

St. Thomas fields a third objection in *SCG*. The objection compares the life of Adam before the Fall with the life of those in heaven. Just as those in heaven are immortal, so Adam led an immortal life and nonetheless was commanded to eat and engage in generative acts.[111] Therefore, there is no inconsistency between an immortal life and an animal life. Therefore, there is no inconsistency in thinking that the saints in heaven enjoy an animal life.

The problem with the third objection, St. Thomas thinks, is that the objection assumes that Adam's immortal life in the state of innocence parallels the immortal life of the saints in heaven. But the life of the saints in heaven differs in some significant ways from Adam's life before the Fall, where such significant differences vitiate the claim in the third objection that Adam's life in the state of innocence parallels heavenly life where bodily life is concerned. First of all, Adam in paradise was commanded to engage in the conjugal act in order to bring about new members of the human species, and in order to do that, had also to take in nourishment (of course, we can add additional reasons God commanded sexual union in the state of innocence, e.g., the conjugal act in

---

110. See, e.g., *In Sent* IV, d. 44, q. 1, a. 3, q.c. 4, ad 4 (*ST Suppl.*, q. 81, a. 4, ad 4). See also *In NE* VII, lects. 12 and 14; X, lect. 7. For a place where St. Thomas also mentions the problematic—because this-worldly—view of certain Jews, Saracens, and the Chiliasts, i.e., Millenarians, see *SCG* IV.83.14.
111. *SCG* IV.83.15.

the garden is a beautiful and fitting sign of the beatific vision in heaven). But the saints in heaven are not under a requirement analogous to that of Adam and Eve to eat, drink, and engage in sexual activity (and after having the vision, there is no longer a desire, let alone a need, to engage in what is a figure of the vision). Indeed, such animal acts have no place in a society such as heaven where there is no need to add to the number of that society.[112] Second, where Adam's immortality was conditional on his freely choosing not to sin and necessarily involved the taking in of nourishment, the immortality and incorruptibility enjoyed by the saints in heaven is such that the saints in heaven cannot die; nor can their bodies in any way suffer dissolution.[113]

Finally, St. Thomas raises a fourth objection in *SCG*, one which notes that the scriptures sometimes speak in a manner that seems to confirm the views of those Jews, Saracens, and Chiliasts who say that there is eating and drinking (and we might think, by extension, sexual union) in the next life.[114] Here is St. Thomas:

> For Isaias (25:6, 8) says: "The Lord of hosts shall make unto all people in this mountain a feast of fat things full of marrow, of wine purified from the lees." And we are to understand this of the state of those who rise, as is clear from the addition: "He shall cast death down for ever: And the Lord God shall wipe away tears from every face." Isaias (65:13, 17) also says: "Behold my servants shall eat, and you shall be hungry; behold, my servants shall drink, and you shall be thirsty." And that this refers to the future life is clear from the addition: "Behold, I create new heavens and a new earth," and so forth. Our Lord also says: "I will not drink from henceforth of this fruit of the vine until that day when I shall drink it with you new in the kingdom of My Father" (Mt. 26:29); and He says in Luke (22:29–30): "I dispose to you as My Father hath disposed to Me, a kingdom; that you may eat and drink at My table in My kingdom." And we read in the Apocalypse (22:4) that "on both sides of the river" which will be in the City of the Blessed, there will be "the tree of life bearing twelve fruits." It also says: "I saw … the souls of them that were beheaded for the testimony of Jesus … and they lived and reigned with Christ a thousand years" (Apoc. 20:4–5).[115] From all of which the opinion of the heretics mentioned seems to be confirmed.[116]

---

112. *SCG* IV.83.18.
113. Ibid.
114. *SCG* IV.83.17. See also *ST* I-II, q. 4, a. 7, obj. 1.
115. Here St. Thomas has in mind the Chiliasts or Millenarians, who believed in a future literal one-thousand-year reign of Christ, and if St. Augustine is right, a kingdom that involves lots of eating and drinking (see *SCG* IV.83.14 and St. Augustine's *The City of God* XX.7).
116. *SCG* IV.83.17 (trans. O'Neil, 317).

According to the fourth objection then, there are a number of passages of scripture that teach, at least on a surface reading, that human persons will eat and drink in the kingdom of heaven. In addition, with scripture teaching that eating and drinking constitute parts of heavenly life, we might also think that heavenly life so closely resembles this-worldly life that it also includes sexual activity as a constitutive part.

St. Thomas thinks that all of these passages can and should be read spiritually (*spiritualiter*), by which he means in this context, not according to a spiritual sense, for example, allegorically, morally, or anagogically,[117] but rather as conveying spiritual truths through sensible things, that is, by way of metaphorical or figurative language. Indeed, as St. Thomas goes on to say in response to the objection, "For divine Scripture proposes intelligible things to us in the likeness of sensible things, 'so that the soul from what it knows may learn to love the things it knows not,'"[118] which is the way St. Thomas speaks about the use of metaphorical language in scripture.[119] In fact, St. Thomas is explicit that talk of eating and drinking in the kingdom is metaphorical in *ST* I-II.[120] So St. Thomas proposes that the talk of eating and drinking in the kingdom of heaven is figurative language for what the blessed experience in heaven, namely, the delight which is in the contemplation of wisdom (*delectatio quae est in contemplatione sapientiae*) and the assumption of intelligible truth in our intellect (*assumptio veritatis intelligibilis in intellectum nostrum*).[121]

Indeed, as St. Thomas points out, scripture makes this comparison between eating and drinking, on the one hand, and the contemplation of wisdom, on the other, explicit in various places in the wisdom literature of the Old Testament. St. Thomas cites the following examples: Proverbs 9:2, 4–5 ("she has mixed her wine, she has also set her table.... To those without sense she says, 'Come, eat of my bread and drink of the wine I have mixed'"); Sirach 15:3 ("She will feed him with the bread of learning, and give him the water of wisdom to drink"), and Proverbs 3:18 ("She is a tree of life to those who lay hold of her; those who hold her fast are called happy").[122]

---

117. On St. Thomas on the three spiritual senses of scripture, see, e.g., *ST* I, q. 1, a. 10, resp.
118. *SCG* IV.83.20 (trans. O'Neil, 318). St. Thomas quotes here from Pope St. Gregory the Great, *Homilies on the Evangelists* I, 11, i.
119. See, e.g., *ST* I, q. 1, a. 9, resp.
120. *ST* I-II, q. 4, a. 7, ad 1.
121. *SCG* IV.83.20. See also *SCG* III.51.6.
122. *SCG* IV.83.20.

But would Christ's original hearers have understood him to be speaking metaphorically?[123] And why does Christ speak metaphorically about such things? As for the first question, perhaps many of Christ's hearers would have been familiar with the comparison of the contemplation of wisdom and feasting in the wisdom literature of the Old Testament mentioned above. Also, Christ would have made clear the metaphorical nature of these sayings when he spoke to the apostles, for example, after his resurrection (see, e.g., Acts 1:3b). As for the second question, as we have seen, St. Thomas would say, perhaps citing Pope St. Gregory the Great, that Christ does so as a good teacher, beginning from what we already know (or what we can imagine) in order to facilitate us learning new things (some of which cannot be imagined).

As for Matthew 26:29, St. Thomas notes that it can be read as referring to Christ's eating with the apostles after his resurrection and before his ascension. Such eating would be "new" because Christ eats with his new, spiritual body, and so not of necessity as he does at the time he utters that statement, although he eats and drinks after his resurrection simply for the sake of proving the resurrection of his body. Such eating will also be "in the kingdom of My Father" because in the resurrection of Christ the kingdom of immortality demonstrably begins.[124]

As for the millennium in Revelation 20, St. Thomas, following St. Augustine,[125] reads "thousand" in these passages as a figure for "perfection," as "one thousand is the cube whose root is ten," so that "the millennium of the Church" signified the time of the perfection of the church, that is, that time from the resurrection of Christ to the end of time. Recall that St. Thomas aims to refute the millennialist interpretation of the kingdom of heaven, as the millennialists speak of the kingdom of heaven as a time of literal eating and drinking. Presumably, St. Thomas thinks that insofar as the millennialist interpretation of "the millennium" has plausibility, so does their understanding of the carnal nature of the kingdom of heaven.

As we have seen, for St. Thomas the *subtlety* of the glorified body is the human body being perfected by the soul having the beatific vision in heaven insofar as the body is perfectly subject to the beatified human soul

---

123. Thanks to Matthew Braddock for raising this good question.
124. *SCG* IV.83.21.
125. *The City of God* XX.6–8.

as substantial form of the glorified body. In addition, for St. Thomas the subtle body is a spiritual body in St. Paul's sense of the term. St. Thomas understands the glorified body being spiritual to mean not only that the body does not hinder the beatific vision of God in heaven, but that the body actually participates in such contemplation of God insofar as that is possible. As the human blessed "are as the angels in heaven," even the bodily life of the saints in heaven is a spiritual rather than an animal one, that is, it is a bodily life that is God-centered, beatific, well-ordered, and wholly contemplative, for example, it involves sensation and movement at the service of contemplating the glory of God. The subtlety of the glorified body is such that the saints in heaven do not—in fact, they have no desire to—engage in the animal activities of eating, drinking, and sexual union.

ON THE AGILITY OF THE GLORIFIED BODY

St. Thomas ascribes the quality of *agility* to the glorified body in a number of places.[126] But what does St. Thomas mean by agility (*agilitas*)? According to his earliest and most detailed treatment, St. Thomas thinks that the glorified body is altogether subject to the will, even as the human body was in the case of Adam and Eve before the Fall; in fact, even more so. The glorified body is more subject to the will of a human person than in the case of Adam's body in paradise because in the former case, but not the latter case, the subjection of the body to the will has among its causes a disposition intrinsic to the agent. This is because the glorified body will share in the perfection of the beatified soul. Now, as I noted above, the human soul is united to the body as form of the body, that is, as the intrinsic formal principle of actual and specific being, and as mover, that is, as principle of movement. As we have seen, the gift of subtlety is the glorified body's subjection and perfection in relation to the beatified soul insofar as the body stands in relation to the soul as matter to substantial form. The gift of agility is the glorified body's subjection and perfection in relation to the beatified soul insofar as the body stands in relation to the soul as thing moved to its mover so that, as a consequence, the body is prompt (*expeditum*) and apt (*habile*) in obeying

---

126. See, e.g., *In Sent* IV, d. 44, q. 2, a. 2, q.c. 1 (*ST Suppl.*, q. 83, a. 1); d. 49, q. 4, a. 5, q.c. 3, resp.; *SCG* IV.86.3; *In 1 Cor* 15, lect. 6, n. 982; *CT* I, chap. 168; *CSA*, a. 11.

the will of the one whose body is.[127] St. Thomas also notes that the gift of agility covers not only local movements, but also acts of sensation and any acts of the body that are required for perfection of the soul's operations.[128]

Although the glorified body has the power to move quickly, St. Thomas considers the possibility that the saints in heaven in fact will never make use of such a power.[129] He rejects this view for a number of reasons. First, Christ ascended into heaven with his glorified body, and as the saints follow the pattern of their Savior in their redemption, they too will ascend into heaven.[130] Therefore, glorified bodies not only have the ability to move, but human persons in heaven actually make use of this power.[131]

Second, St. Thomas argues that it is likely that after rising to heaven, the glorified bodies still actually move, as such motion makes clear the divine wisdom insofar as the saints are activating a power they possess. Indeed, as we will see in chapter 13, St. Thomas thinks that the empyrean heaven is the proper and fitting place for embodied saints in heaven. Nonetheless, St. Thomas also believes it does not diminish the glory of the elect—in fact, in a way it conduces to their glory—if they are sometimes present in other places, for example, the "new heavens and the new earth."[132] But embodied saints sometimes being in the empyrean heaven and sometimes being elsewhere requires that the saints actually move.

In addition, the active use of the gift of agility better enables the saints to cognize God in creatures in "the new heavens and the new earth." This is because, as perfect as the sense faculties are in heaven, their perfect exercise nonetheless requires that the saints move to various places in order to cognize things they cannot cognize (by way of the senses) without so moving.[133]

Notice that St. Thomas sees no incompatibility between motion in

---

127. *In Sent* IV, d. 44, q. 2, a. 3, q.c. 1, resp. (*ST Suppl.*, q. 84, a. 1, resp.). See also *CT* I, chap. 168, and *In 1 Cor* 15, lect. 6, n. 982.

128. *In Sent* IV, d. 44, q. 2, a. 3, q.c. 1, ad 3 (*ST Suppl.*, q. 84, a. 1, ad 3).

129. *In Sent* IV, d. 44, q. 2, a. 3, q.c. 2 (*ST Suppl.*, q. 84, a. 2, resp.).

130. According to St. Thomas, Christ's actions immediately after his resurrection and before his ascension also exemplify what human bodies (can) do in heaven (see, e.g., *CT* I, chap. 237).

131. *In Sent* IV, d. 44, q. 2, a. 3, q.c. 2 (*ST Suppl.*, q. 84, a. 2, resp.).

132. See, e.g., *ST Suppl.*, q. 70, a. 3, ad 8.

133. *In Sent* IV, d. 44, q. 2, a. 3, q.c. 2 (*ST Suppl.*, q. 84, a. 2, resp.) See also *CT* I, chap. 171.

heaven on the part of embodied saints and their enjoyment of God in the beatific vision. For one thing, as St. Thomas notes, Pope St. Gregory the Great teaches that each of the blessed angels is simultaneously on some mission with respect to the world while also having the beatific vision.[134] As we have seen, part of what it means for the body to be glorified is that it in no way hinders the essential reward of human persons. Here, St. Thomas notes that the actual movements of the glorified body in "the new heavens and the new earth" no more hinder the embodied saint's enjoyment of God in the beatific vision than an angel's mission in this life hinders that angel's beatific vision. Indeed, given St. Thomas's principles, the glorified body's agility is one manifestation of the human body's participating in the soul's beatific vision in heaven, the soul's beatification overflowing into the body so that it moves with agility.

But does not the actual movement of the glorified body imply imperfection and need on the part of that which is moved?[135] As the saints are perfected in heaven and have all of their desires sated, why would they move their bodies in heaven?[136] As far as the imperfection of movement is concerned, St. Thomas argues that a thing moving, in and of itself, does not change what is intrinsic to that thing. Therefore, a saint S moving S's body in heaven does not imply an intrinsic imperfection in S, although it does imply that S lacks the perfection of not being present to every place at once. But the ability to be present to every place at once cannot belong to an embodied saint, no more than the perfection of being uncreated can belong to something embodied, as the perfections of being omnipresent and uncreated belong to absolutely perfect God alone.[137]

As far as the objection from desire is concerned, St. Thomas distinguishes two kinds of need, need *simpliciter* and need *secundum quid*. If person S needs P *simpliciter*, then S cannot exist or be perfect without P. Embodied saints do not need to move *simpliciter*, as a saint can exist and be perfectly happy without moving her body. S needs P *secundum quid* if and only if S needs P in order to realize some end (or to do so more perfectly). In St. Thomas's view, the saints moving their bodies is a need *secundum*

---

134. *In Sent* IV, d. 44, q. 2, a. 3, q.c. 2 (*ST Suppl.*, q. 84, a. 2, resp.). See also *CA*, Mt 18, lect. 3, and *In Mt* 18, lect. 1, n. 1505.
135. *In Sent* IV, d. 44, q. 2, a. 3, q.c. 2, obj. 1 (*ST Suppl.*, q. 84, a. 2, obj. 1).
136. *In Sent* IV, d. 44, q. 2, a. 3, q.c. 2, obj. 2 (*ST Suppl.*, q. 84, a. 2, obj. 2).
137. *In Sent* IV, d. 44, q. 2, a. 3, q.c. 2, ad 1 (*ST Suppl.*, q. 84, a. 2, ad 1).

quid, because without moving their bodies they will not be able to show forth the gift of agility.[138]

We can also put St. Thomas's point here in a couple of other ways, given things that he says in other places. For example, we might think that movement is incompatible with the essential reward, but not with the accidental reward. But movement of the glorified body in heaven does not belong to the essential reward (or the attainment of perfect happiness), but rather belongs to the accidental reward (or that which is added to perfect happiness in order to make for the attainment of the well-being of perfect happiness).

For example, in a place within *ST* I-II, St. Thomas distinguishes what belongs to the essence of perfect happiness and what is nonessential to perfect happiness in heaven but is required antecedently for perfect happiness in heaven or follows as a logical consequence of what is essential to heaven.[139] St. Thomas goes on to argue that *perfection* of the body—which includes the glorified body's agility—is not essential to perfect happiness in heaven for human persons. The human person having the beatific vision is perfectly happy, even without her body. But as long as the human person is embodied in heaven, perfection of the body, including agility, is a logical consequence of perfect happiness in heaven.[140] Recall that whenever the soul is embodied in heaven, the soul stands to the matter it informs as mover to thing moved, and what is moved in no way resists, but is in fact perfected by that which moves it, namely, the soul having the beatific vision. Therefore, perfection of the body insofar as it engages in agile activity is simply a logical consequence of the beatified soul being embodied.

In addition, recall the distinction that philosopher Brandon Dahm finds in St. Thomas between *desire-from-fulfillment* and *desire-from-lack*.[141] We can use this distinction to make sense of the distinction between need *simpliciter* and need *secundum quid* in St. Thomas's discussion of

---

138. *In Sent* IV, d. 44, q. 2, a. 3, q.c. 2, ad 2 (*ST Suppl.*, q. 84, a. 2, ad 2). See also *SCG* IV.86.3.

139. See, e.g., *ST* I-II, q. 3, a. 3, resp. See also my discussion of this distinction in chapter 4 above.

140. *ST* I-II, q. 4, a. 6, resp. As we have seen, St. Thomas also talks as follows: there is a difference between the attainment of perfect human happiness and the attainment of the well-being of perfect human happiness; embodiment and its qualities belong to the latter and not the former. Thus agility does not belong to the perfect happiness of the saints in heaven, but it does belong to the saints' well-being of perfect happiness (see, e.g., *ST* I-II, q. 4, a. 5, resp.).

141. See the discussion of Brandon Dahm's work at the end of chapter 9.

the movement of glorified bodies. Recall that a person S's possession of desires-from-lack entails that S is not perfectly happy. On the other hand, desires-from-fulfillment are desires that arise not from a lack in the desirer, but rather from a perfection in the agent. Similarly, the need *secundum quid* for embodied saints to move with agility is not from a desire-from-lack, but rather from a desire-from-fulfillment. The saints desire to move only because such movement is a fitting way for glorified bodies to participate in the beatific vision.

As far as what it means for the glorified body to be agile is concerned, St. Thomas denies that the possession of such a quality by the saints in heaven entails that the saints in heaven can move their bodies from here to there *instantaneously*. The movement of the glorified body from here to there in heaven may *appear* instantaneous—because such bodies move so quickly—but for a local movement to be instantaneous, St. Thomas reasons, is a contradiction in terms.[142] What is interesting for our purposes here is that, because the glorified bodies move, and such bodily movement is not instantaneous, such movement takes time (even if it is not time *as we measure it in this life* by the movements of the heavenly bodies; or as we would say, the movement of the earth in relation to heavenly bodies). Because embodiment in heaven involves movement of glorified bodies that takes time and the accidental reward for human persons is an aspect of heavenly human existence for St. Thomas, it follows that time of some sort is a (sometime) aspect of heavenly human existence according to St. Thomas.

Why should one think that glorified bodies will be agile? We have already seen some reasons that St. Thomas would give. Christ—and so the saints eventually—move their bodies. But if the saints move their bodies, then they have the quality of agility, as perfect movement is agile movement and glorified bodily movement is perfect bodily movement. Therefore, the embodied saints have agility.

St. Thomas has a number of other arguments. First, in contrasting the human body in this life and the glorified body, St. Thomas notes that St. Paul says: "It is sown in weakness, it is raised in power" (1 Cor 15:43b). But according to an authoritative gloss on this text, St. Paul means by *power* that the glorified body will be living and mobile. But mobility must

---

142. *In Sent* IV, d. 44, q. 2, a. 3, q.c. 3 (*ST Suppl.*, q. 84, a. 3).

mean "agility."[143] In addition, there are other passages in scripture that suggest that glorified bodies are mobile (and if glorified bodies are mobile, they are presumably agile rather than sluggish), for example, Isaiah 40:31 ("They shall run and not be weary, they shall walk and not faint")[144] and Wisdom 3:7 ("[The just] shall run to and fro like sparks among the reeds").[145]

St. Thomas thinks that glorified bodies are agile and the saints will make use of this power and actually move their bodies. What are the causes of such agile movement on the part of glorified bodies? As with the qualities of impassibility and subtlety, St. Thomas rejects the view that explains the agility of the saints as due to the glorified body being composed of a heavenly body.[146] Again, the causes of the glorified body being agile are two: the beatified soul is the intrinsic formal cause of the glorified body's agility insofar as the beatified soul's perfection flows over into the body—a consequence of which is that the soul is the perfect moving cause of the body—and God is the efficient cause of the glorified body's agility insofar as it is God who beatifies the soul.[147]

St. Thomas gives the account above of the causes of the glorified body's agility in heaven a couple of slightly different twists in *SCG*. First, he argues there that the soul having the beatific vision has all of its desires sated. But the body is moved because of the soul's desire. Therefore, if the soul having the beatific vision wishes the body to be moved, it will be moved in every way in obedience to the soul's will.[148] Second, a body is weak to the extent that it cannot fulfill the desires of the soul with respect to actions and movements of the body. But such weakness is taken away when power flows over into the body from the soul that is having the beatific vision.[149]

---

143. *In Sent* IV, d. 44, q. 2, a. 3, q.c. 1, s.c. (*ST Suppl.*, q. 84, a. 1, s.c.). See also *SCG* IV.86.3 and *CT* I, chap. 168.
144. See, e.g., *In Sent* IV, d. 44, q. 2, a. 3, q.c. 2, s.c. (*ST Suppl.*, q. 84, a. 2, s.c.), and *In 1 Cor* 15, lect. 6, n. 982.
145. *ST Suppl.*, q. 84, a. 2, s.c. (trans. English Dominicans, 2908; *In Sent* IV, d. 44, q. 2, a. 3, q.c. 2, s.c.). See also *SCG* IV.86.3; *In 1 Cor* 15, lect. 6, n. 982; *CSA*, a. 11.
146. *In Sent* IV, d. 44, q. 2, a. 3, q.c. 1, resp. (*ST Suppl.*, q. 84, a. 1, resp.).
147. Ibid.
148. *SCG* IV.86.3.
149. Ibid.

THE CLARITY OF THE GLORIFIED BODY

In St. Thomas's view, the glorified body also has the quality of *claritatis*.[150] Of course, we can render St. Thomas's *claritatis* as clarity, but also as clearness, brightness, distinctness, radiance, or splendor, even fame, prestige, or good repute.[151] We can also note that St. Thomas either uses the words *lucida*[152] and *luminosum*[153] as synonyms of *claritas*, or else St. Thomas thinks that any glorified body that has the quality of *claritatis* is also *lucida* and *luminosum*. We can render St. Thomas's *lucida* as clear, bright, shining, full of light,[154] or lightsome,[155] and St. Thomas's *luminosum* as full of light, light, or luminous.[156]

St. Thomas thinks that the luminosity of the glorified body does not cancel out the colors that are naturally discerned in seeing the various parts of the human body. This is partly because each of the different parts of the human body, by nature, is differently disposed to receiving the light of glory as an overflow of the glory of the beatified soul and grace does not destroy nature, but perfects it.[157] In addition, the luminosity of the glorified body *adorns* (*superaddetur*)—and so does not cancel out—the natural colors of the body with a glow (*relucere*) or resplendence (*splendore*), just as, he says, bodies sometimes have this effect by way of the sun or some other cause, whether intrinsic or extrinsic.[158]

How bright will the glorified body be? As we will see, each glorified body will be bright or luminous to the extent that the soul that informs it has the virtue of charity. But, in St. Thomas's view, all glorious bodies will be brighter than the sun is now. As St. Thomas notes, Isaiah 30:26 teaches that the brightness of the sun will be greater in the next life than it is

---

150. See, e.g., *In Sent* IV, d. 44, q. 2, a. 4 (*ST Suppl.*, q. 85); d. 49, q. 4, a. 5, q.c. 3, resp.; *SCG* IV.86.2; *In 1 Cor* 15, lect. 6, n. 981; *CTI*, chap. 168; *In Mt* 17, lect. 1, n. 1424; *ST* III, q. 45, a. 1, obj. 3 and ad 3; a. 2, resp.; *CSA*, a. 11.
151. Roy Deferrari, *A Latin-English Dictionary of St. Thomas Aquinas* (Boston: Daughters of St. Paul, 1986), 157. Charles O'Neil renders St. Thomas's *claritatis* as "lightsomeness" (*SCG* IV.86.325). St. Thomas contrasts the *claritatis* of the glorified body with the deformities and miseries of this-worldly bodily life, citing Jb 14:1 in *In 1 Cor* 15, lect. 6, n. 981.
152. *In Sent* IV, d. 44, q. 2, a. 4, q.c. 1, resp. (*ST Suppl.*, q. 85, a. 1, resp.); see also ad 2 (*ST Suppl.*, q. 85, a. 1, ad 2).
153. See, e.g., *In Sent* IV, d. 44, q. 2, a. 4, q.c. 1, obj. 1 and ad 1 (*ST Suppl.*, q. 85, a. 1, obj. 1 and ad 1).
154. Deferrari, *A Latin-English Dictionary*, 609–10.
155. This is the preferred translation of the Fathers of the English Dominican Province.
156. Deferrari, *A Latin-English Dictionary*, 616.
157. *In Sent* IV, d. 44, q. 2, a. 4, q.c. 1, ad 3 and ad 4 (*ST Suppl.*, q. 85, a. 1, ad 3 and ad 4).
158. *In Sent* IV, d. 44, q. 2, a. 4, q.c. 1, ad 3 (*ST Suppl.*, q. 85, a. 1, ad 3).

now. But the glorified bodies will be brighter than the sun in the next life. (This is presumably because glorified bodies will be the brightest bodies in the next life due to the cause of their brightness, the beatified soul, which cause is more perfect than the cause of the brightness of the glorified heavenly bodies, or at least the sun.) Therefore, the glorified bodies will be very bright, even brighter than the sun is now.[159] Despite the degree of the glorified body's brightness, St. Thomas argues that the brightness of glorified bodies will not disturb us (as looking at the sun with a nonglorified body certainly does). This is because the glorified body is glorified not in virtue of its natural component parts but in virtue of the beatified soul that informs it. For clarity caused by the soul does not disturb, but rather delights us (it is clarity caused by bodies that disturbs us).[160]

Finally, St. Thomas also thinks that the glorified body as *claritas* is transparent (*pervium*).[161] St. Thomas notes that the transparency of the glorified body is not inconsistent with its having density, which a *human* body clearly has, as a crystal both has density and transparency (St. Thomas cites Pope St. Gregory the Great here as far as the comparison between the glorified body and a crystal is concerned).[162]

In presenting his case for why we should believe that the glorified bodies have *claritatis*, St. Thomas argues from the authority of scripture, mentioning Matthew 13:43 ("the righteous will shine like the sun in the kingdom of their Father")[163] and Wisdom 3:7 ("The just shall shine, and shall run to and fro like sparks among the reeds").[164] In addition, St. Thomas notes that St. Paul writes in 1 Corinthians 15:43: "It is sown in dishonor, it is raised in glory," which St. Thomas reads as referring to clarity, as evidenced by the immediate context where St. Paul compares the glory of the resurrected bodies of the saints to the clarity of the stars (in 1 Cor 15:41–42: "There is one glory of the sun, and another glory of the moon, and another glory of the stars; indeed, star differs from star in

---

159. *In Sent* IV, d. 44, q. 2, a. 3, q.c. 2, obj. 2 and ad 2 (*ST Suppl.*, q. 85, a. 2, obj. 2 and ad 2). See also *In Mt* 13, lect. 3, n. 1185.

160. *In Sent* IV, d. 44, q. 2, a. 4, q.c. 2, ad 2 (*ST Suppl.*, q. 85, a. 2, ad 2).

161. *In Sent* IV, d. 44, q. 2, a. 4, q.c. 1, ad 2 (*ST Suppl.*, q. 85, a. 1, ad 2).

162. Ibid. St. Thomas also speaks of the glorified body as *fulgentia* (shining) in *In 1 Cor* 15, lect. 6, n. 981.

163. See, e.g., *In Sent* IV, d. 44, q. 2, a. 4, q.c. 1, s.c. (*ST Suppl.*, q. 85, a. 1, s.c.); *SCG* IV.86.2; *In 1 Cor* 15, lect. 6, n. 981; *In Mt* 13, lect. 3, n. 1185; *CSA*, a. 11.

164. *ST Suppl.*, q. 85, a. 1, s.c. (trans. English Dominicans, 2913; *In Sent* IV, d. 44, q. 2, a. 4, q.c. 1, s.c.). See also *SCG* IV.86.2 and *In Mt* 13, lect. 3, n. 1185.

Glorified Bodies 325

glory. So it is with the resurrection of the dead"). Therefore the bodies of the saints in heaven will be lightsome.[165]

As far as the cause of the brightness of the glorified human body is concerned, here, of all places, it is surely tempting to think that the predominance of a heavenly body is the cause of the glorified body's luminosity. But St. Thomas again explicitly rejects such an explanation, calling such an explanation *absurdum*.[166] He prefers the explanation that the clarity of the body is caused by an "overflowing" of the glory of the soul to the body (*causabitur ex redundantia gloriae animae in corpus*).[167]

But how is this supposed to work? St. Thomas explains by starting with what, for him, is an epistemological axiom: if a perfection P is received in x, P is received in x in accord with the mode of x's being (and not in accord with the mode of the source from whence P flows [*per modum influentis*]). For example, as we have seen, God is the efficient cause of the saints' experiencing the beatific vision. But the saints do not receive God according to the mode of God's existence, but according to the mode of a rational creature, albeit one that has been lifted up to new spiritual heights by God's gift of the *lumen gloriae*. In the case of the body of the saint in heaven receiving glory at the resurrection, such glory is received in a corporeal fashion, and not in the mode of the formal cause, that is, spiritually. That being said, as we have seen, St. Thomas thinks that the glory of the beatified body is a true participation in the glory of the beatified soul, and so the clarity of the glorified body is a true reflection of the luminosity of the glorified soul. Now, to speak of the clarity or luminosity of the *soul* is to speak of that soul's *charity*. Therefore, just as the beatified soul is luminous to the extent it is full of charity, the glorified body participates in the soul's charity in a corporeal manner, that is, the glorified body is luminous, or, as scripture has it, human persons with glorified bodies "will shine like the sun in the kingdom of their Father" (Mt 13:43).[168] Interestingly, St. Thomas draws the logical conclusion, given other things we have seen him say, that, because the luminosity of the glorified body is a participation in the luminosity, or charity, of the be-

---

165. See, e.g., *In Sent* IV, d. 44, q. 2, a. 4, q.c. 1, s.c. (*ST Suppl.*, q. 85, a. 1, s.c.); *SCG* IV.86.2; *CT* I, chap. 168. In *In 1 Cor* 15, lect. 6, n. 981, St. Thomas cites St. Augustine's *Tractates on the Gospel of John* as a source for the idea that the expression *resurget in gloria* in 1 Cor 15:43 refers to the clarity of the glorified body.
166. *In Sent* IV, d. 44, q. 2, a. 4, q.c. 1, resp. (*ST Suppl.*, q. 85, a. 1, resp.).
167. Ibid. See also *SCG* IV.86; *CT* I, chap. 168; *In Mt* 13, lect. 3, n. 1185.
168. *In Sent* IV, d. 44, q. 2, a. 4, q.c. 1, resp. (*ST Suppl.*, q. 85, a. 1, resp.).

atified soul, the greater the charity in a soul, the greater the luminosity of that person's glorified body. Therefore, one way of knowing a saint's relative degree of charity—and so perfect happiness or essential reward—is by way of sensing the relative degree of luminosity in that saint's glorified body.[169]

Given the account of Christ in the Gospels, some questions remain. For example, some of St. Thomas's contemporaries wondered whether the clarity of a glorified body could be seen by a nonglorified eye, as if it *could* be, it would seemingly *always* be, unless there was some physical problem with the nonglorified eye. But the disciples did not always see Christ's glorified body as luminous, for example, after his resurrection or on the road to Emmaus, and there is no reason to believe this was because there was some physical problem with their eyes.[170] St. Thomas thinks that the clarity of the glorified body can be seen by a nonglorified body, as Sts. Peter, James, and John saw the transfigured Christ with nonglorified eyes, and the clarity of Christ's glorified body is like the clarity the apostles saw in Christ's transfiguration. In addition, the damned will see the clarity of the beatified.[171]

Nonetheless, someone with well-functioning, nonglorified eyes does not necessarily see the clarity of a glorified body at which that person is looking, as is clear from the fact that the apostles did not always discern such clarity in Christ's resurrected body.[172] St. Thomas explains the fact that the apostles only sometimes get a glimpse of the clarity of Christ's glorified body with their nonglorified eyes by noting that the glorified body's appearing luminous is a function of the merit in the will of the saint whose glorified body it is. As the glorified body is wholly under the power of that person's will, whether a saint's clarity of the body is evident to others is a function of whether the saint whose body it is wills to reveal the clarity of that saint's glorified body.[173]

St. Thomas puts together the notion that the degree of luminosity of a person S's glorified body is a function of S's will and the notion that the luminosity of S's glorified body is a reflection of S's charity in an in-

---

169. Ibid. See also *ST* I, q. 57, a. 4, ad 1. Recall that Dante takes advantage of this implication of St. Thomas's views to great dramatic effect throughout *Paradiso*.
170. *In Sent* IV, d. 44, q. 2, a. 3, q.c. 2, obj. 3 (*ST Suppl.*, q. 85, a. 2, obj. 3).
171. *In Sent* IV, d. 44, q. 2, a. 4, q.c. 2, s.c. (*ST Suppl.*, q. 85, a. 2, s.c.).
172. *In Sent* IV, d. 44, q. 2, a. 4, q.c. 3, s.c. (*ST Suppl.*, q. 85, a. 3, s.c.).
173. See, e.g., *In Sent* IV, d. 44, q. 2, a. 4, q.c. 2, ad 3 (*ST Suppl.*, q. 85, a. 2, ad 3); q.c. 3, resp. (*ST Suppl.*, q. 85, a. 3, resp.); *CT* I, chap. 238; *ST* III, q. 54, a. 1, ad 2; a. 2, ad 1; q. 55, a. 6, ad 4.

teresting way. Given Christ's virtue, St. Thomas argues that Christ, after his resurrection, had to cloak the splendor of his bodily glory in order to provide the apostles with a proof that he had, in fact, risen from the dead. In St. Thomas's view, if Christ had displayed the full splendor of his bodily glory in his resurrection appearances, then this would have made it difficult, perhaps impossible, for the apostles to believe that Christ now possessed specifically the same human nature as he did in this life, or indeed that it was, in fact, Christ risen from the dead.[174]

The glorified bodies of the saints will be impassible, subtle, agile, and luminescent. But just *where* will those bodies be? Before we treat that topic at the end of part 3, St. Thomas has interesting things to say about some of the creaturely communal dimensions of heavenly life, for example, the communion of the saints, the aureoles, and the fruits. It is to those subjects that I now turn.

174. See, e.g., *CT* I, chap. 238, and *ST* III, q. 55, a. 6, ad 4.

12

The Accidental Reward IV

THE COMMUNION OF THE SAINTS, THE AUREOLES, AND THE FRUITS

In the preceding three chapters, I examined what St. Thomas thinks, and why, about human embodiment in heaven. This chapter addresses some other aspects of the accidental reward as St. Thomas understands it, namely, (a) the so-called aureoles, or little golden crowns, (b) the so-called fruit (*fructus*), and (c) friendship with other created persons in heaven, or what we might call the communion of the saints in heaven or the church in heaven.

ST. THOMAS ON SOME SPECIAL ACCIDENTAL REWARDS IN HEAVEN: AUREOLES AND FRUITS

Not to be confused with the *aurea* (a golden crown)—a metaphor for the joy of the essential reward of the saints in heaven[1]—an *aureola* (little golden crown), according to a traditional doctrine, is a metaphorical way of speaking about a special accidental reward enjoyed by saints in heaven who faithfully lived a special kind of Christian life.[2] More specifically, an *aureola* is a metaphorical way of speaking about the joy that certain kinds of saints in heaven take in those good works of theirs in this life that evince a most perfect participation in Christ with respect to his

---

1. See, e.g., *In Sent* IV, d. 49, q. 5, a. 1 (*ST Suppl.*, q. 96, a. 1); a. 2, q.c. 1, resp. (*ST Suppl.*, q. 96, a. 2, resp.); a. 4, q.c. 3, resp. (*ST Suppl.*, q. 96, a. 10, resp.).

2. St. Thomas also notes that there is a more general sense of *aureola* that picks out any reward added to the essential reward, i.e., any aspect of the accidental reward. See, e.g., *In Sent* IV, d. 49, q. 5, a. 1, resp. (*ST Suppl.*, q. 96, a. 1, resp.).

victories over the world, the flesh, and the devil.³ St. Thomas also distinguishes the joy of the *aureola* from the joy some saints know in heaven in virtue of their possessing in this life a disposition to withdraw from the pleasures of sexual congress.⁴ The name for this latter kind of joy or accidental reward in heaven is fruit (*fructus*).⁵ This part of the chapter says something about the fruits and the aureoles as accidental rewards of joy possessed by certain of the saints in heaven.

Let us begin with the fruit as a special kind of accidental reward. Again, the fruit of heaven, in the relevant sense, is the joy accruing to those saints in heaven who, by choice, possess a disposition in this life to withdraw from the pleasures of sexual congress, not because sexual pleasure is bad, wrong, or dirty, but because sexual pleasure is something good sacrificed for the sake of witnessing to the reality of the kingdom of God. The fruit is therefore a kind of joy in heaven in having participated in God's plan in a particularly powerful way. Recall that there is no sexual union in heaven. So to withdraw intentionally from the pleasures of sexual union in this life is to remind human persons in this life of the reality, nature, and importance of heavenly life.

St. Thomas argues that, because there are, more or less, three ways of possessing a disposition to withdraw from sexual congress (i.e., being continent), there are three different kinds of fruit as accidental reward in heaven, each one greater than the last.⁶ The first way of having a disposition to withdraw from sexual pleasure is as one who engages in the pleasures of sexual congress, but does so habitually in accord with right reason. This is the way that chaste married people are continent.⁷ So persons in heaven who were married in this life and habitually acted chastely enjoy the first kind of fruit as an accidental reward.

The second and third ways of being continent are greater than the

---

3. See, e.g., *In Sent* IV, d. 49, q. 5, a. 1 (*ST Suppl.*, q. 96, a. 1); a. 2, q.c. 1, resp. and ad 3 (*ST Suppl.*, q. 96, a. 2, resp. and ad 3); aa. 3–5 (*ST Suppl.*, q. 96, aa. 5–13).

4. See, e.g., *In Sent* IV, d. 49, q. 5, a. 2, q.c. 1, resp. (*ST Suppl.*, q. 96, a. 2, resp.); a. 2, q.c. 2 (*ST Suppl.*, q. 96, a. 3); a. 2, q.c. 3 (*ST Suppl.*, q. 96, a. 4).

5. See, e.g., *In Sent* IV, d. 49, q. 5, a. 2, q.c. 1, resp. and ad 2 (*ST Suppl.*, q. 96, a. 2, resp. and ad 2). St. Thomas recognizes that *fructus* is used in a number of different senses in scripture and tradition, senses that correspond with the various ways that "fruits" can be used metaphorically to describe spiritual things. See, e.g., *In Sent* IV, d. 49, q. 5, a. 2, q.c. 1, resp. and ad 2 (*ST Suppl.*, q. 96, a. 2, resp. and ad 2) and q.c. 2 (*ST Suppl.*, q. 96, a. 3).

6. See, e.g., *In Sent* IV, d. 49, q. 5, a. 2, q.c. 3, resp. (*ST Suppl.*, q. 96, a. 4, resp.), and *ST* I-II, q. 70, a. 3, ad 2.

7. Ibid.

first, as they are "superabundant" when compared with the state of chaste married persons. They are superabundant because they have human persons withdrawing from sexual congress altogether. Such is the case with widows and virgins[8] who habitually live chastely by intention. Widows represent a second way of living continently: they only live a part of their life in a manner that totally withdraws from sexual congress. The virgin's way of life is a third way of living continently, as a virgin's entire life is characterized by sexual abstinence. Therefore, where widows enjoy a kind of fruit of joy as an accidental reward that is greater than that of married persons, virgins enjoy a kind of fruit of joy as an accidental reward that is greater than that of widows.[9]

Let us now turn to what St. Thomas says about the aureoles. Recall that the aureoles of joy are accidental rewards due to someone for having won a signal victory over temptation to evil in this life, evidenced through that person's good works. In particular, virgins, martyrs, and teachers will receive an aureole of joy in heaven for their respective victories over the flesh, the world, and the devil. That is, in addition to the essential reward (and whatever other accidental rewards these saints might enjoy), virgins, martyrs, and doctors have the added joy in heaven of having been especially conformed in their life to Christ insofar as they won special victories for the kingdom of God.[10] For example, virgins (who have willed to give up the great good of sex for the sake of the kingdom of God) win a special kind of victory over the internal assault of carnal concupiscence and so are justly crowned with joy in having done so.[11] Doctors (teachers of the faith) earn an aureole for winning a special kind of victory over the assault of the devil by driving him out of themselves and others by way of their teaching and preaching.[12] Finally, martyrs win

---

8. In this context, St. Thomas takes "virgin" to refer to someone who intentionally wills to live his or her entire life without engaging in sexual congress. As he notes, this can be true of someone who is violated against his or her will (*In Sent* IV, d. 49, q. 5, a. 3, q.c. 1, ad 4; in *ST Suppl.*, q. 96, a. 5, ad 4), and someone who acts internally against the intention to live virginally but returns to it by the end of his or her life (*In Sent* IV, q. 49, q. 5, a. 3, q.c. 1, resp.; in *ST Suppl.*, q. 96, a. 5, resp.). Presumably, then, married persons who act unchastely internally also enjoy a fruit in heaven as a part of their accidental reward as long as they die living chastely.

9. *In Sent* IV, d. 49, q. 5, a. 2, q.c. 3, resp. (*ST Suppl.*, q. 96, a. 4, resp.), and *ST* I-II, q. 70, a. 3, ad 2.

10. See, e.g., *In Sent* IV, d. 49, q. 5, a. 5, q.c. 1 (*ST Suppl.*, q. 96, a. 11).

11. See, e.g., *In Sent* IV, d. 49, q. 5, a. 3, q.c. 1 (*ST Suppl.*, q. 96, a. 5), and a. 5, q.c. 1 (*ST Suppl.*, q. 96, a. 11).

12. See, e.g., *In Sent* IV, d. 49, q. 5, a. 3, q.c. 3 (*ST Suppl.*, q. 96, a. 7) and a. 5, q.c. 1 (*ST Suppl.*, q. 96, a. 11).

a special kind of victory over external threats to the soul, the greatest among these being the fear of death, and they do so for the greatest of motives, out of love for Christ.[13] St. Thomas argues that among the virgins, doctors, and martyrs, martyrs enjoy the greatest aureole of joy, absolutely speaking.[14]

ST. THOMAS ON FRIENDSHIP, THE COMMUNION OF THE SAINTS, AND THE CHURCH IN HEAVEN

So far, I have spoken in detail about the relevance of God, the beatific vision, the beatified soul, beatified acts of will, the body, and particularly courageous ways of living the Christian life for the essential and accidental rewards in heaven. In St. Thomas's view, human persons in heaven also enjoy the good of friendship with other created persons as an aspect of the accidental reward. However, in speaking about friendship in heaven, we could also speak, as the church often does, about the communion of the saints in heaven, or about the "church triumphant," that is, the church in heaven. So what of the church, or the communion of the saints, or friends, in heaven?

---

13. See, e.g., *In Sent* IV, d. 49, q. 5, a. 3, q.c. 2 (*ST Suppl.*, q. 96, a. 6) and a. 5, q.c. 1 (*ST Suppl.*, q. 96, a. 11).

14. See, e.g., *In Sent* IV, d. 49, q. 5, a. 5, q.c. 1 (*ST Suppl.*, q. 96, a. 12). St. Thomas suggests that saints in heaven who were both virgins and martyrs have two aureoles, one for each victory (see, e.g., *In Sent* IV, d. 49, q. 5, a. 3, q.c. 1, ad 4; in *ST Suppl.*, q. 96, a. 5, ad 4). My unpublished paper, "Martyrdom, the Death of Young Children, and the Heavenly Reward: A Thomistic Response to a Difficult Question about Evil," argues that St. Thomas's doctrine of the aureoles, coupled with his distinction between the essential reward and the accidental reward, provides some ways of showing how God is possibly being very good to all martyrs and any child who dies before reaching the age of reason. How so? According to Catholic tradition, the Holy Innocents are a type of martyr. Presumably, the Holy Innocents have no regrets in heaven about dying in the manner they did. Even if this is chiefly because they now see God face to face in the beatific vision, this is also because, as a part of their accidental reward, the Holy Innocents enjoy the aureole of martyrdom. As part of their accidental reward in heaven, the Holy Innocents experience the everlasting joy of their sharing in Christ's passion in a particularly great manner, for, like Christ, they die for the sake of the kingdom of God. But the everlasting joy of their sharing in Christ's passion in a particularly great manner outweighs the evil that the Holy Innocents suffer in this life. Now, according to Catholic Christian tradition, human persons die because of Adam's sin. On a plausible way of distinguishing moral and natural evil, that means that all human deaths are moral evils insofar as they are deaths caused, at least remotely, by evil willing. Just as martyrs enjoy an aureole insofar as they take joy in sharing in Christ's victory in a particularly great way, it makes sense to think that all baptized human persons who die before the age of reason have an accidental reward like an aureole. That is, they take everlasting joy in sharing in Christ's passion in a manner that not every Christian does, namely, like Christ, they possess a human nature and die as a result of moral evil, without ever having actually sinned, where such everlasting joy outweighs the evil those baptized persons suffer who die before the age of reason.

In commenting on the marriage at Cana account in the Gospel of John, St. Thomas notes that marriage has been given a mystical sense by the Apostle Paul (in Eph 5), so that Christ stands in relation to the church as a whole as a husband stands in relation to his wife. St. Thomas goes on to say this mystical marriage begins in the womb of the Virgin "when God the Father united a human nature to his Son in a unity of person." The marriage of Christ and the church was made public "when the Church was joined to him by faith." Finally, and most important for our purposes, St. Thomas speaks of the consummation of this mystical marriage between Christ and the church "when the bride, i.e., the Church, is led into the resting place of the groom, i.e., into the glory of heaven."[15] St. Thomas also cites here a favorite passage from the Book of Revelation: "Blessed are they who are called to the marriage supper of the Lamb" (Rv 19:9). What is important to see for our purposes is that St. Thomas believes that *the church lives on forever in heaven*. Therefore, insofar as the church includes, at the very least, an assembly of created persons, heaven for St. Thomas involves communion between created persons. Although aspects of the wedding feast for St. Thomas are clearly metaphorical, for example, the talk of physical eating and drinking, one of the literal truths communicated by way of the metaphor is that heaven involves a deep communion between Christ and the church, and the church for St. Thomas is itself a perpetual community of human (and nonhuman) persons.[16]

Consider also St. Thomas's comments on Ephesians 4:4. Recall that the chapter begins with St. Paul exhorting the Ephesians "[to] walk worthy of the vocation in which you are called" (4:1b).[17] In the succeeding verses St. Paul goes on to say in some detail what this would look like: "With all humility and mildness, with patience, supporting one another in charity; careful to keep the unity of the spirit in the bond of peace; one body and one spirit; *as you are called in one hope of your calling*" (4:2-4).[18] In commenting on the second clause of 4:4 (italicized above), St. Thomas states:

---

15. *In Jn* 2, lect. 1, n. 338; trans. James A. Weisheipl and Fabian R. Larcher (Lander, Wyo.: The Aquinas Institute, 2013), available at https://aquinas.cc/la/en/~Ioan.C2.L1.n337.2.

16. St. Thomas believes that the angels too constitute a part of the church triumphant. See, e.g., *ST* III, q. 8, a. 4, resp., and *In Heb* 12, lect. 4, n. 707.

17. *In Eph* 4, lect. 1; trans. Matthew L. Lamb (Albany, N.Y.: Magi Books, 1966), 149.

18. Ibid.; emphasis added.

When he says "as you are called in one hope of your calling" he points out the reason for this unity. We notice when persons are called together *to possess something in common and mutually enjoy it*, they usually live and travel together. Thus, in a spiritual way he says: Because you are called to one and the same reality, namely the final reward, you ought to walk together with a unity of spirit "in the one hope of your calling," tending toward the one reality you hope for as a result of your vocation.[19]

In explaining the passage from St. Paul, St. Thomas thus implies that the one hope of a Christian's calling—the final reward in heaven—involves something that the saints "possess in common and mutually enjoy." The saints possess happiness in common; their accidental reward entails mutual enjoyment in God.

St. Thomas has related things to say about heavenly life in his *Commentary on the Apostles' Creed*. For example, St. Thomas thinks (with St. Paul) about the unity of the church by way of analogy with a bodily organism: "Just as we see that in one human person there is one soul and one body, nevertheless in the body there are diverse members, so the Catholic Church is one body and has diverse members."[20] The church is therefore something more than simply a collection of individual Christians for St. Thomas. Just as the human body is not merely an aggregate of material things, so each individual Christian is a member of a whole that is more than the sum of its integral parts. This is important to bear in mind as we examine what St. Thomas says in explaining the Creed calling the church "Catholic." Now let us say that the church is like an organism and so not simply a collection of individuals. One might admit as much and nevertheless think that the church is something that God wills merely as a *temporary instrument* for human salvation, so that the church comes into existence at some point in time but then disappears, for example, with the advent of the blessed life. St. Thomas knows of a position such as this, and he rejects it: "The Church is Catholic, i.e., universal ... with respect to time. For some have said the Church endures until a certain time; but this is false, since ... after the end of the world it will remain in Heaven."[21]

---

19. *In Eph* 4, lect. 1, n. 196 (trans. Lamb, 154; emphasis added). See also the sermon *Beati qui habitant*, introduction, and the sermon *Beata gens* 1.

20. *CSA*, a. 9 (author's translation). For my translations of *CSA*, I have consulted *Catechetical Instructions* (trans. Collins), 3–66, and *The Three Greatest Prayers* (trans. Laurence Shapcote) (London: Burns, Oates, and Washbourne, 1937), 39–89.

21. Ibid. (author's translation). See also *ST* III, q. 8, a. 4, ad 2.

Another passage from the *Commentary on the Apostles' Creed* has St. Thomas explicitly emphasizing the communal nature of the accidental reward in heaven. In explaining what the Creed means by "eternal life," St. Thomas comments that it involves union with God, the perfect sating of desire, superabundant delight, and perfect security.[22] Finally, St. Thomas says about everlasting life:

> It consists of the pleasant society of all the blessed, which society will be maximally delightful, since each one will possess every good with each one of the blessed. For each one will love another as himself, and therefore he will rejoice in the good of another as his own good, where it happens that if the joy and delight of one were to increase, so would the delight of all: *the dwelling in You is, as it were, of all rejoicing* (Ps 86:7).[23]

Part of the saint's accidental reward is rejoicing in the joy of others, so that "if the joy and delight of one were to increase, so would the delight of all."

One last passage will serve to demonstrate St. Thomas's communal conception of the accidental reward in heaven. In the passage in question, St. Thomas is arguing that (most) human persons are born with original sin. In one of the premises of his argument, St. Thomas states, "the end of every rational creature is to arrive at beatitude, and this cannot be save in the kingdom of God."[24] St. Thomas goes on to explain what he means by the kingdom of God: "the ordered society of those who enjoy the divine vision, in which true beatitude consists."[25] Here again we see that St. Thomas thinks that the blessed enjoy God not in an isolated manner, but rather in the company of other human persons, namely, the other living members of the bride of Christ, the church. Furthermore, this society is not simply an aggregate of individuals; it remains the *body* of Christ, an "*ordered* society of those who enjoy the divine vision."[26]

---

22. *CSA*, a. 12.

23. Ibid. (author's translation). See also the prayer attributed to St. Thomas entitled "For the Attainment of Heaven," in *The Aquinas Prayer Book*, 53–55.

24. *SCG* IV.50.10 (trans. O'Neil, 214). For some discussion of the passage, see Henri de Lubac, *Catholicism: A Study of Dogma in Relation to the Corporate Destiny of Mankind* (New York: Mentor-Omega Books, 1964), 72–75. One might think that St. Thomas is teaching that the communion of the saints is an aspect of the essential reward or perfect happiness in this passage. Whether or not that is so, it is clear that St. Thomas, by the time he writes *ST* I-II, thinks that the communion of the saints is part of the accidental reward, necessary not for the attainment of perfect happiness in heaven (the essential reward), but for the attainment of the *bene esse* of perfect happiness. See, e.g., *ST* I-II, q. 4, a. 8, and discussion of this passage below.

25. *SCG* IV.50.10 (trans. O'Neil, 214).

26. For additional argument and textual support for the thesis that St. Thomas has a

As I have argued above, the resurrection of the body presumably has a salutary effect on the degree to which human persons in heaven enjoy direct communion with one another as a part of their accidental reward.[27] This is because recognizing the faces and bodies of our friends is an important part of our relationships. Nonetheless, it is important to stress that, according to St. Thomas, human persons directly know other human persons in heaven even before the general resurrection, that is, as disembodied soul to disembodied soul. This is true even if, at and after the general resurrection, the saint's direct knowledge of human persons is more perfect than before the general resurrection, whether because the saints at and after the general resurrection know in accord with their complete nature, or because they then also know in accord with their natural ways of knowing, or because they then also know other human persons by way of sensation.

As St. Thomas teaches, the soul has one mode (*modum*) of understanding when it is embodied in this life, that is, by turning to phantasms, and another mode of knowing when it is separated from matter.[28] This is because the soul has one mode of being when it shares its being with matter such that the composite human person exists and another mode of being when it exists apart from matter in the interim state.[29] When the human soul is separated from matter, St. Thomas argues that it naturally knows, by way of divinely infused species,[30] all other separated souls perfectly and the angels imperfectly.[31] That is to say, the separated human soul knows other creatures, not by abstracting

---

thoroughgoing creaturely communal conception of the accidental reward in heaven, see, e.g., R.C. Perry, "The Social Character of Heavenly Beatitude according to the Thought of St. Thomas Aquinas," *The Thomist* 7 (1944): 65–79; John Finnis, *Aquinas: Moral, Political, and Legal Theory* (Oxford: Oxford University Press, 1998), 327–34; and Hutter, *Bound for Beatitude*, 437–45.

27. Recall that the saints in heaven know creatures *indirectly* in knowing the essence of God, because creatures as seen in God constitute the secondary object of the beatific vision. The accidental reward involves the saints in heaven knowing one another *directly*.

28. See, e.g., *QDV*, q. 19, a. 1, resp.; *In 1 Cor* 13, lect. 3, n. 791; *QDA*, aa. 15, 17, 18; *ST* I, q. 89, aa. 1–3.

29. See, e.g., *ST* I, q. 89, a. 1, resp.

30. See, e.g., *ST* I, q. 89, a. 1, ad 3 and a. 3, resp.

31. See, e.g., *QDV*, q. 19, a. 1, resp. Because (a) angels are part of the body of Christ, (b) human persons in heaven presumably continue to directly know immaterial angels at and after the general resurrection, and (c) angels are immaterial beings and so cannot be known directly by way of the senses or by way of knowledge derived by sensation, human persons in heaven presumably also continue to know the blessed angels as does the separated soul, even at and after the general resurrection when those human persons resume the power to sense things. For some excellent discussion of St. Thomas's views on the cognition of the separated soul, see Dom Anscar Vonier, *The Human Soul and Its Relations with Other Spirits* (Lexington, Ky.: Assumption Press, 2014), 62–64.

an intelligible species from a phantasm provided by the senses, but by way of concepts put into the soul directly by God. In addition, although separated souls do not know about the goings on of human persons in this life by a *natural* form of *direct* knowledge, they *do* have some such knowledge by way of the testimony of others, whether by way of other souls, angels, or by way of special revelations from God.[32]

We have seen that St. Thomas thinks that, in fact, human persons in heaven enjoy a happy and holy fellowship with other created persons even before the general resurrection. We now turn to the question of the relative importance of human community for attaining human happiness in heaven according to St. Thomas's views in order to demonstrate the way in which those views allow for a middle position between the individualist and social models of heaven (see chapter 1 and PNH-I), one that does not have the problems that attend the models of heaven offered by philosophical theologians such as Grisez, Griffiths, and Rogers.

We can see St. Thomas addressing the question of the relative importance of human community for human happiness in heaven where he discusses, in a late text, the question regarding whether friends are necessary for human happiness.[33] St. Thomas argues that the society of friends is not necessary for perfect happiness, that is, it is not an aspect of the essential reward. This is because "human persons have the entire fullness of their perfection in God" (*quia homo habet totam plenitudinem suae perfectionis in Deo*).[34] Putting the point another way, St. Thomas says: "Perfection of charity is essential to happiness, as to the love of God, but not as to the love of our neighbor. Wherefore if there were but one soul enjoying God, it would be happy, though having no neighbor to love."[35] Rather, the society of friends is an aspect of the well-being of beatitude, that is to say, it is an aspect of the accidental reward.[36]

In commenting on this passage from *ST* I-II, Jacques Maritain notes that a human person's union with God would satisfy the human longing for society because God himself becomes the common good in which the creature comes to share.[37] Of course, such an idea takes on a pro-

---

32. See, e.g., *ST* I, q. 89, a. 8, ad 1, and *ST* II-II, q. 83, a. 11.
33. *ST* I-II, q. 4, a. 8, resp.
34. Ibid.
35. Ibid., ad 3 (trans. English Dominicans, 608).
36. Ibid., resp.
37. *The Person and the Common Good*, trans. John J. Fitzgerald (Notre Dame, Ind.: University of Notre Dame Press, 1966), 21–22.

founder meaning for the Catholic Christian, who believes that God himself is a society of Persons. So Maritain notes that the adage "goods are common among friends" is even true for the solitary human soul who finds itself united to God. Maritain cites a passage from St. Thomas to this effect: "God loves his creatures not only as the artisan loves his work but also with a friendly association, as friend loves friend, in as much as He draws them into the community of His own enjoyment in order that their glory and beatitude may reside in that very thing by which He Himself is blessed."[38]

We have already seen some additional ways to make sense of St. Thomas's view that a human good such as friendship is an aspect of the accidental and not the essential reward. As an aspect of the accidental reward, the society of friends is a fitting or appropriate good.[39] This is because human persons are rational animals, and thus social animals. Even though the human desire for society is more than met in a soul being taking up into the society of the Trinity, it is fitting also to give to human persons in heaven the gift of the society of created persons. In addition, we might say, following Brandon Dahm, that the fellowship of friends satisfies for human persons a desire-from-fulfillment (and not a desire-from-lack) to share their singular participation in the goodness of God with other created persons.[40]

We might also recall that, in having the beatific vision, the saints in heaven have as a consequence of this vision a knowledge of creatures. So human persons in heaven have a most perfect knowledge of created persons not only directly or, in and of themselves, as an aspect of the accidental reward, but also indirectly, and in a way more perfectly, in knowing creatures in virtue of knowing the essence of God, as an aspect—the secondary object—of the essential reward.

Finally, it is worth noting that the accidental joy in the communion of the saints changes, at least until the consummation of the kingdom, as God's kingdom is ever more realized.[41] When the kingdom is completed—

---

38. *In Sent* II, d. 26, a. 1, ad 2 (as translated and quoted in ibid., 22).

39. Recall: a good G is *fitting* or *appropriate* for a creature C if and only if the perfection of C does not require G, but, given C's nature, the possession of G would be a real good for C.

40. For some additional ways of making sense of St. Thomas's view that the society of friends is not necessary for perfect human happiness or the essential reward, but conduces to the well-being of perfect happiness, or is an aspect of the accidental reward, see my "Friendship in Heaven: Aquinas on Supremely Perfect Happiness and the Communion of the Saints," in *Metaphysics and God* (ed. Timpe), 225–48.

41. See, e.g., *In Sent* IV, d. 45, q. 2, a. 2, q.c. 4, ad 3 (*ST Suppl.*, q. 71, a. 8, ad 3); d. 49, q. 2, a. 5,

as Christians pray for when they utter the petition of the Our Father, "thy kingdom come, thy will be done"[42]—the saints in heaven know a special accidental joy in the completeness of the heavenly kingdom, St. Thomas thinks, following St. Augustine.[43]

I will close this chapter by suggesting that the human person participating well in the Mass offers a perfect image of the view of the relative importance of human society for human happiness in heaven, as St. Thomas understands it. Consider the manner of those who worship well at the Mass. Although there are manifold ways to worship God, many of which are easy enough to accomplish as a solitary soul, the Mass is a fundamentally communal act. The people who gather for Mass see one another, and pray in communion with the angels and the saints. Although the Mass thus involves being aware of the presence of other creatures—and particularly other human persons—the attention of the faithful is always directed by the divine liturgy itself ultimately to God.

In addition, consider a fundamental way that human persons receive grace from God according to St. Thomas: through the sacraments. For St. Thomas, the sacraments simultaneously signify something about the past, the present, and the future. They remind us of the ultimate source of the grace that we can receive in the sacraments: Christ's passion. They also indicate to us what it is we receive right now by way of partaking of the sacraments, namely, the grace to live a new life. But the sacraments also point beyond themselves to the heavenly banquet. They thus act, according to St. Thomas, as a prognostic (*prognosticum*) of our future glory in heaven.[44] What St. Thomas says here about the sacraments acting as a prognostic, can be said of the church's Mass too. The Mass acts as a *prognostic*, providing for us an image of the well-being of perfect happiness in the saints: a society of friends who, though joyfully aware of each other's presence, all know that they possess their essential reward in being united intellectually and volitionally to the ultimate creating, saving, and sustaining source of that holy fellowship.

---

resp. (*ST Suppl.*, q. 92, a. 3, resp.); d. 50, q. 2, a. 1, q.c. 6, resp. (*ST Suppl.*, q. 98, a. 6, resp.); *ST* I, q. 62, a. 9, ad 3; II-II, q. 182, a. 2; *QDM*, q. 5, a. 1, obj. 5 and ad 5.

42. *In Mt* 6, lect. 3, n. 586.

43. Ibid. For a lovely meditation on the communion of the saints in heaven, one that goes beyond, but is fully consistent with, what St. Thomas says, see J. P. Arendzen, "Heaven, or the Church Triumphant," in *The Teaching of the Catholic Church* (ed. Smith), 2:1248–82, esp. 1261–75.

44. See, e.g., *ST* III, q. 60, a. 3.

13

The Accidental Reward V

NONHUMAN MATERIAL BEINGS IN HEAVEN

This chapter examines in three sections the views of St. Thomas on heaven insofar as it is a *place* populated not only by embodied human persons, but by nonhuman material beings. The first section treats St. Thomas's views on the different kinds of nonhuman, nonartificial material beings that populate heaven, as well as his reasons for taking these views. The second section examines whether or not artificial things such as clothes, tools, books, and musical instruments are necessary for perfect human happiness according to St. Thomas and whether, even if such things are not necessary for perfect human happiness, the enjoyment of artifact objects might nonetheless be a constitutive part of the accidental reward of the saints, given St. Thomas's principles. The third section raises some objections to some of the views of St. Thomas presented in this chapter, and suggests ways that St. Thomas, or a Thomist, can respond to them.

ST. THOMAS ON NONHUMAN, NONARTIFICIAL MATERIAL BEINGS IN HEAVEN

As Paul Griffiths notes, St. Thomas offers two different kinds of arguments in defense of his views concerning the kinds of material beings that populate heaven.[1] One kind of argument deploys from consideration of the nature of nonhuman material beings, the operative question being: "which kinds of material beings, given their nature, are fit to exist

---

1. See his *Decreation*, 274.

in heaven?" A second kind of argument deploys by showing that some material beings are (or are not) required for the flourishing of human persons where their accidental reward is concerned. I will begin my examination of these two kinds of arguments, and how St. Thomas uses them to establish what sorts of nonhuman, nonartificial material beings exist in heaven, by discussing some of the principles from whence St. Thomas's arguments take their start.

Arguing about Nonhuman, Nonartificial Material Beings in Heaven: Principles

According to St. Thomas, God's providence extends in different ways to *perpetual* or *incorruptible* beings, on the one hand, and to *nonperpetual* or *corruptible* beings, on the other.[2] For God's providence is chiefly exercised toward that which is perpetual or incorruptible, while God's providence extends to nonperpetual or corruptible beings only insofar as their existence is ordered to that which exists perpetually or incorruptibly. Although human persons are corruptible (nonperpetual) in the sense that they can die, they are incorruptible and thus perpetual insofar as their souls are naturally immortal. Therefore, God's providence is exercised differently with respect to human persons than it is with respect to other corruptible beings, such as nonhuman living material things (i.e., nonhuman animals and plants).

As we have seen, St. Thomas distinguishes different ways in which beings can be perpetual or incorruptible. Some beings are naturally incorruptible: there is no sense in which they are corruptible other than God's being able to annihilate them. For example, angels and the heavenly bodies for St. Thomas are incorruptible in this way. Angels are naturally incorruptible as they are wholly immaterial substances. Though the heavenly bodies are composed of matter, each heavenly body is naturally incorruptible because (unlike sublunary material substances) it is composed of a kind of matter that is not in potency to a substantial form other than the one that that heavenly body naturally possesses.[3]

Other material substances are relatively incorruptible. Although the composite of human soul and matter is naturally corruptible, and

---

2. *ST* I, q. 113, a. 3, resp. See also *SCG* IV.97.3–4.
3. For discussion of, and texts from St. Thomas's works on, the different senses of incorruptibility, see chapter 10 above.

so composite human persons in the postlapsarian state before the resurrection can die, the human soul is naturally incorruptible. Indeed, insofar as the human soul is sufficient by itself to preserve the being of the human person, human persons *qua* human persons are naturally incorruptible. Now the quantitative parts that compose human bodies at and after the general resurrection are in and of themselves corruptible. But as we have seen, God confers on all human souls at the general resurrection a preternatural or supernatural disposition that keeps those quantitative parts from corrupting such that the resurrection body is incorruptible.

According to St. Thomas the elements—the fundamental kinds of physical entity—are also relatively incorruptible. St. Thomas sometimes says that, although the elements can be "corrupted in part," that is, individual *instances* of elemental substance-kinds can undergo corruption in this life, they are also incorruptible "according to the whole," that is, the element *kinds* are incorruptible by nature.[4] According to St. Thomas, the element kinds are incorruptible by nature because he thinks, with Aristotle, that if the planets were not in motion, then the four kinds of elements would exist purely and incorruptibly in four concentric rings, with earth at the middle, water on top of earth, air on top of water, and fire on top of air. But the motions of the heavens will cease in the next life, thinks St. Thomas.[5] Therefore, the four elements will exist as complete substances—and not simply as quantitative parts of human bodies—in the new heavens and the new earth as four concentric rings.

So God's providence extends in different ways to perpetual or incorruptible beings and to nonperpetual or corruptible beings. In another place, St. Thomas makes a distinction between God's exercise of providence with respect to intellectual creatures, such as angels and human persons, and his exercise of providence with respect to those things that are nonintellectual creatures, such as planets, nonhuman animals, plants, and minerals:

---

4. See, e.g., *In Sent* IV, d. 48, q. 2, aa. 4–5 (*ST Suppl.*, q. 91, aa. 4–5); *SCG* IV.97; *QDP*, q. 5, a. 7, resp.; *CT* I, chap. 170. Below, I evaluate and develop St. Thomas's views and arguments concerning which kinds of material beings exist in the next life in light of what we know by way of contemporary science.

5. See, e.g., *In Sent* IV, d. 43, q. 1, a. 3, q.c. 1; d. 47, q. 2, a. 2, q.c. 1, resp. (*ST Suppl.*, q. 74, a. 4, resp.); d. 48, q. 2, a. 2 (*ST Suppl.*, q. 91, a. 2); *SCG* IV.97.2; *QDP*, q. 5, a. 5; *CT* I, chap. 171; *In Jn* 6, lect. 5, nn. 939–40; *In Heb* 1, lect. 5, nn. 72–76.

The very way in which the intellectual [*intellectualis*] creature was made, according as it is master of its acts, demands providential care whereby this creature may provide for itself, on its own behalf; while the way in which other things were created, things which have no dominion over their acts, shows this fact, that they are cared for, not for their own sake, but as subordinated to others. That which is moved only by another being has the formal character of an instrument, but that which acts of itself has the essential character of a principal agent. Now, an instrument is not valued for its own sake, but as useful to a principal agent. Hence it must be that all the careful work that is devoted to instruments is actually done for the sake of the agent, as for an end, but what is done for the principal agent, either by himself or by another, is for his own sake, because he is the principal agent. Therefore, intellectual creatures are so controlled by God, as objects of care for their own sakes; while other creatures are subordinated, as it were, to the rational [*rationales*] creatures.[6]

In still other places,[7] we find St. Thomas distinguishing between those creatures that are perpetual or incorruptible in and of themselves, and those creatures that will be made perpetual or incorruptible for the sake of those creatures that are perpetual or incorruptible in themselves. St. Thomas notes that St. Paul teaches about human persons "this corruptible must put on incorruption, and this mortal must put on immortality" (1 Cor 15:53).[8] In addition, all of creation will be similarly changed in light of the change in human persons: "the creature also itself shall be delivered from the servitude of corruption, into the liberty of the glory of the children of God" (Rom 8:21).[9] Therefore, given both that God created nonperpetual and nonintellectual creatures to serve the needs of intellectual creatures, such as human persons,[10] and the medieval maxim *grace perfects nature, it does not destroy it*,[11] there are material beings that exist in heaven which, though corruptible in and of themselves, are *in some manner* made incorruptible insofar as they

---

6. *SCG* III.112 (trans. Bourke, 2:115). See also *CT* I, chap. 148.
7. See, e.g., *In Sent* IV, d. 48, q. 2, a. 5, resp. (*ST Suppl.*, q. 91, a. 5, resp.) and *SCG* IV.97.
8. *ST Suppl.*, q. 91, a. 5, resp. (trans. English Dominicans, 2944–45; *In Sent* IV, d. 48, q. 2, a. 5, resp.).
9. See, e.g., *SCG* IV.97.1 (trans. O'Neil, 347). See also *In Sent* IV, d. 48, q. 2, a. 1, ad 5 (*ST Suppl.*, q. 91, a. 1, ad 5) and *CT* I, chap. 169. Concerning the testimony of the apostles on the difference between this world and the next life, St. Thomas also cites 1 Cor 7:31: "the fashion of this world passeth away." See, e.g., *SCG* IV.97 (trans. O'Neil, 347–48) and Rv 10:9: "[in the next life] time shall be no longer."
10. See, e.g., *In Sent* IV, d. 47, q. 2, a. 1, q.c. 1, resp. (*ST Suppl.*, q. 74, a. 1, resp.); d. 48, q. 2, a. 1, resp. and ad 5 (*ST Suppl.*, q. 91, a. 1, resp. and ad 5); q. 2, a. 3, resp. (*ST Suppl.*, q. 91, a. 3, resp.); q. 2, a. 5, resp. (*ST Suppl.*, q. 91, a. 5, resp.); *SCG* IV.97; *CT* I, chaps. 148 and 170.
11. See, e.g., *ST* I, q. 1, a. 8, ad 2.

serve as instrumental goods for the new incorruptible and immortal life of human persons.[12]

For example, human persons are incorruptible in and of themselves insofar as they have immortal souls. But instances of the kinds *flesh* and *blood* are not incorruptible in themselves. As human persons after the resurrection have human bodies, and human bodies are composed of flesh and blood, instances of the kinds *flesh* and *blood* exist perpetually and incorruptibly in heaven insofar as they are parts of the incorruptible bodies of human persons. On the other hand, if there are some nonperpetual creatures that do not serve a necessary purpose for human persons in an incorruptible life, then those creatures will not exist in the next life. Therefore, we can also distinguish those creatures, nonperpetual in themselves, that nonetheless serve a purpose for human persons in their immortal and incorruptible life (in the next life), and so exist perpetually in heaven insofar as they serve a purpose for perpetual human life in heaven, and those creatures, nonperpetual in themselves, that do not serve such a purpose in the next life and so do not exist in the next life.

The texts that I have examined provide principles that guide St. Thomas's argumentation with respect to the kinds of material beings that populate heaven. Because God shows particular providential care for perpetual or intellectual creatures, some of whom, namely, human persons, require certain nonhuman material beings for their accidental reward, there will be nonhuman material beings in heaven insofar as they too are perpetual by nature or because they serve some need of human persons in heaven. Indeed, insofar as certain kinds of material beings that are nonintellectual and nonperpetual exist in heaven for the sake of human persons, they will themselves be renewed by being prevented, by grace, from corrupting; they will become (parts of) a "new heavens and a new earth."

St. Thomas on Nonliving, Nonartificial Beings in the Next Life

Given St. Thomas's theological principles, what sorts of nonliving beings will exist in the next life? For one, there is the *empyrean heaven*,

---

12. Why not angels too? Because they are wholly immaterial creatures and in no way are served by the material world.

or a place "above all the heavens" (Ephesians 4:10).[13] For St. Thomas, the empyrean heaven, or some place like it, is the highest (most perfect) corporeal place, that place which is beyond motion and fully luminous.[14] Such a place is the fitting and proper place of the blessed angels in the sense that "the angels were created in a corporeal place, not as if depending upon a body either as to their existence or as to their being made.... [but] in order to show their relationship to corporeal nature, and that they are by their power in touch with bodies."[15]

As St. Thomas notes, despite their different views on the empyrean heaven, St. Basil the Great (330–79), the Venerable Bede (672/73–735), and Strabus (ca. 808–49) all agree that the empyrean heaven is also the place of beatified human persons.[16] As St. Thomas himself argues regarding the empyrean heaven:

In the reward to come a two-fold glory is looked for, spiritual and corporeal, not only in the human body to be glorified, but in the whole world which is to be made new. Now the spiritual glory began with the beginning of the world, in the blessedness of the angels, equality with whom is promised to the saints. It was fitting, then, that even from the beginning, there should be made some beginning of bodily glory in something corporeal, free at the very outset from the servitude of corruption and change, and wholly luminous, even as the whole bodily creation, after the Resurrection, is expected to be. So, then, that heaven is called the empyrean, i.e., fiery, not from its heat, but from its brightness.[17]

Indeed, in St. Thomas's view, the empyrean heaven, or a place "above all the heavens," is the proper or fitting place for Jesus in his human nature after his ascension, the Virgin Mary after her assumption, and all blessed human persons, both before and after the general resurrection.[18] Nonetheless, it will not diminish the glory of the elect—in fact, in a way it will conduce to their glory—if they are sometimes present in other places, for example, the "new heavens and the new earth."[19]

How do we know about the empyrean heaven? St. Thomas points out

---

13. Recall that for St. Thomas, *place* in the sense of *where* is one of the ten categories of being (see, e.g., *Expositio Libri Physicorum* [hereafter *In Phys*] V, lect. 5, n. 322).
14. See, e.g., *ST* I, q. 61, a. 4; q. 66, a. 3; q. 68, a. 4, resp.; q. 102, a. 2, ad 1.
15. *ST* I, q. 61, a. 4, ad 1 (trans. English Dominicans, 304).
16. *ST* I, q. 66, a. 3, resp.
17. Ibid. (trans. English Dominicans, 332).
18. See, e.g., *In Sent* III, d. 22, q. 3, a. 1, s.c. and resp.; a. 3, q.c. 1, ad 1; *ST Suppl.*, q. 69, a. 7, ad 10; *SCG* IV.87.1; *In Eph* 4, lect. 3, n. 209; *ST* I, q. 66, a. 3, resp.; q. 102, a. 2, ad 1; I-II, q. 4, a. 7, ad 3; III, q. 57, a. 1, ad 2; aa. 4–5; *In SA*; *CSA*, a. 6.
19. See, e.g., *In Sent* IV, d. 44, q. 3, a. 3, ad 8 (*ST Suppl.*, q. 70, a. 3, ad 8).

that, given its nature, we cannot know about it by way of philosophical or scientific inquiry, for it is not visible to us from earth.[20] Indeed, talk of the empyrean heaven as the fitting place of the blessed, St. Thomas notes, "rests only on the authority of Strabus and Bede, and also of Basil."[21] Nonetheless, whether or not we call it the empyrean heaven, St. Thomas argues based on Ephesians 4:10 there is an abode of the blessed, a place "above all the heavens," one that is incorruptible, immutable, and invisible to us from earth in this life.[22]

In addition to the empyrean heaven, St. Thomas also thinks there will be celestial objects in the next life, such as planets and stars, which celestial objects undergo accidental changes in this life.[23] St. Thomas has a number of arguments for this view. First, there are the scriptures that speak of the next world such that it includes "a new heavens and a new earth," such as Isaiah 65:17 ("For I am about to create new heavens and a new earth; the former things shall not be remembered or come to mind") and Revelation 21:1 ("Then I saw a new heaven and a new earth; for the first heaven and the first earth had passed away").[24] At face value, these scriptures teach not only that the earth and some other celestial objects exist in heaven, but also that such objects somehow share in the glory of heaven, that is, they, like human persons and angels in heaven, exist in the next life as "new creatures."[25]

In a second argument, St. Thomas shows that it follows from the principle that God's providence extends especially to perpetual substances that the planets and other celestial objects visible to us in this life exist in heaven. For according to St. Thomas's cosmology, the planets and other heavenly bodies are perpetual substances. But those substances that are perpetual or have an aptitude for being perpetual will remain in heaven. Therefore, the planets and other celestial objects visible to us in this life exist in heaven.[26]

---

20. See, e.g., *In Sent* II, d. 2, q. 2, a. 1, resp.

21. *ST* I, q. 66, a. 3, resp. (trans. English Dominicans, 332).

22. See, e.g., *In Sent* II, d. 2, q. 2, a. 1, resp.; III, d. 22, q. 3, a. 1, s.c. and resp.; a. 3, q.c. 1, ad 1; *SCG* IV.87.1; *In Eph* 4, lect. 3, n. 209; *ST* I, q. 66, a. 3, resp.; q. 102, a. 2, ad 1; *ST* I-II, q. 4, a. 7, ad 3; *In SA*; *ST* III, q. 57, a. 1, ad 2; aa. 4–5; *CSA*, a. 6.

23. See, e.g., *In Sent* IV, d. 47, q. 2, a. 2, q.c. 1, resp. (*ST Suppl.*, q. 74, a. 4, resp.); d. 48, q. 2, a. 1 (*ST Suppl.*, q. 91, a. 1); *SCG* IV.97; *CT* I, chap. 170.

24. See, e.g., *In Sent* IV, d. 48, q. 2, a. 1, s.c. (*ST Suppl.*, q. 91, a. 1, s.c.); *SCG* IV.97.8 (note that St. Thomas brings the *SCG* to a close by citing these two verses) and *CT* I, chap. 169.

25. See also *In Sent* IV, d. 47, q. 2, a. 1, q.c. 1 (*ST Suppl.*, q. 74, a. 1).

26. See, e.g., *In Sent* IV, d. 48, q. 2, aa. 4–5 (*ST Suppl.*, q. 91, aa. 4–5); *SCG* IV.97; *QDP*, q. 5, a. 7,

A third argument begins with the assumption that likeness is the reason for love. But human persons have a likeness to the universe as a whole, and this is why the human person is called "a little world." Therefore, human persons naturally love the universe as a whole and wish it well. Therefore, it is an aspect of the accidental reward that the universe as a whole, like human persons, be renewed. But the heavenly bodies are essential parts of the universe as a whole. Therefore, the new heavens and the new earth include heavenly bodies.[27]

Here is a fourth argument that the visible heavens and the earth will (exist and) be renewed in the next life.[28] Material substances were made for the sake of human persons, and this for two reasons: (a) to provide for their bodily needs, such as food, drink, and shelter, and (b) to help them know the existence and nature of God. St. Thomas cites, on this score, Romans 1:20: "Ever since the creation of the world his eternal power and divine nature, invisible though they are, have been understood and seen through the things he has made." But glorified human persons will not need material substances for reason (a), as their bodies are impassible, immortal, and incorruptible. In addition, glorified human persons will know the existence and nature of God in the most intimate, clear, and certain manner possible in enjoying the beatific vision. So material substances are not *antecedently* necessary for perfect human happiness.[29] That being said, as we have seen, the beatified soul so configures matter at and after the general resurrection that human bodies in heaven come to participate in the soul's beatific vision to the extent that they are able. But one cannot see God directly with the bodily eye. Therefore, in order that the sense faculties can participate in the beatific vision in a fitting manner, the material substances that can be sensed by way of the glorified senses will be glorified such that the saints can sense, especially *see* with the bodily eye, with manifest clarity and certainty that those material substances are the effects of the Godhead. As St. Thomas notes, this will chiefly occur in the flesh of Christ, but also in the flesh of the saints, and in the new heavens and the new earth.[30]

---

resp.; *CT* I, chap. 170. For a text where St. Thomas entertains the possibility that the visible heavenly bodies are by nature corruptible, see *In Mt* 24, lect. 3, n. 1959.

27. See, e.g., *In Sent* IV, d. 48, q. 2, a. 1, s.c. (*ST Suppl.*, q. 91, a. 1, s.c.).

28. See, e.g., *In Sent* IV, d. 48, q. 2, a. 1, resp. (*ST Suppl.*, q. 91, a. 1, resp.).

29. For more on the notion that *x* pertains to, or is necessary for, *y antecedently*, see chapter 5 above.

30. See, e.g., *In Sent* IV, d. 48, q. 2, a. 1, resp. (*ST Suppl.*, q. 91, a. 1, resp.); q. 2, a. 3, resp. (*ST*

Here is a fifth argument: it is fitting that whatever has an essential relationship to the generation of human persons in this life should exist in the new heavens and the new earth. Just as the elements are material causes of human bodies in this life, so the heavenly bodies, such as the sun, are among the efficient causes of human bodies.[31] Therefore, it is fitting that the heavenly bodies are among the things that exist in the new heavens and the new earth.[32]

A sixth argument begins from the assumption that human persons are part of the material universe. As human persons remain in the next life and a part would not be perfect if a whole to which it belonged did not remain, the material universe as a whole will exist in the next life. But in the material universe, some parts are essential, whereas others simply contribute to the beauty and adornment of the material universe insofar as it is corruptible. The integrity of the whole does not require the nonessential parts but only the essential parts. But the planets (and the elements) are among the essential parts of the material universe, as the whole world machine (*tota mundi machina*) consists of these.[33]

Other than glorified celestial beings, what other sort of nonartificial material things will exist in the new heavens and the new earth according to St. Thomas? Recall St. Thomas's principles: those things exist in heaven that are intellectual or perpetual or are necessary to serve the needs of glorified human persons. Therefore, St. Thomas thinks that the fundamental material bodies that he calls *elements*, for example, instances of earth, air, fire, and water, will exist in the new heavens and the new earth, and this for two reasons. First, the elements are parts of the compound nonliving material bodies that make up glorified human bodies (e.g., flesh, blood, bone, hair, etc.), and so the elements will at least exist by power (*virtute*) as that which make up the compound nonliving bodies that exist as the quantitative parts of glorified bod-

---

Suppl., q. 91, a. 3, resp.); d. 49, q. 2, a. 2 (*ST Suppl.*, q. 92, a. 2); *SCG* IV.97; *CT* I, chap. 170; *ST* I, q. 12, a. 3, ad 2.

31. Recall also that St. Thomas thinks that the motion of the heavenly bodies is an efficient cause of the existence of mixed bodies, including the human body and those mixed bodies that compose human bodies, in this life.

32. See, e.g., *CT* I, chap. 170.

33. See, e.g., *QDP*, q. 5, a. 7, resp., and *CT* I, chap. 170. Because minerals, plants, and nonhuman animals only exist because the heavens are in motion, these kinds of material substances merely contribute to the beauty and adornment of the material universe insofar as it is corruptible; for other arguments that there will be no minerals, plants, or nonhuman animals in the new heavens and the new earth, see below.

ies.[34] Second, recall also that, although elemental substances can be "corrupted in part," that is, individual *instances* of elemental substance-kinds can undergo corruption in this life, elemental substances are incorruptible "according to the whole," that is, each one of the elemental substance *kinds* is incorruptible by nature.[35]

As already mentioned, there will be nonliving compounds or mixed bodies (e.g., bone, flesh, and blood) in the next life insofar as these things exist as quantitative *parts* of the glorified human body. But St. Thomas argues in many places that mixed bodies will not exist in the new heavens and the new earth as *substances*.[36] This last claim requires a bit of explanation.

Following Aristotle's anti-reductionist, anti-atomist metaphysic of material objects, St. Thomas thinks that substances are not composed of substances. The idea here is that a material substance is a unified being of the highest order. A material object composed of substances is not a material substance but rather a mere collection or aggregate or heap of material substances. Although collections, aggregates, and heaps have a degree of unity, they do not enjoy the high degree of unity and being enjoyed by material substances.[37] According to St. Thomas, although mixed bodies exist as quantitative parts of the glorified bodies of the saints, they do not exist as substances in heaven.[38]

Why will there be no substantial instances of minerals or mixed bodies in the new heavens and the new earth according to St. Thomas? Such beings are not perpetual in any sense or necessary for the good of human persons in the new heavens and the new earth. Whereas the elements can exist as substances apart from the motion of the heavens, the mixed bodies exist only insofar as the heavens are in motion. But, according to St. Thomas, the heavenly motions will cease in the next life. In addition, human persons do not require the existence of the mixed bodies

---

34. See chapter 9, note 5 above.
35. See, e.g., *In Sent* IV, d. 48, q. 2, aa. 4–5 (*ST Suppl.*, q. 91, aa. 4–5); *SCG* IV.97; *QDP*, q. 5, a. 7, resp.; *CT* I, chap. 170.
36. See, e.g., *In Sent* IV, d. 47, q. 2, a. 1, q.c. 1, ad 3 (*ST Suppl.*, q. 74, a. 1, ad 3); d. 48, q. 2, a. 5, resp. (*ST Suppl.*, q. 91, a. 5, resp.); *SCG* IV.97; *CT* I, chap. 170.
37. For texts on substances and mixed bodies (or compound nonliving substances) in St. Thomas, see my *Aquinas and the Ship of Theseus*, 87–94.
38. For discussion of St. Thomas on different kinds of parts, see chapter 9 above, the section on St. Thomas's philosophical anthropology. For more detailed discussion of, and texts in, St. Thomas on parts, see my *Aquinas and the Ship of Theseus*, 68–112.

as substances for their accidental reward. Therefore, the mixed bodies *as substances* will not exist in the new heavens and the new earth.[39]

Evaluation and Development of St. Thomas's Thought on Nonliving, Nonartificial Beings in the Next Life

What should we say about St. Thomas's positions and arguments with respect to heavenly beings in the next life, especially in light of contemporary science? One might think that modern cosmology refutes the idea of the empyrean heaven. It does not. As we have seen, St. Thomas thinks that the empyrean is a place beyond change, and so not visible to us from earth. Although we obviously have a very different view of the universe than the medievals and can see much farther into the universe then they could, there surely are places in it we shall never see from earth in this life. Call *the empyrean heaven*, then, that part of the physical universe that (a) is beyond the earth's atmosphere, (b) cannot be sensed by us in this life, even with the most sophisticated instruments we will ever develop (the reasons for this being limited only by one's imagination), (c) is from the beginning of creation free of corruption, thereby anticipating the incorruptibility of "the new heavens and the new earth," and (d) is the proper, if not necessary, abode of the blessed angels, Jesus in his human nature, the Virgin Mary, and all the saints, both before and after the general resurrection.

What of St. Thomas's arguments regarding those heavenly bodies we can observe in this life? For example, we presumably cannot argue, as St. Thomas does, for the existence of the heavenly bodies in the next life in virtue of their natural incorruptibility. Consider, for example, St. Thomas's second argument above that the heavenly bodies exist in the new heavens and the new earth. It apparently will not work as it stands, given contemporary physics.[40] Nonetheless, we might think that Thomas's other arguments for the existence of the heavenly bodies in the next life are plausible.

We might wonder, however, whether the arguments for the existence of the heavenly bodies in the next life that do not mention the perpetu-

---

39. See, e.g., *In Sent* IV, d. 47, q. 2, a. 1, q.c. 1, ad 3 (*ST Suppl.*, q. 74, a. 1, ad 3), and *In Sent* IV, d. 48, q. 2, a. 5, resp. (*ST Suppl.*, q. 91, a. 5, resp.).

40. However, see some of the arguments in chapter 10 above on possible causes of the incorruptibility of next-worldly bodies, even given contemporary physics.

ity of the heavenly bodies—all the arguments save the second—are really meant to deploy independently of the assumption that the heavenly bodies are perpetual. For, given the importance that St. Thomas attributes to a thing's being perpetual or incorruptible in some sense for its existing in the next life, it seems reasonable to assume they do not. In that case, we might think that St. Thomas's second argument argues from the assumption that the incorruptibility of the heavenly bodies is a *sufficient* condition for their existence in the next life. His other arguments suppose, if only for the sake of argument, that the incorruptibility of the heavenly bodies is a *necessary but not a sufficient condition* for their existence in the next life. In that case, St. Thomas's other arguments assume that the incorruptibility of the heavenly bodies, when coupled with other truths about the heavenly bodies, provide jointly sufficient conditions for the existence of the heavenly bodies in the next life. In showing that these jointly sufficient conditions obtain, St. Thomas thereby concludes by such arguments that the heavenly bodies exist in the next life.

For example, consider St. Thomas's fifth argument that the heavenly bodies exist in the next life, an argument that trades on the assumption that whatever plays an essential role in the generation of human persons in this life will fittingly exist in the next. Given that the heavenly bodies *can* exist in the next life, as they are by nature perpetual, by hypothesis such an argument is trying to show the heavenly bodies *do* exist in the next life, as the heavenly bodies are not only perpetual, but play an essential role in the generation of human persons in this life.

That being said, we have seen that St. Thomas thinks there is a reason that the heavenly bodies visible to us in this life exist in the next life besides their incorruptibility: they enable the glorified bodies of human persons to participate in the beatific vision insofar as the glory and wisdom of God in creating the new heavens and the new earth is immediately evident to human persons by way of their sense faculties. As human persons make an active use of their sense faculties in the next life, they need to have something to sense. But the glorified body's participation in the beatific vision does not seem to be a *sufficient* condition for nonhuman material substances existing in the next life for St. Thomas, as such substances also have to be by nature perpetual. Given a contemporary physics that has it that heavenly bodies in this life are not by nature perpetual, and St. Thomas's plausible assumption that being perpetual in some sense is a necessary condition for existing in the next life, none of St. Thomas's arguments that heavenly bodies exist in the next life are sound.[41]

On the other hand, could God not do for stars and planets—and some other nonliving material substances—what he does for human bodies in the next life, namely, confer on such objects a non-natural disposition that enables them to take on the quality of being incorruptible? Perhaps not. For God's causing resurrection bodies to be incorruptible such that those bodies themselves have the intrinsic quality of being incorruptible requires that there be *something* about those bodies that gives them an aptness for incorruptibility. Of course, the aptness of human bodies for incorruptibility is grounded in the natural immortality of human souls. We might think with St. Thomas that, if there is nothing about this-worldly stars, planets, and other nonliving material objects themselves that makes them apt to be incorruptible, then they cannot take on the intrinsic quality of being incorruptible. And in that case, it would not make sense to think that heavenly bodies exist in the next life.

But perhaps we can say that the stars, planets, and nonliving material substances of the new heavens and the new earth have their incorruptibility in a manner similar to that by which Adam and Eve were made preternaturally immortal in Eden,[42] namely, by God as extrinsic principle preserving their bodies from corruption. However, according to St. Thomas, it would not be fitting for a substance to be kept perpetually, merely by extrinsic principle, in a state such that the substance's corruptible nature is not expressed.[43] Adam and Eve's *temporarily* being preserved as immortal in the state of innocence simply by God's power as extrinsic principle is one thing, but keeping substances that are naturally corruptible *perpetually* in a state of incorruptibility by extrinsic prin-

---

41. Indeed, if we assume that St. Thomas's arguments for the existence of the heavenly bodies in the next life (other than the second) deploy independently of the assumption that the heavenly bodies are in some sense incorruptible, then those arguments could be used to argue for the existence of things that are by nature corruptible, e.g., nonhuman animals and plants. For example, St. Thomas's fourth argument could be reformulated to argue for such a conclusion. Because St. Thomas rejects the view that nonhuman animals and plants exist in the next life, this gives us reason to think that St. Thomas's arguments for the existence of the heavenly bodies do not deploy independently of the assumption that the heavenly bodies are by nature perpetual.

42. See, e.g., *ST* I, q. 97, a. 1. See chapter 10 above for a detailed comparison of the impassibility of glorified bodies, the incorruptibility of resurrection bodies *qua* resurrection bodies, and Adam and Eve's preternatural gift of immortality in the state of innocence.

43. See, e.g., *QDP*, q. 5, a. 9, resp.

ciple is quite another. Note that, according to St. Thomas, the state of innocence would not have been perpetual in any case—had Adam and Eve and their progeny not sinned, they would have eventually been translated to heaven.[44] Therefore, stars, planets, and nonliving substances do not perpetually exist in heaven merely by an extrinsic principle, given St. Thomas's principles.[45]

Of course, God could create a *new* heavens and earth such that these material objects are numerically different from any material objects in this life. Such material objects would be, metaphysically speaking, more like celestial objects as Aristotle understands them, that is, they would be incorruptible substances. In that case, we would have the following:

(1) The stars, planets, and earth of the next life are new creations in the sense of being numerically distinct from the stars, planets, and earth of this life.

But is (1) plausible? Scripture does teach there will be "a new heavens and a new earth."[46] However, Catholic Christian tradition also speaks about a *restoration* of the world,[47] which suggests, if it does not entail, the falsity of (1), for example, that the sun in the next life is numerically and thus specifically identical to the sun in this life. Indeed, St. Thomas himself interprets such a renewal of the world to mean that the heavenly bodies are specifically—so they can be numerically—the same as heavenly bodies in this life.[48]

So it seems as if we have a new problem on our hands. On the one hand, it seems as if whatever exists at and after the general resurrection has to be in some sense perpetual. On the other hand, contemporary physics suggests that the heavenly bodies are not in any sense perpetual. Therefore, the heavenly bodies in this life do not exist in the next life. However, according to scripture and tradition, there will be "a new heavens and a new earth." Furthermore, Catholic Christian tradition speaks of the new heavens and the new earth such that the heavenly bodies are *restored*, not

---

44. See, e.g., *QDV*, q. 18, a. 1, ad 6.
45. Someone might think that the operative principle at play here is a principle of St. Thomas's Aristotelian physics. Rather, the operative principle is theological. For God to make a substance S perpetual merely by an extrinsic principle, where S is in no sense perpetual would be for God to set aside S's nature, rather than perfecting it.
46. See, e.g., Is 65:17, 22; 2 Pt 3:13; Rv 21:1.
47. See, e.g., Ott, *Fundamentals of Catholic Dogma*, 495–96.
48. See, e.g., *In Sent* IV, d. 48, q. 2, a. 1, resp. (*ST Suppl.*, q. 91, a. 1, resp.). See also *SCG* IV.97.7 and *CT* I, chap. 169.

replaced. Now, it seems that if object x is in some sense perpetual and object y is in no sense perpetual, then x and y are not specifically, and so not numerically, identical. Therefore, if the heavenly bodies in the next life are in some sense perpetual, then the heavenly bodies in this life are not *restored* in the next life, but *replaced* by specifically, and thus numerically distinct, heavenly bodies. Therefore, we have an apparent contradiction within Catholic Christian tradition regarding the new heavens and the new earth.

Perhaps this problem could be solved by supposing that *all* material substances have an *obediential potency* for incorruptibility, that is, an aptness for incorruptibility unactualized in this life but actualized, perhaps by a miracle, in the next.[49] Although St. Thomas himself does not take up this strategy of making sense of the Catholic belief in "the new heavens and the new earth," he does mention the notion of an *obediential potency* in a passage from *ST* III. The context is his discussion of Christ's knowledge by his human soul, and more specifically, his suggestion that Christ in this life, like the angels and the saints in heaven, has infused knowledge. Here is the passage:

> Now it must be borne in mind that in the human soul, as in every creature, there is a double passive power: one in comparison with a natural agent; the other in comparison with the first agent [i.e., God], which can reduce any creature to a higher act than a natural agent can reduce it, and this is usually called the obediential power [*potentia obedientiae*] of a creature.[50]

Notice that St. Thomas states that this passive power, which he calls the obediential power, is a power to receive a higher act from God, and is common to "every creature" (*qualibet creatura*).

In another text, St. Thomas suggests that the world's future renewal existed in the works of the six days of creation as an obediential potency (*potentia obedientiae*).[51] Although St. Thomas does not help himself to using the notion of obediential potency of all creatures to receive grace in order to defend the perpetuity of a restored new heavens and the new earth, perhaps we can.[52]

---

49. Mark Spencer offered this interesting and helpful suggestion.
50. *ST* III, q. 11, a. 1, resp. (trans. English Dominicans, 2084). For other places where St. Thomas speaks about *obediential powers*, see, e.g., *In Sent* II, d. 15, q. 3, a. 1, ad 8; d. 19, q. 1, a. 5, resp.; III, d. 2, q. 1, a. 1, q.c. 3, resp.; q. 2, a. 2, q.c. 3, resp.; IV, d. 11, q. 1, a. 3, q.c. 3, ad 3; d. 17, q. 1, a. 5, q.c. 1, ad 1; d. 48, q. 2, a. 1, ad 3 (*ST Suppl.*, q. 91, a. 1, ad 3); *QDV*, q. 8, a. 12, ad 4; q. 12, a. 3, ad 18; q. 29, a. 3, ad 3; *QDP*, q. 6, a. 1, ad 18.
51. *In Sent* IV, d. 48, q. 2, a. 1, ad 3 (*ST Suppl.*, q. 91, a. 1, ad 3).
52. Why did St. Thomas not make use of the notion of obediential potency to explain the

If we do take *this* hypothesis seriously, then I will need to revise slightly St. Thomas's way of distinguishing between Adam's incorruptibility in Eden and the incorruptibility of human persons at and after the general resurrection. This is because, by hypothesis, there is an intrinsic principle of incorruptibility in all creatures, namely, an obediential potency to receive an actual grace such that, when activated by God, such creatures are made actually perpetual. But, as we have seen, St. Thomas states that Adam's incorruptibility *qua* composite of soul and matter in Eden was brought about merely by extrinsic principle, whereas the incorruptibility of human persons *qua* composite of soul and matter at and after the general resurrection is caused by an intrinsic principle, namely, a preternatural or supernatural disposition in the soul.

Let us say, then, that all *nonintellectual* material substances, such as the sun and the earth, have an obediential potency for incorruptibility in the sense that they naturally have a passive potency to receive a graced disposition so as to be made incorruptible at and after the resurrection. As for the incorruptibility *qua* composite of soul and matter enjoyed by Adam and Eve in the state of innocence, because they are *intellectual* creatures, they were created with an obediential potency to receive from God a preternatural disposition so as to remain incorruptible even *in this life*. Nonetheless, their keeping this kind of preternatural disposition was contingent upon their remaining obedient to God, which they had the freedom not to do. In contrast to the preternatural incorruptibility *qua* composite of soul and matter given to Adam and Eve in the state of innocence, which could be (and was) lost, both the preternatural disposition given to all human persons at the general resurrection in virtue of the resurrection of Christ and the supernatural disposition given to all the blessed in virtue of their having the beatific vision are *permanent* dispositions, that is, they cannot be lost.

On St. Thomas's Arguments Regarding Fundamental Physical Entities in the Next Life

We might wonder how St. Thomas's theological and philosophical principles apply to the existence of fundamental physical entities in the

---

perpetuity of the new heavens and the new earth? Perhaps he saw no need to do so insofar as the best physics of the time—Aristotle's—posited that the heavenly bodies are actually perpetual by nature.

new heavens and the new earth, given different interpretations of contemporary physics. Where we might think it clear that stars and planets are not perpetual by nature, it is perhaps less clear what to say on this score about fundamental physical entities. For St. Thomas, the elements are perpetual (according to the whole) because there being instances of element-kinds in existence is not, unlike the instances of mixed body-kinds, contingent upon the motion of the heavens. Presumably, if we did think that instances of the fundamental particle-kinds are perpetual (according to the whole), we would give a very different kind of explanation for it. But perhaps the fundamental physical entities, whatever they are, do not exist as *substances* in and of themselves in the next life (or in this life). Those things being said, however we think about the fundamental physical entities, insofar as glorified bodies are human bodies and human bodies are composed of such entities, they at least exist in the next life as the quantitative parts of human bodies and any other compound material substances that exist in the next life.[53]

St. Thomas on Nonhuman Animals and Plants in the Next Life

According to St. Thomas, there will be no nonhuman animals or plants in the new heavens and the new earth.[54] He has a number of arguments across his corpus for this view. A first argument begins with the assumption that, if there are nonhuman animals or plants in the new heavens and the new earth, then either every single nonhuman animal or plant exists there—just as every single human person exists there—or else only some nonhuman animals and plants exist in the next life. However, if all nonhuman animals and plants exist in the next life, then they exist there for the same reason that human persons do, namely, in virtue of having an immortal soul. But the souls of nonhuman animals and plants come to nothing at their deaths. Therefore, it is not the case that every single animal and plant exists in heaven. However, if it is not the case that every single animal and plant exists in heaven, then, as there is no reason for some to remain rather than others, it seems that none remain. Furthermore, the state of the world at the resurrection remains as

---

53. This also goes for nonfundamental, nonliving, nonartificial, noncelestial material entities, e.g., instances of blood, bone, flesh, gold, etc.

54. See, e.g., *In Sent* IV, d. 48, q. 2, a. 5, resp. (*ST Suppl.*, q. 91, a. 5, resp.); *SCG* IV.97; *CTI*, chap. 170.

it is forever. Therefore, there are no—and never will be any—nonhuman animals and plants in heaven.[55]

In a second argument, St. Thomas notes that, if nonhuman animals and plants exist in heaven, their species have to be perpetuated. But the species of wholly corruptible things are perpetuated partly by the movement of the heavens. Nonhuman animals and plants are wholly corruptible things. Therefore, the species of nonhuman animals and plants are partly perpetuated by the movement of the heavens. But the movement of the heavens will cease in the next life.[56] Therefore, the species of nonhuman animals and plants are not perpetuated in the next life. Therefore, there are no nonhuman animals and plants in heaven.[57]

Here is a third argument. If nonhuman animals and plants exist in the next life, then species of nonhuman animal and plants serve the needs of human persons in the next life. However, the species of nonhuman animal and plants serve the needs of human persons in this life only as sources of shelter, food, and clothing. But human persons do not need plants and nonhuman animals for these reasons in the new heavens and the new earth, the resurrected bodies of human persons being incorruptible. Therefore, it is not the case that species of nonhuman animal and plants serve the needs of human persons in the next life. And so it follows that nonhuman animals and plants do not exist in the next life.[58]

A fourth argument begins from the assumption that the renewal of the heavens and the earth is for the sake of human persons in heaven. But, as 1 Corinthians 15:33 points out, "This corruptible must put on incorruption, and this mortal must put on immortality,"[59] that is, the corruptible in human persons ceases (to dominate) after the general resurrection and human persons then live an incorruptible and immortal life. Therefore, anything that does not partake of the incorruptible does not exist in heaven. But nonhuman animals and plants are corruptible with respect to their matter and their souls are not naturally immortal. Therefore, nonhuman animals and plants do not exist in the new heavens and the new earth.[60]

---

55. See, e.g., *In Sent* IV, d. 48, q. 2, a. 5, s.c. (*ST Suppl.*, q. 91, a. 5, s.c.).
56. See, e.g., *In Sent* IV, d. 47, q. 2, a. 1, q.c. 1, ad 3 (*ST Suppl.*, q. 74, a. 1, ad 3); d. 48, q. 2, a. 5, resp. (*ST Suppl.*, q. 91, a. 5, resp.); *SCG* IV.97.1–2; *CT* I, chap. 171.
57. See, e.g., *In Sent* IV, d. 48, q. 2, a. 5, s.c. (*ST Suppl.*, q. 91, a. 5, s.c.), and *QDP*, q. 5, a. 9, resp.
58. See ibid. and *CT* I, chap. 170.
59. *ST Suppl.*, q. 91, a. 5, resp. (trans. English Dominicans, 2944–45; *In Sent* IV, d. 48, q. 2, a. 5, resp.).
60. See, e.g., *In Sent* IV, d. 48, q. 2, a. 5, resp. (*ST Suppl.*, q. 91, a. 5, resp.).

A fifth argument is as follows. Only those kinds of things that are perpetual (or incorruptible) or those kinds that have an aptitude for perpetuity (or incorruptibility) exist in heaven. According to St. Thomas, a kind of substance is perpetual or has an aptitude for perpetuity if it has a part that is incorruptible (St. Thomas uses the expression "incorruptible according to part" to cover these kinds) or it is "incorruptible as a whole," that is, that substance-kind always has some instances existing, whether the heavens are in motion or no. For example, according to St. Thomas, each of the planets is incorruptible in whole and in part, human persons are incorruptible according to part insofar as they have immortal souls, and the elements are incorruptible according to the whole, but not according to the part, as individual instances of elemental kinds can be corrupted, although some instances of the elemental kinds naturally exist in any case. But nonhuman animal kinds and plant kinds are incorruptible neither according to the whole, as their existence depends upon the motion of the heavens, which ceases in the next life, nor according to the part, as their souls are not naturally immortal and their matter is corruptible. Therefore, there are no nonhuman animals or plants in heaven.[61] St. Thomas reads St. Paul as teaching this in 1 Corinthians 7:31: "The fashion of this world passeth away."[62]

Sixth, nonhuman animals and plants have matter that consists of contraries and so is by nature corruptible. Furthermore, their forms are by nature corruptible. Therefore, if nonhuman animals and plants exist forever in heaven, then it would be due merely to an extrinsic principle acting perpetually to keep nonhuman animals and plants from corrupting. But it is not fitting to keep a corruptible nature perpetually from corrupting merely by an extrinsic principle. Therefore, nonhuman animals and plants do not exist in heaven.[63]

A seventh argument is similar to an argument I examined above for why there are planets and elements in heaven, but no mixed bodies. The purpose of nonhuman animals and plants is twofold. One purpose is, as we have seen, the maintenance of the human species in this life. But another purpose is the completion of the universe. With respect to the completion of the material universe, some parts are essential, that is, those parts that complete the material universe in an absolute sense, for

---

61. See, e.g., *SCG* IV.97.4–5 and *CT* I, chap. 170.
62. *SCG* IV.97.5 (trans. O'Neil, 348).
63. See, e.g., *QDP*, q. 5, a. 9, resp.

they exist in the material universe whether or not the heavens are in motion, such as heavenly bodies, elements, and human persons, whereas others are accidental, that is, those parts that exist in the material universe only when the heavenly bodies are in motion, such as mixed bodies, animals, and plants. The perfection of the universe as a whole does not require the nonessential parts, but only the essential parts. But in the next life, the heavens are not in motion. Therefore, there are no nonhuman animals or plants in heaven.[64]

Evaluating and Developing St. Thomas's Views on Nonhuman Animals and Plants in the Next Life

St. Thomas's position that nonhuman animals and plants do not exist in the next life is a hard doctrine for some. What should we think of St. Thomas's arguments for that view? Of course, some of the arguments assume Aristotelian views we now know to be false, namely, the second and the seventh arguments above. But most of St. Thomas's arguments use the assumption that a kind of substance exists in the new heavens and the new earth only if that kind of substance is perpetual (or incorruptible) or it has an aptitude for perpetuity (or incorruptibility). As nonhuman animals and plants are by nature corruptible, and so part of "the fashion of this world [that] passes away" (1 Cor 7:31),[65] they do not exist in the next life.

But why cannot nonhuman animals and plants—especially our pets—be graced such that they become incorruptible? Grace perfects nature; it does not set it aside. But to make, by grace, nonhuman animals and plants incorruptible in the next life, when they are in no sense incorruptible in this life, would seem to have God setting aside their nature. Now, God does indeed sometimes add grace to nature in surprising ways—think of God causing the accidents of bread and wine to exist such that they do not inhere in a substance in the Eucharist.[66] But it is one thing for God miraculously to keep accidents in being without a subject *for a time*,[67] and it is quite another thing for God miraculously to keep nonhuman animals and plants from corrupting *perpetually*. The latter seems like an example of setting aside a thing's nature whereas the former does not.

---

64. Ibid.
65. See, e.g., *SCG* IV.97.5 (trans. O'Neil, 348).
66. See, e.g., *ST* III, q. 77, a. 1. Thanks to Mark Spencer for providing this example.
67. See ibid., ad 1.

Nonhuman animals and plants do not have immortal souls in this life. But what if there are material substances in the new heavens and the new earth that are *like* nonhuman animals and plants, only incorruptible? Call these incorruptible material creatures "nonhuman panimals" and "phlants," respectively. However, as nonhuman panimals and phlants are by hypothesis incorruptible by nature, and nonhuman animals and plants are by nature corruptible, nonhuman panimals and phlants would not be specifically identical to—and so also not numerically identical to—any nonhuman animals or plants in this life. Of course, there may very well be phlants and nonhuman panimals in heaven—immortal material substances that look, and in many ways act, like nonhuman animals and plants, but are *not* nonhuman animals and plants.

On the other hand, I suggested above the possibility that *all* material substances have an intrinsic aptitude for incorruptibility insofar as they are created with an obediential potency for incorruptibility. How would that theory work in the case of nonhuman animals and plants? We might think that when a nonhuman animal or plant dies, because the souls of nonhuman animals and plants are not naturally immortal, nonhuman animals or plants go out of existence for good. Indeed, as St. Thomas thinks about the substantial forms of nonhuman animals and plants, those forms are not naturally immortal concrete things, as in the case of human souls. But we are supposing for the sake of argument that nonhuman animals and plants have an obediential potency for incorruptibility. In that case, if God can miraculously cause the accidents of bread and wine to exist without a subject for a time in the Eucharist, why not think that God could miraculously preserve the existence of the souls of nonhuman and plant souls after death, until those souls can configure matter again at the time of the restoration of creation?

Alternatively, perhaps God does not miraculously preserve the existence of *all* nonhuman animal souls, but only those that have become important for individual human persons. In addition, perhaps God activates the obediential potency of those nonhuman animals and plants existing at the time of the general judgement, so that it is the particular nonhuman animals and plants existing at the time of the general resurrection that primarily populate the new heavens and the new earth.

However, the hypothesis currently under consideration is not without its potential problems. Will any of these restored nonhuman animals and plants prey upon one another? Presumably not, as there can be no death in the next life. However, as St. Thomas plausibly argues, it is part of the very nature of a lion, to take just one example, to hunt and eat flesh.[68] In that case, if there is a creature that looks like a lion in the next life that does not hunt and eat, it will be specifically different from the lions that exist in this life. Such lion lookalikes would not *be* lions.

St. Thomas on Places in Heaven

Before leaving this first section, a few more words about *places* in heaven are in order. As we have seen, one aspect of heaven for St. Thomas is the empyrean heaven, which is the incorruptible, immutable, and luminous proper abode of the blessed angels and saints. In addition, heaven, after the general resurrection, includes the existence of the new heavens and the new earth, that is, the existence of material things. But wherever there are material things there are places in which those material things exist. Therefore, there must exist many different places in heaven. Indeed, given St. Thomas's Catholic Christian confession of faith, heaven must already—in some sense of *already*—include a place or places. This is because both Jesus Christ and the Virgin Mary have human bodies in heaven. But where there are human bodies, there are places. Therefore, places already exist in heaven.

In an article within *ST* I-II, St. Thomas asks whether external goods are necessary for happiness.[69] One of the objections in that article cites Matthew 5:12, where Jesus states: "Your reward is very great in heaven."[70] But to be *in* heaven implies that the external good of place (*locus*) exists in heaven. Therefore, the external good of place is necessary for human happiness in heaven. In responding to the objection, St. Thomas states, following St. Augustine, that the reward of which Christ speaks is a spiritual and not a material reward. But St. Thomas goes on to note that, even if the external good of place is not necessary for perfect happiness in heaven, a bodily place, namely, the empyrean heaven, will be provided for the saints by reason of "a certain fitness and decoration" (*secundum quandam congruentiam et decorum*),[71] that is, it forms an aspect of the accidental reward of the saints, or is part of the well-being of perfect happiness.

---

68. For texts and discussion, see below in this chapter.
69. *ST* I-II, q. 4, a. 7.
70. Ibid., obj. 3 (trans. English Dominicans, 607).
71. *ST* I-II, q. 4, a. 7, ad 3.

Therefore, there will be *bodily* places for the saints in heaven, if not as a part of their essential reward, at least as an aspect of their accidental reward. Insofar as the next life includes "a new heavens and a new earth," and, as we have seen, the saints in heaven have human bodies and have the gift of agility, human persons in heaven will always exist in bodily places, and will be able to go from one place, such as the empyrean heaven, to another, such as the new heavens and the new earth, and back again.[72]

ARTIFACTS IN HEAVEN

In the first section of this chapter, I examined St. Thomas's views regarding nonhuman, nonartificial material beings in heaven. In this second section, I think with St. Thomas about the possibility of there being artifacts in heaven.

Artifacts play important roles in our this-worldly lives. We use them to protect ourselves, in eating and drinking, and in order to increase our happiness. Will there be artifacts in heaven? In one place, St. Thomas argues that human persons do not need to wear clothes in heaven by noting that clothes are necessary in order to protect human persons from suffering pain, for example, from exposure to heat or cold.[73] But the environment of heaven is in no way hostile to glorified human bodies. Therefore, human persons in heaven do not need clothes. In addition, glorified bodies are impassible and agile. Therefore, in the new heavens and the new earth human persons do not need the kinds of tools that are required in this life for the maintenance of the body, or for expeditiously transporting the body from one place to another.

In *ST* I-II, St. Thomas argues that human persons do not need external goods for perfect happiness in heaven, as such goods are necessary only insofar as they support the animal activities of growth, nourishment, and generation. But perfect happiness in heaven, which consists essentially in seeing God and the proper accidents that flow from the vision, is possessed either by the separated soul, which does not have a

---

72. For St. Thomas, as we saw above, the *proper* place for the saints is the empyrean heaven. But, as we also saw above, that does not mean that the saints could not visit other places for a time. Interestingly, St. Thomas notes there is a sense in which even separated souls exist in a place. See, e.g., *In Sent* IV, d. 45, q. 1, a. 1, q.c. 1 (*ST Suppl.*, q. 69, a. 1).

73. *CT* I, chap. 156.

body at all, or the soul united to a body no longer animal but spiritual.[74] As we have seen, by saying that the human body is spiritual, rather than animal, in heaven, St. Thomas means, among other things, that human bodies in heaven no longer require or desire food, drink, or sexual congress.

Although St. Thomas does not mention the possibility, one wonders whether certain artifacts might nonetheless be a fitting constitutive part of the accidental reward for human persons in heaven. Perhaps, for example, there will be fashion in heaven (of course, purified of any motive of self-aggrandizement).[75] Even if we do not need clothes for protection, or for the sake of modesty, clothes could be valued in heaven as something beautiful. Recall that St. Thomas thinks that seeing and taking pleasure in the beauty of the heavenly bodies is a constitutive part of the accidental reward for human persons in heaven. So, just as sensing the beauty of the heavenly bodies is a contemplative-like activity that is a fitting accompaniment to the beatific vision, perhaps so too is the making and wearing of clothes. In addition, perhaps there are novels and musical instruments in heaven. For example, we might think external goods such as playing or listening to jazz and public readings of Tolkien's *The Lord of the Rings* are constitutive parts of the accidental reward in heaven. The saints in heaven do not *need* these things to be perfectly happy, to be sure, but their presence would be fitting sensible signs of the beauty, goodness, and glory of the Lord.

But if there could be the use of musical instruments in heaven, why not the enjoyment of other external goods such as food and drink? The answer: because the enjoyment of food and drink is logically inconsistent with the *incorruptible* lifeworld of heaven, while, one might suggest, the enjoyment of music, reading, or fashion is not. The latter goods, like seeing the beauty of the heavens, can be construed as essentially contemplative activities, or, at the very least, activities that are not essentially tied to the practical life, whereas activities such as eating, drinking, and sexual union are essentially tied to the practical life, partially serving the ends of nutrition and procreation. We might construct the following Thomistic rule for deciding whether a good G is consistent with the incorruptible lifeworld of heaven:

---

74. *ST* I-II, q. 4, a. 7, resp.
75. Thanks to John V. Glass III for this suggestion.

(H) A created good G is compatible with the incorruptible and perfect lifeworld of heaven if and only if (a) G is a purely contemplative activity or the proper accident of a purely contemplative activity, such as the beatific vision and the proper accidents of the vision, or (b) G serves a purely contemplative activity in heaven and G is not essentially tied to practical activity, such as glorified human embodiment and activity, or (c) G is an incorruptible substance in some sense, for example, "the new heavens and the new earth."[76]

In addition, we might think that, if a good G satisfies H, then human persons do (or it would be fitting for human persons to) find G in heaven, at least as a constitutive part of the accidental reward.

It seems that certain artifacts, such as art objects, and instruments for the making of art objects, could satisfy H. Therefore, given St. Thomas's principles (if not anything he explicitly says), the existence, making, and use of art objects and instruments would be a fitting component part of the accidental reward for human persons in heaven.[77]

Recall also Paul Griffiths's winsome suggestion that heavenly life is a purely *liturgical* life, with the perfect heavenly liturgy being repeated perpetually. Given the teaching of St. Thomas, perhaps we could develop Griffiths's view as follows: where the essential reward for the angels and saints consists of the beatific vision and its proper accidents as participated eternity, the accidental reward for created persons in heaven is purely liturgical. Such a purely liturgical accidental reward could, for human persons, involve worship similar to the Mass, but also time for play, which play is itself a form of participation in a purely liturgical

---

76. See, e.g., *SCG* IV.86.4; *ST* I-II, q. 4, a. 7, ad 2; *In Mt* 22, lect. 3, nn. 1798–1800.

77. For St. Thomas, artifacts are not substances, but rather a kind of composite of an accidental form and a material substance or substances. See, e.g., *DPN*, chap. 1; *In Sent* IV, d. 44, q. 1, a. 1, q.c. 1, ad 4 (*ST Suppl.*, q. 79, a. 1, ad 4); q.c. 2, ad 4 (*ST Suppl.*, q. 79, a. 2, ad 4); *In DA* II, lect. 1, n. 218; lect. 2, nn. 235–37; *In Phys* I, lect. 2, n. 14; lect. 12, n. 108; II, lect. 2, n. 149; *In Meta* VII, lect. 17, n. 1680; *ST* III, q. 2, a. 1. Therefore, an artifact's coming into existence or going out of existence is an accidental and so not a substantial change. Just as there is no theological or philosophical problem with accidental changes in heaven after the general resurrection such as St. Paul willing his body to move to the new heavens at *t*, and to the new earth at *t+1*, etc., there is no theological or philosophical problem with artifacts coming into, or going out of, existence. So if God created an incorruptible stuff in heaven out of which the saints could make art-objects and artifacts, the coming into or going out of existence of such objects, if or when it occurred, would be compatible with the *incorruptible* life world of heaven. Such accidental changes would be like the coming into existence or going out of existence of composites such as *running St. Paul*, or *singing St. Paul*. For more on St. Thomas on the ontological status of artifacts, see my *Aquinas and the Ship of Theseus*, 98–103, my "Souls, Ships, and Substances: A Reply to Toner," *American Catholic Philosophical Quarterly* 81 (2007): 655–68; and Brower, *Aquinas's Ontology of the Material World*.

life.⁷⁸ As play and art, both in their making and in their reception, are human goods and certainly ways in which human persons can see the glory of God by way of the senses,⁷⁹ these would seem to be, according to Thomistic principles, fitting aspects of the accidental reward for human persons in heaven. Consider, then, the following hypothesis: human persons in heaven, as aspects of their accidental reward, cycle between (i) participating in perfect liturgical worship analogous to the antiphonal nature of the Mass and (ii) play time as liturgical celebration, which time allows human persons to engage with other saints in common loves and interests, such as writing and reading literature, playing and listening to jazz, or racing from the new heavens to the new earth and back again, to see or hear the beauties of the new heavens and the new earth. Just as the angels before the culmination of the kingdom of God are engaged both in serving the Lord and at the same time enjoy the beatific vision,⁸⁰ so human persons in heaven continually engage in the beatific vision while also enjoying an accidental reward that consists of engaging in a perpetual back and forth between participating in antiphonal liturgical worship and liturgical play.

ST. THOMAS ON "THE NEW HEAVENS AND THE NEW EARTH": OBJECTIONS AND REPLIES

Some may think that St. Thomas's views on the sorts of material things that exist in heaven is too restrictive, or, even if some may agree with St. Thomas's views, they may nonetheless disagree with some of his ways of arguing for those views. Nonetheless, this is not the place to look at all possible positions or arguments that oppose the views of St. Thomas.⁸¹ Instead, the third section of this chapter has three stages. First, I examine some arguments offered by Paul J. Griffiths in his book,

---

78. Thanks to Mark Spencer for the suggestion that play can be a kind of participation in a purely liturgical life. Spencer offered the following this-worldly example: the activities of a parish festival as a form of participation in liturgical life.

79. Recall St. Thomas's affirmation that human persons in heaven enjoy, as part of their *accidental* reward, the knowing of God in heaven by way of the senses insofar as the saints in heaven immediately sense the glory and wisdom of God in the material creatures God has made.

80. See, e.g., *In Mt* 18, lect. 1, nn. 1504–6, and *ST* I, q. 58, a. 2.

81. For some other works that argue that nonhuman animals (or plants) exist in heaven, see, e.g., Trent Dougherty, *The Problem of Animal Pain: A Theodicy for All Creatures Great and Small* (Houndmills: Palgrave Macmillan, 2014) and Shawn Graves, Blake Hereth, and Tyler M. John, "In Defense of Animal Universalism," in *Paradise Understood* (ed. Byerly and Silverman), 161–92.

Decreation: The Last Things of All Creatures. Griffiths argues, in conversation with some of the texts of St. Thomas, that there are nonhuman animals and plants in heaven.[82] Let us call the thesis that there are nonhuman animals and plants in heaven, *the animal and plant thesis* (APT). Second, I examine Griffiths's arguments concerning inanimate substances and artifacts in heaven.[83] Third, as Griffiths's arguments can be construed as objections to St. Thomas's views, I respond to those arguments from a Thomistic point of view.

Griffiths on Nonhuman Animals and Plants in Heaven

Griffiths has two argumentative strategies for defending APT. First, there is what he calls a "broadly Thomistic" strategy, one that argues that nonhuman animals and plants exist in heaven insofar as they fittingly contribute to the accidental reward of human persons in heaven. Second, Griffiths argues for APT insofar as the presence of nonhuman animals and plants in heaven "might glorify the LORD independently of anything they have done, are doing, or might do for humans."[84]

In developing his "broadly Thomistic strategy" for defending nonhuman animal and plant existence in heaven, Griffiths first notes that St. Thomas employs two different kinds of arguments to defend the view that there are no nonhuman animals or plants in heaven. One kind of argument begins from the *nature* of nonhuman animals and plants. A second, anthropocentric kind of argument begins from the premise that nonhuman animals and plants exist in heaven if and only if the happiness of human persons requires it. Interestingly, in developing his own arguments in defense of APT, Griffiths never attempts to rebut those arguments of St. Thomas that nonhuman animals and plants are simply *not the kinds of things* that can exist in an incorruptible new heavens and new earth. Griffiths argues that, as St. Thomas's anthropocentric arguments are not needed if the arguments from the nature of nonhuman animals and plants are sound, St. Thomas must have had doubts about the soundness of the arguments from the nature of nonhuman animals.[85] Griffiths therefore sets aside St. Thomas's arguments from the nature of nonhuman animals and plants and focuses on his anthro-

82. *Decreation*, 267–96.
83. Ibid., 297–312.
84. Ibid., 289.
85. Ibid., 282.

pocentric arguments as St. Thomas's primary reasons for denying APT.

Griffiths argues that (something such as) the following is the general structure of St. Thomas's anthropocentric arguments:

(2) If nonhuman animals and plants are necessary for the perfection of the beatitude of human saints in heaven, then nonhuman animals and plants exist in heaven [assumption].

(3) If nonhuman animals and plants exist in heaven, then nonhuman animals and plants are necessary for the perfection of the beatitude of human saints in heaven [assumption].

(4) It is not the case that nonhuman animals and plants are necessary for the perfection of the beatitude of the saints in heaven [assumption].

(5) Therefore, nonhuman animals and plants do not exist in heaven [from (3) and (4), MT].

As we have seen, St. Thomas accepts (3) and (4), and this is one reason that he accepts (5). Of course, St. Thomas does not need to draw on (2) in order to make his argument for (5). But Griffiths thinks that St. Thomas nonetheless accepts (2), as St. Thomas defends, in other places, premises analogous to it, such as the following:

(2*) If human saints in heaven need to be aware, in heaven, of the suffering of the damned for the sake of the perfection of their beatitude, then the human saints in heaven are aware, in heaven, of the suffering of the damned.[86]

In contrast to St. Thomas's anthropocentric kind of argument that there are no nonhuman animals and plants in heaven, Griffiths's own "broadly Thomistic anthropocentric" argument for APT uses (2) and ignores (3). Because Griffiths thinks that (4) is false, he thereby concludes that heaven is populated with nonhuman animals and plants. Such is the basic structure of Griffiths's "broadly Thomistic, anthropocentric" strategy for defending APT.

But how might nonhuman animals and plants contribute to the accidental reward of the saints in heaven? Griffiths makes two interesting suggestions, and based on each of these suggestions mounts a particular "broadly Thomistic, anthropocentric" argument for APT. Griffiths's first

---

86. See, e.g., *In Sent* IV, d. 50, q. 2, a. 4, q.c. 1 (*ST Suppl.*, q. 94, a. 1). Griffiths quotes this text in *Decreation*, 278.

suggestion is as follows. Reflecting upon the creation narrative in Genesis, he suggests that, in naming the animals, Adam saw them as significantly different from himself, for unlike himself, these creatures were not created in the image and likeness of God. After God creates Eve as a suitable partner for Adam, both Adam and Eve recognize each other as suitable partners, that is, as fellow human persons. They do so, at least partly, by recognizing themselves as distinct from the other visible creatures God had made, and they recognize themselves as distinct from the other visible creatures through the presence of nonhuman animals and plants in Eden. Therefore, on Griffiths's reading of Genesis, the presence of nonhuman animals and plants in the Garden is partly constitutive of Adam and Eve—and so human persons, more generally—knowing that they are especially suited for social relations with other human persons, especially the exclusive social relation that is marriage between a male person and a female person. How so? The presence of nonhuman animals and plants in Eden plays an important role in their recognizing the significant difference between themselves and nonhuman living things.

So, Griffiths continues, for the same reason that sexual difference exists in heaven, there are specific differences among living creatures in heaven. For sexual difference in heaven is not for the sake of marriage or sex in heaven, but rather for the sake of human persons in heaven being aware of the differences between the sexes. This is because "part of what it means to exist as a human male is to be differentiated from the human female, and vice versa"[87] and awareness of this difference is made clear by way of the presence of human persons who differ from one another in their sex. Therefore, an aspect of the accidental reward in heaven for male human persons requires the presence of females, and vice versa. Analogously, there will be nonhuman animals and plants in heaven, not because human persons need such things for food, clothing, etc., but because part of what it means to exist as a human person is to be aware of how human persons are differentiated from other visible creatures. But such awareness requires the presence, and therefore existence, of nonhuman animals and plants in heaven.

Griffiths has a second particular "broadly Thomistic anthropocentric" argument for APT. This argument begins from the assumption that death of all kinds is an effect of the Fall. But human persons, like many

---

87. *Decreation*, 287.

other animals, live, after the Fall, by constantly killing other animals and eating them. According to Griffiths, such a cycle of death is a significant aspect of how God's original creation was, and continues to be, damaged by the Fall.

Now, Griffiths argues that the Christian way of responding to a creature—and so creation—damaged by evil is the *mending* of it, rather than the *ending* of it. But our relations with nonhuman animals and plants are damaged by evil after the Fall insofar as we kill—or are benefitting from the killing of—nonhuman animals and plants. Therefore, in order that creation be completely mended and healed in heaven, Griffiths suggests that the new heavens and the new earth contain not only human persons, but nonhuman animals and plants too. In that way, all living creatures exist in heaven in transfigured and healed relations with each other. That is, in heaven human persons no longer kill nonhuman animals and plants, but rather live with nonhuman animals and plants in peace and harmony.

In addition to these two particular "broadly Thomistic, anthropocentric" arguments for APT, Griffiths also offers a nonanthropocentric argument, a central premise of which is that God wills and loves nonhuman animals and plants for their own sake, and not simply for the sake of meeting the needs and desires of human persons. Why should one think that God wills and loves nonhuman animals and plants in and of themselves, independently of the concerns of intellectual substances? Griffiths offers two reasons. First, there is the nature of God. For *God is love*, and so God loves whatever he creates. But what does it mean for God to love nonhuman animals and plants? Griffiths explains: "The LORD ... not only creates the manifold kinds of plants and animals, but also loves them in their particularity—in their appearance, their constitution, their mode of reproduction, their complex symbiotic relations with other such kinds, and so forth."[88]

According to Griffiths, a second reason to think God wills and loves nonhuman living things in and of themselves is the fact that God has created millions of different kinds of nonhuman animal and plant species, many of which species existed, or went extinct, long before there were any human persons in the cosmos. There is also the possibility that there are living creatures in other parts of the cosmos, parts of the universe

---

88. Ibid., 290.

we will never know about (in this life). All of this suggests that God loves nonhuman animals and plants—that such creatures bring God glory—independently of the concerns, needs, or desires of human persons.

Griffiths's nonanthropocentric argument for the existence of nonhuman animals and plants in heaven would thus seem to have the following form:

(6) If God loves nonhuman animals and plants for their own sake—if such creatures bring God glory independently of the concerns and projects of human persons—then nonhuman animals and plants exist in heaven [assumption].

(7) God loves nonhuman animals and plants for their own sake [assumption].

(8) Therefore, there are nonhuman animals and plants in heaven [from (6) and (7), MP].

Even if we grant premise (7) for the sake of argument, why should one think that premise (6) in the argument above is true? For Griffiths, (6) is true because nonhuman animals and plants die, and the death of anything—even nonhuman animals and plants—is not an aspect of God's antecedent will.[89] As Griffiths says in many places, death is an "artifact" of the Fall. Since the Fall, nonhuman animals and plants are damaged insofar as they die, and in some cases, such creatures kill other creatures, it stands to reason that God, who loves them, wants to see them healed and restored. In other words, the new heavens and the new earth, understood as a healed, and so transfigured, cosmos, contains all creatures as perfected and healed (of the effects) of sin. Now, both the death of nonhuman animals and plants, and nonhuman animals and plants engaging in acts of killing, are effects of sin—of course, not their own sin, as such effects of sin are caused by intellectual substances such as human persons or demons. Therefore, nonhuman animals and plants

---

89. The chapter supplies St. Thomas's distinction between God's will understood *antecedently* and God's will understood *consequently* for the sake of clarity of expression (Griffiths himself does not invoke such a distinction). God's antecedent will is God's will understood as logically prior to what free creatures choose. God's consequent will is God's will understood in light of what free creatures choose. For example, God wills antecedently that "all human persons be saved, coming to a knowledge of the truth" (1 Tm 2:4). But God wills consequent to human persons refusing or not refusing to cooperate with God's grace that human persons get what they choose, whether to be united to God or not to be united to God. See, e.g., *ST* I, q. 19, a. 6, ad 1. For some good discussion of the distinction between God's will understood *antecedently* and God's will understood *consequently* in St. Thomas, see Stump, *Aquinas*, 456–60.

exist in heaven too as healed and restored such that none of them either kill or die.

Griffiths on Nonliving Material Creatures in Heaven

In his discussion of inanimate material creatures, Griffiths makes a distinction between *artifacts*, "those in the making of which human agency is centrally involved," and the so-called *Givens*, those nonliving, nonartificial, material creatures.[90] Concerning the question whether such things exist in the next life, Griffiths takes as a background assumption that inanimate, nonartificial, material creatures too have been negatively affected by angelic sin and the Fall of human persons insofar as they are sometimes destroyed and are themselves sometimes agents of destruction. Admitting that our judgments are fallible when it comes to answering whether a particular act of a nonliving material creature should be classified as a *destructive* act, Griffiths does think it safe to assume that *some* acts of nonliving material creatures are destructive and that such destructive activity is an effect of the Fall.[91]

So, in Griffiths's view, what sorts of inanimate material creatures exist in heaven? In order to articulate his own speculative answers to this question, Griffiths makes use of the two approaches that he employs in order to defend APT, that is, both an anthropocentric and a nonanthropocentric approach. As Griffiths divides the world of inanimate creatures into artifacts and givens, let us take up his eschatological views toward each of these in turn.

Griffiths thinks that no artifacts exist in heaven (call this *the artifact thesis*). This will be true, he thinks, whether we argue nonanthropocentrically or anthropocentrically. For, according to Griffiths, human making is a function of the Fall. That is, human persons only make things because, after the Fall, they have certain kinds of physical and spiritual limitations. After the Fall, human persons are no longer immortal and impassible and so they make houses, clothes, and tools in order to protect themselves from harm.

In addition, because of the Fall, human persons are alienated from one another and from God, and so they make things, including languages, in order to decrease the distance between themselves and other hu-

---

90. *Decreation*, 299.
91. Ibid., 301–2.

man persons, and between themselves and God. Although, at their best, artifacts are certainly beautiful, and such beautiful things can (but certainly do not always) facilitate love between human persons and between human persons and God, artifacts are unnecessary—or, as Griffiths says in some places, *otiose*—in heaven, as knowledge, love, and community in heaven are direct and unmediated.[92] Even artifacts that human persons use in the liturgy have no place in heaven, thinks Griffiths. Just as taking the sacrament of the Eucharist under the species of bread and wine is necessary and fitting in this life, but has no place in the world to come, so use of artifacts in the liturgy, although in this life necessary and fitting, are neither needed nor desired in heaven. Indeed, use of such forms of mediation in heaven would not be sensible, thinks Griffiths, given that human saints in heaven enjoy unmediated relations with God and created persons.

What of the New Jerusalem in heaven, about which both the Book of Revelation and passages in the Old Testament (read according to the anagogical sense) attest? Is not the city of God in heaven a counterexample to the artifact thesis? Griffiths thinks not. Recall that Griffiths defines an artifact as a nonliving creature that is such that an act of human making is central to its existence. But, according to Griffiths, the city of God in heaven, at least in its nonliving aspect, is not made by human hands. Rather, it is wholly of God's making. Therefore, it is not an artifact and so does not serve as a counterexample to the artifact thesis.[93]

In contrast to artifacts, Griffiths thinks that the Givens do exist in heaven (call this *the Givens thesis*). He thinks that this view is defensible on both anthropocentric and nonanthropocentric grounds. As for his anthropocentric defense of the Givens thesis, Griffiths has two arguments. In his first argument, Griffiths asks us to consider that human persons in heaven are embodied. Being embodied in the human way means being *placed*, and so existing in relation to bodies of certain kinds. Even if the relations of human persons with nonhuman animals and plants are more significant than the relations of human persons with inanimate

---

92. See, e.g., ibid., 307.
93. Mark Spencer suggests the following problem for Griffiths's views: Adam named the animals *before* the Fall (see Gn 2:19–20), but language is an artifact. Therefore, contrary to Griffiths, who, of course, accepts the authority of Genesis, there are artifacts before the Fall. Perhaps Griffiths thinks that Adam and Eve, prior to the Fall, employed a purely nonconventional language in a manner analogous to what Plato has Cratylus suggest in his dialogue *Cratylus*.

substances, the latter are still partly constitutive of what it means for human persons to be embodied. Therefore, the Givens exist in heaven.

Griffiths's second anthropocentric argument for the Givens thesis parallels an argument he offers for APT. Recall that Griffiths offers an anthropocentric argument for APT based on the premises that (a) death is an artifact of the Fall and (b) heaven is, at least partly, a recapitulation of the cosmos prior to the Fall, which cosmos enjoyed a harmony of relations between human persons and nonhuman living things. According to Griffiths, not only death, but also *corruption itself* is an artifact of the Fall. As heaven is, at least partly, a recapitulation of the prelapsarian created order, the Givens exist in heaven without their active or passive potency to corruption so that human persons can enjoy harmonized and healed relations with inanimate creatures too.

Griffiths also has a nonanthropocentric argument for the existence of the Givens in heaven. As the existence of the Givens is not an artifact of the Fall, and those things that exist in the Garden of Eden before the Fall also exist in heaven, the Givens exist in heaven, albeit as transfigured and healed from the negative effects of the Fall, such as corruption.

Responding to Griffiths's Arguments for APT

Griffiths's arguments for APT defend a general thesis about *heaven* to which St. Thomas is opposed, namely, that heavenly life includes a recapitulation of the prelapsarian this-worldly life of all natural, material creatures, but it also defends a view that, if true, would significantly alter what St. Thomas calls *the accidental reward of the saints* in heaven. This section responds to Griffiths's arguments as objections to St. Thomas's views regarding the contour of "the new heavens and the new earth," and the nature of the accidental reward for human persons in heaven.

There are a number of problems with Griffiths's arguments. Let us first examine Griffiths's "broadly Thomistic" *strategy* for defending APT. Recall that St. Thomas has two different kinds of arguments for his view that nonhuman animals and plants do not exist in heaven. The first kind is from the nature of nonhuman animals and plants as wholly corruptible and nonintellectual creatures. The second kind of argument begins from the premise that there are nonhuman animals and plants in heaven if and only if the perfection of human beatitude requires such creatures. Given these two kinds of argument, Griffiths argues that:

(9) If St. Thomas thinks that the arguments from the nonintellectual and corruptible nature of nonhuman animals and plants (for the thesis that nonhuman animals and plants do not exist in heaven) are decisive, then he does not offer a different kind of argument, such as an anthropocentric argument, for his view that nonhuman animals and plants do not exist in heaven [assumption].

(10) In addition to his arguments from the nonintellectual and corruptible nature of nonhuman animals and plants, St. Thomas does employ a different kind of argument to show that nonhuman animals and plants do not exist in heaven, namely, the anthropocentric argument [assumption].

(11) Therefore, St. Thomas does not think the arguments from the nonintellectual and corruptible nature of nonhuman animals and plants are decisive [from (9) and (10), MT].

Given (11), Griffiths therefore thinks that he can safely ignore St. Thomas's arguments from the corruptible and nonintellectual nature of nonhuman animals and plants.

The argument consisting of propositions (9)–(11) is not a good one, as premise (9) is false. The fact that St. Thomas offers two kinds of arguments for a thesis T does not show that he thinks either of those arguments is indecisive where T is concerned.[94] For example, St. Thomas is famous for offering, in *ST*, five ways of showing that God exists. Does his use of the second, third, fourth, and fifth way of demonstrating God exists show that St. Thomas does not think the first way, the argument from motion—which in St. Thomas's view most clearly shows God exists—

---

94. Indeed, if the argument consisting of (9)–(11) is a good one, then one could also construct an analogous argument that St. Thomas does not think that his anthropocentric arguments are decisive. In addition, Griffiths posits that St. Thomas's arguments from the nature of nonhuman animals and plants such that those kinds of beings do not exist in heaven are, in St. Thomas's view, *based* on those kinds of things not being made in the *imago dei* and the Christocentric tenor of Christian thinking (see, e.g., *Decreation*, 277–78). Here is Griffiths: "Animals and plants lack . . . a [rational] soul, which is to say that they are not made in the image [of God]. Notice that for Thomas this is not principally, and perhaps not at all, a claim based on evidence about the capacities of various kinds of animal" (277). Now Griffiths neither cites any texts from St. Thomas to this effect, nor does he take into account texts (that Griffiths himself cites) from St. Thomas's corpus that seem to have St. Thomas arguing, for *philosophical* reasons, that nonhuman animals and plants do not exist in heaven because they are neither intellectual nor perpetual creatures. In addition, St. Thomas thinks that the mode of a thing's action shows us its mode of being (see, e.g., *ST* I, q. 75, a. 2, resp.). But nonhuman animals (and by extension, plants) simply act such that they possess a corruptible and nonintellectual mode of being (see, e.g., *ST* I, q. 75, a. 3, resp.). Therefore, St. Thomas thinks, for philosophical reasons, that nonhuman animals and plants are not the sorts of beings that can exist in an incorruptible reality such as "the new heavens and the new earth."

is not, for him, decisive? Hardly. St. Thomas often collects arguments for the positions he adopts. For different arguments for the same thesis often bring out different aspects of that thesis. Consider again the five ways. All are arguments that purport to show that a being "which we call God" exists. The first way brings out one truth about the "being we call God," namely, that God is absolutely immutable. The second way makes explicit the truth about God that God is an uncaused cause of the existence of those beings that have an efficient cause of their existence, etc.

Countless examples of St. Thomas giving a number of different kinds of arguments for a thesis—with no indication from St. Thomas that doing so means he thinks any of these arguments is by itself indecisive—could be given. Consider just one more example. When arguing for his view that there is no sexual union in heaven, St. Thomas offers at least *ten* different arguments. Again, rather than the multiplication of such arguments showing that St. Thomas considers each of these arguments to be indecisive, St. Thomas offers a number of different arguments because each of them brings out a different facet of the thesis under discussion.

For example, one of St. Thomas's arguments that there is no sexual union in heaven makes clear that conjugal relations in heaven make no sense in light of the relationship between the essential and accidental rewards. As the accidental reward is a bodily participation in the essential reward and the essential reward is purely contemplative, the accidental reward involves purely contemplative rather than animal activities. Another argument for the lack of sexual union in heaven makes explicit that life in heaven is a perpetual life, where marriage and sexual union are necessarily connected to a way of life that is temporary.

So Griffiths's decision to ignore St. Thomas's arguments from the corruptible and nonintellectual nature of nonhuman animals and plants is unwarranted. In fact, as we will see, if St. Thomas's arguments that there are no nonhuman animals and plants in heaven from the nature of such creatures stand unrefuted, they provide Griffiths reasons for drawing a different conclusion where APT is concerned. Therefore, given his interest in dialoguing with St. Thomas on APT, Griffiths's strategy to take seriously only St. Thomas's anthropocentric argument is not a good one.

Let us turn now to discussing Griffiths's *particular* arguments for APT, each one of which can be read as an objection to St. Thomas's view on these matters. Recall that Griffiths has two "broadly Thomistic anthropocentric" arguments. The first anthropocentric argument can be formulated as follows:[95]

(12) If Adam and Eve in Eden recognize themselves as suitable partners, that is, relevantly similar to one another so that they both know each other and themselves to be human persons, then there are nonhuman animals and plants in Eden [assumption].

(13) If human persons enjoy the perfection of beatitude in heaven, then human male persons in heaven are aware of the difference between themselves and human female persons in heaven, and vice versa [by analogy from (12)].

(14) Human persons are male or female, and an essential part of what it means to be a human male is to be with human females, and vice versa [from (12)].

(15) Human persons are distinct from other living material creatures and an essential part of what it means to be a human person is to be in relation with nonhuman, living, material creatures, to which human persons are both similar and distinct [by analogy from (14)].

(16) Therefore, if human persons in heaven enjoy the perfection of beatitude in heaven, then human persons in heaven are aware of the difference between human persons, on the one hand, and nonhuman animals and plants, on the other hand [by analogy from (12) and (13)].

(17) If human persons in heaven are aware of the difference between human persons, on the one hand, and nonhuman animals and plants, on the other hand, then nonhuman animals and plants are present, that is, exist, in heaven [assumption].

(18) Therefore, if human persons enjoy the perfection of beatitude in heaven, then nonhuman animals and plants are present, that is, exist, in heaven [from (15); from (16) and (17), HS].

(19) Human persons in heaven enjoy the perfection of beatitude in heaven [Christian doctrine].

(20) Therefore, nonhuman animals and plants are present, that is, exist, in heaven [from (18) and (19), MP].

Griffiths may be arguing for (18)—and so (20)—by way of propositions (12), (14), and (15), or by way of propositions (12), (13), (16), and (17).

95. Because it is not clear (to this reader) whether Griffiths is arguing for APT from (12), (13), and (16)–(20) or from (12), (14), (15), and (18)–(20), both versions of the argument are treated in what follows.

Either way, Griffiths's first anthropocentric argument has problems.

Say we take Griffiths's argument to consist of propositions (12), (14), (15), and (18)–(20). According to that interpretation of the argument, Griffiths is arguing that an essential property of human persons is their existing in relation to nonhuman animals and plants. There are at least three problems with that argument.

First, premise (14) is subject to a counterexample. Surely, Adam was a human person before he entered into a relation with Eve. Because *being a human person* is an essential feature of anything that has that feature, if being in relation to a woman or women is an essential feature of a male human person, then Adam underwent a substantial change when he entered into relation with Eve, going from not being a human person to being a human person. But Adam does not undergo a substantial change when he enters into relation with Eve. For, in scripture, persons undergo a change of name when something significant happens to them. Certainly, a *substantial* change is significant if any change is significant. But Adam is named "Adam" before and after the creation of Eve.

Second, (14) is unmotivated. Adam and Eve may indeed have lacked a degree, even a kind, of self-awareness as human persons apart from one another. But it does not follow that Adam was not a human person at all before the creation of Eve. As (14) is false or unmotivated, that means that (15) and (18) too are unmotivated. But this means that Griffiths's conclusion that there are nonhuman animals and plants in heaven—proposition (20)—is unmotivated too.

Third, even granting (15), it is not clear that (18) follows logically from it. For human persons in heaven could be related to nonhuman animals and plants in heaven by way of human persons *remembering* them, or by way of human persons having the nature of nonhuman animals and plants revealed to them by God, rather than by human persons existing in real relations with them in heaven. A human person, Susan, can recognize herself as importantly similar to and distinct from another being, for example, her cat Cuddles, by remembering Cuddles, even after Cuddles is gone. So, instead of inferring (18) from (15), it seems as though Griffiths's line of reasoning at best supports the following weaker inference from (15):

(18*) Therefore, if human persons in heaven are to enjoy the perfection of beatitude in heaven, then the human persons in heaven know in some way nonhuman animals and plants, for example, by remembering them, or by having their natures revealed to them by God [from (15)].

But (20) does not follow from (18*) and (19). As Griffiths's (18) is unmotivated, so is (20).

There are also two problems with Griffiths's first anthropocentric argument, if it consists instead of propositions (12)–(13) and (16)–(20). First, as on the first reading, it appears as though the mere remembering of nonhuman animals and plants in heaven is sufficient to meet the needs of human persons in heaven. Note that premise (13) states that the beatitude of human males in heaven requires that they see themselves as distinct from human females, and vice versa. But St. Paula can recognize herself as a human female in heaven, even if there is no human male in heaven insofar as she remembers human males and thereby recognizes herself as similar to but different from human males. Analogously, human persons in heaven can remember nonhuman animals and plants in heaven, even if there are no such beings in heaven, thereby enjoying an awareness of themselves as similar to but distinct from such creatures. Human persons recognizing themselves as similar to but distinct from nonhuman animals and plants therefore does not require the actual presence or existence of such creatures in heaven. Therefore, premise (17) is false. But, in that case, (18) is unmotivated, and with it Griffiths's conclusion that nonhuman animals and plants exist in heaven.

Second, certainly God could create nonhuman living creatures in heaven that are incorruptible. Say this genus of incorruptible, nonhuman, living creatures divides neatly into two species, phanimals and phlants (where for any phanimal P, P is not numerically identical to a nonhuman animal, and for any phlant P1, P1 is not numerically identical to a plant). According to the hypothesis under consideration, phanimals and phlants are like nonhuman animals and plants in being nonrational living creatures, but they are unlike nonhuman animals and plants in being incorruptible.[96] In addition, and importantly, phanimals and phlants are like human persons in being incorruptible, but significantly unlike human persons in being nonrational material substances.

---

96. Recall that St. Thomas himself thinks that there are creatures in this life—and the next—that are perpetual or incorruptible and yet nonrational, i.e., the planets and the elements. Although St. Thomas thinks that all intellectual substances are incorruptible (in some sense), he does not think that all incorruptible substances are rational.

Given this phanimal and phlant hypothesis, premise (18) is unmotivated. Let us suppose that Griffiths is correct about the following:

(16*) The perfection of human beatitude in heaven requires that human persons see themselves as similar to, but distinct from, some nonhuman, living creatures.

If God creates phanimals and phlants in heaven, then the requirement for the perfection of human beatitude in heaven in (16*) is satisfied, and without nonhuman animals and plants actually existing in heaven. Given the possibility that God creates phanimals and phlants in heaven and the analogy Griffiths is trying to draw from (12) and (13), the consequent of (16) does not follow logically from its antecedent. As (16) is false, (18) again is unmotivated. Therefore, (20) remains unmotivated.

Perhaps we find ourselves nonetheless sympathizing with the argument that consists of propositions (18)–(20). We recognize that our relations with nonhuman animals and plants in this life are something very good. And that certainly gives us a *prima facie* reason to think that such relations continue in heaven insofar as human persons in heaven, at some point, enjoy the well-being of perfect happiness. However, as Griffiths himself admits, just because we enjoy some good G in this life, it does not follow that G exists in heaven. Marriage, conjugal union, and receiving Christ in the Eucharist under the species of bread and wine are very good things in this life, but, as Griffiths himself admits, none of these very good things exist in heaven.[97] Some good things in this world are simply incompatible with the greater good of heavenly life.

It is just at this point in the dialectic where St. Thomas's arguments from the *nature* of nonhuman animals and plants—arguments Griffiths sets to one side—become very relevant. For just as Griffiths's arguments for why there is no marriage in heaven give us reason to think marriage does not exist in heaven, St. Thomas's arguments from the nature of nonhuman animals and plants give us reasons for thinking that the perfection of the beatitude of human saints does not require relations with nonhuman animals and plants in heaven. Anything that exists in the new heavens and the new earth is, in some sense, a perpetual thing or an intellectual substance. But nonhuman animals and plants are nei-

---

97. *Decreation*, 260–63.

ther incorruptible nor intellectual.[98] Therefore, nonhuman animals and plants cannot exist in heaven. But the blessed do not desire what is impossible. Therefore, the blessed in heaven do not desire relations with nonhuman animals or plants in heaven.

Of course, this is not to say that some human persons *in this life* do not desire to live with (certain) nonhuman animals and plants in perpetuity. In addition, sometimes the correct thing to say to someone who asks whether there will be x in heaven is, "If (a) you go to heaven and (b) you need x in heaven in order to be perfectly happy, then x exists in heaven."[99] But human persons often have false beliefs in this life about what really makes them happy. So from the fact that some human person S, *in this life*, wants something x to exist in heaven, it does not follow that, if S goes to heaven, then x exists in heaven, if only because it does not follow that, if S wants x in this life, then S will want x in heaven.

So much for Griffiths's first anthropocentric argument for APT. What about Griffiths's second anthropocentric argument? This can be formulated as follows:

(21) Although there is more to heaven than exists in the created universe as a whole before the Fall, that is, the fall of some angels from grace and subsequent angelic sin, or the fall of Adam and Eve, heaven includes a recapitulation of the created universe as a whole before the Fall [assumption].

(22) Death, including the death of animals and plants (by way of other animals), is an artifact of the Fall, that is, the fall of some angels from grace and subsequent angelic sin, or the fall of Adam and Eve [assumption].

(23) Therefore, the created universe before the Fall included animals and plants that did not die and did not kill other animals and plants [from (22)].

(24) Therefore, nonhuman animals and plants exist in heaven [from (21) and (23)].

---

98. Alternatively, perhaps they are not the sort of thing that can exist in an incorruptible universe, given the necessary connection between their mode of being and living in a universe of corruptible beings, e.g., if lions are essentially hunters and flesh eaters.

99. This nugget of wisdom (among many others!) comes from Eleonore Stump. Of course, one can affirm the conditional proposition while, at the same time, denying (b) in the antecedent and denying the consequent. In addition, it is sometimes wise not to make explicit one's own denial of both (b) in the antecedent and the consequent, but simply to affirm for someone the truth of the conditional proposition.

What to think of this argument? Both (21) and (22) are unmotivated. Indeed, both (21) and (22) are axiomatic in Griffiths's *Decreation*; he never argues for either of these views. Rather, they are starting points for his eschatological discussions in the work.

But why should we believe either of these propositions? Neither (21) nor (22) is a part of Christian dogma or doctrine. Indeed, from St. Thomas's perspective, both (21) and (22) are false. Consider first proposition (21). St. Thomas thinks of heaven as a state of affairs such that all the things that exist in it are, in some sense, incorruptible. Those things that are by nature corruptible or supervene on a corruptible life have no place in heaven. But, even before the Fall, St. Thomas thinks that there are things corruptible by nature, such as instances of the elements and mixed bodies. We might think with St. Thomas that the material universe in this life is shot through, by nature, with corruption, independently of what rational creatures choose. As there is no more corruption in heaven, the incorruptible life of heaven is quite different from the created, material universe, even prior to the Fall.

Now, take proposition (22). St. Thomas thinks that the death of living things is a natural feature of the material universe, even prior to the Fall. For example, in one place where St. Thomas speaks about the relationship between human persons and other creatures in Eden, he says:

> In the opinion of some, those animals which now are fierce and kill others, would, in that state [of innocence], have been tame, not only in regard to man, but also in regard to other animals. But this is quite unreasonable. For the nature of animals was not changed by man's sin, as if those whose nature now it is to devour the flesh of others, would then have lived on herbs, as the lion and falcon. Nor does Bede's gloss on Gen. i. 30, say that trees and herbs were given as food to all animals and birds, but to some. Thus, there would have been a natural antipathy between some animals.[100]

Note St. Thomas's reason for thinking there is antipathy between some animals. Because such antipathy is natural, for example, the lion has a natural inclination to hunt creatures such as the antelope, and because sin does not change the nature—and so the natural inclinations—of God's creations, it follows that antipathy between animals is not an effect of sin, but is natural to them. Indeed, in one important sense, the sin of in-

---

100. *ST* I, q. 96, a. 1, ad 2 (trans. English Dominicans, 486). See also the texts cited in chapter 2, note 108 above.

tellectual creatures does not even change their own natures. For human persons and angels remain human persons and angels, respectively, after the Fall. Human persons also have the same sorts of *natural* inclinations after the Fall as before, even if they now lack the preternatural gift of integrity, and so suffer concupiscence, which makes it difficult, if not impossible, to act rationally on their natural inclinations apart from grace.[101]

There are additional reasons to reject both (21) and (22). As for (21), there are things that exist in God's creation before the Fall that are not recapitulated in heaven, such as sex, marriage, eating, and drinking. Proposition (21) is therefore subject to good counterexamples. As for (22), we might first wonder how nonhuman animal and plant death could be an artifact of the Fall. For nonhuman animals killed other nonhuman animals and plants and died for millions of years before the Fall of human persons. But to imply that fallen angels change the nature of nonhuman animals and plants so that they are changed from being incorruptible to corruptible, as Griffiths does,[102] seems to give the sin of the fallen angels too much power. Just as St. Thomas says about human sin, "the nature of animals was not changed by man's sin," we should also say about the sins of the fallen angels: "the nature of animals was not changed by their sin."

Second, consider that Griffiths accepts the following proposition concerning the Garden of Eden:

(25) The Garden of Eden, the abode of Adam and Eve in the state of innocence, was preserved from the effects of angelic sin.[103]

But the following proposition follows from (25):

(26) If death, including the death of animals and plants (by way of other animals), is an artifact of the Fall, that is, the fall of some angels from grace and subsequent angelic sin, or the fall of Adam and Eve, then there was no death in the Garden of Eden prior to the fall of Adam and Eve.

Now, death is the corruption of a living thing. But plants are living things. Indeed, so are cells. But plants, and certainly cells, suffered death before

---

101. See, e.g., *ST* I, q. 64, a. 4, and *ST* I-II, q. 82, a. 1.
102. *Decreation*, 134.
103. Ibid.

the Fall of human persons in the Garden of Eden insofar as Adam and Eve ate plants or plant parts there. Therefore, the consequent of (26) is false: there *was* death in the Garden of Eden before the Fall of Adam and Eve insofar as plants or their living parts suffered death. Therefore premise (22), which is the antecedent of (26), is false. Therefore, there are good reasons to think that both (21) and (22) are false. Griffiths's APT remains unmotivated.

As we have seen, Griffiths also has a nonanthropocentric argument for APT. The argument can be formulated as follows:

(27) God is love and God loves in and of itself whatever he creates [assumption].

(28) Whatever God creates brings glory in and of itself to God [assumption].

(29) God creates nonhuman animals and plants [assumption].

(30) God has (a) created millions of different kinds of nonhuman animal and plant species, (b) many of which species existed long before there were any human persons in the cosmos, (c) and many of which species went extinct before there were any human persons in the cosmos. (d) There is also the possibility of there being living creatures in other parts of the cosmos, parts of the universe we will never know about (in this life) [assumption].

(31) Therefore, God loves nonhuman animals and plants in-and-of-themselves, independently of the concerns, needs, or desires of human persons, and nonhuman animals and plants bring God glory in-and-of-themselves, independently of the concerns and projects of human persons [from (27)–(29) and from (30)].

(21) Although there is more to heaven than exists in the created universe as a whole before the Fall, that is, the fall of some angels from grace and subsequent angelic sin, or the fall of Adam and Eve, heaven includes a recapitulation of the created universe as a whole before the Fall [assumption].

(22) Death, including the death of nonhuman animals and plants (by way of other animals and plants), is an artifact of the Fall, that is, the fall of some angels from grace and subsequent angelic sin, or the fall of Adam and Eve [assumption].

(32) If (a) heaven includes a recapitulation of the created universe as a whole before the Fall and (b) death, including the death of nonhuman

animals and plants (by way of other animals and plants), is an artifact of the Fall, then God creates nonhuman animals and plants in heaven in order to restore fully those things in the cosmos that have been damaged by sin, things God loves in and of themselves and that, in and of themselves, bring glory to God [from (31)].

(33) Therefore, God creates nonhuman animals and plants in heaven in order to restore fully those things in the cosmos that have been damaged by sin, things God loves in and of themselves and that, in and of themselves, bring glory to God [from (21), (22), and (32), MP].

(34) If God creates nonhuman animals and plants in heaven in order to restore fully those things in the cosmos have been damaged by sin, things God loves in and of themselves and that, in and of themselves, bring glory to God, then nonhuman animals and plants exist in heaven [self-evident].

(35) Therefore, nonhuman animals and plants exist in heaven [from (33) and (34), MP].

So goes Griffiths's nonanthropocentric argument for APT. There are two main problems with the argument. First, like the second of Griffiths's anthropocentric arguments, his nonanthropocentric argument employs propositions (21) and (22) as premises. I have offered reasons above for thinking that those premises are false, or at least unmotivated. But that means that (33) and so (35)—that is, APT—are unmotivated.

Second, there are problems with Griffiths's inference to (31) from premises (27)–(29) or (30). First, there are problems with the inference to (31) from (27)–(29). Although God *is* love, the second part of proposition (27)—that God loves whatever he creates *in and of itself*—is unmotivated. In fact, that assumption seems to beg the question at issue. Therefore, the argument for proposition (31) from premises (27)–(29) is inconclusive. So far, premise (31) remains unmotivated.

Second, there are also problems for Griffiths's use of (30) as a reason for affirming (31). Here is one problem with using (30) to affirm (31): Griffiths does not rule out the possibility that the millions of existing species of nonhuman animals and plants—as well as the species from the past that have gone extinct—form a web of life such that these very species form conditions necessary for the existence and flourishing of human persons in this life.

There is another problem with the inference from (30) to (31): as St. Thomas points out in a number of places, God not only loves some things in-and-of-themselves (or for their own sake, and not simply for the sake of other things), that is, intellectual creatures, but God loves all things for the sake of the perfection of the universe as a whole.[104] Therefore, (31) does not follow from (30), as even if there are things (call them "the *xs*") that exist independently of the cares, concerns, and needs of human persons, it does not follow that God wills the *xs* in-and-of-themselves, or for their own sake. For God may indeed will these things, not for their own sake or for the sake of human flourishing, but for the sake of the perfection of the universe as a whole. Therefore, premise (31) is unmotivated.

I can now bring this second problem for Griffiths's nonanthropocentric argument for APT to a close. Premise (32) of that argument is supposed to follow from premise (31), but (31) is unmotivated. Therefore, premise (32) is also unmotivated, and that means that (33) too is unmotivated. But APT, found in (35), is inferred from (33) and (34). Therefore, Griffiths's nonanthropocentric argument fails as a defense of APT.

Responding to Griffiths's Arguments for the Artifact Thesis and the Givens Thesis

As we have seen above, Griffiths also offers speculative positions on whether there are nonliving material creatures in heaven. His position has two parts, which parts correspond to two species of nonliving, material creatures, namely, artifacts, that is, those nonliving material creatures the existence of which have human agency as a central cause, and the Givens, that is, those nonliving creatures that are not artifacts. Griffiths thinks that there are no artifacts in heaven (the artifact thesis) but that the Givens do exist there (the Givens thesis).

Griffiths's argument for the artifact thesis is predicated on the assumption that human making—whether tools, languages, music—is an artifact of the Fall and so stands or falls with that assumption. I can only record the intuition that that assumption seems false. It is granted that human making was affected by the Fall, like any other human activity, but that *human making itself* is a function of the Fall seems to forget that we are created in the image and likeness of God, where God himself

---

104. See, e.g., *ST* I, q. 22, a. 2, ad 2.

has freely decided to make a universe. It seems much more plausible to think that human making is a function of being created in the image and likeness of God than that human making is, as Griffiths puts it, "a response to the devastation produced" by the Fall insofar as "the mediation of symbol, image, trope, and ornament ... is ... prompted by and responsive to the facts of opacity and separation," themselves artifacts of the Fall.[105]

Now, St. Thomas is certainly correct to think that human making is not necessary for perfect human happiness or the essential reward—having the beatific vision and its concomitant accidents of love and joy are sufficient for that. However, St. Thomas also thinks that human friendship and seeing the beauty of the new heavens and the new earth are aspects of the accidental reward for the saints in heaven insofar as they are fitting and appropriate ways in which human persons, as embodied, participate in the beatific vision. It seems, for the same kind of reason, that human making—even the contemplating of the truths, goods, and beauties of the great human artifacts of this life—can be an aspect of the accidental reward. Indeed, it seems very fitting that the making and appreciating of art plays some role in the accidental reward of human persons in heaven insofar as human persons are created in the image and likeness of a God who freely decides to create.[106]

What of Griffiths's arguments for the Givens thesis? Recall that Griffiths offers two anthropocentric arguments and one nonanthropocentric argument. Griffiths's arguments for the Givens thesis parallel his arguments for APT, and so are subject to the same problems.

Like one of Griffiths's anthropocentric arguments for APT, his first anthropocentric argument for the Givens thesis contains an unmotivated premise that human existence is essentially related to the existence of some kind of material substance other than human persons, whether nonhuman animals and plants, or, in this case, the Givens. Grant that embodied human persons in heaven need to be in a place, and that the existence of places requires that material things exist other than hu-

---

105. *Decreation*, 306.
106. For beautiful reflections on the theme of the nature of—and potential dangers for—human persons as "subcreators," see J. R. R. Tolkien, "Tree and Leaf," in *The Tolkien Reader* (New York: Ballantine Books, 1966), 33–124, esp. 87–90, and his collected letters in *The Letters of J. R. R. Tolkien*, ed. Humphrey Carpenter and Christopher Tolkien (Boston: Houghton Mifflin, 1995). For some good discussion of Tolkien on human persons as subcreators, see Bradley J. Birzer, *J. R. R. Tolkien's Sanctifying Myth: Understanding Middle Earth* (Wilmington, Del.: ISI Books, 2009).

man bodies, for example, to give the saints spatial orientation. But why should one think that *all* the material substances that exist in this life need to exist in heaven? Perhaps "a new heavens and a new earth" includes only some of those kinds of givens, or includes entirely new kinds, namely, those whose mode of existence is consistent with the incorruptible life of the saints.

Like his second anthropocentric argument for APT, Griffiths's second anthropocentric argument for the existence of the Givens in heaven makes at least two unmotivated, or false, assumptions: first, the corruption of the Givens in this life is an artifact of the Fall, and second, heaven is partly a recapitulation of the created order as a whole prior to the Fall. When treating Griffiths's argument that the death of animals and plants is an artifact of the Fall, I asked how angelic sin could have accomplished (or occasioned) such a thing. Even more difficult to understand is how the corruption of nonliving material substances is itself a function of angelic sin, as Griffiths suggests. Rather, it seems more plausible to suggest, with St. Thomas, that, although God does not will corruption—or death—for its own sake, he does will it *per accidens* for the sake of the beauty of the whole corruptible universe, for the sake of the nourishment and generation of human persons in this life, and for the mending, healing, and refining of the souls of his saints, if they were to fall into sin.[107] For sin, as grievous as its effects are on the created order, is not so powerful so as to destroy or alter the natures or natural inclinations of what God has created. Furthermore, acts of eating, drinking, and reproduction certainly each involve the corruption of *something*, and such activities were part of life in Eden.[108]

Finally, there is Griffiths's nonanthropocentric argument for the Givens thesis, which argument parallels his nonanthropocentric argument for APT. Griffiths's nonanthropocentric argument for the Givens thesis therefore also assumes the problematic—or at least unmotivated—assumptions that corruption itself is an artifact of the Fall and that heaven is, at least partly, a recapitulation of the created order prior to the Fall. In addition, the argument also implicitly contains the unmotivated (and false, at least from a Thomistic perspective) assumption that if God

---

107. See, e.g., *SCG* III.112; *ST* I, q. 49, a. 2; *In Rom* 8, lect. 6. For a magisterial treatment of the problem of suffering and evil from a Thomistic perspective, see Stump, *Wandering in Darkness*.

108. Even if there were *de facto* no acts of reproduction in Eden, God antecedently wills acts of reproduction there (see, e.g., Gn 1:28).

loves x, then God wills x to exist for its own sake. Finally, the argument also contains an invalid inference. Recall that Griffiths seems to assume that if God does not will created thing x for the sake of the existence or flourishing of human persons, then God wills x for its own sake. But, as St. Thomas points out, (it is possible that) God wills all nonhuman material substances to exist, not for their own sake, but for the sake of the perfection of the universe as a whole.

My exposition of St. Thomas's views on the essential reward (part 2 of this book) and the accidental reward (part 3 of this book) in heaven is now complete. The fourth and final part shows how St. Thomas's doctrine on heaven fruitfully bears on the four problems concerning eternal life discussed in part 1.

PART 4

THOMISTIC SOLUTIONS TO FOUR APPARENT PROBLEMS CONCERNING ETERNAL LIFE

14

A Thomistic Solution to PNH-I

THE GOODS OF THE BEATIFIC VISION AND
THE CITY OF GOD, RIGHTLY ORDERED

Part 1 of this book explained four apparent problems concerning traditional Christian accounts of eternal life, canvased some interesting solutions to these problems offered by contemporary theologians and philosophers, and highlighted some problems or limitations for each of these contemporary solutions. Drawing on the exposition of St. Thomas's views on heaven in part 2 (the essential reward) and part 3 (the accidental reward), this final part makes explicit how a Thomist can fruitfully respond to these four apparent problems concerning eternal life.

This chapter takes up a Thomistic response to PNH-I in particular. It shows that a Thomistic response enjoys advantages over the contemporary responses canvased in chapter 1. For, on St. Thomas's view, heaven plausibly can be understood to be both a private communion with God and a participation in a perfected cosmos, where these goods are rightly ordered to one another. For whereas the essential reward in heaven consists in a human person's vision of the essence of God such that she is caught up into the very eternal life of God, a human person's accidental reward consists, among other things, in glorified embodiment, membership in the communion of the saints, and the sensing of the beauties of "the new heavens and the new earth." Such a response is not only consistent with the teaching of authoritative, Catholic Christian tradition, but it avoids the problems or limitations that plague the solutions of Germain Grisez and Katherin Rogers.

SOME CONTEMPORARY RESPONSES TO PNH-I:
A BRIEF REVIEW

Before reviewing the solutions of Grisez and Rogers, recall the four crucial premises concerning the first problem of the nature of heaven:

(1) The notion that (a) *heaven for an intellectual creature consists merely of the beatific vision* is in conflict with the notion that (b) *heaven includes the reality of "the new heavens and the new earth," which itself includes a perfect human community, and, at least eventually, perfected embodiment on the part of human persons in the next life* [assumption].

(2) The notion that (c) *heaven consists merely of a perfect cosmic community, that is, "the new heavens and the new earth," which includes a perfect human community, overseen by a good and gracious God*, is in conflict with the notion that (d) *God is absolutely perfect and infinitely good* [assumption].

(3) (a) or (c) [assumption].

(4) (b) and (d) [assumption].

From premises (1)–(4), we can derive a contradiction; hence, we have PNH-I.

Let us begin with a review of Grisez's solution. Grisez either rejects (2) or (3) of PNH-I, as he rejects (a), accepts (d), and thinks that union with God in heaven is just one of many fundamental goods enjoyed by the saints in heaven, even if union with God is the greatest good enjoyed by the saints. Thus, depending on how we interpret (c), Grisez either rejects (c)—and so rejects (3)—or rejects that (c) and (d) are in conflict—and so rejects (2).

Nevertheless, there are at least two problems with Grisez's solution. First, in treating union with God and union with other created persons as two necessary (and jointly sufficient) conditions for perfect human happiness, Grisez's solution to PNH-I is not consistent with what I have called (in chapter 1) *the Augustinian Intuition*. As St. Augustine says, wisely, in the *Confessions*: "the one who enjoys God has no less than he who enjoys some creature in addition to God."[1] Grisez's solution to PNH-I thus does not do justice to the good of the beatific vision as incommensurate with finite goods.

Grisez's solution has a second problem. He thinks that the commu-

---

1. See, e.g., *Confessions* V.4.

nion of the saints in heaven is partly constitutive of perfect human happiness. This is because Grisez thinks that there are certain "fundamental goods" for human persons, the possession of each of which is necessary for perfect human happiness. According to Grisez, the fundamental goods include *life*, which good itself includes health and bodily integrity, *skillful work, play, knowledge, aesthetic experience, harmony with God, harmony among human beings, harmony between one's own faculties* (e.g., harmony with one's own judgements, choices, feelings, and behavior), *marriage*, and *parenthood*. As grace perfects and does not set aside nature, the graced perfect human life of heaven includes the perfection of all these fundamental goods for human persons, including sexual union and marriage. But according to scripture, there is no marriage in heaven (see, e.g., Mt 22:23–33 and Lk 20:27–40). Therefore, a Grisezean solution to PNH-I is in conflict with the teaching of scripture and authoritative Christian tradition.

Chapter 1 also discussed Katherin Rogers's attempt to split the gap between the individualistic and social conceptions of the nature of heaven. Rogers offers her account of the nature of heaven as an interpretation of St. Anselm's views. Like Grisez's solution to PNH-I, Rogers's solution offers a middle position between the individualistic and social models of heaven. But whereas Grisez's solution is closer to the social model of heaven, Rogers's solution is closer to the individualistic model.

Rogers thinks that St. Anselm has the view that perfect human happiness consists in the beatific vision. Nonetheless, she thinks that a puzzle such as PNH-I presents us with a false dichotomy insofar as intellectual creatures also perfectly know creatures in the beatific vision in virtue of knowing the essence of God in the beatific vision.[2] Rogers's Anselmian solution to PNH-I has a problem. Whatever the saints know of creatures *in God*, it seems as though scripture and authoritative, Catholic Christian tradition teach that the saints in heaven know other creatures *directly*. But knowledge of a creature in virtue of having the beatific vision is an indirect form of knowledge of that creature. Rogers's Anselmian middle way is thus not really a middle way at all but rather has us affirming

---

2. As we have seen, St. Thomas also thinks that, if God is the primary object of the beatific vision, creatures form a secondary object of the vision. See the discussion of this distinction in chapter 6 above. Nonetheless, St. Thomas's account of human happiness is not limited in the way in which Rogers's Anselmian position is, as St. Thomas thinks that human persons in heaven not only know creatures indirectly and mediately in the beatific vision, but also directly and immediately as a part of their accidental reward.

premise (3) of PNH-I. For all that Rogers has said—and admittedly, she is not in her article explicitly addressing PNH-I—we are still stuck with the awkward conclusion that the Christian tradition on heaven entails a contradiction.

ST. THOMAS'S DOCTRINE AND PNH-I

Given the arguments presented in parts 2 and 3 of this book, St. Thomas would accept premises (1), (2), and (4) of PNH-I. But he would reject premise (3) insofar as heaven, for St. Thomas, has different aspects. For example, heaven consists of each saint's essential reward, that is, the vision of the essence of God and the proper accidents following upon that vision, namely, delight, love, and joy. But heaven also consists of each saint's accidental reward. For example, after the general resurrection, the accidental reward for human persons in heaven includes glorified human embodiment, embodied human community, and the direct knowing of bodily creatures, especially the risen body of Christ, scarred for the sake of the salvation of human persons, but also nonrational material creatures in "the new heavens and the new earth."

What allows St. Thomas, reasonably, to have such a capacious view of the heavenly life of the saints? In particular, it is the plausibility of his distinction between the *essential* reward and the *accidental* reward of the saints. As the essential reward consists in the beatific vision and the acts of will that flow from it—the most direct and unmediated form of union with God logically possible for a creature—and God is absolutely perfect and infinite goodness, the essential reward all by itself completely sates human desire. For the saint having the beatific vision is made deiform, thereby participating in God's own happiness in the greatest way possible for a creature. As the elements of the accidental reward are nonetheless genuine human goods, God in his graciousness gives those goods to the saints in heaven too. As heaven essentially consists in a private and most intimate union with God (the beatific vision and the delight that flows from it), (c) is false; but because heaven also fittingly consists of the accidental reward, including the communion of the saints, (a) too is false. Therefore, premise (3) of PNH-I is false.

Assume, for the moment, that the distinction between the essential reward and the accidental reward is coherent. That distinction gives the Thomist a way of gracefully synthesizing the notion that beatific union with God in heaven is incommensurate with other goods—thereby affirming the Augustinian Intuition—with the notion that creaturely goods, such as human embodiment and the communion of the saints, are lesser (but still) fitting and appropriate goods for human persons to have in heaven. The Thomist can therefore affirm both proposition (b) and proposition (d). Therefore, St. Thomas's distinction between the essential reward and the accidental reward of the saints allows the Thomist to accept premise (4) of PNH-I. Thinking about St. Thomas's distinction between the essential reward as the beatific vision and delight in the vision, on the one hand, and the accidental reward as the saint's knowledge and love of creatures in heaven, on the other, can also help us make sense of why some thinkers have accepted (the false) propositions (a) and (c).

As we saw in chapter 1, a reason to accept proposition (a) is that God is perfect being, goodness, and beauty itself. If a view of heaven treats something other than God as constitutive of the essential reward or perfect human happiness, then that view does not do justice to the absolute and infinite perfection of God, that is, proposition (d). Put in a different way, the Augustinian Intuition is true: all other things being equal, the person S who enjoys some creature in addition to beatific union with God is no more perfectly happy than the person S1 who simply enjoys beatific union with God. Without accepting the distinction between the essential reward and the accidental reward, accepting (d) or the Augustinian Intuition leads to accepting (a). If we distinguish perfect human happiness, or the essential reward, and the well-being of perfect happiness (the accidental reward added to the essential reward), then we can accept (d) and the Augustinian Intuition while also rejecting (a).

The intuition behind accepting premise (c) is that creatures, or the finite, have some role to play in the heavenly life of human persons too, that is, proposition (b). But the incommensurate goodness of the beatific vision compared to the goodness of creatures threatens to eliminate creatures entirely from playing a role in human happiness in heaven. So, in order to preserve the humanity of heaven, one is tempted to reject (d) or the Augustinian Intuition. As we have seen, St. Thomas makes sense of the intuition that there are creaturely goods in heaven, without contradicting (d) or the Augustinian Intuition, in two ways.

Sometimes St. Thomas distinguishes the essential reward in heaven and the accidental reward. For St. Thomas, the individual saint's essential reward consists in the beatific vision and the proper accidents that follow on that vision, wherein an absolutely perfect and infinitely good God brings it about that he is the object of the saint's understanding and love. But creaturely goods, goods such as human embodiment at and after the general resurrection, the communion of the saints, and the direct cognition of creatures, to take just a few examples, are constitutive parts of the accidental reward. The creaturely goods that form component parts of the accidental reward are certainly not the focus of heavenly life for human persons; in fact, they are not even necessary for perfect human happiness.

This brings us to a second way St. Thomas sometimes talks about the relative importance of creaturely goods in heaven. Whereas creaturely goods are not necessary for perfect human happiness—the beatific vision and its proper accidents being both necessary and sufficient for perfect human happiness in heaven—certain creaturely goods are necessary for the well-being (*bene esse*) of perfect human happiness in heaven.

I have offered (at the end of chapter 9 above) a number of ways to show that St. Thomas's view that *the essential reward is a good that wholly satisfies human desire and the accidental reward consists of genuine human goods* is coherent. Recall that the beatific vision, along with its concomitant accidents of delight, love, and joy, is sufficient to sate the desire of an intellectual creature. This is because the beatific vision is God's gracing the intellectual creature such that the beatified creature engages in the perfect and simultaneously whole act of seeing the essence of God in the most direct and unmediated way possible for a creature. The beatified creature is thereby made *deiform*, like unto God, in the greatest logically possible way. For the beatified creature is taken up into God's own perfect eternal life and happiness so as to actively and immutably participate in it. In addition, in virtue of knowing the essence of God in the beatific vision in this intimate way, the intellectual creature is also granted a great knowledge of creatures. The goodness of the beatific vision is simply incommensurate with any other creaturely good. Therefore, if a human person S with a degree of charity C enjoys the good of union with God in the beatific vision, and a human person S1 with a degree of charity C has the good of union with God in the beatific vision *and* some creaturely good G, S1 is not more intensely happy than S (and, we might also say, using another way that St. Thomas speaks, that S1 is no more perfectly happy than S, keeping in mind the real difference between perfect happiness, on the one hand, and the well-being of perfect happiness, on the other). St. Thomas thus preserves what we have called the Augustinian Intuition about God and human happiness.

That being said, Christian tradition teaches that the saints in heaven enjoy goods other than God in heaven, including human embodiment and the communion of the saints. As Ezra Sullivan puts it, these goods are not, however, necessary for perfect human happiness; they are rather *gratuitous* goods. I suggested that a *gratuitous* good G is a good that a person S would not miss if S did not possess G, but S is nonetheless thankful for G if or when S does possess G. For example, your friend invites you to go out for drinks after work. You suggest drinks at your house instead (not only is your bar well-stocked, but your friend will not have to pay for anything). Your friend could have paid for his drinks that day. But given your insistence, he is happy to receive this gratuitous good.

I also spoke in a second way of those goods that are aspects of the accidental reward—or make for the well-being of perfect happiness. Because we are animals of a certain sort, some of the goods that are aspects of the accidental reward are *fitting* or *appropriate* goods for creatures such as ourselves to enjoy in heaven, even if they are not necessary for perfect happiness. I said that a good G is *fitting* or *appropriate* for a creature C if and only if the perfection of C does not require G, but, given C's nature, the possession of G would be a real good for C.[3] For example, Sam could live a good human life even if he never sees the Grand Tetons. But seeing the Grand Tetons is a genuine good for Sam because Sam is a rational animal, sensible beauties bring him pleasure, and this mountain range is a particular sensible beauty the seeing of which is quite pleasant. Thus, seeing the Grand Tetons is a fitting or appropriate good for Sam.

Given the notions of a gratuitous good and a fitting or appropriate good, we can make sense of the relative goodness of the component parts of the accidental reward—or goods that make not for perfect happiness but the well-being of perfect happiness—as follows. Because the beatific vision is a good that is simply incommensurate with any other good, a

---

3. Recall that "fitting" is being used here in a slightly weaker sense than St. Thomas's *conveniens*, which is often translated as "fitting" (see, e.g., *ST* III. q. 1, a. 2).

saint in heaven can be perfectly happy without any aspect of the accidental reward, for example, embodiment. For even without her body in heaven, Sally (a human person) enjoys an intellectual and loving union with God that is as direct and unmediated—as intimate—as is logically possible for a creature. But having a human body is a gratuitous good and a fitting or appropriate good for an animal such as Sally.

As we saw in chapter 9, we can make sense of the distinction between the good of the essential reward in heaven for human persons and the good that is the accidental reward for human persons in heaven in still another way, by drawing upon the work of philosopher Brandon Dahm. We saw that Dahm distinguishes between *desires-from-fulfillment* and *desires-from-lack*. *Desires-from-lack* are the more ordinary sort of desires. A person S's possession of such desires entails that S is not perfectly happy. Although all human persons in this life suffer desires-from-lack, no human persons having the beatific vision in heaven suffer such desires, including human persons who do not currently possess all the aspects of their accidental reward, for example, human persons without their bodies. That is to say, the essential reward satisfies the desires-from-lack in the saints in heaven.

On the other hand, *desires-from-fulfillment* are desires that arise not from a lack in the desirer, but rather from a perfection in the agent such that she wills to share the perfection she has. Dahm's this-worldly example of a desire-from-fulfillment is the father who rushes to tell his family and friends—even any strangers he happens to meet along the way—about the birth of his first child. He does so, not so much out of an unsatisfied need, but rather because he desires to share a great good with others. The saint having the beatific vision, and so enjoying the essential reward or perfect happiness, who desires a component part of the accidental reward—or a creaturely good that makes for the well-being of perfect happiness—has a desire-from-fulfillment. For example, the saint wishes for her body, or other saints, to participate in some way in the incommensurate good of the beatific vision.

Given St. Thomas's coherent distinction between the essential reward as sating all desire (from lack) on the part of the person who possesses it and the accidental reward as consisting of genuine human goods, St. Thomas can reasonably reject (3) in PNH-I. Although the beatific vision is the essential and central aspect of heavenly life for created persons, it is not the only aspect of heaven. For there is also the accidental reward.

In addition, the essential reward consists not only of the intellectual act that is the beatific vision, but also the proper accidents of the vision, such as love, joy, and delight. Therefore, according to St. Thomas, proposition (a) is false not only because there is the accidental reward in addition to the essential reward but for another reason: the essential reward itself does not simply consist of the beatific vision, for it also consists of the proper accidents of the vision, which are the volitional aspects of perfect human happiness, such as delight, love, and joy.

According to St. Thomas, it is also the case that those aspects of heavenly life that fall under the accidental reward are not classified as goods in the same sense that the essential reward is good. Indeed, the saint having the essential reward without the accidental reward is perfectly happy. Therefore, the Thomistic solution to PNH-I, unlike Grisez's solution to PNH-I, is consistent with the Augustinian Intuition.

With St. Thomas's distinction between the essential reward and the accidental reward, he can also affirm premise (4). For his view of what the accidental reward consists in allows him to affirm both propositions (b) and (d). Although the most glorious activity in which the saints are involved in heaven is the beatific vision and the proper accidents of love, joy, and delight that flow from that vision, according to St. Thomas, experience, even activity, in heaven has multiple facets. It also includes sensation, and the knowing and loving of creatures, such as Christ in his human nature, the Virgin Mary, the angels, the saints, and the nonrational creatures that constitute "the new heavens and the new earth." This communion of created goods in heaven, unlike Rogers's Anselmian view, involves direct and unmediated union between created persons and other creatures, and not simply the saints' knowing and loving of creatures in virtue of having the beatific vision.

Unlike Grisez's solution to PNH-I, St. Thomas can solve that problem without rejecting (d) or the Augustinian Intuition. In addition, a Thomistic solution, given the distinction between the essential reward and the accidental reward, is also consistent with the truth of proposition (b), unlike Rogers's solution. St. Thomas's model of beatitude thus allows him to make sense of a wider variety of sources and intuitions about God, human persons, heaven, and blessedness in the Christian tradition than the models of Grisez or Rogers.

15

A Thomistic Solution to PNH-II

TRANSFIGURED HUMAN EMBODIMENT

A second apparent problem concerning eternal life suggests there is a tension in the Christian tradition regarding the degree to which eternal life is continuous with this-worldly life. The Christian tradition's otherworldly account of heaven, particularly in its emphasis on the beatific vision and human life as incorruptible, seems to be at odds with the Christian tradition's affirmation that human persons in heaven are eventually embodied, where the bodies of human persons in heaven are numerically identical to the bodies human persons possess in this life. This apparent problem was referred to as PNH-II, above.

LYNNE RUDDER BAKER AND PNH-II

Recall that I formulated the second problem concerning the nature of heaven as follows:

(1) The notion that (*e*) *heaven is otherworldly insofar as it involves the beatific vision, that is, an immaterial union between immaterial God and the immaterial soul*, is in conflict with the notion that (*f*) *human persons are essentially temporal beings* or the notion that (*g*) *the resurrected bodies of the saints in heaven are numerically and specifically the same as the bodies human persons have in this life, e.g., bodies that are constantly changing, are corruptible, take up space, etc.* [assumption].

(2) The notion that (*h*) *heaven is otherworldly insofar as the resurrected bodies of the saints in heaven are spiritual, incorruptible, and immortal in heaven* is in conflict with (*g*) [assumption]

(3) Proposition (f) is true [assumption].

(4) Authoritative, Christian tradition affirms (e), (g), and (h) [assumption].

(5) Therefore, the Christian tradition's account of heaven entails a contradiction [from (1)–(4)].

As we saw in chapter 1, Lynne Rudder Baker thinks that there is a conflict between propositions (g) and (h). She accepts (h) but rejects (g). Why does she think those things? On the strength of the words of St. Paul, Rudder Baker thinks that resurrection bodies are immortal and incorruptible (1 Cor 15:53). But our bodies in this life are mortal and corruptible. Therefore, our bodies in this life and our bodies at and after the general resurrection are not specifically identical and so not numerically identical.

In speaking about the resurrection of the body, Rudder Baker is careful to talk about time-honored traditions with respect to the doctrine of the resurrection of the body. For example, she argues that a Christian way of speaking about the next life must include three elements. First, Christian belief about the next life requires belief that persons in this life are numerically identical to persons in the next; *psychological similarity* is not enough. Second, our life in the next world, whether in heaven or in hell, involves embodiment. Plato is wrong to think the afterlife for some is wholly immaterial. Third, the resurrection of the dead is not something natural, but miraculous.

Although Rudder Baker clearly defends traditional Christian beliefs about the next life, her traditionalism, at least from a Catholic point of view, is also clearly selective. This is because authoritative Catholic Christian tradition also clearly teaches that our bodies at and after the resurrection are specifically and numerically the same as our bodies in this life.

A THOMISTIC SOLUTION TO PNH-II

Given what I have said about St. Thomas's views in previous chapters, how can a Thomist reasonably respond to PNH-II? We have seen that St. Thomas has a very exalted view of the beatific vision of the saints in heaven. Such a vision makes the saints in heaven *deiform*, like unto God, in such a way that they come to participate in God's own eternal life and happiness such that their essential reward cannot be measured by time or aeveternity. St. Thomas thinks that the beatific vision is a graced *activity*. Although not identical to God's eternal act, the beatific vision is nonetheless a participation therein, enabling those saints to be as closely united to God as is logically possible (given the degree of charity possessed by each of those intellectual creatures when their beatific vision begins). On such an exalted view of the beatific vision, it may look as though a Thomist needs to accept premise (1) of PNH-II insofar as there is indeed a conflict between the notion that the saints in heaven have the beatific vision and the notion that human persons are essentially temporal beings.

But a Thomist might very well wonder whether we should accept premise (3). Of course, in this life, all of our experience is colored by the passage of time. Indeed, we may think that bodily being is necessarily a temporal mode of being. But Thomists think that human persons are not simply bodily beings. Human persons, insofar as they have intellectual souls as parts, are, by nature, spiritual beings too. Indeed, St. Thomas sometimes compares the nature and characteristic activity of the human soul with angelic existence and activity.[1] From a Thomistic perspective, then, (3) is ambiguous because (f) is ambiguous. For example, here are two things that (f) could mean:

(f*) Human persons are essentially temporal beings insofar as (i) human matter is an essential part of human persons, and (ii) although human persons need not be embodied, it is *natural* or *normal* for them to be embodied such that they have human matter as a metaphysical part, and (iii) anything with human matter as a metaphysical part is such that its actions are temporal.

(f**) Human persons are essentially temporal beings insofar as (i) human matter is an essential part of human persons, and (ii) although human persons need not be embodied, it is *natural* or *normal* for them to be embodied such that they have human matter as a metaphysical part, and (iii*) anything with human matter as a metaphysical part is such that *some* of its actions are temporal, that is, its bodily acts.

---

1. See, e.g., the preface to the treatise on human persons in *ST*: "Post considerationem creaturae spiritualis et corporalis, considerandum est de homine, qui ex spirituali et corporali substantia componitur." See also *In Sent* III, d. 31, q. 2, a. 4; IV, d. 50, q. 1, a. 1; *QDV*, q. 19, a. 1; *SCG* II.81.11–15; *In 1 Cor* 13, lect. 3, nn. 790–91; *ST* I, q. 89, aa. 1–2; *QDA*, a. 15; *QDSC*, a. 1; *QQ* III, q. 9, a. 1; XII, q. 9, a. 12; *ST* I-II, q. 67, a. 2, ad 3. For some thoughtful discussion of St. Thomas's views on human persons as spiritual beings, see Vonier, *The Human Soul and Its Relations with Other Spirits*.

St. Thomas rejects (f*) because human persons are composed of a part, the intellectual soul, whose nature is aeveternal, and so human persons—even when composed of human matter—at and after the general resurrection may be capable of actions that are measured not by time but aeveternity.

Also, St. Thomas certainly thinks that human persons composed of human matter can engage in the nontemporal act that is the beatific vision. The possibility of human persons engaging in such an act is not only a function of human persons having intellect, but because God, by his grace, confers on human persons in heaven the light of glory (*lumen gloriae*) so as to raise up the human intellect to engage in the nontemporal, nonaeveternal act that is the beatific vision. In addition, as we have seen in chapter 11, the human body that is part of a human person having the beatific vision is *glorified*, that is, it comes to participate in the soul's beatific vision as far as it can, taking on the properties of impassibility, subtlety, agility, and luminosity. Particularly relevant here is the glorified body's property of *subtlety*. Recall that in St. Thomas's view, the subtlety of the glorified body is the human body being perfected by the soul having the beatific vision insofar as the glorified body is subject to the soul as substantial form of the glorified body. In addition, for St. Thomas, the subtle body is a spiritual body in St. Paul's sense (1 Cor 15:44). And St. Thomas understands that to mean that not only does the body not hinder the contemplation of God in heaven, but the body actually participates in such timeless contemplation in what it does, insofar as that is possible, rather than being engaged in characteristically animal activities.

On the other hand, St. Thomas can accept (f**), rightly understood. First, at and after the general resurrection, the human person can engage in temporal acts, such as moving one's body from the new heavens to the new earth, and back again, even while engaging in the nontemporal acts that constitute the essential reward, that is, the beatific vision and delighting in, taking joy in, and loving God as possessed by way of the vision. But, as we saw above in chapter 11, there is no necessary incompatibility between a human person S engaging in an act that is nontemporal insofar as it is a graced activity of the intellect and will and S also engaging in temporal acts insofar as S does things with S's body. Therefore, a proper understanding of (f) as (f**) can be true, making premise (3) true and proposition (f) compatible with (e).

Recall that I mentioned that St. Thomas can accept (f**), rightly understood. The importance of the caveat lies in the fact that St. Thomas thinks that time will cease in the next life.[2] He cites a number of scriptural passages to defend this view. For example, St. Thomas cites the Vulgate translation of Revelation 10:6 that "time shall be no longer" (*tempus amplius non erit*).[3] St. Thomas also cites Isaiah 60:20 ("Your sun will never set again, and your moon will wane no more")[4] and 1 Corinthians 7:31 ("For this world in its present form is passing away").[5]

It seems clear that by saying *time will cease* St. Thomas means that *time will cease as we now experience it* as the measure of change with respect to before and after, *where the standard of measure is the motion of the heavens*. For, as we have seen, St. Thomas thinks that the motion of the heavens will cease at the general resurrection. In addition, he thinks that the natural mode of being of the angels and the graced mode of being of human persons after the general resurrection is aeveternity. But aeveternity involves a relation to time *in the general sense* that it is a measure of change with respect to before and after.[6] To see this, recall that the natural mode of the substantial being of the angels is aeveternal. But some of their activities are measured by time (in the general sense specified above), because sometimes an angel is acting at this place and time, for example, Gabriel's delivering a message to Zechariah, while sometimes acting at another place and time, for example, Gabriel's delivering a message to the Virgin Mary. So, when it comes to human persons in heaven, in those aspects of the accidental reward that involve cognition and movement, human personal activity in heaven is measured by time (in the general sense).

Indeed, we do not have to share St. Thomas's Aristotelian cosmology to admit that time, as we now know it and experience it, will cease insofar as there is "a new heavens and a new earth," or insofar as human lives and bodies will be immortal and incorruptible. Certainly, there is no need to accept proposition (f) or proposition (iii*) in (f**)—and so (f**)—

---

2. See, e.g., *In Sent* IV, d. 47, q. 2, a. 2, q.c. 1, resp. (*ST Suppl.*, q. 74, a. 4, resp.); d. 48, q. 2, a. 2 (*ST Suppl.*, q. 91, a. 2); *CT* I, chap. 171; *SCG* IV.97; *QDP*, q. 5, a. 5; *In Jn* 6, lect. 5, n. 940; *In Heb* 1, lect. 5, n. 72.

3. See, e.g., *In Sent* IV, d. 48, q. 2, a. 2, s.c. (*ST Suppl.*, q. 91, a. 2, s.c.); *SCG* IV.97.2; *QDP*, q. 5, a. 5, s.c.

4. *In Sent* IV, d. 48, q. 2, a. 2, s.c. (*ST Suppl.*, q. 91, a. 2, s.c.).

5. See, e.g., *SCG* IV.97.5 and *CT* I, chap. 171.

6. See, e.g., *QQ* X, q. 2; *QDP*, q. 3, a. 14, ad 18; *ST* I, q. 10, a. 5.

if we understand (f) or (iii*) in (f**) to mean that experiencing time *as we do now* is essential to being an embodied human person.

As I have said, St. Thomas's exalted understanding of the beatific vision need not be seen as conflicting with (f**) understood in such a way that human persons in heaven engage in temporal acts that are not measured in the same way we measure temporal acts in this life. Nonetheless, human temporal acts in heaven will involve before and after. Insofar as St. Thomas is committed to the doctrine that grace does not destroy or set aside nature, but rather perfects it, he does not think that the grace of beatific activity in heaven sets aside or destroys human nature. This includes the aeveternal dimension of a human person's substantial being or the temporal acts of cognition and the human body that are aspects of the accidental reward. Rather, we should say, with St. Thomas, the following:

(6) The mode of *substantial* being of any intellectual creature, including the angels and saints having the beatific vision, is aeveternal.[7]

(7) The acts of the human person in soul and body that are aspects of the accidental reward are temporal (in a general sense).

(8) The created act that is the beatific vision is neither measured by time (in any sense) nor aeveternity, as the beatific vision is the intellectual creature's graced participation in God's own eternal life and perfect happiness.[8]

The Thomist can therefore reasonably affirm that there is no conflict between (e)—even when it includes St. Thomas's exalted position with respect to the beatific vision—and (f), plausibly understood as (f**). So far, a Thomist can reasonably say that premise (1) of PNH-II is false.

To answer the question regarding whether (e) and (g) are compatible, we can simply ask if (h) and (g) are compatible. For, as we have seen, St. Thomas thinks that the characteristic qualities of human bodies in heaven are caused by the soul's beatific activity in heaven and so there is no inconsistency between the beatific activity of the saints and the saints possessing glorified bodies. Therefore, if we can show that glorified human bodies can be numerically identical to human bodies in this life, we

---

7. Or perhaps more precisely: the mode of the substantial being of the angels is aeveternal, the mode of the substantial being of human persons *qua* intellectual soul is aeveternal, the mode of the substantial being of human persons *qua* composite is temporal (in a general sense).

8. See, e.g., *ST* I, q. 10, a. 5, ad 1.

thereby also show that there is no conflict between the saints having the beatific vision while, after the general resurrection, also possessing bodies that are numerically identical to the bodies they possessed in this life.

So, are propositions (h) and (g) compatible? That question leads naturally to the argument of Lynne Rudder Baker's examined in chapter 1, which we can formulate as a defense of (2) and, because St. Thomas accepts (g) and (h), as an objection to the views of St. Thomas. St. Thomas's response to this objection brings this chapter to a close.

Recall that Rudder Baker argues that the bodies of the saints in heaven cannot be numerically identical to the bodies we possess in this life, as the bodies of the saints in heaven will be immortal and incorruptible whereas human bodies in this life are mortal and corruptible. For the persistence conditions of a thing are an essential feature of that thing. If objects x and y have different essential properties, then x and y are not numerically identical. Because human bodies in this life and the bodies of the saints in heaven have different persistence conditions, they are not numerically identical.

As we have seen, Rudder Baker resolves this conflict by denying that we have *human* bodies in the next life. That is, she rejects (g). But St. Thomas cannot do that, as he thinks with authoritative, Catholic Christian tradition that (g) is true. Furthermore, St. Thomas agrees that heavenly life is otherworldly. Not only is St. Thomas's view of the essential reward quite otherworldly, but so is his account of the accidental reward. For, according to the tradition that St. Thomas inherits, human bodies in heaven are *glorified* bodies; the glorified human body participates in the beatific vision such that it is impassible, subtle, agile, and luminescent. So we might wonder (with Rudder Baker), how can a human person's glorified body—one that is impassible, subtle, agile, and luminescent—be a *human* body, let alone numerically the same human body that that person had in this life?

St. Thomas entertains a similar objection in his commentary on 1 Corinthians.[9] In that text St. Thomas mentions an objection to human bodies being numerically identical at the resurrection based on the Pauline text that "the corruptible will put on the incorruptible" (15:53). The objection begins by positing that corruptible things and incorruptible things differ by genus. But if x and y differ in genus, then x and y are not

---

9. *In 1 Cor* 15, lect. 9, n. 1015.

numerically the same. Because St. Paul teaches that resurrection bodies are incorruptible and human bodies in this life are obviously corruptible, it follows that human bodies at the resurrection will not be numerically the same as human bodies in this life.

St. Thomas responds to this objection by admitting that, if a body's incorruptibility were caused by its nature, then that incorruptible body would differ in genus from a body that, by nature, is corruptible, as a thing's genus and species are derived from its own nature and not from that which is extrinsic to its nature. But St. Thomas thinks that the Christian faith teaches that the incorruptibility of the resurrection body is brought about by causes extrinsic to its nature. First, the incorruptibility of human bodies at and after the general resurrection is brought about by the power of God. For, according to St. Thomas, the power of Christ's resurrection is applied to all human bodies at and after the general resurrection to make all human bodies incorruptible,[10] while the grace of the beatific vision is an additional extrinsic cause of the incorruptibility of human bodies in heaven. Second, although all human persons have incorruptible bodies by some sort of preternatural or supernatural disposition in their souls—merely a preternatural disposition in the souls of the damned and both supernatural and preternatural dispositions in the souls of the blessed—human bodies at and after the resurrection remain, in and of themselves, corruptible. Therefore, there is no reason to affirm the premise of the objection that says that incorruptible human bodies at and after the resurrection and corruptible human bodies in this life differ in genus.[11]

Note, then, how St. Thomas would respond to Rudder Baker's contention that the resurrection bodies of the saints in heaven are numerically distinct from our human bodies in this life. Recall that Rudder Baker argues for this view as follows:

(RB1) The resurrection bodies of the saints in heaven and our human bodies in this life have different persistence conditions—the latter are corruptible whereas the former are incorruptible.

(RB2) A thing's persistence conditions are among its essential properties.

---

10. See, e.g., *SCG* IV.86.1.
11. *In 1 Cor* 15, lect. 9, n. 1015.

(RB3) If x and y have different essential properties, then x and y are not numerically identical.

(RB4) Therefore, the resurrection bodies of the saints in heaven are not numerically identical to human bodies in this life.

St. Thomas would respond to this argument by noting that a thing's essential properties are derived from its nature, and not because of circumstances or qualities in the soul extrinsic to its nature. The incorruptibility of the bodies of the saints in heaven is due to the beatified soul configuring matter after the resurrection, and the beatification of the soul is itself due to God as extrinsic source of the graces of the beatific vision and the *lumen gloriae* in the souls of the beatified. Therefore, RB2 is ambiguous. It can mean either of the following statements:

(RB2*) A thing's persistence conditions based on its nature or kind are among its essential properties.

(RB2**) A thing's persistence conditions based on something extrinsic to its nature or kind, for example, a graced disposition in the soul making that thing have a certain set of persistence conditions, are among its essential properties.

If RB2 is read as RB2**, then RB2 is false, St. Thomas thinks, because a thing's species—its set of essential features—is derived from its nature, and not from something extrinsic added to that nature, such as a superadded grace that makes a corruptible body incorruptible. Given that RB2 should be read as RB2**, Rudder Baker's argument that the resurrection bodies of the saints in heaven are not numerically identical to the human bodies those saints possessed in this life has a false premise.

But if we read RB2 as RB2*, then, given St. Thomas's view that the glorified body is glorified, not on account of its nature, but because of God's beatifying the soul in the beatific vision, Rudder Baker's argument is invalid. For it may be true that the persistence conditions of our bodies in this life differ from those of resurrection bodies (RB1), but given RB2* and RB3, it would not follow, for all that, that the resurrection bodies of the saints and the bodies that the saints possess in this life have different essential properties. This is because it may be—as St. Thomas thinks is the case—that the resurrection bodies of the saints in heaven and the bodies they possess in this life are intrinsically the same in the relevant respects. Although the resurrected bodies of the saints are incorruptible, they are not incorruptible by nature, that is, because of the essential properties of the saint's body, but rather the resurrected bodies of the saints are incorruptible by the action of God giving to the human body through the body's soul certain qualities, such as incorruptibility and impassibility. And so it would not follow that the resurrected bodies of the saints in heaven are specifically different—and so numerically distinct—from the bodies that the saints possess in this life. According to St. Thomas, this-worldly human bodies and resurrection bodies are specifically (i.e., essentially) the same, but they differ in their accidents, that is, this-worldly bodies are the bodies of human persons that lack an accidental disposition that would make their bodies incorruptible and so such bodies are corruptible, whereas the resurrection bodies of the saints in heaven are the bodies of human persons who have, for example, the accidental disposition of the *lumen gloriae* and the accident of engaging in the act of the beatific vision, and the bodies of such human persons are incorruptible.

Because (g) and (h) are consistent with one another, premise (2) is false. As I said above, (e) is consistent with (h). The glorified human body in heaven has its characteristic features in virtue of the soul's having the beatific vision; apart from the beatified soul's influence on the human body in heaven, the human body in heaven would be passible, carnal, sluggish, and darksome (as are human bodies in this life and as are resurrected human bodies in hell, according to St. Thomas). Therefore, as (e) and (h) are consistent with one another, and (h) and (g) are consistent with one another, it follows that (e) and (g) are also consistent with one another. Because I showed above that (e) and (f) are also consistent with one another, premise (1) of PNH-II is also false.

As we have seen, St. Thomas's exalted understanding of the human person's beatific vision in heaven is fully compatible with there being a temporal dimension to human activity in heaven (in the broad sense of *temporal* as change that can be measured with respect to before and after). Furthermore, a Thomist can defeat a Rudder Baker-like objection to the view that the incorruptible bodies of the saints in heaven are numerically identical to the bodies those saints had in this life. Now St. Thomas affirms that human person S's body in heaven is numerically identical to S's human body in this life. As authoritative, Catholic Christian tradition has it that human bodies in heaven are numerically identical to human bodies in this life and Rudder Baker rejects that part of Christian tradition, St. Thomas's solution to PNH-II therefore has an advantage over Rudder Baker's solution. For St. Thomas's view, but not Rudder Baker's, is fully compatible with the teaching of authoritative, Catholic Christian teaching on heaven. In addition, insofar as St. Thomas's views make clear in what sense human persons are temporal beings, and how that sense of being temporal is compatible with traditional Christian doctrine about the otherworldliness of the beatific vision in heaven, a Thomistic solution to PNH-II also has great explanatory power.

16

A Thomistic Solution to PNH-III

HEAVEN AS PERFECTLY DYNAMIC

As noted above, the third problem concerning the nature of heaven (PNH-III) is an apparent problem concerning the nature of eternal life. Recall that, drawing on the work of philosopher Eric Silverman, I defined *static views of heaven* (or SV*) and *dynamic views of heaven* (DV**) as follows:

(SV*) *Conceptions of heaven that portray paradise as a place or state of existence where* there is no further moral change or progress *and* there is no further aesthetic change or progress *and* there is no further epistemological change or progress *and* there is no further relational change or progress *and* there is no other change or progress *for the creaturely inhabitants of heaven.*

(DV**) *Conceptions of heaven that depict paradise as a place or a state of existence where* there are moral changes or progress *or* there are aesthetic changes or progress *or* there are epistemological changes or progress *or* there are relational changes or progress *or* there are other changes or progress *for the creaturely inhabitants of heaven.*

Note that SV* and DV** are logical contraries. According to PNH-III, Christian tradition includes assumptions that entail that heaven is both static and dynamic in the senses specified above. These are the assumptions of PNH-III that lead to a contradiction:

(1) The notion that (*i*) *heaven is static* is in conflict with the notion that (*b*) *heaven includes the reality of "the new heavens and the new earth," which itself includes a perfect human community, and, at least eventually, perfected embodiment on the part of human persons in the next life* and the notion that (*j*) *if there is a human person S in heaven, then S is flourishing* [assumption].

(2) The notion that (k) *heaven is dynamic, that is, not static*, is in conflict with the notion that (a) *heaven for intellectual creatures consists merely in the beatific vision* and the notion that (l) *human persons in heaven are perfectly happy* [assumption].

(3) (i) is true or (k) is true [assumption].

(4) [(b) is true or (j) is true] and [(a) is true or (l) is true] [assumption].

SOME CONTEMPORARY RESPONSES TO PNH-III: A BRIEF REVIEW

Chapter 2 examined works by two contemporary authors, Eric J. Silverman and Paul J. Griffiths. Let us begin with a Silvermanian response to PNH-III. Silverman can solve PNH-III in two ways, depending on his ultimate attitude toward proposition (l) in premise (2). First, if Silverman accepts proposition (l), he can reject premise (2) by making sense of it not being the case that (k) entails the falsity of proposition (l). As we saw in chapter 2, Silverman thinks that even a perfect human existence in heaven is consistent with human persons engaging in different activities at different times. Second, if Silverman rejects proposition (l), he can reject premise (4) as he also rejects proposition (a). Why would he reject proposition (l)? Silverman shows some sympathy for the notion that an absolutely perfect human existence is a contradiction in terms insofar as *human* happiness in heaven could always be improved upon, for example, by adding another person to the communion of the saints, the presence of whom would increase every human participant's enjoyment of heaven.

As we saw in chapter 2, Silverman also shows some sympathy for a *totally dynamic* (TD) view of the nature of heaven. Recall that a TD view has it that human persons in heaven undergo perpetual moral, aesthetic, epistemological, and relational progress in heaven, not only with respect to other creatures, but with respect to God as well.

I noted four potential problems for the TD view of the nature of heaven.[1] First, the view is incompatible with an important traditional Catholic Christian account of the relation between one's degree of charity (or merit) at death and one's degree of beatitude that has among its defend-

---

1. In addition, chapter 2 above offers defeaters for arguments in defense of the TD view of heaven that are not repeated here.

ers St. Thomas Aquinas, Ludwig Ott, Karl Adam, and Dom Anscar Vonier. According to that Catholic theological tradition,

(16) If human persons in heaven have the ability to get ever closer to God in heaven, that is, advance in the beatific vision or the essential reward, then human persons in heaven have the ability to undergo moral improvement in heaven, that is, they can merit in heaven.

In addition, according to this Catholic theological tradition, no one can grow in merit or charity in the next life. Therefore, the antecedent of (16) is false. Because the TD view has it that the antecedent of (16) is true, the TD view is inconsistent with this important traditional Catholic theological tradition.

Second, assume that if a human person S in heaven can get closer to God in heaven, as the advocate of the TD view believes, then the way S does so is by making good morally relevant free choices in heaven, that is, choices to act in a supererogatory fashion. However, if the way S gets closer to God in heaven is by making good morally relevant free choices, then the importance of the choices S makes during S's preheavenly existence, *at least where those choices have an effect on the degree to which S is happy in heaven*, would be problematically minimized. For, what human persons choose in this life, at least where those choices have an effect on the degree to which S is close to God in heaven, will be eclipsed by the morally relevant choices the saints in heaven make *over the course of an infinite amount of time*. But the free choices that S makes in this life are significant where the degree to which S is happy in heaven is concerned. Therefore, human persons do not make morally relevant choices in heaven. In that case, human persons do not get closer to God in heaven and the TD view is false.

Third, assume that the essence of beatitude in heaven for a human person is the beatific vision of God and the love of God that results from that vision. We might think (with, for example, St. Thomas) that the beatific vision is as direct and unmediated a union with God as is logically possible for a creature, a union in which God raises up the intellect of the human person so as to unite the human person with himself such that God himself functions, as it were, as that by which the essence of God is apprehended. That is to say, the essential reward of the saints in heaven is a participation in God's own eternal life. Accordingly, just as God's life is perfect and simultaneously whole, the human person united intellectually and volitionally with God in heaven is made deiform, like unto God, thereby engaging in acts of knowledge and love that are simultaneously whole and as perfect as it is logically possible for a creaturely act to be, given the degree of that person's charity at the time of her death. Like God, the acts that constitute the essential reward are immutable. Therefore, if we accept such a view of the beatific vision, then persons in heaven do not get ever closer to God in heaven. But that would mean that the TD view of heaven is false.

Fourth, if the TD view of heaven is correct, then every dimension of heavenly existence, including one's relation with God, is *perpetually* developing, changing, and growing in heaven. But, in that case, heaven is in no sense a *novissimum* (a last thing), a reality in which the human person is *quietus* (at rest). But heaven, among other things, is that reality where our hearts are at rest. Therefore, the TD view of heaven is not correct.

Chapter 2 also examined a response to PNH-III based on Griffiths's view that heaven consists in a perpetually repeated perfect liturgy, central to which, at least for angels and human persons, is the beatific vision of God, which beatific vision itself consists in both an unmediated intellectual apprehension of the Trinity and a sensitive apprehension of the flesh of Christ the Lord. Nonetheless, the heavenly liturgy is also social, involving human persons knowing and loving the saints, angels, non-human animals, and plants. Griffiths thinks that the perfect liturgy exists in systolic (nonmeasurable) time, and repeats itself without end. Although each cycle of the heavenly liturgy involves change, for example, it has a beginning, middle, and end (or perhaps a Gloria, Credo, Sanctus, etc.), each token of the type, *heavenly liturgy*, is indiscriminable from any other token, with the ending of each token of the liturgy perfectly transitioning into the beginning of the next token. As it is metronomic or measurable time that leads to boredom, and the perpetual heavenly liturgy exists not in metronomic but systolic time, the repetitive stasis of heaven cannot be boring, but rather produces the delight of perfect rest. Finally, the human experience of knowing and loving God and creatures in the heavenly liturgy—that is, the human experience of the beatific vision and relations with creatures—is devoid of second-order or self-referential experience, according to Griffiths, the actions of the saints in heaven being perfectly habitual and thus other-directed.

How can Griffiths respond to PNH-III? Given the way that I have defined *static* and *dynamic* views of heaven, Griffiths's view counts as a dynamic view. In addition, Griffiths clearly thinks that proposition (k) is not in conflict with (l). Although the saint in heaven is undergoing changes within each cycle of the heavenly liturgy, she is not happier in one moment of the cycle than at another moment. It is participating in the systolic liturgical cycle that makes the saint perfectly happy. Furthermore, each reiteration of the liturgy is specifically identical to the one that comes before. So she is not, for example, happier (or less happy) in the second reiteration of the liturgy than in her first participation in it. And the same goes for the third reiteration, etc. Because the changes that human persons in heaven undergo are not directed at obtaining further perfections on their part, Griffiths can accept that heaven is a changing reality without rejecting the view that human persons in heaven are perfectly happy. Griffiths therefore rejects premise (2) of PNH-III.[2]

There is an important problem for Griffiths's views, namely, he underestimates the extent to which intellectual creatures such as angels and human persons are glorified in heaven. There are two ways to see this limitation in Griffith's account. First, Griffiths thinks that human life in heaven is, at least in part, a recapitulation of Edenic life, where scripture and Catholic Christian tradition teach that human life in heaven is really a *transfiguration* of human life, even human bodily life. For even prelapsarian life was shot through with corruption, death, and biological growth and decay (if not *human* death and decay), for example, there was clearly the death of many sorts of things in paradise before the fall of Adam and Eve, and Adam and Eve, prior to the Fall, ate, drank, and were commanded, like the other creatures, to generate new members of the species. But bodily life in heaven is entirely immortal and incorruptible. As St. Thomas puts it, the saints in heaven no longer live an *animal* life of eating, drinking, and sexual union; rather, our bodily life is *spiritual*, and so part of a wholly *contemplative* life.

Second, Griffiths thinks that the beatific vision is of a temporal duration, and, taking a cue from St. Thomas, we might rather think that intellectual creatures, in having the beatific vision, come to participate in the eternal life of God. On that Thomistic supposition, the beatific vision is not a temporal duration or even an aeveternal one. Rather, the be-

---

2. See chapter 2 for another way that Griffiths might argue for the falsity of premise (2).

atific vision is a participated eternity, in itself the simultaneously whole and immutable intellectual activity of seeing the essence of God. Again, Griffiths underestimates the glory of heaven as a radically incorruptible kingdom, the created persons of which become deiform, living a godlike rather than an animal life.

ST. THOMAS'S DOCTRINE AND A THOMISTIC RESPONSE TO PNH-III

How would St. Thomas respond to PNH-III? It is first worth mentioning again[3] an assumption implicitly made by many (if not all) contemporary analytic philosophers discussing a problem such as PNH-III, namely,

(I) An immutable existence is a kind of static existence.[4]

But given that:

(II) A static existence is an *imperfect* mode of existence compared to a dynamic mode of existence.

It then follows from (I) and (II) that:

(III) An immutable existence is an imperfect mode of existence compared to a dynamic mode of existence.

Let us grant proposition (II) for the sake of argument. But why should one think that proposition (I) is true if we accept some version of classical theism? For example, if we think with Aristotle, St. Augustine, Boethius, St. Anselm, and St. Thomas Aquinas (among others) that God is absolutely perfect, absolutely immutable, and timeless, then, given (II), we are not going to think of God's being and activity as static. For God's inability to change exemplifies a perfection in God and not a limitation. Therefore, if we think about God's timelessly eternal and absolutely immutable being and activity as a form of pure dynamism, then we will reject proposition (I), a proposition, it seems, that is doing a lot of work in discourse on heaven within contemporary philosophy of religion.

But if we also think with St. Thomas that the beatific vision is a crea-

---

3. See also the discussions of dynamism and mutability in chapters 2, 4, and 7 above.
4. See, e.g., Silverman, "Conceiving Heaven as a Dynamic Rather than Static Existence," for a good example of a contemporary philosopher that assumes proposition (I).

turely participation in God's own eternal life and perfect happiness, namely, an immutable and timeless knowing (and so delighting) in God's perfect being, then we are not going to think of the immutable beatific vision either as something static. Rather, we will think of the beatific vision as the most perfect sort of dynamism possible for a creature.[5] In that case, we are going to define the terms in premises (1) and (2) in PNH-III quite differently (and admittedly, I have been taking a cue from the implicit common practices of contemporary analytic philosophers in defining *static* and *dynamic* views of heaven).

Given that God's absolutely immutable and timelessly eternal mode of being and the beatific vision as an immutable and timelessly eternal participation in God are *the most dynamic of realities*, we should reconsider SV* and DV** (see the beginning of this chapter) as follows:

(Static views of heaven [SV**]): conceptions of heaven that portray paradise as a place or state of existence where there is no moral *activity* and there is no aesthetic *activity* and there is no epistemological *activity* and there is no relational *activity* and there is no other *activity* in the creaturely inhabitants of heaven.

(Dynamic views of heaven [DV***]): conceptions of heaven that depict paradise as a place or a state of existence where there is moral *activity* or there is aesthetic *activity* or there is epistemological *activity* or there is relational *activity* or there is other *activity* in the creaturely inhabitants of heaven.

So the first thing to note about a Thomistic solution to PNH-III is that the character of such a solution will depend upon how we define *static* and *dynamic* conceptions of heaven.

If we accept the revised definitions of *static* and *dynamic views of heaven* in SV** and DV***, then St. Thomas can reject premise (2) of PNH-III, and for two reasons. First, in that case there would be no incompatibility between heaven being dynamic and heaven consisting only of the beatific vision. Therefore, a Thomist could reject that (k) entails the falsity of (a) insofar as heaven would be the most dynamic of realities if it consisted merely of the beatific vision. Second, on these assumptions, whether or not (a) is true, the Thomist could also reasonably say that a human person's being perfectly happy—even *immutably* and perfectly happy—in heaven is

---

5. See also Rogers, "Anselmian Mediations on Heaven," 38–39.

compatible with heaven's being dynamic insofar as the beatific vision, understood as an immutable, nontemporal, nonaeveternal participation in God's own eternal life, is the most dynamic of creaturely activities, and one that sates all rational human desire. Therefore, neither does (k) entail the falsity of (1) given St. Thomas's views and DV*** as a conception of dynamic views of heaven.

But even if we rather accept SV* and DV** as descriptions of static and dynamic views of heaven, respectively, a Thomist can still reject premise (2), although for different reasons. For given DV**, St. Thomas still thinks that heaven is a dynamic reality. Recall that St. Thomas thinks that human happiness in heaven consists of both the essential reward and the accidental reward. Admittedly, the essential reward is static in the sense of SV*, because it consists of the immutable acts of the beatific vision and the delight, joy, and love that follow upon that vision. Therefore, on this reading of static and dynamic views of heaven, (k) and (a) are logically inconsistent.

However, according to St. Thomas, the accidental reward consists of a number of dimensions, many of which involve human persons undergoing changes in heaven, for example, human persons with glorified bodies moving their bodies from the new heavens to the new earth, or sometimes turning their bodies to see *this* saint's body rather than *that* saint's body, or moving their bodies to just the right place in order to take in the full beauty of Mars. According to St. Thomas the human person with the essential reward is perfectly happy, having all of her desires-from-lack sated. Any goods that are aspects of the accidental reward do not add to the intensity of the essential reward of the beatific vision and the delight that flows from it; at best, they provide for the well-being of perfect happiness, gratuitous or fitting or appropriate complements to the saint's essential reward. Therefore, heaven being dynamic in the sense of DV** is not incompatible with human persons being perfectly happy. As (k) does not entail the falsity of (1) on St. Thomas's views, a Thomist can reject premise (2) of PNH-III.

Given what we have seen of St. Thomas's views, I can also add an additional criticism, or perhaps a development, of Griffiths's view that human experience in heaven is exclusively an experience of a perpetual, ever-repeating, perfect liturgy, where such an experience involves no self-reference. Rather, let us imagine a view of heaven that involves a greater variety of human activities, including a greater variety of activities involving change, than the model Griffiths puts forward. First, the essential reward or perfect happiness for human persons in heaven—the beatific vision and the love, joy, and delight that flows from that vision—is the most intimate intellectual and volitional union with God that is logically possible for a creature. Second, let us assume that participation in the perfect liturgy of heaven is *the accidental reward* of the saints in heaven. Third, given that we are created in the image of God, who created the universe, it is fitting that, *pace* Griffiths, the accidental reward can be split into two parts, between which two parts the saints cycle back and forth.

The first part is participation in perfect liturgical worship analogous to the antiphonal nature of the Mass. The second part is a time of play as liturgical celebration, which time allows human persons to engage with other saints in common loves and interests, such as writing and reading literature, playing and listening to jazz, or racing from the new heavens to the new earth and back again, to see or hear the beauties of the new heavens and the new earth. Just as the angels before the culmination of the kingdom of God are engaged both in serving the Lord and at the same time enjoy the beatific vision,[6] so human persons in heaven continually engage in the beatific vision while also enjoying an accidental reward that consists of engaging in a perpetual back and forth between participating in antiphonal liturgical worship and liturgical play. As St. Thomas's account of heaven is consistent with this happy amendment of Griffith's views, we have another reason for preferring St. Thomas's account of heaven to that of Griffiths.

Finally, neither the Silvermanian totally dynamic view of heaven nor Griffiths's view make room for St. Thomas's sublime and beautiful doctrine that the essence of the essential reward is a vision of the essence of God such that human persons having that vision become deiform, being graced with the power to participate in God's own timelessly eternal, absolutely immutable, and perfect life. If the beauty of a doctrine is an argument for its truth, then St. Thomas's doctrine of the beatific vision is itself also a good reason for preferring a Thomistic response to PNH-III over the contemporary views that I have examined.

---

6. See, e.g., *ST* I, q. 58, a. 2, and *In Mt* 18, lect. 1, nn. 1503–6.

17

A Thomistic Solution to the Problem of the Tedium of Heavenly Immortality

Contemporary philosopher Bernard Williams has argued that an immortal life—even a heavenly one—will eventually become tedious for persons such as ourselves, persons who habitually desire and enjoy limited goods such as movies, songs, books, trips, conversations, and gelato. Philosopher Brian Ribeiro has developed Williams's argument in a way that takes aim at the kind of otherworldly account of heaven we find in St. Thomas. That brings us to the final apparent problem concerning eternal life, the problem of the tedium of heavenly immortality (PTHI).

ST. THOMAS ON PTHI: OVERTURE

As we saw in chapter 3, some contemporary theologians and philosophers suggest that our experience of boredom in this life is in fact reflective either of the timeboundedness of the goods that are central to human experience in this life (Chappell and Meilaender) or the nature of time as we experience it in this life (Griffiths). But insofar as we begin to have a taste of the eternal in this life—for example, insofar as we follow St. Paul's admonition in Colossians 3:2 ("set your minds on things that are above, not on things that are on earth")—we already desire and have some experience in this life of that unlimited good the experience of which is incompatible with boredom.

St. Thomas's rich and detailed expression of the doctrine that the saints in heaven participate in God's own timelessly eternal life insofar as the saints have the beatific vision provides a solution to PTHI to which the work of the contemporary thinkers I have examined merely point the way. If it is correct that a human person S's immortal life is characterized as boring or tedious as a whole only if S's immortal life is focused upon finite, temporal goods, then St. Thomas's view that the essence of the essential reward for the saints is the beatific vision, a timelessly eternal participation in God's own eternal life and happiness, provides us, all other things being equal, with a powerful solution to PTHI. For it shows that it is conceptually impossible for the saints in heaven to experience boredom, let alone have a life that is characterized by boredom as a whole.

Other aspects of St. Thomas's baroque view of the heavenly life of the saints, a view that takes into account *all* that the Christian tradition hands down with respect to heaven, provide additional reasons to think that the immortal life of human persons in heaven is a perfectly happy one, free of any threat of boredom or tediousness. For example, I noted in chapter 6 that a logical entailment of a human person's having the beatific vision is that such a person has a specific knowledge of all of God's creatures. In this way, the natural human desire for knowledge of creatures is perfected in the greatest way logically possible. That human persons enjoy such a good in heaven underscores that, for St. Thomas, God graces human persons in heaven with a *participation* in God's own perfect life, which life, for God, includes God's knowledge of creatures insofar as those creatures are reflections of his own perfect being, goodness, and beauty.

As we have seen, St. Thomas thinks that the human saint's participation in God's perfect life in heaven also *extends* to, even if it is not made more intense by, the saint's *human* body at and after the general resurrection. The human person in heaven having a glorified body is that person's bodily participation in the beatific vision. Such a glorified body is impassible, subtle, agile, and luminescent. Embodied human persons in heaven have human bodies that are as perfect as it is logically possible for them to be. For these bodies cannot be harmed, and their sense faculties are glorified such that the saints with such faculties can immediately sense the glories of God and the other saints in the objects of sense. Chief among the objects of sense are the bodies of Christ, the Virgin Mary, the other saints, and the beauties of the "new heavens and the new earth."

Furthermore, the bodily inclinations of these glorified bodies are such that they are perfectly integrated with, so as to fully support, the soul's beatific activity, which, again, is the essential activity of the saints in heaven. As glorified bodies are human bodies, they not only move, but also do so with agility. In fact, the saints in heaven can move their bodies so quickly that their movement from one part of the new heavens to the new earth appears to be instantaneous. Finally, glorified human bodies in heaven are luminescent, shining and showing forth the degree of glory and charity characterizing the souls of those saints. Such bodies are gloriously beautiful, all the more so insofar as they make sensibly present the virtues of the saints, while also casting in grave relief the beautiful scars of those who won the ultimate victory in this life of being killed for the faith.

In addition to the glory of the body, the happiness of the saints, as St. Thomas describes it, casts out any threat of boredom or tediousness in heaven insofar as the saints are part of the glorified church in heaven, composed of angels and saints. As we have seen, St. Thomas thinks that the angels and saints in heaven have a deep knowledge of each other indirectly in virtue of having the beatific vision. That is to say, one saint S knows another saint S1 in virtue of S having a participated knowledge of God's knowledge of S1 in S's beatific vision. But the happiness of heaven, for St. Thomas, is excessive. So, as a part of their accidental reward, embodied human persons also know one another directly, as one creature to another, in a graced perfection of the ways that human persons know one another in this life.

Of course, even if St. Thomas's ascribing to human persons in heaven a God-like happiness in the beatific vision entails that the life of those persons is not tedious, Williams would surely remind us of the other horn of his dilemma: persons engaged in such beatific activity in heaven cannot be personally identical to human persons in this life whose desires are predominantly mundane and ordinary, for example, wanting to watch a football game or to try out a new restaurant in town. As we saw in chapter 3, philosopher Brian Ribeiro argues with particular force and clarity that persons in heaven having the beatific vision cannot be personally identical to human persons in this life. I called this development of Williams's PTI, one that is specifically aimed at an otherworldly conception of heaven as we find in St. Thomas, PTHI. I now turn to a presentation of a Thomistic solution to that problem.

A THOMISTIC SOLUTION TO PTHI

Recall my formulation of PTHI:

(1) A human person S and a human person S1 are personally (and so numerically) identical only if there is psychological continuity between the psychological stages of S and the psychological stages of S1 [assumption].

(2) There is psychological discontinuity between the psychological stages of any human person S in this life and the psychological stage or stages of any person in heaven enjoying the beatific vision, when the first stage of S's intellectual life is S's rationally desiring, that is, willing, things in this life [assumption].[1]

(3) Therefore, no human person in this life who rationally desires (i.e., wills) things is personally—and so numerically—identical to a person having the beatific vision in heaven [from (1) and (2)].

(4) Therefore, no human person in this life who rationally desires things can go to heaven [from (3)].

(5) But it does not make sense for a human person to wish for something impossible, once that person is made aware of its impossibility [assumption].

(6) Therefore, no human person S in this life can sensibly desire to go to heaven, once S becomes aware of an argument consisting of propositions such as (1)–(6) [from (4) and (5)].

Recall also that Ribeiro defends (2) as follows:

(7) The psychological change that a human person S who rationally desires things in this life would have to undergo in order to become a person S1 who enjoys the beatific vision in heaven is unmixed, instantaneous, and radical [assumption].

(8) A psychological change that is unmixed, instantaneous, and radical is a discontinuous change [assumption].

As I noted in chapter 3, I am granting premises (1) and (5) of PTHI to the objector, if only for the sake of argument.[2] The key premises, then,

---

1. On the phrase "when the first stage of S's intellectual life is S's rationally desiring things in this life," see chapter 3, note 3 above.
2. Some Thomists will want to insist that premise (1) of PTHI is false because the following proposition is true: (1*) For a human person S and a human person S1, S is numerically and

in PTHI are (2), (7), and (8). If St. Thomas's doctrine can make sense of the rejection of premises (7) or (8), then that doctrine gives us reason to think that PTHI fails to establish its conclusion. For (2) is a proposition that requires argumentative support if Ribeiro is to make his case regarding the irrationality of wanting to go to heaven. Indeed, as we will see, St. Thomas's doctrine also gives us reason for thinking that premise (2) is false. Therefore, St. Thomas's doctrine gives us reason to think that PTHI is unsound.

Before examining a distinctively Thomistic response to PTHI, let us examine some possible counterexamples to (8) that do not trade on Thomistic assumptions. These counterexamples are interesting in their own right, but they will also serve as a first glimpse of how St. Thomas's doctrine provides reasons for thinking that there are problems with premises (7) or (8) of PTHI, as well as problems with its premise (2).

Consider the following proposed counterexample to (8). Some people who try to kill themselves, and fail in the attempt, report feeling very differently about their desire to die immediately after they have set in motion what they take to be their final action, for example, after jumping off a bridge.[3] Before they make the suicide attempt, they want to die. But immediately after setting in motion their suicide, they have a very strong desire to remain alive. The change here is radical—going from wanting to die, to not wanting to die. It is also clearly instantaneous. Indeed, the change also appears to be unmixed (and directed from without). In addition, the person immediately before the suicide attempt is personally identical to the person immediately after the suicide attempt. However, if a change that is radical, unmixed, and instantaneous is a discontinuous change, that is, if premise (8) is true, then the person immediately before the suicide attempt is not personally identical to the

---

personally identical with S1, if S and S1 have numerically the same intellectual or rational soul. Given (1*), a person S and a person S1 could have numerically the same intellectual soul and therefore S is personally and numerically identical to S1, even though there exists psychological discontinuity between S and S1. (Thanks to Mark Spencer for raising this point.) I do not deny (1*), although there is a complication regarding (1*) that cannot be discussed here (see the discussion of St. Thomas on numerical, specific, and personal identity beyond death in chapter 10 above for the details). But Ribeiro thinks that (1*) is obviously false and St. Thomas's doctrine has the resources to show that PTHI is unsound without assuming (1*). Therefore, for the sake of engaging in this chapter with philosophers such as Ribeiro who take (1*) to be false, I do not assume or draw upon (1*) in offering here a Thomistic solution to PTHI.

3. See, e.g., Lisa Firestone, "Busting the Myths about Suicide," *Psych Alive*, available at www.psychalive.org/busting-the-myths-about-suicide/.

person immediately after the suicide attempt. Therefore, premise (8) is false.

Notice that it would not matter for present purposes if at some point in the future the person who survives his suicide without regret does not feel as strongly about wanting to live as he does immediately after initiating an action he thinks will lead to his death. For the fact of the matter is that at time t, he wants to die, and, in the next moment, $t+1$, he does not want to die. In fact, that is all he is thinking about. At t life is intolerable, whereas at $t+1$ life is a great good. That change is instantaneous, radical, and unmixed. But he is numerically the same person immediately before and immediately after the suicide attempt and so there is no psychological discontinuity between the person immediately before the suicide attempt and immediately after the attempt. Again, premise (8) is false.

Consider an additional potential counterexample to (8): St. Augustine's own lucid and psychologically rich account of his conversion to Christianity in the *Confessions*. That conversion, as St. Augustine relates it, is itself composed of a number of microconversions: for example, St. Augustine changes his mind about the rationality of Catholic Christianity (before coming to Milan, he thinks Catholic Christianity absurd; later, after hearing St. Ambrose preach, St. Augustine finds it quite plausible); later St. Augustine moves from being agnostic about Manichean beliefs to rejecting those beliefs as false; still later, Augustine moves from thinking that Catholic Christianity is merely plausible to thinking that it is true. Finally, he goes through the change of thinking Catholic Christianity true, but not giving himself wholly to God, to willing that he give himself wholly to God in the sense that St. Augustine wills to give up those practices he takes to be incompatible with his newfound Catholic Christian beliefs.

For St. Augustine, it is that last mentioned change that constitutes the decisive *psychological* moment in his conversion to Catholic Christianity.[4] It is also the change that counts as a counterexample to (8). For this last microconversion event is a change that is, arguably, unmixed, radical, and instantaneous. For the change is (we might think, with St. Augus-

---

4. *Confessions* VIII. Of course, there is also St. Augustine's going from not being baptized to being baptized as a Catholic in Milan (see *Confessions* IX), which, St. Augustine would perhaps say, is the decisive *metaphysical* moment in his conversion insofar as it is in this change that St. Augustine goes from not being, to being, an adopted son of the Father.

tine) all for his good, and so is unmixed; one moment he is not willing to give himself wholly to God, and the next moment he wills to give himself wholly to God. However, this change is also both a radical and instantaneous change.

Granted, St. Augustine's macroconversion to Catholic Christianity is a radical and non-instantaneous change. For, we might say, with St. Augustine, that it begins with his reading Cicero's *Hortensius*, reaches a climax with his peaceful acceptance of God's will after reading Romans 13:13–14 in the garden, and ends with his baptism in Milan. However, the microconversion to Catholic Christianity that is his change of will with respect to being obedient to God in the garden is an instantaneous, unmixed (from a Catholic Christian perspective), and radical change. In addition, there is no reason to think that this microconversion of St. Augustine's involves a loss of personal identity. Therefore, as St. Augustine's personal identity is lost going through the change in question if St. Augustine's psychology on the two sides of the change is discontinuous, St. Augustine's microconversion to Catholic Christianity constitutes a good counterexample to premise (8).

Whatever we think of these two counterexamples, they are useful for setting up a Thomistic solution to PTHI. It is to examining the details of such a solution that we now turn.

A Thomistic Response to PTHI

In general terms, St. Thomas agrees with Ribeiro that, if human persons exist in the next life, then there needs to be personal continuity between human persons in the next life and human persons in this life. For example, in one place St. Thomas states, "at the resurrection the soul will ... be either entirely borne away to the heavenly life *to which it adhered while living in the world*, or will be cast down into the life of the brutes, *if it lived as a brute in this world*."[5] In addition, we might sympathize with Ribeiro that a person could undergo psychological changes so drastic that it would lead to the annihilation of the person who undergoes them.

But given St. Thomas's views (a) that any human person needs to be prepared by grace in this life and the next in order to enjoy the beatific vision in heaven, and (b) the ways God *does* prepare human souls for

---

5. *ST Suppl.*, q. 79, a. 1, obj. 2 (trans. English Dominicans, 2877; emphasis added). See also *In Sent IV*, d. 44, q. 1, a. 1, q.c. 1, obj. 2. In his answer to the objection, St. Thomas does not reject this aspect of the objector's argument.

the beatific vision before they get to heaven, both premises (7) and (8) in Ribeiro's argument need to be disambiguated. When we do that work of disambiguation, the versions of (7) and (8) that are relevant for human persons transitioning from this life to heaven do not entail (2). In fact, St. Thomas's account of the beatific vision, his theology of grace, his views on the manner in which some human persons undergo moral transformation in this life, and his views on how many, perhaps most, human persons undergo moral transformation in purgatory together provide for a powerful way of solving PTHI. For, given those Thomistic background assumptions, either premise (7) or premise (8) is false, and premise (2) is false.

St. Thomas on Grace Perfecting Nature

Nothing can act beyond its power to do so; thus says St. Thomas.[6] Furthermore, that nothing can act beyond its power to do so stems from "an institution of divine providence" (*ex institutione divinae providentiae*).[7] Although it is logically possible that God create a world such that creatures do nothing on their own but only act because God acts in them or by them—one may think of that possible world that occasionalists such as Nicholas Malebranche take to be actual—St. Thomas thinks that, given God's goodness and power, it is fitting that God creates and sustains the world such that creatures are true secondary causes of things that happen in the world. Although God could move creatures in a manner that does not allow them to participate in such movement, God does not create and move them thusly. Rather, God freely confers on creatures "the dignity of causality" (*dignitatem causalitatis*).[8]

St. Thomas also thinks that creatures have *natural abilities* or powers that correspond with their God-given natures. For example, God creates plants such that all mature and healthy plants have the natural ability to nourish themselves, grow, and contribute to the reproduction of the species to which they belong. Mature and healthy animals have the generic natural abilities that belong to plants plus the natural abilities to cognize

---

6. See, e.g., *ST* I-II, q. 114, a. 2, resp.
7. Ibid.
8. *ST* I, q. 23, a. 8, ad 2; see also *ST* I, q. 22, a. 3, resp. Thanks to Michael Rota for these references. See his paper "The Problem of Evil and Cooperation," in *Evolution, Games, and God*, ed. Martin Nowak and Sarah Coakley (Cambridge, Mass.: Harvard University Press, 2013), 362–74. See also *SCG* III.76–77, 83, 94; *CT* I, chaps. 130–31; *ST* I, q. 103, a. 6, resp.

the world by way of the senses. Mature and healthy human persons naturally have the generic powers that plants and nonhuman animals have, plus the intellectual and volitional powers.

That being said, human persons after the Fall—even biologically mature and healthy ones—apart from grace find it difficult, if not impossible, habitually to act well.[9] Now, according to St. Thomas's Catholic views, God created Adam and Eve with the supernatural endowment of sanctifying or habitual grace (which endowment made them fit for heaven) and the preternatural[10] gifts of impassibility,[11] negative immortality,[12] and integrity.[13] Integrity is the preternatural gift that counteracts the natural tension in human persons between spirit and matter. In possessing that gift, it was therefore (a) easy for Adam and Eve in the state of innocence freely to will to maintain their graced relationship with God (e.g., to act in accord with reason), and (b) difficult for them to freely decide to satisfy the desires of the flesh that conflict with the dictates of reason. When Adam and Eve fell from grace, they and their progeny lost the preternatural gifts of immortality, impassibility, and integrity, along with sanctifying grace.

All this means that, unless God preserves a person from coming into the world with a lack of sanctifying grace and the preternatural gift of integrity, a human person S after the Fall that reaches the age of reason experiences the tension between spirit and matter so that it is difficult

---

9. This is because human persons are naturally composites of spirit and matter. For *spirit*, the principle by which human persons are created in the image and likeness of God (Gn 1:26–27), is a principle by which human persons are naturally inclined to know and love God above creatures, while *matter*, although not evil in itself, is a principle by which human persons are naturally inclined to preserve their bodily integrity at all costs, without regard for whether doing so—or the manner in which human persons do so—would be against reason. Therefore, according to the order of nature apart from grace, spirit and matter "pull against" each other, making it difficult for an intellectual creature, apart from grace, habitually to act well. This natural "tug of war" between spirit and matter is what the Catholic Christian tradition calls *concupiscence*.

10. See chapter 2, note 109, above for a definition of *preternatural gift*.

11. See, e.g., *ST* I, q. 97, a. 2. See also *In Sent* II, d. 19, a. 3, and IV, d. 44, q. 2, a. 1, q.c. 4, ad 1 (*ST Suppl.*, q. 82, a. 4, ad 1).

12. See, e.g., *ST* I, q. 97, a. 1. Negative immortality is immortality such that it is due merely to God's extrinsic efficient causality keeping the soul and the body from naturally separating (in circumstances where soul and body would naturally separate), which immortality lasted only as long as Adam and Eve did not sin. As we have seen, St. Thomas contrasts the negative immortality of Adam and Eve with, e.g., the positive immortality of the saints in heaven, which latter immortality is caused not only by God acting as extrinsic efficient cause but also by the beatified soul as intrinsic formal cause. See also *In Sent* II, d. 19, q. 1, a. 2; IV, d. 44, q. 3, a. 1, q.c. 2 (*ST Suppl.*, q. 86, a. 2); *QDV*, q. 24, a. 9, resp.; *CT* I, chap. 152; *ST* I, q. 76, a. 5, ad 1; *QDM*, q. 5, a. 5; *In Rom* 5, lect. 3.

13. See, e.g., *ST* I, q. 95, aa. 1–2. See also *In Sent* II, d. 20, q. 2, a. 3; d. 29, q. 1, a. 2; *QDV*, q. 26, a. 8; *QDM*, q. 4, a. 2.

for S freely to will what reason commands and easy for S freely to will what contradicts the declarations of reason. In St. Thomas's view, however, God has not simply left humanity in this graceless state. Rather, God freely gives supernatural assistance to human persons in virtue of the passion, death, resurrection, and ascension of Jesus Christ, making the grace of Christ available to human persons by faith, the sacraments of the church, prayer, and good works done from the virtue of charity. Now God has not granted to most human persons in this life the (equivalent of the) preternatural gift of integrity. That means that baptized and otherwise graced human persons nonetheless experience concupiscence, that is, the inclination to satisfy desires for material goods over against the dictates of reason. Nonetheless, God does give sanctifying grace, the infused virtues, and the gifts of the Holy Spirit to the baptized, all of which make it possible for Christians to live a life characterized by virtuous—even perfectly virtuous—actions in this life.

Thus when Ribeiro imagines there to be a great psychological gulf between an ordinary (ungraced) human person and his habits of responding to sinful inclinations and a human person in heaven lacking such inclinations altogether,[14] he is, according to St. Thomas's Catholic views of nature and grace, quite correct. Indeed, if a creature is to act in a manner that exceeds her ordinary and natural powers, then God must give her the power to do so, not simply as a power that comes from outside the creature, but as a power that is possessed by the creature. According to St. Thomas, God does give to certain human persons such power, power that enables those human persons to become fit for heavenly activity: this power is a special quality called *grace*. In addition, because "grace does not destroy nature, but perfects it,"[15] God transforming ordinary human persons into children of God fit for heaven by grace preserves personal identity through such a transformation. Before explaining how God does that, in St. Thomas's view, I should say a bit more about grace itself according to St. Thomas.

St. Thomas on the Nature and Effects of Grace

In the Christian tradition, grace is said in many ways.[16] One sense of grace that is relevant for my purposes is *sanctifying grace*. According to

---

14. See his "The Problem of Heaven."
15. *ST* I, q. 1, a. 8, ad 2 (trans. English Dominicans, 6).
16. See, e.g., *ST* I-II, q. 111.

St. Thomas, sanctifying grace is that quality of the essence of the soul that God confers upon a created person S (e.g., when S is baptized or receives the sacrament of reconciliation) such that S comes to "participate in the Divine Nature, after the manner of a likeness, through a certain regeneration or re-creation."[17] Though by nature human persons are rational creatures and so are created in the image and likeness of God (Gn 1:26–27), in receiving sanctifying grace, the nature and powers of human persons become deiform[18] (i.e., like unto God), so that it is right to consider such human persons children of God.[19] St. Thomas is fond of citing 2 Peter 1:4 on this score: "He hath given us most great and most precious promises; that by these you may be made partakers of the Divine Nature."[20] The human person with sanctifying grace has a deified nature and deified rational powers of intellect and will, although all of this is in proportion to the receptiveness of the subject. The caveat is important, as it shows that God does not annihilate the personality of the person who receives grace; grace is given to a human person in such a way that perfects that person's nature and does not set it aside. Furthermore, if a human person S does not cooperate with the grace S possesses, but instead develops natural vices such as cowardice, self-indulgence, etc., S inhibits the working of God's grace in S.[21]

As human persons naturally go through different stages of life in this life—birth, adolescence, adulthood, maturity, death—and God bestows grace in a manner proportionate to our human nature, St. Thomas thinks there are, in this life, different stages of the spiritual life too. In addition, he thinks there are a number of different spiritually age-appropriate instruments for God's bestowal of grace into the human soul in this life, which stages and instruments are analogous and proportionate to the instrumental causes by which human persons naturally undergo development. First, human persons are spiritually born in baptism. Second, some human persons live long enough freely to cooperate with grace in this life as human persons who can actually reason and choose. Human persons do this especially by faithful reception of the

---

17. *ST* I-II, q. 110, a. 4, resp. (trans. English Dominicans, 1135).
18. See, e.g., *ST* I, q. 4, a. 3, s.c.; q. 12, a. 5, resp.; I-II, q. 112, a. 1, resp.; III, q. 79, a. 8, s.c.
19. See, e.g., *SCG* IV.4.2; *ST* I-II, q. 110, a. 3, resp.; III, q. 37, a. 3, ad 2.
20. See, e.g., *ST* I-II, q. 110, a. 3, resp. (trans. English Dominicans, 1134); q. 112, a. 1, resp.; III, q. 1, a. 2, resp.; q. 62, a. 1, resp.
21. See, e.g., *ST* I-II, q. 65, a. 3, ad 2.

Eucharist, participation in the Mass, prayer, study, and works of love. Third, some human persons reach a stage of perfection in this life such that they habitually use this life as a kind of purgatory. Such persons consider the things of this world as nothing compared to the love of God and neighbor. Fourth, some human persons reach a stage of spiritual perfection in this life that St. Thomas calls "the summit of perfection,"[22] a stage that sufficiently prepares them for the transition from this life to the activity of the beatific vision in heaven. Such human persons are, as it were, living this life as though they were already in heaven. Fifth, some human persons are prepared for the transition to heaven in the next life by losing their excessive attachments to creatures in purgatory.[23] By way of bringing human persons through these various stages of grace perfecting nature in this life and the next, St. Thomas thinks that God brings human persons from this life to heaven in a manner that respects their created human natures. God thereby preserves their personal identity through such changes.

What does all of this have to do with responding to PTHI? Ribeiro has trouble imagining how typical human persons in this life could be personally identical to persons in heaven, where those persons in heaven, for example, do not engage in lustful thoughts, and who would be content with the contemplation of divine truth. Part of the problem here is that Ribeiro assumes that persons in heaven are numerically identical to human persons who have not been given grace in this life.[24] In fact, God prepares ordinary human persons such as Ribeiro describes for heaven by giving them grace, which grace makes them—or at least goes some distance toward making them—fit for heaven.

Because there are different stages of the spiritual life, we can also speak of transitions between these different stages. I will now discuss

---

22. *ST* I-II, q. 61, a. 5, resp. See also the detailed discussion of this stage of spiritual development below.

23. It should be mentioned that, in order to make possible beatific activity in heaven, the saints, upon entrance to heaven, are also given the grace of the *lumen gloriae*, a final gift of grace which is the fitting culmination of graces given to human persons in earlier stages of the spiritual life. Chapter 8 above discusses the importance of the *lumen gloriae* for making sense of the beatific vision and perfect happiness in heaven in some detail. Finally, see also the discussion of the dowries (*dotes*) of the blessed conferred by Christ on the church as his bridegroom in order to facilitate the delight of the saints in the beatific vision in chapter 8, note 40, above.

24. Thanks are due to participants at a session on St. Thomas Aquinas at the 2014 International Congress for Medieval Studies in Kalamazoo, Michigan, and an anonymous reviewer, for emphasizing the need to talk about grace in this context.

each of these stages and the transitions between them in some detail in order to show their relevance for a Thomistic response to PTHI.[25]

According to St. Thomas, human persons—with one important exception[26]—are not born with sanctifying grace. St. Thomas thinks it fitting, therefore, that the ordinary manner in which human persons receive sanctifying grace so as to become deiform or children of God is through the sacrament of baptism in infancy. For, in that case, it is near the beginning of their natural lives that human persons are spiritually born, thereby receiving the benefits of sanctifying grace, the infused virtues of faith, hope, and charity, and the gifts of the Holy Spirit. Those who have not yet reached the age of reason have these infused virtues and the gifts of the Holy Spirit as actual habits or qualities that are not (yet) in second act.[27]

When baptized human persons reach the age of reason—or, as happens in some cases, when human persons are baptized as adults—such human persons are able to begin freely cooperating with the grace of God. In doing so, they bring the infused virtues and the gifts of the Holy Spirit to second act, thereby both activating acts of faith, hope, and charity, and acting such that they, to use St. Paul's winsome phrase, "live by the Spirit" (Gal 5:16). Such persons can also receive an additional outpouring and strengthening of the Spirit for the life of grace in the sacrament of confirmation.[28]

Now, human persons who thus cooperate with sanctifying grace in this life still struggle with concupiscence (God in his wisdom does not restore the preternatural gift of integrity through baptism). Nonetheless, those human persons who receive sanctifying grace are empowered by grace to act virtuously in two ways that surpass those human persons who have not been made deiform and so do not have the infused virtues and the gifts of the Holy Spirit. First, graced human persons can engage in acts that make them fit for eternal life in heaven whereas human persons without grace cannot. According to St. Thomas, human persons, for example, cannot engage in acts of the theological virtues of faith, hope, and charity without grace, as such acts require the possession of pow-

---

25. For a recent detailed study of grace as a preparation for the beatific vision, see, e.g., Hutter, *Bound for Beatitude*.
26. See, e.g., *ST* III, q. 27, a. 4, resp.
27. See, e.g., *ST* III, q. 69, aa. 4–6.
28. See, e.g., *ST* III, q. 72, a. 7.

ers that exceed our natural human powers.[29] Second, because human nature without grace is damaged and extremely limited, it is easier for graced human persons to acquire those virtues and engage in actions that lie within the natural power of human persons.[30]

Before moving on to the next stages of the spiritual life, and the transitions between them, let us take stock of the relevance of these initial stages of the spiritual life for a Thomistic solution to PTHI. Ribeiro argues that the unmixed, radical, and instantaneous change that is the transition from an ordinary human life to (something like) a life of beatific activity in heaven would annihilate the personality of the human person undergoing that change, so that no human person in this life could rationally want to go to heaven. But given what I have said about the significance of grace as that which prepares human persons for heaven according to St. Thomas, I can disambiguate (7) and (8) as follows:

(7*) The following psychological change would be unmixed, instantaneous, and *extremely* radical: going from being a human person S who rationally desires things in this life such that S does so *without grace as a preparation for beatific activity in heaven*, to being a person who enjoys the beatific vision in heaven [assumption].

(7**) The following psychological change would be unmixed, instantaneous, and *non-extremely* radical: going from being a human person S who rationally desires things in this life such that S does so *with sanctifying grace such that S is made deiform and engages in graced action in this life so as to be prepared for beatific activity in heaven*, to being a person who enjoys the beatific vision in heaven [assumption].

(8*) A psychological change that is unmixed, instantaneous, and *extremely* radical, where a human person is not prepared by grace for that change, is a discontinuous change [assumption].

(8**) A psychological change that is unmixed, instantaneous, and *non-extremely* radical, where a human person S is prepared by grace for that change such that, in this life, God causes (a) the soul of S to be deiform, (b) the soul of S to possess the infused virtues of faith, hope, and charity, and (c) the soul of S to possess the gifts of the Holy Spirit, and (d) the soul of S freely to cooperate with God's grace such that S activates those virtues and gifts, is a discontinuous change [assumption].

---

29. See, e.g., *ST* II-II, q. 6, a. 1; q. 23, a. 2.
30. See, e.g., *SCG* I.4; *ST* I, q. 1, a. 1, resp.; I-II, q. 68, a. 2; II-II, q. 23, a. 7.

Notice, first, that I have distinguished an extremely radical, instantaneous, and unmixed change from a non-extremely radical, instantaneous, unmixed one. It is difficult to define an extremely radical change, but perhaps an example will suffice. In fact, I will employ an example Ribeiro himself gives of a radical and instantaneous change:[31] a saint going from living a life of sanctity one moment, to being (*per impossible*) demon-possessed the next. Assume with Ribeiro that a human person could not survive such a change and that this is a good example of an extremely radical change. Now, a non-extremely radical change is one that is radical but not extremely radical. Let it remain an open question for now whether a person can survive a change that is instantaneous, unmixed, and non-extremely radical. For example, think of the potential counterexamples to (8) mentioned above, which we might think are good examples of unmixed, instantaneous, and non-extremely radical changes.

Second, suppose what St. Thomas proposes is true with respect to God's (ordinary, if not only) way of giving grace. A human person S receives grace initially through baptism and then later through reception of other sacraments such as the Eucharist and confirmation, as well as by way of the actualization of the deiform character of the soul and its infused virtues and gifts of the Holy Spirit in this life. Now, becoming deiform in this life is a necessary condition for going to heaven (if a human person S1 who goes to heaven does not receive grace in this life in the ordinary ways mentioned above, then S1 receives the graces requisite for life in heaven in some extraordinary way). Therefore, propositions (7*) and (8*) are not relevant where the transition from this life to heaven is concerned for human persons. However, premises (7**) and (8**) are relevant for the transition between this life and beatific action in heaven. This is because God prepares human persons for beatific action in heaven by way of (a) making the human soul in this life deiform and, sometimes, (b) enabling human persons to cooperate with grace in this life such that they activate infused virtues and the gifts of the Holy Spirit.

That being said, we may think that premise (8**) is false. That is, given the help of God's grace mentioned in (8**), we may think that the change described in (8**) is *not* discontinuous. Of course, if (8**) is false and (8*) and (8**) are the correct ways to disambiguate (8), because (8*)

---

31. It seems the change being unmixed is not relevant here.

is not a relevant interpretation of (8), it follows that (8) is false. Therefore, we may already think that Ribeiro's argument for premise (2) is unsound, as at least one of the premises of the right sort in an argument for (2) will turn out to be false. In fact, given what I have said about the ways God prepares by grace human persons in this life for the beatific vision in heaven, we already have good reasons to think that premise (2) of Ribeiro's argument is false too.

But say that we still have our doubts about the falsity of a premise such as (8**). St. Thomas has more to say about grace and infused virtue that is relevant for God bringing a typical human person from this life to heaven such that the personal identity of that person is preserved through the change. So far, I have spoken about the first two stages of a spiritual life and the transitions between these stages. But St. Thomas also mentions some additional stages of the spiritual life that are relevant for an evaluation of PTHI. These additional stages of the spiritual life are characterized by perfections of infused virtuous activity in this life and, for those who require it, the purging of sinful inclinations in purgatory. These additional stages of the spiritual life have something in common: they both involve transforming a human person such that she goes from living a typical human life that is preoccupied with many ordinary things that exist in time to living a supernatural life that is focused on the one thing necessary that exists outside of time. That is to say, these additional stages of the spiritual life involve transforming a human person from living a life full of practical activity to living a life that is essentially contemplative, that is, focused on thinking about and delighting in God. Or, to put the point still another way, St. Thomas has a number of ways of explaining how God's grace at work in human persons in this life turns Marthas into (perfect) Marys.[32] As the human activity that is the beatific vision in heaven is a timeless contemplation of the essence of God, according to St. Thomas, we need to see the significance of the connection between contemplation and timelessness.

Consider that contemplation itself is an activity that is timeless or, at the very least, an activity that tends toward timelessness. That is to say, insofar as a being is engaged in contemplative activity, that being is either timelessly contemplating some truth or engaging in an act such that the person is not, or tends not to be, aware of the passage of time while

---

32. See Lk 10:38–42. See also St. Thomas's reflection on this passage in *SCG* IV.83.24.

she is engaged in such contemplative activity. Therefore, insofar as the life of a human person *in this life* is characterized to some extent by contemplative virtues and activity, there can exist psychological continuity between such a person in this life and the numerically same person in heaven who is essentially engaged in the timeless contemplative act of the beatific vision.

As for the (tending toward) timelessness of contemplation, consider the testimony of the saints. Perhaps the most famous such attestation comes from St. Augustine's *Confessions*, where he recalls an intimate conversation with his mother, St. Monica, which culminated in an act of contemplation that allowed both of them, if only briefly, to leave the cares of this life—and even time—behind:

> Our colloquy led us to the point where the pleasures of the body's senses, however intense and in however brilliant a material light enjoyed, seemed unworthy not merely of comparison but even of remembrance beside the joy of that life, and we lifted ourselves in longing yet more ardent toward *That Which Is*, and step-by-step traversed all bodily creatures and heaven itself, whence sun and moon and stars shed their light upon the earth. Higher still we mounted by inward thought and wondering discourse on your works, and we arrived at the summit of our own minds; and this too we transcended, to touch that land of never-failing plenty were you pasture Israel for ever with the food of truth. Life there is the Wisdom through whom all these things are made, and all others that have been or ever will be; but Wisdom herself is not made: she is as she always has been and will be forever. Rather should we say that in her there is no "has been" or "will be," but only being, for she is eternal, but past and future do not belong to eternity. And as we talked and panted for it, we just touched the edge of it by the utmost leap of our hearts; then sighing, and unsatisfied, we left the first-fruits of our spirit captive there, and returned to the noise of articulate speech, where a word has a beginning and end. How different from your Word, our Lord, who abides in himself, and grows not old, but renews all things.[33]

The ordinary experience of people also attests to the fact that contemplation tends toward unity and timelessness. People often speak of "losing track of time" when they are spending time with someone with whom they are enamored, when they are thinking deeply, reading an absorbing book, listening to great music, and, sometimes, when they are praying in earnest. Indeed, for Catholics, the Mass in particular is where

---

33. *Confessions* IX.10.24, trans. Maria Boulding (New York: Vintage Books, 1998), 188.

human persons are called to a contemplative, corporate worship that has human persons practicing for eternal life.[34] Although human persons do not experience absolute timelessness and unity of focus in this life, some contemplative activities that we experience in this life tend toward a timeless, unified human activity.

With this talk of the nature of contemplation in the background, I can begin speaking of a third and a fourth stage of the spiritual life whereby God prepares human persons for eternity. I will begin by examining a text by St. Thomas which suggests human persons can begin to live contemplatively, even in a habitual way, in this life. The context of the text is a discussion of how to distinguish the different species of cardinal virtues in *ST* I-II. Discussing a text from the Roman statesman, Macrobius (fl. ca. 400 A.D.), who himself is citing Plotinus and Plato, St. Thomas distinguishes between *exemplar* cardinal virtues (*virtutes exemplares*), *political* or *human* cardinal virtues (*politicas*), *purgative* cardinal virtues (*purgatorias*), and the cardinal *virtues of the purified soul* (*purgati animi*).[35]

St. Thomas notes in this text that Christ teaches that we should be perfect even as the heavenly Father is perfect (Mt 5:48). It follows, then, that there are cardinal virtues that lie between political or human virtues, which virtues have to do with bringing our passions to a relative mean, and the exemplar virtues, which are the virtues as they are found in God, and so have nothing at all to do with passion, as there is no passion in God.[36] Between the political or human virtues and the exemplar virtues are both the *purgative* virtues and the *virtues of the purified soul*. St. Thomas describes *purgative virtues* as the virtues of those who are on their way toward and tending to divine similitude.[37] Human persons characterized by the purgative virtues in this life regard their passions for earthly things as nothing compared to the love of God and neighbor. To take an example of a purgative cardinal virtue, St. Thomas describes purgative *prudence* this way: "by contemplating the things of God, [pur-

---

34. See chapters 2 and 16 above for discussion of Paul Griffiths's helpful view that the Mass is where the systolic time of heaven breaks into the metronomic time of this life, thereby habituating us for life in heaven.

35. *ST* I-II, q. 61, a. 5, resp. and ad 2. See also *In Sent* III, d. 33, q. 1, a. 4, ad 2; d. 34, q. 1, a. 1, ad 6; *QDV*, q. 26, a. 8, ad 2; *In Mt* 5, lect. 2, nn. 407 and 435–38; *ST* I-II, q. 63, a. 4, resp.; *In NE* X, lect. 11, nn. 2103–10.

36. *ST* I-II, q. 61, a. 5, ad 2. For texts and discussion on the reality of love, delight, and joy in God, yet without emotion, passion, or feeling, see the discussion of the nature of God in chapter 4 above.

37. *ST* I-II, q. 61, a. 5, resp.

gative prudence] counts as nothing all things of the world, and directs all the thoughts of the soul to God alone."[38] Someone who habitually activates the purgative virtues has reached the third stage of the spiritual life.[39]

According to St. Thomas, the *virtues of the purified soul* are the infused virtues possessed by the blessed in heaven and *those in this life* who have reached "the summit of perfection." For example, St. Thomas says that the cardinal virtue of prudence in the purified soul "sees nought else but the things of God."[40] Thus, he suggests here that a human person S might reach a level of perfection in virtue, even in this life, such that S goes beyond habitually regarding everything naturally good, for example, pleasure in eating, drinking, and conversation about temporal matters, as nothing compared to the love of God and neighbor, as in the third stage of the spiritual life. In this fourth stage of the spiritual life, S actually has no desire for those things.[41] S might engage in such activities, but S does so simply for the sake of the love of God and neighbor, and not because of delight in those things themselves. As we saw in chapter 11 above, St. Thomas thinks that blessed human persons in heaven are "like the angels in heaven," which means, among other things, that the blessed in heaven no longer experience bodily passions for food, drink, and sex (and we might add, politics). Therefore, human persons in this life who, by the grace of God, possess the virtues of the purified soul, even if they engage in temporal affairs, do so without any passion for them.[42] To put the point another way, human persons in this life who act in accord with the virtues of the purified soul are living, in essence, this life as though they were already in heaven. This is the fourth stage of the spiritual life.[43]

Consider some ways of making sense both (a) of the possibility that some human persons reach the summit of perfection in this life, and (b) of

---

38. Ibid. (trans. English Dominicans, 850). One also thinks of the attitude that St. Paul expresses in Phil 3:5–8.

39. The argument here assumes that God can gracefully bring a human person S from the second to the third stage of the spiritual life such that there is psychological continuity in S throughout that transition so that S's personal identity is preserved through such a transition.

40. *ST* I-II, q. 61, a. 5, resp. (trans. English Dominicans, 850). One also thinks of the attitude that St. Paul expresses in 2 Tm 4:6–8.

41. *ST* I-II, q. 61, a. 5, ad 2.

42. For additional relevant texts and discussion, see chapter 11 above on St. Thomas on the impassibility, subtlety, and spirituality of the glorified body.

43. The argument here assumes that God can gracefully bring a human person S from the third to the fourth stage of the spiritual life such that there is psychological continuity in S throughout that transition so that S's personal identity is preserved through such a transition.

The Tedium of Heavenly Immortality

the view that such a way of life is a good one. First, compare the activity of such persons with angelic activity aimed at bringing about goods for human persons in this life. For some of the angels having the beatific vision, although unaffected by passion, are nonetheless expressing love for God and created persons in the world in concrete ways, for example, by delivering a revelation, guiding someone to do the right thing, or comforting the afflicted.[44] Second, compare the activity of the human persons in this life who reach the summit of perfection with embodied saints in heaven, as St. Thomas thinks about them. As we saw in chapters 10 and 11 above, embodied saints in heaven will move their bodies and make use of their sense faculties. As these comparisons are designed to illustrate, human persons with the virtues of the purified soul in this life are not psychically and physically inactive, uninvolved, or indifferent to temporal affairs, no more, to take another example, than an immaterial God is inactive, uninvolved, or indifferent to what happens in this world.

In addition, in order to make the idea of a human person living in the fourth stage of the spiritual life more concrete, consider the examples of saints who perhaps reached the fourth stage of the spiritual life—the summit of perfection—in this life: one thinks, of course, of the Virgin Mary, but also Pope St. John Paul II, St. Catherine of Siena, St. Teresa of Avila, St. Thérèse of Lisieux, and St. Thomas himself.[45]

Given that contemplation is timeless or tends toward timelessness and St. Thomas's account of infused moral virtue in this life, Ribeiro is wrong to assume that no human persons could be personally identical—because not psychologically continuous—with persons in heaven who are having the beatific vision. For we are now armed with a number of ways of showing that premise (2), (7), or (8) of PTHI is false. To see why, note that there are a number of additional ways of disambiguating both propositions (7) and (8):

---

44. See, e.g., Mt 18:10.

45. See, e.g., *SCG* IV.54: "since, the perfect beatitude of man consists in the enjoyment of God alone ... necessarily every man is kept from participation in the true beatitude who cleaves as to an end to these things which are less than God... And we look upon this consequence of God's Incarnation: a large part of mankind passing by the cult of angels, of demons, and all creatures whatsoever, spurning, indeed, the pleasures of the flesh and all things bodily, have dedicated themselves to the worship of God alone, and in Him only they look for the fulfillment of this beatitude; and so the Apostle exhorts: 'Seek the things that are above where Christ is sitting at the right hand of God. Mind the things that are above, not the things that are upon the earth' (Col 3:1–2)" (trans. O'Neil, 228–29). St. Thomas also notes in this chapter that Christ's incarnation itself shows it is possible for possessors of human nature to have the beatific vision.

(7*) The following psychological change would be unmixed, instantaneous, and *extremely* radical: going from (a) being a human person S who rationally desires things in this life such that S does so without grace as a preparation for beatific activity in heaven, to (b) being a person who enjoys the beatific vision in heaven [assumption].

(7***) The following psychological change would be unmixed, instantaneous, and *non-extremely* radical: going from (a) being a human person S who rationally desires things in this life such that S does so with sanctifying grace so that S is made deiform and engages in graced action in this life, for example, S's activity expresses *purgative* virtues so as to be prepared for beatific activity in heaven to (b) being a person who enjoys the beatific vision in heaven [assumption].

(7****) The following psychological change would be unmixed, instantaneous, and *non-extremely* radical: going from (a) being a human person S who rationally desires things in this life such that S does so with sanctifying grace so that S is made deiform and engages in graced action in this life, for example, S's activity expresses virtues of the *purified* soul so as to be prepared for beatific activity in heaven to (b) being a person who could enjoy the beatific vision in heaven [assumption].

(8*) A psychological change that is unmixed, instantaneous, and *extremely* radical, where the person is not prepared by grace for that change, is a discontinuous change [assumption].

(8***) A psychological change that is unmixed, instantaneous, and *non-extremely* radical, even where a human person S is prepared by grace for that change such that, in this life, God causes (a) the soul of S to be deiform, (b) the soul of S to possess the infused *purgative* virtues of faith, hope, and charity, (c) the soul of S to possess the gifts of the Holy Spirit, and (d) the soul of S freely to cooperate with God's grace such that S activates those virtues and gifts, is a discontinuous change.

(8****) A psychological change that is unmixed, instantaneous, and *non-extremely* radical, even where a human person S is prepared by grace for that change such that, in this life, God causes (a) the soul of S to be deiform, (b) the soul of S to possess the infused virtues of faith, hope, and charity such that they are *the virtues of the purified soul*, (c) the soul of that person to possess the gifts of the Holy Spirit, and (d) the soul of S freely to cooperate with God's grace such that S activates those virtues and gifts, is a discontinuous change.

Given what I have said about contemplative activity and St. Thomas's views on purgative virtues and the virtues of the purified soul—along with the assumption that some human persons can embody such virtues in this life—one may reasonably reject Ribeiro's argument for (2) by accepting propositions such as (7***) and (7****) but rejecting propositions such as (8***) and (8****). Given that God prepares by grace human persons in this life for the beatific vision in heaven by bringing them to the third or fourth stages of the spiritual life, we have good reason to think that premise (2) of Ribeiro's argument is false too.

However, St. Thomas's account of the virtues of the purified soul gives the Thomist a second way of responding to Ribeiro's argument. Recall that Ribeiro thinks that the change from this life to heaven would have to be radical, unmixed, and instantaneous. If St. Thomas is right that some human persons in this life act in accord with the virtues of the purified soul, those human persons do undergo a radical change in their relationship to earthly desires, but they do so gradually over time, so that, at the end of their earthly life, the change that is moving from life in this world to having the beatific vision in heaven, although an instantaneous one, is not radical at all. Therefore, premise (7****)—and so premise (7)—is false. That means Ribeiro's argument for (2) is unsound. Indeed, given the truth that some human persons can practice heaven-like contemplation in this life, and that God has gracefully brought them to that position without destroying their human personalities, it follows that premise (2) of the Ribeiro-like objection is false.

Of course, many human persons will not reach the summit of perfection in this life. So what about the rest of us? Can we make sense of the possibility of psychological continuity between a human person who, at best, both periodically contemplates poorly in this life and has disordered desires for things other than God, on the one hand, and a person enjoying the beatific vision in heaven, on the other? St. Thomas's talk of purgative virtues suggests a fifth possible stage of the spiritual life, and, given the real effects of original sin on human persons, perhaps a more typical way in which God's grace completes the preparation of human persons for the beatific vision in heaven.

Many human persons who really have charity for God in this life will not be psychologically ready for eternity when they die—having not sufficiently practiced in this life an activity analogous to the activity in which perfect human happiness essentially consists in heaven.[46] In many cases, this could be partly a moral failing. For, as St. Thomas notes, possessing the moral virtues is a prerequisite for engaging in the contemplative life insofar as passions can both keep us from engaging in contemplation in the first place and can disturb our contemplation once we begin.[47] Therefore, insofar as human persons die still having venial sinful kinds of attachments to the passions and pleasures of earthly life, such a condition can and must be healed by suffering in purgatory. Let us suggest that, given enough time in purgatory, God can preserve psychological continuity between a human person with typical sorts of earthly desires in this life and a person in heaven who is focused on contemplating the divine essence.

For example, imagine that Jane dies with a desire to be with God forever such that she will go to heaven. To be with God forever is to have eternal life, which, as we have seen, for St. Thomas consists in an intellectual and joyful timeless participation in God's non-successive life. Imagine also that when Jane dies, she is not quite psychologically and morally ready for an eternal life that consists essentially in contemplating the essence of God, as she retains venial sinful desires for timebound, earthly things. Purgatory—building on the graces and nature given to Jane by God in this life—finishes Jane's preparation for heaven. While in purgatory, Jane's psyche undergoes a radical change, but never so drastically, or quickly, so as to annihilate Jane's self. Sufficient time in purgatory ensures that God's gift of eternal life does not destroy Jane's nature, but rather perfects it, as Jane's passions to satisfy sinful desires gradually fall away, no longer being desirous for her. Eventually, all that is left is her desire, present in this life in perhaps only a sapling-like form, that her life be characterized such that, essentially, she contemplates and loves the essence of God, and, accidentally, she contemplates and loves creatures in God and for the sake of contemplating and loving God.

Spending time in purgatory, then, is perhaps the way that God prepares many, perhaps most, human persons for eternity, given how many

---

46. Again, as the examples of Christ, the Virgin Mary, and the lives of many saints make clear, one can live a contemplative life in the midst of a very active life. In fact, St. Thomas's own life, involving as it did much teaching and preaching, is a model of a contemplative life that is also active. The fact that human persons in this life can live a life that is both contemplative and active, however, does not contradict the theological fact that heavenly beatitude is purely contemplative, as in this life we always remain wayfarers whereas beatitude in heaven entails the fulfillment of desire.

47. See, e.g., *ST* II-II, q. 180, a. 2, resp.

human persons only make little more than a beginning in this life at putting into practice St. Paul's admonition that we "set [our] minds on things that are above, not on things that are on earth" (Col 3:2). This way of God's preparing human persons for beatitude in purgatory, if coherent, provides us another reason for thinking that premise (7) is false. For some persons make the transition from this life to beatific activity in heaven through time in purgatory, thereby undergoing a radical and unmixed change, although not instantaneously.

Again, given the ways that God can preserve the personal identity of human persons transitioning between this life and heaven that I have mentioned, not only does St. Thomas give us reasons for thinking that premise (7) is false, but he also gives us reasons for thinking that premise (2) is false as well. For God can preserve the personal identity of human persons through the transition(s) from ordinary this-worldly life to beatific activity in heaven by taking such human persons through a number of different intermediate stages of the spiritual life, which intermediate stages begin (and, for some saints, end) in this life and culminate (for some) in purgatory.

Let us assume that I have shown that (2) is false. Given the possibility that God completes the preparation for heaven for most human persons in purgatory, Ribeiro cannot even retreat to the following weaker claim:

(2a) In the case of *most* human persons who die possessing the virtue of charity, there is psychological discontinuity between those human persons in this life and the psychological stage or stages of any person in heaven who enjoys the beatific vision in heaven, when the first stage of those human persons in this life are those persons rationally desiring, that is, willing, things in this life [assumption].[48]

Ribeiro is left without reason for affirming—and the Thomist has reasons for rejecting—(2a) because it may be that, among human persons who go to heaven whose first psychological stage is rationally desiring things in this life, *most* of those human persons will spend time in purgatory and the suffering they undergo there will duly prepare them for eternity.[49]

---

48. Recall that psychological continuity between person S and person S1 requires that there be psychological continuity between the psychological stages of S and the psychological stages of S1, e.g., John at two years old and John at twenty years old are psychologically continuous only if John's psychological stages between two and twenty are continuous.

49. Indeed, nothing that the Catholic church teaches rules out that some canonized saints had to spend some time in purgatory before they were recognized to be saints in heaven.

We may think such time in purgatory does indeed involve those human persons undergoing a change that is extremely radical; nonetheless, such an extremely radical change will not be instantaneous. Although the change that consists in going from not having the beatific vision in the last stage of human life in purgatory to having the beatific vision in heaven for any given human person S will be instantaneous, it will not constitute an extremely radical psychological change for S, given the efficacy of purgatorial cleansing.

Finally, we might think about the way that a human person in this life is partly transformed through sufferings in purgatory into someone fit for the beatific vision such that she retains psychological continuity throughout in another way. Consider the possibility that the change that is going from suffering purgatorial cleansing to beatific activity in heaven is indeed, mixed, instantaneous, and non-extremely radical, but that it is false that such a change represents a discontinuous change. For God has prepared the person for the beatific vision by distributing to that person grace in this life and in purgatory. Therefore, this change is not an extremely radical change, but a non-extremely radical one, and such a change is not an example of a discontinuous change. We can therefore make a good case, in at least two different ways from the teaching of St. Thomas on grace, that even the weaker premise (2a) is false.

To conclude, texts in St. Thomas give us a number of ways of solving PTHI. St. Thomas's theology of grace and his account of the various stages of the spiritual life allow one reasonably to reject key premises in PTHI, namely, premise (2) and either (7) or (8). The doctrines of St. Thomas provide a powerful defeater for the problem of the tedium of heavenly immortality.

Conclusion

St. Thomas's teaching on heaven recommends itself both by way of its beauty and its explanatory power. According to St. Thomas, heaven is that reality where human hearts are no longer restless, because they find their fulfillment in knowing and loving God in the most intimate way logically possible for creatures: knowing the essence of God in the beatific vision, and as a logical consequence, perfectly loving and enjoying what they know. St. Thomas goes so far as to speak of this essential reward, consisting of supernaturalized acts of intellect and will, as a participated eternity, beyond both time and aeveternity. Enabled by the grace of the *lumen gloriae* to see the essence of God and fittingly love what they see, the saints in heaven become perfectly deiform. That is, the saints in heaven come to participate in the greatest logically possible way in God's own eternal life, the timelessly eternal knowing and loving communion of the Father, the Son, and the Holy Spirit.

According to St. Thomas, the blessed in heaven also have a profoundly intimate knowledge and love of creatures just in virtue of having the beatific vision. While God himself is the primary object of the vision, creatures form the secondary object. But St. Thomas's account also takes into account the reality and proper place for human embodiment in heaven, as well as the good of a direct knowledge and love of creatures by way of the body, especially in the communion of the saints in heaven. St. Thomas treats these aspects of heavenly glory (among others) as aspects of the accidental reward of the saints in heaven. Such human goods are gratuitous, or fitting, or appropriate aspects of heavenly life for human persons. But they are not essential to perfect human happiness in heaven, given the following Catholic doctrines: (a) God is infinite and absolutely perfect being, goodness, beauty, and truth; (b) human persons are created in the image and likeness of God and so are intellectual creatures whose hearts are restless until they rest in God; and (c) God raises up the saints in heaven to participate in God's own eternal life.

Aside from their great beauty, St. Thomas's views on heaven also have great explanatory power, for they allow us to solve four apparent problems concerning eternal life. The Thomistic solutions to these apparent problems have a set of intellectual virtues not shared by the contemporary theological and philosophical accounts of heaven examined in this volume. For example, we might think that, all other things being equal, if there are two theories A and B about some aspect of heaven, and A is consistent with authoritative, Catholic Christian tradition whereas B is not, then we should prefer A. Where St. Thomas's views are consistent with authoritative, Catholic Christian tradition—indeed, in some cases, they are an important source of the development of that tradition—many of the contemporary theological and philosophical views that I have examined in this volume conflict with such tradition.

Indeed, St. Thomas thinks that (1) the essential reward consists in the beatific vision and the delight that flows from it, which makes the blessed perfectly deiform; that (2) the next life—even in its accidental and bodily dimension, particularly for the blessed—is a new and transfigured life and not simply a perfected continuation of this life; and that (3) Christians in this life are nonetheless personally identical to human persons in the next, even to the extent that both their charity at the end of this life follows them into the next and their bodies in this life are numerically the same human bodies they possess at and after the general resurrection. These views of St. Thomas's are consistent with, and obviously inform, the following judgment of the Sacred Congregation for the Doctrine of the Faith:

> Christians must firmly hold the two following essential points: on the one hand, they must believe in the fundamental continuity, thanks to the power of the Holy Spirit, between our present life in Christ and the future life (charity is the law of the kingdom of God, and our charity on earth will be the measure of our sharing God's glory in heaven); on the other hand, they must be clearly aware of the radical break between the present life and the future one, due to the fact that the economy of faith will be replaced by the economy of fullness of life: we shall be with Christ and "we shall see God" (1 Jn 3:2), and it is in these promises and marvelous mysteries that our hope essentially consists. Our imagination may be incapable of reaching these heights, but our heart does so instinctively and completely.[1]

---

1. Letter (on Certain Questions concerning Eschatology), *Recentiores Episcoporum Synodi*, no. 4659 (May 17, 1979), in DH 1028.

But St. Thomas's views on the nature of heaven also have *philosophical* advantages over contemporary views. St. Thomas's distinction between the essential reward and the multifaceted accidental reward can make better sense of the transcendent and immanent dimensions of heavenly existence, as those dimensions are spoken about in scripture and Christian tradition, than can the views, for example, of Germain Grisez, Katherin Rogers, Paul Griffiths, Lynne Rudder Baker, and Eric Silverman. Grisez's attempt to show that this-worldly goods are constitutive of heavenly life fails to take seriously enough the transcendence and infinite goodness of God. Rogers's account of human happiness does not make a place for direct human contact in heaven. The accounts of heaven in the work of Griffiths and Silverman do not do justice to the greatness and glory of heaven insofar as it consists essentially in a direct union with God, a union that transcends time and aeveternity. Rudder Baker's account of bodily life in heaven is founded on a kind of dualist philosophical anthropology that divorces our personal identity from our human nature.

However, according to St. Thomas, heaven is a reality that transcends this-worldly life insofar as it consists primarily of the most direct and immediate intellectual and volitional union with God that is logically possible for a creature. This beatific vision, and the charity, delight, and joy that follow from it, makes its possessor perfectly happy. But heaven for human persons nonetheless contains all those this-worldly goods—human embodiment, sensation, movement, human community—that are logically consistent with heaven for human persons being a human life of participated eternity with God. Although these accidental goods are not necessary for perfect human happiness, they are fitting and appropriate ways for human persons *qua* embodied social beings to participate in the knowing and loving of the Father, the Son, and the Holy Spirit.

Finally, some work by contemporary theologians and philosophers offers helpful, if underdeveloped, responses to PTHI. Building on the work of contemporary thinkers Timothy Chappell, Gilbert Meilaender, and Paul Griffiths, I noted that a Thomistic solution to that apparent problem—one that takes seriously St. Thomas's account of the beatific vision, his theology of grace, the different stages of the spiritual life, and the Catholic doctrine of purgatory—can defeat even the most potent version of PTHI. St. Thomas's teaching on heaven thus allows us to solve four apparent problems concerning eternal life, and in ways that are preferable to, or improve upon, the contemporary theological and philosophical solutions that I have addressed here. We do well to take St. Thomas as our theological and philosophical guide where thinking intelligently about heaven is concerned.

SELECTED BIBLIOGRAPHY

Adam, Karl. *The Spirit of Catholicism*. Translated by Dom Justin McCann. Garden City, N.Y.: Image Books, 1954.

Alarcon, Enrique, ed. *Corpus Thomisticum*. Available at www.corpusthomisticum.org.

Alighieri, Dante. *The Divine Comedy*. Translated by Allen Mandelbaum. New York: Alfred A. Knopf, 1995.

Anzulewicz, Henryk. "*Aeternitas – Aevum – Tempus*. The Concept of Time in the System of St. Albert the Great." In *The Medieval Concept of Time: Studies on the Scholastic Debate and its Reception in Early Modern Philosophy*, edited by Pasquale Porro, 83–130. Leiden: Brill, 2001.

Aquinas, Thomas. *The Aquinas Prayer Book: The Prayers and Hymns of St. Thomas Aquinas*. Translated by Robert Anderson and Johann Moser. Manchester, N.H.: Sophia Institute Press, 2000.

———. *Catechetical Instructions of St. Thomas Aquinas*. Translated by Joseph B. Collins. Fort Collins, Colo.: Roman Catholic Books, 1939.

———. *Catena Aurea. Commentary on the Four Gospels, Collected Out of the Works of the Fathers by St. Thomas Aquinas*. Translated by St. John Henry Newman. 4 vols. Boonville, N.Y.: Preserving Christian Publications, 2009 (1841–45).

———. *Commentary on Aristotle's* Metaphysics. Translated by John P. Rowan. Notre Dame, Ind.: Dumb Ox Books, 1995.

———. *Commentary on Aristotle's* Nicomachean Ethics. Translated by C. I. Litzinger. Notre Dame, Ind.: Dumb Ox Books, 1993 (1964).

———. *Commentary on the Gospel according to St. Matthew*. Translated by Paul M. Kimball. Camillus, N.Y.: Dolorosa Press, 2012.

———. *Commentary on Isaiah*. Translated by Joshua Madden. Lander, Wyo.: The Aquinas Institute, 2017. Available at aquinas.cc/la/en/~Isaiah.C11.L2.v11.2.

———. *Commentaries on the Letters of St. Paul to the Corinthians*. Translated by F. R. Larcher, B. Mortensen, and D. Keating. Edited by J. Mortensen and E. Alarcón. Lander, Wyo.: Aquinas Institute for the Study of Sacred Doctrine, 2012.

———. *Commentary on Saint Paul's Epistle to the Ephesians*. Translated by Matthew L. Lamb. Albany, N.Y.: Magi Books, 1966.

———. *Commentaries on St. Paul's Epistles to Timothy, Titus, and Philemon*. Translated by Chrysostom Baer. South Bend, Ind.: St. Augustine's Press, 2007.

———. *Light of Faith: The* Compendium of Theology. Translated by Cyril Vollert. Manchester, N.H.: Sophia Institute Press, 1993 (1947).

———. *On Evil* (Disputed Questions on Evil). Translated by Jean Oesterle. Notre Dame, Ind.: University of Notre Dame Press, 1995.

———. *On Love and Charity: Readings from the* Commentary on the *Sentences* of Peter Lombard. Translated by Peter A. Kwasniewski, Thomas Bolin, and Joseph Bolin. Washington, D.C.: The Catholic University of America Press, 2008.

———. *On the Power of God* (*Quaestiones disputatae de potentia dei*). Translated by the English Dominican Fathers. Eugene, Ore.: Wipf and Stock, 2004 (1932).

———. "Online Text Viewer." Aquinas Institute. Available at aquinas.cc/173/513/~182.

———. *Opera Omnia*. Edited by Leonine Commission, S. Thomae Aquinatis Doctoris Angelici. Rome: Vatican Polyglot Press, 1882–.

———. *Opera Omnia Project*. The Aquinas Institute. Available at aquinas.cc/173/513/~182.

———. *Quaestiones Quodlibetales*. Edited by Raymundi Spiazzi. Turin: Marietti, 1956.

———. *S. Thomae De Aquino Opera Omnia*. Corpus Thomisticum. Edited by Enrique Alarcon. Available at www.corpusthomisticum.org/iopera.html.

———. *St. Thomas Aquinas's Works in English*. Available at isidore.co/aquinas/.

———. *Summa contra gentiles*. Translated by Anton C. Pegis (Book I), James F. Anderson (Book II), Vernon J. Bourke (Book III), and Charles J. O'Neil (Book IV). 5 vols. Notre Dame, Ind.: University of Notre Dame Press, 1975.

———. *Summa theologiae*. Edited by Petri Caramello. Turin: Marietti, 1950.

———. *Summa Theologica*. Translated by the Fathers of the English Dominican Province. 5 vols. Allen, Tex.: Christian Classics, 1981 (1911).

———. *Super Pslamos*. The Aquinas Translation Project. Available at hosted.desales.edu/w4/philtheo/loughlin/ATP/index.html.

———. *Thomas Aquinas: The Academic Sermons*. Translated by Mark-Robin Hoogland. The Fathers of the Church: Medieval Continuation 11. Washington, D.C.: The Catholic University of America Press, 2010.

———. *The Three Greatest Prayers*. Translated by Laurence Shapcote. London: Burns, Oates, and Washbourne, 1937.

———. *Treatise on Happiness*. Translated by John A. Oesterle. Englewood Cliffs, N.J.: Prentice Hall, 1964.

———. *The Treatise on Happiness/The Treatise on Human Acts: Summa Theologiae I-II 1–21*. Translated by Thomas Williams. Commentary by Christina Van Dyke and Thomas Williams. Indianapolis, Ind.: Hackett, 2016.

———. *The Trinity and the Unicity of the Intellect* (St. Thomas' *Commentary on Boethius's* De trinitate). Translated by Rose E. Brennan. St. Louis, Mo.: B. Herder, 1946. Available at isidore.co/aquinas/english/BoethiusDeTr.htm.

———. *Truth* (*Quaestiones disputatae de veritate*). Translated by Robert W. Mulligan (QQ I–IX), James V. McGlynn (QQ. X–XX), and Robert W. Schmidt (QQ. XXI–XXIX). 3 vols. Indianapolis, Ind.: Hackett, 1994 (1954).

Selected Bibliography

Arendzen, J. P. "Heaven, or the Church Triumphant." In *The Teaching of the Catholic Church*, edited by George D. Smith, 2:1248–82. New York: Macmillan, 1949.

Aristotle. *Nicomachean Ethics*. Translated by Terence Irwin. Second edition. Indianapolis, Ind.: Hackett, 1999.

Ashley, Benedict, OP. "Integral Human Fulfillment according to Germain Grisez." In his *The Ashley Reader: Redeeming Reason*, 225–69. Naples, Fla.: Sapientia Press, 2006.

Augustine of Hippo, St. *The City of God*. Translated by Marcus Dodds. New York: Barnes and Noble, 2006.

———. *Confessions*. Translated by Maria Boulding. New York: Vintage Books, 1998.

———. *Confessions*. Translated by Frank Sheed. Indianapolis, Ind.: Hackett, 2006.

———. *The Trinity*. Translated by Edmund Hill. Hyde Park, N.Y.: New City Press, 2012.

Badham, Linda. "Problems with Accounts of Life after Death." In *Philosophy of Religion: Selected Readings*, edited by Michael Peterson, William Hasker, Bruce Reichenbach, and David Basinger, 469–75. New York: Oxford University Press, 2001.

Baker, Lynne Rudder. "Persons and the Metaphysics of Resurrection." *Religious Studies* 43, no. 3 (2007): 333–48.

Barr, Stephen M. *Modern Physics and Ancient Faith*. Notre Dame, Ind.: University of Notre Dame Press, 2003.

Benedict XII, Pope. *Benedictus Deus*. Apostolic Constitution. January 29, 1336. In DH 302–3.

Birzer, Bradley J. *J.R.R. Tolkien's Sanctifying Myth: Understanding Middle Earth*. Wilmington, Del.: ISI Books, 2009.

Boethius, Anicius Manlius Severinus. *Boethius: The Theological Tractates and the Consolation of Philosophy*. Loeb Classical Library 74. Cambridge, Mass.: Harvard University Press, 1973.

Bonin, Therese. *Thomas Aquinas in English: A Bibliography*. Available at aquinas-in-english.neocities.org.

Bradley, Denis. *Aquinas on the Two-Fold Human Good: Reason and Human Happiness in Aquinas's Moral Science*. Washington, D.C.: The Catholic University of America Press, 1997.

Brower, Jeffrey E. "Matter, Form, and Individuation." In *The Oxford Handbook of Aquinas*, edited by Brian Davies and Eleonore Stump, 85–103. Oxford: Oxford University Press, 2012.

———. *Aquinas's Ontology of the Material World: Change, Hylomorphism, and Material Objects*. Oxford: Oxford University Press, 2014.

Brown, Christopher M. "Aquinas on the Individuation of Non-Living Substances." *Proceedings of the American Catholic Philosophical Association* 75 (2001): 237–54.

———. *Aquinas and the Ship of Theseus: Solving Puzzles about Material Objects*. London: Continuum, 2005.

———. "Souls, Ships, and Substances: A Reply to Toner." *American Catholic Philosophical Quarterly* 81, no. 4 (2007): 655–68.

———. "Friendship in Heaven: Aquinas on Supremely Perfect Happiness and the Communion of the Saints." In *Metaphysics and God: Essays in Honor of Eleonore Stump*, edited by Kevin Timpe, 225–48. London: Routledge, 2009.

———. "Making the Best Even Better: Modifying Pawl and Timpe's Solution to the Problem of Heavenly Freedom." *Faith and Philosophy* 32, no. 1 (2015): 63–80.

———. "Some Advantages for a Thomistic Solution to the Problem of Personal Identity beyond Death." In *Paradise Understood: New Philosophical Essays about Heaven*, edited by T. Ryan Byerly and Eric J. Silverman, 228–62. Oxford: Oxford University Press, 2017.

———. "Martyrdom, the Death of Young Children, and the Heavenly Reward: A Thomistic Response to a Difficult Question about Evil" (unpublished manuscript).

———. "St. Thomas Aquinas on the Nature of Miracles" (unpublished manuscript).

Brown, David. "No Heaven without Purgatory." *Religious Studies* 21, no. 4 (1985): 447–56.

Budziszewski, J. *On the Meaning of Sex*. Wilmington, Del.: ISI Books, 2012.

Byerly, T. Ryan, and Eric J. Silverman, eds. *Paradise Understood: New Philosophical Essays about Heaven*. Oxford: Oxford University Press, 2017.

Bynum, Caroline Walker. *The Resurrection of the Body in Western Christianity, 200–1336*. New York: Columbia University Press, 1995.

Catechism of the Catholic Church. Second edition. Vatican City: Libreria Editrice Vaticana, 1994.

Cessario, Romanus. *Introduction to Moral Theology*. Revised edition. Washington, D.C.: The Catholic University of America Press, 2013.

Chappell, Timothy. "Infinity Goes Up on Trial: Must Immortality Be Meaningless?" *European Journal of Philosophy* 17, no. 1 (2009): 30–44.

Code of Canon Law: Latin-English Edition. Washington, D.C.: Canon Law Society of America, 1999.

Condic, Samuel B., and Maureen L. Condic. *Human Embryos, Human Beings: A Scientific and Philosophical Approach*. Washington, D.C.: The Catholic University of America Press, 2018.

Cooper, John W. *Body, Soul, and Life Everlasting: Biblical Anthropology and the Monism-Dualism Debate*. Grand Rapids, Mich.: Eerdmans, 1989.

Corcoran, Kevin J., ed. *Soul, Body, and Survival: Essays on the Metaphysics of Human Persons*. Ithaca, N.Y.: Cornell University Press, 2001.

———. *Rethinking Human Nature: A Christian Materialist Alternative to the Soul*. Grand Rapids, Mich.: Baker Academic, 2006.

Council Lateran IV. "The Catholic Faith." In DH 266.

Council of Carthage XV (or XVI). In DH 82–85.

Council of Florence. Session 6. July 6, 1439. In Tanner (ed.), *Decrees*, 527–28.
Council of Lyon II. "Profession of Faith of Michael Palaeologus." In Dupuis, *The Christian Faith*, 17–21.
Council of Toledo XI. *Symbol of Faith*. In Dupuis, *The Christian Faith*, 940–41.
Council of Trent. *Decree on Original Sin*, no. 1511. June 17, 1546. DH 372.
———. *Decree on Justification*, canon 32, no. 1582. January 13, 1547. DH 388.
Council of Vienne. Decree, no. 28. In Tanner (ed.), *Decrees*, 383.
Council Vatican I. *Dei Filius*. April 24, 1870. Available at www.vatican.va.
Council Vatican II. *Lumen Gentium*. November 21, 1964. Available at www.vatican.va.
———. *Gaudium et Spes*. December 7, 1965. Available at www.vatican.va.
Cross, Bryan R. "A Thomistic, Non-Ableist Conception of Impairment and Disability." *The National Catholic Bioethics Quarterly* 20, no. 2 (2020): 233–42.
Cushing, Simon, ed. *Heaven and Philosophy*. Lanham, Md.: Lexington Books, 2018.
Dahm, Brandon. "Distinguishing Desire and Parts of Happiness: A Response to Grisez." *American Catholic Philosophical Quarterly* 89, no. 1 (2015): 97–114.
Daley, Brian E. *The Hope of the Early Church: A Handbook of Patristic Eschatology*. Cambridge: Cambridge University Press, 1991.
Davies, Brian. *The Thought of Thomas Aquinas*. Oxford: Clarendon Press, 1992.
Deferrari, Roy. *A Latin-English Dictionary of St. Thomas Aquinas*. Boston: Daughters of St. Paul, 1986.
De Lubac, Henri. *Catholicism: A Study of Dogma in Relation to the Corporate Destiny of Mankind*. New York: Mentor-Omega Books, 1964.
Denzinger, Heinrich. *Compendium of Creeds, Definitions, and Declarations on Matters of Faith and Morals*. Edited by Peter Hunermann, Robert Fastiggi, and Anne Englund Nash. 43rd edition. San Francisco, Calif.: Ignatius Press, 2012.
Devine, Arthur. *A Manual of Ascetical Theology; Or, the Supernatural Life of the Soul on Earth and in Heaven*. New York: Benzinger, 1902.
Dewan, Lawrence. "The Individual as a Mode of Being according to Thomas Aquinas." *The Thomist* 63, no. 3 (1999): 403–24.
———. "St. Thomas, Norman Kretzmann, and Divine Freedom in Creating." *Nova et Vetera* (English edition) 4, no. 3 (2006): 495–514.
Doolan, Gregory. *Aquinas on the Divine Ideas as Exemplar Causes*. Washington, D.C.: The Catholic University of America Press, 2014.
Dougherty, Trent. *The Problem of Animal Pain: A Theodicy for All Creatures Great and Small*. Houndmills: Palgrave Macmillan, 2014.
Dupuis, Jacques, ed. *The Christian Faith in the Doctrinal Documents of the Catholic Church*. Sixth edition. New York: Alba House, 1996.
Eberl, Jason T. "Do Human Persons Persist between Death and Resurrection?" In *Metaphysics and God: Essays in Honor of Eleonore Stump*, edited by Kevin Tempe, 188–205. New York: Routledge, 2009.
Ehrman, Terrence. "Disability and Resurrection Identity." *New Blackfriars* 96, no. 1066 (2015): 723–38.

Eitenmiller, Melissa. "On the Separated Soul according to St. Thomas Aquinas." *Nova et Vetera* (English edition) 17, no. 1 (2019): 57–91.

Farrell, Walter. *A Companion to the Summa*. London: Sheed and Ward, 1942.

Feingold, Lawrence. *The Natural Desire to See God according to St. Thomas and His Interpreters*. Second edition. Naples, Fla.: Sapientia Press, 2010.

Feser, Edward. *Aquinas*. Oxford: Oneworld, 2009.

———. "In Defense of the Perverted Faculty Argument." In his *Neo-Scholastic Essays*, 378–415. South Bend, Ind.: St. Augustine's Press, 2015.

———. *Five Proofs of the Existence of God*. San Francisco, Calif.: Ignatius Press, 2017.

———. "Aquinas on the Human Soul." In *The Blackwell Companion to Substance Dualism*, edited by Jonathan J. Loose, Angus J. L. Menuge, and J. P. Moreland, 88–101. Oxford: Wiley Blackwell, 2018.

———. *Aristotle's Revenge: The Metaphysical Foundations of Physical and Biological Science*. Neunkirchen-Seelscheid: Editiones Scholasticae, 2019.

Finley, John. "The Metaphysics of Gender: A Thomistic Approach." *The Thomist* 79, no. 4 (2015): 585–614.

Finnis, John. *Aquinas: Moral, Political, and Legal Theory*. Oxford: Oxford University Press, 1998.

Firestone, Lisa. "Busting the Myths about Suicide." *Psych Alive*. Available at www.psychalive.org/busting-the-myths-about-suicide/.

Fischer, John Martin. "Why Immortality Is Not So Bad." *International Journal of Philosophical Studies* 2, no. 2 (1994): 257–70.

Fischer, John Martin, and Benjamin Mitchell-Yellin. "Immortality and Boredom." *The Journal of Ethics* 18, no. 4 (2014): 353–72.

Gaine, Simon Francis. *Will There Be Freewill in Heaven? Freedom, Impeccability, and Beatitude*. London: T and T Clark, 2003.

Garrigou-Lagrange, Reginald. *Life Everlasting*. Translated by Patrick Cummins. St. Louis, Mo.: Herder, 1952.

———. *Beatitude: A Commentary on St. Thomas' Theological Summa, Ia IIae, qq. 1–54*. Translated by Patrick Cummins. St. Louis, Mo.: Herder, 1955.

Gasser, Georg, ed. *Personal Identity and Resurrection: How Do We Survive our Death?* Surrey: Ashgate, 2010.

Graves, Shawn, Blake Hereth, and Tyler M. John. "In Defense of Animal Universalism." In *Paradise Understood*, edited by T. Ryan Byerly and Eric J. Silverman, 161–92. Oxford: Oxford University Press, 2017.

Griffiths, Paul J. *Decreation: The Last Things of All Creatures*. Waco, Tex.: Baylor University Press, 2014.

Grisez, Germain. *Way of the Lord Jesus*, vol. 2, *Living a Christian Life*. Quincy, Ill.: Franciscan, 1993.

———. "Natural Law, God, Religion, and Human Fulfillment." *American Journal of Jurisprudence* 46, no. 1 (2001): 3–36.

———. "The True Ultimate End of Human Beings: The Kingdom, Not God Alone." *Theological Studies* 69, no. 1 (2008): 38–61.

Hereth, Blake, and Kevin Timpe, eds. *The Lost Sheep in Philosophy of Religion: New Perspectives on Disability, Gender, Race, and Animals*. New York: Routledge, 2020.

Hibbs, Thomas. "Transcending Humanity in Aquinas." *Proceedings of the American Catholic Philosophical Association* 66 (1992): 191–202.

Hofer, Andrew. "Deification in the Dominican Tradition: Albert, Thomas, and Catherine." In *Called to be Children of God: The Catholic Theology of Human Deification*, edited by David Meconi and Carl E. Olson, 101–17. San Francisco, Calif.: Ignatius Press, 2006.

Homiak, Marcia L. "Feminism and Aristotle's Rational Ideal." In *A Mind of One's Own: Feminist Essays on Reason and Objectivity*, edited by Louis M. Antony and Charlotte Witt, 3–20. Second edition. New York: Routledge, 2018.

Hontheim, J. "Heaven." In *The Catholic Encyclopedia*. New York: Robert Appleton Company, 1910. Available at www.newadvent.org/cathen/07170a.htm.

Hopkins, Gerard Manley. *The Major Works*. Oxford: Oxford University Press, 2002.

Hutter, Reinhard. *Dust Bound for Heaven: Explorations in the Theology of Thomas Aquinas*. Grand Rapids, Mich.: Eerdmans, 2012.

———. *Bound for Beatitude: A Thomistic Study in Eschatology and Ethics*. Washington, D.C.: The Catholic University of America Press, 2019.

Jensen, Steven. *The Human Person: A Beginner's Thomistic Psychology*. Washington, D.C.: The Catholic University of America Press, 2018.

John Paul II, Pope St. (Karol Wojtyła). *Man and Woman He Created Them: A Theology of the Body*. Translated by Michael Waldstein. Boston: Pauline Books and Media, 2006.

Jurgens, William A., ed. and trans. *The Faith of the Early Fathers*. 3 vols. Collegeville, Minn.: Liturgical Press, 1979.

Kretzmann, Norman. *The Metaphysics of Theism: Aquinas's Natural Theology in* Summa contra gentiles *I*. Oxford: Clarendon Press, 1997.

———. *The Metaphysics of Creation: Aquinas's Natural Theology in* Summa contra gentiles *II*. Oxford: Clarendon Press, 1999.

Lamb, Matthew L. "Eternity and Time in St. Thomas Aquinas's Commentary on the Gospel of John." In *Reading John with St. Thomas Aquinas: Theological Exegesis and Speculative Theology*, edited by Michael Dauphinais and Matthew Levering, 127–39. Washington, D.C.: The Catholic University of America Press, 2005.

Lauinger, William A. "Eternity, Boredom, and One's Part-Whole-Reality Conception." *American Catholic Philosophical Quarterly* 88, no. 1 (2014): 1–28.

Leget, Carlo. *Living with God: Thomas Aquinas on the Relation between Life on Earth and 'Life' After Death*. Leuven: Peeters, 1997.

Levering, Matthew. *Jesus and the Demise of Death: Resurrection, Afterlife, and the Fate of the Christian*. Waco, Tex.: Baylor University Press, 2012.

Liturgy of the Hours according to the Roman Rite. New York: Catholic Publishing Group, 1975.

Maritain, Jacques. *The Person and the Common Good*. Translated by John J. Fitzgerald. Notre Dame, Ind.: University of Notre Dame Press, 1966.

McDannell, Colleen, and Bernhard Lang. *Heaven: A History*. New Haven, Conn.: Yale University Press, 1988.

Meilaender, Gilbert. *Should We Live Forever? The Ethical Ambiguities of Aging*. Grand Rapids, Mich.: Eerdmans, 2013.

Meixner, Uwe. "The Indispensability of the Soul." In *Die menschliche Seele: Brauchen wir den Dualisms?*, edited by Bruno Niederberger and Edmund Runggaldier, 19–40. Heusenstamm: Ontos Verlag, 2006.

Middleton, J. Richard. *A New Heaven and a New Earth: Reclaiming Biblical Eschatology*. Grand Rapids, Mich.: Baker Academic, 2014.

Miller, Lisa. *Heaven: Our Enduring Fascination with the After-Life*. New York: HarperCollins, 2010.

Nevitt, Turner. "Survivalism, Corruptionism, and Intermittent Existence in St. Thomas." *History of Philosophy Quarterly* 31, no. 1 (2014): 1–19.

———. "Aquinas on the Death of Christ: A New Argument for Corruptionism." *American Catholic Philosophical Quarterly* 90, no. 1 (2016): 77–99.

Nichols, Terence. *Death and Afterlife*. Grand Rapids, Mich.: Brazos Press, 2010.

Nussbaum, Martha. *The Therapy of Desire: Theory and Practice in Hellenistic Ethics*. Princeton, N.J.: Princeton University Press, 1994.

Oderberg, David S. *Real Essentialism*. New York: Routledge, 2007.

———. "Survivalism, Corruptionism, and Mereology." *European Journal for Philosophy of Religion* 4, no. 4 (2012): 1–26.

Ott, Ludwig. *Fundamentals of Catholic Dogma*. Translated by Patrick Lynch. Rockford, Ill.: TAN Books, 1974.

Overall, Christine. *Aging, Death and Human Longevity: A Philosophical Inquiry*. Los Angeles: University of California Press, 2005.

Pakaluk, Michael. "Grisez's Critique of Aquinas on the Ultimate End of Human Life." Lecture at Duke University, April 11, 2019. Available at https://www.academia.edu/38785923/Grisez_Critique_of_Aquinas_on_the_Ultimate_End_of_Human_Life.

Pasnau, Robert. *Thomas Aquinas on Human Nature: A Philosophical Study of* Summa theologiae Ia. 75–89. Cambridge: Cambridge University Press, 2002.

Paul VI, St. Pope. *Solemni Hac Liturgia*. Apostolic Letter. June 30, 1968. Available at www.vatican.va.

———. *Lumen Ecclesiae*. Apostolic Letter. November 20, 1974. Available at www.vatican.va.

Pawl, Timothy. *In Defense of Conciliar Christology: A Philosophical Essay*. Oxford: Oxford University Press, 2016.

———. *In Defense of Extended Conciliar Christology: A Philosophical Essay*. Oxford: Oxford University Press, 2019.

Pawl, Timothy, and Kevin Timpe. "Incompatibilism, Sin, and Free Will in Heaven." *Faith and Philosophy* 26, no. 4 (2009): 398–419.

———. "Paradise and Growing in Virtue." In *Paradise Understood: New Philosophical Essays about Heaven*, edited by T. Ryan Byerly and Eric J. Silverman, 97–109. Oxford: Oxford University Press, 2017.

Pelser, Adam C. "Heavenly Sadness: On the Value of Negative Emotions in Paradise." In *Paradise Understood: New Philosophical Essays about Heaven*, edited by T. Ryan Byerly and Eric J. Silverman, 113–35. Oxford: Oxford University Press, 2017.

Perry, R. C. "The Social Character of Heavenly Beatitude according to the Thought of St. Thomas Aquinas." *The Thomist* 7, no. 1 (1944): 65–79.

Peter, C. J. *Participated Eternity in the Vision of God. A Study of the Opinion of St. Thomas Aquinas and His Commentators on the Duration of the Acts of Glory*. Analecta Gregoriana 142. Rome: Gregorian University Press, 1964.

Phan, Peter C. *Responses to 101 Questions on Death and Eternal Life*. New York: Paulist Press, 1997.

———. "Roman Catholic Theology." In *The Oxford Handbook of Eschatology*, edited by Jerry L. Walls, 215–32. Oxford: Oxford University Press, 2008.

Pieper, Josef. *Happiness and Contemplation*. Translated by Richard Winston and Clara Winston. South Bend, Ind.: St. Augustine's Press, 1998.

Pius IX, Pope. *Ineffabilis Deus*. Papal Bull. December 8, 1854. In DH 573–75.

Pius XI, Pope. *Studiorum Ducem*. Encyclical Letter. June 29, 1923. Available at www.vatican.va.

Pius XII, Pope. *Mystici Corporis*. Encyclical Letter. June 29, 1943. Available at www.vatican.va.

———. *Munificentissimus Deus*. Apostolic Constitution. November 1, 1950. In DH 808–9.

Plantinga, Alvin. *God, Freedom, and Evil*. Grand Rapids, Mich.: Eerdmans, 1977.

Plato. *Symposium and Phaedrus*. Translated by Benjamin Jowett. New York: Dover, 1993.

Plested, Marcus. *Orthodox Readings of Aquinas*. Oxford: Oxford University Press, 2012.

Rahner, Karl. "The Intermediate State." In his *Theological Investigations*, vol. 17. New York: Crossroads, 1981.

Ribeiro, Brian. "The Problem of Heaven." *Ratio* 24, no. 1 (2011): 46–64.

Robinson, James M., ed. *The Gospel of Thomas*. Translated by Thomas O. Lambdin. In *The Nag Hammadi Library*. Revised edition. San Francisco, Calif.: HarperCollins, 1990. Available at www.earlychristianwritings.com/text/thomas-lambdin.html.

Rogers, Katherin. "Anselmian Meditations on Heaven." In *Paradise Understood: New Philosophical Essays about Heaven*, edited by T. Ryan Byerly and Eric J. Silverman, 30–47. Oxford: Oxford University Press, 2017.

Rota, Michael. "The Problem of Evil and Cooperation." In *Evolution, Games, and God*, edited by Martin Nowak and Sarah Coakley, 362–74. Cambridge, Mass.: Harvard University Press, 2013.

Russell, Jeffrey Burton. *A History of Heaven: The Singing Silence*. Princeton, N.J.: Princeton University Press, 1997.

Sacred Congregation for the Doctrine of the Faith. *De Persona Humana*. Declaration. December 29, 1975.

———. *Recentiores Episcoporum Synodi*, no. 4659. Letter (on Certain Questions concerning Eschatology). May 17, 1979. In DH 1028.

Scannell, T. "Supernatural Gift." In *The Catholic Encyclopedia*. New York: Robert Appleton Company, 1909. Available at www.newadvent.org/cathen/06553a.htm.

Schmisek, Brian. *Resurrection of the Flesh or Resurrection from the Dead*. Collegeville, Minn.: Liturgical Press, 2013.

Silverman, Eric J. "Conceiving Heaven as a Dynamic Rather than Static Existence." In *Paradise Understood: New Philosophical Essays about Heaven*, edited by T. Ryan Byerly and Eric J. Silverman, 13–29. Oxford: Oxford University Press, 2017.

Spencer, Mark K. "The Personhood of the Separated Soul." *Nova et Vetera* (English edition) 12, no. 3 (2014): 863–912.

———. "What Is It Like to Be an Embodied Person? What Is It Like to Be a Separated Soul?" *Angelicum* 93, no. 1 (2016): 219–46.

———. "The Phenomenology and Metaphysics of Spiritual Perception: A Thomistic Framework." *New Blackfriars* 97, no. 1072 (2016): 677–92.

Spezzano, Daria. *The Glory of God's Grace: Deification According to St. Thomas Aquinas*. Ave Maria, Fla.: Sapientia Press, 2015.

Stenberg, Joseph. "Aquinas on the Relationship between the Vision and Delight in Perfect Happiness." *American Catholic Philosophical Quarterly* 90, no. 4 (2016): 665–80.

Stump, Eleonore. *Aquinas*. London: Routledge, 2003.

———. "Resurrection, Reassembly, and Reconstitution: St. Thomas on the Soul." In *Diemenschliche Seele: Brauchen wir den Dualismus?*, edited by Bruno Niederberger and Edmund Runggaldier, 151–71. Heusenstamm: Ontos Verlag, 2006.

———. *Wandering in Darkness: Narrative and the Problem of Suffering*. Oxford: Clarendon Press, 2010.

———. *The God of the Bible and the God of the Philosophers*. Marquette, Wis.: Marquette University Press, 2016.

Sullivan, Ezra, OP. "Seek First the Kingdom: A Reply to Germain Grisez's Account of Man's Ultimate End." *Nova et Vetera* (English edition) 8, no. 4 (2010): 959–95.

Taliaferro, Charles. "Why We Need Immortality." *Modern Theology* 6, no. 4 (1994): 367–77.

Talking Heads. *Fear of Music*. Sire Records SRK-6076, 1979, compact disc.

Tanner, Norman P., ed. *Decrees of the Ecumenical Councils*. 2 vols. London / Washington, D.C.: Sheed and Ward / Georgetown University Press, 1990.

Selected Bibliography

Timpe, Kevin. "Defiant Afterlife: Disability and Uniting Ourselves to God." In *Voices from the Edge: Centering Marginalized Perspectives in Analytic Theology*, edited by Michelle Panchuk and Michael Rea, 206–31. Oxford: Oxford University Press, 2020.

Tolkien, J.R.R. "Tree and Leaf." In his *The Tolkien Reader*, 33–124. New York: Ballantine Books, 1966.

———. *The Letters of J.R.R. Tolkien*. Edited by Humphrey Carpenter and Christopher Tolkien. Boston: Houghton Mifflin, 1995.

Tollefsen, Christopher O. "First- and Third-Person Standpoints in the New Natural Law Theory." In *Subjectivity: Ancient and Modern*, edited by R. J. Snell and Steven F. McGuire, 95–113. Lanham, Md.: Lexington Books, 2016.

Toner, Patrick. "Personhood and Death in St. Thomas Aquinas." *History of Philosophical Quarterly* 26, no. 2 (2009): 121–38.

———. "St. Thomas on Death and the Separated Soul." *Pacific Philosophical Quarterly* 91, no. 4 (2010): 587–99.

———. "St. Thomas Aquinas on Gappy Existence." *Analytic Philosophy* 56, no. 1 (2015): 94–110.

Torrell, Jean-Pierre. *Saint Thomas Aquinas: The Person and His Work*, vol. 1 of *St. Thomas Aquinas*. Translated by Robert Royal. Revised edition. Washington, D.C.: The Catholic University of America Press, 2005.

Van Dyke, Christina. "Human Identity, Immanent Causal Relations, and the Principle of Non-repeatability: Thomas Aquinas on the Bodily Resurrection." *Religious Studies* 43, no. 4 (2007): 373–94.

———. "Aquinas's Shiny Happy People: Perfect Happiness and the Limits of Human Nature." *Oxford Studies in the Philosophy of Religion* 6 (2014): 269–91.

Velde, Rudi te. *Aquinas on God: The "Divine Science" of the* Summa Theologiae. London: Routledge, 2006.

Vigilius, Pope. *Profession of Faith*, nos. 412–15. DH 145–46.

Vonier, Dom Anscar. "Death and Judgment." In *The Teaching of the Catholic Church*, edited by George D. Smith, 2:1101–40. New York: Macmillan, 1949.

———. *The Human Soul and Its Relations with Other Spirits*. Lexington, Ky.: Assumption Press, 2014 (1913).

Waddell. Michael. "Thomas Aquinas and the Resurrection of the (Disabled) Body." *The Saint Anselm Journal* 12, no. 2 (2017): 29–51.

Walls, Jerry. *Heaven: The Logic of Eternal Joy*. Oxford: Oxford University Press, 2008.

Weinandy, Thomas. *Does God Suffer?* Notre Dame, Ind.: University of Notre Dame Press, 2000.

Wilhelm, Joseph, and Thomas B. Schannell. *A Manual of Catholic Theology Based on Scheeben's "Dogmatik."* 2 vols. Second edition. New York: Benziger Brothers, 1899.

Williams, A. N. *The Ground of Union: Deification in Aquinas and Palamas*. New York: Oxford University Press, 1999.

Williams, Bernard. "The Makropulos Case: Reflections on the Tedium of Immortality." In his *Problems of the Self*, 82–100. Cambridge: Cambridge University Press, 1973.

Wippel, John F. *The Metaphysical Thought of Thomas Aquinas: From Finite Being to Uncreated Being*. Washington, D.C.: The Catholic University of America Press, 2000.

Wojtyła, Karol (Pope St. John Paul II). *Love and Responsibility*. Translated by H.T. Willetts. San Francisco, Calif.: Ignatius Press, 1993.

Wright, N.T. *Surprised by Hope: Rethinking Heaven, the Resurrection, and the Mission of the Church*. New York: HarperOne, 2008.

Zaleski, Carol. "In Defense of Immortality." *First Things* 105 (September 2000): 36–42.

SCRIPTURAL INDEX

Gn 1:26–27: 258, 428n9, 430
Gn 1:28: 386n108
Gn 1:30: 380
Gn 2:19–20: 371n93
Gn 15:1: 98n42

Ex 33:20: 135, 139

Dt 32:4: 248

2 Sm 6:5: 30n1

1 Kgs 10:12: 30n1

1 Chr 13:8: 30n1
1 Chr 15: 30n1
1 Chr 16:5: 30n1
1 Chr 25:1–7: 30n1

2 Chr 5: 15n28
2 Chr 5:12: 30n1
2 Chr 9:11: 30n1
2 Chr 20:28: 30n1
2 Chr 29:25: 30n1
2 Chr 30:1–26: 15n28

Neh 12:27: 30n1

1 Mc 3:45: 30n1
1 Mc 4:54: 30n1
1 Mc 13:51: 30n1

Jb 14:1: 323n151
Jb 19:25–27: 235–36
Jb 19:26: 301
Jb 19:26–27: 251
Jb 22:26: 102

Ps 15:5: 98n42
Ps 15:10: 102
Ps 15:16: 98n42
Ps 33:2: 30n1

Ps 33:12: 98n42
Ps 35:10: 188n43
Ps 43:4: 30n1
Ps 48: 15n28
Ps 57:8: 30n1
Ps 65: 15n31
Ps 71:22: 30n1
Ps 72:25–8: 98n42
Ps 81:1–2: 30n1
Ps 84:5: 98n42
Ps 86:7: 334
Ps 87: 15n28
Ps 92:1–4: 30n1
Ps 94:12: 98n42
Ps 102:5: 98n42
Ps 108:2: 30n1
Ps 137: 15n28
Ps 143:15: 98
Ps 144:9: 30n1
Ps 147:14: 98n42

Prv 3:18: 315
Prv 9:2–5: 315
Prv 10:24: 102
Prv 16:4: 98n42

Eccl 1:4: 176

Wis 3:7: 102, 322, 324
Wis 5:5: 102
Wis 7:11: 98n42

Sir 15:3: 315
Sir 24:29: 223
Sir 39:12–15: 30n1
Sir 51:12: 15n28

Is 11:1–16: 73n108
Is 11:6: 14n21
Is 25:6: 314
Is 25:8: 261n127, 314
Is 30:26: 323

Is 33:20: 15n28
Is 40:31: 322
Is 60:14: 15n28
Is 60:20: 404
Is 65:13: 314
Is 65:17: 14n20; 15: 345; 352n46
Is 65:17–18: 245
Is 65:25: 73n108

Hos 13:14: 261n127

Mi 4:10: 15n28

Zec 8:3: 15n28

Mt 5:8: 135, 136, 140, 185
Mt 5:12: 360
Mt 5:48: 437
Mt 9:5: 15n33
Mt 11:27: 137
Mt 13:43: 324, 325
Mt 13:44–5: 98n42
Mt 16:17: 137
Mt 18:10: 135, 136, 140, 439
Mt 19:12: 307n91
Mt 20:10: 191
Mt 22: 42
Mt 22:1–14: 41
Mt 22:23–33: 1n1, 393
Mt 22:30: 23n53, 192, 279, 283, 284, 291n42, 310, 311
Mt 25: 42
Mt 25:14–30, 41
Mt 25:21: 98n42
Mt 25:41: 168
Mt 26:29: 314, 316

Mk 2:19: 15n33
Mk 12:18–27: 1n1
Mk 12:25: 23n53, 279

461

Lk 5:34: 15n33
Lk 10:32: 130
Lk 10:38–42: 435n32
Lk 10:42: 13: 308, 309
Lk 12:36: 15n33
Lk 20:27–40: 1n1, 393
Lk 20:35–36: 23n53, 192, 279
Lk 22:29–30: 314
Lk 24:39: 243, 244, 250–51, 252, 301
Lk 24:43: 280

Jn 1:18: 135, 136, 139, 140
Jn 4:24: 11n10, 136
Jn 9:4: 44
Jn 14:2: 191
Jn 14:8: 98n42
Jn 14:21: 252n94
Jn 14:23: 252n94
Jn 17:3: 98n42, 135, 136, 140, 167, 176
Jn 20:19–26: 302
Jn 20:27: 252
Jn 21: 280

Acts 1:3b: 316
Acts 10:40–41: 280

Rom 1:20: 346
Rom 5:9: 261 n127
Rom 6:9: 243, 261n127
Rom 8:9: 245
Rom 8:17: 242n44
Rom 8:21: 245, 342
Rom 13:13–14: 426

1 Cor 2:11: 164
1 Cor 7:31: 342n9, 357, 358, 404
1 Cor 7:38: 307n91
1 Cor 13: 154
1 Cor 13:12: 10n8, 135, 136, 140, 154
1 Cor 13:13: 83n17

1 Cor 15: 16n35, 41
1 Cor 15:12–58, 27n60
1 Cor 15:21–22: 262
1 Cor 15:26: 261n127
1 Cor 15:33: 356
1 Cor 15:40: 242, 245n62
1 Cor 15:41: 191
1 Cor 15:41–42: 324
1 Cor 15:42: 284
1 Cor 15:42–53: 26n59, 28
1 Cor 15:43: 284, 285, 321, 325n165, 324
1 Cor 15:44: 242, 245n62, 298, 299n68, 300, 403
1 Cor 15:48: 287
1 Cor 15:50: 242, 244, 245, 251, 301n75
1 Cor 15:53: 74: 236, 261, 262, 342, 401
1 Cor 15:54: 264, 268

2 Cor 5:6–8: 212–13
2 Cor 5:10: 16n35, 16n37. 44n30
2 Cor 12:3: 139

Gal 5:16: 432
Gal 6:10a: 44n30

Eph 4:1–4: 332
Eph 4:10: 344, 345
Eph 4:13: 254
Eph 5: 332

Phil 2:5: 294n53
Phil 3:5–8: 438n38
Phil 3:20–21: 242n44
Phil 3:21: 244, 250, 287

Col 3:1–2: 439n45
Col 3:2: 420, 443

1 Tm 2:4: 369n89
1 Tm 6:16: 135, 136, 140

2 Tm 4:6–8: 438n40

Heb 12:22: 15n30

2 Pt 1:4: 430
2 Pt 3:13: 14n20, 15, 352n46:

1 Jn 3:2: 10n9, 135, 154, 136, 140, 179, 186, 446
1 Jn 4:8: 119n128, 120n130
1 Jn 4:12: 135
1 Jn 4:16: 119n128, 120n130

Rv 3:12: 15n30
Rv 3:21, 242n44
Rv 4: 41
Rv 4:8–11: 41
Rv 5: 15
Rv 5:8: 30n1
Rv 5:10: 102
Rv 7:16 284
Rv 10:6: 404
Rv 10:9: 342n9
Rv 14:2: 30n1
Rv 14:13: 98n42
Rv 15:2: 30n1
Rv 19: 15n33
Rv 19:9: 332
Rv 20: 316
Rv 20:4–5: 314
Rv 21: 15n30
Rv 21:1: 14n20, 15, 245, 345, 352n46
Rv 21:4: 16n36, 73, 261, 284
Rv 21:1–4: 26n59
Rv 21:1–5: 80
Rv 21:23: 188n43
Rv 22: 41, 42
Rv 22:4: 314
Rv 22:5: 188n43
Rv 22:13: 98n42

GENERAL INDEX

abstinence, sexual, 333. *See also* continence; virginity; virgins

accidental feature, 117, 175

accidental reward in heaven, 2, 106–9, 133n44, 218, 222, 224, 226, 227, 276, 328–31, 333, 334, 335, 336; change and, 108, 318–21, 404, 418; cognitive acts that take place in time (in some sense) as part of, 225n73, 291–92, 294n54; direct knowledge and enjoyment of creatures as part of, 335, 337, 393n2, 394, 396, 422, 445; embodiment wholly a part of, 130, 212–33, 304, 396, 445; engaging in common loves and interests as part of, 364, 419; essential reward and, 2, 44n29, 57, 89–90, 104, 106, 108–9, 121, 122, 201, 294n54, 344, 391, 394, 395, 396, 398–99, 418, 447; experiencing the passage of time (in some sense) as a part of, 175n14, 321, 404–5; glorified human embodiment as part of, 2, 108, 282–327, 391, 394; as including goods that are contemplative, are proper–accidents of contemplative activities, or sub-serve contemplative activities, 312, 362–63, 374; as including goods that are gratuitous, or fitting, or appropriate, 228–30, 233, 396–98; joy in sensing the beauty of the "new heavens and the new earth" as a part of, 2, 150, 283, 288–94, 346, 362, 385, 391; movement as a part of and consistent with, 319–21, 404; music-making as a part of, 276, 363–64; seeing God indirectly in glorified bodies, especially Christ's glorified body, but also in the "new heavens and the new earth," as a part of, 107, 218n52, 346, 364n79. *See* desire; essential reward in heaven; heaven; resurrected body; well-being (*bene esse*) of perfect human happiness. *See also* animals, non-human; aureoles; communion of the saints; friends; friendship; fruit; liturgy; places; plants

accidents: concomitant, 105, 127, 128, 129, 182, 183, 193, 214, 215, 228, 230, 385, 396; individuation of, 239–40; inseparable, 106, 107, 259; kinds of, 106, 240, 258; nonproper, 106, 107, 217, 218; proper 2, 105, 106, 107, 128, 161, 175, 180, 191, 206, 214, 218n52, 224, 225n73, 228, 232, 258, 259, 286, 291, 292, 294n54, 361, 363, 394, 396, 399; separable, 106, 107, 259

act: of being (*actus essendi*), 117, 153, 200–201; pure, 113, 119; three ways of being in, 123. *See* intellectual activity. *See also* volitional activity

action(s), 35, 48n49, 49, 67, 83, 91, 95, 114, 117, 169, 199, 210n37, 216, 235, 236n21, 247n68, 250, 271, 279, 286, 308, 312, 313, 318n130, 402, 403, 414, 429, 433

active life, 130n33, 308, 309, 442n46

activity: aesthetic, 417; bodily, 11, 124, 125, 181; brain, 125; contemplative, 95, 132, 138, 363, 435, 436, 441; as dynamic, 114; epistemological, 417; immutable, 61, 75, 177, 178; moral, 417; mundane, 114; nontemporal, 28, 403, 418; relational, 417; spiritual, 299. *See* glorified body; intellectual activity. *See also* volitional activity

actuality, 110, 112, 113, 119

Adam and Eve: as causing death in the state of innocence by eating, 73; and cognition of God before the Fall, 147, 149; created with sanctifying grace and the preternatural gifts of impassibility, negative immortality, and integrity, 428; death in paradise before the Fall of, 415; did not have the beatific vision in the Garden of Eden, 74; as enjoying the preternatural gift of immortality before the Fall, 74, 351, 354; Griffiths on animals and plants in the Garden and, 365–68, 374–77, 379–83; Griffiths on the significance of the naming of the animals and, 367, 371n93; and the human body entirely subject to the

Adam and Eve: (*cont.*)
  will before the Fall in, 317; and immortality in the state of innocence as differing from the immortality of the saints in heaven, 313–14, 354; as not having the beatific vision in the Garden, 74, 138n70, 155; and original sin, 262; would have been translated to heaven eventually had they not sinned, 74, 352
Adam, Karl, 44–46, 413
Adoro te devote (hymn of St. Thomas), 98n41, 306n89
Advent, 65
aeveternal being, 172, 174, 178, 403, 404, 405
aeveternity (*aeviternitas*), 115–19, 167–79, 183, 402–5, 445, 447. *See also aevum*
aevum, 167n1, 168–69. *See also* aeveternity (*aeviternitas*)
affections (*affectiones*), 118n124, 177
afterlife, 1, 14n25, 41, 242, 253n100, 272, 273, 401
age: of reason, 78n3, 94n17, 143, 331n14, 428, 432; of the risen, 254–55
agent, 90, 91, 125, 132, 151, 155, 159, 178, 230, 249, 250, 287, 289, 317, 321, 342, 353, 398
agility of the glorified body, 108, 138n69, 187n40, 247, 282, 296, 299n68, 317–22, 361, 403, 422. *See* glorified body; resurrected body
aging, 8n2, 81, 82
air, 265, 293, 295, 301, 302, 341, 347
Albert the Great, St., 167n1, 186n39
Ambrose of Milan, St., 425
analogy, 52, 53, 111, 151, 152, 153, 232, 291, 333, 375, 378
ancestors, 76
angels: and the beatific vision, 74, 163, 217, 414, 439; blessed, 7, 16n35, 63, 73, 75, 94, 103, 160; as cared for by God for their own sake, 341; changeableness of intelligence, affections, and acting in places, 118n124; composed of act and potency, 112; as created in a state of grace without the beatific vision, 174; and the empyrean heaven, 264n139, 344, 349, 360; fallen, 379, 381–82; and the general judgement, 16n35; in heaven enjoy both the essential and an accidental reward, 217, 363; in heaven enjoy multiple modes of cognition, 291, 294n54; in heaven are glorified, 415; in heaven are a model for human happiness in heaven, 23, 131–32, 138n67, 192, 283, 307, 310–11, 317, 364, 419, 438; in heaven more or less happy insofar as they have a greater or lesser beatific vision, 163, 192; in heaven as "new creatures," 345; as immutable with respect to their substance but mutable with respect to their accidental features, 117–19, 155, 174, 176; as incorruptible substances, 74n109, 114, 117, 262, 264, 340; and infused knowledge, 353; natural knowledge of God and, 149; as not the object of perfect human happiness, 133n44; as part of the social world of human persons in heaven, 64, 68, 229, 332n16, 335, 336, 399, 414, 422; and their beatific vision as a participated eternity, 176–77; and their enjoying the beatific vision consistent with their being simultaneously on mission, 135, 319, 364, 419; and their relation to time and change, 64, 117–18; and their substantial being not measured by time but aeveternity, 115, 174, 404–5; as wholly immaterial beings, 343n12
the animal and plant thesis (APT), 365–70, 372, 374, 375n95, 379, 382, 383, 384, 385, 386
animals, nonhuman, 64, 68, 73, 119, 162, 340, 341, 347n33, 351n41, 351, 355–60, 364n81, 364–70, 371, 372–84, 385, 414, 428; in heaven, 64, 68, 347n43, 351n41, 355–60, 364–70, 371, 372–84, 414, 447
annihilation, 65, 67, 73, 426
Anselm of Canterbury, St., 9, 24, 393, 416
answers, 160
Anzulewicz, Henryk, 167n1
Aphraates the Persian Sage, 50n53
apostles, 147, 250, 280, 301, 302, 316, 326, 327, 333, 334, 342n9
appetite(s): intellectual, 181; sensitive, 181. *See* will. *See also* emotions; feelings; passions; volitional activity
Aquinas, St. Thomas: action theory of, 90–92; on Aristotle on happiness, 94, 95, 104, 216; as the Common Doctor, 3, 47n44; on death before the Fall, 73, 380; on desiring something as entailing one does not possess that something, 35n11; as Dominican theologian and priest who preaches and

teaches the Word of God, 96; five ways of, 373; on God alone as the object of perfect human happiness, 97–103; on his account of heaven being more consistent with authoritative Catholic Christian Tradition than alternative accounts of heaven, 409–10; on his account of heaven having great explanatory power, 410, 446–47; on his account of heaven taking into account more Christian data about God, blessedness in heaven, and human persons, than alternative accounts, 394–99; and his commentaries on Scripture as fruits of understanding as a gift of the Holy Spirit, 149; his philosophical anthropology, 198–204; on grace perfecting nature, 427–29; on the natural antipathy between some animals, 380; on the nature of the sacraments, 306, 338; on no meriting in heaven, 45–46; on personal identity between human persons in this life and in heaven, 2n3, 173n12, 201–204, 235–45, 253n100, 423n2, 427–44; on purgatory, 431, 435, 442–44, 447; on sanctifying grace making created persons deiform, 429–31; on the stages of spiritual and moral transformation, 430–31; on the ultimate end of human persons, 83n17, 90–94. *See* accidental reward in heaven; beatific vision according to St. Thomas; essential reward in heaven; God; heaven; human happiness, perfect

Arendzen, J. P., 338n43

argument from disquiet in the will, 210, 224, 225

argument from first perfection, 210–11, 219–20

argument for the imperfect happiness of the separated soul (AIHSS), 208, 211, 220

argument from imperfect and perfect operation (AIPO), 206, 207, 208, 211, 219–22, 227

argument from the natural union of the soul and body, 208, 220

Aristotle: on accounts of human immortality, 261; action theory of, 91n2; on the essence of happiness versus the decoration of happiness, 104, 216; on god-like virtue, 95n18; on God as absolutely immutable, 416; on his account of the best kind of human life as neither masculine nor feminine, 257n114; on human beings as creatures that wonder, 133; on human happiness as imperfect in this life, 94; on incorruptible substances, 261, 352; on the incorruptibility of the elements, 341; on *makarios* versus *eudaimonia*, 93n10; on the nature of heavenly bodies, 111n105, 352; on the nature of human happiness, 95, 97, 311–12; on spiritual pleasures as pleasures absolutely speaking, 310, 312–13; on time, 114; on the universe as interminable, 115

art, 30, 39, 248, 363, 364, 385. *See* heaven

artifacts, 361–63, 365, 370, 371, 384, 385; in heaven, 361–64, 370–71, 384–85; as (not) a part of the accidental reward in heaven, 339, 361–64, 384–85. *See* heaven

the artifact thesis, 370, 371, 384

artists, 93n13

Ashley, Benedict, 19n39

athletes, 95n18,

"For the Attainment of Heaven" (prayer of St. Thomas), 334n23

Augustine of Hippo, St.: on accounts of human immortality, 261; on the beatific vision as an immutable cognition, 34, 290; on candidates for human happiness, 97; on chiliasm, 314n115; on Christ ascending into heaven with his scarred body, 252; on Christ rising from the dead in a youthful age, with a body about thirty years old, 254; on desire for something as entailing that one does not possess that something, 35n11; on a figurative reading of the millennium spoken about in Revelation 20, 316; on the general resurrection, 236; on the glorification of the body in heaven as "overflowing" from the soul having the beatific vision, 308n93; on God as the perfect good, 98; on heaven as a place of *quies*, 66; on his conversion as recounted in Confessions as composed of a number of micro-conversions, 425–26; on John 14:2, 191; on the heavenly reward as a spiritual rather than a material reward, 360; on Luke 10:42, 309; on perfect human happiness as a transcendent good, 82, 84, 97; on the saints in heaven knowing a special accidental joy in the completeness of the heavenly kingdom, 338; on the separated soul's desire for

Augustine of Hippo, St.: (cont.)
embodiment, 209, 217, 222–23, 226; on the separated soul as existing in an imperfect state, 268; on seeing God indirectly in "the new heavens and the new earth," 290n39; as teaching the classical understanding of God, 9, 416; on union with God by itself as sufficient to satisfy human desire, 11–13, 102–103, 165, 392

Augustinian Intuition, 12, 23, 228, 392, 395, 397, 399

aurea (golden crown): as a metaphor for the joy of the essential reward, 328

aureoles (little golden crowns), 83, 108, 276n168, 327, 328–29, 330–31. See accidental reward in heaven

authority, 11, 45, 47n44, 53n60, 62, 63, 97, 135n53, 212, 213, 250, 258, 268, 324, 345, 371n93

Baker, Lynne Rudder, 28, 29, 400–401, 406–410, 447

baptism, 44n28, 50n53, 426, 430, 432, 434

the baptized, 143, 147, 429

Barr, Stephen M., 272n159

Basie, Count, 77

the beach, 77

beatific vision: and Dante, 36n15, 110n101; as looking at the face of the beloved, 81n10; according to St. Anselm and Katherin Rogers, 24, 393, 399. See beatific vision according to St. Thomas; Griffiths, Paul J.; Grisez, Germain

beatific vision according to St. Thomas, 103, 122–140, 141, 142–50, 182; as direct and unmediated a union with God as is possible for a creature, 11, 26, 103, 124, 126, 138, 140, 143, 147, 154, 228, 298, 306, 336, 394, 396, 398, 413, 447; does not involve a medium by which (quo), 152–54; as a dynamic reality, despite being immutable, 61, 416–17; entails right-willing and the inability to sin, 74, 180, 181, 183–84; as greater in some than others, 180, 191–93, 205; as immutable, 108, 167, 168, 173n12, 176, 177, 178, 212, 225n73, 291, 414, 416, 417, 418; as impossible to lose, 173–74, 178; and the Incarnation, 439n45; as incommensurate compared to other creaturely goods, 57, 58, 228, 392, 395, 397, 398; as knowing God in the Word, 163n95; as a non-comprehensive knowledge of God, 135–36, 156–60, 164; not greater after the resurrection than before, 212–27; not possible for a human person with an animal body, 137–38; not a seeing God directly with the corporeal eye, 136; as a participated eternity, 78, 109, 118n124, 167–79, 363, 416, 445; the proper accidents of, 2, 105–7, 128, 175, 180–84, 191, 206, 214, 218n52, 224, 225n73, 228, 232, 291, 292, 294n54, 361, 363, 394, 396, 399; as sufficient for the attainment of the essence of perfect human happiness, 134–35; understanding of the Trinity and the Incarnation and, 149; as vision of the essence of God, 53, 122, 139, 152, 155, 183, 193, 287, 391, 394, 419. See creatures; essential reward in heaven; God; heaven; human happiness, perfect. See also light of glory; the Trinity

beatitude: accidental, 104; essential, 104

Beatitudes, 21, 99, 185

beatitudo, St. Thomas on different senses of, 92–97. See accidental reward in heaven; essential reward in heaven; human happiness, perfect. See also felicitas

beauty, 10, 40, 182, 216, 229, 252, 253, 280, 299, 305, 308, 313, 347, 362, 385, 386, 395, 397, 418, 419, 421, 445, 446; in heaven, 10, 40, 229, 252, 253, 280, 299, 305, 308, 313, 362, 385, 418

Bede the Venerable, St., 252, 344, 345

being: aeveternal, 174; contingent, 112, 130, 160; eternal, 119, 168, 169; first, 113; immaterial, 7, 11, 16, 26, 126, 136; material, 153, 339–87; natural, 205, 219, 222; temporal, 25, 26, 400, 402, 410; uncaused, 113. See angels; God; human persons; substance(s)

being risible, 102, 123n6, 126. See also risibility

belief(s), 3, 18, 26n59, 29, 41, 55, 60, 84, 93, 146, 147, 257, 290, 353, 379, 401, 425

Benedict XII, Pope, 11, 16n37, 21, 27n63, 53n60, 67, 78n3

Benedictus Deus (Pope Benedict XII), 11, 16, 21

benevolence (benevolentia), 181

birth of a child, 230

Birzer, Bradley J., 385n106

bishops, 102

the blessed in heaven, 38, 43, 145, 146, 147,

General Index

149, 150, 153, 154, 155, 156, 158, 174, 176, 188n43, 209, 223, 246, 247, 248, 253, 265, 266, 279, 282, 283, 285, 288, 292n43, 294, 297, 299n68, 300, 301, 303, 311, 312, 314, 315, 317, 334, 345, 354, 379, 407, 431n23, 438, 445, 446

blood, 34, 64, 137, 237, 238, 242, 243, 244, 245, 246, 247, 250, 251, 253, 286, 301, 343, 347, 348, 355n53

body: animal, 137, 138, 300; spiritual, 138n69, 242, 298, 299, 300, 316, 317, 403. *See* glorified body; heaven; human body. *See also* mixed bodies

bodily organs, 199, 241
bodily states, 118n124, 121
Boethius, 9, 65, 97, 114, 119, 312, 416
Bonaventure, St., 9
bones, 238, 243, 244, 251, 301
books, 339, 420
boredom, 26, 41, 68, 76, 80, 81, 85, 414, 420, 421, 422; as impossible in, 26, 41, 80, 81, 85, 414, 420, 421, 422. *See also* tedium
Braddock, Matthew, 81n12, 316n123
Bradley, Denis, 19n39, 94n15
brain, 82, 125, 126, 238, 246, 253
bread, 315, 358, 359, 371, 378
brightness, 296, 323–25; 344
brothers, 1, 23, 66
Brower, Jeffrey E., 203n16, 239n28, 363n77
Brown, David, 34
Budziszewski, J., 276n166
Bynum, Caroline Walker, 7n1, 282n1
Byrne, David, 30

calendar, liturgical, 65–66
Capek, Karel, 76
Carthage, Fifteenth (or Sixteenth) Council of, 74n110
Catena Aurea (St. Thomas), 309
Catherine of Siena, St., 186n39, 439
Catholic dogma on heaven, 11, 16, 21, 27n63, 44, 47n44, 53n60, 67, 78n3, 156n61, 193n60, 234n1
Catholic moral teaching, 227
causality: dignity of, 427; efficient, 428n12; formal, 12, 297; principle of, 99
cause(s): efficient, 99, 101, 248, 274; exemplar formal, 99, 100, 101; final, 248; formal, 12, 99, 100, 101, 105, 106, 182, 198, 199, 203n19, 237, 238, 248, 249, 273, 274, 287, 288, 296, 297, 317, 322, 428n12;

intrinsic formal, 198, 199, 203n19, 237, 238, 288, 317, 322, 325, 428n12; primary, 99, 101, 113, 141, 264n140; secondary, 99n54, 427

Celestial Hierarchy (Dionysius the Areopagite), 192

Cessario, Romanus, 11n15
change: accidental, 111, 112, 117, 119, 174, 345, 363n77; in heaven, 3, 33, 34, 38, 44, 55, 56, 58, 67, 224, 296, 317, 319, 320, 321, 322, 404, 422; substantial, 111, 112, 116, 117, 174, 363n77, 376. *See also* psychological changes
Chappell, Timothy, 8on4, 81, 84, 420, 447
charity (*caritas*), 2, 44n29, 46, 50, 52, 56, 59, 82, 83n17, 85, 95, 108, 148n35, 166n107, 168n3, 181, 192, 193, 214, 216, 228, 231, 275, 276, 323, 325, 326, 332, 336, 396, 402, 412, 413, 414, 422, 429, 432, 433, 440, 441, 443, 446, 447; as determining the relative perfection of a soul's beatific vision, 192–93. *See* accidental reward in heaven; beatific vision according to St. Thomas; clarity of the glorified body; essential reward in heaven
chastity, 329–30
children, 10, 33, 102, 179, 186n39, 245, 255, 274, 276, 278, 331n14, 342, 429, 430, 432
Christ. *See* Jesus Christ
Christmas, 65, 70
the church: as bride of Christ, 186n40, 334; Catholic, 11n13, 16n34, 27n63, 44, 193n60, 333, 338n43, 443n49; as a community of human persons and angels, 332, 422; in heaven, 328, 331–38, 422; lives on forever in heaven, 332; triumphant, 108, 331, 332n16, 338n43; as a whole that is more than the sum of its integral parts, 333. *See also* communion of the saints
Cicero, 97, 426
City of the Blessed, 314
City of God (St. Augustine of Hippo), 98, 254
clarity of the glorified body: as an aspect of the glorified body in heaven, 108, 247, 282; as the body being subject to the beatified soul as principle of movement with respect to changing degrees of brightness, 296–97; as brighter than the sun in this life, 323–24; causes of, 325–26; as delightful, not disturbing to the eyes, 324; does not cancel out colors in the body, 323; as a dowry of the body in heaven, 187n40;

clarity of the glorified body: (*cont.*)
and 1 Corinthians 15:41: "Star differs from star in glory," 191–92; greater in some than others, 192; problematic views of, 325; may or may not be revealed by the person having a glorified body, 326; as relative to the amount of charity in the beatified soul, 192; reveals the degree of a person's charity, 325–25; as transparent, although not lacking in density, 324. *See* glorified body

classical theism, 9, 32, 61, 416

clearness, 323

clerics, 102

clothes in heaven, 361–62

cognition: in heaven human persons have multiple modes of, 225n73, 291–92, 294n54; of universals, 125–26. *See* God; knowledge

Commentary on the Apostles' Creed (*Collationes in Symbolum Apostolorum*, St. Thomas), 333–34

Commentary on Aristotle's Nicomachean Ethics (*Sententia Libri Ethicorum*; St. Thomas), 109, 216

Commentary on Boethius's De trinitate (*Expositio super librum Boethii De trinitate*; St. Thomas), 239–40

Commentary on Matthew (*In Matthaeum*; St. Thomas), 283

Commentary on the Sentences (*Scriptum super libros Sententiarum*; St. Thomas), 105, 165, 167–68, 204, 206, 207, 211, 217, 221, 226, 232, 236, 274, 294, 304

Commentary on St. Paul's First Letter to the Corinthians (*Expositio et lectura super Epistolas Pauli Apostoli*; St. Thomas), 244–45, 268, 298, 406

communion: of created goods, 399; of the Father, the Son, and the Holy Spirit, 445; with God, 7, 8, 391; between God, the blessed angels, and blessed human persons, 103; in God's kingdom, 20; with other creatures, 107

communion of the saints, 2, 8, 23n54, 24, 42, 43, 44n29, 57, 104, 108, 130, 218, 228, 229, 231, 276, 289, 306, 327, 328, 331–38, 391, 394, 395, 396, 397, 412, 445. *See* the church; communion

community: and facial recognition, 256–57; in heaven, 7, 8, 9, 15, 17, 22, 31, 42, 71, 257, 332, 336, 337, 371, 392, 394, 411, 447; monastic, 66. *See* communion; church

Compendium theologiae (*Compendium of Theology*, St. Thomas), 174

composing and dividing, 142

composite: of accidental form and material substance, 363n77; of essence and *esse*, 187; of goods, 227; of matter and form, 124, 153, 220; of soul and body, 268n152; of soul and matter, 263, 340, 354. *See* composition; human persons; substances

composition: of act and potency, 110, 111n104, 112; of *actus essendi* and form or essence, 112; is not identity, 201n14, 202; of soul and prime matter, 201. *See* composite

computers, 144n11

concepts, 37, 55, 62, 185, 186, 336. *See also* species

concupiscence, 118n124, 330, 381, 428n9, 429, 432

Condic, Maureen L., 190n50, 238n24

Condic, Samuel B., 190n50, 238n24

Confessions (St. Augustine of Hippo), 11, 392, 425, 436

comprehendere, 156n64

confirmation, sacrament of, 432

conjugal act, 102, 276, 303, 306, 307n90, 309, 310, 311, 313. *See* heaven; resurrected body. *See also* conjugal love; lovemaking; marriage; procreating; sexual activity; sexual congress; sexual union; spirituality of the glorified body; subtlety of the glorified body

conjugal love, 82. *See* heaven; resurrected body. *See also* conjugal act; lovemaking; marriage; procreating; sexual activity; sexual congress; sexual union; spirituality of the glorified body; subtlety of the glorified body

consummation, 175, 306, 307, 332, 337

contemplation, 27, 81, 131, 132, 133n44, 134, 138, 299, 307, 308, 313, 315, 316, 317, 403, 431, 435, 436, 437, 439, 441, 442. *See* intellectual activity. *See also* contemplative life

contemplative life, 130n33, 308, 309, 313, 415, 442. *See also* contemplation

continence, 329–30

conveniens, 229n80, 397n3

conversation, 81, 276, 299, 385, 436, 438; in heaven, 276, 299

General Index

conversion(s), 425
Cooper, John W., 14n25
Corea, Chick, 229–30
corruptible order of this life, 303. *See also* incorruptible order of the next-life
corruptible things. *See* things
corruption: as an artifact of the Fall (Griffiths), 74, 372, 386; in Aristotelian cosmology, 270; before the Fall, 268n150, 380, 415; composite of soul and matter, 263–65; does not occur in the next-life, 260–73, 280–84, 380; existence, 263–65; as going out of existence, 54, 221, 245, 253, 263–64, 267, 268n150, 270, 272, 273, 284, 287, 341, 342, 344, 348, 349, 351, 372, 380, 386, 415; of human persons, 199n7, 263; principles of, 272–73, 351; in the thought of St. Paul, 245, 284, 342. *See* incorruptibility. *See also* impassibility of the glorified body
corruptionism, 202n15, 202n16, 203n18
cosmology, 264, 270, 271, 295, 345, 349, 404
courage, 83, 95, 216
Cratylus (Plato), 371n93
created thing(s), 18, 98, 100, 102, 120, 151, 163, 164, 290n38, 342, 387. *See* creatures
creation, 162n91, 176n19, 225n73, 245, 258, 264n139, 290, 313, 342, 344, 346, 349, 353, 359, 367, 368, 376, 381
creator *ex nihilo*, God as, 10n3, 13n19, 100, 101, 110, 116, 151, 158, 169, 188, 260, 264n140, 293
creatures: as essentially spatial and temporal (Griffiths), 64; intellectual, 12, 13, 31, 42, 71, 72, 73, 75, 98, 124, 134, 140, 153, 154, 159, 160, 162, 163, 180, 185, 187, 188, 190, 191, 263, 341, 342, 343, 354, 384, 393, 402, 412, 415; material, 7, 144, 146, 339–87, 394; as the secondary object in the beatific vision, 133n44, 141, 160–66, 276, 335n27, 337, 445; spiritual, 118n124, 177. *See also* created thing(s)
Credo, 414
Cross, Bryan R. 254n100
Cross, Richard, 254n100
crowns, 108, 328. *See also* aurea; aureoles

Dahm, Brandon, 19n39, 203n16, 230, 231, 320, 337, 398
Damascene, St. John, 236
damned, the: the fallen angels among, 118, 174; and the blessed in heaven's awareness of, 108, 366; as enduring perpetually, 168; enjoy some perfection or they would not exist, 246–48, 265; God's care for, 277n170; as having bodies that are passible, carnal, heavy, and darksome, 247, 282n2, 299n68, 311n104; have bodies that are incorruptible, 266, 271n158, 283n8, 407; possess the R properties, 246, 282n2, 303; and the possibility of annihilation (Griffiths), 67n94; as subject to inclinations that contradict the inclinations of God or reason, 297; will see the clarity of the beatified, 326
damnation, 46
Dante, 36, 50n53, 110n101, 326n169
Davies, Brian, 202n16, 239n28
Da Vinci, Leonardo, 39
Day of Judgment, 212
death, 2n3, 10n5, 11, 14n25, 16, 44, 46, 50, 53n60, 59, 64, 65, 67, 73, 74, 79, 82, 83, 120, 136, 153, 193, 199, 200, 201, 202, 203, 204, 221, 235, 236, 238, 240, 241n36, 243, 253, 261, 262, 263, 264, 268n150, 269, 270, 279, 284, 285, 306, 309, 314, 331, 359, 360, 367, 368, 369, 372, 379, 380, 381, 382, 386, 412, 414, 415, 424n2, 425, 429, 430
Decreation: The Last Things of All Creatures (Paul J. Griffiths), 63, 365, 380
deiformity, 12n17, 186n39. *See also* theosis
Deferrari, Roy, 323n51
De Fide Catholica (Lateran Council IV, Dogmatic Constitution 1215), 234n1
delight (*delectatio*): act as immutable, 114, 417, 418; as candidate for the object of human happiness, 97; as concomitant accident of the beatific vision, 103, 129, 182, 183, 193, 206, 215, 228, 396; as contrasting with desire, 181; as a fitting decoration of the beatific vision, 182; as a form of love involving inclination to that which one possesses, 120, 121; in God, 437n36; in the justice of God, 108; as part of the essential reward in heaven, 44n29, 50, 57, 105, 127, 130, 180, 184, 186n40, 307, 309, 315, 334, 395, 399, 403, 418, 419, 431n23, 446, 447; as a proper accident of the attainment of perfect human happiness in the beatific vision, 2, 105, 106, 107, 127, 128, 129, 180, 182, 183, 191, 214, 394, 399; as related to the beatific vision as effect to its formal

delight (*delectatio*): (*cont.*)
  cause, 181–82; as a resting in the ultimate end as attained, 181, 414; as supervening on the beatific vision, 182; in those who have the virtues of the purified soul, 438; as unmixed good, 102. *See* desire
demonstration, philosophical or scientific, 133n45, 145n17, 146
desire: for created goods, 218, 224; from-fulfillment, 230, 231n82, 233, 320, 321, 337, 398; for a good that is part of the accidental reward in heaven, 225–26, 228n7; to go to heaven, 77–78, 423; for greater union with God, 35n11; in heaven for many this-worldly goods there is a lack of, 311, 438; human, 3, 11, 17, 18, 21n50, 99, 104, 134, 228, 337, 394, 396, 418, 421; for a knowledge of created things, 165, 421; from-lack, 230, 231n82, 233, 320, 321, 337, 398; for perfect goodness, 3, 134, 225; in Plato's Symposium, 35n11; in the separated soul in heaven, 223, 224; for society, 337; for the ultimate end, 92, 128, 291. *See* delight
De trinitate (Boethius), 239
devil, the, 329, 330
Devine, Arthur, 104n64, 141n1
Dewan, Lawrence, 239n28
difference (in logic), 142
dimensions: terminated quantity under three, 239; unterminated quantity under three, 239–40
Dionysius the Areopagite, 9, 192, 227n74, 311n104
disabilities in heaven, 253n100
disease, 15, 16
dispositions, 95, 186n40, 191n51, 270, 284, 285, 354, 407. *See also* preternatural disposition(s) or power(s); supernatural disposition(s)
Disputed Questions on the Power of God (*Quaestiones disputatae de potentia*; St. Thomas), 208, 209, 211
Disputed Questions on Truth (*Quaestiones disputatae de veritate*; St. Thomas), 151, 164, 165
distinctness, 323. *See* clarity of the glorified body
doctors, 93n13, 108, 330, 331. *See also* teachers
doctrine, 16n37, 24, 27, 27n63, 29, 50n53, 57, 112, 113, 120n128, 148, 186n39, 191, 192n56, 193n60, 245n37, 246, 251, 273, 328, 331n14, 358, 375, 380, 387, 394, 401, 405, 410, 416, 419, 420, 424, 446, 447
dogma, Catholic, 44, 78n3, 136, 380
Doolan, Gregory, 13n18
Dougherty, Trent, 364n81
dowries: of the body, 186n40; of the soul, 186n40, 431n23
drinking, 74, 76, 96, 124, 235, 245, 247n68, 248, 251, 273, 274, 279, 284, 293, 299, 303n85, 304, 305, 307, 308, 309, 310, 311, 312, 313, 314, 315, 316, 317, 332, 361, 362, 381, 386, 415, 438; in heaven there is no desire for, 273–81, 303–17
duration: aeveternal, 115–16, 415; eternal, 65; infinite, 50; measurable, 64–65; of participated eternity, 167n1; temporal, 50, 64–65, 74, 85, 115, 415
Duns Scotus, Blessed John, 9
dwarfism, 256

earth, 10n3, 44, 104n64, 120n129, 176, 235, 265, 295n57, 321, 341, 345, 346, 347, 349, 352, 354, 385n106, 420, 436, 439n45, 443, 446. *See also* "the new heaven(s) and the new earth"
Easter, 65, 70, 91
eating: as an activity essentially tied to the practical life, 362; animals, 368; as an animal action, 235n13, 299, 303, 415; and artifacts, 361; by Christ after the resurrection and before the ascension, 280; in the Garden of Eden, 73–74; 268n150; in heaven there is no (desire for), 247n68, 284, 438; as a metaphor for spiritual communion, 332; as not an aspect of life in heaven, 124, 245, 251, 293, 299, 303–17, 381, 415; as not an aspect of the next life, 235, 247n68, 249, 273–81, 303; primary purpose(s) of, 274–75, 279–80; secondary purpose(s) of, 274–75; as tied to corruption, 386. *See also* drinking; sexual union
Eberl, Jason T. 202n15
Eden, Garden of, 65, 73, 351, 354, 367, 372, 375, 380, 381, 382, 386. *See also* prelapsarian state; state of innocence;
Eitenmiller, Melissa, 203n16, 292
elements: as among the essential parts of the material universe, 347, 348, 355, 357–58; as composing compound or mixed material substances, 265, 347; as fundamen-

General Index

tal kinds of material substance for St. Thomas, 198n5, 341, 347; as incorruptible according to the whole but corruptible in part, 341, 348, 355, 377n96, 380; in heaven, 285–87, 341, 347–48, 354–55, 357, 358, 377n96; remain in human bodies after the general resurrection, 286–87, 347; St. Thomas as relying on Aristotle's theory of the, 285n16, 295n57. See heaven

Ellington, Duke, 77

embryo(s), 190n50, 237n24

embryology, 190n50; 237n24

emotions, 68, 80n7, 118n124, 121, 181, 284. See also feelings; passions

empyrean, 264n139, 318, 343–45, 349, 360, 361. See heaven

end: actual realization of the ultimate, 93–94; last, 70, 93; natural, 95n18; notion of ultimate, 93; supernatural, 147; an ultimate, 92; the ultimate, 18n38, 19n39, 23n52, 83n17, 90, 92–93, 97–98, 128, 129, 162, 181, 211, 229n79, 230n81, 291, 292, 304

engineers, 93n13

enjoyment (*frutio*), 53n60, 180–81, 227n74, 319, 439n45

Erhman, Terrence, 253n100

eros (in Plato's *Symposium*), 120. See desire

escalator analogy, 52–53

eschatological sense, reading scripture according to the, 254. See also scripture

eschatology, 2n3, 14n23, 14n24, 17n37, 20, 27n63, 446n1

essence. See God; essential reward in heaven

essential reward in heaven: beatific vision as the essence of, 105, 107, 122–35, 140, 141, 151, 152, 211, 214; as consisting of the beatific vision and the acts of will that flow from the vision as proper accidents, 44, 105, 106, 107, 127, 129, 180–82, 184, 214, 218, 363, 394, 399; as dynamic reality, 417–18; as equivalent to the attainment of perfect happiness, 109, 227, 374, 394; as equivalent to becoming perfectly deiform, 419; as fixed upon the uncreated good, 109; as greater in some than others insofar as some have a greater beatific vision, 191–93; and the intellect, 124–34; knowledge of creatures as the secondary object of the beatific vision as an aspect of, 337; as a logical part of *beatitudo*, 89, 418; as the most intimate intellectual and volitional union with God logically possible for a creature, 394, 398, 413, 419, 447; as no greater before the resurrection than at and after the resurrection, 212–27; as not changing in the saints, 43–54, 108, 212, 413, 414, 446; as not more intense after the general resurrection than before, 226, 232; as a participated eternity, 90, 109, 363, 413, 421, 445; plus the accidental reward makes for the attainment of the well-being of perfect human happiness, 227–32; as purely contemplative, 309, 374; the same for all the saints in terms of the object of, 191; as sating all desires-from-lack, 394, 418; and sensation, 124–27; the separated soul can enjoy, 201; as transcending time and aeveternity, 175, 183, 401–2, 403, 445; as true beatitude, 109; and the will, 127–30. See accidental reward in heaven; eternal life; glorified body; human happiness, perfect

eternality of God, 1on3, 65, 71, 110n100, 114–19, 169, 176, 436.

eternal life: in beatified creatures as participated eternity, or participation in God's eternal life, 90, 122, 167–79, 209, 401, 405, 413, 415, 417, 418, 420, 421, 442, 445–46; of God, 75, 90, 109–21, 228, 334, 391, 396; and John 17:3, 135, 176; as graced acts in this life as making one fit for, 432; problems concerning, 1–3, 7–29, 30–75, 76–85, 89, 391–99; 400–410; 411–19; 420–44; 446–48; and practicing for, 437; and purgatory, 442. See beatific vision according to St. Thomas; essential reward in heaven; eternity; human happiness, perfect

eternity: St. Augustine and St. Monica and the momentarily shared vision of, 436; the beatific vision and its proper accidents (the essential reward in heaven) as a participated, 65, 109, 118n24, 167–79, 363, 416, 445, 447; contemplation in this life as a preparation for, 437; and the definition of Boethius, 114–20; and immutability, 115–19; as interminable, 114; as meaningful, 41; as perfect possession of life, 119–20; persons in, 51, 53; purgatory as a preparation for, 441–44; psychological readiness for, 441; as simultaneously whole (*total simul*), 115–19, 172,

eternity: (cont.)
175; as temporal infinity, 50, 85, 231n86; as transcending time and aeveternity, 115–19, 175. See beatific vision according to St. Thomas; essential reward in heaven; eternal life. See also eternality of God

the eternity of choices in heaven eclipses the choices of this life objection, 47–53

etiquette, 69

Eucharist, 305, 306, 358, 359, 371, 378, 431, 434

eudaimonia, 93n10

evangelical counsels, 48

evidence, 146, 218, 219, 225n73, 250, 373n94

evil, 16n35, 37, 39, 47, 48, 74n111, 100n48, 178, 222, 251, 268, 277, 285, 291, 292, 313, 330, 331n14, 368, 386n107, 427n8, 428n9; in heaven there is no, 313

existence, 7, 28, 31, 32, 33, 34, 37, 38, 39, 40, 43, 50, 55, 56, 57, 58, 59, 63, 64, 65, 74, 99n54, 100, 101, 111, 112, 113, 116, 117, 118, 120, 121, 144, 149, 155, 172, 173, 174, 175, 183, 198, 199, 200, 201, 202n16, 203, 232, 238, 241n36, 244, 257, 261n125, 262, 263, 264, 265n144, 280, 286, 301, 312, 321, 325, 333, 340, 344, 346, 347n31, 348, 349, 350, 351n41, 354, 355, 357, 359, 360, 363, 365, 367, 369, 371, 372, 374, 377, 383, 384, 385, 386, 387, 402, 411, 412, 413, 414, 416, 417, 447

experience: aesthetic, 20, 393; beatific vision as an immutable and timeless, 170, 172, 173n12; of boredom, 80, 85, 420–21; categorical layering of, 69; of concupiscence, 429; and contemplation, 436–37; of creatures as media for knowing God, 151; of Dante the traveler, 36n15; direct, 24; of emotions, or passions, or feelings, 283–84; of a happy human person, 34; in heaven, 26, 68–69, 80, 83, 175n14, 283–84, 290, 293, 313, 315, 331n14, 399, 404, 414, 418, 420–21, 436; in an immutable cognition, 34; of negative psychological states, 80; novel, 290; of old age, 254; of ourselves, 26; out-of-body, 26; of pain and suffering, 285; of pleasure in the conjugal act, 309–10; possessive layering of, 69; and qualia, 68; of rapture, 139; second-order, 68–69, 414; static, 34; subjective, 24; of systolic time, 66; in this life, 420, 436; of

time, 26, 64n80, 175n14, 402, 404, 437; what is essential to human, 37n16, 60n72

external goods in heaven, 360–64

eyeglasses, 144n11

faces, 255, 257, 335

face to face (1 Cor 13:12), 10, 11, 16, 53n60, 135, 154, 306n89, 331n14

faith: act of, 53n60, 146, 216, 429, 432; being killed for the, 422; the Catholic Christian, 11n13, 16n35, 16n37, 27n63, 53n60, 57, 74n110, 143, 148, 149, 271, 330, 360, 407, 422, 446; confession of, 360; divine, 145, 146, 147, 149; economy of, 446; knowledge of God by, 24, 133n45, 142, 145–47, 148, 272; lack of, 253, 270n156; light of, 145n17, 146, 175n15; person of, 149, 150; Sacred Congregation for the Doctrine of the, 446; science and making sense of the, 271; teachers of the, 330; union with God by, 306, 332; virtue of, 53n60, 83n17, 95, 147, 150, 429, 432, 433, 440; walking by (2 Cor 5:7), 212–13; what comes directly under, 148; what comes indirectly under, 148. See also martyrs

the Fall, 65, 68, 70, 73, 74, 85, 143, 147, 149, 155, 188, 313, 317, 367, 368, 369, 370, 371n93, 372, 379, 380, 381, 382, 383, 384, 385, 386, 415, 428. See also sin

fame, 97, 323

family, 1, 33, 230, 398

farmers, 93n13

fashion in heaven, 362

Father, God the, 12, 16n35, 135, 137, 252n94, 253, 314, 316, 324, 325, 332, 338, 425n4, 437, 445, 447. See God. See also the Lord; the Trinity

fathers, 93

Fathers, Church, 35n11, 140n80, 193n60, 236, 252

Fathers of the English Dominican Province, 323n155

fear, 30n2, 33, 83n17, 178, 331,

feast, 15, 314, 332. See also supper

feelings, 20, 68, 118n124, 121, 181, 284, 393. See also emotions; passions

Feingold, Lawrence, 19n39, 270n156

felicitas, 92n10, 207. See also *beatitudo*, St. Thomas on different senses of

General Index

female, 257, 258, 259, 260n122, 280, 367, 375, 377. *See also* male
Feser, Ed, 91n2, 111n104, 113n109, 126n14, 203n18, 276n166, 277n171, 278n172
fetus, 237n24
Finley, John, 251n121, 260n122
Finnis, John, 335n26
fire, 265, 341, 347
Firestone, Lisa, 424n3
Fischer, John Martin, 80
flesh, 137, 242
Florence, General Council of, 27n63, 44n28, 50n53, 193n60
flourishing, 232
form: accidental, 111–12, 239, 258, 363n77; as ascribed to God, 151, 153, 154; composite of matter and, 153, 220, 265n144; immanent, 139; individual, 106; as intellectual species, 125, 146, 151, 152; intentional, 152, 153; as matter to, 249; as participated in, 153; as sensible species, 125, 155; substantial, 106, 112, 116–17, 124, 151, 153, 198, 199, 200, 210, 219, 220, 237, 238, 240, 241, 243, 248, 249, 259, 263, 264, 265, 266, 267, 269, 270n156, 273, 287, 295, 296, 297, 298, 299, 317, 340, 403
free choices in heaven: morally weighty, 47, 49, 74n111; morally trivial, 47; no morally significant, 47–48; non-morally significant, morally relevant, 48, 49, 50, 53, 413
freewill, libertarian, 35n11, 47, 48n48, 49n50, 161n87, 183n27, 184n33, 292n43, 369n89
friends, 52, 127, 218, 230, 231, 232, 331, 335, 336, 337, 338, 398. *See* accidental reward in heaven. *See also* communion of the saints; well-being (*bene esse*) of perfect human happiness
friendship, 39, 57, 81, 82, 100, 166n107, 257, 274, 275, 276, 278, 279, 310, 328, 331, 337, 385. *See* communion; the church
fruit (*fructus*), 83, 108, 329–30
fruit of the Holy Spirit. *See* Holy Spirit, God the
future, 33, 53n60, 67, 82, 160, 161, 162n91, 223, 306, 309, 314, 338, 353, 425, 436, 446

Gabriel, 119, 404
Garrigou-Lagrange, Reginald, 104n64, 141n1

Gaudium et Spes (Vatican Council II), 15n34, 16n36
gender, 253n100, 258, 259, 260n122. *See also* sex, biological
general judgment. *See* resurrection
general resurrection. *See* resurrection
generation, 74, 257, 274, 280, 298, 299, 309, 347, 350, 361, 386
genus, 48, 123n6, 142, 236n21, 377, 406, 407
ghost, 244, 280, 301
gifts of the Holy Spirit. *See* Holy Spirit, God the
gifts, preternatural. *See* preternatural gifts
gifts, supernatural. *See* supernatural gifts
the Givens thesis, 371, 372, 384, 385, 386
Glass III, John V., 362n75
Gloria, 414
glorified body: as beautiful, 422; does not hinder the beatific vision, 319; as a function of the body's participation in the soul's beatific vision, 223, 232n86, 296, 308, 325, 350, 374, 421; as an overflowing of the beatific vision of the soul into the body, 223, 231, 307, 312, 319, 323, 325; as a reflection or participation of the soul's beatific vision in heaven, 307, 309; and sensation, 288. *See* clarity of the glorified body. *See also* agility of the glorified body; impassibility of the glorified body; spirituality of the glorified body; subtlety of the glorified body
glory: acts of, 167n1; beauty of, 252; of the bodies of the martyrs in heaven, 252–53; of the body in heaven, 138n67, 191–92, 206, 218, 223, 224, 284, 344; of the children of God, 342; of Christ's resurrected body, 242, 244, 250, 252, 327; divine, 84; of the elect in heaven, 318; as fame, 97; of God, 188n43, 290, 294n53, 313, 317, 350, 362, 364, 369, 382–83, 446; of God's grace, 186n39; of heaven, 73, 74, 223, 302, 306, 332, 345, 416, 445, 447; in heaven a twofold, 344; of perfect happiness, 109; of the resurrected bodies of the saints, 108, 245, 324, 325, 422; of souls in heaven, 206, 218, 223, 296, 297, 323, 325, 337, 338; spiritual, 344; vision of, 118n24, 177. *See* beatific vision according to St. Thomas; glorified body. *See also* light

God: as common good in which created persons come to share in heaven, 336–37; as conferring on creatures "the dignity of causality," 427; as distinct from the world, 13n19; as a dynamic being, 61, 113–14, 173, 416–17; as exemplar formal cause of creatures, 99, 100, 101; freedom in creating of, 13n19; as infinitely exceeding man's desires, 102; as intelligible species, as it were, of the saints' beatific vision in heaven, 145, 151, 152, 153, 155, 188, 190; as living, 10n3, 119–20; as loving intellectual creatures for their own sake, 342; nature of, 22, 90, 110, 149, 154, 346, 368, 437n36; as object or cause of perfect human happiness, 97–103; no passions in, 118n24, 121; as not a composite of matter and form, 124; as primary efficient cause of all creaturely goods, 99, 101; as primary object of the beatific vision, 141–60, 170, 183, 393n2, 445; as supremely happy in Himself, 13n19, 173; as the uncreated good, 109, 134; as the unparticipated good, 134; will as antecedent and will as consequent in, 369n89; as willing creatures to exist, 232. *See* eternal life; infinity; knowledge. See *also* creator *ex* nihilo, God as; eternality of God; Father, God the; goodness; Holy Spirit, God the; immateriality of God; immeasurability of God; immutability; incomprehensibility of God; Jesus Christ; the Lord; love; omnipotence of God; omnipresence of God; omniscience of God; oneness of God; perfection; simplicity of God; Son, God the; the Trinity; wisdom

good: apparent, 184; of the body, 97; human, 19n39, 20, 21, 91, 94n15, 98, 233, 337; perceived, 120; perfect, 98, 106, 121, 132, 134, 180, 227n74; repute, 323; of the soul, 97; universal, 98; works, 85, 268, 328, 330, 429

goodness, 3, 10, 12, 13n19, 37, 39, 42, 57, 99, 100, 120, 121, 164, 183, 184, 227n74, 228, 230, 231, 232, 269, 291, 297, 305, 306, 308, 337, 362, 394, 395, 396, 397, 421, 427, 445, 447; of God, 9, 12, 17, 18, 22, 23, 35n11, 99, 100, 101, 121, 155, 159, 228, 231, 392, 394, 396, 445, 447.

goods: created, 24, 399; external, 360, 361, 362; fitting or appropriate, 229, 230, 233, 337, 385, 395, 397, 398, 418, 445, 447; of fortune, 104; genuine, 13, 99, 103; gratuitous, 228–29, 230, 397, 398, 418, 445; Grisez on fundamental, 20, 21, 22, 23, 392, 393; instrumental, 343; of marriage, 307; mixed, 100–101; particular, 98; Silverman on heavenly, 38, 39, 55, 62, 63; transcendent, 84; timeless, 84; unmixed, 100–101

Gospel of Thomas, 257, 258

G properties. *See* properties

grace: the beatific vision as a, 126, 137, 140, 150, 188, 266, 402, 403, 405, 419; God's ordinary versus extraordinary ways of giving, 434; gratuitous, 143, 150; habitual, 147, 428, as necessary for being made fit for heavenly life, 429; as needed in this life as preparation for the beatific vision, 426–44; as perfecting nature, not setting it aside or destroying it, 20, 37n16, 190n50, 358, 393, 427, 430, 431; sanctifying, 428, 429, 430, 432, 433, 440

Grand Tetons, 397

Graves, Shawn, 364n81

the greater relation, 205n24

Gregory the Great, Pope St., 50n53, 130n33, 191, 236, 252, 302, 309, 315n118, 316, 319, 324

Gregory of Nyssa, St., 35n11, 45, 47n44, 231n86

Griffiths, Paul J., 21n50, 54n62, 63–75, 84–85, 336, 339, 363, 364–87, 412, 414–16, 418, 419, 420, 437n34, 447

Grisez, Germain, 18–23, 98n41, 227, 229n79, 230n81, 336, 391, 392–93, 399, 447

growth: biological, 248, 255, 299, 361, 415; in charity or merit in heaven, 46, 52; in deiformity, 186n39; moral 40, 46, 51, 52, 58, 82

habit, 50, 69, 124, 192

halos, 108

Hancock, Herbie, 229–30

happiness: adornment (*decorum*) of, 216n45; common conceptions of, 42; created and participated, 94n15; enrichment of, 216n45; essence of, 127, 128, 216; general characteristics of, 94; imperfect, 94–95, 208, 216, 219, 304, 305; in this life, 42, 60, 93n10, 94–95, 104, 312; the soul's activity expressing virtue as the essence of, 95, 96, 104, 216; and Stoicism, 97; this-worldly, 33, 42, 95, 96; true, 213; ultimate, 207, 211;

General Index

as uncreated and unparticipated in God, 94n15; well-being (*bene esse*) of, 216n45. *See* accidental reward in heaven; Aristotle; essential reward in heaven; heaven; human happiness, perfect. *See also* friendship; well-being of perfect human happiness

health, 20, 33, 216, 293, 393

heart, 10, 89, 135, 185, 211, 236, 246, 253, 309, 446

heaven: empirical studies and, 37; as epektatic, 35n11, 36, 40–42, 43–63, 66, 231n86; fear of, 76; gifts of the Holy Spirit in, 148n35; individualistic model of, 13, 14, 18, 21n50, 35, 393; a non-TD dynamic account of, 40, 41, 42, 43, 55, 56, 60, 61, 62, 63; the saints can't get closer to God in, 43–54; the saints enjoy multiple modes of cognition in, 225n73, 291, 294n54; social model of, 14, 18, 22, 393; static views or models of, 30–75, 411–12, 416–18; things as incorruptible or perpetual in, 340–43; a totally dynamic (TD) account of, 36, 37, 40, 41, 42, 43, 54, 55, 56, 59, 60, 61, 62, 63, 412, 413, 414; as unqualifiedly good, 37, 38, 39, 55, 56, 58, 59; as wedding feast, 15, 332; as wholly contemplative for intellectual creatures, 337, 415. *See* accidental reward in heaven; angels; beatific vision according to St. Thomas; change; clarity of the glorified body; elements; essential reward in heaven; glorified body; glory; God; goods; human happiness, perfect; suffering. *See also* agility of the glorified body; artifacts; beauty; boredom; Catholic dogma on heaven; clothes in heaven; communion of the saints; conversation; disabilities in heaven; drinking; eating; empyrean; evil; external goods in heaven; fashion in heaven; heavenly bodies in heaven; impassibility of the glorified body; jazz; Jesus Christ; liturgy; marriage; merit(ing); mixed bodies; moral character; *novissimum*; pets in heaven; place(s); planets; plants; prayer(s); reading in heaven; sensation; sexual union; spirituality of the glorified body; sin; stars; subtlety of the glorified body; time; virtue(s); worship

heavenly bodies in heaven, 345–47, 349–54

Hegelianism, 232

hell, 36n15, 46, 64, 76, 85, 118, 234, 277, 279, 282, 401, 409

heresy, 300

heretics, 242, 314

Hereth, Blake, 253n100, 364n81

Hibbs, Thomas, 83n16

Hilary of Poitiers, St., 311n104

hills, 176

hoc aliquid (this something), 200, 203, 247

Hofer, Andrew, 186n39

Holy Innocents, the, 331n4

Holy Spirit, God the, 12, 148, 149, 164, 191n51, 245, 429, 432, 445, 446, 447; inspirations of, 147; gifts of, 95, 142, 147, 148, 149, 191n51, 216, 429, 432, 433, 434, 440. *See* God. *See also* the Lord; the Trinity

home run, 99, 101

Homiak, Marcia L., 257n114

honor, 97, 102

Hontheim, J., 104n64, 141n1

hope, 14n25, 53n60, 83n17, 95, 216, 223, 224, 332, 333, 432, 433, 440, 446

Hopkins, Gerard Manley, 306n89

Hortensius (Cicero), 426

house, 152n50, 299, 309, 397

human body: animal or this-worldly, 137, 138, 298, 300; as essentially changing and moving, 33–34; identity conditions for, 238–41; meaning of, 236–38; as pertaining to the essential reward in heaven consequently, 127; as spiritual in heaven, 138n69, 242, 298–99, 300, 316, 317, 403. *See* clarity of the glorified body; glorified body; resurrected body. *See also* agility of the glorified body; impassibility of the glorified body; spirituality of the glorified body; subtlety of the glorified body

Humanae Vitae (Pope St. Paul IV), 277n171, 278n173

human embodiment. *See* accidental reward in heaven; essential reward in heaven; glorified body; human body; resurrected body

human faces, 255. *See* resurrected body

human flourishing, 81n10, 83, 85, 384

human happiness, perfect, 1, 8, 11n15, 12, 13, 14, 17, 19, 20, 21, 22, 30n1, 35n11, 57, 59, 71, 72, 90, 94, 95, 96, 97, 98, 99, 101, 103, 104, 107, 121, 122, 123, 131, 132, 133, 134, 152, 166n107, 172, 173, 177, 182, 184, 191, 192n56, 197, 207, 209, 210, 212, 214, 215,

human happiness, (cont.)
216, 219, 225n73, 227, 229, 230, 294n54, 304, 305, 311, 312, 320n140, 337n40, 339, 346, 385, 392, 393, 395, 396, 397, 399, 442, 445, 447; the attainment, possession, use of, 96–97, 103–104, 122; essence of, 104, 106, 122, 123, 124, 129n30, 131, 132, 133, 134, 177, 178, 182, 214, 215, 217, 218, 290, 320; greater in some than others, 191–93; the object of, 96, 97–103, 122. *See* beatific vision according to St. Thomas; essential reward in heaven

human organisms, 198n3

human persons: as composed of soul alone in the interim state, 139, 201, 202, 263; as created in the image and likeness of God, 84, 367, 384, 385, 419, 428n9, 430, 445; as naturally and normally, if not necessarily, a composite of substantial form and prime matter, 74n109, 153, 176, 198, 200, 201, 206, 220, 221, 263, 264, 265n144, 268n152, 335, 340, 341, 354, 405n7, 428n9; and identity conditions at a time, through time and change, and beyond death, 173n16, 198–99, 201, 202–203, 221, 235–45, 253n100, 263, 423n2, 426, 429, 431, 435, 438n49, 438n43, 443; as naturally loving the universe as a whole, 346; as naturally and normally, if not necessarily, embodied, 198, 219, 221, 237; as not treated by God as mere instruments, 191n51, 342; principle of individuation for, 239–40, 244; ultimate end of, 18–21, 90–94, 97, 162, 229n79, 230n81, 304. *See* incorruptibility. *See also* corruptionism; survivalism

human soul: act of being (*actus essendi*) numerically the same as the act of being of the human composite in, 200–201; existence is sufficient for preserving the existence and the identity of the human person of which it is a part in, 200–204; as the formal cause, insofar as it is beatified, of the body's being glorified, 287–88, 296, 322; as the formal cause, insofar as it is perfected, of the incorruptibility of the resurrected body, 273; as having its own act of being, which it can share with matter, 153; as having one mode of understanding in this life, and a different mode of understanding when separated from matter, 335–36; as a *hoc aliquid*, 200; and identity conditions for, 238, 240; and individuation of the, 238–40; as intrinsic formal cause of the human person, 198–99, 203n19, 237, 238; as naturally immortal, 200, 238, 240, 269, 270n156, 340, 351; as substantial form, 153, 198, 199, 200, 210, 219, 220, 237, 238, 240, 241, 243, 248, 249, 259, 266, 267, 269, 270n156, 273, 287, 296, 299, 316–17, 403; as *sui generis* as a kind of part, 199–201. *See* essential reward in heaven; human persons. *See also* corruptionism; survivalism

humility, 332

husband, 33, 332,

Hutter, Reinhard, 2n3, 140n80, 335n26, 432n25

hylomorphism, 198, 203n16, 241n36

ideas, 13n18, 100, 144n9

identity: numerical, 203n19, 235–45, 424n2; personal, 2n3, 1on5, 84, 153n51, 173n12, 202, 235–45, 253n100, 261n125, 423n2, 426, 429, 431, 435, 438n39, 438n43, 443, 447; specific, 235–45

ignorance. *See* heaven

illumination, 145n17, 176n19

image, 15, 69, 84, 165, 338, 367, 373n94, 384, 385, 419, 428n9, 430, 445. *See* human persons

imagination, 30, 98, 289, 349, 446

immobility, 175, 193n58. *See also* immutability

immateriality of God, 7, 11, 16, 25, 26, 118n24, 119, 124, 126, 136, 144, 214, 400, 439; immeasurability of God, 1on3

immortality: as a preternatural gift in Adam and Eve, 74, 267, 314, 351n42, 428; of the resurrected body, 74, 236, 260–73, 314, 316, 342, 356. *See* human persons; human soul; preternatural gifts(s). See also the problem of the tedium of immortality (PTI); the problem of the tedium of heavenly immortality (PTHI); resurrected body

immutability, 110, 115–19, 174–76; of God, 13n19, 110–14

impassibility: four meanings of impassibility, 282–84. *See* glorified body; preternatural gift(s). *See also* supernatural disposition(s); impassibility of the glorified body

General Index

impassibility of the glorified body, 108, 187, 247, 266, 283–84, 296, 322, 351n42, 403, 409, 438n42; arguments for the, 284–85; as the body subject to the beatified soul as principle of movement with respect to sensation, 296; causes of, 285–88; as a gift (*dos*), 286; and sensation in heaven, 288–94. *See* glorified body

impediment, 299

Incarnation. *See* Jesus Christ

incomprehensibility of God, 10n3

incorruptibility: absolute, 264n140; as caused by God hindering the principles of corruption, 272–73; as caused by God removing the cause of corruption, i.e., the movement of the heavenly bodies, 270–72; contemporary physics and, 271–73; as due to form, 264–66; as due to matter or a lack of matter, 262–64; as due merely to an efficient cause miraculously acting upon matter, 266–67; existence, 263–64. *See* corruption; resurrected body

incorruptible order of the next life, 303. *See also* the corruptible order of this life

incorruptible beings: according to the part, 357; according to the whole, 341, 348, 355, 357; naturally, 262, 263, 264, 265, 267, 268, 340, 341; relatively, 340–41. *See also* perpetual beings

individuation, 239, 240, 244

infant(s), 94n17, 237n34

Inferno (Dante), 36n15

infinity: of God's power, 159; of God's will, understanding, and every perfection, 10n3, 156, 158, 159, 445

innocence, state of. *See* state of innocence

instruments, 191, 249, 250, 339, 342, 349, 362, 363, 430; musical, 339, 362

integrity, preternatural gift of. *See* preternatural gifts

intellect, 11, 91, 98, 118, 125, 127, 128, 129, 130, 131, 132, 134, 137, 138, 139, 142, 145n17, 146, 148, 151, 153, 154, 155, 156, 158, 159, 162, 163, 164, 165, 169, 170, 171, 172, 174, 175, 183, 185, 186, 187, 188, 190, 191, 192, 193, 198, 209, 214, 215, 219, 220, 231, 241, 242, 290n39, 292, 294n54, 295, 315, 403, 413, 430, 445; created, 139, 153, 156, 158, 159, 163, 164, 170, 171, 172, 183, 186, 187, 188, 190, 191; as different in kind from the senses, 241; speculative versus practical, 130–31

intellectual activity: as activity of a living thing, 172; and brain activity, 125–26; contemplative, 132; as in and of itself not making use of a bodily organ, 125; natural human, 125; practical, 132; as scientific inquiry, 132; and simple apprehension, 125; speculative, 132; and the will, 91, 199. *See* accidental reward in heaven; beatific vision according to St. Thomas; cognition; essential reward in heaven

interim state, 201, 202, 203, 204, 207, 240, 263, 335. *See also* intermediate state

intermediate state, 204n21. *See also* interim state

intimacy, 21, 154

irascible power, 83n17

Irwin, Terence, 93n10

James the Greater, St., 326

jazz, 229; in heaven, 362, 364, 419

Jensen, Steven, 91n4

Jerome, St., 50n53, 148, 311n104

Jesus Christ, 10, 14n25, 16, 23, 27, 53n60, 121n139, 130, 135, 136n56, 148, 167, 234n3, 250, 257, 261n127, 294n53, 307, 309, 314, 344, 349, 360, 429; ascension of, 16n35, 65, 66, 243, 252, 254, 316, 318, 344, 429; blood of, 250; Catholic Christian understanding of, 136n56; church as body of, 334; church as bride of, 186n40, 279n174, 332, 334, 431n23; death of, 11, 53n60, 65, 202n16, 306, 331n14, 429; flesh of, 346, 414; as having the beatific vision from the moment of conception, 137n65; heaven as consummation of the mystical marriage with, 332; human knowledge of, 162–63, 291, 294n54, 353; human will of, 291n43; judgement seat of, 16n37; passion of, 11, 53n60, 65, 288n28, 306, 331n14, 338, 429; resurrection of, 16, 65, 242, 252, 261n127, 266, 267, 306, 316, 327, 354, 429; second coming of, 234; transfiguration of, 326. *See* resurrection. *See also* Son, God the; the Lord; the Trinity

John the Apostle, St., 10, 120, 179, 186, 326

John Chrysostom, St., 311n104

John Paul II, Pope St., 276n166, 307n90, 307n92, 439

John, Tyler M., 364n81

joy (*gaudium*): as an aspect of the accidental reward in heaven, 2, 83, 108, 328, 329–331, 334, 337, 338; as an aspect of the essential reward, 2, 27, 44n29, 57, 103, 105, 128, 129, 180, 181, 183, 206, 211, 214, 215, 228, 306, 328, 385, 394, 396, 399, 403, 418, 419, 436, 437n36, 447. *See* accidental reward in heaven; essential reward in heaven. *See also* aureoles; fruit

judgment: general, 11, 16, 53n60, 65, 103, 108, 204, 212; as the second act of intellect, 199. *See* resurrection

justice: of God, 108, 268; virtue of, 95, 216

kingdom, 19, 20, 102, 228, 301, 314, 315, 316, 337, 338, 416; of my Father, 314, 316; of their Father, 324, 325; of God, 18, 20, 21n50, 22, 65, 73n108, 83, 242, 244, 245, 251, 306, 307, 329, 330, 331n14, 334, 337, 364, 419, 446; of heaven, 15, 257, 315, 316

kings, 102

knowledge: direct, 144, 335, 336, 445; by faith, 24, 142, 145–47, 148, 272; as fundamental good, 20; God's, 100, 132, 136, 155, 156, 157, 158, 159, 160, 161; indirect, 143, 290n39, 393; intellectual, 144, 185; natural, 138, 146, 149, 294n54; by philosophical argument, 142, 143–44; by preternatural gift prior to the Fall, 143, 149; by prophetic inspiration, 143, 150; by rapture, 143, 150; sense, 91n4, 149, 199, 298, 299; as sometimes involving a medium by which (*quo*), 144, 145, 146, 149, 150, 152, 154, 155, 156, 158, 171, 185, 187, 188, 189; as sometimes involving a medium from which (*a quo*), 144, 145, 146, 185, 188, 189; as sometimes involving a medium under which (*sub quo*), 144, 145n17, 155, 156, 158, 180, 185, 188, 189, 191; supernatural, 138, 155, 185, 186, 187, 191, 192, 294n54, 445; by understanding as a gift of the Holy Spirit, 142–43, 147–49

Kretzmann, Norman, 110n100, 113n109

labor, 309
Lang, Bernhard, 7n1, 14
last thing(s), 21n50, 63, 64, 66, 67, 365
Lateran Council, Fourth, 16n35, 16n37, 234n1
Lauds, 66
lawyers, 93n13
laymen, 102

laypersons, 93n13
Leget, Carlo, 120n129, 217n49
Leo XIII, Pope, 27n63
Levering, Matthew, 14n25
life: and change, 61; and dynamism, 61. *See* God; eternal life. *See also* active life; contemplative life
light, 135, 144, 155, 185, 187, 188, 323, 436; of faith, 146, 175;
light of glory (*lumen gloriae*), 139, 156, 158, 160, 163, 172, 180, 184–91, 192, 193, 296, 306n89, 323, 325, 403, 408, 409, 431n23, 445
light of reason, 144, 145n17, 145n18, 146, 147
lightsomeness, 323n151
likeness, 12, 13, 84, 109, 151, 152, 153, 171, 185, 297, 315, 346, 367, 384, 385, 428n9, 430, 445
Literal Commentary on Genesis (St. Augustine), 222
liturgy, 68, 69, 70, 85, 338; of the hours, 15, 66; heavenly, 63, 68–73, 84, 363, 371, 414, 415, 418, 419; and play, 363–64, 419
The Liturgy of the Hours according to the Roman Rite, 15n31
living thing(s), 16n35, 119, 173, 199, 219, 237, 248, 262, 334, 340, 367, 368, 372, 375, 377, 378, 380, 381, 382
the Lord, 10n3, 11, 16n35, 23n54, 53n60, 68, 71, 72, 98, 212, 213, 261n127, 299, 309, 314, 362, 364, 365, 368, 414, 419, 436. *See* God. *See also* Father, God the; Holy Spirit, God the; Jesus Christ; Son, God the; the Trinity
The Lord of the Rings (J. R. R. Tolkien), 362
love, 118, 120, 121, 166n107, 168n23, 181, 276, 336, 368, 371, 382, 383, 395, 431, 437, 438, 439; as an act of will, 121; *amare*, 181; *delectio*, 181; as an emotion, feeling, or passion, 121; in God, ; as a proper accident of the beatific vision, 57, 83n17, 103, 105, 128, 129, 180, 183, 191, 215, 228, 385, 394, 396, 399, 413, 414, 418, 419, 445. *See also* charity (*caritas*)
lovemaking, 81. *See* heaven; resurrected body. *See also* conjugal act; conjugal love; marriage; procreating; sexual activity; sexual congress; sexual union; spirituality of the glorified body; subtlety of the glorified body
Lubac, Henri de, 334n24
Lumen Gentium (Vatican Council II), 15n34, 16n36

General Index

lumen gloriae. See light
luminosity, 323, 325, 326, 407. *See* clarity of the glorified body
Lyons, Second Council of, 16n35, 16n37

Macrobius, 437
makarios, 93n10
maladies, 256
male, 123n6, 257, 258, 260n122, 278n172, 280, 367, 375, 377. *See also* female
Malebranche, Nicholas, 427
man, 250
Maritain, Jacques, 336–37
marriage, 276, 279, 367; at Cana, 332; carnal, 18n40, 279; as a fundamental good, 20, 23n54, 393; in heaven there is no carnal, 23, 279, 311, 374, 378, 381, 393; sacrament of, 305, 306; and sexual union as pointing to the consummation of the kingdom of God in the beatific vision, the resurrection of the body, and the communion of the saints, 305, 306, 307; in the spiritual or mystical sense between Christ and the Church or Christ and the individual soul in heaven, 279n174, 332
married persons, 330n8
Martha of Bethany, St., 130, 308, 309, 435
martyrdom, 108, 252, 253, 331n14
martyrs, 108, 238n25, 252, 253, 330, 331
Mary, Blessed Virgin, 19, 119, 344, 349, 399, 404, 421, 439, 442n46; as already embodied, 16n37, 103, 127, 204, 234, 235, 344, 349, 360; Assumption of, 16n37, 344
Mary of Bethany, St., 130, 308, 309, 435
Mass, 65, 66, 70, 85, 338, 363, 364, 419, 431, 436, 437n34
materialism, 197, 204; Democretian, 198
material substances. *See* substances
matter: designated, 238, 239, 240, 241, 244, 259, 287; *ex qua*, 243n48; and natural tension with spirit, 428; other-worldly, 286, 287n21, 295, 301, 302; prime, 112, 116, 153, 198, 199, 201, 203, 237, 238, 239, 240, 243. *See also* concupiscence
McDannell, Colleen, 7n1, 14
means (to an end), 83n17, 90, 91, 92, 94, 95, 96, 131, 132, 214, 249, 274
mechanics, 93n13
medium by which (*quo*): *see* knowledge
medium from which (*a quo*): *see* knowledge

medium under which (*sub quo*): *see* knowledge
Meilaender, Gilbert, 8, 81, 82, 83, 84, 420, 447
Meixner, Uwe, 28n65
merit(ing), 44, 45, 46, 49, 50n53, 52, 59, 273, 326, 412, 413; in heaven there is no, 44–47, 412–13
metaphor, 41, 60, 164, 165, 308n93, 328, 332
Metaphysics (Aristotle), 133
Middleton, J. Richard, 14n24
mildness, 332
Miller, Lisa, 30n2
mind, 27, 69, 138n67, 151, 178, 198n3
minerals, 341, 347n33, 348. *See also* mixed bodies
miracle(s), 139n75, 140, 236n21, 267, 286, 303, 353
mirror, 135, 144, 154, 164, 165, 185, 188
Mitchell-Yellin, Benjamin, 80n4
mixed bodies, 198n5, 265, 285n16, 286, 347n31, 348–49, 355, 357, 358, 380; in heaven, 347–49. *See also* minerals
mobility, 321
moderation, 95
molecule(s), 198, 200, 247
Molina, Louis de, 161n87
Monica, St., 436
mood, 93n10
moon, 188n43, 324, 404, 436
moral character, 44; in heaven, 44, 47–48
moral growth, 40, 51, 82
mortality, 83, 245
Moses: and his rapture, 138n69, 139, 150
mothers, 93n13
motion, 168, 270, 373, 424; empyrean as the place beyond, 344; of glorified bodies, 318; of heavenly bodies, 176n19, 270, 271, 341, 347, 348, 355, 357, 358, 404. *See* accidental reward in heaven; glorified body. *See also* agility of the glorified body
motive(s), 331, 362
mountain(s), 77, 176, 314
movement, 33, 34, 44, 46, 115, 128, 178, 296, 320, 356, 404, 427, 447; bodily, 3, 317, 319, 320–22, 422. *See* accidental reward in heaven; glorified body. *See also* agility of the glorified body
Munificentissimus Deus (Venerable Pope Pius XII), 16n37

music, 30n2, 69, 77, 230, 276, 299, 362, 384, 436
musicians, 95n18
music-making, 276
mutability, 34, 113, 416n3. *See also* immutability

nature of heaven, the first problem concerning the (PNH-I), 8–25, 104, 336, 391–99
nature of heaven, the second problem concerning the (PNH-II), 25–29, 400–410
nature of heaven, the third problem concerning the (PNH-III), 30–75, 411–19
need(s), 342, 346, 347, 356, 369, 377, 382, 384; *simpliciter* versus *secundum quid*, 319
neighbor, 69, 166n107, 336, 431, 437, 438
neo-Platonism, 84, 232
Nevitt, Turner, 202n16, 280n179
newborn, 237n24
"new creatures," 345
"the new heaven(s) and the new earth," 2, 3, 8, 9, 14, 17, 22, 26, 30–31, 42, 71, 107, 150, 202, 218n52, 229, 245, 264n139, 272, 283, 290, 294n54, 299, 308, 313, 314, 318, 319, 341, 343–56, 358, 359, 360, 361, 363, 364, 365, 368, 369, 372, 373n94, 378, 385, 386, 391, 392, 394, 399, 403, 404, 411, 418, 419, 421, 422
New Jerusalem, 15, 371
Nicomachean Ethics (Aristotle), 94, 109, 216, 312
nourishment, 137n63, 235n13, 299, 313, 314, 361, 386
novels, 69, 362
novissimum, 54, 64, 66, 67, 414; heaven as, 54, 66–67, 414
Nussbaum, Martha, 83

obediential potency or power, 353–54, 359
object of a power, 91n4
object of perfect human happiness. *See* human happiness, perfect
Oderberg, David S., 202n15, 203n18
offspring, 275, 276, 278
omnipotence of God, 10n3, 81
omnipresence of God, 319
omniscience of God, 132
O'Neil, Charles, 323n151
oneness of God, 10n3, 13n19
operation, 109, 123, 124, 127, 130, 169, 176, 200, 205, 206, 207, 214, 217, 218, 219n56, 221, 222, 249, 250, 311, 318
order, 251, 253, 291, 292, 348; created, 13n19, 372, 386; divine, 308n93; of grace, 163; of nature, 163, 190, 428n9; the old, 284; of the universe, 161. *See also* corruptible order of this life; incorruptible order of the next life
organism, 119, 198n3, 237n24, 241n36, 248, 249, 333
organ(s), 125, 126, 198n5, 199, 237, 238, 241, 249, 250, 260, 279, 311; generative, 249–50, 260, 279–80, 303, 311; sense, 125, 288, 289, 293
Ott, Ludwig, 44, 45, 46, 104n64, 352n47, 413
Our Father, 338
Overall, Christine, 82

pain, 38, 283, 284, 285, 361, 364n81
Pakaluk, Michael, 97n41, 229n79
"panimals," non-human, 359
paradise, 2n3, 25, 31, 32, 35n11, 36, 37, 38, 40, 41, 55, 62, 80n7, 313, 317, 411, 415, 417
Paradiso (Dante), 36, 50n53, 84, 110n101, 276n168, 326n169
parenthood, 20, 393
participation, 2, 63, 65, 70, 71, 72, 85, 94n15, 98, 134, 227, 363, 364, 391, 415, 419, 431, 439n45; in Christ, 328; in God's eternal and immutable life by having the beatific vision 3, 28, 54, 71, 90, 109, 167–79, 209, 337, 413, 416–17, 418, 421, 442; in God's perfect happiness, 13, 94n15, 405; of the human body in heaven in the beatified soul, 232n86, 296, 308, 325, 350, 374, 402, 421; nature of, 12, 13, 297
parts: act and potency as, 110–11; metaphysical, 198, 200, 201, 237, 241n36, 402; quantitative, 110, 198, 199, 200, 201, 235, 237, 238, 241n36, 246, 247, 249, 253, 260, 265, 266, 270, 271, 302, 303, 341, 347, 348, 355; stuff, 247, 260. *See* form; matter
Pasnau, Robert, 10n4, 202n16
passion(s), 118n124, 121, 139, 181, 283, 284, 285, 286, 311, 437, 438, 439, 442. *See also* emotions; feelings
passion of Jesus Christ. *See* Jesus Christ
past, 161, 162n91, 169, 338, 383, 436
patience, 332
Paul VI, Pope St., 16n36, 27n63, 47n44, 277n17, 278n173

General Index

Paul of Tarsus, St., 10, 27, 28, 83n17, 154, 164, 191–92, 212, 242, 244, 245, 250, 251, 254, 261, 262, 268, 297, 300, 321, 324, 332, 333, 342, 357, 401, 407, 438n38, 438n40; on celibacy, 307; on his rapture, 138n69, 139, 150

Pawl, Timothy, 2n3, 31n3, 35n11, 45, 46, 47, 48, 51, 52n58, 136n56, 183n27, 184n33

peace (*pax*), 181, 332, 368

Pelser, Adam, 80n7

Pentecost, 66

perfection, 81n10, 114, 148, 163, 205, 207, 208, 229, 230, 232, 247, 248, 316, 319, 321, 325, 337n39, 393, 397, 398, 431, 438, 439, 441; the attainment of perfect happiness in heaven a human person's supreme, 123, 134n47, 141–42, 178–79; of beatitude in heaven, 366, 372, 375, 376, 378; of charity in heaven, 166n107, 336; as contrasted with perfectionism, 81n10; in creatures as pre-existing in some manner in God, 99–103, 144; final, 210–11; first, 210–11, 219, 220, 304–305; of friendship, 274; of God, 10, 13n19; 100–101, 113, 119, 395, 416; of happiness in heaven relative to the perfection of charity in the soul at death, 193; of human persons in heaven as a perfect participation in God's perfection, 121, 162; of immobility in heaven, 175; of martyrdom, 253; of a power, 133, 148, 217, 221; of possessing the complete nature of the species, 222, 249; of the soul in heaven, 266, 318, 322; of the universe as whole, 358, 384, 387. *See* essential reward in heaven; glorified body; goods; human happiness, perfect; resurrected body. *See also* accidental reward in heaven; beatific vision according to St. Thomas; heaven

perpetual beings, 340, 341, 342, 343, 345, 347, 350, 351n41, 352, 353, 354, 355, 357, 373n94, 377n96, 378. *See* incorruptible beings

Perry, R. C., 335n26

persistence conditions, 28, 406, 407, 408

persons, human. *See* human persons

pertaining relation, 126; pertaining antecedently, 126–27; pertaining consequently, 127; pertaining essentially, 126

Peter, C. J., 167n1

Peter the Apostle, St., 138n69, 326

pets in heaven, 358

Phaedrus (Plato), 10

Phan, Peter C., 14n23, 14n25, 14n26

phantasms, 125, 137, 138, 151, 214, 335, 336

philosopher(s), 2, 7, 8, 9, 14, 15, 29, 31, 32n6, 34, 35n11, 36, 37n16, 49, 57, 59, 61, 66, 76, 77, 80, 81, 82, 84, 85, 89, 91n2, 93n10, 110n100, 113, 120, 143, 176n19, 187, 230, 236, 241, 242, 254n100, 286n20, 320, 391, 398, 411, 416, 417, 420, 422, 424n2, 447

philosophical theology, 110

philosophy, 2n3, 7, 20, 30, 35n11, 65n85, 69, 76, 80n4, 81, 123, 143, 154, 167n1, 198, 202n15, 202n16, 243, 248, 253n100, 294n54, 416

"phlants," 359, 377, 378

physical entities, 341, 354, 355. *See* accidental reward in heaven; elements; heaven; substance(s). *See also* minerals; mixed bodies

physics, 264, 271, 272, 273, 349, 350, 352, 354n52, 355

piano, 126, 229

Pieper, Josef, 96

Pius XI, Pope, 47n44

Pius XII, Venerable Servant of God, Pope, 16n37, 27n63

place(s), 7, 30, 31, 32, 36n15, 41, 45n35, 65, 66, 118n124, 174, 225n73, 239, 264n139, 296, 318, 319, 332, 339, 344–45, 349, 360–61, 371, 385, 404, 411, 417, 418; in heaven,

planet(s), 268n150, 341, 345, 347, 351, 352, 355, 357, 377n96; in heaven, 345–47, 349–54. *See also* stars

Plantinga, Alvin, 47

plants, 64, 68, 73, 116, 119, 162, 268n150, 340, 341, 347n33, 351n41, 355–60, 364n81, 365–70, 371, 372–84, 385, 386, 414, 427, 428; in heaven, 64, 68, 347n43, 351n41, 355–60, 364–70, 371, 372–84, 414, 447. *See* accidental reward in heaven; heaven

Plato, 10, 27, 29, 35n11, 120, 198n3, 237, 257n114, 371n93, 401, 437

Platonism, 203

play, 20, 76, 363–64, 393, 419l in heaven, 20, 30, 299, 362, 363–64, 393, 419

pleasure(s), 82, 92, 97, 99, 102, 105, 106, 283, 309, 310, 312–13, 329, 362, 397, 436, 438, 439n45, 442

Plotinus, 9, 437

position, 252,

General Index

power(s), 13n19, 83n17, 91, 97, 100, 116, 117, 124, 127, 130, 133, 137, 142, 159, 161, 162, 164, 168, 179, 183, 185, 186, 187, 198n5, 199, 201, 219, 236, 237, 241, 250, 253, 265, 266, 267, 273, 285, 286, 287, 288, 289, 290n39, 292, 293, 294, 295, 296, 303, 311, 318, 321, 322, 326, 335n31, 344, 346, 347, 351, 353, 381, 407, 419, 427, 428, 429, 430, 433, 446. *See* will. *See also* intellect; obediential potency or power; senses.
praise (*laus*), 71, 181
prayer(s), 15n31, 39, 63, 66, 81, 85, 98n41, 333n20, 334n23, 429, 431; in heaven, 39
preaching, 96, 330, 442n46
prelapsarian state, 155. *See also* Eden, Garden of; state of innocence
present, 161, 162n91, 338
prestige, 323
preternatural disposition(s) or power(s), 190, 265, 266, 267, 270, 273, 341, 354, 407. *See* preternatural gift(s)
preternatural gift(s): of immortality, 73–74, 263n137, 267, 351n42, 354, 428; of impassibility, 428; of integrity, 381, 428, 429, 432; of knowledge, 143, 149; nature of, 74n109. *See also* preternatural disposition(s) or power(s)
priest(s), 93, 96, 102, 307
prime matter. *See* matter
the problem of heavenly freedom, 2n3
the problem of personal identity beyond death, 2n3, 10n5, 153n51, 202n15
the problem of the tedium of immortality (PTI), 40n24, 76–77, 78, 80, 81, 82, 83, 84, 422
the problem of the tedium of heavenly immortality (PTHI), 40n24, 77–85, 420–44
procreating, 235n13. *See* heaven; resurrected body. *See also* conjugal act; conjugal love; lovemaking; marriage; sexual activity; sexual congress; sexual union; spirituality of the glorified body; subtlety of the glorified body
progeny, 74, 352, 428
prognostic, 338
properties, 116, 117, 198n5, 237, 253n100; characteristic of glorified bodies, i.e., G, 187n40, 247n69, 282, 296, 297, 403; essential, 28, 406, 407, 408, 409; resurrection, i.e., R, 234, 235, 282
prophetic inspiration, 143

propositions, 57n65, 145n17, 146, 147, 199
providence, 340–41, 345, 427
prudence, 437–38
the Psalms, 15
Pseudo-Athanasian Symbol, *Quicumque*, 16n37
Pseudo-Chrysostom, 311n104
psychological changes, 79–80, 423, 426; directed from without, 79; extremely radical, 433, 444; instantaneous, 79–80, 423, 433, 440; non-extremely radical, 433, 440, 444; radical, 79–80, 423, 440; unmixed, 79–80, 423, 433, 440
psychological continuity, 78, 423, 436, 438n39, 438n43, 441, 442, 443n48, 444; and personal identity, 78, 423, 438n39, 438n43
psychological stage(s), 78, 423, 443
psychological state(s), 78n3, 80
psychology, philosophical, 91n4
punishment, 108, 168, 178, 279
Purgatorio (Dante), 36n15
purgatory, 34n9, 36n15, 51, 108, 427, 431, 435, 442–44, 447

quantity, 239, 251, 253, 295
quiddity, 125
quietus (at rest), 54, 414

radiance, 323
rapture, 139, 143, 150
rational being, 91, 97, 134, 312
reading in heaven, 362, 364, 419
reason: age of, 78n3, 94n17, 143, 331n14, 428, 432; natural human, 2n2, 19n39, 57n65, 63, 83n17, 97, 144, 145n17, 145n18, 146, 147, 212, 257n114, 268, 270, 297, 299, 307, 312, 428, 429; right, 95n18, 329
Recentiores episcoporum synodi (Letter [on Certain Questions concerning Eschatology]; Sacred Congregation for the Doctrine of the Faith), 17n37, 27n63, 446n1
reincarnation, 242
rejoicing, 108, 257, 334
relationship, 12, 13, 14, 39, 40, 42, 47, 57n68, 105, 113, 129n30, 148, 170, 216, 256n112, 276n168, 285, 297, 335, 344, 347, 374, 380, 428, 441
religious, 93n13, 307
remembering, 250, 376, 377
the removal of one of the ends of eating and

sex argument (REA), 274–75, 279; development of (DREA), 275–79
Republic (Plato), 257n114
R properties. *See* properties
requiescat in pace, 54, 67
restoration of the world, 352
resurrected body: as a body of a perfect age, 235, 254–55;; as contributing to the perfection of the communion of saints, 335; and identity of biological sex, 235, 257–60; as immortal, 25, 26, 28, 29, 260–62, 275; as incorruptible, 25, 26, 28, 29, 251, 252n97, 260–73, 275, 281, 343; as mature and healthy, 238, 246, 248, 253; as not giving rise to animal actions such as eating, sleeping, drinking, and sexual union, 273–80, 281; and numerical identity of stature, 235, 255–57; as a perfect human body, 246, 247, 248, 249; as possessed by both the damned and the beatified after the general resurrection, 246, 247, 248, 266, 270n158, 282n2, 299n68, 311n104, 326, 407; and the scars of martyrdom, 251–53; as specifically and numerically identical to that human person's body in this life, 234, 235–45; and specific integrity of parts, 234, 245–53. *See also* properties
resurrection: general, 16, 17, 19, 67, 68, 124, 127, 138n70, 176, 181, 201, 204, 205, 206, 207, 208, 211, 212, 223, 224, 226, 227n74, 231, 233, 235, 240, 246, 248, 251, 253, 258, 259, 260, 261, 262, 263, 266, 268, 269, 270, 271, 272, 273, 274, 279n175, 280, 292, 294n54, 335, 336, 341, 344, 346, 349, 352, 354, 356, 359, 360, 363n77, 394, 396, 401, 403, 404, 406, 407, 421, 446; as miraculous, 29, 236, 270n156, 401. *See* Jesus Christ; judgment; resurrected body
revelation, divine, 57n65, 63, 439
reward, heavenly, 104, 107, 175n14, 331n14. *See* accidental reward in heaven; essential reward in heaven
Ribeiro, Brian, 77, 78, 79, 420, 422, 423, 424, 426, 427, 429, 431, 433, 434, 435, 439, 441, 443
riches, 99
risibility, 106, 107, 127, 128, 182, 258, 259. *See also being risible*
river(s), 176, 314
Rogers, Katherin, 24–25, 32n6, 61n75, 336, 391, 392, 393, 394, 399, 417n5, 447

Rota, Michael, 427n8
Russell, Jeffrey Burton, 7n1

sacrament(s), 250, 305–6, 338, 371, 429, 430, 432, 434. *See also individual sacraments by name*
Sacred Congregation for the Doctrine of the Faith, 16n37, 27n63, 446
Sadducees, 1, 23
Sagan, Carl, 264
saints, in heaven. *See* accidental reward in heaven; communion of the saints; glorified body; glory; heaven; the essential reward in heaven
salvation, 46, 96, 148, 333, 394
Sanctus, 67, 414
Scannell, T., 74n109
scars, of the martyrs in heaven, 252–53, 422
SCG. See Summa contra gentiles
science, 19n39, 110n100, 111n104, 127n18, 133n44, 341n4, 349
scripture, 2, 8, 14, 15, 19, 24, 27, 28, 30n1, 41, 44, 80, 98, 121n139, 135, 136, 147, 149, 154, 167, 188n43, 191, 215, 223, 227, 242, 244, 245, 248, 252, 254, 261, 280, 284, 287, 293, 298, 308, 314, 315, 322, 324, 325, 329n5, 345, 352, 376, 393, 404, 415, 447; allegorical sense of, 315; anagogical (or eschatological) sense of, 315, 371; Hebrew, 15; the literal sense of, 15n32; metaphors in, 60; metaphors for heaven in, 11, 15, 41, 60, 121n139, 154, 245, 315–16, 329n5, 332; moral (or tropological) sense of, 315; New Testament, 10, 15, 16, 20; on seeing God, 135–40; spiritual senses of, 15n32
self-absorption, 69
sensation, 3, 138, 144, 283, 288, 289, 290, 294n54, 317, 318, 335, 399, 447; in heaven, 288–94. *See also* impassibility of the glorified body; senses
senses, 72, 124, 125, 126, 127, 137, 138, 139, 140, 143, 241, 289, 292, 293, 294, 318, 335n31, 336, 364, 428, 436; external, 125, 237; glorified, 346; interior, 125, 290; spiritual, 294 n53. *See also* impassibility of the glorified body; sensation
servants, 314
sex, biological, 235, 246, 253, 257, 258, 260. *See* resurrected body. *See also* gender
sexual activity, 274, 310, 314, 315. *See* heaven; resurrected body. *See also* conjugal act;

sexual activity, *(cont.)* conjugal love; lovemaking; procreating; sexual congress; sexual union; spirituality of the glorified body; spirituality of the glorified body; subtlety of the glorified body

sexual congress, 99, 100, 101, 245, 329, 330, 362. *See* heaven; resurrected body. *See also* conjugal act; conjugal love; lovemaking; procreating; sexual activity; sexual union; spirituality of the glorified body; subtlety of the glorified body

sexual union, 235, 249, 251, 260, 273–79, 281, 284, 299, 303–314, 317, 329, 362, 374, 393, 415; in heaven there is no (desire for), 273–81, 303–17. *See* resurrected body. *See also* conjugal act; conjugal love; lovemaking; procreating; sexual activity; sexual congress; spirituality of the glorified body; subtlety of the glorified body

shapes of bodies, 255, 257

signs, 70, 305, 306, 362

Silverman, Eric J., 2n3, 31, 32, 33n7, 36–43, 54, 55, 56, 57, 58, 60, 61, 62, 411, 412, 416n4, 419, 447

Silvermanian argument in defense of the TD account of heaven, 54–63

similitude, 151, 170, 192, 437

simplicity of God, 13n19, 113, 142, 151, 155, 159, 187.

sin, 35n11, 44n28, 47n45, 47n47, 48n48, 49n50, 50n53, 267, 314, 331n14, 369, 370, 379, 380, 381, 382, 383, 386, 428n12; as impossible in heaven, 47–48, 74, 178, 183, 184; original, 74n110, 268n150, 334, 441; venial, 108. *See also* the Fall

sisters, 66, 309

sleeping, 235, 313

society, 336; of the blessed in heaven, 188n43, 314, 334; of created friends, 218, 336, 337, 338; of creatures, 3; in God, 337; human, 338. *See* accidental reward in heaven; community. *See also* communion of the saints

Son, God the, 12, 137, 332, 445, 447. *See also* Jesus Christ; the Lord; the Trinity

soul: of Christ, 162, 163, 190n48; embodied, 208, 209, 211, 221, 226; separated, 37n16, 139, 197, 202n16, 203n17, 205–11, 215, 222, 224, 225, 226, 227n75, 231, 232, 268n152, 291, 292, 335n31, 361. *See* human soul.

space, 25, 64, 239, 253n100, 276n166, 303n85, 400

speaking, 69

species, 3, 33, 48, 68, 101, 102, 106, 107, 123, 128, 142, 146, 151, 152, 161, 162, 170, 171, 182, 203, 221, 222, 237, 240, 243, 249, 258, 259, 274, 275, 277, 278, 310, 313, 356, 357, 368, 371, 377, 378, 382, 383, 384, 407, 408, 415, 427, 437; *infima*, 123, 199, 236n21; infused, 335; innate, 176n19; intelligible, 125, 144, 145, 146, 151, 152, 153, 155, 185, 188, 190, 214, 336; sensible, 125, 144, 145, 151, 155, 289, 290

Spencer, Mark, 11n14, 12, 13, 21n50, 35n11, 37n16, 46n42, 54n63, 59n70, 60n72, 114n111, 118n124, 119n128, 128n29, 203n17, 231n86, 235n13, 270n156, 294n53, 297, 305n87, 353n49, 358n66, 364n78, 371n93, 423n2

Spezzano, Daria, 186n39

spirit(s), 11, 27, 74n109, 136, 164, 243, 250, 257, 280, 287n27, 296, 297, 299n68, 300, 301, 332, 333, 335n31, 402n1, 428, 436. *See also* Holy Spirit, God the

spirituality of the glorified body, 138n69, 242, 294, 298–99, 300, 301, 303, 438n42. *See also* subtlety of the glorified body

spiritual life, stages of the, 430–33, 435–39

splendor, 323, 327

sports, 69

ST. See Summa Theologiae

star(s), 191, 192, 264, 324, 345, 351, 352, 355, 436; in heaven, 345–47, 349–54. *See also* planets

stargazing, 276

state of innocence, 73–74, 138n70, 149, 263n137, 266–68, 313, 351, 352, 354, 381, 428. *See also* Eden, Garden of; prelapsarian state

stature, 235, 254n102, 255–57, 302

Stenberg, Joseph, 129n30

study, 39, 63, 66, 81, 85, 431

Stump, Eleonore, 21n50, 110n100, 144n11, 192n56, 198n6, 202n15, 203n18, 239n28, 277n170, 289n33, 369n89, 379n99, 386n107

subject, 106, 111, 190, 199, 259, 300, 358, 359, 430

substance(s): composite, 153; corruptible, 116, 117, 119, 261; immaterial, 117, 151, 187, 198, 237, 295, 300, 340; incorruptible,

General Index 485

116n122, 117, 352, 377n96; material, 107, 111, 112, 114, 198, 199, 238, 239, 240, 247, 261n125, 262, 263n137, 264, 265, 340, 346, 347, 348, 350, 351, 353, 354, 355, 359, 363n77, 377, 385, 386, 387; as not composed of substances, 348; potential, 198n4; separate, 133n45; spiritual, 13n19, 177; as unified beings of the highest order, 348. *See* things

substance dualism, 197, 198, 204; compound, 198n3; Platonic, 203; simple, 198n3; St. Thomas's philosophical anthropology not a species of, 203

subtlety of the glorified body, 108, 187, 247, 282, 294–317; as the body being *spiritual* in St. Paul's sense of the term, 298–99; as the body being subject to form as a benevolent lord, 296; causes of, 296–97; and different kinds of arguments for why there is no sexual union in heaven, 303–17; heretical or otherwise problematic ways of thinking about the, 300–303; and Jesus passing through locked doors after his resurrection as miraculous, 302–3; and the palpability of the glorified body, 301, 302–3; precise description of the, 299; as primary sense in which the body is perfectly subject to the glorified soul, 296, 297. *See* glorified body; resurrected body. *See also* spirituality of the glorified body

suicide, 424–25

Sullivan, Ezra, 19n39, 228, 229n79, 397

suffering: in heaven there is no, 16, 83n17, 283–88, 361

Summa contra gentiles (St. Thomas) 93, 152, 154, 170, 171, 172, 173, 174, 187, 207, 208, 242, 250, 268, 285, 291, 308, 313, 314, 322

Summa Theologiae (St. Thomas), 89, 90, 93, 175, 219, 312; *Prima Pars* (First Part), 46, 176, 214, 215; *Prima Secundae* (First Part of the Second Part), 89, 90, 177–78, 197, 207, 212, 213, 214, 215, 216, 217, 219, 220, 222, 223, 224, 226, 227, 232, 315, 320, 437

sun, 155, 187, 188n43, 323, 324, 325, 347, 352, 354, 404, 436

supererogatory actions, 48, 49, 50, 51, 52, 53, 413

supernatural disposition(s), 185, 186, 191, 266, 267, 273, 341, 354, 407. *See also* supernatural gifts.

supernatural gift(s), 74n109, 155. *See also* supernatural dispositions

supper, 332. *See also* feast

survivalism, 202n15, 202n16, 203n17, 203n18

Symposium (Plato), 35n11, 120

table, 314, 315

Taliaferro, Charles, 81n10

teachers, 93, 126, 330. *See also* doctors

teaching, 108, 127n18; Catholic Christian, 44n34, 136n56, 193n60, 202, 277, 338n43, 391, 393, 410; Christian, 8, 25; of Dionysius the Areopagite, 192; scriptural, 136, 393; of St. Paul, 251, 287; of St. Thomas, 2n3, 15n34, 89, 178, 204, 363, 444, 445, 447

tears, 314

technology, 144n11

tedium, 40n24, 55, 60, 76, 77, 79, 81, 420, 444. *See* heaven; *See also* boredom; the problem of the tedium of immortality (PTI); the problem of the tedium of heavenly immortality (PTHI)

temperance, 216

temporal being(s), 25, 26, 145, 172, 400, 402, 410

Teresa of Avila, St., 439

Te Velde, Rudi, 110n100

theologian(s), 2, 7, 8, 9, 14, 15, 20, 26n59, 30, 31, 36, 44, 45, 46, 49, 57, 59, 61, 62, 63, 66, 67, 80, 85, 89, 96, 104, 113, 141, 143, 215, 227, 236, 268n150, 286, 300, 301, 302, 336, 391, 420, 447

theology, 7, 11n15, 14n23, 14n25, 14n26, 30, 76, 81n10, 104n64, 110, 141n1, 175n15, 186n39, 253n100, 306n90, 427, 444, 447

theosis, 54. *See also* deiformity

Therese of Lisieux, St., 439

things: corporeal, 290n39; corruptible, 359, 406; desirable, 99; incorruptible, 406; individual, 161, 240, 247. *See also* last thing(s); living thing(s)

Thomist(s), 36n15, 110n101, 125, 202, 202n16, 203n18, 239n28, 259n121, 305, 334n26, 339, 391, 395, 401, 402, 405, 409, 417, 418, 423n2, 441, 443

thoughts, 176, 290, 438; lustful, 431; secret, 160, 161, 163

time, 28, 35, 44, 46, 50, 51, 52, 53, 59, 71, 76, 81, 84, 111, 114, 116, 117, 118, 119, 123, 126,

time (*cont.*)
167, 168, 169, 170, 171, 172, 173n12, 174, 175, 176, 177, 178, 179, 183, 193n59, 198, 204, 212, 225n73, 239, 241n36, 248, 256, 265, 267, 303, 316, 359, 361n72, 363, 401, 402, 403, 405, 413, 435, 436, 436, 441, 442, 443, 444, 445, 447; according to Aristotle and St. Thomas, 115; beginning of, 13n19; certain mundane activities not in, 114; cosmic, 64, 73; in Eden, 73, 74; end of, 16n35, 16n37, 115, 234, 316, 333, 342n9, 404; experience of, 26; after the fall in this life, 7; in heaven, 70, 74, 85, 318, 321; as measure of a being that is in no way immutable, 115–16; metronomic, 64–66, 70, 74, 85, 414, 437n34; mutability and, 115; psychic, 64n80; systolic, 64–67, 70, 71, 73, 84, 85, 414, 437n34; terminus of, 168; as we experience it in this life, 321, 404, 405, 420. *See* heaven

Timpe, Kevin, 2n3, 31n3, 35n11, 45, 46, 47, 48, 51, 183n27, 184n33, 253n100

Toledo, Eleventh Council of, 16n35

Tolkien, J.R.R., 362, 385n106

Tollefsen, Christopher, 21n50

Toner, Patrick, 202n16, 363n77

tools, 154, 339, 361, 370, 384

Torrell, Jean-Pierre, 90n1, 216n46, 268n152, 270n158

Tractates on the Gospel of John (St. Augustine of Hippo), 325n165

tradition: authoritative, Catholic Christian, 2, 10, 15, 16, 19, 23, 24, 25, 27, 28, 29, 34, 43, 45n35, 46, 50, 53, 74, 156, 173, 187, 227, 235, 331n14, 352, 353, 391, 393, 415, 421, 428n9, 446; Catholic, 104, 186n40, 193n60, 282, 286, 293, 294, 329n5, 401, 406, 409–10, 413; Christian, 2n2, 7, 8, 11, 18, 24, 25, 26, 27, 29, 47, 55, 60, 62, 89, 186n40, 228, 236, 254, 264n139, 279, 394, 397, 399, 400, 411, 421, 429, 447; Dominican, 186n39; Jewish-Christian, 41; philosophical, 63; religious, 63; Thomistic commentary, 167n1

transformation, spiritual or moral, 36n15, 73n108, 427, 429

tree of life, 314, 315

Trent, Council of, 44n28, 74n110

triangularity, 114, 126, 157

Triduum, 65

the Trinity, 57, 121n139, 143, 148, 149, 306, 337, 414; and the beatific vision, 110n101, 306, 414

true, universal, 98

truth, 28, 77, 84, 102, 130, 131, 132, 162n9, 165, 202, 315, 369n89, 374, 419, 431, 435, 436, 445

understanding, 10n3, 91, 114, 133, 142, 176n19, 335, 396; as gift of the Holy Spirit, 147–49, 150. *See* intellectual activity

union, 3, 7, 8, 10, 11, 12, 13, 16, 17, 18, 21, 22, 25, 26, 35n11, 41, 54, 56, 57, 81, 102, 103, 104, 118, 120, 124, 133, 134n47, 136n56, 137, 139, 140, 152, 153, 160, 178, 184, 186n39, 186n40, 208, 226, 228, 234n3, 235, 237, 241, 249, 251, 260, 273, 274, 275, 276, 277, 278, 279, 281, 284, 287, 297, 298, 299, 303, 304, 305, 306, 307, 308, 309, 310, 311, 312, 313, 329, 334, 336, 362, 374, 378, 392, 393, 394, 395, 396, 398, 399, 400, 413, 415, 419, 447; of soul and body, 219, 220, 243. *See* beatific vision according to St. Thomas; essential reward in heaven. *See also* sexual union

unity, 204, 241, 332, 348, 436, 437; of the church, 332–33

universals, 125, 126, 187

universe, 12, 115, 161, 346, 347, 349, 357, 358, 368, 379, 380, 382, 384, 385, 386, 387, 419

Van Dyke, Christina, 202n16, 253n100, 294n54

Vatican Council I, 10n3, 13n19

Vatican Council II, 15n34, 18, 20

victories, 83, 108, 329, 330,

Vienne, Council of, 156n61

Vigilius, Pope, 74n110

vigor, 182

vine, 314

virginity, 108

virgins, 108, 330, 331

virtue(s), 2, 31n3, 35n11, 45n38, 47n45, 48, 51, 52, 83, 92, 93n13, 95, 219, 250, 275, 276, 278, 433; acquired, 95n18, 248n75; cardinal, 83n17, 95, 437; as central to human happiness, 95, 104, 216; in Christ, 327; contemplative, 436; degrees of, 56, 59; exemplar cardinal, 437; formal aspects of, 83n17; god-like, heroic, or

General Index 487

superhuman, 95n18; in heaven, 53n60, 83, 148n35, 248n75, 422, 436, 437–41; human, 95n18; infused, 95n18, 96, 147, 150, 248n75, 429, 432, 433, 434, 435, 439, 440; infused as habits, 94n17; intellectual, 446; material aspects of, 83n17; as a means to the end of perfect happiness, 95, 96; moral, 83, 148n35, 439, 442; political cardinal, 437; purgative cardinal, 437–38, 440, 441; of the purified soul, 437–39, 440, 441; theological, 53n60, 83n17, 95, 147, 148n35, 150, 223, 224, 323, 429, 432, 433, 440; as they exist in heaven, 83n17, 148n35, 422, 438–39. *See also individual virtues by name*

vision: of beauty itself in heaven, 10; of glory, 118n124, 177. *See* beatific vision; beatific vision according to St. Thomas

volitional activity, 199; as wholly immaterial, 199, 215. *See* will

voluntary poor, 108

Vonier, Dom Anscar, 44, 45, 46, 47, 287n27, 335n31, 402n1, 413

Waddell, Michael, 254n100
Walls, Jerry, 14n22, 14n23
water, 138n69, 265, 315, 341, 347
wayfarers, 45n35, 442n46
wealth, 92, 97, 99
Weinandy, Thomas, 113, 114, 119
well-being, 20, 93n10
well-being (*bene esse*) of perfect human happiness, 109, 215, 216, 220, 222, 225, 226, 228, 232, 304–305, 312, 320, 360, 378, 396, 397, 398, 418; as an Aristotelian way of speaking, 216; and embodiment as a part of, 197, 215, 216, 217, 218, 304, 320; as the essential reward in heaven plus the accidental reward, 109, 217, 227, 230, 231, 294n54, 395; and human friendships as a part of, 218, 338; some modes of cognition and some acts of will as parts of, 255n73. *See* accidental reward in heaven; essential reward in heaven; goods; human happiness, perfect

whole, 17, 92, 110, 115, 161, 169, 172, 175, 179, 200, 201, 205, 207, 208, 210, 215, 219, 220, 221, 228, 263, 332, 333, 341, 346, 347, 348, 355, 357, 358, 379, 382, 384, 386, 387, 414, 416, 421

"Why Immortality Is Not So Bad" (John Martin Fischer), 81
widows, 330
wife, 1, 23, 332
will: delighting as an act of, 121, 128, 181–84, 199, 214; delight, love, and joy in heaven as concomitant accidents of the beatific vision as acts of, 180–84, 214, 399; desiring as an act of, 78, 128, 423, 443; in heaven human persons have multiple modes of acts of, 225n73, 291–92, 294n54; proper accidents of the beatific vision as acts of, 127, 128, 129, 175, 180–84, 292, 399; rectitude of the (*rectitudo voluntatis*), 95, 181
Williams, A. N., 186n39
Williams, Bernard, 40, 55, 60, 76, 77, 78, 81, 82, 84, 85, 420, 422
Williams, Scott, 254n100
wind, 242, 295, 301
wine, 250, 314, 315, 358, 359, 371, 378
Wippel, John F., 239n28
wisdom, 95, 120, 216, 254, 315, 316, 322, 324, 379n99; of God, 164, 225n73, 250, 260, 293, 294n53, 309, 313, 318, 350, 364n79, 432, 436
Wojtyla, Karol. *See* John Paul II, Pope St.
woman, 250
work, 20, 33, 39, 41, 44, 66, 70, 90n1, 127, 161, 248, 312, 337, 342, 393, 397
world, 13n19, 119, 160, 283, 319, 329, 330, 344, 346, 347, 370, 427, 428, 439; devastated, 70; end of the, 270, 333; external, 283–84; of heaven, 363n77; the human person as a little, 346; machine, 347; material, 203n16, 283, 343n12, 363n77; next, 36n15, 257, 345, 355, 371, 401; possible, 10, 161n87, 427; restoration or renewal of the, 352; this, 65, 74, 257, 307, 309, 342n9, 357, 358, 378, 404, 426, 431, 438, 439, 441
worship, 15, 30n1, 39, 41, 276, 338, 363, 364, 419, 437, 439n45; in heaven, 15, 30, 39, 41, 276, 363–64, 419
Wright, N.T., 14n25
writing, 69, 364, 419

youth, 182, 254, 255

Zaleski, Carol, 76, 81n10
Zechariah, 119, 404
zygote, 201, 237n24

Eternal Life and Human Happiness in Heaven: Philosophical Problems, Thomistic Solutions was designed in Mrs Eaves XL Serif Narrow with Carre Noir and Mrs Eaves display type and composed by Kachergis Book Design of Pittsboro, North Carolina. It was printed on 55-pound Natural Offset and bound by Maple Press of York, Pennsylvania.